JAMES MONROE

Courtesy of Mr. Laurence Gouverneur Hoes

JAMES MONROE

From a portrait by Rembrandt Peale, painted while Monroe was in the White House. It is now the property of the James Monroe Law Office in Fredericksburg, Virginia.

JAMES MONROE

By

W. P. CRESSON

ARCHON BOOKS
1971

© 1946 by The University of North
Carolina Press. Reprinted 1971 with
permission in an unaltered and unabridged
edition by The Shoe String Press, Inc.,
Hamden, Connecticut 06514.

ISBN 0-208-01089-0
Library of Congress catalog card number 75-124098

Printed in the United States of America

TO

J. H. G. *and* M. E. G.

The Truest of Friends

Introduction

BY M. A. DE WOLFE HOWE

An entry in a diary holding only two lines for a single day reminds me that on December 19, 1931, I saw William Penn Cresson for the last time. It was in December of 1929, I learn from the same source, that we began in Washington to make an acquaintance which ripened soon into a friendship. At the invitation of a friend of many years, Dr. Herbert Putnam, I had then begun a term of service at the Library of Congress under the impressive title of "Consultant in Biography." Mr. Cresson was one of the workers in biographical fields who sought such counsel as I could provide on the conduct of their labors. He was working at the time on his biography of Francis Dana, the first United States Minister to Russia.

In the winter and spring of 1929-1930 I saw him frequently, and again through the early months of 1931 when I was back at the Library. I did not know what had more recently befallen him till he lunched with me in Boston when last we met. It was at the Tavern Club, in a large room of which, if my memory serves me right, we were, strangely enough, the only occupants. It seemed a pity that there were none to share his most agreeable company, for his native gifts and charm, ripened by much experience, set him apart from the common run of men. Of all our talk as we lunched together, I have—apart from his habitual gaiety of spirit—but one vivid memory, and that bears directly upon this book.

"Tomorrow," he said, in effect, "I am going to Baltimore for an operation, which may well be fatal. My biography of James Monroe is far on its way to completion, but if I do not live, and if the book is to be published, the final work of revision which I have planned to put into it must be done by somebody else. May I count on you for friendly offices to see that this is done?"

There was but one reply to make, and I assured my friend that the interest I already felt in his book would, at the desperate need he suggested, be continued. His death did not follow immediately upon the operation he underwent, but his work as a writer, curtailed as the end drew near by failing health, was finished. From the hospital he was taken to New York, and thence to Stockbridge, Massachusetts, where he died on May 12, 1932.

Penn Cresson, as he was commonly called, must have reported our conversation to his wife, for in the summer following his death, she wrote to me about the unfinished manuscript. By reason of my occupation with other work and, still more, because of my unfamiliarity with the period involved in a life of James Monroe, I felt quite incapable of bringing the book to completion. It was, however, within my power to tender such help as I could give towards finding a scholar equipped to take the unfinished work in hand. He was found in the person of Mr. Scott Hurtt Paradise, (B.A. Yale, B.A. and M.A. Oxford), Instructor in English, Phillips Academy, Andover, Massachusetts. Mrs. Cresson and he were brought into relations preceding his own undertaking the extensive task of revision, checking authorities, verifying quotations, and the like. His academic duties and an impairment in his own health protracted the work far longer than had been anticipated. Finally, in 1942, he had to abandon all extra-curricular engagements. Unable to see this piece of work to completion, he was unwilling to share that considerable credit for the book which might naturally have been acknowledged by the appearance of his name on the title-page.

More work on the manuscript was then done by a former helper of Mr. Cresson's before it came to The University of North Carolina Press. There the essential value of the manuscript, as the first extended study of President Monroe's services to his country, was recognized. The editors of the Press subjected it to a final revision and scholarly documentation which brought the book to the form in which it is now published.

The "List of References" at the end of this volume will indicate the wide range of impersonal sources drawn upon. Under the heading "Manuscripts" there is an entry, "The Gouverneur-Hoes MSS,"

Introduction

now in the Library of the James Monroe Law Office, Fredericksburg, Virginia, to which more than an impersonal allusion should be made. To Mrs. Gouverneur Hoes and her son, Mr. Laurence Gouverneur Hoes, inheritors of many papers of James Monroe, Mr. Cresson himself, while at work upon this book, had many and quite special occasions for gratitude.

The biography is thus seen to be the product of more than a single hand. Those who have taken part in its preparation, however, would not have it otherwise than that the name, "W. P. Cresson," should stand alone on the title-page, for entirely in conception and largely in execution, it is indeed his—in fitting culmination of a series of historical writings.

Since it stands as something of a monument to a writer, a word should be said not only about the name on the title-page, but also about him who bore it. His full name of William Penn Cresson was his grandfather's, and it might well have been used in all the five books that preceded this one. That it was not was due to his own reluctance to assert any of the implications of Pennsylvania inheritance, historical, industrial, and artistic, which the unabridged name might suggest. He was born, September 17, 1873, at Claymont, in the neighboring State of Delaware. For two years he attended the University of Pennsylvania, and in 1897 entered the École des Beaux Arts in Paris to study architecture. Before beginning to practise that profession at Washington, he studied also in Paris at the École des Sciences Politiques. Cresson was one of those who do not find their ultimate direction at the first attempt. Two years of architecture in Washington were followed by two years on a cattle-ranch in Nevada. Then in 1907 he entered the diplomatic service, and for ten years held secretarial posts at legations and embassies in Lima, Quito, Panama, Lisbon, Petrograd, and London. In 1917 he entered the Air Service of the Signal Officers Reserve Corps, in which he became a captain the next year. In the course of the First World War, one of his assignments was that of Chief of the American Military Mission attached to Belgian General Headquarters.

Nearly fifteen years of life remained to him when the War ended. Almost all of his work as a writer fell within that period. One earlier book, *Persia—The Awakening East* (1908) had been described by the London *Morning Post*, not given to indiscriminate praise, "as a

JAMES MONROE

refreshing little oasis among travel books of today." Eleven years later, in 1919, came *The Cossacks—Their History and Country*, a by-product of his diplomatic term in Russia.

Back in the United States, he won a Ph.D. at Columbia in 1922, taught international law at Princeton, Georgetown, and Tufts, served as diplomatic secretary at international conferences, and published his three others books, *The Holy Alliance—The European Background of the Monroe Doctrine* (1922), *Diplomatic Portraits* (1923), and *Francis Dana—A Puritan Diplomat at the Court of Catherine the Great* (1930). In the study leading to the first of these three books there was much to qualify him for writing a life of Monroe. In the second, he declared of that President that he "has become today, a curiously misunderstood and shadowy figure." The present volume was plainly designed to change all that.

These introductory remarks have dealt almost exclusively with Penn Cresson's background and achievements as a writer. It must be added that his own life in its entirety could not have been the rounded, fulfilled life that it was, but for his marriage in 1921 to Margaret French, the daughter of Daniel Chester French, the sculptor, herself a distinguished practitioner of her father's art. Her devoted interest in this book, from its earliest to its latest stages, has found symbolic expression in her portrait busts both of her husband and of President Monroe.

Boston
July, 1946

CONTENTS

	Introduction by M. A. De Wolfe Howe	vii
1	Williamsburg in Virginia - 1774	3
2	"The Sword Is Now Drawn"	10
3	James Monroe Crosses the Delaware	19
4	"A Brave, Active, and Sensible Officer"	31
5	"A Farewell to Arms"	46
6	Assemblyman, Councillor, Congressman	63
7	Champion of the West	73
8	"The Most Interesting Connection"	91
9	The New Roof	96
10	Senator from Virginia	110
11	Prologue to the First French Mission	119
12	First Mission to France	127
13	Diplomatic Disappointments	137
14	Recall from France	148
15	The Reynolds Affair	155
16	Governor of Virginia	170
17	Louisiana Purchase, 1803	183
18	London Mission, 1803-1804	198
19	Spanish Mission	208
20	Return to London	215
21	Politics and Policies	218
22	The "Chesapeake" Incident	230

23	Homecoming of an Envoy	236
24	Monroe and the New Republicans	240
25	Secretary of State	244
26	Declaration of War	254
27	The British in Washington	261
28	Secretary of War	273
29	President James Monroe	281
30	The Seminole War and the Florida Treaty	302
31	The Banking Crisis	327
32	The Missouri Compromise	339
33	The Monroes and Washington Society	354
34	Jackson and the Governorship of Florida	377
35	Roads, Bridges, Canals	385
36	Recognition of South American Republics	399
37	Relations with Russia	412
38	European Background of the Monroe Doctrine	417
39	Formulation of the Monroe Doctrine	433
40	The End of a Dynasty	451
41	Last Years of a Great American	469
	Appendix: James Monroe's Ancestry	503
	Notes	509
	List of References	549
	Index	561

Illustrations

James Monroe. *From a portrait by Rembrandt Peale*   Frontispiece

Between pages 18-19

William and Mary College, Williamsburg, Virginia

Washington and Lafayette at Valley Forge. *From an engraving after a painting by W. H. Powell*

The Battle of Monmouth. *From an engraving after a painting by A. Chappel*

Stage from Baltimore to Washington. *From an original lithograph*

Between pages 34-35

James Monroe. *From a bust by Margaret Cresson*

Mrs. James Monroe. *From a miniature by Sené*

Monroe's Law Office in Fredericksburg, Virginia

The Desk on Which the Monroe Doctrine Was Signed

Between pages 194-195

James Monroe's Home on Monroe Hill, The University of Virginia

The Signing of the Louisiana Purchase Treaty. *From a painting by André Castaigne*

Celebration of the Louisiana Purchase. *From a lithograph furnished through the Jefferson Bicentennial Commission*

The Destruction of the City of Washington by the British. *From a print by Beale*

Between pages 210-211

President James Monroe. *From a portrait by John Vanderlyn*

Mrs. James Monroe. *From a portrait by Benjamin West*

The White House and St. John's Church. *From a drawing by Latrobe in 1816*

The White House during Monroe's Administration. *From an original lithograph*

JAMES MONROE

Facing page

The Birth of the Monroe Doctrine. *From a painting by Clyde Osmer De Land*   450

A Page from Monroe's Message to Congress, December 2, 1823   451

Oak Hill, Monroe's Home in Loudoun County, Virginia   482

The Entrance Hall of Oak Hill   483

One of the Marble Mantels given to Monroe by Lafayette   483

A Driveway Laid Out by Monroe   483

JAMES MONROE

≈ 1 ≈

Williamsburg in Virginia - 1774

IN WILLIAMSBURG, colonial capital of Virginia, on August 1, 1774, revolution was in the making. Outwardly the town was its lively and hospitable self, as befitted the "chief city of the Colony." Along the broad, straight, dusty mile that was the Duke of Gloucester Street, extending from the Capitol at its east end to the College of William and Mary on the west, the people of the town and countryside went about their affairs in the sweltering sun. Handsome coaches, drawn by four or six horses, churned up the already ankle-deep sand. Frontiersmen threaded their way on horseback among the vehicles. Pedestrians, keeping in the shade of trees and buildings, went busily from shop to shop. Business was booming for the apothecary, the wigmaker, the gunsmith, the silversmith, the saddler, the printer, the snuffmaker, the tavern keeper—all who had goods or services to sell. On the Court House Green and in Market Square, talk and laughter mingled with the noise of traffic. Williamsburg enfolded all these people in a peace of its own. The spire of Bruton Parish Church, beside the Palace Green, pointed tranquilly to the burning blue of the August sky. Peace hung deep over the beautiful gardens behind the Governor's Palace and in the fragrant orchards.

But there was a tenseness among the people, and eyes were momentarily turned to the great Capitol at the east end of Gloucester Street. Usually, at times like these, its courtyard was crowded with vehicles, and its windows were open to catch the least cooling breeze. Through its wrought-iron gates and triple-arched entrance Virginia's leaders came and went. Now its doors were closed, its windows blank and ominous.[1]

As the people of Virginia well knew, the Capitol had been shut and locked since May 26, when the Royal Governor, Lord Dunmore, had dissolved the Assembly because of the Burgesses' protest against the Boston Port Bill and their setting aside of June 1, the day on which the bill was to go into effect, as "a day of Fasting, Humiliation, and Prayer."[2] It was well known, too, that the Burgesses, including George Washington, had observed that day by fasting and by attending Bruton Parish Church in Williamsburg.[3]

The people knew also that on May 27, the day after the Governor had dissolved the Assembly, the Burgesses reassembled in the Apollo Room of the Raleigh Tavern; and there, with Peyton Randolph in the chair, they formed an Association against the East India Company and proposed "a general Congress at such place annually as shall be thought convenient; there to deliberate on those general measures which the united interests of America may from Time to Time require."[4] At that same meeting on May 27, the Burgesses also called for an election of delegates from all the counties to the First Virginia Convention to meet in Williamsburg on August 1, 1774, for the purpose of electing delegates to the proposed general Congress of all the colonies.

Now, on August 1, this first Virginia Convention was meeting in the Raleigh Tavern, and passers-by loitering within earshot, or the more frankly curious who peered in at the windows, heard plenty of verbal fireworks from Patrick Henry and others and the frequent clink of glasses as the perspiring Burgesses strove to quench their thirst. For six days the gathering remained in session, with Peyton Randolph as president. In the oppressive heat of early August, this notable assembly, acting independently of their Royal Governor and as direct representatives of the people, strengthened their previous Association against commerce with England and elected as delegates to the Continental Congress, to meet in Philadelphia in September, Peyton Randolph, Richard Bland, Edmund Pendleton, Benjamin Harrison, George Washington, Patrick Henry, Thomas Jefferson, and Richard Henry Lee. Revolution had begun in Virginia.[5]

With the Capitol closed, it is no wonder that the white-clapboarded and dormer-windowed Raleigh Tavern, with its beau-

Williamsburg in Virginia - 1774

tiful garden and its gracious interior—scene of many a "genteel dinner" and gay rout—became increasingly the center of the town's social and political life. As Lord Dunmore's prestige waned and as state balls in the Governor's Palace became a thing of the past, more and more the leaders of the colony assembled in the hospitable taproom of the Tavern, danced in the candlelight of the great chandeliers, or sat around the long, gleaming table of the Apollo Room to talk till dawn of the days ahead.

The Raleigh Tavern, in the late summer days of 1774, also saw students arriving to begin the first semester of the College of William and Mary and was host to these youthful hotheads, already eager to show their mettle in colonial affairs. That these affairs were in a turmoil they well knew, for the insubordination of the Burgesses was no new thing. Almost ten years before, in May, 1765, Patrick Henry, standing in the richly paneled Hall of the House of Burgesses in the Williamsburg Capitol, had offered a series of radical resolutions, one of which denied the right of Parliament to tax the colonies. And this resolution he had defended with the famous words, "Caesar had his Brutus, Charles the First his Cromwell, and George the Third—may profit by their example!" Governor Fauquier at once prorogued the Assembly and rescued the unfortunate Mercer, sent to distribute the stamps, from an angry crowd of the colony's leading citizens gathered in front of the Raleigh Tavern.[6] Meantime, Patrick Henry's speech had been heard around the world, and the Stamp Act was repealed. Whereupon Williamsburg rejoiced—somewhat prematurely—with fireworks, bonfires, and bell-ringings.

Again, in 1769, the House of Burgesses passed strong resolutions against Parliament's right to tax the colonies, as provided in the Townshend Acts, and Lord Botetourt, the Governor, immediately prorogued the Assembly. The Burgesses then, as later, adjourned to the Raleigh Tavern and there adopted a non-importation agreement.

Thus, when the college students came to Williamsburg in 1774, revolution was in the air, and had been for most of their lives. "The reigning spirit in Virginia," said Philip Fithian in a letter written at Nomini Hall on August 21, 1774, "is liberty—And the universal topic politicks. . . . God Almighty knows where these civil tumults will end; presumably not without War & Blood!"[7]

But not all of the students of William and Mary in 1774 were of one mind. Governor Dunmore's three sons were students at the College during these same months, and Tories enough could be found among the seventy-odd older students to provide plenty of argument. Where exquisitely tailored scions of wealthy planters rubbed shoulders with the more soberly clad sons of merchants and carpenters, there would be found adherents of both camps, and in each camp would be representatives of all classes.

In the faculty, too, the rift between patriot and royalist was widening hourly. President Camm and Professors Gwatkin and Henley were loyal to the Crown from the beginning. George Wythe, the distinguished Professor of Law, and James Madison,* Professor of Natural Philosophy and Mathematics, led the patriot faction.

The atmosphere of the College, sharing as it did in the exciting events of the town, was not conducive to study. Even the tall, rawboned, shy sixteen-year-old who registered at the College in 1774 as James Monroe, of Westmoreland County in the Northern Neck of Virginia, must have been aware of the ferment that was stirring in the colonies, whipping up excitement in Boston, Philadelphia, Annapolis, and Williamsburg. He had been seven years old when Patrick Henry, in 1765, made his famous protest in the House of Burgesses against the Stamp Act. In 1766, when he was eight, and just beginning to understand a little of such events, young James had stood looking after his father, Spence Monroe, hurrying to the small tobacco post of Leeds, on the Rappahannock, where the patriots of Westmoreland County were gathering in answer to Richard Henry Lee's summons to affix their signatures to a pledge to import no more English goods until the Stamp Act was repealed. The nature of his journey reveals Spence Monroe as a patriot, and his young son can be imagined to have absorbed his father's ideas and sympathies.[8]

Spence Monroe, James's father, appears to have been apprenticed as a carpenter, in 1743, to one Robert Walker, of King George, a joiner. In his day, however, it was possible to be a carpenter and a gentleman at the same time. Even the Carys of Warwick County, who, tradition affirms, scorned Washington's bid for one of the Cary girls, signed themselves "carpenters" as well as "gentlemen."[9]

James's mother, too, came of a family important in the life of the colony. She was Elizabeth Jones, daughter of James Jones, of King

*Cousin of President James Madison.

Williamsburg in Virginia - 1774

George County, who was an "undertaker in architecture," and sister of Joseph Jones, of Fredericksburg, Judge of the Virginia General Court, who at different times was member of the House of Burgesses, the Virginia Committee of Safety, the committee that framed the Virginia Declaration of Rights and the State Constitution, and the Continental Congress. He was a "confidential friend" of Washington and on intimate terms with Jefferson and Madison. Elizabeth Jones Monroe is known, in family tradition, as "particularly well educated for colonial days." [10]

Spence Monroe, although he was a gentleman, was not one of the wealthy planters of the countryside. In a neighborhood of sixty-thousand-acre estates manned by a hundred Negroes or more, where house parties and balls, horse racing and cockfighting, drinking and hunting kept the great landowners and their families amused, the Monroes lived "within a stone's throw of . . . a virgin forest," in a frame, two-storied house whose "rafters and beams," writes a descendant, "showed plainly the unskilled art of the craftsmanship of the labor of the period." At Nomini, home of the Carters, and at Stratford, home of the Lees, the gentry of the Northern Neck sat down to dinner in formal dining rooms. The Monroes dined in their "large living room, in which an old-time fireplace with a broad hearth was particularly conspicuous with its pots and pans hanging on cranes over a slow wood fire." The young Carters, Masons, Lees, Harrisons, and Pages learned their Latin and English, arithmetic and writing in the plantation schoolroom, taught by tutors (imported from abroad or brought down from some northern college) before going on to Cambridge or Oxford. Young James Monroe, like the slightly older John Marshall, who learned his classics from his father by their frontier cabin hearthside in Fauquier County,[11] left his home early in the morning to tramp several miles through the primeval forest to Parson Campbell's school. During James's last year at Parson Campbell's, he had the companionship in his morning walk of John Marshall, who had been sent back to Westmoreland for schooling. Each boy carried his books under one arm and had a gun slung over his shoulder, "for these were pioneer days and children were taught self-protection from the cradle." Family tradition makes James out a "fine shot," with a reputation for keeping the Monroe table comfortably supplied with game, but on their way down the leafy arch

JAMES MONROE

of Parson's Lane (the name of the road cut for several straight miles through the forest for the use of the Parson's pupils) the boys did not loiter to look for game. Archibald Campbell was "a power in what was then called Washington Parish," writes one of James Monroe's descendants. "He was a disciplinarian of the sternest type, and he made the school days all work and little play. . . . His pupils were regarded as especially well grounded in mathematics and Latin . . . and in their various subsequent careers they were noted for solidity of character."[12]

Few men had such "solidity of character" as James Monroe. As a man he did not laugh easily. If the child is really father of the man, James must have been a solemn sort of boy. As a youth he left no bright echoes of frivolity, as did his friend, the fun-loving Marshall, in letters to his school fellow. It would be hard to find a more matter-of-fact correspondence than that of James Monroe, whether the letters date from the exciting years of the Revolution, the turbulent era which saw the unfolding of his own political career, the happy time of his honeymoon, or the kaleidoscopic days of his diplomatic adventures, the war of 1812, the terms of his presidency.

The tall boy from the Northern Neck who rode into Williamsburg some time during the most stirring period of that city's history will always remain a stranger. We know he could swim and climb, fish and hunt with the best of the lads who knew every pine- and cedar-tree haunt of Virginia's birds, every hiding place of dove or partridge. His mother never lacked squirrels for brunswick stew or wild pigeons for a pie. He could tell where canvasback could be found feeding in the lee of the shore, mimic the "ur-ouk" of Canada geese, the trumpeting of the wild swan, never miss the flash of white breast, the flare of rust-colored neck that betrayed a wild fowl feeding among the yellow-brown reeds and wild rice along the shores of the Chesapeake. He could not have escaped from Parson Campbell's school without a sound foundation in the classics, a respect for the factual exactness of mathematics, and an understanding of such words as loyalty, honesty, honor, and devotion.

In short, we know little more of James Monroe at this time than that he was solid, even at sixteen. What was to follow his registration at William and Mary would vitalize, not shake him.

Of Monroe's impressions when he rode into Williamsburg from

Williamsburg in Virginia - 1774

the Northern Neck, there is no record. Although Thomas Jefferson described the college buildings as "rude misshapen piles," which looked like "brick-kilns,"[13] it is highly probable that this fine scorn was not shared by young Monroe, fresh from the forest-fringed plantation on Monroe Creek in Westmoreland. The College of William and Mary at this time enjoyed great prestige throughout the colonies. This despite Robert Carter's complaint that the Professors played cards all night and were often seen drunken in the streets.[14] It was Monroe's good fortune that the presidency of the College, after the departure of President Camm, fell to Professor Madison, who instituted a liberal and patriotic regime. Into his teachings he is said to have woven much "sound revolutionary doctrine."[15]

All too little is known of James Monroe's college life. The Bursar's Book discloses that after his father's death his bills were paid by his uncle, Judge Joseph Jones, of Fredericksburg, member of the House of Burgesses, intimate friend of Washington, Jefferson, and Madison, and lifelong adviser of Monroe. The only recorded episode of the boy's student career shows that he did not yet take his own signature very seriously. Eight students, including Monroe, signed a petition addressed to the college authorities complaining that the "Mistress of the College" was giving the students "scarce and intolerable" food, at the same time that she was feeding her brother on the fat of the land and supplying him with candles from the public stores. There were other charges—a long list—but the complainers, when called upon to substantiate their claims, were unable to do so, and as for James Monroe, "he never read the petition & consequently could not undertake to prove a single article."[16] A trivial affair to be recorded when so much of greater moment is lost.

But the rising tide of Revolution was slowly flooding College and town, obliterating, as it rolled in, everything in its way. How could a student sit quietly and con the lines describing the march of Xenophon's thousands when he knew that up and down the tidewater peninsulas the minute men were drilling?

2

"The Sword is Now Drawn"

NEAR THE center of Williamsburg, in Market Square south of the Duke of Gloucester Street, stands the Powder Horn, a stout little brick structure hexagonal in shape, with a cone-like roof and a high encircling wall pierced with a low-arched door. Built by Governor Spotswood in 1714, it guarded for decades the arms and ammunition of the colony's militia.

On the night of April 19, 1775, Massachusetts Minute Men, shot by the redcoats, were lying dead in Lexington and Concord. The news of the battle had not yet reached Williamsburg, but when it did, the response would be as instant and fiery as it had been when Boston's port was closed, for the colonies were now of one mind, North and South.

On the following night, April 20, the King's armed schooner *Magdalen* was lying in the James River, not far from Williamsburg. Upon orders from the Governor, Lieutenant Collins, commanding the *Magdalen*, led a stealthy squad of her seamen through the darkness and into the sleeping town. Quickly rifling the powder magazine, they carried the colony's gunpowder away and stored it aboard the British man-of-war *Fowey;* "but though it was intended to have been done privately," wrote Lord Dunmore to the British Secretary of State, "Mr. Collins & his Party were observed & Notice was given immediately to the Inhabitants of the Place; Drums were sent through the City.—The Independent Company [militia] got under Arms. All the People assembled, & during their Consultation continual Threats were brought to my House, that it was their Resolution to seize upon

"The Sword Is Now Drawn"

or massacre me, & every Person found giving me Assistance if I refused to deliver the Powder immediately into their Custody."[1]

Why had Lord Dunmore ordered the removal of the powder? In his letter to the British Secretary of State he said that he feared the colonial militia daily increasing in numbers and training in the various counties as a result of Patrick Henry's speech of March 23 and the subsequent bill to raise an armed colonial force.

But he told the angry people of Williamsburg that he feared a slave uprising—an obvious subterfuge which angered them further. Mob violence threatened, as citizens and college boys crowded into the Palace Green. It was only the earnest pleas of such conservative leaders as Peyton Randolph and Robert Carter Nicholas that induced them to disperse and await the result of pending negotiation.

Nine days later, the news of Lexington and Concord reached Williamsburg, and the *Virginia Gazette* issued a broadside closing with the words, "The sword is now drawn, and God knows when it will be sheathed."[2]

It is inconceivable that James Monroe, the tall athletic boy from the Northern Neck, was not involved in all this excitement. After the Powder Horn incident, according to a descendant, he, "along with all the other students, returned to his quarters, . . . Rumors ran wild from dormitory to dormitory, and when the day was done, under cover of darkness, a military corps was formed."[3]

The students of William and Mary were organizing fast now, and more than one military company was formed. The Palace Green was a favorite drill ground, and there they marched and wheeled and practiced the manual of arms under the very nose of Lord Dunmore. One account says that "the youth of Williamsburg formed themselves into a military corps and chose Henry Nicholson for their Captain; that on Dunmore's flight from Williamsburg, they repaired to the magazine and armed themselves with blue painted stock guns, kept for the purpose of distribution among the Indians—and equip'd as the minute men were in military garb, that is to say—with hunting shirts—Trousers—bucktails—cockades, and 'Liberty or Death' appended to their breasts as their motto—That they could and did perform all the evolutions of the manual exercise, far better than the soldiers who were daily arriving from the adjacent counties. That their Captain . . . was then about Fourteen years old."[4]

JAMES MONROE

Besides this "Youth's Corps" there were the "College Company" and the "Williamsburg Volunteers." The captain of the latter was James Innis, one of the signers of the complaint against the Mistress of the College, which Monroe had also signed. Since Monroe had been associated with Innis in this college prank, he may have belonged to Innis's company. That he drilled with one of the companies is certain for not long thereafter he became a member of the Virginia line, with every evidence of being a competent soldier.

After the Powder Horn incident, Peyton Randolph and others had been able to quiet the enraged citizenry of Williamsburg, but in the counties it was a different matter. When news that Dunmore had taken the colony's powder reached Fauquier, Culpeper, and adjacent counties, armed men gathered in Fredericksburg in such alarming numbers that Mann Page rode from there to Williamsburg in a single day to get Peyton Randolph's advice; and it took the combined efforts of Randolph and Edmund Pendleton to persuade the assembled troops to delay action.[5]

In Hanover County Patrick Henry was convinced that Dunmore's seizure of the powder was part of a general plan to disarm the colonies. He therefore put himself at the head of the militia he had been training and marched to Williamsburg. As he marched, minute men everywhere flocked to his banner. The news of this approaching band of fighting men raced ahead to Williamsburg. They had reached Doncastle's ordinary, some fifteen miles outside of the town, when an alarmed Governor sent a messenger with £330 to pay for the powder.[6] Patrick Henry, yielding reluctantly to conservative pressure,[7] accepted it (though a part of the money was later refunded), and turned back without entering the capital.

Lord Dunmore, relieved of his immediate apprehension, charged Patrick Henry with extorting money from the Crown and declared him an outlaw. He ordered the people not to aid or abet him.[8] But the people heartily approved of their hero, whose eloquence had supplied them with flaming slogans; and when, not long after, he left for the First Continental Congress in Philadelphia, his admirers accompanied him to the Potomac River with marching troops, military music, and salutes from guns.

With all this fencing between the Governor and the people, Williamsburg passed from one excitement to another. On June 1 Dun-

"The Sword Is Now Drawn"

more called together the prorogued Assembly in an attempt to regain control. It was worse than useless. On June 5 the Burgesses appointed a committee to inspect the powder magazine, as a result of ugly rumors and suspicions, among them the Governor's reputed threat to arm the slaves, which, more than anything else, enraged the people.[9]

Then one day Williamsburg was invaded by a band of horsemen from the piedmont. They rode into town carrying long rifles, wearing "hunting shirts, homemade, homespun, and home-woven, with the words 'Liberty or Death' in large white letters on their breasts. In their hats were buck-tails. In their belts they carried tomahawks and scalping knives."[10] The townfolk, said one of them later, "seemed as much afraid of us as if we had been Indians."[11] They were the "shirt men," as Lord Dunmore contemptuously called them because of their long hunting shirts.

At the head of this easy-riding band of Culpeper Minute Men rode a tall, handsome youth whom James Monroe knew well. It was John Marshall, his schoolmate at Parson Campbell's. "Silver Heels" he was called along the frontier because he excelled in the backwoods sports of high jumping and foot racing. The two boys now met in Williamsburg as fellow soldiers, who were soon to fight in the same battles for "Liberty or Death."

This last invasion of the Capital City was too much for Lord Dunmore's nerves.[12] He fled to His Majesty's man-of-war, the *Fowey*, lying at Yorktown. From the safety of this armed ship he declared martial law throughout the colony and offered freedom to all servants and slaves who would join him. With what troops he could raise by such means, plus a company of regulars, he harassed the Chesapeake shores and threatened to burn Norfolk.[13]

During his last months in Williamsburg, Dunmore had made the Palace something of an arsenal. In it were stored a quantity of arms, and it was even rumored that the powder magazine had been mined so that it could be blown up if the militia companies approached it to secure weapons. Dunmore had been requested by the colonial authorities to return the arms to the magazine, but he had refused to do so. On June 24, after his flight to the *Fowey*, a party of twenty-four men entered the Palace (still manned by servants), and removed the arms to the powder magazine. Among these men, and perhaps the

JAMES MONROE

youngest of them, was seventeen-year-old James Monroe.[14] Three of his companions in the adventure were Theoderick Bland, in his early thirties, Richard Kidder Meade, around twenty-nine, and Benjamin Harrison, Jr., of Berkeley, considerably older, an important member of the House of Burgesses until its dissolution the preceding month, and now on the Committee of Safety.

The act of this small, highly selected group was probably planned to forestall more violent action on the part of the soldiers and minute men who now thronged the streets of the once peaceful city of Williamsburg. In the transfer of arms from the Palace to the Powder Horn, the tall, shy boy from Westmoreland took part in an adventure requiring steadiness, resourcefulness, and not a little courage.

Williamsburg, by the summer of 1775, had become an armed camp. Patrick Henry, commander of all the forces now gathering to defend the colony, organized the two regiments of regular troops and the companies of minute men authorized by the Virginia Convention of July 29, 1775. In addition to being commander of all the colony's forces, Patrick Henry was also colonel of the first regiment, and William Woodford held the command of the second. On September 20 Henry selected a place for an encampment behind William and Mary, and barracks were built there for the troops.[15]

More regiments were now organized, and on September 28, 1775, James Monroe was made second lieutenant in the Third Virginia Regiment.[15-a] He was not yet quite eighteen, but he was tall and strong, an excellent horseman and a fine shot.

As the autumn passed and Dunmore's depredations became more flagrant, the Committee of Safety, of which Edmund Pendleton was president, reluctantly became convinced of the futility of trying to deal legally with their absentee governor and finally dispatched troops to the Chesapeake region. There, on December 9, 1775, a battle was fought at Great Bridge, near Norfolk, and Dunmore's troops were routed. The Virginia force consisted of the Second Virginia Regiment and the Culpeper Minute Men, and both fought under the command of Woodford.[16]

James Monroe was almost certainly not present at "Virginia's Bunker Hill." The two Marshalls, "Silver Heels" and his father Thomas, were there as officers, fighting with the Culpeper Minute Men, but probably Monroe remained with his regiment at Williams-

"The Sword Is Now Drawn"

burg, where Patrick Henry (whom the Committee of Safety had displaced in favor of Woodford) "ingloriously idled . . . with a command put to no more serious labor than guard-mounting."[17]

By January of 1776, six more regiments beyond the first two had been recruited, and Congress accepted Virginia's eight regiments on the Continental line. But Patrick Henry was deeply offended at having been passed over in favor of Woodford for the expedition to Great Bridge, and on February 28 he resigned his commission. On March 1, Congress commissioned Frederick Lewis, brigadier general, to take command of the forces stationed at Williamsburg. Lewis was a fine old Indian fighter and an excellent officer, but Patrick Henry was the people's hero and his soldiers adored him. He had planned to leave for Hanover at once, after a farewell dinner at the Raleigh Tavern with his officers, who were to form a guard of honor and escort him out of town, but the soldiers stormed the Tavern and demanded their discharge if they were to lose their leader. So instead of leaving dramatically and at once, Patrick Henry spent another twenty-four hours in Williamsburg and visited the men in their barracks.[18] That night, behind the College, he must have used his eloquence to good purpose, for no more was heard of discharges.

Throughout the year of 1775 and the early months of 1776, young Monroe (still on the college roll as the Bursar's Book shows), drilled and studied and thought and talked in an atmosphere so explosive that a spark could have set it off. There was still vast difference of opinion, and not even war can kill politics. But the arguments for independence were becoming formidable. When Dunmore burned Falmouth and Norfolk, Washington called them "flaming arguments" for independence. In January, 1776, Thomas Paine's pamphlet *Common Sense* was published and soon reached Virginia readers to reinforce the "flaming arguments" supplied by Dunmore.[19]

The news from the North, brought to Williamsburg by couriers riding in relays, clicked off the events of the first year of war. On July 3, 1775, George Washington, long a familiar figure in Williamsburg, took command of the Continental Army at Cambridge and spent the rest of the year in accumulating supplies and in replacing with new men soldiers whose enlistments were expiring and who would not reinlist. Among the new recruits were rifle companies from Virginia, picked woodsmen armed with rifles, "that deadly weapon

[15]

JAMES MONROE

as yet practically unknown in New England."[20] They are said to have marched six hundred miles in three weeks, without the loss of a single man through sickness.[21]

While Washington struggled to reconstruct his army, the British occupied Boston. But early in 1776, Washington seized and fortified Dorchester Heights commanding Boston, and on March 17 the British abandoned the city and Howe sailed away. Washington, convinced that Howe was headed for New York, hastened to get there first. This was important in Williamsburg, for before many months Virginia regiments were to join Washington's forces in New York. And James Monroe was to be in one of them.

So far, the South had taken care of itself rather well, but early in March, 1776, Sir Henry Clinton started southward with a small fleet to attack the southern coast and to reinforce the royalist governors of Virginia and the Carolinas, who were having a tough time of it with the patriots. Immediately Major General Charles Lee, second to Washington in command, was ordered south to organize the defense of the region. He reached Williamsburg on March 29 and made the town his headquarters.[22]

It was May 12 before he realized that Clinton's main point of attack was to be Charleston instead of the Virginia coast, and on that date he hastened away to help South Carolina's defense.[23] But meanwhile for a month or so this soldier of fortune added color to the life of Williamsburg. This is worth dwelling upon briefly, for later, in a darker hour, he somewhat unaccountably retained the friendship of James Monroe, who, with other young officers in Williamsburg, must have learned something of his picturesque career and felt the magnetism of his presence.

This British-born soldier had fought in the French and Indian War. Later he returned to England, fought in Portugal, Poland, and Russia, and was almost frozen to death on a mission that took him through the Balkans. In 1773, as trouble loomed in America, he returned to the colonies, took up land in Berkeley County, Virginia, and allied himself tempestuously with the patriot cause. His election as major general in the Continental Army was the result of his reputation as an officer in the French and Indian War, his obvious experience and ability, and his equally obvious flair for self-promotion.

When this tall, long-nosed, oddly dressed, slovenly officer ap-

[16]

"The Sword Is Now Drawn"

peared in Williamsburg with his entourage of officers and dogs, he made something of a stir. He went to work energetically at organizing the defense of the southern colonies, and he tried to raise a much-needed cavalry force but was unable to secure arms for it. It is said that he tried to train men in the use of the spear, but nothing came of it. The soldiers in Williamsburg knew him as a warm-hearted, hard-drinking, hard-swearing, impulsive man (the Indians had named him Boiling Water), who had taken up land in Virginia, and all this, together with his high rank and wide jurisdiction, would have attracted the younger men. We shall see more of him later.

Williamsburg, on May 6, 1776, was host to the Virginia Convention which on May 15 passed the historic resolution that "the Delegates appointed to represent the Colony in General Congress be instructed to propose to that respectable body to declare the United Colonies free and independent States, . . ." The people of Virginia regarded this resolution as an actual declaration of independence,[24] and copies of it were scattered throughout the colony and read from the mountains to the sea. In Williamsburg the British flag on the Capitol was struck, and the Continental Union flag run up in its place. Troops marched on the Duke of Gloucester Street, and salutes were fired with artillery and small arms. In the Raleigh Tavern toasts were drunk to the Congress of the United States, to George Washington (himself a notable drinker of toasts in the Raleigh Tavern), and to the Continental Army.[25]

The same convention, on June 12, approved a Bill of Rights. On June 29 it adopted "the first constitution of a free and independent State," and elected Patrick Henry the first governor of that state. On July 5, 1776, the Convention (not yet informed of the historic act of July 4) adjourned, to meet as the first House of Delegates under the new Constitution on the first Monday of the following October.[26]

"Yesterday," declared the *Virginia Gazette* on July 26, "agreeable to an order of the Hon. Privy Council, the Declaration of Independence was solemnly proclaimed at the Capitol, the Courthouse, and the Palace, amidst the acclamations of the people, accompanied by firing of cannon and musketry, the several regiments of continental troops having been paraded on that solemnity."

There were no boys now in the classrooms and corridors of William and Mary. Loyalist professors and students had departed in haste,

JAMES MONROE

and the patriots were about their country's business. It had become clear that the only career left for a young Virginian with red blood in his veins was the bearing of arms in the cause of his country's liberty. And Lieutenant James Monroe, like the rest of them, was ready to go.

WILLIAM AND MARY COLLEGE, WILLIAMSBURG

These buildings—the Sir Christopher Wrenn Building in the center, Brafferton Hall (for Indian students) on the left, and the President's House on the right—formed William and Mary College when Monroe matriculated there in the fall of 1774. The Botetourt Statue, seen dimly in this old engraving, was moved to William and Mary from its original position in front of the Capitol after it had been knocked from its pedestal during the Revolution.

Brown Brothers

WASHINGTON AND LAFAYETTE AT VALLEY FORGE

By the time the nineteen-year-old Monroe reached Valley Forge, he had retreated with Washington's army through New Jersey, had crossed the Delaware, had been wounded at Trenton, had fought at the Brandywine and at Germantown, and had been promoted to major. He spent the Valley Forge winter as aide to Lord Stirling, and at Valley Forge he knew such men as Washington, Lafayette, Hamilton, Wayne, Marshall, and Von Steuben. From an engraving after a painting by W. H. Powell.

Brown Brothers

THE BATTLE OF MONMOUTH

In this engagement Monroe, in the early morning hours of Sunday, June 28, 1778, acted as a scout for Washington; and later, in the thick of the battle, he took over as Stirling's adjutant general. From an engraving after a painting by A. Chappel.

L. C. Handy Studios

STAGE FROM BALTIMORE TO WASHINGTON

Monroe was an inveterate traveller when stage, packet, and horseback were the only means of conveyance. As a member of Congress he made innumerable trips up and down the eastern seaboard between northern cities and his Virginia home, and he made two trips to the Indian country, going west by the Great Lakes, thence south to the Ohio, and back to Richmond "through the wilderness." As President he spent several months touring New England and the South. When Mrs. Monroe accompanied him, he usually traveled in his own carriage. From the original lithograph.

❧ 3 ❦

James Monroe Crosses the Delaware

IN AUGUST, 1776, First Lieutenant James Monroe, now eighteen, left Williamsburg with his regiment, the Third Virginia Infantry. With other regiments it had been ordered north by the Continental Congress to enable Washington to carry out the Congress's instructions to hold the line in New York after the defeat on Long Island. Washington's position in New York was desperate. He himself believed it untenable.[1] The month before, during the first week of July, the Brothers Howe had appeared off Sandy Hook—Sir William down from Nova Scotia, where he had been waiting since his flight from Boston, and Lord Richard just in from England, convoying the first of his transports loaded with Hessian grenadiers and a British regiment. They were now prepared to execute the plan of their ministerial strategists to cut off New England from the rest of the colonies by taking New York and holding the line of the Hudson.

As the big British convoy sailed up the Narrows, New York braced itself behind its bristling defenses, but for a month the British made no attempt to attack. The huge convoy landed on Staten Island and the troops went into camp. When the rest of Lord Howe's transports were in and when Lord Clinton, returning from his Charleston expedition, joined them on August 1, they numbered around thirty thousand men, well trained and well equipped.[1-a]

Washington had been preparing for them since April. He had fortified Brooklyn Heights on Long Island, overlooking New York City, and had strengthened the entrenchments below the Heights. To oppose Howe's thirty thousand disciplined troops, he had some sixteen thousand poorly equipped and untrained men. And he had no control of the waters around New York. The result of the battle of Long Island on August 27, therefore, was easy to predict—defeat for the Americans. But, although defeated, Washington still held Brooklyn Heights, and Howe took time out to prepare a siege before attacking and this gave Washington a chance. On the night of the 29th, favored by an unusually heavy fog, he directed a masterly retreat across the river to Manhattan Island and thus escaped Howe for the moment.[2]

But on September 7, with the British on Long Island preparing to cross the East River to take New York, Washington realized that he could not hold the city against their combined sea and land forces. He therefore on September 12 planned to withdraw northward up Manhattan Island to Harlem Heights.[3] He had already begun to transfer his wounded men and stores, when, on Sunday, September 15, the British crossed the river and landed at Kip's Bay (now at the foot of East 34th Street). The heavy fire from the enemy frigates caused sheer panic among Washington's inexperienced troops, and although he tried, in bitter anger, to rally them for a brief delaying action, the rout was complete. As night fell, after that long, intensely hot Sunday, the weary runaway troops slept in the safety of Harlem Heights.[4]

It was at this point that James Monroe joined Washington's army. For the better part of a month the Third Virginia Regiment, under the command of Colonel George Weedon, of Fredericksburg,[5] had been making its way northward in the summer heat, over back roads and through sparsely settled country. Lieutenant James Monroe marched in the Seventh Company under the immediate command of Captain William Washington, kinsman of the General.[6] In the same regiment were Lieutenant Colonel Thomas Marshall and First Lieutenant John Marshall.[7] These Virginia troops were seasoned men. Some of them had already fought against the British at Great Bridge and elsewhere along the Chesapeake. They had all gone through months of drilling at Williamsburg as militia or minute men before joining the Continental Line. They were experienced woodsmen and could ride and shoot and live off the country on their long trek northward. They were probably pretty fit, although very tired, when

James Monroe Crosses the Delaware

they finally joined Washington's battered forces on September 15.[8]

The next morning they heard an exultant peal of bugles ring out from the British camp on the rocky heights of what is now the northern end of Central Park, sounding insolently the fox-hunters' "Fox in sight and on the run!" Washington, a fox-hunter, as were many of his men, was not slow to understand the insult. A healthy wave of anger stirred the American camp. Washington, meantime, had sent out a reconnoitering party of one hundred twenty men under Knowlton, to feel out the British positions. This party stirred up a British force of three hundred men and Washington decided to cut them off. This manoeuver was unsuccessful, but in the ensuing skirmish, since known as the battle of Harlem Heights, Howe's attack on the American center was repulsed and Howe was driven back with heavy loss.[9] As he was preparing to attack in force, Washington withdrew. There was no pursuit. A detachment of Monroe's regiment fought in this engagement,[10] and he may or may not have seen action; but at any rate he was now in the front lines and within reach of the enemy's fire.

Monroe's first three weeks with Washington's army saw no further skirmishes with the enemy. Washington was engaged in strengthening his position at Harlem Heights, and the British were settling themselves snugly into New York. Two dramatic incidents colored, for Monroe as for others, the period of waiting. Nathan Hale, sent by Washington to spy out the British positions, was caught and executed in New York, and on the day of his execution a great fire broke out in the city. Driven by high winds, it consumed four or five hundred buildings in a devastating conflagration.

The first week in October, the British began to move. They sent two frigates up the Hudson to cut off Washington's supplies from the back country, and troops marched northward to threaten the rear of the American position. Washington was thus forced to withdraw from Harlem Heights to New Rochelle, but he left a force to hold Fort Washington, which commanded New York.[10-a] Again pursued by Howe, the Americans withdrew to White Plains, where the British attacked on October 25. Monroe fought in this brief, bloody battle, where the British loss was so heavy and Washington's new position at Northcastle so strong that Howe retreated southward to New York. But he captured Fort Washington on his way. Less than

[21]

a week later, Fort Lee, on the west bank of the Hudson, was evacuated by General Greene, just ahead of the entering British troops.[11]

Washington now moved the major portion of his army, including Monroe's regiment, across the Hudson and encamped near Hackensack, New Jersey. He sent out repeated calls for reinforcements, but received none. On November 10 he ordered Major General Charles Lee, still in command of the rear guard at White Plains, east of the Hudson, to join him in New Jersey, but Lee unaccountably delayed. It was now late in November and bitterly cold. Enlistments were expiring, and men were deserting. Hunger and cold stalked in the camps. Monroe was seeing war.

Thus began the winter retreat across New Jersey. Most of the men were ill-fed and poorly clothed. Treachery and incompetence marched with them across the desolate country. And now the British were following close. Washington was barely out of Hackensack when the British appeared on the east bank of the Hackensack River. Washington's rear guard burned the bridge to keep them from crossing.

Pausing when he could to raise additional troops—and invariably failing—Washington retreated to Newark, where he halted his sadly diminished army to care for the sick and to seek reinlistments. On November 22 he left Newark, and, as he left, the advance guard of the enemy marched in. His next stop was to be Brunswick, on the Raritan River. Brigadier General Lord Stirling had been sent on in advance with a small body of troops to guard against a possible British landing at Brunswick or Amboy. In Lord Stirling's brigade was the Third Virginia Regiment,[12] and Monroe may well have been in this advance guard.

The desertions continued, and again Washington begged General Charles Lee to join him before it was too late, but that picturesque soldier of fortune, for reasons best known to himself, stayed where he was. As the diminishing American troops made their slow and difficult way across New Jersey with the British at their heels, Washington somehow managed, at every turn, to make the British think he was stronger than he was, and they hesitated to attack without the reinforcements momentarily expected to land on the Jersey coast.

Washington at last realized that he could expect no aid, and he

James Monroe Crosses the Delaware

made his last desperate plan to save his troops and to gain time. From Brunswick, on December 1, he ordered that all boats on the Delaware River should be collected and secured opposite Trenton. Then, as the British approached the Raritan River to cross by the bridge into Brunswick, the American army partly destroyed the bridge and retreated toward Princeton, passed through it, and pushed on to Trenton.

But the British, as usual, did not follow immediately, and Washington ordered two brigades under Lord Stirling (including Monroe's regiment), to return to Princeton to watch the enemy and to cover the removal of stores and baggage to the west bank of the Delaware. Within a week, Washington's entire army was concentrated in Trenton, and he had time to gather more boats, especially the large Durham freight boats, which could carry whole companies of men. He also accumulated provisions on the west bank of the Delaware. At last his matériel was safely across the river, but his men were still on the east bank.

How long would Washington remain in Trenton with his army before taking it to safety? The situation was tense. The British were known to be approaching in several columns, and still Washington waited. Colonel George Weedon, who commanded Monroe's regiment, wrote a friend in Fredericksburg that "General Howe had a mortgage on the rebel army for some time, but had not yet foreclosed it." [13]

At last Washington gave the order, and during the afternoon and night of December 7 and the early morning of December 8 the troops were transferred across the river. They were barely landed when the Hessian grenadiers entered Trenton with great pomp and circumstance—flags flying and music playing. But not a boat could they find to carry them over the river. Again Washington had escaped for the moment.

In the past three weeks Monroe had taken part in the remarkable retreat of a ragged, barefoot little army. They had gone through hostile country, and they had suffered greatly from hunger and cold. Thomas Paine, who was with them, said, "With a handful of men, we sustained an orderly retreat for nearly a hundred miles, brought off our ammunition, all our fieldpieces, the greatest part of our stores, and had four rivers to pass. None can say that our retreat was precipitate, for we were three weeks in performing it, that the country might have time to come."[14]

Colonel Johann Gottlieb Rall, commanding the Hessians across the river in Trenton, was, as Trevelyan calls him, "a brave, proud, stupid man." Through the reports of spies, including the famous Honeyman, Washington was aware that the Hessian general was averse to winter fighting. Rall had given out that he was waiting for "a bridge of ice to cross to the Pennsylvania side," and so take Philadelphia. Meanwhile he made plans to fortify the site of a probable attack from across the river, but put it off from day to day. Urged by his officers to dig the proposed entrenchments, he declared finally that "the rebels were such a miserable lot" that they did not merit such precautions and could be dealt with suitably with bayonets.[15] With blind confidence in the superiority of his trained troops over the despised "farmers," he went ahead with plans for a Christmas celebration that should enhance the German reputation for making Christmas cheer. When the ice formed on the river, he would cross over and wind up this pitiful affair in short order.

But Washington was making other plans. While the Hessians were enjoying themselves in their comfortable quarters in Trenton, he was skillfully marshalling his meagre forces on the west bank of the Delaware. Among the officers he trusted were Greene, Mercer, Stirling, St. Clair, Knox, Hand, Monroe,[16] Stephen, Hamilton, and Sullivan, recently down from New York with the remnant of Charles Lee's troops, that recalcitrant general being currently in the hands of the British.

It was clear to all now that, with the enemy at Trenton, Philadelphia was seriously threatened, and the population there was thrown into panic with fears of a royalist uprising. Washington placed Major General Israel Putnam in command of the city with orders to defend it at all costs. Congress, now sitting in Philadelphia, had a change of heart, with the British drawing near, and began to heed Washington's reiterated pleas for a larger and more stable army. But on December 11 they were so despairing of the American cause that they decreed a day of fasting and humiliation and two days later they left Philadelphia for Baltimore.

Washington, alert to every possibility, kept patrols out scouting the British movements, picking up all boats on the river and all lumber

James Monroe Crosses the Delaware

that could be made into boats. To guard the Delaware fords he sent four brigades up the river under Stirling, Mercer, Stephen, and De Fermoy. Stirling was quartered at the home of Robert Thompson, whose mill was commandeered to grind flour for the soldiers. Captain William Washington and Lieutenant James Monroe were quartered at the house of William Neely, in Solebury.[17]

Washington's army was now little more than a remnant. It was mid-December and the men still lacked clothing and food. Many of them were barefoot, although the ground was frozen and often snow-covered. The region was strongly royalist, or, in the Quaker communities, pacifist. When pleas were made for clothing and food for the soldiers, they went unheeded; if such things as blankets were furnished, an exorbitant price was charged for them. Calls were still being sent out for reinforcements, but they met with little response. Meanwhile, British soldiers and Hessian grenadiers, supremely confident, sat in their warm quarters in Trenton. It was, they thought, only a question of time. So, too, thought many of the patriots.

We have no way of knowing what young James Monroe thought, as he scouted along the Delaware with other men of Lord Stirling's brigade, guarding the fords, looking for boats, riding on scouting missions east of the Delaware, perhaps even creeping up close to Trenton to see what the enemy was up to. He was not yet nineteen, and a good deal of the work he was called upon to do must have reminded him of his boyhood activities along the Potomac and the Rappahannock and in the forests of Westmoreland County. He may have had enough of a boy's confidence in his fellow Virginian as commander-in-chief not to have worried greatly about the outcome. Or he may have had a boy's absorption in the deed of the moment.

On December 18 Washington wrote to his brother, "You can have no idea of the perplexity of my situation. No man, I believe, ever had a greater choice of difficulties, and less means to extricate himself from them. However, under a full persuasion of the justice of our cause, I cannot entertain an idea that it will finally sink...."[18]

Sometime during this period Washington made his "choice of difficulties." He had already decided to do what his good friend Colonel Joseph Reed recommended when he wrote on December 22,

"We are all of the opinion, my dear General, that something must be attempted to revive our expiring credit, . . . Will it not be possible . . . for your troops . . . to make a diversion, or something more, at or about Trenton? . . . Our affairs are hastening fast to ruin if we do not retrieve them by some happy event."[19]

Washington replied on the 23rd: "Christmas-day, at night, one hour before day, is the time fixed upon for our attempt on Trenton. For Heaven's sake keep this to yourself. . . . Necessity, dire necessity will, nay must, justify an attempt. . . . I have now ample testimony of their intentions to attack Philadelphia, so soon as the ice will afford the means of conveyance."[20]

Washington had one asset which today would be called propaganda but which on the wintry bank of the Delaware in 1776 had no opprobrious label. Among the aides of General Nathanael Greene was Thomas Paine, who, during the intervals of his military duties, wrote and published pamphlets in picturesque, emotion-charged language. His latest utterance had been written in camp on the Delaware and was printed in a Philadelphia paper on December 19.[21] Before the march on Trenton, Washington ordered it read at the head of each regiment.[22] Half-starved, half-clothed, swept by cold winter winds, the men who listened so intently were no "summer soldiers," and they knew what Paine was talking about. "These are the times that try men's souls. [*Who knows it better than we?*] The summer soldier and the sunshine patriot will, in this crisis, shrink from the service of his country, but he that stands it now [*We will stand!*] deserves the love and thanks of man and woman. Tyranny, like hell, is not easily conquered . . . it would be strange indeed if so celestial an article as Freedom should not be highly rated. . . ."

Washington divided his troops into three separate corps and took command of one himself. As it turned out, his was the only corps that crossed the river on Christmas night. The others were blocked by large masses of floating ice. The Delaware had been clear of ice on December 23 and 24, but on the 25th it was filled with floating cakes which had formed in the intense cold of December 20 in the upper branches of the river and which were now being carried down on the swift current.[23]

At six o'clock in the afternoon of Christmas Day, immediately after parade, Washington's corps marched to the river to embark

James Monroe Crosses the Delaware

at McKonkey's Ferry, where boats had been assembled. The men were provided with three days' cooked rations, and each carried forty rounds of ammunition.²⁴ It had been snowing since eleven in the morning, and the barefoot men left bloody marks on the snow as they went down to the river. Major James Wilkinson, who had been sent to Philadelphia, returned to camp after the men had left and said that he could trace their march to the river by their bloody footprints in the newly-fallen snow.

Washington, on horseback, watched the boats push off into the dark river. The sharp, jagged ice struck the boats repeatedly, and only the skill of the Marblehead fishermen who formed one of the regiments enabled the heavily loaded boats to cross. A man was stationed in the bow of each boat with a boat-hook to keep off the ice, and the crash of the ice-cakes and the roar of wind and water almost drowned out the commands. Fortunately, the loud, booming voice of General Knox, who repeated Washington's orders, could be heard above the stormy tumult.²⁵

As soon as Stephen's brigade was across, and had thrown a guard around the landing place, Washington dismounted and with his staff crossed the river. When he reached the Jersey side, he stood "calm and collected but very determined" and superintended the landing of the troops. It took nine weary hours to ferry them over. Part of the time, it is said, Washington sat on an old empty beehive, his cloak wrapped around him, his eyes, watchful and sombre, on the hail-swept river.

James Monroe was among the first to cross. There is no famous painting of him in the act, and it is not known that he ever recorded his impressions of the event, but for him, as for all, it was a strange and grim experience. Immediately upon landing, he, with Captain William Washington's company, had been ordered to proceed at once to the Pennington Road to guard it until the troops should come up. On this duty he spent the whole of a bitterly cold and stormy night. We have his own account of one incident. He said, "After crossing the river, I was sent with my command (a piece of artillery) to the intersection of the Pennytown (now Pennington) and Maiden Head (now Lawrenceville) roads, with strict orders to let no one pass until I was ordered forward. Whilst occupying the position, the resident of a dwelling, some distance up the lane, had his attention directed to some unusual commotion by the barking of dogs. He came out in the dark to learn the cause, and encountered my command, and supposing we were from the British camp ordered us off. He was violent and determined in his manner and very profane, and wanted to know what we were doing there such a stormy night. I advised him to go to his home and be quiet or I would arrest him. When he discovered that we were American soldiers, he insisted that we should go to his house, and not stay out in the storm, and he would give us something to eat. I told him my orders were strict and we could not leave, when he returned to the house and brought us some victuals. He said to me, 'I know something is to be done, and I am going with you. I am a doctor, and I may help some poor fellow.' When orders came for us to hasten to Trenton, the doctor went with me."[26]

At three o'clock in the morning of the 26th, all the men were over, and the boats went back for the artillery. They were three hours behind schedule. The storm had changed to sleet, and the wind was cutting like a knife, as the last cannon was being loaded.[27]

Meantime, the Hessian grenadiers, full of food and drink, were sleeping the sleep of the supremely confident. They had had a very merry Christmas, and in the evening Colonel Rall and his officers had dined at the home of Abraham Hunt, a wealthy merchant of Trenton, where they had a highly convivial time and drank and played cards well into the night. Rall had not been without various and emphatic warnings, but he ignored them all. In fact, in his pocket after his death was found the unopened note brought to him at Mr. Hunt's during Christmas night by a Bucks County Tory, who had risked his life to warn the Hessians of possible attack.[28]

At four o'clock on the morning of the 26th, Washington's men, now all across the Delaware, gathered at Bear Tavern, a mile from the river, to start their march on Trenton. "Victory or Death!" was the watchword, and the men were warned to be profoundly quiet—not hard after their sleepless night and in the smothering snow. It was still dark, and icy blasts swept over the weary lines, but the wind was now mainly at their backs.

Soon the troops were separated into two columns. Sullivan's took the lower river road, and Washington went with Greene's column along the upper road from Pennington to Trenton. With it marched

James Monroe Crosses the Delaware

young Alexander Hamilton, captain of artillery, with his battery.[29] Lord Stirling's brigade was in this division, and it was soon joined by Captain Washington and Lieutenant Monroe, who now rejoined the troops after their all-night guard duty on the Pennington road.

"It was broad daylight," wrote one of Washington's staff officers, "when we came to a house where a man was chopping wood. He was very much surprised when he saw us. 'Can you tell me where the Hessian picket is?' Washington asked. The man hesitated, but I said, 'You need not be frightened. It is General Washington who asks the question.' His face brightened and he pointed toward the house of Mr. Howell."[30]

A Hessian came out of the house and yelled to his fellows, who rushed out with guns. They fired, but the bullets went high. The picket guard, now aroused, tried to form and fire, but some broke and ran toward the town.

Then Washington heard the boom of a cannon from the river road and knew that Sullivan was approaching. Captain Forrest unlimbered his guns, and Washington gave the order to advance on the junction of King and Queen streets in the heart of Trenton. Lord Stirling's brigade was now at the head of King Street. Colonel Weedon's regiment (the Third Virginia) was in the advance. Captain William Washington of that regiment and his lieutenant James Monroe, seeing the enemy mobilizing for action, led their men in a charge down the street and took the two brass three-pounder guns of the Rall regiment.

Of this lightning-quick performance General Wilkinson said in his memoirs, "These particular acts of gallantry have never been noticed, and yet could not have been too highly appreciated, for if the enemy had got his artillery into operation in a narrow street, it might have checked our movement and given him time to reflect and reform."[31]

In this brilliant and effective dash, both officers were badly wounded, Captain Washington injured in both hands and James Monroe hit in the shoulder by a ball, which cut an artery. It seems clear that the young lieutenant would have bled to death on the spot if the doctor who had challenged him in the early morning hours had not been at hand, to take up the artery, as Monroe phrased it.[32]

Rall appeared presently and tried to rally his badly confused forces, but he was fatally wounded and the Hessians were forced to surrender. If all three of Washington's corps could have crossed the river as planned, they might well have driven the British out of New Jersey. Even as it was, Washington's victory at Trenton was complete. It turned the trick of revitalizing the cause and rousing the fainting spirit of the patriots. In the words of a staff officer who saw the whole thing, Washington had "pounced upon the Hessians like an eagle upon a hen. . . . If he does nothing more he will live in history as a great military commander."[33] Tradition says that when Washington's men charged into Trenton they yelled, "These are the times that try men's souls!"

That night Washington recrossed the Delaware at McKonkey's Ferry, where the boats awaited him, and before night his troops were safely landed on the western side. Monroe later wrote that after his captain was wounded, "the command fell on me and soon after, I was shot through by a ball which grazed my breast. I was carried by two or three soldiers, for I fell, to the room where Captain Washington was under the care of two surgeons by whom my wound was also dressed. I was removed that night to Mr. Coryell's where I remained ten days, kindly treated, when I was removed to Mr. Wynkoop's where I remained for nine weeks and was attended by a physician from Newtown, three miles distant."[34]

Monroe was still four months short of his nineteenth birthday, but already he had "drunk delight of battle" with his peers, and as he lay recovering from his wound in the comfortable home of the Pennsylvania judge, he confidently looked forward to more of it.

❧ 4 ❧

"A Brave, Active, and Sensible Officer"

WHILE WASHINGTON struck and pierced the enemy lines at Princeton early in January, 1777, and then went into winter camp at Morristown, where he could threaten the British positions and keep the redcoats from overrunning New Jersey, young Monroe lay *hors de combat* in the home of Judge Wyncoop, by all accounts a pleasant place to be. He stayed there for over two months,[1] and if tradition can be trusted he fell in love with Christine Wyncoop, a daughter of the house, who helped to care for the young Virginian in his illness. But she was already pledged to another, and so James Monroe's first romance fell through.[2]

When he left the Wyncoop home, he was a captain without a company. Washington had rewarded him for his bravery at Trenton by promoting him to a captaincy in one of the companies expected to be formed in the near future.[3] But the difficulty of getting enlistments, which darkens all accounts of the war at this time, was too great, and no company for the young captain was forthcoming.

When Monroe returned to Washington's headquarters in August, he took with him a letter written by his uncle, Judge Joseph Jones, to General Washington. This letter, dated August 11, 1777, shows that when Monroe left Judge Wyncoop's, he went to Virginia and tried to help in the raising of troops. Judge Jones writes, "Captain Monroe leaving town this evening I cannot avoid informing you by him that as far as his conduct has fallen under my observation, and I have not been inattentive to it, he has been diligent in endeavoring to raise men; but such is the present disposition of the people in Virginia, neither Capt. Monroe or any other officer preserving the character a Gent'm ought to support can recruit men. Some men have indeed been raised, but by methods I could not recommend, and I should be sorry he should practice." Judge Jones then laments "the high bounty given by the militia exempts," which had disorganized the whole business of replacement, and ends with the suggestion, "I wish Cap'n. Monroe could have made up his company on his own account, as well as that of the public. . . ."[4]

But although he had failed to raise a company, Monroe had no intention of remaining on the sidelines, and soon he was acting as volunteer "additional aide" to Lord Stirling, although by so doing he lost his rank in the Continental line and became again plain James Monroe, Esquire.

Monroe had known Lord Stirling as commander of the brigade containing his own regiment, the Third Virginia, all the way from Harlem Heights to Trenton. After Trenton, Stirling had been promoted from brigadier general to major general, as a reward for his distinguished services in taking the Hessian stronghold. Monroe's close association with him as aide for a year or more gives him importance in this story. His Lordship was a paradox of the times, a claimant to a peerage fighting in the army of the young Republic. The first Earl of Stirling, of Scotland, had been given an immense grant of land in North America. Lord Stirling's father, a descendant of this first earl, had emigrated to America after the Rebellion of 1715 and had attained professional and political prominence in New York and New Jersey. Lord Stirling himself was born in New York City. He fought in the French and Indian War, spent some time abroad, but returned ultimately to marry the sister of Governor William Livingston of New Jersey and to win wealth and distinction. Although claiming the title of sixth Earl of Stirling, he identified himself entirely with America and was an ardent supporter of the patriot cause. Washington trusted him both as friend and as soldier, and early in the war put him in charge of preparing the defenses of the New York area. Captured, after a gallant defense, in the battle of Long Island, he was quickly exchanged and accompanied Washington on the retreat through New Jersey. In New Jersey he was in his own bailiwick, for he owned a handsome estate at Baskenridge,

"A Brave, Active, and Sensible Officer"

not far from Morristown, where, before the outbreak of the war, he interested himself in iron mining, grape culture, and hemp raising, with a view to demonstrating these projects as suitable for enriching America.[5] He was a handsome, soldierly, magnetic man around fifty years old when Monroe joined his staff, which, to judge from the date of Judge Jones's letter, must have been in the latter part of August, 1777, shortly before the battle of the Brandywine.

On August 25 Sir William Howe, sailing up Chesapeake Bay, landed his troops at Elkton and started overland for Philadelphia. Washington marched to intercept him, and took up his position along Brandywine Creek. In this engagement, fought on September 11, Monroe took part. Stirling's division was stationed on the right wing, commanded by Sullivan. Howe, by a bold manoeuver, separated his army into two columns, and, while the strong American center was kept occupied by Lieutenant General Knyphausen's men, Lord Cornwallis, in a wide turning movement, marched eighteen miles to outflank the American right. Stirling had come up only in time to plant his cannon and draw up his line of battle before the British column fell upon him. He made a stout fight of it even when driven back and partially surrounded. Eventually he was swept with the tide of retreat back to Birmingham Church, where Monroe ministered to the wounded Lafayette and began a friendship which was to last as long as these two men lived. Monroe's old regiment, the Third Virginia, was conspicuous in this battle and was commanded by Colonel Thomas Marshall, the father of Monroe's schoolboy friend.[6]

On September 26 the British marched into Philadelphia. This was where John Adams wanted them to be. He had written his wife from Philadelphia on August 30, 1777, "For my own part I feel a secret wish that they might get into this city, because I think it more for our interest that they should be cooped up here than that they should run away again to New York."[7] The British headquarters and some troops were now in Philadelphia, but the greater part of the army was encamped at Germantown, about six miles from the city. The enemy forces were thus divided, and Washington decided to strike at Germantown. Here, too, Monroe was actively engaged. Washington planned a night march and a surprise attack on October 4 along each of the four roads leading into Germantown. But something went wrong, and with dawn came a heavy fog which confused the attacking forces. Some of the hottest fighting took place around the Chew House, a massive stone and brick structure in which a party of British had entrenched themselves. Around this building Stirling threw his reserve division, which attempted to dislodge the enemy, and Monroe, as aide-de-camp, saw and took part in that attempt. Under his eyes, perhaps, the young Virginian, Lieutenant Matthew Smith, may have fallen, shot down as he approached the British under a flag of truce. He may have seen the courageous officer who seized an armful of straw and a torch and succeeded in actually reaching the hostile walls before he was shot. He may have made out the figure of the Chevalier du Plessis as he clambered through a window and then miraculously escaped from the beleaguered redcoats. And he may have seen the failure of Colonel John Laurens to storm the principal entrance with his New Jersey troops, and of the light American artillery to batter down the walls.[8]

Thomas Paine gave a vivid account of the retreat that followed the failure at Germantown. Paine had left Philadelphia on September 21, and was on his way to Washington's camp when he found himself involved with the retreating American army. He described the scene in a letter to Benjamin Franklin in Paris: "Nobody hurried themselves. Every one marched his own pace. The Enemy kept a civil distance behind, sending every now and then a Shot after us, and receiving the same from us. That part of the Army which I was with collected and formed on the Hill on the side of the road near White Marsh Church; the Enemy came within three quarters of a mile and halted. . . . The Army had marched the preceding night 14 miles and having full 20 to march back were exceedingly fatigued. They appeared to me to be only sensible of a disappointment, not a defeat, and to be more displeased at their retreating from German Town than anxious to get to their rendezvous. . . . I breakfasted next morning at Genl. W. Quarters, who was at the same loss with every other to account for the accidents of the day. I remember his expressing his Surprise by saying that at the time he supposed every thing secure, and was about giving orders for the Army to proceed down to Philadelphia; that he most unexpectedly saw a Part (I think of the Artillery) hastily retreating. This partial retreat was, I believe, misunderstood, and soon followed by others. The fog was frequently very thick, the Troops young and unused to breaking and rallying,

JAMES MONROE

Bust by Margaret Cresson, sculptor. Now in the Monroe Law Office, Fredericksburg, Virginia.

Courtesy of Mrs. Gouverneur Hoes

MRS. JAMES MONROE

Formerly Elizabeth Kortright, of New York. From a miniature painted in Paris by Sené in 1794, while Monroe was Minister to France.

Courtesy of Mr. Laurence Gouverneur Hoes

MONROE'S LAW OFFICE IN FREDERICKSBURG, VIRGINIA

After Monroe's marriage in New York and at the end of his term in Congress, he returned to Virginia and settled in Fredericksburg, where he began the practice of law. His law office is now a national shrine.

Courtesy of Mr. Laurence Gouverneur Hoes

THE DESK ON WHICH THE MONROE DOCTRINE WAS SIGNED

Monroe bought this desk in France in 1794, while he was Minister there. It is now in the James Monroe Law Office in Fredericksburg, Virginia. Photograph taken while desk was on exhibition in the Library of Congress in 1946.

"A Brave, Active, and Sensible Officer"

and our men rendered suspicious to each other, many of them being in Red."[9]

After the battle Washington withdrew to White Marsh, about fifteen miles from Philadelphia, from which he could protect his hospitals and stores in Bethlehem and Reading. For the next few weeks the British and the Americans fought for the control of the Delaware, without which Howe could not be at ease in Philadelphia. Washington had already fortified the river to prevent the advance of the British up the broad estuary. Three rows of chevaux-de-frise (up-ended stakes of heavy timber strengthened and tipped with iron) had been sunk across the channel, and two forts had been built, Fort Mifflin on Mud Island and Fort Mercer on the high bluff called Red Bank. In an attempt to hold these forts, picked officers and men gave their lives, but on November 15, Fort Mifflin fell under the weeklong British bombardment from ships below and batteries above, and on November 18 Fort Mercer was evacuated. Washington, meanwhile, had strengthened his position at White Marsh, where he still hoped to be joined by the victorious Gates from the North. Howe tried to lure Washington from the security of White Marsh, but after three unsuccessful feints he withdrew into Philadelphia and settled down for the winter.[10]

Monroe's name does not appear in the accounts of the desperate defense of the river forts, but two days after the evacuation of Fort Mercer, Washington, at White Marsh on November 20, promoted him from additional aide to Lord Stirling, with no military rank, to official aide-de-camp with the rank of major.[11] Lord Stirling's headquarters were now at Reading, Pennsylvania,[12] up the Schuylkill River from Valley Forge, and Major James Monroe was a member of his official family there.

It was at Reading and to a member of Stirling's staff that James Wilkinson, aide-de-camp to General Horatio Gates, babbled while "under the influence of Monogahela whiskey" the fateful words said to have been written to Gates by Major General Thomas Conway, which brought out into the open the underground opposition to Washington: "Heaven has been determined to save your country, or a weak general and bad counsellors would have ruined it." Wilkinson, on his way from General Gates's headquarters to Congress now sitting in York, Pennsylvania, with news of Gates's victory at Saratoga on October 17, stopped over in Reading. At table with Stirling's staff after dinner, he repeated the explosive gossip which startled Stirling's aides into shocked sobriety. Major McWilliams, to whom the remark was made, reported it at once to Stirling, who communicated it to Washington. The Commander-in-Chief then wrote Conway "the shortest letter he ever wrote" merely repeating what had come to him.[13]

Monroe could not have been unaware of the whole dirty intrigue carried on by what has since been known as the Conway Cabal, which had ramifications in Congress and plotted to place Gates above Washington. With the publicity resulting from the Conway affair, the whole thing blew up. Congress had been a strong supporter of the popular Irishman Conway and had appointed him inspector general of the army, but in April, when Conway, thinking himself unjustly treated, resigned, Congress surprised him by accepting the resignation. In May, Congress, as if to cleanse the air of intrigue and treachery before the beginning of the spring campaign, ordered Washington at Valley Forge to administer the oath of allegiance to all the officers of the army. The oath of Stirling, Monroe's chief, was administered by Washington on May 12, 1778,[14] and that of his aide-de-camp James Monroe was administered by Stirling on May 16.

Meantime, during the late fall and early winter of 1777 Monroe must have spent considerable time at his chief's headquarters in Reading. Lord Stirling was in frequent communication with Washington at White Marsh. Important decisions were being made concerning the disposition of the troops for the winter, and Monroe may well have carried confidential messages back and forth. From the all-too-few flashes which reveal the young officer in action, he seems to have excelled in scouting and in courier duty rather than in the secretarial work which burdened so heavily the military headquarters of the day. Little is known of the social life of Lord Stirling's official family at this time. Aaron Burr, in later years, said that Monroe's principal war service consisted in keeping his Lordship's tankard plentifully supplied with ale and listening to his long-winded stories.[16] But contemporary annals give no such impression of either Stirling or his young aide-de-camp. At Reading there were extensive iron works, and cannon were being manufactured there for the Revolutionary army.

"A Brave, Active, and Sensible Officer"

The town was also an important depot for military supplies, and Lord Stirling, a brilliant artillerist, was in his native element there, both in building up and protecting the military stores for the next campaign and in keeping a watchful eye upon the Delaware Valley to the north and east.

In late December Washington moved the American army to Valley Forge on the Schuylkill, only twenty miles away from the enemy snugly ensconsed in Philadelphia. With this move, the war entered upon a phase of hardship which has made the name Valley Forge synonymous with cold and hunger. On the steep slope of the hills rising bare and bleak above the river bank, the men felled trees and built rude huts. Until the huts were completed, they slept without coats or other covering, or sat up all night by fires, as Washington wrote the President of Congress in a letter of December 23, 1777.[17]

It was a severe winter, with heavy snows and storms of wind and sleet. The men were wretchedly clad. Their clothing was torn and tattered. There were very few blankets. Some men lacked shirts, others breeches, and some had so little covering that they were unable to appear at parade. Washington wrote a friend that the men could be tracked by their bloody footprints in the snow, and just before Christmas he wrote of "few men having more than one shirt, many only the moiety of one and some none at all. . . . We have a field-return this day no less than two thousand, eight hundred and ninety-eight men now in camp unfit for duty because they are barefoot and otherwise naked."

The food, what there was of it, was unspeakably bad, most often a "fire-cake" made of dirty, soggy dough warmed over smoky fires and washed down with polluted water. Meanwhile, wagon loads of provisions rolled into Philadelphia from the surrounding countryside. The British paid good prices in gold. Washington wrote bitterly explicit letters to Congress about the state of the troops, but that inexperienced body, greatly troubled as it was by both practical and ideological difficulties, seemed too involved in its own brand-new red tape to do anything about it.

In the crowded huts, tar, pitch, and powder had to be burned to counteract the noisome stench. One of the soldiers encamped in that frozen hell wrote, "Poor food—hard lodging—Cold Weather—

fatigue—Nasty Cloaths—nasty Cookery—Vomit half my time—Smoak'd out of my senses—the Devil's in it—I can't Endure it—Why are we sent here to starve and freeze. . . . Here comes a bowl of beef soup—full of burnt leaves and dirt, sickish enough to make a hector puke—away with it, Boys. . . ."[18]

Thomas Paine wrote to Franklin of the first days at Valley Forge: "I was there when the Army first began to build huts; they appeared to me like a family of Beavers; every one busy; some carrying Logs, others Mud, and the rest fastening them together. The whole was raised in a few days, and is a curious collection of buildings in the true rustic order."[19] In some cases the soldiers hitched themselves to wagons, because of the lack of horses, and so pulled loads of logs into position. Washington's headquarters were in the two-story stone house of Isaac Potts near the confluence of Valley Creek and the Schuylkill River.[20] Mrs. Washington was there for a time, and Washington's favorite secretary and aide-de-camp, Alexander Hamilton, also lived in the Potts house.[21]

There were great names among the men who wintered with Washington at Valley Forge. John Marshall, now Deputy Judge Advocate of the Army, was there, and his buoyant spirit lessened the gloom of the suffering camp.[22] General Anthony Wayne, who felt acutely the wretched condition of his men, begged Congress repeatedly to supply clothing for them and, when that body of "virtuous sages," as Henry Lee called them,[23] did nothing, gave money out of his own pocket to fill the need.[24] But, next to Washington, the most important man at Valley Forge was the German-American General, Frederick William, Baron von Steuben, sent to America by Beaumarchais, Franklin, and Silas Deane in Paris to train America's revolutionary army. When he reached this country and reported to Congress, he was at once sent to Valley Forge as inspector general to train the troops. He reached there on February 23, and with little knowledge of English, performed a miracle in the effective training of the ragged, undisciplined men. Everyone liked and trusted him, from Washington down, and the army that left Valley Forge in mid-June to fight at Monmouth was a testimonial to him as well as to the spring sunshine and the improved working of the quartermaster department under General Nathanael Greene.[25]

On April 23, Major General Charles Lee, the soldier of fortune

"A Brave, Active, and Sensible Officer"

whom Monroe had first seen in Williamsburg, arrived at Valley Forge. For fifteen months he had been in British hands. He was still very popular with Congress and with the public, and he was received at Valley Forge with an ovation. He left there immediately to report to the Congress at York, returned to Valley Forge for duty on May 20, and was given command of the First Division of the Army.[26]

This intransigent general, about whose bizarre figure dark clouds were beginning to gather, had, it will be remembered, refused to come to Washington's aid in the retreat through New Jersey and had dallied so long and so casually in getting to the Delaware that he had been captured by the British outside his headquarters at Baskenridge, under circumstances later regarded as suspicious. But in spite of his insubordination, Washington felt the need of him and had worked hard to get him exchanged.[27] The British were in Philadelphia. The winter was over. The American army, under Steuben's inspired training, was as good as it ever would be. It was time to go

The spring of 1778 had indeed brought a crisis in the affairs of the war. On March 13, France announced that she had formed an alliance with America, which put England and France at each other's throats. And early in June, England, looking for an exit, sent peace commissioners to America to capitalize upon the deplorable state of the country's financial and military affairs and the strong royalist sentiment which had been so conspicuous throughout the gay British winter in Philadelphia.[28]

But meantime Sir William Howe had been recalled at his own request from his Philadelphia command. Sir Henry Clinton took his place and immediately carried out the instructions given him to evacuate Philadelphia and hasten to New York to join the British forces there and help repel the approaching French fleet under Count d'Estaing. England's peace commissioners arrived while preparations for the evacuation of Philadelphia were under way.[29] Everything was in the greatest confusion, for the royalists in Philadelphia were afraid to stay and face their outraged countrymen, and refugees crowded the available shipping.

At eight o'clock on the evening of June 17, 1778, Clinton started to transport artillery and commissary stores over the Delaware at Cooper's Ferry. At three in the morning of June 18, the transports containing the British troops were ordered to push off for the New

JAMES MONROE

Jersey side. British craft, under Admiral Richard Howe, protected the line of transports. The British left Philadelphia very quietly, but toward the end very hastily, so that it was said that "they did not go away, they vanished."[30] By noon they were on their way northward.

At the crack of dawn, an American scouting party, headed by Captain Allen McLane, who had observed the enemy withdrawal, entered the city and captured some belated British officers and men. The news was at once dispatched by express rider to Washington at Valley Forge, and by eleven o'clock that morning the camp was vibrant with the hope of action.[31]

The decision to attack the British column on its way northward through New Jersey was immediate and Washington issued his orders. Major Benedict Arnold was to occupy Philadelphia and preserve order there. Scouts were sent out to observe the British column and bring in reports of their movements. Monroe did this sort of thing at Trenton, and he did it later at Monmouth. It is more than likely that he was thus engaged now. At any rate he was in the tense excitement of that June day which saw the end of the long winter's inaction.

The army at Valley Forge was ordered to march north to Coryell's Ferry on the Delaware, a few miles above Trenton, and there cross into New Jersey.

Clinton was marching with an immense baggage train of fifteen hundred wagons[32] and a swarm of camp followers including hundreds of women, who were such a nuisance that Clinton issued daily orders for their control without appreciable effect. This tremendous train of baggage and armament, which when fully on the march extended for more than eight miles, and Clinton's erroneous belief that the baggage was the Americans' main objective were later controlling factors at Monmouth.

The record of Monroe's part in the campaign which culminated at Monmouth is again a matter of brief, clear pictures—small parts in the larger action. As aide-de-camp to Lord Stirling, he was with the Fifth Division, commanded by his chief, composed largely of Virginia and Maryland troops. To follow him, one must follow Stirling.

When, on June 18, Washington ordered the army out of Valley

"A Brave, Active, and Sensible Officer"

Forge, two advance detachments went out that same afternoon. First marched Major General Charles Lee, with three brigades, leaving at three o'clock. Next went General Wayne's division, also with three brigades, leaving two hours later. Both detachments were ordered to cross the Delaware at Coryell's Ferry and camp on strong ground across the river in New Jersey.

The main army broke camp at Valley Forge early the next morning, Friday, June 19, and marched north under Washington's immediate command. Stirling's division (and, of course, Monroe) was with this main army and thus was not with the advance corps. This relative position was maintained throughout the action as will be seen later. The heavy rains, which were to be a feature of this dramatic week, impeded the march of all the divisions, and the main army did not get across the Delaware with its baggage until Monday the 22nd. On that day, Washington's headquarters were at Coryell's Ferry, and there he issued orders that Lee was to command the right wing and Stirling the left.[33] On Tuesday, the 23rd, the entire army was near the village of Hopewell, about eight miles from Princeton. Here the army rested through the 24th, cleaning firearms and cooking two days' extra rations. It was intensely hot, with heavy thunder showers.

On Thursday, June 25, the army marched ten miles to Kingston. From there Washington sent Wayne out with a thousand men to harass the British column. Lafayette, now in charge of all the advance corps, accompanied Wayne, and Alexander Hamilton, Washington's aide, went along to send back reports to his chief. It was at Kingston that Washington was presented with the superb white horse which fell at Monmouth—a gift from Lord Stirling's brother-in-law, Governor William Livingston of New Jersey.

On the evening of the 25th, Washington ordered a quick night march toward Monmouth, and the watchword that night was "Monmouth." The next morning they reached Cranbury, about ten miles on their way, but heavy rains and extreme heat prevented further advance. And now came the first hint of trouble from General Lee. He resented Lafayette's commanding the advance corps and asked Washington to be placed in command because of seniority. Washington, greatly troubled, made an adjustment to satisfy Lee's pride, without detaching Lafayette from the forces assigned to him. Lafayette generously accepted the change. But, with Lee in command,

JAMES MONROE

Washington had instrusted an important movement to a man who said that he did not believe it could be successful.

On Saturday, June 27, Washington marched from Cranbury to Englishtown, where Lee was encamped with the advance forces. At noon he instructed Lee to attack, (at his discretion), the British column the next morning. Accordingly, early on Sunday, June 28, the advance forces, under Lee, started across the rough, heavily wooded country, cut by ravines and swamps, toward Monmouth Court House, where the British were encamped.

It was in the early hours of that Sunday morning that Monroe appears briefly. During the hot and sultry night, Washington had been receiving reports of scouting parties, and at four o'clock in the early morning Major Monroe wrote him the following note:

"June 28, 1778

"Sir, Upon not receiving any answer to my first information and observing the enemy inclining toward your right I thought it advisable to hang as close on them as possible—I am at present within four hundred yrds. of their right—I have only about 70 men who are now fatigued much. I have taken three prisoners—If I had six horsemen I think If I co'd serve you in no other way I sho'd in the course of the night procure good intelligence w'h I wo'd as soon as possible convey you.

"I am Sir your most ob't Serv't

"Ja^s. Monroe.

"L^t. Col^o. Basset is with me and wishes the same.

"4 o'clock."[34]

It was at about four o'clock in the morning of the 28th that Clinton's forces withdrew from Monmouth Court House, except for a small covering party, later reinforced with more troops under Cornwallis when the severity of the American attack became apparent. It may have been a part of this withdrawal that Monroe observed and reported to Washington.

The story of General Lee and the men he commanded on that historic Sunday is a strange and confused one. The heat was intense— "96 degrees in the shade"—and the moisture from the heavy rains steamed up from the wet ground around the perspiring men. Mosquitoes tortured them unmercifully. Clinton, still believing that the

"A Brave, Active, and Sensible Officer"

impending American attack was mainly an attempt to capture the baggage train, had no thought of meeting the enemy except in rearguard action. Lee, apparently thinking the British too strong for him, and failing utterly to give clear commands to his subordinates, seemed content to do little except watch what was happening. The result was a confused, though unhurried, retreat, in which men dropped exhausted from the heat or wandered bewildered in the surrounding marshes and ravines. There is even some indication that Lee himself was affected by the intense heat,[35] as was Aaron Burr, who was said to have had "a slight sunstroke on the blistering field of Monmouth."[36]

Finally, in desperation, Lafayette began to send urgent messages to Washington, begging him to come at once, as did also Lieutenant-Colonel Laurens, Washington's aide. Washington was still at Englishtown bringing up the main army. He had no idea that everything was not going well with the advance contingents and could not believe that they were in retreat. He sent out two aides and followed immediately himself. Soon they began to meet the retreating troops, some barely able to walk in the oppressive heat and some suffering fearfully from thirst. When Washington saw Lee, his anger and scorn were scorching. An aide informed him that the British were pressing hard and would be up in about fifteen minutes. Washington took command and in a magnificent display of personal force and magnetism, he rallied the retreating troops, turned them around, and checked the British advance. For the moment, the men forgot the heat and their overpowering thirst, but Washington's beautiful white horse fell dead from heat and exhaustion, and Billy Lee, Washington's body servant, had to bring up the brown horse that had already served him well.

The main army now came up, with Stirling in command of the left wing, and Greene of the right. Lafayette was in command of the second line.

The British attacked Stirling's wing first, but were met by "the severest artillery fire ever heard in America." Washington himself rode up and down the lines, and General Steuben encouraged the men and with his familiar commands brought discipline to the hard-fighting ranks. The conflict was terrific for nearly an hour, and in the thick of it James Monroe appears. When Lieutenant Colonel Francis

JAMES MONROE

Barber, one of Stirling's aides, was badly wounded, Major James Monroe took his place and acted as Stirling's adjutant general during the rest of the engagement.[37]

Failing with Stirling's left wing, the British attacked the American right under General Greene. Cornwallis led this attack, but was repulsed by the remarkably accurate gunfire of the Continentals. They next tried to storm the American center, but there to meet them was Mad Anthony Wayne. Three times they came, but each time were driven back with heavy casualties.

It was now about quarter to five in the afternoon, and Washington prepared to pursue, but night fell before his men could cross the difficult terrain between the Americans and the British. So the weary soldiers slept on the field of battle, intending to attack in the morning. But that night the enemy slipped away in the dark. The battle of Monmouth was over.

General Charles Lee, deeply insulted by Washington's treatment of him at Monmouth, asked for and received a court-martial, at which Lord Stirling presided. There were twenty-six sessions, held at intervals on the army's march from Brunswick, New Jersey, where they spent the Fourth and celebrated with a *feu-de-joie* of firearms, to North Castle, New York. On August 12, Lord Stirling announced the decision: Lee was guilty of disobedience to orders, misbehavior before the enemy, and disrespect to the Commander-in-Chief. His sentence was to be "suspended from any command in the Armies of the United States for the term of twelve months."[38]

This court-martial still remains something of a mystery. There was no accusation of treachery, with which Lee has since been generally associated. Yet the charges were grave, and the penalty absurdly light. There was much contemporary dissatisfaction with the decision, and considerable difference of opinions as to Lee himself. The point here is that Monroe remained his friend, as extant letters show. And other officers rallied to his support, among them Generals Mercer, Muhlenberg, Knox, Greene, and "Light Horse Harry" Lee.[39] John Marshall, too, "did not condemn him utterly," and later, as Chief Justice, gave "both sides of the controversy" with characteristic impartiality.[40] It may be that these men, most of whom had known Lee in Virginia, sensed an essential honesty in his odd character, and that Monroe was fundamentally right in his loyalty to an old friend.

"A Brave, Active, and Sensible Officer"

James Monroe was now twenty years old. He had not succeeded in getting himself written into the annals of the period except in the briefest passing reference, but when Washington wrote one of his rare letters of recommendation to Archibald Cary, he said of the young Virginian, "He has in every instance, maintained the reputation of a brave, active, and sensible officer."[41]

5

"A Farewell to Arms"

AFTER THE AFFAIR at Monmouth and the Fourth of July celebration at New Brunswick, Washington's army marched north by easy stages through Scotch Plains, Springfield, Paramus, and Haverstraw. On July 17, 18, and 19 they crossed the Hudson at King's Ferry. On the 24th they joined Gates's army at White Plains, north of New York City.[1]

James Monroe, not yet twenty-one and still an aide-de-camp to Lord Stirling, found himself back at the point where he had first joined Washington's army. But now the positions were reversed. It was the British, in New York City, who were "reduced to the use of spade and pick-axe for defense," as Washington wrote a friend,[2] and the Continentals who had the whip-hand. It was true that the British still controlled the harbor, but Count d'Estaing, with a French fleet of six frigates and twelve ships of the line had arrived off the Delaware Capes on July 7, had conferred with Washington's aides at Sandy Hook, and had planned to attack the British fleet in New York Harbor. No one knew what a fiasco the French aid was to be at this time. On August 24, D'Estaing, thwarted by a heavy storm, withdrew to Boston and later sailed away to fight the enemy in the West Indies. Thus Washington was left without the means to launch a strong offensive.

In August, Lord Stirling, in camp at White Plains, obtained permission for his wife and younger daughter, Lady Catharine Alexander, to pass the British lines and visit his elder daughter, Lady Mary, in New York City. Mary had married Mr. Robert Watts, who had remained neutral and lived quietly in the City during the British occupation. Lady Catharine (better known, after her marriage to William Duer in 1779, as Lady Kitty Duer), wrote her father a lively account of the visit and said that her sister was "perfectly rebellious" and very tired of living under the British.[3]

With armies on the march in New Jersey, Lady Stirling and her daughters spent a good deal of time in Elizabethtown with Lady Stirling's brother, William Livingston, Governor of New Jersey. The Governor himself had daughters, and war could not entirely suppress the gay doings of the young people in the Governor's mansion, "Liberty Hall." When the British came too near, the ladies withdrew to Governor Livingston's more secluded country home, not far away. Lord Stirling's estate, Baskenridge, was within easy riding distance, as was also Paramus, where the popular Mrs. Prevost, later the wife of Aaron Burr, lived in her "little Hermitage."[4]

At least one letter written by the youthful Monroe shows that the tall young Virginian with the gray-blue eyes and the serious face—which, according to his contemporaries, lighted up marvellously when he smiled—was an intimate member of this cosmopolitan little group in the Jerseys. In fact, he seems to have formed an attachment for one of the girls which approached the seriousness of a formal engagement.[5] A letter of which she is the subject, addressed by Monroe to Mrs. Prevost, reveals her as somewhat temperamental and not a little possessive. From Philadelphia, on November 8, 1778, he writes, with a half-humorous consternation at the insistence of this "fond, delicate, unmarried lady," who resents his slightest attention to anyone else, even his writing to Mrs. Prevost, and who objects vigorously to his carrying out his intention of going to France. This letter is quoted in full, for it contains the only information available as to what was going on in the mind of twenty-year-old James Monroe:

"A young lady who either is, or pretends to be, in love, is, you know, my dear Mrs. Prevost, the most unreasonable creature in existence. If she looks a smile or a frown, which does not immediately give or deprive you of happiness (at least to appearance), your company soon becomes very insipid. Each feature has its beauty, and each attitude the graces, or you have no judgment. But if you are so stupidly insensible of her charms as to deprive your tongue and eyes of every expression of admiration, and not only to be silent

[47]

respecting her, but devote them to an absent object, she cannot receive a higher insult; nor would she, if not restrained by politeness, refrain from open resentment.

"Upon this principle I think I stand excused for not writing [to you] from B. Ridge [Baskenridge, Lord Stirling's estate]. I proposed it, however; and, after meeting with opposition in ———, to obtain her point, she promised to visit the little 'Hermitage' [Mrs. Prevost's home at Paramus], and make my excuses herself. I took occasion to turn the conversation to a different object, and plead for permission to go to France. I gave up in one instance, and she certainly ought to in the other. But writing a letter and going to France are very different, you will perhaps say. She objected to it, and all the arguments which a fond, delicate, unmarried lady could use, she did not fail to produce against it. I plead the advantage I should derive from it. The personal improvement, the connexions I should make. I told her she was not the only one on whom fortune did not smile in every instance. I produced examples from her own acquaintance, and represented their situation in terms which sensibly affected both herself and Lady C. [probably Catharine, Lord Stirling's daughter]. I painted a lady [Mrs. Prevost] full of affection, of tenderness, and sensibility, separated from her husband, for a series of time, by the cruelty of war—her uncertainty respecting his health; the pain and anxiety which must naturally arise from it. I represented, in the most pathetic terms, the disquietude which, from the nature of her connexion, might possibly intrude on her domestic retreat. I then raised to her view fortitude under distress, cheerfulness, life, and gayety, in the midst of affliction.

"I hope you will forgive me, my dear little friend, if I produced you to give life to the image. The instance, she owned, was applicable. She felt for you from her heart, and she has a heart capable of feeling. She wished not a misfortune similar to yours; but, if I was resolved to make it so, she would strive to imitate your example. I have now permission to go where I please, but you must not forget her. She and Lady C—— promise to come to the Hermitage to spend a week or two. Encourage her, and represent the advantage I shall gain from travel. But why should I desire you to do what I know your own heart will dictate? for a heart so capable of friendship feels its own pain alleviated by alleviating that of others.

"A Farewell to Arms"

"But do not suppose that my attention is only taken up with my own affairs. I am too much attached ever to forget the Hermitage. Mrs. Duvall, I hope, is recovering; and Kitty's indisposition is that of my nearest relation. Mrs. de Visme [Mrs. Prevost's sister-in-law] has delicate nerves. Tell me her children are well, and I know she has a flow of spirits, for her health depends entirely on theirs.

"I was unfortunate in not being able to meet with the governor [Governor Livingston]. He was neither at Elizabethtown, B. Ridge, Princeton, nor Trenton. I have consulted with several members of Congress on the occasion. They own the injustice, but cannot interfere. The laws of each state must govern itself. They cannot conceive the possibility of its taking place. General Lee [probably General Charles Lee, then in Philadelphia] says it must not take place; and if he was an absolute monarch, he would issue an order to prevent it.[6]

"I am introduced to the gentleman I wished by General Lee in a very particular manner. I cannot determine with certainty what I shall do till my arrival in Virginia.

"Make my compliments to Mrs. and Miss De Visme, and believe me, with the sincerest friendship,
"Yours,
"James Monroe."[7]

No one reading Monroe's letter to Mrs. Prevost can believe that his heart was deeply involved in this romantic episode. Indeed, he implies that the lady herself may have been pretending to be more in love than she was. The young Virginian is obviously more interested in going to France, in returning to Virginia, in securing interviews with influential people, than in courting any girl in the Jerseys, however charming she may be.

The outcome of the affair is revealed in a letter written by Monroe the following May, in which he says that Lord Stirling "behaved with great politeness and kindness to me, giving me an honorable recommendation to present to the [Virginia] Assembly, and in a letter to my uncle [Joseph Jones] approved of the part I have acted with respect to the young lady."[8]

In Monroe's letter to Mrs. Prevost, written in Philadelphia in November, 1778, he said, in closing, "I cannot determine with certainty what I shall do till my arrival in Virginia." He had evidently resigned as aide to Lord Stirling and was headed for home.[8-a] Reasons for this can readily be conjectured. His embarrassing love affair may have had something to do with it, but probably the main reason was his impatience with the static condition of his affairs and his distaste for the long winter which Washington's army was to spend on the west side of the Hudson, with little to do except to keep an eye of the British, while news from the South became more and more ominous. It was a financial burden, too, to serve as aide to Lord Stirling. Monroe paid his own expenses, as he did throughout most of his service in the Continental army,[9] and he may have felt the need of retrenchment.

Whatever the reason, he seems to have made his headquarters in Philadelphia, seat of the Continental Congress (of which his uncle, Joseph Jones, was a member), until May, 1779, when he left for Virginia, armed with letters of warm recommendation from Washington's favorite military aide Alexander Hamilton, from Washington himself, and from Lord Stirling.

Hamilton's letter is addressed to Lieutenant Colonel John Laurens and dated May 22, 1779. "Monroe is just setting out from Head Quarters," Hamilton writes, "and proposes to go in quest of adventures to the Southward. He seems to be as much of a knight errant as your worship, but as he is an honest fellow, I shall be glad he may find some employment that will enable him to get knocked on the head in an honorable way. He will relish your black scheme if anything can be done for him in that line. You know him to be a man of honor, a sensible man and a soldier. This makes it unnecessary for me to say anything to interest your friendship for him. You love your country too and he has zeal and capacity to serve it."[10]

The "black scheme" of which Hamilton speaks, refers to the plan of enlisting slaves to fight on the side of the colonists, suggested in February, 1799, by Henry Laurens, President of Congress, and his son, Lieutenant Colonel John Laurens.[11] On March 29, Congress "recommended South Carolina and Georgia to arm 3,000 slaves, for whose freedom Congress would pay." There were not enough troops to oppose the invading British, and both Lincoln and Greene urged the use of blacks. But South Carolina indignantly rejected the proposal, and so the "black scheme" referred to by Hamilton as a

"A Farewell to Arms"

possible opening for Monroe as officer of colored troops, failed to materialize.

Washington's letter, recapitulating Monroe's career and revealing the Commander in Chief's estimate of his young fellow Virginian, is dated May 30, 1779, and is addressed to his long-time associate in Virginia affairs, Colonel Archibald Cary. Washington writes:

"I very sincerely lament that the situation of our service will not permit us to do justice to the merits of Major Monroe, who will deliver you this, by placing him in the army upon some satisfactory footing.[12] But as he is on the point of leaving us and expresses an intention of going to the Southward, where a new scene has opened, it is with pleasure I take occasion to express to you the high opinion I have of his worth. The zeal he discovered by entering the service at an early period, the character he supported in his regiment, and the manner in which he distinguished himself at Trenton, when he received a wound, induced me to appoint him to a Captaincy in one of the additional regiments. This regiment failing from the difficulty of recruiting, he entered into Lord Stirling's family, and has served two campaigns as a volunteer aid to his Lordship. He has, in every instance, maintained the reputation of a brave, active, and sensible officer. As we cannot introduce him into the Continental line, it were to be wished that the State could do something for him, to enable him to follow the bent of his military inclination, and render service to his country. If an event of this kind could take place, it would give me particular pleasure; as the esteem I have for him, and a regard for his merit, conspire to make me earnestly wish to see him provided for in some handsome way."[13]

When Monroe reached home in the late spring of 1779, Virginia, after a period of relative quiet, was again being engulfed in the main currents of war. Sir Henry Clinton, in New York, had resolved, as soon as D'Estaing sailed for the West Indies, to attack "the weakest portion of the Union" (that is, Georgia and South Carolina), and in late November, 1778, had dispatched Lieutenant Colonel Campbell, with three thousand troops, to conquer Georgia. Savannah had fallen on December 29, 1778, and Augusta on February 1 following. The American commander, Major General Robert Howe, the victim of these reverses, was replaced by Major General Lincoln, who meantime had reached Charleston and was pushing rapidly toward the

JAMES MONROE

Georgia line. The British forces in South Carolina, under Brigadier General Prevost, greatly outnumbered Lincoln's troops, of whom only a third were trained soldiers. But bands of partisans, under the leadership of such men as Andrew Pickens, Francis Marion, and Thomas Sumter, harried the British unmercifully, and Governor John Rutledge inspired South Carolina patriots with a burning zeal which staved off destruction for the moment. Meantime Virginia and North Carolina were implored to send troops to repel the British in the South, and Washington detached Bland's and Baylor's regiments of horse to be sent south and also certain companies recently recruited in Virginia.[14]

Sir Henry Clinton now decided that if he could destroy Virginia's resources, he would be "cutting into the roots of resistance in the South," and in this idea he was right, for Virginia, close to the southern theatre of war and as yet relatively unscathed, was the main source of supply for the fighting armies. Early in May, 1799, Clinton dispatched a portion of the British fleet under Sir George Collier, with two thousand men commanded by Brigadier General Matthews, and on May 9, they anchored in Hampton Roads and seized Portsmouth, Norfolk, and Gosport. Quickly they took on board all military supplies that they could carry and destroyed the rest. Before the end of May, they sailed back to New York, leaving Virginia's much needed military stores greatly depleted.[15]

It was shortly after this disaster that Monroe approached the Virginia Assembly, meeting in Williamsburg. He was armed with the almost mandatory recommendation of the Commander-in-Chief of the American army, and the Assembly dutifully appointed him Lieutenant Colonel of one of the regiments of militia which, it was hoped, would be raised soon. But Virginia's treasury was empty. Virginia troops had been fighting since 1775, and companies had recently been recruited for fighting on the southern front. No new companies were forthcoming, and James Monroe's military career, except for sporadic fighting during the British invasion the following year, came to an end.

It is clear from letters written later by Monroe that this period of uncertainty and lack of direction was a trying one for him. He had written Mrs. Prevost that he wanted to go to France—a recurring theme in his letters of the period. He was an experienced officer, with

"A Farewell to Arms"

all the energy of his twenty-one years and with a frame built for muscular activity and endurance—noted in practically every contemporary description of him—and he must have felt almost unbearably thwarted by the circumstances that denied him military service in the Continental line or in the state militia in the time of Virginia's greatest danger.

In a confused and baffling time, he acted wisely. He stayed in Williamsburg, perhaps with the intention of studying law under George Wythe, Jefferson's teacher, newly appointed to "the first chair of law in an American college," at William and Mary,[16] or perhaps with the thought that he might be on hand for any opening that might appear.

In a way, both things happened. He was appointed aide to Governor Jefferson, and he embarked on the study of law under that brilliant and kindly mentor. A fellow aide, who was also a pupil of Jefferson, was John Francis Mercer, another Continental officer, afterward Governor of Maryland.

Even in these busy wartime days, the indefatigable Governor found time to give the two young men instruction in the law, using a system he had himself evolved.[17] This system, including many of the features of the "case-method" procedure now used in leading schools of law, was superior to that used by such well-known teachers as George Wythe, who taught the law by assignments in Blackstone and other textbooks. Jefferson asked his pupils to analyze the reports of decided cases and make abstracts of them, using for this purpose his large private collections of law reports, which he had gathered with the idea of reforming the colonial system in use in the Virginia courts.

During these months of close association with Jefferson, James Monroe found himself. As he wrote Jefferson the following year, when his "plan of life" was "perplexed" and he was "exposed to inconveniences" which "almost destroyed" him, "you became acquainted with me & undertook the direction of my studies ... My plan of life is now fix'd, has a certain object for its view & does not depend on other chance or circumstance further than the same events may affect the public at large."[18]

From the North, in July, came the cheering news of Anthony Wayne's capture of the fort at Stony Point, and in August, news of the successful surprise attack of Henry (Light-Horse Harry) Lee, on Paulus Hook, the present Jersey City. These brilliant exploits, together with the constant threat of Washington's army at their back, kept the British on tenterhooks until, late in September, D'Estaing left the American coast and sailed for France.[19] With the French fleet out of the way, and with the frozen winter of the North immobilizing Washington's army, Sir Henry Clinton decided to attack Charleston. On the day after Christmas, 1779, he, with Cornwallis and over seven thousand troops, set sail for the South Carolina coast. And in December Virginia sent practically her entire line to South Carolina, under Woodford and Scott.

In Virginia, with British invasion threatening, the last meeting of the General Assembly to meet in Williamsburg was held on December 24, 1779, and early in 1780 the Capital was moved to Richmond.[20] This posed a problem for James Monroe. Should he follow Jefferson to Richmond, or should he pursue his study of law in Williamsburg under George Wythe? He seems to have asked the advice of his uncle, Joseph Jones, for he received the following reply, dated March 7, 1780:

"This post will bring you a letter from me, accounting for your not hearing sooner what had been done in your affairs. If your overseer sends up before next post-day you shall hear the particulars. Charles Lewis, going down to the college, gives me an opportunity of answering, by him, your inquiry respecting your removal with the governor, or attending Mr. Wythe's lectures. If Mr. Wythe means to pursue Mr. Blackstone's method I should think you ought to attend him from the commencement of his course, if at all, and to judge of this, for want of proper information, is difficult; indeed I incline to think Mr. Wythe, under the present state of our laws, will be much embarrassed to deliver lectures with that perspicuity and precision which might be expected from him under a more established and settled state of them. . . . The governor [Jefferson] need not fear the favor of the community as to his future appointment, while he continues to make the common good his study. I have no intimate acquaintance with Mr. Jefferson, but from the knowledge I have of him, he is in my opinion as proper a man as can be put into the office, having the requisites of ability, firmness, and diligence. You do well to cultivate his friendship, and cannot fail to entertain a grate-

"A Farewell to Arms"

ful sense of the favors he has conferred upon you, and while you continue to deserve his esteem he will not withdraw his countenance. If, therefore, upon conferring with him upon the subject, he wishes or shows a desire that you go with him, I would gratify him. Should you remain to attend Mr. Wythe, I would do it with his approbation, and under the expectation that when you come to Richmond you shall hope for the continuance of his friendship and assistance."[21]

Monroe evidently followed this wise—and worldly-wise—advice. At a later day (September 6, 1792), he wrote Lord Stirling, "I submitted the direction of my time and plan to my friend Mr. Jefferson, one of our wisest and most virtuous republicans, and under his direction and aided by his advice, I have hitherto till of late lived."[22]

In January, 1780, Washington ordered Major General Peter Muhlenberg to Virginia to take command of the forces of the state and to organize them for defense, but because of heavy snows Muhlenberg did not reach Virginia until March. He "entered upon his new command without a single regiment and almost destitute of the necessary munitions of war." Governor Jefferson was absent at the time of Muhlenberg's arrival, "on a visit to Albemarle," to attend to his property there. Upon his return he informed Muhlenberg that "there is no money in the treasury to carry on the recruiting business properly."[23]

On May 12 Charleston fell, and the British army began to roll northward across the Carolinas. Congress, after long delay, thoroughly alarmed at the news from the South, had at last sprung into action. Baron de Kalb had been sent South with some two thousand men and on June 20 he reached Hillsborough, North Carolina, where he waited for the Virginia and North Carolina militia to join him.[24]

Monroe was now to see active service. In June, 1780, he received the following communication, dated Richmond, June 10:

"The executives have occasion to employ a gentleman in a confidential business requiring great discretion, and some acquaintance with military things. They wish you to undertake it if not inconvenient with your present pursuits. It will call you off some weeks, to the distance of a couple of hundred miles, expenses will be borne at a reasonable premium. Will you be so good as to attend us immediately for further communications."[25]

The "confidential business" proved to be the establishing of com-

[55]

munications between the Governor's Council and the Southern troops, and the office carried with it the title of Military Commissioner from Virginia to the Southern Army. This threw Monroe back into military life and enabled him to make friends among the officers of the Virginia militia and to renew acquaintance with such men as William Washington, now a colonel, Henry Lee, and Generals Morgan and Muhlenberg.

On June 26, 1780, about ten days after his appointment, Monroe wrote to Jefferson a long detailed report from Cross Creek (Fayetteville), North Carolina, a highly strategic point from which to keep an eye on Cornwallis and Tarleton. The letter shows that, in selecting Monroe for the purpose of establishing communications with the army in the South, Jefferson knew his man. It reads in part:

"Sir,—Some days since I arrived here [Cross Creek] & trust I have so arranged the line of communication between us, that whatever alterations the course of events may effect in my own situation, I shall have it in my power to make it subservient to my wishes. I expected I should more effectually put in execution your Excellency's orders by coming immediately here, the source from which Governor Nash at Newberry or Baron de Kalb at Hillsborough get their Intelligence, than by taking my route to either of those posts & I have had the good fortune in meeting Governor Nash here to approve my determination. The Governor was on his route to Baron de Kalb & called upon General Caswell here with a view of making himself acquainted with his force and object, . . . I have it not in my power to give your Excellency, at present information upon all the points you require, but an event we are informed has taken place of such importance in its probable consequences to the State of Virginia, as to make it necessary I should immediately inform you of it. We have it from authority we cannot doubt, that an embarkation has taken place at Charlestown and sailed some days since under the command of General Clinton, consisting of about 6000 men.[25-a] The remainder of their army, supposed upwards of 4000, with their cavalry forming a corps of 600 under Col. Tarleton, are left behind under Lord Cornwallis. General Caswell has repeatedly had information, they had embarked, but never 'til today that they had sailed, & today, I examined myself two men of Woodford's brigade, lately escaped from Charlestown, who confirm it. A Garrison of about 800

"A Farewell to Arms"

are said to be left at Charlestown; 2500 at Camden; . . . What may be the object of those who have sailed or of those who remain is uncertain . . .; but . . . we must conclude they mean to land somewhere in Virginia, and by directing their armies to the same object endeavour to Conquer all these Southern States. . . . What again would induce this belief . . . is the universal scarcity of all kinds of provisions, except meat, which prevails in this country. Upon this account the army under General de Kalb at Hillsborough and that under General Caswell here, are no longer able to hold those stations and are in that dilemma that they have only the alternative of advancing shortly on the enemy or retiring to Virginia. This however will in a great degree be remedied when the harvest comes in. What plan General de Kalb may take to oppose them I cannot determine, . . . Only 1500 militia are collected here under General Caswell & about 1,100 under Brig. Rutherford, west of the enemy, who hold the position I could wish Baron de Kalb to take with the Continental troops at least. At Charlotte, Salsbury or Chatham the country is better able to support an army & when Harvest comes in will be more so, while that near here or towards the coast is much exhausted. Between here and Halifax . . . I could scarcely get provisions for myself & men & in many instances could not procure corn for my Horses at any rate. . . . At Governor Nash's request I shall attend him tomorrow to where Baron de Kalb may be, or if the Governor does not go himself, shall perhaps go up on the business I have referred to & in my next shall have it in my power to inform your Excellency of the plan Baron de Kalb may take for his future operations, with the probability of success, or what effect it may have on the movements of the enemy. . . .

"I cannot inform you where Porterfield is; but expect somewhere near the Baron. Colonel Armand's Corps are here under the command of General Caswell. We have had reports a French fleet are off C. Town but not from such authority as to give assent."[26]

This letter implies that Monroe continued for a time as Military Commissioner, and, by the "line of communication" he had "arranged," kept Jefferson informed of events in the Carolinas during the early summer of 1780.

In response to a strong public demand, Washington (who would have preferred Nathanael Greene), dispatched Gates, "the hero of

Saratoga," to Hillsborough, where, on July 25, he took command of the forces assembled there.[27]

The summer of 1780 wore on, with an intensity of heat that caused Cornwallis to linger in Charleston, postponing his invasion of North Carolina until fall. But he surprised Gates at Camden on August 16, and "the hero of Saratoga" fled the field, with tremendous loss of men and equipment. On September 8, Cornwallis started north for Charlotte, the "agreeable village" in a "damned rebellious country," and while there heard of the Battle of King's Mountain (October 7)—news which drove him precipitately back into South Carolina. On December 2, Nathanael Greene took command of the southern army at Charlotte.[28]

Once again Monroe was to take arms against the British—this time in defense of his native state. When Clinton heard of Gates's defeat at Camden in August, he considered Virginia ripe for the harvest and ordered General Leslie to the South. Leslie landed at Portsmouth in October with three thousand men, probably more for establishing contact with Cornwallis than for raiding.[29]

A little army of "old soldiers, recruits, and deserters" had been gathered at Chesterfield Court House by General Muhlenberg. These troops, together with volunteers who flocked to the defense of the Tidewater district, formed the nucleus of a little army, lacking in numbers and discipline but determined to oppose the invader by the methods of guerrilla warfare.[30]

Jefferson now sent to Muhlenberg's assistance all the troops, both militia and regular, which his efforts were able to gather from the Virginia back country. This little force was commanded by General Weedon, formerly of Monroe's regiment in the Continental Line, and Generals Nelson and Stevens of the Virginia militia. With them marched Monroe,[31] now Colonel of an "emergency regiment" largely recruited through his own efforts among his neighbors of Prince George County. General Muhlenberg now had eight hundred regulars and was able to march against the enemy, hoping at least to prevent General Leslie's invading forces from "ravaging the lower counties with impunity."[32] General Nelson was detached from the main body with another force of about eight hundred men, nearly all Virginia militia, to operate on the north of the James River. To this latter division "Colonel James Monroe's regiment was attached."[33]

[58]

"A Farewell to Arms"

Leslie reëmbarked his forces on November 28 to join Cornwallis, but the respite for Virginia was to last only a few weeks. On December 30, another formidable British expedition entered the Virginia Capes and boldly sailed up the James. At the head of this new invasion was the most hated man of the Revolutionary War. The traitor Arnold, now a British subject, had prepared a campaign of terrorism by which he hoped to overawe the Virginia patriots. His first exploit was the burning of the capitol at Richmond, which he reached on January 5, 1781.[34] In the operations directed by Generals Steuben and Muhlenberg Monroe was attached to the latter as a staff officer.

Washington, especially anxious to capture Arnold, sent Lafayette with a force of regulars to aid in the defense of Virginia. An amusing picture has been drawn of the difficulties confronting the gallant young French officer conducting a campaign wherein he was obliged to depend upon the unruly Virginia militia, whose ideas of discipline were entirely different from those of the Continental line. Horses, he wrote to Washington, were regarded as sacred animals by their owners, and were almost impossible to obtain, and the slow-moving oxen which drew the transports were never able to keep up with the rapid movements of the troops. Yet the detestation in which Arnold was held throughout Virginia enabled Lafayette to carry on an able campaign. When Lord Cornwallis, manoeuvered out of the Carolinas by the masterly tactics of Nathanael Greene, invaded Virginia, reaching Petersburg on May 20, the situation became desperate. It was mainly, however, Lafayette's spirited defense that induced the British to take up their fatal position in the lower Tidewater around Yorktown.[35]

On April 29, Lafayette reached Richmond and camped among its smoking ruins.[36] Cornwallis now set about the conquest of the Old Dominion in deadly earnest, but first he had to annihilate Lafayette. "The boy cannot escape me," he wrote exultingly to Clinton. "I am not strong enough even to be beaten," was the Marquis's graceful answer to this boasting as he retired toward the West. Then taking a strong position at Ely's Ford on the Rapidan, he placed himself in the path of the British troops marching towards Fredericksburg.

In these manoeuvers Monroe apparently had no direct part, but an incident of Arnold's invasion was seriously to affect the fortunes of his friend Jefferson during the last days of his term as Governor.

Refraining from pursuit, Cornwallis sent the dashing Light-Horseman Tarleton on a sweeping ride around Lafayette's flank to Charlottesville, where, in the shadows of Jefferson's mountains, the refugee Assembly of Virginia was holding its sessions. Cornwallis's idea was further to shatter Virginia's morale by capturing her Governor and the Assembly. Before the Americans knew what was going on, Tarleton had reached Louisa, a small village about forty miles from Charlottesville. Fortunately an American Captain, John Jouett, spending the night at the Cuckoo Tavern in Louisa, saw the British horsemen pass through the town and realized their objective. In a perilous ride over mountain trails, he reached Monticello just in time to warn the Governor.

Whatever criticism may be levelled at Jefferson's lack of military capacity during the invasions of his state, the sudden approach of the British cavalry gave him an opportunity for a display of calmness that completely vindicated his personal courage. Until five minutes before McLeod's white-coated dragoons (who had been charged by Tarleton to secure his person) broke into the front court of Monticello, Jefferson was "calmly sorting official papers." Then, slipping out a rear door, he mounted his horse (standing ready) and rode away. The Assembly escaped also, and reassembled in Staunton, where they voted "an elegant sword and a pair of pistols" to Captain Jouett.[37]

Concerning Jefferson's narrow escape, Monroe, writing him on June 18 from Fredericksburg, said,

"Dear Sir,—I some time since address'd a letter to you from a small estate of mine in King Georges whither I had retir'd to avoid the enemy from the one I lately dispos'd of on the Potommack river. I had then the pleasure to congratulate you on the safe retreat from Richmond to Charlottesville & anticipated the joy yourself & family must have felt on your arrival at Monticello from which the misfortune of the times has long separated you. I lament your felicity on that head was of but short duration. I hope howe'er that neither yourself nor Mrs. Jefferson has sustain'd injury from these obtrusions of the enemy."[38]

In the same letter Monroe informed Jefferson of his continued efforts to obtain military employment. Writing from Fredericks-

"A Farewell to Arms"

burg, the home of General Weedon, he said that he had set out "to join the Marquis' Army to act in any line either himself or Council wo'd employ me in. Being confin'd here some few days with small indisposition, Gen'l Weedon has requested of me to sit out this Ev'g to manage the British flag on its way to Alexandria. So soon as I disengage myself from this affair, I shall join the army & serve till the enemy leave this State." After that event he hoped to "leave for the Continent."

On October 1, he again wrote that he had "waited on Governor Nelson and solicited some command in the militia," only to be informed that "the Militia in the field was officer'd & of course that I co'd procure none whatever. This wo'd have mortified me much had I not discover'd during my continuance with the army that Gen'l W. had under his command 15000 regular troops, a force certainly very sufficient to reduce the post at York."[39]

We have no word of Monroe's whereabouts during the heroic Yorktown period. On the first day of October—the month of Cornwallis's surrender—he wrote Jefferson from Caroline that having failed to secure from Governor Nelson a command in the militia and having learned that Washington (who had reached Williamsburg on September 14) had "a force certainly very sufficient to reduce the post at York," he was taking advantage of an opportunity to go to France with a certain "Colonel Josiah Parker [who] has a ship just ready to sail to France." He added that he had been living "a very sedentary life upon a small estate I have in King Georges," and had read "all the books you mention on the study of law."[40]

At the time this letter was written, Cornwallis was in Yorktown, trapped between De Grasse by sea and Washington and Lafayette by land. About three weeks later, on October 19, Yorktown surrendered.

On the November 11 following Cornwallis's surrender, there was a great Peace Ball in Fredericksburg, said "by well founded tradition" to have been held in Weedon's Tavern. To this ball came the officers of the French and Continental armies. "Mrs. Mary Ball Washington attended, entering on the arm of her illustrious son. . . .

"Among the dignitaries known to have attended the Peace Ball were: Colonel George Mason and his daughter Miss Anne Mason; Colonel James Monroe, General Gustavus Browne Wallace; General William Woodford; Hon. Richard Henry Lee, General Harry Lee,

[61]

JAMES MONROE

General Baron Von Steuben; General Anthony Wayne; Capt. William Browne Wallace; Admiral Count de Grasse; Count de Estaing, Count Deux Pont; . . . Colonel John Laurens; . . . Mrs. Isabella Gordon Mercer, widow of General Hugh Mercer who fell at Princeton . . . Mrs. Willis of Willis Hill; Colonel Torbet Lewis and Miss Lewis; . . ."[41]

So here among his fellow Virginians and fellow officers we find James Monroe, now twenty-three, with a touch of shyness controlled by the assurance the last few years had given him, with a gentle friendliness and a rather endearing awkwardness, as he joined in the heartfelt celebration of a Peace which he himself had done what he could to bring about.

6

Assemblyman, Councillor, Congressman

WHEN MONROE wrote Jefferson in the fall of 1781 that he planned to go abroad with Colonel Josiah Parker, who "had a ship just ready to sail to France," he expressed, in the same letter, his intention to prepare himself for public service. "Altho' I shall most probably be glad some time hence," he wrote, "to acquire more by the practice of the law ... I wou'd still wish to prosecute my studies on the most liberal plan to qualify myself for any business I might chance to engage in. This, if not profitable will be agreeable, for surely those acquirements qualify a man not only for publick office, but enable him to bear prosperity or adversity ... with greater magnanimity & fortitude. ..." He also asked Jefferson for advice regarding the place of residence he should fix on abroad, whether "altogether in the South of France" or "a year at the Temple in London."[1] The latter—somewhat extraordinary though not impossible in view of the loose views of neutrality held at the time—was favored by Monroe. He either anticipated an early peace or a surprising magnanimity on the part of the benchers of the famous Inns of Court.

These plans, however, were interrupted by an earlier opportunity to hold "publick office" than young Monroe had anticipated. He had sold his estate in Westmoreland and had been living on "a small estate I have in King Georges." It was probably the prestige and popularity of his uncle, Joseph Jones, and his own military career that induced his neighbors in King George County to send him, in spite of his youth, as their representative to the General Assembly in 1782.

JAMES MONROE

Of great concern to him at this time was Jefferson's withdrawal from public office because of the harsh criticism of his conduct of Virginia's military affairs during the war. Not long after Monroe took his seat in the Assembly, he wrote to his older friend urging him, with engaging naïveté, to return to the service of his country: "As I have had an opportunity since I wrote last of being better inform'd of the sentiments of those whom I know you put the greatest value on, I think it my duty to make you acquainted therewith. It is publickly said here that the people of y'r county inform'd you they had frequently elected you in times of less difficulty & danger than the present to please you, but that now they had call'd you forth into publick office to serve themselves. . . . The present is generally conceiv'd to be an important era w'ch of course makes y'r attendance particularly necessary, & as I have taken the liberty to give you the public opinion & desire upon this occasion, & as I am warmly interested in whatever concerns the publick interest or has relation to you, it will be unnecessary to add it is earnestly the desire of, Dear Sir, y'r sincere friend & servant. . . ."[2]

Jefferson replied from Monticello on May 20, thanking Monroe for his friendly letters and congratulating him upon his election. He said, in answer to his friend's protest, "I have examined my heart to know whether it was thoroughly cured of every principle of political ambition." He found "no lurking particles." Because of his thirteen years of public service he felt sure of his "right to withdraw," and felt his duty to be towards his family. He felt that he had been "suspected and suspended" in the eyes of the world as though charged with "a treason of the heart" rather than "merely a weakening of the head." He doubted, in short, whether in America "the state could command public service" and hinted that "public service and private misery are linked together."[3]

Monroe clearly attributed his political preferment to the letters of commendation he had brought with him when he sought a command in the Virginia forces. In September he wrote his former chief, Lord Stirling: "Lately I have taken part in the civil line of the State, and have been elected to the Legislature—and afterwards by the Legislature into the Executive Council of the State, which last office I at present fill. I am happy to make my acknowledgments to your Lordship and to his Excellency General Washington, for your and

Assemblyman, Councillor, Congressman

his friendly letters to this State in favour of my conduct while an aid in your family, without which I could not have expected, among so many competitors, at my age, to have attained, in this degree, the confidence of my countrymen. I cannot forget your Lordship's kindness to me. . . ."[4]

And he had already written to Washington from Richmond on August 15 that although Washington's letter had failed of its immediate purpose, it had helped greatly "in another line."[5]

Also elected to the Executive Council on which Monroe served was John Marshall, representative from his home county of Fauquier.[6] The Council, an administrative body of eight, chosen by the legislature from among its own members or from the people at large, was an important unit in the state government, for, since the outbreak of the Revolution, the jealousy with which the Governor's prerogatives had been regarded caused the Executive to consult more and more frequently with his Council on all important matters. Their new position thus afforded Monroe and Marshall invaluable experience in government. Contemporary critics, however, regarded them as too young for the honor.

Alexander Macaulay, a Scotch merchant of Yorktown, who met Monroe at the home of Mrs. Craig, of Williamsburg, in February, 1783, wrote of him in a letter that "he appear'd to be a modest, well-behav'd Man, but Rather young for a Councillor,"[7] and Edmund Pendleton, Judge of the High Court of Chancery and President of the Court of Appeals, had written to Madison of the other young councillor, "Young Mr. Marshall is elected a Councillor. . . . He is clever, but I think too young." This criticism was a more serious one, for, because of it, Marshall was moved to resign his position.[8]

The two young men became at this time boon companions in the enjoyment of such minor dissipations as the somewhat primitive opportunities of the Virginia capital afforded. Marshall's "Account Book" gives an amusing glimpse of their youthful prodigalities. Since he was married to the beautiful "Polly" Ambler, Marshall offered his more sober companion diversions strictly within the limits imposed by a happy marriage, chiefly some mild card-playing, a little betting on the horses, and occasional visits to the theatre.

Marshall, later to be won over to the more conservative Washingtonian clique, was in full accord with Monroe, the pupil of Jefferson, at this period in their political development—a fact revealed in their correspondence of the time. This was concerned with such matters as the "Commutable bill," allowing taxes to be paid in tobacco, hemp, flour, and deerskins, and with plans for public defense and similar subjects.

The Virginia legislature, as Monroe first knew it, was a body more likely to arouse amusement or scorn than awe. Johann David Schoepf, in his *Travels in the Confederation in 1783 and 1784*, gives a vivid description of the scene in which Monroe moved in these early days of the Republic:

"The Assembly had just now come together for its half-yearly winter session; a small frame building serves the purpose, used also on occasion, with change of scene, for balls and public banquets. It is said of the Assembly: It sits, but this is not a just expression, for these members show themselves in every possible position rather than that of sitting still, . . . During the visit I made I saw this estimable assembly quiet not 5 minutes together. . . . At the open door of the hall stands a door-keeper, who is almost incessantly and with a loud voice calling out for one member or another. In the ante-room . . . they amuse themselves zealously with talk of horse-races, run-away negroes, yesterday's play, politics, or it may be, with trafficking. . . . In the same clothes in which one goes hunting or tends his tobacco-fields, it is permissible to appear in the Senate or the Assembly. There are displayed boots, trowsers, stockings, and Indian leggings; great coats, ordinary coats, and short jackets, according to each man's caprice or comfort, and all equally honorable."9

Indeed, Virginia's legislature was no longer the courtly assemblage it once had been. The war, after all, was not yet over, and the untidy little capital of the state still bore the marks of Arnold's last visit.

In June, 1783, Monroe's term in the Assembly came to an end with his election to the Fourth Congress of the Confederation for a one-year term that began the first Monday in November. He was to remain away longer, however, and to serve in the two succeeding Congresses as well. But he did not allow his new office to break his connections with the state legislature; he kept posted on Virginia affairs through an unbroken correspondence with Marshall, then deep in a struggle to secure an honorable solution to the question of debts owed British creditors by Virginia merchants.

Assemblyman, Councillor, Congressman

The Congress of which Monroe, at the age of twenty-five, now found himself one of the youngest delegates, was principally occupied with the ratification of the treaty with Great Britain which brought the war to an end with its signing on July 27, 1783. As a member of Congress Monroe took part in the ceremonies at Annapolis when Washington, after the more familiar scene at Fraunces Tavern in New York, resigned his commission as Commander-in-Chief. With sheathed sword he made a brief appearance before Congress and then hastened off to Mount Vernon. The picture of the scene painted by Rembrandt Peale shows Monroe and Madison, seated just in front of the Father of their Country, wearing their cocked hats in imitation of the British Parliamentary privilege—while other members, more respectful in the Great Presence, sat bare-headed.

Monroe felt deeply the responsibility of his position. "I am called," he wrote from Congress on December 16, 1783, to Richard Henry Lee, "on a theatre to which I am a perfect stranger. There are before us some questions of the utmost consequence that can arise in the councils of any nation: . . ."[10]

Congress met in the fall of 1783 in Annapolis, to the dissatisfaction of some and the discomfort of all of its members. Many had hoped that Philadelphia or New York—with their more developed social life—would be chosen, and that the practice of crowding half a dozen men into a tavern room or into even less desirable boarding houses might be stopped. For, in addition to scanty "wages" and long hours, the "Gentlemen of Congress" suffered not a little actual hardship in the discharge of their legislative duties. Congress was a peripatetic body, meeting from session to session according to its own resolves. To young Monroe, accustomed to the hazards of the camp, this was probably a matter of indifference, but the older members were loud in their complaints.

Monroe and Jefferson messed together during their months in Congress and were served by a French caterer, Partout, who perhaps softened considerably the discomforts of Annapolis life and who seems to have furnished Monroe an opportunity to practice his French. When Jefferson, on May 7, 1784, was appointed minister plenipotentiary to serve in France with Franklin and Adams in the negotiating of treaties of commerce, and left Annapolis, Monroe wrote him, "I very sensibly feel your absence not only in the solitary situation in w'h you have left me but upon many other accounts," and added that he was working out a "cypher" for their future correspondence.[11]

In spite of the grumblings of the legislators, Annapolis was not without advantages as the seat of national government. It had been ambitiously laid out by the Lord Proprietor of Maryland to be the metropolis of the Chesapeake, and had been a center of colonial gaiety and splendor rivaling the Virginia capital at Williamsburg. It had several fine mansions, notably the Chase and Harewood houses, excellent examples of the domestic architecture of America. With its "College of St. John" and its fine State House, where the national legislature now met, it was one of the social and intellectual centers of America. But any attempt to make it the permanent residence of Congress was frustrated by the jealousy between the states of the "Eastern and Southern tiers."

The Virginia delegates were eager to have Georgetown chosen for the national capital. In a letter of Jefferson, written May 25, 1784, Monroe mentions this choice. He speaks of going that evening to view Georgetown as a possible site and says, "Our report will be in favor of the Maryland side and of a position near the town."[12]

To Monroe, his uncle, Judge Joseph Jones, wrote: "There can be no doubt the object of Maryland will be to continue Congress at Annapolis. This is evident by her not having yet made any tender of Georgetown or its vicinity which the offer of Virginia presented to their view. By aiming at too much, they may and do hazard losing all. The Eastern Gentlemen I think will never consent to remaining in Annapolis from apprehensions of danger from its contiguity to the Bay in case of a War and from an opinion it cannot be a healthy situation."[13]

The Judge was right. The committees which were optimistically appointed from time to time to view sites for a permanent federal town continued to meet in vain, for the rivalries of the different delegations prevented any choice. When action was finally taken, the hopes of the Virginia delegates were temporarily dashed. In a letter to Jefferson dated April 12, 1785, Monroe writes of the proposed federal buildings, "Our dependence for their erection at Georgetown had been on the Southern States and as soon as Congress conven'd, we found they had given it up." Congress passed resolutions to

Assemblyman, Councillor, Congressman

lay out "a district of not less than two nor exceeding three miles square, on the banks of either side of the Delaware . . . for a federal town," and to enter into contracts to erect "in an elegant manner a federal house for the accommodation of Congress." Houses were also to be built for the secretaries of war, foreign affairs, and marine, and for the officers of the Treasury. The Virginians evidently refused to accept this as final and did not rest until Congress had rescinded its action and chosen the site the Virginia delegation had suggested, where Washington now stands.[15]

It throws an interesting light upon the inefficiency of this early Congress to realize the difficulty with which they accomplished the most pressing business before the session—the ratification of the treaty of peace. At first only six states were in attendance, whereas nine were needed for ratification. Letters were sent to governors requesting that their delegates appear. Almost a month was spent in futile discussion of whether seven states could ratify as well as nine, and it was not until January 14, a delegate from Carolina having arrived, that the treaty was ratified without a dissenting vote.[16]

In addition to these domestic difficulties there were complications from abroad. The conflicting interests of the eastern and the southern states were played upon by foreign agents. Judge Jones's almost weekly letters to Monroe (in the valuable Gouverneur-Hoes MSS) are full of warning at this time concerning British influence and the underground activities, in Richmond, of exiled loyalists now creeping home to recover what they could of their confiscated estates. From Spring Hill, Jones writes on December 20, 1783: "I have no reluctance to a return of friendly intercourse with Britain but I feel a reluctance to hold out lures or encouragements to return and live among us to those whose services we had a right to expect in our defence and who instead of yielding us their service, went away and left us in the hour of danger and distress and have exerted every faculty to oppress and destroy us. . . . I have on the same coat I set out with and will wear it while I live."[17]

The double duty of federal legislator and devoted Virginian set Monroe a pretty problem in loyalty. He chose loyalty to the new nation, and he never wavered from it. His own words as a member of the national Congress are clear:

"There are before us some questions of the utmost consequence that can arise in the councils of any nation: the peace establishment; the regulation of our commerce, and the arrangement of our foreign appointments; whether we are to have regular or standing troops to protect our frontiers, or leave them unguarded; whether we will expose ourselves to the inconveniences, which may perhaps be the loss of the country westward, from the impossibility of preventing the adventurers from settling where they please; the intrusion of the settlers on the European powers who border on us, a cause of discontent and perhaps war. . . ."[18]

In the premonition here expressed (which a few years later, and treated from another angle, was to become a factor in the famous Doctrine), Monroe referred to a matter which had cost Jefferson and himself many anxious hours of study and consultation. Legislation concerning the "back country" and relations with Spain on the Mississippi had, indeed, become their chief interest. The vast hinterland covered by Virginia's former "Lieutenant-Governorship beyond the Mountains" had long presented problems which called for the exercise of the highest, most constructive statesmanship. The widespread conflicting claims to the "Western Waters" held by Virginia, Pennsylvania, and—through a curious intrusion resulting from the generous and vague terms of their charter—the New England states as well, infinitely complicated an already difficult problem.

Compared with the compact development of the tidewater counties and the piedmont near the Alleghenies, the sprawling, scattered settlements of the transmontane wilderness were like another civilization. Even during the early days of the Revolution, the frontiersmen were imperatively bringing their difficulties before the Virginia Assembly.[19] In contrast with the earlier colonies, now transformed into the home-counties, very little supervision had been exercised by England over the pioneers who had first pushed through the western passes. Settlement had at one time (1763) actually been forbidden except on land bordering the shores of rivers "running into the Atlantic."[20] But this measure, enacted to avoid conflict with the claims of France—and later of Spain—had been disregarded with the same buoyant indifference that the frontier population has shown for the rights of the Indians, the claims of jurisdiction advanced by neighboring colonial governments, and the protests of grantees holding vague title by royal patents. On the frontiers, as travelers fre-

Assemblyman, Councillor, Congressman

quently remarked, were to be found the first "real Americans." Their mode of life, their struggles with the un-European forces of the wilderness differentiated them so completely from the English, French, and Dutch of the Atlantic seaboard that they seemed a race apart.[21] In many ways they were what Jay somewhat contemptuously called "white savages."[22] Yet a set of customs—the rude "laws" and practices of the frontier—had held them from complete lawlessness. Their courts of justice, if rarely in session, were held under their chosen "judges or triers." The lesser crimes of civilization were rare in a community so widely scattered; and where men went constantly armed, the regulating force of the law was less frequently invoked.[23] Here, too, was a real democracy, in which the Negro slavery that, William Byrd complained, "blows up the power and ruins the industry of all but the few" in the older colonies, was almost unknown. King's Mountain showed the quality of the frontiersmen.

Concerning the future relations of the vast transmontane country to the new Confederation, several theories obtained. New York, as early as 1782, decided on the cession of the back country to the jurisdiction of Congress. But a strong party in Virginia and Pennsylvania believed that the future importance of their states might be augmented by retaining jurisdiction over the frontier. Washington, who was deep in his Potomac-Ohio development, and Madison also, seem to have cherished this theory. Patrick Henry wished to hold the settlements as a "nursery of soldiers." Jefferson and his followers, however, leaned to another solution. This was the "New States" movement, which began in the early 1780's. In February, 1784, Jefferson was writing in favor of "cession": "It is for the interest of Virginia to cede so far immediately, because the people beyond that will separate themselves, because they will be joined by all our settlements beyond the Alleghany if they are the first movers."[24]

Monroe, in an interesting letter to George Rogers Clark on October 19, 1783, frankly sides with the generally expressed wishes of the pioneers to form separate state governments of their own. He writes, "Of this you may rest assur'd that the object of this part of the State, an object wh. will govern in all our Councils, will be to effect a separation & erect an independ't State westw'd as it will enable us to oeconomize our aff'rs here & give us greater strength in the federal councils."[25]

JAMES MONROE

From the beginning, James Monroe, a former militia man, who had served beneath the Rattlesnake Flag with the pioneers, was by instinct and sympathy a "Man of the Western Waters." From the frontiersmen he was to draw much of his political strength and, in return, was to serve them with all the ability and energy at his command.

7

Champion of the West

THE LEADING part taken by Monroe in the great question of the western lands was, in a measure, the result of the interest shown in this important matter by his uncle, Joseph Jones. The year 1780 saw the rise of a party in Virginia devoted to the liberal and patriotic policy of cession. In these efforts Judge Jones was the prime mover.[1] In June he wrote to Jefferson: "Could Virginia but think herself, as she certainly is, already full large for vigorous government, she too would moderate her desires, and cede to the United States, upon certain conditions, her territory beyond the Ohio."[2] George Mason later gave form to the cession proposals—stipulating that two states should be erected and Virginia indemnified for the cost of Clark's conquering expeditions, which had given valid claim to the territory. Washington echoed the proposal and upon resigning his commission (1783) suggested the territory as an asylum for the disbanded veterans of his army. In Monroe's letter to Clark, already mentioned, he urged that a new state be set up with the traditions of Virginia, "so that the old commonwealth, now becoming aware of her isolation among her sisters, might have an efficient ally in the federal councils."[3]

As the Revolution drew to its close in 1783, the problem of rewarding the devotion of the patriot troops appealed with especial force to ex-officers who, like Monroe, were in a position to exercise legislative influence in favor of their old comrades. Nor was the debt owing to these men merely one of gratitude. The pay actually earned by the Continental line was shamefully in arrears. The militia, so often implored to serve in the most desperate emergencies, and so often sent home unthanked and unhonored when the danger had passed, was in an even more disgraceful plight as to their pay.

These "Legionnaires of '76" can hardly be blamed for taking into their own hands the situation confronting them. The misery and discontent of the troops, mostly regulars, who were awaiting disbandment on the Hudson at Newburgh, had resulted in demands that caused alarm among the "rich and great" who filled the seats of the Continental Congress.

In May, 1783, the officers of the Continental Army formed the hereditary Society of the Cincinnati, both "that they and their sons might properly remember . . . the hardships and glories of the revolution," and that, by implication, they might strengthen their own situation in the succeeding peace.[4] Following their example, the rank and file also organized to defend their rights. The next month General Rufus Putnam headed a movement among the soldiers and non-commissioned officers. With the approval of many officers, the men now demanded that Congress make just requital for their services by distributing among them the lands of the great unsettled frontiers. Washington himself forwarded their memorial with his endorsement to Congress. These statesmen received the request with mingled feelings of relief and apprehension. The founding of a "Soldier State" on the frontier might appear ominous in civilian eyes, but the means it offered through payment in land to satisfy the importunities of these clamorous heroes furnished a solution to a problem fast becoming a menace. At a moment when Congress could no longer force upon the army its depreciated currency—this "Western Movement" of pioneer comrades-in-arms took on an irresistible force and vigor. In Monroe and Jefferson the "Ohio Associates," later formed by these pioneers, found their best and most constructive patrons. Jefferson had already drafted a plan for the distribution of the public lands along the frontiers during the winter of 1783-84. On March 22 it was delivered to the Virginia Assembly. According to Paul Leicester Ford, it ranks as a public document "next to the Declaration of Independence."[5] Superseded by the "Ordinance of 1787" it nevertheless contained all the important provisions contained in that famous document. It was signed by Jefferson, S. Hardy, Arthur Lee, and James Monroe, and it read in part:

Champion of the West

"Resolved, that so much of the territory ceded or to be ceded by individual states to the United States as is already purchased or shall be purchased of the Indian Inhabitants & offered for sale by Congress, shall be divided into distinct states ... which shall remain forever part of this Confederacy of the United States of America, that in their persons, property & territory they shall be subject to the Government of the United States in Congress Assembled."[6] The states were to have a republican form of Government and to admit no person to be a citizen who held "any hereditary title." It was provided by the authors that, after 1800, in all the vast area, "there shall be neither slavery nor involuntary servitude" except as punishment for misdemeanor.

In matters of detail, Jefferson revelled in geographical formulae, measuring off the vast territory into states which were given names borrowed from antiquity, in the classical taste of the time. The present state of Michigan was divided between two states to be named Cherronesus and Metropotamia. North of Virginia lay Polypotamia and Pelisipia, and the more familiar name of Washington was attached to the smallest of the proposed new commonwealths.

After Jefferson's departure for France (he sailed from Boston July 5, 1784) Monroe continued his interest in the frontier settlements, and frequent reference to these matters in his correspondence with Jefferson shows the importance he attached to the subject. Soon after Congress adjourned he set out on a long-contemplated journey to see for himself that land of promise and opportunity where so many of his comrades-in-arms were already carving out their future homes. To Jefferson he wrote from King George on July 20:

"The day after to-morrow I sit out upon the route thro the western country. I have chang'd the direction & shall commence for the westward upon the No. River, by Albany &c. I shall pass through the lakes, visit the posts, & come down to the Ohio & thence home. The route will necessarily take me all the time during the recess of Congress. ... I may perhaps acquire a better knowledge of the posts w'h we sho'd occupy, the cause of the delay of the evacuation of the Brit'h troops, the temper of the Indians tow'd us, as well as of the soil, waters & in gen'l the natural view of the country. Capt'n Tenny, whom we saw at Annapolis, accompanies me. I am sensible of the fatigue I shall undergo but am resolv'd to sustain it."[7]

JAMES MONROE

And a little over two weeks later he wrote from New York: "I am so far on my way in performance of my trip thro' the lakes, rivers, &c. . . . I have chang'd my route & commence for the Westw'd here up the No. river, thence to the Ohio—from the Ohio home. Upon the Ohio I purchase horses. Perhaps I may visit Montreal. Had I a month more to spare, I wo'd go to Boston, up the Kennebeck river, to Quebec & thence on. I will certainly see all that my time will admit of. It is possible I may lose my scalp from the temper of the Indians, but if either a little fighting or great deal of running will save it I shall escape safe."[8]

The dangers which Monroe half-humorously anticipated were really no joke. In a letter to Jefferson from Trenton, November 1, 1784, Monroe wrote:

"Two days since I arriv'd here after performing a tour up the North River by fort Stanwix down the wood-creek, thro' the Oneida Ontario & (by the Niagara falls) part of lake Erie, thence back to Niagara thro' the Ontario by Coolton Island thro' the St. Lawrence to Montreal & from Montreal over Lake Champlain by Albany to N. York again. You find I have taken a route different from the one I intended, as my object was to take in my view the practicability also of a communication from Lake Erie down the Potowmack. But from this I was dissuaded by an accident wh. happen'd to some of the party upon Lake Erie, with whom I came from fort Stanwix to Niagara. I had separated from them by accident three days before the event. They landed near some Indian huts (a Mr. Teller from Schenactady with four men in a batteau) & were fir'd on by those Indians, Mr. Teller & two men killed & a 4th wounded; the latter with the 5th made their escape. The Indian chiefs highly reprehended the act & were, at the earnest instigation of the gentlemen of the Brit'h garrison, endeavoring to detect & bring the villains to justice. Upon advice of this disaster Colo. Depeister, commanding at Niagara, sent an Express to me just entering upon Lake Erie advising my return, with wh. I complied & took the above route to this place. My excursion hath been attended with great personal exposure & hardship & much greater expence than I had expected."[9]

Monroe traveled by packet, stage, and horseback, and the latter part of the journey was "through the wilderness," with hasty camps

Champion of the West

for food and sleep and with constant watchfulness against arrows and tomahawks. Even Monroe, who was made of tough and enduring stuff, might well be exhausted after such a trip—and yet he always seemed eager for excursions into the western lands. In his letters he urges Madison and others to accompany him on his jaunts, describing the comfort and speed of the packets and stages, but apparently the invitations were rarely accepted.

By October 30 he was back in Trenton for the opening of Congress, whence he wrote to Governor Harrison of Virginia concerning "some of the measures adopted by the British Government" which he "conceived highly interesting." Great Britain, he believed, was preparing to retain the posts "which fell within our lines by the treaty" and "many of the vessels on the lakes were again put in commission."[10] To Jefferson he wrote, November 1, "If I were to estimate the present or the probable future value of Canada to the Brit'h dominion, considered in a commercial light—and compare it with the expense necessarily incurr'd if they keep up a military establishment in supporting it, I sho'ld think Britain would act a politic part in relinquishing it, and the not doing it satisfies me she either has or will have other objects." He made many recommendations looking toward a possible commercial treaty. He desired a firm attitude in Congress respecting Canada, although he admitted that "we are in a poor condition for War."[11]

Monroe had returned from his journey somewhat disillusioned. No more than five states, he believed, could be planned where Jefferson had laid out twice as many. He also favored natural boundaries rather than the "astronomical survey" proposed by Jefferson, who still saw danger in too many large states.

Not the least of the young Congressman's troubles at this time was the difficulty he encountered in collecting his salary. Marshall wrote him, "The exertions of the Treasurer & of your other friends have been ineffectual. There is not one shilling in the Treasury & the keeper of it could not borrow one on the faith of the government." He added that he himself was "pressed for money," and said that Monroe's "old Land Lady Mrs. Shera begins now to be a little clamorous. . . . I shall be obliged, I apprehend, to negotiate your warrants at last at a discount. I have kept them this long in hopes of drawing money for them from the Treasury."[12]

JAMES MONROE

In contrast with the "easy and almost boundless generosity" of the legislature respecting gifts of land was their policy regarding the payment of salaries in hard cash. Judge Jones wrote Monroe on December 21, 1783, that, from the Treasurer's report, he doubted "whether he [the treasurer] will be able to pay the delegates ten pounds each cash on account their wages and he fears much unless the House gives some express direction for supplying the delegation to Congress they will suffer for want of money, as the commutable bill which has passed the Senate (the bill last brought in) will deprive the Treasury payments from the Sheriffs till the Spring...."[13]

Monroe, like the other federal congressmen, embraced every opportunity to return home. During the congressional recess of the winter of 1784, he made several visits to Richmond, where his favorite companion, John Marshall, was already established. The future Chief Justice of the United States had cast off the shackles of public office and was beginning his career as a lawyer. Like Monroe he was tormented by a lack of ready money. Each was possessed of considerable holdings of land besides the grants obtained from the state for their services in the army.[14] But ready money for their daily expenses was a commodity which even men far more comfortably situated than they found difficult to obtain. In December 28, 1784, Marshall writes to Monroe: "I do not know what to say to your scheme of selling out. If you can execute it you will have made a very capital sum, if you can retain your lands you will be poor during life unless you remove to the western country, but you have secured for posterity an immense fortune."[15]

The same letter shows the easy intimacy of these two men who were later to find themselves so often in disagreement in larger matters:

"The excessive cold weather," writes Marshall, "has operated like magic on our youth. They feel the necessity of artificial heat & quite wearied with lying alone, are all treading the broad road to Matrimony....

"Tabby Eppes has grown quite fat and buxom, her charms are renovated & to see her & to love her are now synonymous terms. She has within these six weeks seen in her train at least a score of Military and Civil characters....

Champion of the West

"The other Tabby is in high spirits over the success of her antique sister & firmly thinks her time will come next. . . . Lomax is in his county. Smith is said to be electioneering. Nelson has not yet come to the board. Randolph is here & well. . . . Farewell, I am your J. Marshall."

Jefferson, Madison, Monroe, and the other men whose political philosophy directed the early policy of the future Democratic-Republican party were the first to realize the implications of America's sublime geography. They thought in terms of future expansion at a time when the Federalist leaders were only too ready to sacrifice the frontiers to the "Eastern" interests.

When, after his long journey through the back country, Monroe reached Trenton for the sessions of Congress, he was able to discuss the questions arising from the debates over the western territory with an authority denied nearly all of his colleagues. He was among the few men who had "been there." When he wrote to Madison in November, 1784, concerning the garrisons necessary to hold the military posts which, it was hoped, Great Britain would evacuate in the spring, he was able to say, "Many of the West'rn Posts I have seen & think 1200 the smallest number we should think of."[16] He drafted the report of the committee to which had been referred his own motion to instruct the American Minister to express the "dissatisfaction" of the United States "at the delay of the Court of Great Britain" in complying with the articles of the treaty respecting the withdrawal of the King's troops.[17] His experience on his travels had also enabled him to form definite opinions on another important matter which was to occupy much of the time of the federal legislators—the right of the settlers to navigate the Mississippi, secured to them by the Treaty of 1783 with Great Britain.[18]

It was a critical time for the future of the West, with its vastly important lands between the Alleghenies and the Mississippi. Nor is it possible, even today, to affirm that the destiny of the West was at that time so inevitably fixed as certain later historians somewhat complacently affirm.

In the struggle for this greater empire, which now forms the might and glory of the Republic, no statesman of his time played a more significant part than James Monroe. As the champion in Congress of the still-undefined rights of the United States to the lands ceded by the Treaty of 1783 and to the free navigation of the Mississippi, he performed a service for which credit has too often been denied him. When Jefferson left for France, it was Monroe who took his place as the champion of the "Men of the Western Waters." His authority in these matters was recognized by his contemporaries and they elected him to the chairmanship of the two important committees chiefly concerned with western interests—the committee dealing with the negotiations for the free navigation of the Mississippi (August 25, 1785) and the committee to form a temporary government for the western lands (May 10, 1786).

The dispute with Spain reached its crisis in the summer of 1786—nor were the Spanish pretensions to control of the lower waters of the Mississippi either ill-founded or advanced with unreasonable arrogance. A secret article of the treaty between Great Britain and her former colonies had purposely left vague the southern boundary of the territory ceded to the United States. In the negotiations a notable area of Florida, then a Spanish possession, was calmly apportioned between the late combatants at the expense of the Spanish crown.[19] When the Ministers of Charles and Ferdinand became aware of this diplomatic enterprise, their indignation was both deep and understandable. Moreover, in order to secure the commercial treaty which the merchants of New England and New York so ardently desired, the "Easterners" were ready to sacrifice the vital interests of the backwoodsmen in the use of the Mississippi, the great avenue of western trade.

Monroe's distrust of Jay[20] and the group of what he termed "flagitious" statesmen,[21] who represented the eastern states, may today appear both exaggerated and provincial. Yet, as he had soon realized after his arrival in Congress, the moral tone of that body, never highly esteemed by the army, was, in some respects, more deplorably low than ever. This was notably the case with the conduct of foreign relations. Before the signing of the Treaty of Peace, the "underground" influence of Great Britain and of France was apparent in the votes taken respecting such matters as the appointment of commissioners to arrange peace. France had aimed at nothing less than dictating the instructions which were to control this negotiation.[22] In later years, Morris, in conversation with Jay himself,

Champion of the West

did not hesitate to qualify his fellow members of the Second Congress as "a set of damn scoundrels,"[23] a verdict which few modern historians have seen fit to dispute.[24]

The difficulties which Monroe and his colleagues of the southern states were called upon to face were soon apparent. Many Southerners, even the great Washington himself, were at first opposed to "Western predominance." These tidewater statesmen, while friendly to the men of the expanding frontier, desired to maintain the dependence of the pioneers upon the older colonies. It was a renewal of the old struggle between the lordly Westmoreland planters and the "men of the Forest." Furthermore, Washington had a favorite land project of his own. Immediately after the declaration of peace, he traveled through western Virginia almost to the Ohio. His favorite scheme at this time was the development of a "Potomac Company," which, by connecting the upper waters of the Ohio with the Potomac, "would direct the trade of the new settlements forever to the East."[25] Yet Washington's plan was by no means developed to the point of serving the "Eastern" interests—or the commercial schemes of the merchants of Boston and New York, whose spokesman, John Jay, was one of the chief negotiators of the peace of 1783 and had succeeded Livingston as secretary for foreign affairs. Personifying the contending parties of the East and the South, Jay and Monroe developed an antagonism that was almost inevitable. During Monroe's congressional career, it was to continue as an almost personal duel.

Monroe's concern for the "New Virginia" growing up on the western frontier is understandable. Nor was his solicitude confined to the southern frontiersmen. He was equally aware that the farmers of western Pennsylvania found it to their advantage to ship their produce by way of New Orleans rather than to entrust it to the "axle-breaking roads" that led across the Alleghenies to Philadelphia.[26]

It was mainly about the problems of the frontier that Monroe, waiting in Trenton for a congressional quorum to assemble, wrote to James Madison, recently a member of Congress and at this date a member of the Virginia Assembly. The lifelong friendship between the two men is said to have begun at their meeting in Richmond in 1783, when Monroe took Madison's place in the Virginia legislature. Monroe was younger than Madison by seven years.[27]

As early as December, 1784, Monroe (having previously sent

JAMES MONROE

Madison a "small cypher"), wrote to him, "The conduct of Spain respecting the Mississippi &c. requires the immediate attention of Congress."²⁸ A few weeks later he wrote to Jefferson, "From Spain we expect a Mr. Gardoqui in quality of chargé des affrs. All our measures with that court have of course ceas'd untill his arrival wh. is weekly expected."²⁹

During the summer of 1785, the Court of Spain, in spite of its refusal to recognize a republic on a basis of equality, sent Don Diego de Gardoqui as envoy to the United States, with the sonorous but empty title of *Encargado de Negocios,* which puzzled Congress considerably. Monroe wrote, "We have had some difficulty in regulating the etiquette respecting him. . . . A letter from the King with full powers I sho'd suppose constituted the minister, be the term or stile what it may."³⁰ Gardoqui now discussed with Jay, the new Secretary for Foreign Affairs, "the right of the United States to their territorial bounds and free navigation of the Mississippi."

Jay, unduly influenced by his experiences with the proud and unbending Spanish Court in 1779, was also fully alive to the fact that the merchants of the New England states greatly preferred a favorable treaty with Spain to the outlet to the Gulf so ardently desired by the frontiersmen. It was Jay's honest opinion that the situation justified a surrender of the right of navigation on the Mississippi for a period of twenty-five or thirty years.

Monroe, of course, bitterly opposed this view. He was convinced that such a surrender of any American rights was fraught with the most dangerous possibilities. Nor, in the light of subsequent developments, can it be denied that his view was by far the more statesmanlike and farsighted.

To understand the part played by Monroe in the controversy over the navigation of the Mississippi, it is necessary to realize the vital importance he attached to this issue. He believed that the whole development of the Union was at stake. The solution of this problem would be the touchstone in both foreign and domestic affairs, and would decide, once for all, whether the United States was to constitute a nation or was to repeat, upon a new continent, the petty and complicated state system of Europe. With the development of party, or, as it was first called, "factional" feeling, in Congress, the Mississippi question was to transcend all others.

Champion of the West

Monroe's letters of this period to Madison and Jefferson show his growing distrust of Jay. To Madison, on February 1, 1785, he had written of Jay's proposal to Congress that " 'all foreign letters & papers wh. may be laid before Congress sh'd *in the first instance* be *referred* to him.' " And Monroe added, "Whether it will be the sense of the Committee to make it a matter of right in the minister of foreign aff'rs to advise Congress in the first instance upon the various subjects of his department & preclude themselves from a previous consideration, or will consider the office in a different point of view, consulting when necessary & referring or declining to refer to him, at pleasure, any of the subjects before them, is yet to be determin'd." [31]

But in spite of his doubts as to Jay's intentions, Monroe wrote to Madison a few weeks later that "the arrangement of our foreign affairs begins at last to assume some form." And he was relieved to find that the Spanish envoy was, as he wrote Jefferson, "a polite and sensible man." On July 20, 1785, acting in committee with Gerry and Johnson, Monroe agreed to confer on Jay, as secretary for foreign affairs, "the power to negotiate treaty with Don Diego de Gardoqui." [32]

As Jay soon discovered, his tact and diplomacy had to be exercised not only toward Gardoqui but also toward Monroe and the other members of Congress who opposed his plans for an accommodation with the Spanish Court. On May 31, 1786, Monroe wrote an important letter to Madison expressing his views of the situation. Jay had reported that "difficulties had taken place in his negotiation" and requested " 'that a Committee be appointed without instructions to direct & controul the said negotiations.' It was immediately perceived that his object was to relieve him from the instruction respecting the Mississippi & to get a Committee to cover the measure." Monroe thought that he might "enter into an engagement, at least for a certain term," for the "occlusion" of the Mississippi and a "reciprocal guaranty" of Spain's and America's "respective possessions, . . . in consideration for which we are to be reciprocally, they into our ports here & we into theirs in Europe, upon an equal footing with our citizens and subjects respectively." Monroe reiterated his own opinion that "from the best investigation that I have been able to give the subject I am of opinion . . . that it will be for the benefit of the U S. that the river should be opened." He again asserted his belief that the arrangement that Jay proposed might separate the people—"I mean all those Westw'd of the mountains,—from the Federal Government & perhaps throw them into the hands eventually of a foreign power." He also stated that "a reciprocal guaranty stipulates an important consideration to them without a return." He closed his letter with a somewhat pessimistic review of the interests involved, "as important as they are intricate," and of the motives of the members likely to support Jay's proposal. His one hope, he suggested, lay in the opposition of King, who "hath married a woman of fortune in N. Y. so that if he secures a market for fish and turns the commerce of the Western country down this river he obtains his object."[33]

Finally, in an important and often quoted letter to Patrick Henry, Governor of Virginia, written from New York on August 12, 1786, Monroe makes clear the dangers of the situation and his own increasing conviction that his stand is right. After outlining the course of events in Congress, he says, "It appears manifest that they have 7 states & we 5, Maryland inclusive, with the southern states. Delaware is absent. It also appears that they will go on under 7 states in the business & risque the preservation of the confederacy on it. We have & shall throw every possible obstacle in the way of the measure, protest against the right of 7 either to instruct or ratify, . . . This is one of the most extraordinary transactions I have ever known, a minister negotiating expressly for the purpose of defeating the object of his instructions, and by a long train of intrigue & management seducing the representatives of the states to concur in it."

Monroe's fear for the Union is also expressed in this letter. He continues, "This however is not the only subject of consequence I have to engage your attention to. Certain it is that committees are held in this town of Eastern men and others of this State [New York] upon the subject of a dismemberment of the States east of the Hudson from the Union & the erection of them into a separate govt. To what lengths they have gone I know not, but have assurances as to the truth of the above position, with this addition to it that the measure is talked of in Mass: familiarly, & is supposed to have originated there. . . . I am persuaded these people who are in Congress from that State (at the head of the other business) mean that as a step toward the carriage of this, as it will so displease some of them as to prepare the

Champion of the West

States for this event." The "other business" that Monroe mentions is the matter of the Mississippi, which, he fears, the "Eastern" commercial interests may use toward the dismemberment of the Union. And he adds the poignant statement:

"I am thoroughly persuaded the govt. is practicable & with a few alterations the best that can be devised. To manage our affairs to advantage under it & remedey these defects, in my opinion, nothing is wanting but common sense & common honesty, in both of which necessary qualifications we are, it is to be lamented, very defective. I wish much your sentiments upon these important subjects. . . . Let me hear from you . . ."[34]

This letter induced Henry to exert himself to "defeat the proposed treaty." It was characteristic of Monroe that, having done so much to build up a powerful opposition to the measures he deplored, he should next seek to formulate a compromise that might satisfy all the parties to the dispute. To James Madison he wrote from New York on August 14, 1786: "It has occurred to G. [Grayson] & myself to propose to Congress that negotiations be carried on with Sp'n upon the following principles 1. That exports be admitted thro' the Mississipi to some free port—perhaps N. Orleans, to pay there a toll to Sp'n of ab't 3 pr centm. ad valorem & to be carried thence under the regulations of Congress. . . . That imports shall pass into the western country thro. the ports of the U.S. only. 3. That this sacrifice be given up to obtain in other respects a beneficial treaty. I beg of you to give me y'r opinion on it. It is manifest here that Jay & his party in Congress are determin'd to pursue this business as far as possible, either as the means of throwing the western people & territory without the gov't of the U. S. and keeping the weight of population & gov't here, or of dismembering the gov't itself, for the purpose of a separate Confederacy. There can be no other object than one of these & I am from such evidence as I have, doubtful which hath the influence. I write in Congress & therefore am deprived of the advantage of the cypher, but am so desirous of y'r sentiments as to risque mine without that cover."[35]

Another of Monroe's anxieties concerning the free navigation of the Mississippi was the defection of at least one important member of the Virginia delegation—Henry Lee. And behind Lee loomed the great First Citizen's disapproval of Monroe's efforts. On January 19,

1786, Monroe had written to Jefferson deploring the death of a favorite colleague, Hardy, and mildly complaining that in the delegation as transformed, "I am unacquainted with those added to it, Colonel Carrington and Henry Lee of the horse."[36] In spite of the instructions of the Virginia Assembly, the redoubtable "Light-Horse Harry" held a private opinion that Monroe attached too much importance to the Mississippi question and that the main interest was to secure an accommodation with Spain. In this he was privately supported by no less an authority than General Washington, who wrote Lee from Mount Vernon:

"If I stopped short of your ideas respecting the navigation of the Miss[issippi], or of what may be the opinion of Congress on the subject, it was not from want of coincidence of sentiments, but because I was ignorant, at that time, of the rubs which are in the way of your commercial treaty with Spain, and because I thought some address might be necessary to temporize with Kentucky and keep that settlement in a state of quietness. At this moment it is formidable and the population is rapidly increasing."[37]

Washington's own very practical scheme for binding the western settlements to the tidewater by means of canals connecting the Potomac with the rivers flowing into the Ohio led him to deprecate a policy that would furnish an alternate outlet for western traffic toward the Gulf of Mexico and would tend further to detach the "Men of the Western Waters" from all dependence on the commercial ports of the Atlantic coast. Although Monroe found himself supported by the political sentiment of Virginia (and, as it turned out, Lee was to lose his seat in consequence of a too honest expression of views) the discovery that the powerful influence radiating from Mount Vernon was tending to support the position of the eastern states must have been disconcerting to him.[38]

Meanwhile Monroe's prestige in Congress had increased considerably. In accordance with his report as chairman of a committee dealing with the Mississippi matter, Congress had instructed Jay (August 25, 1785) "particularly to stipulate the right of the United States to their territorial bounds, and the free navigation of the Missisipi from the source to the ocean, as established by their treaty with Great Britain; and that he neither conclude nor sign any treaty, compact or convention, with the said encargardo de negocios until

Champion of the West

he hath previously communicated it to Congress and received their approbation."[39] This measure, in the final outcome of the negotiation, was to become the main factor in the situation, and was to furnish the parliamentary basis for the rejecting or "postponement" of the entire matter. Monroe, with the added influence of his chairmanship of the committee on commercial treaties, was now in a position to checkmate the plans of the Secretary for Foreign Affairs and the demands of the eastern states that Spain should be placated, at all costs, in the interests of the shipping trade.

Monroe's final action respecting the Mississippi question was to draft and present the motion of the Virginia delegates, whose immediate interest in the ceded territories (settled mainly by citizen of Virginia) gave them a right to remonstrance which even the most ardent proponents of "occlusion" were bound to respect. This somewhat repetitious document (dated August 29, 1786), set forth and reviewed at length the whole course of the committee's dealings with Jay, and concluded: "As to the surrender or forbearance of the use of the navigation of the Mississippi, for the term proposed, for the consideration proposed . . . it is inadmissable. . . ."[40]

A good part of Monroe's last year of service in Congress was taken up with the problems of the relations of the Indians and the settlers on the frontier. For some years the tide of immigrants had been flowing strongly down the Ohio. At the close of 1785 there were estimated to be something like fifty thousand west of Pittsburgh, mostly of English, Scotch-Irish, and German stock. But the Indians were restless. They had agreed, by the Treaty of Fort Stanwix (1768) that the Ohio should be their southern boundary, and under the leadership of Joseph Brant and emissaries of the British at Detroit, they were ready to resist further encroachment. The situation required careful handling, and a commission was appointed to meet with the Indian chiefs and prepare for a further treaty. The indefatigable Monroe accompanied the party—for "private considerations," his opponents maintained. These "considerations," however, as the sequel shows, were his wish to do something for the much-neglected men who had fought in the Revolution. A treaty was finally signed January 31, 1786, with the Indians leaving hostages for good behavior, and the way was at last open to further settlement in the western lands.

JAMES MONROE

Monroe wrote to Jefferson about the trip, saying that it was his intention "to take a view of the Indian treaty to be held at the mouth of the big Miami, and of the country lying between lake Erie, and the head waters of the James or Potom'k rivers, with those w'h empty from either side into the Ohio." But unfortunately "the danger from the Indians made it imprudent for me to pass the river, and the delay at fort Pitt, and upon the Ohio, the water being low," was so long that he was obliged to give up his plan and "take my course directly thro' the Kentucky settlements & the wilderness to Richmond."[41]

On May 10, 1786, a committee of which Monroe was chairman reported to Congress concerning the "Plan of a Temporary Government" for the western states.[42] He was deeply interested, too, in the plan of General Benjamin Tupper, of Massachusetts, who was studying the western country with an eye to its colonization by his former comrades-in-arms. General Rufus Putnam was an enthusiastic ally of Tupper in working out the project. The closing chapters of this adventure do not strictly belong to Monroe's story, for he was no longer a member of the Federal Congress when on July 13, the celebrated "Ordinance of 1787" was finally passed—the last constructive act of a somewhat futile legislature soon to be transformed by the adoption of the Constitution. From his retirement, however, he must have felt satisfaction in the accomplishment of an objective he had so long worked for—the adoption of a system for the West which permitted the veterans of the Revolution to set up their Soldier State upon the nation's frontiers.

Throughout this period, Monroe was concerned with still another issue—the right of the Confederation to regulate commerce. American trade had fallen on evil days, mainly because of the inability of Congress to reconcile the divergent interests of various sections of the country. In 1785 John Adams was in London protesting in vain against the Navigation Acts and threatening reprisals which the British knew only too well must, under the Confederation, be mere mouthings. In the meantime the once lucrative trade between the States and the West Indies was carried on perforce only in British ships, while the cargoes of American ships trading with Great Britain were limited to articles produced in the particular states of which their owners were citizens. It was, actually, a continuation, along commercial lines, of the war which the Treaty of 1783 had sup-

Champion of the West

posedly brought to a victorious conclusion for the United States.

But instead of uniting against Great Britain, the common enemy, the states were engaged in a bitter trade war among themselves. In 1785, ten states voted power to Congress to regulate commerce for the ensuing thirteen years, but the acts by which this power was granted were such a jumble of incongruities that Congress was forced to refer them back to the several state legislatures with a request that some measure of uniformity be given them.[43] Meanwhile, Massachusetts, New Hampshire, and Rhode Island passed navigation acts of their own against Great Britain, while Connecticut perversely opened her ports at once to British ships but laid duties upon imports from Massachusetts. Pennsylvania waged commercial war on Delaware as well as on New Jersey, and New York City put import duties on goods from New England and New Jersey.

This was the situation facing Monroe when he took charge of the Committee on Commerce, consisting of Spaight of North Carolina, Houston of Georgia, King of Massachusetts, and Johnson of Connecticut.[44]

On March 28, 1785 the committee submitted a report, recommending that the ninth Article of Confederation be altered so as to grant Congress right and power of regulating the trade of the states with foreign nations as well as with each other. To Jefferson Monroe commented: "If the report sho'd ultimately be adopted it will certainly form the most permanent and powerful principle in the confederation. At present the alliance is little more than an offensive and defensive one, . . . On the other hand, the effect of this report w'd be to put the commercial economy of every state entirely under the hands of the Union, the measure necessary to obtain the carrying trade, to encourage domestic by a tax on foreign industry, or any other ends which in the changes of things become necessary, will depend entirely on the Union. . . . This will give the Union an authority upon the States respectively which will last with it & hold it together in its present form longer than any principle it now contains will effect."[45]

Quoting from Adam Smith's *Wealth of Nations*, Monroe continues his letter to Jefferson by expressing the hope that "the giving of our own citizens a show in the carrying trade . . . will turn what is called the 'balance of trade' in our favor." At the same time he records the opinion of "a Mr. Smith on the wealth of nations that the balance of trade is a chimera...."[46]

In a letter of March 26, 1785, Joseph Jones had inquired anxiously, had "Congress been authorized by the states to regulate commerce for fifteen years, and what is proper to be done to counteract the British policy?"[47] The question was premature, but on June 2, as chairman of the Committee on Commercial Treaties, Monroe drafted a report giving authority to the commissioners appointed to negotiate such treaties to make trade agreements.[48]

These broad questions regarding the control of commerce and the formation of commercial arrangements with foreign nations were, however, beyond the power of a loosely formed Confederation to settle with any degree of certainty or satisfaction. But the spadework done by Monroe as chairman of the important commerce committee did much to prepare the way for their solution five years later.

8

"The Most Interesting Connection"

THE SPRING of 1785 had not been a particularly happy one for Monroe. Somewhere in the last of March he had contracted a bad "ague and fever" and was "very ill." Monroe was often troubled in later life by vicious attacks of what he called "rheumatism." On April 15, 1785, his uncle is writing to say how happy he is to hear his nephew is "so soon over a very dangerous disorder."

Monroe was also plagued by indecision on the subject of his private career. Judge Jones, in April, 1785, had written advising him that, if ". . . your real design is to undertake the Law, the sooner you did it the better." Mercer and Marshall, he warns, are about to fix their residence and establish their practice just where Monroe was thinking of hanging out a shingle, and, says the Judge, ". . . as they . . . are by no means destitute of abilities for their standing at the Bar, especially the last named, you will find it a disadvantage to come after them. You shod. seriously consider and determine the point, wheth. to undertake the law or not—if you determine to make that an object, you shod. pretermit all others, and as a man engages to do with a woman he marries, cleave only unto her. . . . It is high time you fixed your course for life, if you mean to adhere to any particular pursuit, and not rove at large depending on expedients and contingencies."[1]

By May, Monroe had evidently made up his mind to settle down to a law practice in Fredericksburg, for from another of the Judge's letters[2] we learn that young James has been corresponding with a

JAMES MONROE

Mr. Maury and a Mr. Dawson about a lot and house "on the hill" in that town. He nevertheless intended continuing in politics. "I had some conversation with Col. Taliaferro," writes Judge Jones sometime in 1785, "respecting your offering your service for the County the coming year, and it was his opinion it wod. be indispensably necessary you shod. be in the County before the election and attend it when made."[3]

The winter of 1786 found Monroe in New York, attending the session of Congress and involved in a whirl of activities. He was active in affairs of state, associating daily with the most important men in the nation. His social life was spent with his old friends of the war days, the Stirlings and the Duers, both representative of the city's glittering best families. And his private life was even more exciting. James Monroe was in love.

"There is a report circulating in this neighborhood," wrote John Taliaferro to Monroe in February, 1786, "that a certain member was lately wounded in New York by the little God Cupid. As the Belle Dame is in this city, can you tell me what is the gentleman's name?"[4]

Taliaferro did not need to be told either the belle dame's or the gentleman's name. Their circle of acquaintance was already buzzing with the astonishing news that the beautiful Elizabeth Kortright, whose reputation for exclusiveness, to be maintained to her dying day, was already firmly established in New York society, had consented to marry the "not particularly attractive Virginia Congressman, Monroe."[5] He was not unattractive, with his well-formed, rawboned figure just short of six feet. Someone once called him "respectable looking."[6] His eyes, according to another critic, had "more kindness than penetration."[7]

Elizabeth Kortright, it is said, always awed people. She had the hauteur of the born aristocrat and was something of the grande dame even in her girlhood. It was reported by Mrs. Burton Harrison that Miss Kortright's friends, when they heard of her marriage, "twitted her with the amiable reflection that she was expected to have done better."[8] Nevertheless it proved to be an unusually successful marriage.

Monroe, for some time before the wedding, had been corresponding on the subject of marriage with Judge Jones, who advised his nephew thus: "You will act prudently so soon as you determine to fix

"The Most Interesting Connection"

yourself to business to form the connection you propose with the person you mention or some other as your inclination and convenience shall dictate. Sensibility and kindness of heart, good nature without levity, a modest share of good sense with some portion of domestic experience and economy will generally if united in the female character bring that happiness and benefit which result from the marriage state, and is the highest human felicity a Man can enjoy...."[9]

The good Judge's rather astringent treatment of so warm a matter failed, evidently, to dampen the young man's impetuosity. Under date of March 2, 1786, Monroe informed his uncle that "... on the Thursday ensuing I was united to the young lady I mentioned. To avoid the idle ceremonies of the place we withdrew into the country for a few days. We have been several days since return'd to her father's house since which I have as usual attended Congress."[10]

He also told his uncle of his intention to take his bride back to Virginia with him "the latter end of Sepr. next," in the meantime attempting to fix on a place of residence. He still could not decide whether it should be Fredericksburg or Richmond.

In a letter of April 20, 1786, Monroe's uncle again addressed him: "When I shall relinquish my present state," he says, "I know not ... nor need it interfere with your settlement in Fredericksburg, as you proposed. If I do not reside there I shall be much with you and ... make your situation as easy and convenient as I can." He ends, "If a chariot can be had, neat and light in Philadelphia," it is to be purchased for a sum not to exceed 220 pounds and his nephew is to use it to transport his wife to Fredericksburg.[11]

On May 11 Monroe could write definitely to Jefferson telling him that in the "fall ... we remove to Fredericksb'g in Virg'a. where I shall settle for the present in a house prepar'd for me by Mr. Jones to enter into the practice of the law."[12] And on May 15 his letter of resignation from Congress was presented. He continued to serve until the late fall, and he wrote Jefferson from New York on October 12, "I am wearied with the business in w'h I have been engag'd. It has been a year of excessive labour & fatigue & unprofitably so."[13]

It was his uncle's advice that finally persuaded Monroe to settle in Fredericksburg. And it was in his uncle's house, one which the Judge had "lately bought of Mr. Bowdoin"[14] that he was to live.

[93]

JAMES MONROE

Monroe would have preferred Albemarle, where he could have had his good friend Jefferson as neighbor. To the latter he wrote in August: "Believe me I have not relinquished the prospect of being your neighbour. The house for which I have requested a plan may possibly be erected near Monticello—to fix there & to have yourself in particular, with what friends we may collect around, for society is my chief object, or rather the only one which promises to me, with the connection I have formed, real & substantial pleasure, . . ."[15]

But these plans were not to be realized, and Monroe had to satisfy himself with the society of the citizens of Fredericksburg. Actually, outside of Richmond and Williamsburg, Fredericksburg was the most desirable site for Monroe's purposes. It offered a busy and litigious community of Scotch merchants and factors that promised a good harvest of cases for a young lawyer. In October, 1786, Monroe was admitted to the bar of the Courts of Appeal and Chancery and, in the following April, to the General Court. And, in his law office in Charles Street,[16] the newly fledged attorney began his practice.

A letter to Madison, written May 23, 1787, shows that Monroe was already chafing at the narrow scope of his activities: "My leisure furnishes me with the opportunity but the country around does not with the materials to form a letter worthy your attention. The scale of my observations is a narrow one & confin'd entirely within my room: & the subjects of my researches in which I am but seeking to make some proficiency, as I sho'd only detail to you the sentiments of others, give me nothing to supply the deficiency."[17]

But he was not long to be restricted to the narrow confines of private life. Through Judge Jones, he won election to the town council (on which his single recorded act was to vote in favor of prohibiting a company of players from giving a performance), and soon he found himself eligible for a seat in the Virginia Assembly. He wrote Jefferson on July 27, 1787, "Mrs. Monroe hath added a daughter to our society who tho' noisy, contributes greatly to its amusement.... With the political world I have had little to do since I left Congress. My anxiety however for the gen'l welfare hath not been diminished. The affairs of the federal government are, I believe, in the utmost confusion."[18]

Throughout the years 1785 and 1786—the twilight hours of the

"The Most Interesting Connection"

Confederation—the proposed changes in the national government occupied Monroe's close attention and formed the subject of a steady correspondence with Jefferson and Madison. No personal relationships founded on common interests, opinions, and loyalties such as united these three men—Jefferson, Madison, Monroe—has ever more profoundly affected the political life of a nation. In 1786 the ties were strongest between Jefferson and Monroe. "I look forward with anxiety," wrote Jefferson to Monroe in August of that year, "to the approaching moment of your departure from Congress. I know not to whom I may venture confidential interests when you are gone."[19] In this triumvirate Monroe played a subordinate part. He was inferior to Madison in intellectual capacity, but his genius for friendship drew him closer to Jefferson's heart than Madison ever was. "He is a man whose soul might be turned wrong side outwards," said Jefferson, "without discovering a blemish to the world."

9

The New Roof

THE AUTUMN of the fateful year 1787 found Monroe in Richmond accompanied by his wife and her sister awaiting the opening of the Virginia Assembly. The Constitutional Convention had finished its monumental labors in Philadelphia on September 17. Monroe's absence from that notable gathering may well have involved a certain disillusion. The leading part he had taken in Congress concerning the issues most likely to affect Virginia's stand towards the proposed new form of government made him in many respects a logical member of the delegation. But Edmund Randolph, the energetic young Governor, had decided, in view of the importance of the occasion, to attend in person, and in the face of his popularity and prestige Monroe's claims to share in the Constitutional debates fell to the ground. Monroe's disappointment was the more bitter because of his disposition to project his private friendships into the imponderable and treacherous associations of the political arena. In a letter to Jefferson (July 27) he complained that "the Governor, I have reason to believe, is unfriendly to me & hath shewn (If I am well inform'd) a disposition to thwart me"; and, even more serious, "Madison, upon whose friendship I have calculated, whose views I have favor'd, and with whom I have held the most confidential correspondence" is "in strict league" with the Governor.[1] To a man who placed so high a value on personal loyalty, these defections were hard to bear. They were, moreover, the first disillusion of a public career until now fortunate, even beyond the deserts of young Monroe's talents or experience. The support of his uncle,

The New Roof

Judge Jones, of Jefferson, and of Madison had played a part that the young Congressman was inclined, perhaps pardonably, to ascribe too exclusively to his own merits and good intentions.

Monroe anticipated a spirited contest over the Constitution in his native state and was no little excited by it. On October 13 he wrote to Madison from Richmond: "The report from Phil'a. hath presented an interesting subject. . . . It will perhaps agitate the minds of the people of this State more than any subject they have had in contemplation since the commencem't of the late revolution, for there will be a greater division among the people of character than then took place, provided we are well informed as to the sentiments of many of them. It is said that Mr. Henry, Gen'l. Nelson, Harrison & others are against it. This insures it a powerful opposition more especially when associated with that of the 2 dissenting deputies.[2] There are in my opinion some strong objections agñst the project w'h I will not weary you with a detail of. But under the predicament in w'h the Union now stands & this State in particular with respect to this business, they are over balanc'd by the arguments in its favor."[3]

It is probable that Monroe's views were, far more than either Madison's or Randolph's, those generally held by Virginians. As Beveridge has pointed out, the people at large were in no frame of mind for any government that meant federal power, taxes, and the restrictions implicit in a scheme of organized national life. These were principles supported solely by commercial and financial interests, by what Washington referred to as "mercantile persons," and which represented the industrial East. The agricultural South was strongly opposed. So, too, was the agricultural element even in the East. In Massachusetts, the rural population of the Berkshires joined hands with Kentucky and Tennessee frontiersmen in openly defying the tax-collector. In "Shays's Rebellion," these grievances found dangerous expression. Jefferson actually expressed sympathy with this movement and his influence on Monroe's opinions in this question must not be neglected as a potent factor in the stand the latter took.

Monroe's part in the Virginia Ratifying Convention, to which he had been elected as delegate from Spotsylvania County, is shown in two of his literary ventures, the first in the shape of a program addressed to his constituents of Spotsylvania;[4] the second a more or

JAMES MONROE

less autobiographical review of the debates, his stand on the various questions and the reasons for it. Washington, who was furnished with a copy of the first, wrote to Monroe: "However I may differ with you in sentiment . . . I am pleased in discovering so much candour and liberality as seem to predominate in your style and manner of investigation."[5] From the second composition (sometimes attributed to Madison),[6] a summary of Monroe's views as he expressed them at the convention can be obtained.

Although the opening of the convention on June 2, 1788, coincided with the annual Jockey Club races, a crowd of spectators was nevertheless attracted, probably by the prospect of seeing assembled all the most famous men in Virginia's recent stirring history. No event since the Revolution had called forth such a brilliant assemblage.

Among the one hundred and seventy attending, a majority were probably anti-Federalist. But the advocates of the Constitution had prepared the ground carefully and had managed, by their superior strategy, to turn many from the course which they had planned and which their constituents had depended on them to take. Those opposed to the Constitution placed their hopes on the flaming eloquence of Patrick Henry, who, whenever he spoke, filled the galleries with breathless listeners and drew back to their seats on the floor the delegates who were only too wont to be in the anteroom, where they preferred to transact their business.

Until the opening of the debate Randolph, like Monroe, had taken a middle course. Of him Washington had written to Lafayette, "The governor, if he approves it at all, will do it feebly."[7] But by Washington's adroit persuasion and Madison's convincing arguments, Randolph was finally induced to become Henry's chief opponent. His change of front was, in the fashion of the time, imputed to improper motives, a charge which his subsequent appointment as first attorney general under the new Constitution did nothing to mitigate. To Monroe, who believed that the Governor had been elected to the Constitutional Convention as a critic rather than as a proponent of the Constitution, this sudden conversion must have been especially distasteful. But the arguments of Madison he found even more disturbing. He was shaken and bewildered to find himself opposed to this friend, whose intellect he so admired.

The New Roof

Madison, fresh from his labors with Hamilton as propagandist for the Constitution in the pages of the *Federalist*, rose to speak in support of his convert Randolph. Handsome in blue and buff costume carefully contrived to make up in impressiveness what he lacked in height, his hair combed forward to hide his premature baldness, Madison drew from his hat the first pages of a long and superbly logical address that was to continue, despite the interruptions of the debate, to its remorseless climax during the closing days of the session. He began to speak, and it did not take long for his hearers to realize that in him, a master of political science, the Constitutionalists had their most competent spokesman. Monroe, shaken if not convinced, later wrote to Jefferson that to his mind Madison overshadowed all who took part in that memorable occasion.

When Patrick Henry rose to speak in an attempt to offset Madison's telling address, it had become apparent that the success or failure of the Constitutionalist bloc hinged on the votes of the thirteen frontiersmen in homespun who represented Kentucky. Addressing himself particularly to these delegates, as well as to those from the backwoods of the tidewater, Henry outlined the dangers inherent in the Constitution threatening the navigation of the Mississippi, arguing that the preponderance given the eastern states, notably in the Senate, would doom this most cherished right. He revealed publicly for the first time that only the determination of the six southern states to preserve western rights had thwarted the aim of the seven northern states that had voted for occlusion. Had the Senate devised under the Constitution been in control of this issue, he argued, the West's cause would have been lost. Corwin's masterly summary of Henry's argument briefly presents his chief thesis as follows: "The treaty-power could 'dismember the Empire,' by which he meant particularly that it could surrender the Mississippi country; second, that it could sacrifice personal rights and inflict unusual punishments for the violation of treaties; third, that the treaty-power was paramount not only to State laws and constitutions but also to the acts of Congress...."[8] Henry closed his telling address by calling upon Monroe and the other members of the Continental Congress, who now sat on the floor of the Convention, to bear him out in his interpretation.

It was the soldierly ardor of Harry Lee, a defender of the Constitution, that momentarily prevented the immediate testimony which

Henry thus demanded. Leaping to his feet at the close of Henry's address, he injected into the discussion a new issue concerning the militia of the Commonwealth, in which Henry, like Jefferson, saw the chief palladium of every Republic. Lee now taunted the last speaker with passing judgment on the conduct of the Continental regulars without having himself shown a soldier's spirit during the Revolution. Randolph contributed further interruption by launching a bitter, a personal attack on Henry.

Both these interruptions were in the Constitutionalists' favor but had little bearing on the subject in hand. It was not until the next morning that the debate resumed its logical course, with Monroe's rising to speak in corroboration of Henry's statements regarding the voting on the Mississippi question.

Monroe was an ideal champion for the cause he had been chosen to advocate, a cause that had a direct appeal for him. In his first speech, made on June 10, he had cautiously declared that he came "not as the partisan of this or that side of the question, but to commend where the subject appears to me to deserve commendation; to suggest my doubts where I have any; to hear with candor the explanation of others. . . ." In this, his second speech, he took a more decisive stand. And if his halting eloquence scarcely rose to the level of that of other orators, his sincerity and open-mindedness were enough to secure careful attention. In response to Henry's call, he reviewed his long battle in Congress to prevent the occlusion of the Mississippi. He said, in effect, that "in spite of the strenuous opposition of the Southern States, the seven Easternmost States had voted to repeal the instructions which made the free navigation of the Mississippi a *sine qua non* of the treaty," and declared "that the interest in the western country would not be as secure, under the proposed Constitution, as under the Confederation; because, under the latter system, the Mississippi could not be relinquished without the consent of nine states; whereas, by the former, a majority of seven states could yield it."[9]

The Federalist chosen to reply to Monroe's argument was his boyhood friend, later the country's foremost jurist and interpreter of the document over which the two men differed. Marshall, at this point of his career, was celebrated mainly for his oratorical gifts. Since their Richmond days, the two men had followed divergent ways. Monroe

The New Roof

had already begun the difficult ascent to public achievement; Marshall had been enjoying a quiet success at the bar. At the convention their paths crossed, and they met, as they were many times again to meet, in political battle.

As Marshall subsequently admitted, the people who had elected him to the convention were opposed to the Constitution. It was his personal popularity which had won the votes, not any promise to depart from his course of championing the New Plan. Urging that the power of taxation be given Congress, he reasoned, brilliantly, that "The friends of the constitution are as tenacious of liberty as its enemies. . . . Our inquiry here must be, whether the power of taxation be necessary to perform the objects of the constitution and whether it be safe, and as well guarded as human wisdom can do it. What are the objects of the national government? To protect the United States and to promote the general welfare. Protection in time of war is one of its primal objects. Until mankind shall cease to have avarice and ambition, wars shall arise. There must be men and money to protect us. How are armies to be raised? Must we not have money for that purpose? But the honorable gentleman says that we need not be afraid of war. Look at history, . . ."[10]

Monroe, in his address, had wisely attacked the Constitutionalists at their weakest points: the Mississippi issue and the absence from the proposed Constitution of a Bill of Rights. On the former, Marshall, himself a product of the frontier and the leglislative agent for the men of Kentucky, could speak with authority. "How," he asked, "were the liberties of the frontiers to be preserved by an impotent central Government? Was the Mississippi safe in the hands of the Confederation? Could the ends sought by the frontier be secured by retaining that weak Government which has hitherto kept it from us? No! Only by providing an instrument of Nationality, sufficiently strong to make our just cause respected by Great Britain and Spain could this great result be achieved."[11] The issue of the Bill of Rights, eloquently brought forward by Patrick Henry as well as Monroe, held surprisingly little interest for the men who deliberated that day in Convention Hall, and Marshall could safely pass quickly to a subject on which he could use his eloquence to advantage, the proposed federal judiciary. "The debate on the Judiciary," comments Beveridge, "was the climax of the fight."[12] Neither Monroe, always indifferent to legal questions, nor Madison took an important part in this debate. It was Henry who undertook the battle. "The purse is gone; the sword is gone," he thundered, and now the scales of justice were to slip from the hands of the state. "Shall Americans," he asked, referring to trial by jury, "give up that which nothing could induce the English people to relinquish? The idea is abhorrent to my mind." Equally abhorrent to him was the supremacy of a national court. Characteristic was his threat, "Old as I am . . . I may yet have the appellation of *rebel*. . . ." Closing his arguments to the accidental accompaniment of crashing thunder, he left the breathless audience again a thrall to his matchless tongue.

But Marshall had not fallen under the spell. He rose, and shattered the objections of the opposition, recapturing the field. The anti-Federalists, sensing defeat, expended their final efforts in securing consideration at some future time of the amendments that even the most fanatic Constitutionlists admitted to be necessary. Tyler did make a last attempt to alter the New Plan by insisting on a Bill of Rights, but Madison protested that it could be secured by the action of the proposed federal Congress in the future. On the final count, the Constitution was adopted by the slender majority of ten.

Monroe, although properly counted among the anti-Constitutionalists, experienced no sharp disappointment at the defeat of his faction and was one of the first to accept the Constitution as a *fait accompli*. As he wrote a few weeks later to Jefferson, "All parties had acknowledged defects in the federal system, and been sensible of the propriety of some material change." He admitted to no inclination to enlist himself on either side, in fact. The amendments for which he had argued at the convention, he felt, would not fail to be passed by Congress. A great deal of his confidence stemmed from the trust he put in General Washington. "Be assured," he wrote, "his influence carried this Government; for my own part I have a boundless confidence in him nor have I any reason to believe he will ever furnish occasion for withdrawing it."[13]

In the sessions of the Virginia Assembly, which met in October, 1788, was fought the final battle over a second Constitutional Convention, championed by the anti-Federalists as the means of securing a revision of the New Plan. The guiding spirit of the movement was Patrick Henry, whose power can be judged by Washington's com-

The New Roof

ment to Madison that Henry's ". . . edicts . . . are enregistered with less opposition [i.e. by the Virginia Assembly], than those of the Grand Monarch are in the Parliament of France. He has only to say, let this be Law, and it is Law."[14] Henry was honestly convinced that "four fifths of our inhabitants are opposed to the new scheme of government," and declared his intention of seeking its revision "in a constitutional way."[15] The weeks that passed between the Constitution's adoption by the convention and the Assembly meetings Henry employed in systematic agitation for amendment. He pursued that goal until the first ten amendments embodying the Bill of Rights were finally passed by Congress on the fifteenth of December, 1791. He had left little to chance. Madison, when he prophesied to Washington that Henry would "get a Congress appointed in the first instance that will commit suicide on their own authority,"[16] knew whereof he spoke. Henry dictated the nomination of two senators by the Virginia Assembly, Richard Henry Lee and William Grayson, seeing to it that Madison was defeated. That done, he set about forestalling Madison's election to Congress by the people at large. Resorting to the plan which in Massachusetts became famous as "Gerrymandering," in tribute to one of its most astute practitioners, Elbridge Gerry, Henry drew the lines of the federal districts so as to secure everywhere a majority of anti-Federalist votes. But for once the ruse did not succeed. Madison was elected by a majority of 300. The man he defeated was James Monroe.

It was an odd contest. The platforms of the candidates were identical. The men themselves were friends. After it was over, Monroe found himself almost apologizing to Jefferson: "It wo'd have given me concern to have excluded him [Madison], but those to whom my conduct in publick life had been acceptable, press'd me to come forward in this Govt. on its commencement; and that I might not lose an opportunity of contributing my feeble efforts, in forwarding an amendment of its defects, nor shrink from the station those who confided in me wod. wish to place me, I yielded. As I had no private object to gratify so a failure has given me no private concern."[17]

Jefferson, in Paris observing apprehensively the gathering storm of the French Revolution, answered the letters of Monroe and Madison in a vein of philosophic detachment, the result, no doubt, of the perspective of home affairs his distance from them gave him. On the Constitutional question, he held to middle ground. He looked with favor on "a declaration of rights," but the fanaticism of a Patrick Henry was impossible for a thoughtful spectator in the Paris of the 1780's. "We were educated in Royalism," he wrote to Madison, "no wonder some of us retain that idolatry still."[18] He would lose his tolerance once he found himself back in the scenes that vividly recalled his own country's epic struggle with "Royalism," but for the moment he walked between the pro-Federalist Madison and Monroe, the disciple of fervently democratic Patrick Henry.

The letters that brought Virginia into Jefferson's Paris study and Jefferson's warm presence into Monroe's little office in Fredericksburg continued and deepened the extraordinary friendship between these two men. Monroe, writing of his desire to settle near Jefferson's Albemarle home, was gratified with the older man's reply: "It would indeed be a pleasant circumstance to me to see you settle in the neighborhood of Monticello."[19] And some time before, he had written: "I find friendship to be like wine, raw when new, ripened with age, the true old man's milk and restorative cordial. . . . I wish to heaven, you may continue in the disposition to fix . . . in Albemarle. Short will establish himself there, and perhaps Madison may be tempted to do so. This will be society enough, and it will be a great sweetener of our lives. Without society, and a society to our taste, men are never contented."[20]

Finally, Jefferson was informed by his friend that the desired change of residence had been made: "It has always been my wish to acquire property near Monticello. I have lately accomplish'd it by the purchase of Colo. G. Nicholas improvements in Charlotteville & 800 acres of land within a mile, on the road to the R. fish Gap— . . . Whether to move up immediately or hereafter when I shall be so happy as to have you as a neighbour I have not determin'd. In any event it puts it within my reach to be contiguous to you when the fatigue of publick life shod. dispose you for retirement, and in the interim will enable me in respect to your affairs, as I shall be frequently at Charlotteville as a summer retreat, and in attendance on the district court there, to render you some service."[21]

In August, 1789, he wrote again to Jefferson, saying: "We may move on Monday next to Albemarle, having already sent up the

The New Roof

principal part of our furniture &c.—You will address me in the future by the way of Richmond."[22]

The Monroes first occupied a house and farm in Charlottesville, which still stand on ground now a part of the University of Virginia campus. This house he enlarged, and made use of a neighboring small building as an office. Later he purchased the plantation close to Monticello and built there the first section of his "cabin-castle," which today is probably the rear portion of Ash Lawn. In Monroe's absence in France, Jefferson supervised construction for him.[23] In a letter to Jefferson sent from Paris in November, 1795, Monroe writes: "I accept with great pleasure your proposal to forward my establishment on the tract adjoining you, in the expectation, however, that you will give yourself no further trouble in it than by employing for me a suitable undertaker who will receive from you the plan he is to execute, that you will draw on me for the money to pay him, & make my plantation one of the routes you take when you ride for exercise, at which time you may note how far the execution corresponds with the plan. With this view I shall look out for a model to be forwarded you as soon as possible, subjecting it to yr. correction, & give you full power to place my house, orchards, &c. where you please. . . ."[24]

On January 20, 1796, he wrote to James Madison: "Mr. Jefferson proposes to have a house built for me on my plantation near him & to wh. I have agreed under conditions that will make the burden as light as possible upon him. For this purpose I am about to send 2 plans to him submitting both to his judgment, & contemplate accepting the offer of a skilful mason here who wishes to emigrate & settle with us, to execute the work. I wish yrself & Mr. Jones to see the plans & council with Mr. Jefferson on the subject."[25]

Nothing is known of the plans sent from Paris, or of Jefferson's later corrections.

Here in Albemarle Monroe made his home until he became president, when he built "Oak Hill," and here were spent the happiest and most prosperous years of his busy career. Jefferson, from his mountaintop, looked down upon the good earth and rhapsodized: "Where has nature spread so rich a mantle under the eye? mountains, forests, rocks, rivers. With what majesty do we ride above the storms! How sublime to look down into the workhouse of nature, to see her clouds, hail, snow, rain, thunder, all fabricated at our feet! and the glorious sun when rising as if out of a distant water, just gilding the tops of the mountains, and giving life to all nature!"[26] Monroe was less articulate, but no less appreciative.

Abandoning the East when he came to Charlottesville, Monroe abandoned also what it lived and thought by—the "Atlantic tradition." He was leaving behind him the aristocratic interests of the "hard-drinking, fox-hunting imitators of the English squires," and dedicating himself to the interests of the "hard-working, hard-thinking men who wrestled with nature as with their consciences," building "churches in the woods and school houses in the clearings." Like Jefferson, Monroe loved the men of the West whose break with the traditions of Europe, which the Tidewater planters copied so faithfully, was complete. In Congress, where he had long fought their battles, he had done as much as any statesman to secure the titles to their lands through the Ordinances of 1784 and 1787 and to maintain their rights to a free navigation of the Mississippi. It was, he felt, not as a stranger, but as their tried and experienced champion that he came to the foothills of the tall Allegheny chain that was the geographical boundary between these people of the West and the aristocrats of the older Virginia.

Jefferson, returning from his European "exile," hastened to Albemarle. From Monticello he wrote on the fourteenth of February in 1790, telling the President that he would "no longer hesitate to undertake" the office of Secretary of State that Washington had urged upon him the previous November.[27] On March 21, he had arrived in New York. In June, Monroe heard from him. "Congress has been long embarrassed," wrote Jefferson, "by two of the most irritating questions that ever can be raised among them: 1. the funding the public debt, and 2. the fixing of a more central residence. After exhausting their arguments & patience on these subjects, they have for some time been resting on their oars, unable to get along as to these businesses, and indisposed to attend to anything else till they are settled. And, in fine, it has become probable that unless they can be reconciled by some plan of compromise, there will be no funding bill agreed to, our credit (raised by late prospects to be the first on the exchange at Amsterdam, where our paper is above par) will burst and vanish, and the states separate, to take care every one of itself."

The New Roof

A passage in this same letter that seems to have caused Monroe some anxiety foreshadowed the celebrated and much criticized arrangement with Hamilton: "I have been, and still am of their opinion, that Congress should always prefer letting the States raise money in their own way, where it can be done. But in the present instance, I see the necessity of yielding to the cries of the creditors in certain parts of the Union; for the sake of union, and to save us from the greatest of all calamities, the total extinction of our credit in Europe."[28]

There are historians who persist in making Monroe the echo of Jefferson in ideals and policies. No more emphatic denial can be made than that implicit in the correspondence in which Monroe at this time attempted to recall both Jefferson and Madison to a stand which both were later to take. "The assumption of the State debts is dislik'd here," Monroe protested to Jefferson, "and will create great disgust if adopted under any shape whatever."[29]

Again, in a letter written July 18 from Albemarle: "The more I have reflected on the subject, the better satisfied I am of the impolicy of assuming the State debts. The diminishing the necessity for State taxation will undoubtedly leave the national gov^t. more at liberty to exercise its powers & increase the subjects on w^h. it will act. . . ."[30]

Monroe's stand reflected well the view held by the great majority of his fellow Virginians. Their wealthy state had, on the whole, met its debts, unlike the "Eastern" states, notably Massachusetts. Monroe suspected the "probable inefficiency of the National gov^t. comparatively with those of the States in raising the necessary funds," and believed that "even in our time we may hope to see the whole debt extinguish'd—or nearly so." He feared "the weight of all the State creditors thrown into the national scale" might produce "some disorders in the system" of the new government, and impressed upon both Jefferson and Madison the peril of acceding to a "tyrannous sacrifice of the interests of the minority to that of the majority." The proper mode and means of payment could only be determined, he asserted, "by gradual operation & gentle experiments, which the assumption . . . will entirely prevent."[31]

There was much to cause Monroe disquiet in Jefferson's temporizing conduct since the latter had entered Washington's Cabinet. Madison, moreover, besides writing to Pendleton in favor of Hamilton's

Report, had recommended a modified plan which would at least protect the rights of the original creditors.[32] Monroe wrote to him, opposing his stand. "No proposition that I have seen removes my objections to it, for at best, if it does not compel the industrious & complying States to pay the debts, or a part of the debts, of those who have been less deserving, it prefers the exercise of taxation in the hands of the national to those of the State governments, w'h I cannot approve. And for w'h I can see no necessity, unless it shall be shewn me, that the national gov't is answerable for the debts of the individ'l State, w'h of course I conclude they are not, till they assume them. . . ."[33]

Madison's own plan, a modification of Hamilton's, had already been presented to Congress and been defeated by a Federalist coalition and by speculators anxious to protect the tremendous profits Hamilton's plan promised them. Madison's proposal, however, had rallied to his banner those who stood to lose much by Hamilton's plan: the old soldiers of the Revolution and the poor farmers who because of financial pressure had been forced to dispose of their holdings of the depreciated State obligations at a low price. Madison wanted to restore to these defrauded "original holders" the face value of their original holdings. The Hamiltonians accused him of "treason," though many "respectable characters," including Massachusetts' representative, Judge Dana, supported his honest solution.

Madison, disillusioned, wrote to Monroe, "The Eastern members . . . avow, some of them at least, a determination to oppose all provision for the public debt which does not include this Assumption, and intimate danger to the Union from a refusal to assume."[34]

Monroe, chafing at his absence from the scene of battle, suggested to Jefferson in a letter employing a cypher so cryptic as to baffle the latter's best efforts to decode it, the desirability of becoming a candidate for the office of senator from Virginia. On October 20, 1790, he wrote more openly to his patron: "After the most mature reflection I have at length yielded to my inclinations to suffer my name to be mention'd for a publick appointment. If it takes place, unless some unpleasant reflections on probable future events sho^d. press on me, it will contribute greatly to my own & the gratification of Mrs. M. as it will place us both with & nearer our friends. But to be candid there is not that certainty in the event we seem'd to suppose. M^r.

The New Roof

Harvie, Mann Page, Walker & Govr. Harrison are in or rather will be in the nomination, and as some of them are active in their own behalf it is extremely doubtful how it will terminate."[35]

Although his election was opposed by his old friend John Marshall, now completely won over to Federalist tenets, Monroe succeeded in winning the senatorship. But months before he took his seat in the Senate the cause of Assumption had been won—and through the complaisance of Jefferson. The latter had concluded the curious bargain by which, in return for Federalist acquiescence to fixing the permanent capital on the banks of the Potomac, the recommendations of Hamilton's *Report* had been allowed to pass both Houses.[36]

10

Senator from Virginia

THE DECEMBER of 1790, when Monroe, now thirty-two years old, took his seat in the third session of the First Congress, was a critical time in the history of the federal government. The brief final session saw Hamilton's proposals for such unpopular measures as excise and the national bank accepted by Congress, as was also his proposal for a mint at Philadelphia. Vermont was admitted as a state; and a preliminary act was passed admitting Kentucky to statehood. The new senator from Virginia found that in more than one respect he was treading on dangerous ground, because Hamilton's excise act would at home loose a horde of excise men upon a people whose doctrines of liberty were too brightly novel to permit them to accept such tyrannies without energetic protests. By voting for Hamilton's excise bill, which taxed distilled liquors, Madison had, in the lower house, distinctly added to the unpopularity caused by his stand on Assumption.[1] Moreover, Hamiltonian prosperity, somewhat circumscribed in its benefits after raising Hamilton's reputation to the skies, was to end in an orgy of speculation and stock-gambling. Finally, the red peril of the revolution looming across the Atlantic was to call forth in Congress debates peppered with strife and ill-feeling.

Monroe's first term as senator was a busy, though inconspicuous one. His proved capacity for good sense and hard work won him a place on committees to consider many diverse matters: the memorial of the Kentucky Convention; the report of the Secretary of State on coins, weights, and measures; bounty lands; a mint; the admission

Senator from Virginia

of Vermont; land offices; a Revolutionary land warrant; the protection of the frontiers; the settlement of loan office accounts; and national defense.

The Second Congress met in Philadelphia on October 24, 1791. Among Monroe's colleagues in the Senate was Aaron Burr, recently elected from New York by grace of one of those political combinations of which he was a master craftsman. With Madison in the lower house, the new tendency towards a liberal party was strengthened by the addition of William B. Giles to the Virginia delegation. His election, like that of Monroe, had placed him in the first Congress "too late to attract attention." As James Schouler observes, Giles, "like his industrious and high-spirited co-worker in the Senate," now "advanced Virginia ideas with vigor and boldness."[2] Virginia's representatives were engaged in a sharp criticism of the Treasury Department and its management. Jefferson, already at odds with Hamilton despite the famous bargain which had traded Assumption for the national capital, was, with Madison, preparing the opposition to Hamilton which was to make this session of Congress memorable. Both southerners knew how much that transaction had damaged their position with fellow Virginians, and both realized the value of such organized publicity as a battle royal with the hated Federalists.

As Fisher Ames, a Federalist, complained, "faction" was glowing "like a coal pit" beneath the "tranquillity" that had "smoothed the surface" of the debates.[3]

It was the opposition provoked by the Virginia delegation that caused Hamilton's report on manufactures to be laid aside without action. Then followed a reorganization of congressional representation, based on the first census (1790). Virginia's part in this struggle was to enlarge the lower house to make it a "surer counterpoise" to the Senate.[4]

When questions of procedure subsequently arose, the senators from Virginia, Monroe and Lee, further aroused the ire of the Federalist faction by an attempt, though unsuccessful, to abolish secret sessions. On February 21, 1791, Monroe moved: "That it be a standing rule, that the doors of the Senate Chamber remain open whilst the Senate shall be sitting in a legislative capacity, except on such occasions as, in their judgment, may require secrecy; and that this rule shall commence and be in force on the first day of the next session of Congress. That the Secretary of the Senate request the Commissioners of the City and County of Philadelphia to cause a proper gallery to be erected for the accommodation of the audience."[5] Monroe was optimistic. It was to be three years—until February 20, 1794,—before the doors of Congress, which had been closed to the public since its first meeting, were opened.

Federalist historians frequently make the charge that the Virginia-inspired and -conducted opposition (the "Republican" bloc in Congress) was seizing upon every pretext to attack the group surrounding the President. It is undoubtedly true that the crisis facing the new government demanded unity of action and the subordination of faction and party spirit. But, as Monroe wrote to Jefferson, the paramount issue in the eyes of the Virginia delegation was the growing attempt to centralize power in the hands of the central government. "Upon political subjects we perfectly agree," he wrote, "& particularly in the reprobation of all measures that may be calculated to elevate the government above the people, or place it in any respect without its natural boundary. To keep it there nothing is necessary but virtue in a part only (for in the whole it cannot be expected) of the high publick servants, & a true develop'ment of the principles of those acts wh. have a contrary tendency. The bulk of the people are for democracy, & if they are well informed the risk of such enterprizes will infallibly follow."[6]

During the summer of 1791, Monroe was a member of a committee to amend the Virginia constitution, an appointment which was "neither wished nor expected."[7] Jefferson had seen with dismay the growing tendency of the general government towards "monarchy" and concluded that the remedy lay in having each state erect "such barriers at the constitutional line as cannot be surmounted either by themselves or by the General Government."[8] It was to Jefferson's plan to strengthen the state governments as the strength of the federal government increased that Monroe gave his time.

The annoyance we may suppose Monroe felt at this demand upon him was increased by a domestic complication which had occurred earlier in the year, one which must have seemed inexcusable to his well-ordered mind. He described it to Jefferson in a letter of March, 1791, written at Charlottesville:

"From a desire to place my brother without the reach of bad

Senator from Virginia

example, in a quiet good family & where he might pursue his studies to the best advantage, I engag'd lodgings for him with old Mr. Jas. Kerr. The genl. opinion of my acquaintance here, was in favor of this preference for his house & society, wh. was the more confirm'd on my part, from a knowledge, that I had render'd him services, & had a claim to his attention. You will readily conceive my astonishment when you hear that on my way up yesterday, I was inform'd he was married to Mr. Kerr's daughter. . . . Believe me this has been the most heartfelt & afflicting stroke I have ever felt. If his education had been complete & himself establish'd in life, able to take care of a family, to me it wod. have been a matter of indifference with whom he connected himself."[9]

Meanwhile Jefferson, accompanied by Madison, was absent on his famous tour of the New England states. The intimacy between these two men had grown even closer during the Philadelphia sessions of Congress. There was no attempt to exclude Monroe from their councils, but the lonely widower and the little bachelor of Montpelier quite naturally saw more of each other than the more domesticated member of their group. Jefferson was occupying lodgings in the suburbs and suggested that Madison "come and take a bed and plate with me. . . . to me it will be a relief from the solitude of which I have too much."[10] Jefferson's letter suggests that his friend would be glad to be relieved of the society of Hamilton and Colonel Bodsmith, the British agent, whose influence on Madison the older man perhaps feared was becoming too great. But when the sessions of the House of Representatives began, the Federalist leaders complained that the Virginia delegation was generating a distrust of the Treasury Report.[11] And, in fact, as Federalism became more and more dogmatic in its devotion to a centralized government and as the methods of the Hamiltonian clique revealed ever more clearly an intention to override the liberties of the people, Madison found himself more willing to subscribe to the program for which the partisan Monroe and the leader of southern democracy were already laying foundations. A letter from Monroe to Jefferson, written at Richmond June 17, 1792, shows that there was growing opposition to Federalist policies and a corresponding hope for the Jeffersonian ideals:

"I find the general sentiment of the people, of this State against the fashionable doctrines of some persons in & about the government; ... I have not seen nor have I heard of any display of passion but in the sober exercise of their reason they disapprove of them. I mean those doctrines which may be deemed anti-republican or which inculcate or furnish the means for the support of a government by corrupt influence, or indeed by any other than the pure interest of those who formed it."

Monroe was turning more and more to politics, to the neglect of everything else. He continued: "The length of the last session has done me irreparable injury in my profession, as it has made an impression on the general opinion, that the two occupations are incompatible. ... I ... have determined to withdraw from those courts where an interference might take place, and in general to make such an arrangement in my business, as will in other respects leave me more at liberty to discharge the duties of the other station."[12]

He now discovered, too, that the role of gentleman-planter dependent upon the income of his estates was incompatible with public life.[13] He wrote complainingly to Jefferson, "My plantation in Alb: [Albemarle] is not such as I could wish it"; he wrote to Madison also: "I found my farm in every respect in the most miserable state that it could be. At best but little can be said in its favor, but less industry had been used to improve its natural deformities or make it yield what it is really capable of, than might have been. Time & patience have been immemorially prescribed, as the only source of relief in difficult cases. Whether the practise of these virtues will produce in the present instance the desired effect, is questionable. Admit it might, it would notwithstanding be infinitely more agreeable independent of the profit, to apply the same labor to a more grateful soil."

Necessity, as well as his secret but consistent inclination, was turning Monroe into an inveterate office-holder. The political situation required that a man cherishing such ambitions should not only represent the opinions of his constituents but also enter into the electoral arena with every determination to master the strategy of party battles. It was a fortunate circumstance for the junior senator from Virginia that he shared Jefferson's confidence at a time when the latter needed a lieutenant capable of rendering just such service to the party's cause. Monroe was one of the earliest American professional statesmen, a part for which his gift for friendship eminently fitted him.

Senator from Virginia

In building up the organization and machinery of the new party which was to oppose the well entrenched forces of Federalism, the Republican leaders soon realized that their principal task lay in stirring the apathy of the masses. The sullen resentment of the "unlearned" against the brilliant financial coups of the Hamiltonians had been largely inarticulate. While every tavern held its muttering group of aggrieved tax-payers and every crossroads meeting ended in political debate, no reasoned protest had been raised by humble men outside the walls of Congress. Public opinion must be created.

To Jefferson, Monroe expressed his opinions of the situation in the spirit of a party man: "Whether things have reached their height in the division of parties, relative to govt. in America, and will have a regular course hereafter in favor of the principles of either seems doubtful. That the partisans for monarchy are numerous & powerful, in point of talents and influence is in my estimation certain. Even the list of those who have been & perhaps still are active is formidable.... To be passive in a controversy of this kind, unless the person had been bred a priest in the principles of the Romish church, is a satisfactory proof he is on the wrong side."[14]

Both parties were soon to be drawn into a wordy war of propaganda which preceded by many months the battle at the polls. Jefferson's trenchant pen was early employed upon this business in letters to high and low. Madison, whose successful *Federalist* papers had established his reputation as a controversialist, was more reluctant to enter the arena, his scholarly and fastidious mind recoiling from the rough and ready methods of pamphleteering. Monroe, who was later in his career to have a sad experience of printers' bills and to indulge in a veritable orgy of literary "vindication," confined himself at first to the useful task of collecting and forwarding to his friends such political news of the Virginia countryside as might serve as ammunition for the cause.

Jefferson soon realized the necessity of obtaining some facile writer to offset the flood of Hamiltonian propaganda pouring from Fenno's Federalist press. With this purpose in view, he began to patronize the poet-editor Freneau by securing for him a minor post as translator in the new Department of State. For the same reason, he welcomed the reappearance in the arena of an almost forgotten champion of the people's liberties, Thomas Paine.

JAMES MONROE

In 1791, Paine had launched an appeal to the English liberals in his eloquent defense of the principles of the French Revolution—*The Rights of Man*. It was, in substance, an answer to Burke, the most eloquent British statesman and writer of the time, who had been driven to a reactionary stand by the crimes of the terrorists. In America, Burke's arguments had been eagerly approved by the Federalists and later turned to account by another convert to conservatism, John Adams, in his *Discourses on Davila*. To Monroe, in Virginia, Jefferson wrote from Philadelphia on July 10, 1791: "The papers which I send Mr. Randolph weekly, & which I presume you see, will have shown you what a dust Paine's pamphlet has kicked up here. My last to Mr. Randolph will have given an explanation as to myself, which I had not time to give when I sent you the pamphlet. A writer, under the name of Publicola, in attacking all Paine's principles, is very desirous of involving me in the same censure with the author. I certainly merit the same, for I profess the same principles; but it is equally certain I never meant to have entered as a volunteer into the cause. My occupations do not permit it. Some persons here are insinuating that I am Brutus, that I am Agricola, that I am Philodemus, &c., &c. I am none of them, being decided not to write a word on the subject, unless any printed imputation should call for a printed disavowal, to which I should put my name. . . . A host of writers have risen in favor of Paine, and prove that in this quarter, at least, the spirit of republicanism is sound." [15]

Thus, perhaps fortuitously, the result desired by the liberal leaders had been attained. *The Rights of Man* was everywhere read in the small towns and villages of the land, and grumbling discontent was changed to discussion. To Paine, Jefferson wrote "that the controversy had awakened the people, shown the 'monocrats' that the silence of the masses concerning the teachings of 'Davila' did not mean that they had been converted 'to the doctrine of king, lords, & commons,' and that they were 'confirmed in their good old faith.'" [16]

Monroe, as a letter to Madison written September 18, 1792, indicates, was also trying his somewhat heavy hand in the pamphleteering war: "I sent off on Saturday the packet to Dunlap so that on Thursday night it will be rec'd & may be published on Saturday next. I inserted the paragraph I had first written, & made the conclusion rather more pointed introducing the extracts, making the writer & the person to whom written perfectly passive in regard to the publication stating indeed that I had obtained them from the latter & wo'd make them accessible to others if necessary. The continuation sho'd immediately follow but I am greatly oppressed with the fatigues of the journey . . . & shall not be able to turn the incident to that acc't in every view its importance wo'd of. Whether pointed allusions to the Sec'y of the tre'y wo'd be proper & dignified as relating to the subject, the character to be vindicated, or derogatory, is a question of some delicacy." [17]

The line between Republican and Federalist was now definitely marked. The correspondence passing among Jefferson, Madison, and Monroe was almost entirely related to matters of party strategy. The political figures throughout the country were carefully appraised and their abilities as leaders weighed in the balance. Concerning Burr and his possible candidacy for vice-president in 1792, Monroe wrote to Madison from Albemarle, September 18, 1792: "My opinion is briefly this; that if Mr. Burr was in every respect inexceptionable it would be impossible to have him elected. He is too young, if not in point of age, yet upon the public theatre, to admit the possibility of an union in his favor. If formed at all, it must be upon the recommendation & responsibility of particular characters in the several States; & if this c'd succeed, it wo'd be an unpleasant thing to those who would stand as sponsors. But for an office of this kind it could not, nor sho'd it succeed. Some person of more advanc'd life and longer standing in publick trust sho'd be selected for it, and particularly one who in consequence of such service had given unequivocal proofs of what his principles really were. A person who had marked a line of conduct so decisively that you might tell what he would be hereafter by what he had been heretofore. To place this gent'n, or any other of his standing in the chair of the present incumbant, wo'd not be well thought of in America; nor wo'd it produce the desired effect; for some compunction always attends the rejection of an old servant, especially when accompanied with any kind of reproach." [18]

The final session of the Second Congress, to which the Monroes, accompanied by Madison, journeyed to Philadelphia in a new post-chaise, opened on November 5, 1792. This session, in contrast to the preceding one, was barren of important legislative results, but the political aspect of the debates revealed the rise of a disciplined party of opposition. The actions of Congress were largely confined to the House, where Giles and Madison were already leading a spirited attack on Treasury policies that forced Hamilton to a brilliant and, on the whole, successful vindication of his course. The Senate, dignified spectators of this party battle, gave consideration to the President's message with its anxious references to the excise troubles now distracting the western settlements. But more interest was aroused by the Jefferson-Hamilton quarrel—daily growing more personal—which was being carried on in the columns of Fenno's and Freneau's rival newspapers.

As an outcome of this situation, Monroe was drawn into a personal incident with Hamilton which was to have an important effect upon his own reputation later on. As a member of a senatorial committee to inquire into rumors that Hamilton had been engaged in a shady money transaction with a clerk of the Treasury Department named Reynolds, Monroe mortally offended the proud Federalist leader, once his comrade-in-arms. In order to clear his financial reputation, Hamilton was obliged to make embarrassing avowals that brought to light an intrigue with Reynolds' wife and revealed himself to be the foolish victim of an unscrupulous blackmailer. The climax of this unpleasant business was not to be reached until some years later, when Monroe returned from his French mission, but the bad blood thus unfortunately engendered between these two men further embittered the quarrel between Hamilton and Jefferson.

11

Prologue to the First French Mission

THE CONVENTION in Paris, anticipating England's intention to begin hostilities after the execution of Louis XVI, had, on the first of February, 1793, included George III of England among the encircling enemies of France.

Monroe, in Virginia the following May for a vacation, wrote to Jefferson that enroute from Philadelphia he had found scarcely a man unfriendly to the new rulers of France. "Many," he remarked, "regret the unhappy fate of the Marq: of Fayette, and likewise the execution of the King. But they seem to consider these events as incidents to a much greater one, & which they wish to see accomplished."[1] In another letter he commented on the growing interest felt on this side of the Atlantic in the "European war," and declared that Genêt, the French envoy, whom he had passed on the road between Fredericksburg and Richmond, "had made a most favorable impression on the inhabitants of the latter city."[2] He did not say whether he had had an interview with Genêt, who was to play a curiously important role in the events of the ensuing summer which prefaced Monroe's French mission.

In spite of the sinister impression that the execution of the French king had at first made on all classes in America, Genêt, on his landing in Charleston, had been given an enthusiastic welcome by the Republicans. Described by one of Hamilton's correspondents as a "good person ... quite active ... always in a bustle," Genêt had a novel diplomatic technique, which was "to laugh us into war."[3]

News of the declaration of hostilities had reached the President while he was resting at Mount Vernon, and he hastened back to Philadelphia to debate with his Cabinet a series of questions concerning what course the administration should pursue.

Genêt's triumphal progress towards Philadelphia was fortunately delayed by the banquets, speeches, and ovations planned by the enchanted Republicans. Before he reached the Capital, two questions demanded settlement by the administration.[4] Should Genêt be received? What attitude should the country adopt towards the belligerents? In view of the now embarrassing Treaty of Alliance of 1778 with France, the two questions must be considered together. Hamilton, spokesman for the interests still financing commercial operations with London credits, naturally favored an answer that would please the British.[5] Jefferson, on the other hand, argued the obligations assumed under the French treaty and emphasized the threat to the United States from a power that still used her mastery of the seas to impress American seamen and, in spite of treaty agreements, retained her fortified posts within American territory.[6]

In the end, a compromise was arrived at. The Cabinet agreed to a proclamation warning American citizens against warlike acts,[7] yet recognizing the new regime in France by receiving Genêt. They reserved for future consideration the binding force of treaties, however.[8]

Jefferson, later explaining his part in these proceedings, indicated that only the necessity for a compromise induced him to agree to such half-measures.[9] To Madison he wrote that the wiser course would have been to declare openly a "manly neutrality, claiming the liberal rights ascribed to that condition." Only the "penchant of the President . . . and above all, the ardent spirit of our constituents" he said, could prevent its becoming "a mere English neutrality."[10]

Washington's stand on neutrality was not the least famous of his credos. Yet Jefferson, the leader of the liberal forces, in another letter to Madison, spoke of the "pusillanimity" of the proclamation announcing the neutral course the government would take,[11] and declared that it revealed the Federalist "fear lest any affection should be discovered" in it. Of course, Jefferson accused, not the President, but "his counsellors" of an unholy love for Great Britain, especially Hamilton. Indeed, he wrote to Monroe, Hamilton was at this time "panic-struck if we refuse our breach to every kick which Gr. Brit.

Prologue to the First French Mission

may choose to give it. He is for proclaiming at once the most abject principles, such as would invite and merit habitual insults. And indeed every inch of ground must be fought in our councils to desperation, in order to hold up the face of even a sneaking neutrality, for our votes are generally 2½ against 1½. Some propositions have come from him which would astonish Mr. Pitt himself with their boldness. If we preserve even a sneaking neutrality, we shall be indebted for it to the President & not to his counsellors."[12]

Yet Jefferson had agreed, in the matter of the treaties, with the convenient solution proposed by Hamilton: that the Cabinet "refer to future consideration and discussion the question whether the operation of the treaties ... ought not to be temporarily suspended."[3]

Even Monroe, partisan though he was, could see the wisdom of a neutral stand. His belief was that Great Britain, rather than France, had most to gain by forcing an open rupture with the United States. A pro-French policy, he wrote to Jefferson, would "injure that nation, & ourselves, but benefit the party we meant to injure. Freed from any embarrassing questions respecting the rights of neutrality, our commerce would be her lawful plunder, and commanding as I presume she will the seas, but little would escape her." Indeed, he would not be surprised, he wrote, to find England attempting to involve the United States in the war by "every species of insult and outrage...."[14]

A month later, however, his attitude underwent some modification. He had thought, he said, that Washington's proclamation of neutrality was "harmless" at the time it was issued, but that the more recent statements resulting from it, particularly the "order for the prosecution of two marines who had embarked in a privateer licensed by the French Minister"[15] seemed to indicate that the Executive was claiming "the right to say we shall be neutral," and this would imply that he also had the right to say "that we sho'd war." Monroe considered this "both unconstitutional & impolitick." The privateers had taken several prizes, and orders had been issued to all ports to prevent the equipping of privateers by anyone.[16]

These restraints, Monroe asserted, could not be properly imposed on privateers—men acting with letters of marque. Taking as an example the practice of hiring mercenaries, he argued that if the Hessian depredations had not given the American government a claim upon the sovereign of these mercenaries for damages during the Revolution, how could Great Britain now demand reparations for similar practices on the sea? Moreover, permission "to fight in the service of one Prince agnst another was never denied . . . to anyone." [17]

But even Jefferson was inclined to stretch to its limits the conveniently elastic neutrality. When, in the case of the *Little Sarah*, Knox and Hamilton had proposed to erect batteries to sink the privateer should she attempt to depart against the express orders of the government, Jefferson had protested against extreme measures, arguing that "it is inconsistent for a nation which has been bearing for years the grossest insults and injuries from their late enemies to rise at a feather against their friends and benefactors." [18]

It was not until Genêt, the French envoy, had overstepped all diplomatic bounds in the matter of the privateers, threatening to "appeal from the President to the people" and to use the expected arrival of three ships of the line "to do justice to his country," [19] that even the Republican leaders lost patience.

"You will perceive," wrote Jefferson to Madison in a letter of August 25, ". . . that Genêt has thrown down the gauntlet to the President . . . and is himself forcing that appeal to the public, & risking that disgust which I had so much wished should have been avoided. The indications from different parts of the continent are already sufficient to shew that the mass of the republican interest has no hesitation to disapprove of this intermeddling by a foreigner. . . ." [20]

Monroe, however, continued for some time to plead Genêt's cause. To John Brackenridge he complained, in a letter written at Albemarle, August 23, 1793, that the "monarchy party . . . has seized a new ground whereon to advance their fortunes. The French minister has been guilty, in the vehemence of his zeal, of some indiscretions, slighting the President of the U. States, and instead of healing the breach, this party have brought it to the publick view & are labouring to turn the popularity of this respectable citizen, agnst the French revolution, thinking to separate us from France & pave the way for an unnatural connection with Great Britain." [21]

A month later, having learned of Jefferson's own differences with Genêt, Monroe joined the quickly filling ranks of the envoy's critics. Genêt's conduct, he wrote to Jefferson, "fills me with extreme concern. That he shod. not have implicitly follow'd yr. advice in all the

Prologue to the First French Mission

affrs. of his country is to me astonishing, as well from yr. known attachment to that nation & her cause as his having mentioned that fact in Richmond on his way to Phila. With respect to him he must follow the fortune he has carved out for himself."[22] At the same time, Monroe told his patron that though the Federalists of Richmond had lost no time in making political capital out of the conduct of the Republican party's pet, Genêt, he felt sure that "the sense of the community" would be "9. to 1. in favor of the French cause...."[23]

Even before Genêt's recall, Washington had in his hands Jefferson's resignation from the Cabinet.

Jefferson had realized that the leadership of the great opposition party could best be exercised by a man not hampered by the restraints of official position. And he knew, too, that if ever the young liberal party needed strong leadership it was now, in the moment of crisis precipitated by Genêt's ill-advised patriotism. By the middle of October, Jefferson was back in Virginia and in full control of the local situation. At Monticello, the spermaceti candles burned late into the night as Jefferson sat with Monroe and Madison discussing the strategy to be followed in Philadelphia and Richmond.

The new apportionment bill and public dissatisfaction with the administration's meekness in the face of English aggression brought to Philadelphia on December 2, 1793, a largely Republican Congress. Muhlenberg, Monroe's friend, took the Speaker's chair that had been the Federalist Sedgwick's. But the Senate seats were equally divided.

The plan of campaign hatched at Monticello was, as a letter of Monroe reveals, to begin the session ". . . by some act, connected with the present state of our affrs. founded on the publick sentiment, and which shod. at the same time vindicate our rights & interests, and likewise shun all possible pretext for war, on the part of the power it was meant to affect...."[24] The first move was the introduction in the House by Madison of a series of resolutions meant to carry out the provisions of a report made by Jefferson shortly before his retirement. These resolutions proposed additional duties on the products and shipping of countries having no commercial treaties or "alliances" with the United States. The Federalists, of course, saw in this move a renewed attack on Great Britain "in the interest of France."[25] Debate was bitter and acrimonious, and ended in the first notable Republican victory in the House.

JAMES MONROE

In the Senate, meanwhile, Monroe and the other liberals were waging a desperate fight for the control upon which so much now depended. The central point of issue was the seating of the new senator from Pennsylvania, Albert Gallatin, who had come to the States only fourteen years before from his native Switzerland, and whose length of citizenship was in question.[26] In the same session Monroe scored a point in obtaining the adoption of a measure, which he had first advocated in 1791, the opening to the public of all sessions of the upper house except those in which there should be taken up "any business which may, in the opinion of a member require secrecy." A motion, moved and seconded, would be necessary to close the doors. But this innovation was to await ". . . the end of the present session of Congress . . ." and the construction of "suitable galleries."[27]

Before this could be accomplished, international developments had brought a new crisis. In the Straits of Gibraltar hordes of predatory Algerian pirates were loosed upon American commerce, and the new British Orders in Council of November 6 closed the French West Indies to American trade by isolating these islands with a hostile fleet of British cruisers.

The upshot of these grave developments was the birth of the United States Navy. On March 27, 1794, the construction of four forty-four-gun ships and two thirty-six gun vessels was authorized and provision made for their officers and crews.[28]

The "opposition," who, as Monroe wrote to Jefferson, from Philadelphia on March 16, 1794, had begun its congressional activity by ". . . the most open declaration in favor of G. Britain, justifying her in all her enormities . . . latterly has assumed a new tone passing into the opposite extreme." Sedgwick, in fact, brought forward a proposal to raise fifteen thousand provisional troops for "defense against a possible invasion . . . considering the unfriendly conduct of G. B. towards us for some time past." Monroe at first suspected this to be a counter-move designed to defeat Madison's resolutions as inadequate to the emergency and a strategic attempt "to remove . . . the impression" that Federalist partiality for England "had created among their constituents." Later, he saw in it an even darker purpose ". . . the foundation of measures more destructive to the publick happiness."[29] Monroe saw in a regular army an ever-present threat

Prologue to the First French Mission

to republican government and to the concepts of liberty and freedom which he cherished.

No sooner had the spectre of a regular army begun seriously to haunt him, than there appeared another Federalist-inspired threat to Monroe's peace of mind. This time, it was the proposal, in the face of "the agressions of Great Britain," to send an envoy extraordinary to the Court. And, worse, Hamilton was urged for the post by his party. Jay and King were also candidates, either of whom, Monroe feared, would "answer to bind the aristocracy of this country stronger & closer to that of the other."[30] Hamilton's obtaining the post must be stopped at all costs, and to this end Senator Monroe appealed directly to the President. "Sir," he wrote to Washington on April 8, "Having casually heard that it was requested by many of Colo. Hamilton's political associates, that you would nominate him as Envoy to the Court of Great Britain, and as I should deem such a measure not only injurious to the publick interest, but also especially so to your own, I have taken the liberty to express that sentiment to you & likewise to observe farther, that in case it is your wish I should explain to you more at large my reason for this opinion, I will wait on you at any hour you may appoint for that purpose."[31]

To this letter, which for the first time raised the question of the propriety of criticism by a senator of a nomination before its formal submission to the Senate, Washington dispatched a most diplomatic reply. Passing over Monroe's suggestion of a personal interview, he merely requested that the specific objections to the appointment be communicated in writing.[32] Monroe complied with alacrity. On the score of Hamilton's pro-British party affiliations, he prophesied that, "Should a person ... of such character and principles be sent to England and upon an occasion so attractive of the publicke notice, it would not only furnish an opportunity for political intrigue against republicanism here, and against our connections with France, but as I have reason to believe, be regarded in a light unfavorable to the authority appointing." He was particularly concerned with French reaction, which, he claimed, would be so unfavorable as to create a situation "as mortifying as it would be alarming" in the event of her friendship and coöperation being required by the United States.[33]

The appointment of John Jay rather than Hamilton did nothing to allay Monroe's apprehension. He desired no envoy to England,

JAMES MONROE

certainly no envoy from Federalist ranks. To Jefferson he described the measure as "the most submissive . . . that cod. be devised, to court (England's) favor & degrade our character." And, wrote he, "sending an envoy to negotiate with Engld. at the time that the Minister of France, on the ground & cloathed with similar powers, is only amused with acts of civility, shews that a connection with the former power is the real object of the Executive." [34]

ᶈ 12 ᶍ

First Mission to France

THE HARASSED administration had yet another pressing problem, that of finding a man for the important Paris post to succeed the aristocratic Gouverneur Morris, whose recall the French government had demanded. As Monroe remarked in a letter to Jefferson, the task of selecting a man from the ranks of the opposition—for the French would find another Federalist no more to their taste than Morris—was no easy one. Robert R. Livingston, Monroe had heard, had been offered the place, and Burr was another, though a remote, possibility.[1]

The twenty-sixth of May brought its surprises. Early in the morning, Monroe had written from Philadelphia to tell Jefferson that the post had been offered to and declined by Madison and Livingston, leaving Burr the strongest candidate. He made the observation, also, that Washington "supposes he lays [the Republican party] under obligations to him for the nomination, for I am persuaded in addition to other considerations he really surmounts some objections of a personal nature in making it. . . ."[2]

Hardly had he sent off his letter before Randolph, the Secretary of State, called on him. His purpose, it soon became clear, was to ask whether Monroe would accept appointment as minister to France. Burr, Randolph said, had been rejected by Washington because, Livingston having declined the offer, it would seem that only New Yorkers were being considered. Monroe insisted, however, that since he had supported Burr, he could not think of replacing him unless he were definitely out of the running. Randolph promised to "satisfy the friends of Colo. Burr on this head," and only after "this point of delicacy" was removed did Monroe set about consulting Madison and some other of his friends. He finally decided to accept "upon the necessity of cultivating France; & the uncertainty of the person upon whom it might otherwise fall."[3]

In coming to this decision, Monroe had relied heavily on Madison, to whom he had entrusted settlement of the matter with Randolph. "If it has not the approbation of my few friends & yourself in particular," he wrote Madison, "I certainly will decline it. . . ."[4]

The nomination was confirmed promptly by the Senate, and, an early departure being insisted upon by the administration, June 18 saw Monroe and his family on shipboard, watching the Baltimore shore-front disappear in the summer haze. He had not even been able to go to Virginia for a farewell visit with Jefferson.

The twenty-nine day voyage, "free from storms"[5] and other excitements (he was seasick only "an hour or two") gave him ample opportunity to study his official instructions. "The President has been an early and decided friend of the French Revolution," ran the document, "and whatever reason there may have been, under our ignorance of facts and policy, to suspend an opinion upon some of its important transaction; yet he is immutable in his wishes for its accomplishment; incapable of assenting to the right of any foreign prince to meddle with its interior arrangements; persuaded that success will attend their efforts; and particularly, that union among themselves is an impregnable barrier against external assaults." Monroe was further instructed to "show our confidence in the French Republic, without betraying the most remote mark of undue complaisance. You will let it be seen, that in case of war, with any nation on earth, we shall consider France as our first and natural ally."

The passage that was to prove most interesting of all, in view of subsequent events, concerned Jay's mission to London. "We have," it declared, ". . . pursued neutrality with faithfulness. . . . We mean to continue the same line of conduct in future; and to remove all jealousy with respect to Mr. Jay's mission to London, you may say, that he is positively forbidden to weaken the engagements between this country and France. *It is not improbable that you will be obliged to encounter, on this head, suspicions of various kinds. But you may declare the motives of that mission to be, to obtain immediate com-*

First Mission to France

pensation for plundered property, and restitution of the posts." (Monroe's italics.)

Monroe probably paid more heed, however, to the sentences phrasing what positive action he was to take, namely, to bring to the attention of the French government the claims of American citizens that arose *inter alia* from the seizure of American ships by the French, in violation of the treaties of commerce and alliance made in 1778. And, further, "Among the great events with which the world is now teeming, there may be an opening for France to become instrumental in securing to us the free navigation of the Mississippi. Spain may, perhaps, negotiate a peace, separate from Great Britain, with France. If she does, the Mississippi may be acquired through this channel, especially if you contrive to have our mediation in any manner solicited."[6]

Though not free from ambiguity, the instructions justify an inference that the Administration wished to maintain close and friendly relations with France. They similarly imply restrictions on Jay's powers that would make French fears groundless. At least, they served to allay Monroe's own earlier suspicions of the English mission.

The third of August found the newly arrived Monroes established in Paris lodgings. Morris was away from the city, and the new envoy had to find his own way about. The way was not an easy one. Monroe had come to Paris at a critical time. Barely a week before, Robespierre had gone to his death, together with Saint-Just, Couthon, and others. "The fall of Robespierre," wrote Monroe to Madison, "had thrown a cloud over all whom it was supposed he had any connection with or in whose appointment he had been in any wise instrumental.... I did not know the ground upon which the Americans stood here, but suspected as the acquisition of wealth had been their object in coming, they must have attached themselves to some preceding party & worn out their reputations."[7]

Monroe therefore decided to wait until Morris should return. When he did, the two went to the Foreign Affairs Office, where Morris formally notified the Commissary of his recall and of Monroe's succession. The new envoy left a copy of his credentials, with a request for the earliest possible reception.

The troubled state of internal affairs in France was not the only hurdle in Monroe's path. French distrust of the attitude of the American government had been growing deeper. The Genêt affair had done nothing to dissipate it. Nor were cordial relations much furthered by the uncompromisingly aristocratic attitudes struck by the elegant Gouverneur Morris. Indeed, it was being rumored in governmental circles that the administration's confidence in Morris was undiminished, despite the demand for his recall by France.[8]

It was not too surprising, therefore, that ten days elapsed without a word from the executive body, the Committee of Public Safety. Monroe spent the period in restless speculation. Perhaps, he suggested in a letter to Madison, the Commissary was associated with Robespierre and was therefore out of favor with the Committee of Public Safety.[9] Or perhaps it was the political upheaval, he suggested to Randolph, that might be keeping the Committee from acting.[10] Later, he wrote to Randolph that the Committee may have reasoned that as "my principles were with them, I ought on that account to be the more dreaded; for if they confided in me, I should only lull them asleep as to their true interest, in regard to the movements on foot; and under this impression I was viewed with a jealous eye, and kept at the most awful distance."[11] Long after, when he had returned to America, Monroe expressed the opinion that it was Jay's mission that may have aroused the Committee's distrust.[12]

Whatever the reason for the delay, Monroe's impatience could await the Committee's pleasure no longer. It had been suggested to him by certain persons familiar with the workings of the governmental machinery that an appeal be made directly to the legislative body, the National Convention. So, on August 13, Monroe sent a letter to the President of the National Convention, expressing his desire to be received.[13] This communication was read in the Convention, and, as Monroe wrote Randolph, "was immediately taken, by a member present, to the committee of public safety, by whom a report was made in two hours afterwards to the Convention, and a decree adopted by the latter body for my reception by the Convention itself at two the following day."[14]

The scene on the morrow would have pleased the most ardent American partisan of the French cause. In the Journal of the National Convention of August 15, 1794,[15] it is recorded that "Citizen Monroe, Minister Plenipotentiary of the United States of America near the French Republic is admitted to the hall at the sitting of the

First Mission to France

National Convention. He takes his place in the midst of the representatives of the people, and remits to the President of the Convention a translation of his discourse addressed to the National Convention. It is read by one of the secretaries. The expressions of fraternity and union between the two peoples, and the interest which the United States takes in the French Republic are heard with a lively sensibility and with applause. The letter of credence of Citizen Monroe is also read, as well as those written by the American Congress and addressed to the President of the National Convention and to the Committee of Public Safety. In witness of the fraternity which unites these two peoples, French and American, the President gives the *accolade* [fraternal embrace] to Citizen Monroe."

The congressional letters referred to in the record were replies to a communication that the Committee of Public Safety had sent on the tenth of February, 1794, to Congress.[16] In its missive, the Committee had joyfully related the great victories won by the French and had expressed the hope "of drawing closer more than ever the bonds of friendship which unite the two great generous and free nations." Randolph, in communicating the replies of the Senate and House, had been far from reserved in his expressions of good will, assuring the French nation that the "Senate . . . tender to the Committee of Public Safety, their zealous wishes for the French Republic; they learn with sensibility every success which promotes the happiness of the French nation; and the full establishment of their peace and liberty will be ever esteemed by the Senate as a happiness of the United States and to humanity. And for the House of Representatives as follows: That the letter of the Committee of Public Safety of the French Republic . . . be transmitted to the President of the United States, and that he be requested to cause the same to be answered on behalf of this House, in terms expressive of their sensibility for the friendly and affectionate manner in which they have addressed the Congress of the United States; with an unequivocal assurance, that the Representatives of the people of the United States, have much interest in the happiness and prosperity of the French Republic. . . . Yes, Representatives of our ally, your communication has been addressed to those who share in your fortunes, and who take a deep interest in the happiness and prosperity of the French Republic."[17]

JAMES MONROE

Monroe emulated the tone of the Secretary's rather florid effusions. "Citizens, President and Representatives of the French People," he began, "My admission into this Assembly . . . to be recognized as the Representative of the American Republic, impresses me with a degree of sensibility which I cannot express. I consider it as a new proof of that friendship and regard which the French nation has always shewn to their ally, the United States of America. . . . America had her day of oppression, difficulty, and war, but her sons were virtuous and brave and the storm which long clouded her political horizon has passed and left them in the enjoyment of peace, liberty, and independence. France, our ally and our friend and who aided us in the contest, has now embarked in the same noble career; and I am happy to add that whilst the fortitude, magnanimity and heroic valor of her troops command the admiration and applause of the astonished world, the wisdom and firmness of her councils unite equally in securing the happiest results. . . ."[18]

The reply to this oratorical bouquet was delivered by the President of the convention, who used equally glowing terms, and after the ceremony of the kiss and the embrace had taken place "in the midst of universal acclamations of joy, delight, and admiration,"[19] the following decree was passed:

"The reading and verification being had of the powers of Citizen James Monroe, he is recognized and proclaimed minister plenipotentiary of the United States of America near the French Republic. . . . The letters of credence of Citizen James Monroe . . . those which he has remitted on the part of the American Congress . . . the discourse of citizen Monroe, the response of the President of the Convention shall be printed in the two languages, French and American, and inserted in the bulletin of correspondence. . . . The flags of the United States of America shall be joined with those of France, and displayed in the hall of the sittings of the Convention in sign of the union and eternal fraternity of the two people."[20]

The enthusiasm with which the reports of this reception was received across the Channel was understandably restrained. The English reaction was described by Jay in a letter of September 13, 1794, to Washington as "disagreeable."[21] Washington's reply showed that he himself disapproved of Monroe's speech and of Randolph's letter: "Considering the place in which they were delivered and the

First Mission to France

neutral policy the country had to pursue, it was a measure that does not appear to have been well devised by our minister." But he saw a possible beneficial result: "Yet, under the existing circumstances, the expression of such reciprocal good will was susceptible of two views, one of which even in the pending state of negotiations (by alarming as well as offending the British Minister) might have no unfavorable operation in bringing matters to a happy and speedy result."[22]

The official rebuke came from Randolph, and was directed against the speech Monroe had made before the National Convention. Remarking that the administration had expected Monroe's reception would take place privately and that his accompanying speech would be "oral and therefore not exposed to the rancorous criticism of nations at war with France," Randolph deplored that the Envoy had not acted so "as to leave heart-burnings nowhere," regretted the "extreme glow of some parts" of the address, hoped that he would henceforth "cultivate the French Republic with zeal but without any unnecessary éclat"![23]

Monroe felt the reprimand to be unjust, though a letter of his to Madison two months before Randolph penned his criticism shows him to have anticipated some displeasure from "many in America." Excusing himself on the grounds that he had had "but little time to prepare," he argued the expediency of cementing Franco-American relations by a show of "interest which every department of our government took in their success and prosperity. . . ." He foresaw that his critics would protest that "it was intended that these things should have been smuggled in secretly and as secretly deposited afterwards." But, he retorted, they are deceived if they suppose me capable of being the instrument of such purposes. On the contrary, I have endeavored to take the opposite ground. . . ."[24] He denied Randolph's accusation that his speech had in content exceeded his instructions.[25]

In a letter of September 4, 1794, to Joseph Jones, Monroe enclosed a copy of his speech and one of the President's reply, with this comment: "I thought it my duty to lay those papers before the Convention as the basis of my mission—containing the declarations of every department in favor of the French revolution, or implying it strongly. My address you will observe goes no further than the declrs. of both Houses."[26]

[133]

JAMES MONROE

Two days after Randolph had written his first, formal letter of official reprimand, he sent off a more interesting private letter to Monroe in which he seems to have anticipated Monroe's arguments. Replying in advance to them, he wrote soothingly, "We are fully sensible of the importance of the friendship of the French Republic. Cultivate it with zeal, proportioned to the value we set upon it. Remember to remove every suspicion of our preferring a connection with Great Britain or in any manner weakening our old attachment to France. The caution suggested in my letter of the 30th ultimo arises solely from an honorable wish to sustain our character of neutrality, in a style which may be a pattern for the morality of nations."[27]

Not only was Monroe hurt by the official censure, but, as he later wrote Madison, "surprised," since he had not thought that "it would be avowed that it was wished" he should make secret use of the congressional resolutions. In other words, he was surprised at what he considered a frank intent on the part of the opposition party that he should "become the instrument of that party here, thereby putting in its hands my own reputation to be impeached hereafter in the course of events." Quite to the contrary, he was glad of the opportunity offered to publish "the covenant which subsisted between them and me; by the publication they are bound to the French nation & to me to observe a particular line of conduct. If they deviate from it they are censurable and the judicious part of our countrymen as well as posterity will reward them accordingly."[28]

Here, then, was the crux of the whole matter. Far from acting with the administration, it would seem that Monroe was acting with France. As Bond puts it, "An inference might be drawn from this letter that in so publicly announcing the resolution of Congress, Monroe had purposely attempted to force the pro-British party to a closer alliance with France, or else to a decided avowal of its real policy." And, although unwilling to draw a definite conclusion from this letter, Bond does state that in his opinion Monroe exceeded his instructions: "Carried away by his sentiments in favor of the Revolution, . . . he had definitely departed from the path of strict neutrality, and had committed the United States to a warm predilection for France."[29]

In September, Monroe began his ministerial work in earnest.

First Mission to France

On the third of the month, he delivered a note to the Committee of Public Safety summarizing his country's grievances against France. French seizures of British goods on American ships were violations of Article 23 of the Treaty of 1778, which provided that "free ships shall also give a freedom to goods." Seizures of provisions had violated the twenty-fourth Article, which expressly declared provisions to be non-contraband. "We are allies," cautioned Monroe, "and what is more interesting, the friends of France." He admitted, however, that he was "under no instruction to complain of, or request the repeal of the decree authorizing a departure from the 23rd and 24th articles of the Treaty of Amity and Commerce; on the contrary I well know that if, upon consideration, after the experiment made, you should be of opinion that it produces any solid benefit to the Republic, the American government and my countrymen in general will not only bear the departure with patience but with pleasure. It is from the confidence alone which I entertain that this departure cannot be materially beneficial to you, and that the repeal would produce the happiest effect, in removing every possible cause of uneasiness and conciliating still more and more toward each other the affections of the citizens of both republics, and thereby cementing their union, that I have taken the liberty, as connected with other concerns, to bring the subject before you."[30]

Nothing could have been more gentle than this polite request. Expressly asked by the government whether he insisted on the execution of the treaty, Monroe told them "in the most explicit terms, that I was not instructed by the President to insist on it; that their compliance would certainly be highly beneficial to my country, but that in my observations I had considered the proposition merely in relation to France, and wished them to do the same, since I was satisfied that the true interest of France dictated the measure...."[31]

Both Randolph[32] and Washington[33] were again provoked at his leniency. Monroe had justified his stand by the way his instructions on this point had been framed. They read: "But you will go farther and insist upon compensation for the captures and spoliations of our property, and injuries to the persons of our citizens by French cruisers."[34] And Randolph's letter to him of July 30, 1794, had expressly said, "In regard to the spoliation of our commerce, you are therefore charged to make this your special and immediate business, and to press the right of our citizens in a manner which indicates that we cannot waive the justice due us."

As it happened, on January 7, 1795, a decree was passed which restored to force the 23rd and 24th Articles of the treaty, but it was an act which the French could claim as a favor done, rather than a duty performed.

The important issue of obtaining, through French assistance, the privilege of navigation on the lower Mississippi from Spain still remained to be negotiated. The first opportunity to bring the matter up arose in a strange way. In October Monroe received a curious request from Gardoqui, Spain's minister of finance, asking him to coöperate with one of the French foreign affairs officials, M. Otto, in soliciting permission for the Spaniard to visit certain baths in France. Monroe knew that the season for the health resorts was already over, and that, moreover, Gardoqui could find others more conveniently situated than those within the Republic. Through the thin disguise he perceived the true object—"to open the door . . . to . . . a negociation for peace" between Spain and France. Such a peace, at such a moment, Monroe saw, was prejudicial to his country's interests. Instead of delivering the enclosed message to Otto, or even answering that to himself, he laid Gardoqui's correspondence before the Committee with his "free comments upon them." He likewise "told them explicitly that in [his] opinion, it was the wish of the Spanish Court to commence a negociation, and that it had addressed itself through him to inspire a distrust . . . by creating a belief that the United States were more friendly to Spain and Britain than to France."

A decision was finally reached that Monroe should reply to Gardoqui, advising him to apply directly to the Committee. It was then that the government approached Monroe on a subject nearer their hearts, the possibility of financial aid from the United States in their coming campaign against England. Monroe now had a bargaining point for enlisting French aid in securing the desired concessions to America from both Spain and England.[35]

13

Diplomatic Disappointments

AFFAIRS in Paris were moving smoothly towards a successful conclusion for Monroe. French confidence was won and the way cleared for satisfaction of American grievances. Across the Channel, John Jay was also very busy. Conference after conference with Lord Grenville was held, all shrouded in darkest secrecy. And though the summer was unclouded by suspicion, autumn found Monroe increasingly uneasy about what was going on in London.

The French government had for many months been bristling with distrust of Jay's negotiations. Monroe wrote Madison how embarrassing to his aims had been Jay's reported activity, and said that French doubts concerning the real motive of the London talks were producing in Paris ". . . a repellant disposition towards me not from any real distrust in me, but from a distrust of the Ex: adm'n." He admitted failure in dispelling that distrust.[1]

When the rumor percolated through official circles that Jay was crossing to Paris to propose, at England's insistence, a mediation of peace on the part of the United States, Monroe immediately sought out the Committee of Public Safety to assure them that "the object of Mr. Jay's mission to England was confined strictly to the procuring compensation for the depredations committed on our trade, and obtaining the surrender of the western posts."[2]

But French resentment was unallayed. Monroe's own desire to believe the best was no proof against rumor. To Madison he finally sent off a letter in which his animadversions on Jay were freely (and indiscreetly) aired. Three copies were enclosed, one for Randolph and the other two for whomever Madison thought best. Monroe suggested that "one . . . be addressed to Langdon, & the other either to Burr, Butler, or Ross." He could readily conceive, he wrote, that Jay would be "well disposed" to work with the English towards weakening Franco-American ties, "and that in pursuit of this object he would not be over nice or scrupulous as to the means." But, he added, he took comfort in "unshaken confidence in the integrity of the President and in the veracity of the instructions given me to declare that he had no such power."[3]

On November 19, 1794, the Jay Treaty was signed in London. Five weeks later, Monroe received an official request from the Committee of Public Safety to allay disquieting reports of its terms by communicating to them "as soon as possible the treaty whereof there is a question."[4]

Monroe had just received two letters from Jay. The first, dated November 24, pointed out reassuringly enough that the treaty "expressly declares that nothing in it shall be construed to operate contrary to existing treaties between the United States and other powers," a statement paraphrasing the third section of Article XXV of the Jay Treaty.[5] The second letter, written only a day later, contained an important sentence: "As the treaty is not ratified, it would be improper to publish it."

Concluding that Jay had told him all he intended to, and that full information would be forthcoming from Philadelphia,[6] Monroe made a fatal misstep. Informing the committee of Jay's letters, he told them, "I am altogether ignorant of the particular stipulations of the treaty, but I beg leave to assure you that as soon as I shall be informed thereof I will communicate the same to you."[7]

January 16 brought another letter from Jay in which the envoy spoke of ". . . communicating . . . the principal heads of the treaty confidentially."[8] The "confidentially" disturbed Monroe, as well it might after his rash promise. He dispatched a special messenger to Jay, requesting that the terms of the treaty be given him and expressly signifying his intention of communicating them to the French government. He justified this move by arguing that "as nothing will satisfy this government but a copy of the instrument itself, and which, as our ally, it thinks itself entitled to so it will be useless for me to make to it any new communication short of that."[9]

Diplomatic Disappointments

Jay's reply was acid. "You must be sensible," he wrote, "that the United States, as a free and independent nation, have an unquestionable right to make any pacific arrangements with other powers which mutual convenience may dictate, provided those arrangements do not contradict or oppugn their prior engagements with other states. . . ." Jay's anger mounted beyond the limits of tact. "It does not belong to ministers who negotiate treaties," he declared, "to publish them even when perfected, much less treaties not yet completed and remaining open to alteration or rejection. . . ." And with iron finality, ". . . my obligations will not permit me to give, without the permission of their government, a copy of the instrument in question to any person, or for *any purpose;* and by no means for the purpose of being submitted to the consideration and judgment of the councils of a *foreign nation,* however friendly."[10]

Monroe's indignation brimmed over into a hot letter to Randolph, to whom he protested that Jay himself had made the first offer to communicate the treaty's terms and that the latter "wished me to compromise my character, and through me that of the United States with this nation upon the contents of his treaty, without letting me see it; or placing in this government or myself the least confidence in regard to it. . . ."[11]

But now a strange change of heart took place in Jay. On February 19 he sent to Monroe by one Colonel Trumbull a letter conveying the surprising information that the bearer, "who had copied and knew the contents of his treaty with the English government," was instructed to communicate the treaty to Monroe, because the latter "was an *American Minister* and in which character it might be *useful*" to him. However, he "must receive it in *strict confidence*, and under an injunction to impart it to no other person whatever. . . ."[12]

Monroe was naturally surprised. But he clung stubbornly to his stand in the matter. "The line of propriety," he later wrote to Randolph, ". . . appeared to me to be a plain one. I was bound to use such information as Mr. Jay might think fit to give me in the best manner possible, according to my discretion, to promote the public interest: But I was not bound to use any artifice in obtaining that information, or to violate any engagement by the use of it. My duty to the public did not require this of me, and I had no other object to answer. As soon, therefore, as I had made a decision on the subject, I apprized Colonel Trumbull, that I could not receive the communication proposed, upon the terms on which it was offered."

But Trumbull's presence in Paris aroused the suspicions of the French that Monroe was coöperating with Jay in keeping the treaty a secret. Monroe decided he must communicate to the Committee of Public Safety his correspondence with Jay. He also assured its members again that he "was satisfied the treaty contained in it nothing which could give them uneasiness; but if it did, and especially if it weakened our connection with France, it would certainly be disapproved in America."[13]

Further and further Monroe found himself entangled in the unfortunate web his strong partisanship had woven. Here was a diplomat, ostensibly at his post to maintain his country's neutrality, in its best interests, yet acting in a manner likely, as Bond points out, "to range him with the French government as the aggrieved party in opposition to Jay and, consequently, to the government of the United States."[14]

The embassy mail at this time was full of surprises. A few days after Trumbull's arrival, an astonishing letter came from an American resident in Paris, a Mr. Hichborn. "In some free conversation with Colonel Trumbull," he wrote, "on the subject of the late treaty between Great Britain and America, I could not avoid expressing the uneasiness I felt at the disagreeable effects, which had already shewn themselves, and the still more serious consequences which might result from that negociation. And I must confess, I experienced a very agreeable surprise when he assured me upon his honor, that the treaty had for its object, merely the adjustment of some matters in dispute between the two nations,—that it secured to the Americans some rights in commerce . . . that it provided a compensation with those of either nation who had been injured—and finally settled all controversy respecting the boundary line and the western posts." Even more interesting, Hichborn assured his correspondent that "the treaty did not contain any separate or reciprocal guarantee, of any rights, privileges, or territory, or an engagement on either part to afford aid or supplies of any kind to the other, under any circumstances whatever." Trumbull, according to Hichborn, had declared that the treaty merely was an assurance of continued peace

Diplomatic Disappointments

between England and the United States and specified how "the matters of controversy between them shall be finally settled."[15]

Monroe immediately suspected Jay's hand behind this strange communication. Bond has no doubt that the note was inspired by Jay and showed "to just what extent it was considered safe to enlighten Monroe and, incidentally, the French government."[16] Trumbull, it seems, was doing his work thoroughly. To Jay he wrote that he thought it "prudent to remain as long as my business required, contenting myself with repeating on all occasions that the treaty contained nothing contrary to the engagements of existing treaties. . . ."[17]

In a letter he sent to Randolph we learn how Monroe handled the situation. "I was . . . possessed of the paper in question; and it was my duty," he wrote, "to turn it to the best account for the public interest, that circumstances would now admit of. It was, it is true, the most informal of all informal communications, and one, of course, upon which no official measure could be taken; yet the character of the parties entitled it to attention. Upon mature reflection, therefore, and the more especially as I did not wish to meet the committee again on that point, until I heard from you, lest I should be questioned why this new mode of diplomatic proceeding was adopted, I thought it best to send the paper in by my secretary, Mr. Guavain . . . instructing him to assure the members, on my part, that they might confide in the credibility of the parties. The paper was presented to Merlin de Douay . . . and since which I have neither heard from the committee, Colonel Trumbull, nor Mr. Jay on the subject."[18]

The French held their peace throughout that spring, distrustful, awaiting more definite developments.[19] Meantime, across the Atlantic sailed the vessel carrying two letters from Randolph to the waiting Monroe. One, dated February 15, informed him that by the Jay treaty ". . . our commercial intercourse has been also regulated," and advised him to tell the French that "a treaty has been concluded for commerce, also: France will enjoy all the advantages of the most favored nation . . ."[20] The other, also arriving on the same May day, and written on March 8, told Monroe that the treaty would be kept secret until June. But, wrote Randolph, ". . . so far as a cursory perusal of the treaty enabled him to speak, he discovered no reasoned ground for dissatisfaction in the French Republic."[21]

JAMES MONROE

On April 25, 1795, new Orders in Council were issued again authorizing seizure by British vessels of provisions on American ships destined for French ports. Monroe wrote Jefferson, pointing out this as proof of "how little confidence we ought to place in treaties" with Great Britain.[22] Again, he warned that ". . . if we do nothing when it is known in America, but abuse the English and drink toasts to the success of the French revolution, I do not know what step they [the French] will take in regard to us."[23] And to George Logan, Aaron Burr, and Thomas Beckley he dispatched notes stressing the advisability of close relations with France rather than with England. Supposedly confidential, these nevertheless were in part reprinted in American newspapers.[24]

August brought an end to speculation. In the Paris newspapers, for all to read, appeared the news of the passage through the United States Senate of the Jay Treaty, and the terms of the agreement.[25]

No protest came from the French government. And Monroe also bided his time, resolving "to take no step without the particular instruction of the Secretary of State."

Privately, Monroe, in a letter to Madison, attacked the treaty paragraph by paragraph. He could not find a single stipulation in his country's favor contained in it, nor one which improved the American position. He did, however, find in it "a series of stipulations . . . extremely unfavorable and disgraceful, & others at best indifferent." He believed Washington would refuse to ratify it. So incensed was he that he advocated seizure of British possessions and property—Bermuda, and British posts, and perhaps an invasion of Canada.[26]

Bond points out that Monroe did not see that such action "would precipitate the very war which the President was trying so strenuously to avoid."[27]

October brought a letter from Randolph in which the Secretary maintained that the United States had pursued a path of strict neutrality. As for the controversial issue of the instructions given Monroe, he insisted these were "literally true." He did admit, however, that Jay had been authorized to negotiate a further commercial treaty to be kept secret until the grievances over the British posts and depredations had been permanently settled.[28]

In the same post was another letter from Randolph, expressing

Diplomatic Disappointments

some doubt whether, in view of popular opposition, Washington would ratify the treaty.[29]

Monroe was understandably uncertain about what step to take next. Shortly after the arrival of Randolph's letter, he called on Jean de Brie, who was the Committee of Safety's American affairs head. Monroe found him absorbed in a copy of the Jay Treaty. This the Frenchman proceeded to discuss "with great asperity," adding that he was preparing a letter for Monroe on the subject. Monroe finally prevailed upon him to postpone further action until he had read the Randolph-Adet correspondence, which would be immediately sent him.

Unfortunately for himself, Monroe failed to report this incident to Philadelphia for nearly a year, losing the chance to refute the charge made to Washington that French indignation over the Jay Treaty were fabrications of his imagination.

By November, Paris knew definitely that Washington had ratified the treaty on August 18. Official notification came to Monroe on the first of December from Pickering, the new Secretary of State. The new Secretary took this occasion to outline his reasons for believing that the treaty could not be a legitimate grievance of France. He later took the stand that Monroe should have immediately made use of these arguments to put an end to French dissatisfaction. But Monroe hoped that time would ease the situation, and he felt that pressing the matter would only make French feeling more bitter. Nor had he given up the hope that further British depredations would prevent the treaty's execution.[30]

Notwithstanding the treaty trouble, Monroe was able to exact considerable aid from the French in solving the knotty problem of Mississippi navigation. The French diplomat sent to negotiate the peace between the Republic and Spain had been "expressly instructed," Monroe was informed by the Committee of Public Safety, "to use his utmost efforts to secure . . . the points in controversy between the United States and that power."[31] Monroe's services were being made use of by the French as intermediary in the Spanish negotiations, which had been opened by a letter sent by him to the Spanish government.[32]

The Spaniards had also requested him to act as intermediary, promising in return to adjust American demands. This was the situation Monroe carefully explained to the new envoy extraordinary to Spain, Thomas Pinckney, when he arrived in Paris that May. His advice was that Pinckney should go to the Committee of Public Safety, request their aid in his negotiations with Spain, "satisfying them, at the same time, that they were not injured by Mr. Jay's treaty." But Pinckney was cautious—argued that "he could not request such aid without having previously exposed to . . . view Mr. Jay's treaty." This he did not choose to do, "for considerations," wrote Monroe, "delicacy forbade me to inquire into. . . ."[33]

And so Pinckney left for Spain, taking the Spanish business out of Monroe's hands. Pinckney found the Spanish, especially the prime minister, Godoy, in a conciliatory frame of mind, induced, probably, by a healthy respect for the new rapprochement between America and England. And, too, the French envoys were insisting on Spanish concessions to the United States.[34] Negotiations proceeded smoothly to a satisfactory conclusion in the Treaty of San Lorenzo el Real, signed on October 27, 1795. By its terms, the United States obtained freedom of navigation on the Mississippi and the privilege for three years of using New Orleans as a shipping point, duty-free.[35]

Meanwhile, Monroe was busy seeking French assistance in clearing up the Algerian situation. A considerable number of American seamen were languishing in Algerian prisons, victims of the Dey of Algiers' inconvenient habit of making a prize of almost any ship that ventured into the Mediterranean. Most European powers were familiar with His Supreme Highness's weakness, and had as a necessity proffered him "gifts." Monroe had instructions from Philadelphia "to buy peace" in the same manner.[36] Monroe had taken no affirmative steps, however, awaiting the arrival of Colonel Humphreys, United States Minister at Lisbon, who had been appointed envoy to the Dey and who arrived in Paris with an $800,000 gift.

In July, Monroe dispatched a letter to the Committee of Public Safety, announcing Humphreys' arrival and requesting "its good offices and influence" with the Dey.[37] The French assured him that "the aid desired should be given in the most efficacious manner that it could be,"[38] and arrangements were completed for the negotiations with Algiers to be pursued by Mr. Joel Barlow, "with the full aid of France."[39] But before Barlow had even left the shores of France, news came that on September 5 a treaty had been signed with the

Diplomatic Disappointments

Dey by "a Mr. Donaldson, whom Colonel Humphreys had left at Alicante with a conditional power, but in the expectation that he would not proceed in the business till he heard further from him." And so the business was settled without benefit of French intervention, somewhat to Monroe's chagrin.[40] Indeed, he seemed to be more concerned about improving Franco-American relations by using the French government's good offices in the Algerian affair than he was about reaching an understanding with the Dey. To Madison he wrote expressing his fear that France would get no credit in the matter.[41] And he lost no time making a full report of his negotiations with the French, rather pointedly hinting that Donaldson had exceeded his powers.[42]

A February afternoon in 1796 found Monroe in the office of the Minister of Foreign Affairs. He had come to press some American claims of minor importance. Again, as on a previous visit, he had, instead, to listen to a monologue on the Jay Treaty. The French government had not become reconciled to it. In the interim since its ratification, the Foreign Office had been busy planning a retort, and it was ready. The Directory, Monroe was informed, had at length decided how to deal with the matter. The alliance between France and the United States was broken, and an envoy extraordinary would be forthwith sent to America to apprize the former ally of France of this development.[43]

Monroe tried his best to forestall such a move. He argued and pleaded with the Minister that such a step would produce the "most serious ill-consequences," that the enemies of both countries would welcome it with delight, and their friends "behold the spectacle with horror."

The Minister countered with the argument that even aside from any treaty with Great Britain the French had "much cause of complaint," that the treaty was a gesture of absolute unfriendliness, and justified rupture of the alliance between the two countries. Nevertheless, concluded the Minister, Monroe's arguments were "strong and weighty with him," and he would present them to the Directory, "by whom, he doubted not, all suitable attention would be paid to them."[44]

Monroe deduced from the whole situation that the "minister, the government, preferred to have us as open (enemies) rather than perfidious friends."[45] This comment leaves no question as to where his sympathies lay.

On March 10 Monroe was able to write to Pickering the good news that the Minister had assured him of the government's decision to abandon the project of sending an envoy extraordinary and "to make its representations through the ordinary channel."[46] But almost immediately the information reached him that the Directory still had under consideration the sending of a special envoy. He lost no time in asking and obtaining an audience with the Directory, which he requested to authorize the Minister of Foreign Affairs to present to him the French complaints. He asked that the government "in the interim would suspend any decision in regard to the merit of the complaints, or the mission spoken of. . . ."[47] Nothing, replied the Directory, was more reasonable than Monroe's request, which would be granted.

On March 11 Monroe was presented a note outlining the French objections to the Jay Treaty.[48] Its terms, maintained the French, indicated a complete acquiescence on the part of the United States in the English interpretation of the rules of international maritime law. Particularly offensive to the French were the clause placing ship supplies in the contraband class and the absence of a definite statement as to the status of provisions. The latter left the French with the impression that the United States had "tacitly acknowledged the pretensions of England to extend the blockade to our colonies and even to France, by the force of a proclamation alone."[49]

The task of replying to these charges was a particularly difficult one for Monroe, since he had, in effect, the same accusations to make against the treaty.[50] The assistance he had had from Philadelphia in formulating a defense was negligible, limited chiefly to Pickering's letter of September 13, 1795. Upon this communication he nevertheless drew heavily in composing his reply to the Directory. First, he argued, the unsettled state of the law of nations had made it impossible for the United States to get better terms from Great Britain. As to the clause placing ship supplies in the contraband class, to which the French so strongly objected, he said that "it was . . . deemed expedient for the time to relinquish a point we could not obtain; suffering the ancient law of nations to remain unchanged in any respect." And in reply to the objection involving the article which

Diplomatic Disappointments

France contended would prohibit the shipment of provisions from the United States to France, he argued that "no such prohibition is to be found in it or other stipulation which changes the law of nations in that respect: On the contrary, that article leaves the law of nations where it was before; authorizing the seizure in those cases only, where such provisions are contraband, 'by the existing law of nations,' and according to our construction, when carrying to a blockaded port; and in which case payment is stipulated; but in no respect is the law of nations changed, or any right given to the British to seize other than they had before; and such, I presume, you will agree, is the true import of that article."[51] It was good legalistic argument. But it convinced neither the Minister of Foreign Affairs nor the members of the Directory.

Although the French government delayed putting into effect retaliatory measures,[52] the rumors grew more persistent that it was definitely going to act.[53] On July 7, the Minister of Foreign Affairs announced to Monroe the Directory's final decision. Since the United States by the Jay Treaty had abandoned the neutrality principles laid down in the Treaty of 1778 with France, especially the "free ships make free goods" rule, "the Directoire considers the stipulations of (the) treaty of 1778, which respects the neutrality of (the) flag as altered and suspended by this act; and that it would think itself wanting in its duty if it did not modify a state of things which would never have been consented to but upon the principles of strict reciprocity."[54]

On July 2, also, had been passed a decree providing that the French would treat neutral vessels "in the same manner as they suffer the English to treat them."[55] The crowning blow was the recall of the French minister to the United States, Adet. No successor was appointed. Monroe appealed in vain to the Directory. Paris regarded the matter closed.[56]

14

Recall from France

OFFICIAL difficulties were not the only clouds darkening Monroe's horizon. His characteristic generosity was again proving a boomerang. This time, it had been lavished on no less a personage than Thomas Paine, who, since his association with the young Monroe of Revolutionary days, had met with many adventures. Not the least colorful of them had been his participation in the French Revolution as an elected member of the National Convention. The experience had not been fortunate; and Monroe, not many months after his arrival in Paris, received a letter from Paine entreating the new envoy to secure his release from the Luxembourg prison, where he had long been confined as a result of incurring extremist anger for his opposition to the King's execution.[1]

Immediately busying himself, Monroe first began informal negotiations for his former colleague's release. Then he took the bull by the horns and officially requested that Paine be either tried or released. Two days later came an order for the prisoner's release, and Monroe lost no time in installing the ailing, unhappy Paine in his own home.

On September 15, 1795, Monroe wrote to his uncle, Judge Jones, that his and Mrs. Monroe's plans to spend a month or two enjoying the beautiful autumnal weather at St. Germain, where their daughter Eliza[2] was at school, had had to be abandoned, "on account of the ill health of Mr. Paine who has lived in my house for abt. 10 months past. He was upon my arrival confined in the Luxemburg & released on my application, after wh. being sick he has remained with me: for sometime the prospect of his recovery was good: his malady being

Recall from France

an abscess in his side, the consequence of a severe fever in the Luxemburg, but more latterly the symptoms have become worse, & the prospect now is that he will not be able to hold out more than a month or two at the furthest. I shall certainly pay the utmost attention to this gentln. as he is one of those whose merits in our revolution were most distinguished."[3]

In return, all Monroe asked of Paine was that he refrain from writing on public affairs as long as he remained a guest of the American Minister. But no sooner had the man regained his health and the favor of the French government than he merrily proceeded to violate the promise his host had finally and with difficulty extracted from him. To Pinckney, who had stopped off at Paris enroute from Spain, Paine entrusted a letter containing an extract from one to Frederick Muhlenburg of Philadelphia "upon engl. & american affairs & which he intended should be published with his name." Pinckney wisely declined, on learning its contents, to be its bearer. Monroe, learning of Paine's defection, again remonstrated with the irrespressible pamphleteer, who observed "he was quite surprised" at the envoy's concern.[4]

But worse was to come. When Paine finally left Monroe's home, he at once busied himself with an attack "of the most virulent kind"[5] against the President, who, Paine was sure, "had winked at his imprisonment, and wished he might die in goal." Nothing Monroe could say to stop Paine availed. Gloomily he prophesied in a letter to Madison that despite his "efforts to prevent it Paine will probably compromise me by publishing some things which he picked up while in my house. It was natural unaided as I have been or rather harassed from every possible quarter that I talked with this man, but it was not so to expect that he would commit such a breach of confidence as well as ingratitude."[6]

Nowhere is the generosity which, lavished on Paine brought such a bitter harvest, better seen than in Monroe's letters written during his Paris days to Joseph Jones. In these pages is recorded, too, a remarkable testament of the man's loyalty—in this case, loyalty to family. His less fortunate brothers and sister were never out of his mind. Letter after letter, full of solicitude for their needs and happiness, bombarded Monroe's uncle, to whom he had entrusted the execution of his wishes while abroad.

JAMES MONROE

Although he was in the midst of the early difficulties surrounding his recognition by the French government, he found time to write, in September, 1794, instructing the Judge to guard his sister's and brothers' welfare: "You recollect," he wrote, "that I promised to educate a son of hers & supply her with what she might want to the amount of £15 annually or such pt. as might be useful to her; an attention due only on acct. of the negligence of her husband and her sufferings in consequence of it for he is rich enough. You likewise remember my promise to Joseph of supplies &tc. I wish you to settle with him. . . . I intend likewise to do some friendly office for Andrew by assisting him in the purchase of some land, gift of a servant, or aid in the education of a child."[7]

A letter bearing the date, September 15, 1795, mentions Monroe's determination "to pay the balance (between £200 & 300) of Joseph's debts in Scotland." And, he writes, the news that his sister's son was "educating" at his expense would be welcome indeed. He adds, also, that, since it is his wish to do everything in his power for Joseph, he is offering his brother the use of his house and what food supplies it contains.

Again, in a letter of June 20, 1795, he wrote: "I mean to pay (Joseph's) debts & otherwise assist him all in my power. I wod. even help him in addition to the above to the amt. of 500. or six hundred dollrs. to be paid in 12. mos. or sooner if possible in the purchase of a tract of land. . . . You know my wishes with respect to my sister & one of her children—upon these points be so kind as write me."[8]

Monroe abhorred debts, his brother's as much as he would have his own, had he ever allowed himself to contract any. But Joseph had the typical ne'er-do-well's nonchalance in matters of money, whether his own or his brother's or his neighbor's.

"Joseph," Monroe wrote despairingly to Judge Jones the fall of his recall from France, "writes me he has lost the acct. of Forbes, or forgets he ever had it, but will draw on me for the amt. of his debts . . . abt. 200. exclusive of interest. It is easy for him to pay off his debts in that manner but hard for me to do it. . . . He informs me that he has made away with the money for his own land—that he makes nothing by his profession . . . asking finally that I will be so kind as put him in the way to make money. . . ."[9] Monroe could never bring himself to give Joseph up as hopeless.

Recall from France

Busy as he was with pressing diplomatic business, Monroe found time to write nostalgic letters full of plans for the planting on his estate, instructions about servants, private money matters. Nothing is more characteristic than this concern over the details of a country-house's management while in the midst of one of the most exciting periods of Paris history and of his own public life.

The spring of 1796 found a movement afoot in Philadelphia to recall the Minister to France. Monroe had long been expecting some such intrigue on the part of his enemies at home and claimed to be staying on at his post only to deprive the Federalists of the satisfaction of a resignation.[10]

In June he had received a stern letter from Pickering reprimanding him for his "silent and inactive" stand during the period that elapsed between ratification of the Jay Treaty and the French government's official announcement of its objections. The tone of the Secretary's letter, wrote Monroe to Madison, was that "from an overseer on the farm to one of his gang." Pickering took the stand that if Monroe had presented to the French the arguments supplied him by Philadelphia, the Directory would have been safely muzzled; that the whole deplorable misunderstanding with the French was due to Monroe's "misconduct" in suppressing the letter from the State Department. "It will occur to you," wrote Monroe, "that I could not defend the treaty until there was a charge brought against it and to prevent which was always the object of my efforts."[11]

In May, Pickering transmitted Monroe's correspondence to Washington with the comment that the best man to take Monroe's place, ". . . should the President finally resolve on a change of the minister at Paris," was John Quincy Adams."[12] In June, Wolcott, the Secretary of the Treasury, was writing to Hamilton about the advisability of Monroe's recall.[13] Hamilton's reply was that Monroe must be replaced in order to check French disquietude.[14]

Washington first considered sending a special envoy to France to deal with the rising French discontent, and asked his Cabinet, and Hamilton also,[15] whether "the Executive, in the recess of the Senate, has power, in such a case . . . to send a special character to Paris, as Envoy Extraordinary to give and receive explanations?"[16] Pickering, speaking for the Secretaries of the Treasury and War as well as for himself, replied that the President in their opinion had no such power. They suggested, instead, that Monroe be removed and a more acceptable person be appointed in his stead.[17]

In a joint letter elaborating this opinion, the three members of the Cabinet said, "Altho the present minister plenipotentiary of the United States at Paris has been amply furnished with documents to explain the views and conduct of the United States, yet his own letters authorize us to say that he omitted to use them, and thereby exposed the U. States to all the mischiefs which could flow from jealousies & erroneous conceptions of their views and conduct. Whether this dangerous omission arose from such an attachment to the cause of France as rendered him too little mindful of the interests of his own country, or from mistaken views of the latter, or from any other cause the evil is the same."

As evidence of "the expediency of recalling Mr. Monroe," there was enclosed a letter Monroe had written to Dr. George Logan on the political situation in France. Monroe had sent it with the understanding that it was to be published. Concerning this letter the three secretaries said, "A minister who has thus made the notorious enemies of the whole system of the government his confidential correspondents in matters which affect that government, cannot be relied on to do his duty to the latter.—This private letter we received in confidence."

Monroe was also accused of having a hand in the anonymous letters from France written to Thomas Blount and others. "These anonymous communications from officers of the U States in a foreign country on matter of a public nature," went on the letter to Washington, "and which deeply concern the interests of the United States, in relation to that foreign country, are proofs of sinister designs, and shew that the public interests are no longer safe in the hands of such men."[18]

To this was added the opinion of Hamilton that "though ... there are weighty reasons against it," Monroe should be recalled, "if a proper man can be found."[19] He had come to this conclusion after conferring with Jay.

And so, on July 8, Washington informed Pickering that after giving the subject the serious consideration it deserved, he had determined to recall Monroe and to appoint in his place someone who would "promote, not thwart, the neutral policy of the government."[20]

When Pickering received Monroe's account of his answer to the

Recall from France

French objections to the Jay Treaty, he wrote to Washington that the arguments with which the minister to France had been furnished should have given Monroe material for "a more forcible explanation . . ." to the French. Moreover, he was convinced "that the ominous letters of Mr. Monroe composed a part of a solemn farce to answer certain party purposes in the U. States."[21] With this interpretation, Washington was in full agreement, saying he was glad to find that "more smoke than fire is likely to result from the representation of French discontents," and that "it was far from being impossible, that the whole may have originated in a contrivance of the opposers of the government, to see what effect such threats would work."[22]

Washington reasoned that if French "suspicions, doubts, and discontentment" were as real as Monroe's account of them to Philadelphia, then all the more reason why he should have hastened to allay them before the French made official announcement of their displeasure with the treaty.[23]

In November, Monroe received his letter of recall, sent by Pickering on the twenty-second of the preceding August. It was brief, giving as reasons for the President's action his "uneasiness and dissatisfaction," and a further consideration of Monroe's reports on the French situation, together "with other concurring circumstances."[24]

Charles Cotesworth Pinckney, appointed to take Monroe's place, reached Paris in early December. But the sudden announcement of the French minister of foreign affairs that the Directory would "no longer recognize nor receive a minister plenipotentiary from the United States, until after a reparation of the grievances demanded of the American Government . . ."[25] left Pinckney cooling his heels.

On December 30 Monroe made his formal farewell speech, restrained in tone, to the French government, expressing his gratitude for the courtesy shown him during his tenure of office and the hope that relations between the two countries would soon become more harmonious.

President-Director Barras was not conciliatory in his reply. He said, in part:

"By presenting today the letters of recall to the executive directory, you gave to Europe a very strange spectacle.

"France rich in her liberty surrounded by a train of victories, strong in the esteem of her allies, will not abase herself by calculating the consequences of the condescension of the American government to the suggestions of her former tyrants. Moreover the French republic hopes that the successors of Columbus, Raleigh and Penn, always proud of liberty, will never forget that they owe it to France. ... Assure the good American people, sir, that like them we adore liberty; that they will always have our esteem, ... As for you, Mr. minister plenipotentiary, you have combatted for principles. You have known the true interests of your country. Depart with our regret. In you we give up a representative to America, and retain the remembrance of the citizen whose personal qualities did honour to that title." [26]

On January 8, Monroe wrote to Madison: "... you will perceive it was impossible unless I exposed myself & family to the danger & inconvenience of a winter voyage, to depart hence before the beginning of April next, which we propose to do in case a suitable passage can be obtained from any of the ports of France. ... I mean to take a trip into Holland in the interim with Mrs. M. to see some other parts of Europe before our return, & which I was not able to do before, for I never saw things in such a state here after my arrival to be able to absent myself from Paris more than 24 hours at a time, without apprehending real danger to my country & in consequence never went further from Paris ... than Saint Germain." [27]

And so, in the spring of 1797, Monroe sailed for home, a deeply angered and embittered man. Misled by the deception of Randolph in regard to the Jay Treaty, hampered by Pickering's narrowness, his task made difficult by the paucity of correspondence from Philadelphia, he felt that his best efforts in the cause of his country's good name had been nullified and his reputation needlessly ruined by the intrigue and stupidity of the Philadelphia administration. And his greatest service, that of postponing for so long French action on the Jay Treaty, had gone entirely unacknowledged.

That the administration might have cause for complaint he could not or would not see. That he might have committed some diplomatic *faux pas*, that his devotion to France had rendered him incapable of coöperating with Washington's wise policy of reserved friendliness with both England and France, that he was too much influenced by the tenets of his party were possibilities that never suggested themselves to him as he paced the deck on the long voyage home.

15

The Reynolds Affair

FROM THE MOMENT Monroe, accompanied by his family, set foot on his native shore, incidents and events began to occur that could not but deepen his depression. At the landing stage in Philadelphia, the port officials—of Federalist persuasion—summarily ordered the Monroes back on board until "the usual formalities" had been observed. Once disembarked, it did not take Monroe long to observe how the wind blew. Everywhere, scandal-mongers were merrily busy with the stories of his part in the Paine episode. They were also deriving boundless delight from the affair of the toast to Washington at a dinner, arranged by the American colony in Paris, celebrating American independence. This toast to Washington, proposed by a guest, had been opposed by certain gentlemen not in favor of the Jay Treaty, until Monroe suggested changing the subject of the toast to "the executive." When, subsequently, a persistent pro-treaty guest proposed a toast to "General Washington," such opposition was provoked as must have hugely entertained the French officials who were present. Monroe himself drank the toast and retired, but the harm was done.

It was obvious that Monroe's doings in France had become a football of party politicians, and now that he had returned, it was inevitable that he become involved in the factional disputes between Federalists and Republicans. Had Monroe, seeing how matters stood, sought out Pickering and Washington immediately on his arrival instead of conferring as he did with the Republican leaders, he might have been able to prevent much of the ill-feeling that he was to incur.

JAMES MONROE

But it is understandable that he should seek solace in the bosom of his own party. And, too, he was avid for news of the latest political developments.

The first his party members were quick to oblige him with. Gallatin was convinced from his "conversation with Monroe, from his manner and everything about him" that the man "was possessed of integrity superior to all the attacks of malignity, and that he had conducted himself with irreproachable honor and the most dignified sense of duty."[1] On June 30, Gallatin wrote to his wife, "We give to-morrow a splendid dinner to Monroe at Oelkr's hotel, in order to testify our approbation of his conduct and our opinion of his integrity. Jefferson, Judge McKean, the governor, and about fifty members of Congress will be there...."[2] At this dinner Livingston proposed a toast to "Monroe the virtuous citizen, who, to keep the peace of the country, refuses to do justice to himself."

It was unfortunate that the resolution implied in this toast was one which, if Monroe did make at the time, he did not persist in. But in extenuation of his failure to do so, let it be said that such a course was rendered difficult, if not impossible, by the political code of the time and by the resuscitation of the Reynolds affair.

To understand the Reynolds affair, from which stemmed the bitter feud between Hamilton and Monroe which raged that summer of 1797 and almost led to a duel, the pages of their personal histories must be turned back to the year 1792.

In that year, James Reynolds and Jacob Clingman, the latter once a clerk of former Speaker of the House Frederick Muhlenberg, were being prosecuted for a criminal offense rising out of certain speculations in government funds. Reynolds was in jail. Clingman, less seriously involved, was at liberty, and came to his former employer, Muhlenberg, appealing for help in obtaining his own and Reynolds' release or discharge from the prosecution. Muhlenberg "promised so far as respected Clingman, but, not being particularly acquainted with Reynolds in a great measure declined, so far as respected him." Indeed, he "could not undertake to recommend Reynolds," whom he "verily believed ... to be a rascal" and described him as such to the comptroller of the Treasury. But Clingman persisted in his attempts to free Reynolds also. Muhlenberg's report unfolds the story: "Clingman, unasked, frequently dropped hints to me, that Reynolds

The Reynolds Affair

had it in his power very materially to injure the Secretary of the Treasury, and that Reynolds knew several very improper transactions of his. I paid little or no attention to those hints, but when they were frequently repeated, and it was even added that Reynolds said he had it in his power to hang the Secretary of the Treasury, that he was deeply concerned in speculation, . . . it created considerable uneasiness in my mind, and I conceived it my duty to consult with some friends on the subject. Mr. Monroe & Mr. Venable were informed of it yesterday morning."[3]

The two new figures in the drama continue the story in their statement: "Being informed yesterday in the morning, that a person of the name of Reynolds from Virginia (Richmond) was confined in jail upon some criminal prosecution relative to certificates, and that he had intimated he could give some intelligence of speculations of Mr. Hamilton which should be known, we immediately called on him, . . . he informed us that he could give information of the misconduct in that respect, of a person high in office, but must decline it for the present until relieved, which was promised him that evening: that, at ten today, he would give us a detail of whatever he knew on the subject. He affirmed he had a person in high office in his power . . . and, in fact, expressed himself in such a manner as to leave no doubt he meant Mr. Hamilton."

In a third statement, signed by Monroe and Muhlenberg, it was disclosed that Mrs. Reynolds was the next to be questioned. She reluctantly gave further damning evidence, confessing to burning, at Hamilton's request, a considerable number of letters from him to her husband and displaying several anonymous notes which she believed were from Hamilton and were so endorsed by Reynolds. She admitted Hamilton had offered Reynolds "something clever" to leave these parts and not be seen again, a request which she was satisfied came not from friendship but because Reynolds "could tell something that would make some of the heads of departments tremble."

This, and much more evidence of a like nature, together with Clingman's statements, wove about Hamilton's name and person a net of questionable behavior and suspicious traffic with shady characters that grew stronger with every clue that was uncovered.

Finally, on the evening of December 15, 1792, Muhlenberg, Venable, and Monroe called on Hamilton himself, then living in the

Pemberton Mansion. Five persons were present at that strange interview: the three Republicans, Hamilton, and his friend Wolcott, whose notes on the episode tell us what happened there:

"The conference was commenced on the part of Mr. Monroe by reading certain Notes from Mr. Hamilton, and a Narrative of conversations which had been held with the said Reynolds and Clingman. . . ."[4]

The story Hamilton told that night to his astonished and absorbed listeners was, after all, not an unusual one. Later he wrote substantially the same narrative in a pamphlet published to vindicate himself:

"Some time in the summer of the year 1791, a woman called at my house in the city of Philadelphia, and asked to speak with me in private. I attended her into a room apart from my family. With a seeming air of affliction she informed me that she was a daughter of a Mr. Lewis, sister to a Mr. G. Livingston of the State of New York, and wife to a Mr. Reynolds, whose father was in the Commissary Department during the war with Great Britain; that her husband, who for a long time had treated her very cruelly, had lately left her to live with another woman, and in so destitute a condition that, though desirous of returning to her friends, she had not the means; that knowing I was a citizen of New York, she had taken the liberty to apply to my humanity for assistance. . . . In the evening I put a bankbill in my pocket and went to the house. I enquired for Mrs. Reynolds and was shown upstairs, at the head of which she met me and conducted me into a bedroom. I took the bill out of my pocket and gave it to her. Some conversation ensued from which it was quickly apparent that other than pecuniary consolation would be acceptable.

"After this I had frequent meetings with her, most of them at my own house; Mrs. Hamilton with her children being absent on a visit to her father. In the course of a short time, she mentioned to me that her husband had solicited a reconciliation, and affected to consult me about it. I advised to it, and was soon after informed by her that it had taken place."[5]

The effect of these painful and undesired confidences upon the humorless and strait-laced Monroe must have been deplorable. Muhlenberg, a clergyman, was probably shocked. Venable, a free-living Virginian, was less sensitive; Wolcott records that he im-

The Reynolds Affair

mediately "requested Mr. Hamilton to desist from exhibiting further proofs," but the latter grimly "insisted upon being allowed to read such documents as he possessed. . . ."[6]

Whereupon there was presented to the three gentlemen a collection of missives distinguished as much by poor English as by passion. "I have kept my Bed these two days," Hamilton's inamorata wrote, "and now rise from My pillow wich your Neglect has filled with the shorpest thorns." Another note bore the injunction "Reade this all," followed by this message: "In a state of mind wich know language can paint I take up the pen . . . I have woes to relate wich I never expected to know accept by the name Come therefore tomorrow sometime or Els in the Evening do I beg you to come gracious God had I the world I would lay It at your feet." And again, "I only do it to Ease a heart which is ready Burst with Greef."[7]

Hamilton did admit conversations with Mrs. Reynolds and her husband, also, which were more like those the self-appointed investigating committee had expected to hear. He said, "She told me . . . that her husband had been engaged in speculation, and she believed could give information respecting the conduct of some persons in the department which would be useful. I sent for Reynolds who came to me accordingly.

"In the course of our interview, he confessed that he had obtained a list of claims from a person in my department which he had made use of in his speculations. I invited him, by the expectation of my friendship and good offices, to disclose this person. After some affectation of scruple, he pretended to yield, and ascribed the infidelity to Mr. Duer. . . . Mr. Duer had resigned his office sometime the seat of government was removed to Philadelphia. . . ."

This revelation had no small interest for Hamilton's listeners, for Duer, until the doors of a debtors' prison had closed upon him, had been known to use his friendship with Hamilton to hover about the Treasury long after his resignation in 1790.[8] Although it appears certain today that Hamilton was himself innocent of the charge of using his knowledge for corrupt purposes, his father-in-law, General Schuyler, was believed by the Republican leaders to belong to the "ring of speculators" who had profited by their inside knowledge to gamble in bank scrip and public securities. New York, that stronghold of an aristocracy closely related by intermarriage, was a hotbed of such speculation. Hamilton himself probably entertained doubts of Duer's conduct, for he explained that "this discovery, if it had been true, was not very important—yet it was the interest of my passions to appear to set value upon it, and to continue the expectation of friendship and good offices."

At this time Reynolds went for a time to Virginia and on his return came to Hamilton asking employment as a clerk in the Treasury Department. "The knowledge I had acquired of him," Hamilton's account states, "was decisive against such a request. I parried it by telling him, what was true, that there was no vacancy. . . ." Mrs. Reynolds, too, was making difficulties. "Her conduct made it extremely difficult to disentangle myself," wrote Hamilton, whose ardor had cooled. "All the appearances of violent attachment, and of agonizing distress at the idea of a relinquishment, were played with a most imposing art."

In brief, the affair had sunk to a common blackmailing adventure. Reynolds, indeed, had kept a meticulous record of these disbursements. Hamilton had kept one of Reynolds' acknowledgments, couched in terms of extravagant gratitude.

At the conclusion of the interview, the deportment of the three inquisitors was such as to convey the impression that their apprehensions and worst suspicions had been allayed. Indeed, Wolcott records that Monroe, Muhlenberg, and Venable "severally acknowledged their entire satisfaction, that the affair had no relation to Official duties" and that after leaving Hamilton's house Venable repeated to Wolcott that "the explanation was entirely satisfactory. . . ."[9]

Hamilton, indeed, was later to offer strong proof of his financial integrity by dying penniless. But it is evident from the report of the interview drawn up by his three visitors on that fateful night that Hamilton had not entirely satisfied them on the score of his official blamelessness: "Last night we waited on Colonel Hamilton when he informed us of a particular Connection with Mrs. Reynolds; The period of its Commencement & Circumstances attending it—His vissiting her at In Skeep's; the frequent supplies of Money to her & her Husband, on that Account; his duress by them, from fear of a disclosure, and his anxiety to be relieved from it and them. To support this he shewed a great number of letters from Reynolds & herself commencing early in 1791. He acknowledged all the letters in

The Reynolds Affair

a disguised Hand in our possession to be his—We left him under the impression our suspicions were removed—He acknowledged our Conduct toward him had been fair and liberal—He could not complain of it—We brought back all the Papers even his own Notes, nor did he ask their Destruction." [10]

With characteristic complacency, Hamilton seems to have believed that he had handled the situation with dignity and finality. At a later date, he described the affair as a conspiracy "against honest fame," implying that he had been guilty only of a "little foible or folly." [11] The self-constituted committee he called a "Jacobin Scandal Club."

The affair was not, however, closed. Among the documents pertaining to it appears a notation dated January 2, 1793, and signed by Monroe alone: "Mr. Clingman called on me this Evening and mentioned that he had been apprised of Mr. Hamilton's Vindication by Mr. Wolcott a Day or two after our Interview with him—He further observed to me that he communicated the same to Mrs. Reynolds, who appeared much shocked at it and wept immoderately. That she denied the Imputation and declared that it had been a Fabrication of Colonel Hamilton: and that her Husband had joined in it, who had told her so, and that he had given him Receipts for Money and written letters so as to give countenance to the Pretence—that he was with Colonel Hamilton the Day after he left the Jail when we supposed he was in Jersey—He was of Opinion she was innocent and that the Defence was an Imposition." [12]

And it was this particular memorandum in Monroe's hand that was to figure with particular prominence in the next scene of the drama, which was not to be played until several years later.

In the spring of 1797, when Monroe was preparing to leave Europe and his name on this side of the Atlantic was in the mouths of scandal-mongers and political enemies, a bombshell was hurled into the ranks of the Hamiltonians in the shape of a curious narrative entitled *History of the United States for 1796*, brought out in Philadelphia over the name of one Callender.

This was nothing more or less than an exposition of the entire Reynolds affair, based on "an attested copy, exactly conformable to that, which, at his own desire, was delivered to Mr. Hamilton himself," of the principal papers drawn up by the committee of three—

Muhlenberg, Venable, and Monroe. Actually, the evidence contained was incomplete, notably in regard to Mrs. Reynolds' part in the affair, but on the whole sufficiently correct to convince Hamilton that one of that committee had betrayed his trust. Which one of the three it was, he was not slow to decide. The preamble of this extraordinary work was in itself sufficiently damning: "Attacks on Mr. Monroe have been frequently repeated from the stock-holding presses. They are cowardly, because he is absent. They are unjust, because he displayed, on an occasion that will be mentioned immediately, the greatest lenity to Mr. Alexander Hamilton, the prime mover of the federal party."

Yet as early as June 24, 1797, almost a month before Hamilton was to face Monroe and charge him with breach of faith, Theodore Sedgwick, writing to Hamilton's intimate, informed him that John Beckley had not been reëlected clerk by the House of Representatives, that "this was resented not only by himself but the whole party [Republican], and they were rendered furious by it. To revenge, Beckley has been writing a pamphlet mentioned in the enclosed advertisement. The 'authentic papers' there mentioned are those of which you perfectly know the history, formerly in the possession of Messrs. Monroe, Muhlenberg, and Venable. This conduct is mean, base and infamous."[13] This Beckley was an ardent Republican, an adherent of Jefferson, who had often been entrusted by the Virginia members of the party and those in the capital with important documents and other messages. Now Monroe, as he later declared, had left the papers from which Callender's *History* had been assembled "sealed with his friend in Virginia," the friend remaining unnamed, but almost certainly Jefferson. Jefferson knew and was later a patron of Callender, who in 1797 was in communication with a group of Virginia Republicans.[14]

It is not too difficult to link the names of Beckley, Jefferson, and Callender into a chain of evidence that gives us a simple solution of the case.[15] Hamilton, however, was convinced that Monroe was responsible for the attack upon him and was determined to obtain satisfaction. Thus stood matters when Monroe, newly arrived from abroad, journeyed from Philadelphia to New York. The day after his arrival, Monroe received a visitor at ten in the morning. Hamilton, accompanied by his brother-in-law, Mr. Church, entered the

The Reynolds Affair

room, where Monroe sat with David Gelston, a Republican congressman. The last-named, whose account of the encounter pictures vividly what occurred that memorable day, relates that "Col. Hamilton appeared very much agitated upon his entrance into the room." He recapitulated the events of five years before and it was not long before "some warmth appeared in both gentlemen." Gelston describes the ensuing moments in great detail:

"Col. Monroe then began with declaring it was merely accidental his knowing anything about the business at first he had been informed that one Reynolds, from Virginia, was in Gaol. He called merely to aid a man that might be in distress, but found it was a Reynolds from New York, and observed that after the meeting alluded to, at Philadelphia, he sealed up his copy of the papers mentioned and sent or delivered them to his friend in Virginia. He had no intention of publishing them and declared upon his honor that he knew nothing of their publication until he arrived at Philadelphia from Europe, and was sorry to find that they were published. Col. Hamilton observed that as he had written to Col. Monroe, Mr. Muhlenberg, and Mr. Venable, he expected an immediate answer to so important a subject in which his character, the peace and reputation of his family was so deeply interested. Col. Monroe replied that if he, Col. Hamilton, would be temperate or quiet for a moment, or some such word, he would answer him candidly: That he received his, Col. Hamilton's letter, at 10 o'clock that night; that he had determined to leave Philadelphia next morning, and actually did leave it for New York; that immediately, at a late hour that night, after receiving the letter, he went to Mr. Venable's quarters; that it was impossible to meet Mr. Muhlenberg and Mr. Venable, and that at the meeting before alluded to they were all present (upon which Mr. C. took out of his pocket two pamphlets in which was a statement signed by Mr. Muhlenberg, by Mr. Venable and Col. Monroe) and all had signed it; that he thought it most proper for them all to meet and return a joint answer to Col. Hamilton's letter, which he meant to do on his return to Philadelphia. . . . Col. Monroe then proceeded upon a history of the business printed in the pamphlets and said that the packet of papers before alluded to he yet believed remained sealed with his friend in Virginia."

Hamilton snapped, "This as your representation is totally false!"

Monroe rose from his chair, "Do you say I represent falsely? You are a scoundrel."

Hamilton was on his feet too. "I will meet you like a gentleman," he retorted.

"I am ready," said Monroe quietly, "Get your pistols."

Church and Gelston both interposed, stepping between the taut figures.

"Gentlemen, gentlemen, be moderate," cried Church.

Whereupon the men seated themselves again. Hamilton remained agitated but Monroe, who had cooled, repeated his entire ignorance of the publication and the surprise with which he learned of its appearance. It was finally agreed to "let the whole affair rest until Col. Monroe returned to Philadelphia and a meeting could be had with Mr. Venable and Mr. Muhlenberg and a joint letter or answer be given as Col. Monroe had proposed . . . and it was decided that all present would proceed to Philadelphia where the matter would be resumed on the following Sunday."

As the gentlemen rose to go, Mr. Church observed that in view of the forthcoming explanation to be offered by Muhlenberg, Venable, and Monroe, "any warmth or unguarded expression that had happened during the interview should be buried and considered as though it never had happened.

"In that respect," said Monroe, "I shall be governed by Col. Hamilton's consent."

Colonel Hamilton then agreeing that "any intemperate expressions should be forgotten," the visitors took their leave, and the encounter was over.[16]

Six days later, Monroe and Muhlenberg wrote a joint reply to the charges in which the entire situation was carefully analyzed. That the "original papers" had been "deposited in the hands of a respectable character in Virginia where they now are" was reiterated, despite the fury that statement had evoked in Hamilton during his interview with Monroe. All connection with Callender's publication was disavowed, the two men declaring that they had had "no agency in or knowledge of the publication of these papers till they appeared, so of course we could have none in the comments that were made on them." To support this contention, they pointed out "the difference which appears between the papers which preceded our inter-

The Reynolds Affair

view and those contained in No. 5 of the publication." Their own records, having been intended "only as memoranda" and without a view "to any particular use," were "entered concisely and without form," while those in the published version were in more polished style. The letter concluded with the protest, already advanced by Venable in his letter to Hamilton, that the Federalist *Gazette of the United States* had been inaccurate in making the charge that "two very profligate men" had from a prison cell sought to obtain their liberation "by favor of party spirit," since Clingman "was never imprisoned for any crime alleged against him."[17]

It was in one of the two replies[18] of Hamilton to this letter that he made evident his purpose to put all of the blame on Monroe alone, basing his charges on the final memorandum signed by Monroe alone and containing Clingman's statement that Mrs. Reynolds had denied any affair between herself and Hamilton and insisted that the latter's guilt was solely on the score of misuse of his office as Secretary of the Treasury. This memorandum now became the subject of a bitter epistolary battle.

To Hamilton's attack on this memorandum, Monroe, who was at this same period crossing swords with Pickering over the matter of his recall, replied in a letter in which we can detect a harassed, impatient, exasperated frame of mind. He wrote, "It is impossible for me to trace back at this moment, occupied as I am with other concerns, all the impressions of my mind at the different periods at which the memoranda were made . . . but I well remember that in entering the one which bears my single signature, although I was surprised at the communication given, yet I neither meant to give nor imply any opinion of my own as to its contents . . . I simply entered the communication as I received it, reserving to myself the liberty to form an opinion upon it at such future time as I found convenient, paying due regard to all the circumstances connected with it."[19]

Here was exactly the admission that Hamilton was waiting for: that Monroe had allowed Clingman's word to outweigh his own. Hamilton pressed for an even more definite expression of the fact "that the information of Clingman had revived the suspicions which his explanation had removed."[20] What Monroe offered was: "I can only observe that in entering the note which bears my single signature, I did not convey or mean to convey any opinion of my own, as to the faith which was due to it, but left it to stand on its own merits, reserving to myself the right to judge of it, as upon any fact afterwards communicated according to its import and authenticity."[21] This was diplomatic enough, but Hamilton, reading in it only what he wished to find, was in his next letter inveighing against the "sanction of credit" Monroe had given the word of Clingman and the Reynoldses and declaring that it merited "epithets the severest I could apply."

Monroe, provoked by Hamilton's high-handed tone, rejoined irritatedly with: " 'Tis proper also to observe that we admitted your explanation upon the faith of your own statement, and upon the documents you presented, though I do not recollect they were proved, or that proof was required of them.

"You will remember that in this interview in which we acknowledged ourselves satisfied with the explanation you gave, we did not bind ourselves not to hear further information on the subject, or even not to proceed further in case we found it our duty so to do. This would have been improper. . . ."[22]

At last Monroe had laid himself open to the action Hamilton was obviously eager to take. He replied on the following day, after having "maturely considered" Monroe's letter, which had been "delivered at about nine" the previous night. He complained that Monroe's explanation gave no "cause of satisfaction," further expressed his displeasure on the score of the "countenance" given Clingman's testimony, and declared he was being driven to "a formal defence." "You have been," he accused, "and are actuated by motives towards me malignant and dishonorable; nor can I doubt that this will be the universal opinion, when the publication of the whole affair which I am about to make shall be seen."[23]

In the code of the day, this was tantamount to a challenge. It was characteristic of the choleric Hamilton to precipitate such a situation. It was equally characteristic of sober-minded, sensible Monroe to react to it by attempting to inject a little sane reasoning into an affair that was getting out of hand. With wisdom, and very honestly, he wrote to Hamilton:

"Why you have adopted this style I know not. If your object is to render this affair a personal one between us, you might have been more explicit, since you well know, if that is your disposition, what

The Reynolds Affair

my determination is, and to which I shall firmly adhere. But if it is to illustrate truth, and place the question on its true merits, as I have always been disposed to do, it appears illy calculated to promote that end ... I have constantly said and I repeat again, that in making an entry which appears after our interview with you, and which ought to have been signed by the other gentlemen as well as myself, I never intended to convey an opinion upon it, nor does it convey any opinion of my own, but merely notes what Clingman stated, leaving it upon his own credit only. But you wish me to state that this communication made no impression on my mind, and this I shall not state, because in so doing I should be incorrect."[24]

To interpret these words, as Hamilton's biographers have done, as a cowardly attempt to avoid an encounter on the field of honor is possible only if one omits the second sentence and the two final ones, or reads them all with eyes blinded by bias. The final sentences could not state more explicitly Monroe's courageous refusal to do the very thing that would have avoided resort to pistols or swords. His letter of a few days later was equally clear in meaning: "I have stated to you that I have no wish to do you a personal injury. The several explanations which I have made accorded with truth and my ideas of propriety. Therefore I need not repeat them. If these do not yield you satisfaction, I can give you no other, unless called on in a way which, for the illustration of truth, I wish to avoid, but which I am ever ready to meet."[25]

Hamilton replied to this by a letter informing Monroe that he had "authorized Major Jackson to communicate with you and to settle time and place."[26] He chose to interpret Monroe's reply as a challenge, although he himself was the aggrieved party and had certainly provoked the whole thing. But public opinion, even at that time, held the aggressor responsible for the consequences of a duel, and Hamilton was careful to avoid any possible criticism on that score.

Monroe was aghast at the outcome, and appealed to Colonel Burr for guidance in this matter, which was like nothing his past experience had taught him to handle. To him he wrote, "I enclose you a copy of my correspondence with Colo. Hamilton since my return to this city which I hope you will immediately peruse. I send likewise a letter to him in reply to his last which after reading & sealing I wish you to present him. I have written this last letter as you will perceive to dem'd whether he meant his as a direct challenge on his part or as the acceptance of one on mine (the latter being the idea of Major Jackson), or of an invitation on my part. If the former be the case, then you will accept it of course. If the latter then the expl'n which I give ends the aff'r; as I never meant to give him a challenge, on acc't of what has passed between us, seeing no cause to do so; having conceded nothing w'h as a man of honor and truth I ought not: and in the stile followed his example, especially when our interview at New York is also notic'd: an example however which ought not to have been given."

But the whole affair held little importance for Monroe, in comparison with the subject of his recall from France, which was throughout this same period holding his attention. The letter to Burr continues:

"If the aff'r takes the first course, then time must be given me on acc't of my publication, the adjustment of my family aff'rs—having been long absent and they requiring much attention, especially when it is considered that in case of accident I sho'd leave Mrs. M. almost friendless in Virg'a, she being of New York. For the whole of this ab't three months wo'd be necessary—two wo'd be for the publication only. The place I sho'd wish to be ab't or near the Susquahanna, but on this head I sho'd not be to vigorous. As you have a child & a family I wo'd not trouble you unless in y'r neighborhood, but shall calculate on the aid of Mr. Dawson. However 'tis probable I sho'd be forced to ask y'r aid, as I [mutilated] much confidence in you.

"You will explain to him, if he asks expln., why I referred him to you and did not adjust it with Major Jackson, that I supposed it wo'd be more agreeable to him to have you authorized to represent me fully in the aff'r for the purpose of closing it at once with him on the spot: and that to me it was an object of importance, since being much occupied in other concerns and meaning soon to leave town, I wished to have my time and mind free from interruption.

"I hope you will settle this disagreeable aff'r finally so that we write no more either to the other on it. Nor need I observe that as I have entire confidence in your judgment, honor and friendship for me, so I could equally confide that you will close it in such a manner, as duly observing that a certain result, ought always to be avoided whilst it can with propriety, especially by a person with a family, yet it is not to be avoided by any the slightest sacrifice or con-

The Reynolds Affair

descention ... Indeed I was never averse to the simple question "did you mean to give any opinion of y'r own as to the credibility due to the entry bearing your single signature"? to answer "that I did not but meant it to stand on the credibility of the man." This wo'd have been perhaps of some service to him, but he w'd never ask'd it in that form, always endeavoring to get more from me than in conscience I w'd give. Nor sh'd I now hesitate (provided you approved it) after the aff'r is settled (if settled amicably) to give such an answer to such question: observing that the aff'r be first settled, before any other (be undertaken)."

Monroe in this letter also voiced the opinion that Hamilton had been "pushed on by his party friends here, who to get rid of him, wo'd be very willing to hasard him. Of this I have many reasons to be well assured of." He closed the letter with these words: "I had no hand in the publication, was sorry for it—and think he has acted, by drawing the publick attention to it, & making it an aff'r of more consequence than it was in itself, very indiscreetly."[27]

That he was willing to accept a challenge, but refused to be the challenger, is clearly stated in the letter he enclosed for Hamilton: "Seeing no adequate cause, by anything in our late correspondence, why I should give a challenge to you, I own it was not my intention to give or even provoke one by anything contained in those letters. I meant only to observe that I should stand on the defensive, and receive one if you thought fit to give it. If, therefore, you were under a contrary impression, I frankly own you are mistaken. If, on the other hand, you meant this last letter as a challenge to me, I have then to request that you will say so, and in which case, have to inform you that my friend, Col. Burr, who will present you this, and who will communicate with you on the subject, is authorized to give my answer to it, and to make such other arrangements as may be suitable in such an event."[28]

But Hamilton also refused to assume the odious role of aggressor, and the crisis was resolved by the brief note he penned to Monroe on August 9 stating that as Monroe had not intended to make "an advance towards a personal interview [*i.e.*, challenge], any further step ... would be improper" because "inconsistent with the ground I have heretofore taken."[29] Instead, he vindicated his "fiscal honor" by publishing his pamphlet on the whole Reynolds affair, in which he set forth his version of the tale in startlingly frank style.

16

Governor of Virginia

IT WAS on July 11 of the summer of Monroe's return from Europe that Hamilton called on him in New York, and on August 9 that Hamilton wrote the note which officially brought the affair to an end as far as Monroe was actively concerned. Over almost exactly the same period there was raging an epistolary battle between Monroe and another adversary, Timothy Pickering, the Secretary of State, of whom Monroe was demanding the reasons for his recall from France.

The latter was by far the more important of the two controversies to Monroe. It will be remembered that in issuing his instructions to his second, Colonel Aaron Burr, Monroe demanded that before meeting Hamilton on the field of honor he be allowed at least two months for finishing the article he was writing in vindication of his diplomatic actions. The tone of his letters to Hamilton was one of annoyance, like that of a man who, engaged in a closely fought duel—in this case, a duel of wits—is exasperated by the persistent attack of a wasp.

Monroe's first letter to Pickering was written almost immediately upon his return to the States. In it he asked Pickering to elaborate on the reasons for his recall beyond the vague reference to his correspondence and "other concurring circumstances" mentioned in Pickering's official note. This the Secretary of State refused to do, on the grounds that the President could remove a public official without giving any reasons. Monroe, for all his native restraint, could not help giving expression to the rage and bitterness that he had carried in his heart so long: "If you supposed that I would submit in silence to the injurious imputations that were raised against me by the administration you were mistaken. I put too high a value upon the blessing of an honest fame, & have too long enjoyed that blessing, in the estimation of my countrymen, to suffer myself to be robbed of it by any description of persons, and under any pretence whatever.

"Nor can I express my astonishment which the present conduct of the administration excites in my mind; for I could not believe till it was verified by the event, after having denounced me to my countrymen as a person who had committed some great act of misconduct, & censured me for such supposed act by deprivation from office, that when I called upon you for a statement of the charge against me, with the facts by which you support it, I should find you disposed to evade my demand & shrink from the inquiry."[1]

Pickering was adamant in refusing to concede that the President must give reasons for recalling a minister. But in his reply to Monroe's second letter he lists the reasons that might lead to the recall of any diplomatic agent, such as want of confidence, deficiency in judgment, skill, or diligence, insincerity of his views, "intimate and improper correspondence on political subjects, with men known to be hostile to the government he represents and whose actions tend to its subversion," and countenancing and inviting, "from mistaken views of the interests of his own country ... a conduct in another, derogatory from its dignity and injurious to those interests." Pickering vouchsafed this, too, that recall of a minister did not necessarily imply actual misconduct but rather "want of ability," and that it might "imply only a change in political affairs which demands, or renders expedient for the public good, the substitution of a different character."[2] Thus, without giving Monroe the satisfaction of an official reply to his demands, Pickering yet managed to convey to him with unmistakable clarity why he had been recalled.[3] He even offered, in a note written a day later, to give Monroe an unofficial statement of the reasons for his recall.

Monroe understood the implications of Pickering's words, but he refused to plead guilty to any of the charges against him. He replied angrily:

"Permit me to premise that in any discussion which has or may take place between us, I have not nor shall I consider you in any other than your official character, having yet to learn what your pretentions are to confidence as an individual citizen, or the weight which your opinions ought to have as such, especially in the present case. . . . Indeed knowing what my own conduct was, and what your views are, . . . I had no expectation of obtaining from you any thing like a candid answer. . . .

"But I think proper to make a few comments upon the hints & innuendos contained in your letter of the 24th and with a view to place them (and your conduct in making them) in their true light. . . ."[4]

In this letter Monroe did not hesitate to admit that he had engaged in a wide political correspondence. But in his eyes this was not open to the charge of indiscretion because, as he explains, his own integrity and that of his correspondents were unquestionable. His reply to the charge that out of a mistaken idea of his country's best interests he had provoked France to injurious actions shows that he thought he knew better than the administration what was in his country's interests. It is easy to understand how Monroe, knowing that he acted with the best of intentions and with an honest desire to act wisely, found the attitude of Pickering and the administration completely incomprehensible, unless it was explained as a deliberate and malicious party-move to malign him and the Republican party. The intensely personal note struck in his communications to Pickering bears out this view.

By the end of July, Monroe came to the conclusion that he could get nowhere by writing to Pickering. An appeal for justice to the administration would get no answer. He determined now to vindicate his conduct in France by appealing to his fellow-citizens instead. In doing so, he was acting according to the fashion of the day, which saw nothing wrong in the public confessional of written vindications and explanations. It was not a tenet of eighteenth-century political philosophy that *qui s'excuse, s'accuse.*

In September he was settled at Albermarle, with two thirds of the writing completed on the pamphlet which was to present his cause to the public. A month later he was discussing with Jefferson what title he should give his work, and on December 2, 1797, was finally published *A View of the Conduct of the Executive, in the Foreign Affairs of the United States, connected with the mission to the French Republic, during the years 1794, 5, & 6.* This tract of

Governor of Virginia

more than a hundred pages recounted the events that occurred in the course of the author's mission to France with great faithfulness, although there was a certain amount of judicious omission. It ended with a bitter denunciation of the administration's policy. The interpretation of the facts was, of course, colored by Monroe's passionate devotion to France, and the reader was left with the impression that both the United States and its minister to France had been betrayed by the Federalist administration for the sake of a connection with England.

The *View* enjoyed a wide circulation, its reception varying with the political affiliations of its readers. It immediately provoked counter-attacks of every description. The most notable was that of Uriah Tracy, of Connecticut, who entered the arena under the nom de plume of Scipio.[5] We can today read with a smile Monroe's fretful complaint to Jefferson that "I have repeatedly thought I would answer the flimsy scurrilous papers of Scipio, but whenever I took up the subject it really laid me up with a headache." But for Monroe it was no laughing matter. Washington, although he did not make public his reaction to the *View*, unburdened himself in caustic annotations in the margins of his copy.[6] And John Adams, who had in that year succeeded Washington to the presidency, in a public speech pointed out that the words of praise with which France had officially taken leave of Monroe upon his recall were an "insult of farewell from the Directory to this government." "To you, my fellow citizens," he harangued his audience, "I will freely say, that the honor done, the publicity and solemnity given to the audience of leave to a *disgraced minister, recalled in displeasure for misconduct*, was a studied insult to the government of my country."[7]

It was a dark period in Monroe's life and one that almost left him permanently warped in mind and spirit. Nothing shows this more clearly than the rough drafts he outlined for three possible retorts to this address of Adams. In infinite detail they present the alternatives of calling on Washington, "the original aggressor," on Adams, "who has thus made himself responsible," or of taking "a seat in the Republican ranks . . . ready to answer what may be said."[8]

Fortunately for his peace of mind and the interests of his country, the third alternative was to be the one his destiny dictated. The power of the Federalist party was on the wane. The beginning of 1799 saw

JAMES MONROE

the first signs of Republican ascendancy. Monroe, just past forty, who the previous year had decided to shun public life and return to his law practice, began to reconsider. Finally, in obedience to the "public will as expressed by the Assembly" of his fellow Virginians, he entered the political lists again and emerged Governor of Virginia.

The news of his victory reached Mount Vernon on a chill, snowy evening in December. Washington had just come in from a walk. The melting snow falling from his wig, he sat in his wet clothes discussing the news heatedly and not without anger. A few hours later, struck down by a sudden chill, he took to his bed, from which he was never again to rise.[9] Thus a celebrated controversy claimed its last and most distinguished victim.

Monroe's first term in the executive mansion at Richmond was marked by at least one important crisis, which he met with a levelheadedness and quick decision like the soldier he had been. Virginia, in the summer of 1800, was rife with disquieting rumors of an imminent Negro rising, filling plantation owners with uneasy apprehension and recalling to the minds of all the tales of terror told nine years before by refugees fleeing the horror of black conquest in San Domingo. By 1800, indeed, the fame of Toussaint L'Ouverture had spread to every corner of the Old Dominion. Around the cabin fires of slave-quarters, excited Negro voices repeated again the saga of this black hero who had defied Napoleon himself to free his people and made himself an emperor whom the great government at Washington had not only recognized, but even helped to fight the French. It may have been such stories as these that fired the imagination of the Negro Gabriel, a slave on the Prosser plantation at Richmond, and his lieutenant, one Jack Bowler, a black giant of a fellow, to plan a revolt. There is also to be weighed the not-too-remote possibility that these black puppets were manipulated by strings held in the clever hands of a man who was much occupied with American affairs at the moment, a man who hated the new republic as much as he hated his task of the moment, which was to make peace with her, a man whose name spells diplomatic intrigue of just such a kind—none other than the great Talleyrand himself. No one would have liked better than he to see the South aflame with black revolt. But of his implication there is no proof.

Governor of Virginia

Whatever the reason for its inception, the insurrection was undoubtedly on the point of execution when Monroe was warned by a Negro, Pharaoh, who had slipped away from the conspirators and found his way, against great odds, to the capital. A letter from Monroe to John Drayton, Lieutenant-Governor of South Carolina, tells what happened: "Fortunately the plot was discovered, about two o'clock in the afternoon of the day on which the stroke was to have been given, in consequence of which measures were taken to avert the danger. Much embarrassment too was occasioned to the authors of the conspiracy, by a rain which fell about the time appointed for the rendezvous of the different parties, which prevented the meeting of many who were engaged in it. Being thus checked, the Government had time to act with effect, which it did, for from that period it had the entire command of the affair."

What Monroe did was to warn the surrounding towns, call out the militia, and place Richmond in a state of siege. The leaders and most active insurgents were apprehended and executed, although Monroe disliked imposing such a severe penalty. His reluctance to invoke the law of capital punishment led him to discuss with Jefferson a plan for banishing insurgent slaves and other criminals of similar stamp, a scheme which was uppermost in his mind for some years to come. On June 15, 1801, he wrote to Jefferson: "I enclose you a resolution of the General Assembly of this Commonwealth, of the last Session, by which it is made my duty to correspond with you on the subject of obtaining by purchase lands without the limits of this State, to which persons obnoxious to the laws or dangerous to the peace of society may be removed. This resolution was produced by the conspiracy of the slaves which took place in this city and neighbourhood last year, and is applicable to that description of persons only. The idea of such an acquisition was suggested by motives of humanity . . . to provide an alternate mode of punishment for those . . . doomed to suffer death."[11]

Simultaneously with the insurrection, a personal tragedy was being enacted. Monroe's only son, suffering a series of what the father described as "those diseases of childhood," was fighting a child's pitiful battle with death. In vain Mrs. Monroe was traveling with him in the hope that a change of air and scenery might bring about some improvement, but in the last days of September a letter to Jefferson shows that Monroe was expecting the worst, and on the night of the twenty-eighth of that month, the child was dead.

National affairs were meanwhile taking a turn that held the attention of Monroe and the other Republican leaders. The battle between President Adams and Alexander Hamilton for the control of the Federalist party was being fought to the bitter death, with no quarter given. Determined to preserve his dignity in the struggle, the President took a step which sacrificed to that end the Federalist machine. In the fall of 1799 he executed the diplomatic *coup d'état* which ended the quasi-war with France but with the same stroke removed the issue that gave Federalism its chief hold on the electorate. Against the emphatic protest of the Hamilton men in his Cabinet, Adams suddenly determined to send a second commission to France to arrange an understanding, thereby at once astonishing, outraging, and appalling his own party. The Federalists had emphatically made the pronouncement that they did not desire peace with France and would not make it. Again, on May 5, 1800, Adams moved suddenly, removing two of Hamilton's adherents in the Cabinet, McHenry and Pickering. Wolcott, a Hamilton man, later resigned. But by thus cleaning house, Adams was also putting the axe to the supports that held that house up. It was an intensely human act for him to remove those of his own party who were planning to forestall his reëlection, but, politically, it was short-sighted. As Beveridge remarks, "he should have struck sooner or not at all."[12]

In Virginia, where Monroe, sick with anxiety over his child's illness, was coping with the Negro insurrection, the only brightness in his horizon was the knowledge that Federalist prestige was sinking lower with every hour and the sun of his own party beginning to rise.

John Marshall, the new Secretary of State, was unable, despite a brilliant performance of official duty which embraced the signing of the treaty of peace with France, to stem the tide of Republican victory. The Federalist candidate who attempted to obtain the congressional seat Marshall had just vacated was beaten by "an immense majority ... grossly insulted ..." in spite of the new Secretary's influence.[13]

Hamilton met Adams' offensive with a plot of his own which was

Governor of Virginia

to fail and end his own career as leader of the Federalist party. This scheme was to "support Adams and Pinckney *equally*," which, he wrote Sedgwick, was the only way to save the party "from the fangs of Jefferson." But he was temperamentally unequal to such an equivocal and trying game and it was to bring him nothing but discredit among his own party members, who eyed such tactics askance. From the beginning, he met with failure. In New York, he approached Governor Jay, with a plan for offsetting the Federalist fiasco by calling the legislature in extra session, with the "object the choosing of electors by the people"; in this way they would "secure a Federalist majority" in spite of the expressed will of the electorate. The letter in which Hamilton set forth this scheme, Jay left unanswered, merely endorsing it, "Proposing a measure for party purposes which it would not become one to adopt."[14]

In October, his spleen against Adams getting the better of his judgment, he dropped the mask of equal support of Adams and Pinckney and in a "confidential" pamphlet attempted to turn the wavering party favor toward Pinckney, away from Adams. In it he denounced Adams' "extreme egotism ... terrible jealousy ... eccentric tendencies" and assailed his French peace.[15] Intended for private circulation in South Carolina alone, it was captured by Burr and published in the Republican *Aurora* and *Bee*.[16] Even Hamilton's closest political allies failed to support him. Troup, to whom Hamilton appealed for corroboration, adamantly said, "Not a man ... but condemns it." Needless to say, the Republican pamphleteers, to whom Hamilton was fair game, tore the unfortunate man limb from limb.

And now the harvest of tares which the Federalists had been so busily sowing was ripe for the reapers; sweeter fruits were in store for the leaders of the party that was to succeed to the political crown and sceptre awaiting in Washington. In the arena where Federalist and Republican did battle, Monroe was very active. Jefferson's position as vice-president kept him in a measure aloof, though he was the most concerned in the outcome. Madison, the theorist, instinctively held back from the foray. But Monroe was the general in the field and the party's chief tactician.

Upon the choice of electors, in whose hands lay the decision regarding the presidency, was centered the attention of both parties. The Republicans, united in single allegiance to Jefferson, had the advantage over the Federalists, whose ranks were split by petty intrigue, dissension, and jealousies. But Monroe was not easy in his mind. He worried over South Carolina and Pennsylvania and the unexpected strength of the Federalists in his own legislature. He was even more disturbed by Aaron Burr's rising popularity among northern Republicans, about which only his distrust of the mails restrained his full expression in his letters of that period. So distrustful of the Federalist machine was he that even after Republican victory was a certainty he was fearful of some last-minute Federalist manoeuver that might upset the apple-cart. He was quite right in this conjecture.

On January 6 of the year that was to see a new president inaugurated, Monroe wrote an urgent message to Jefferson concerning a new development of grave import:

"Some strange reports are circulating here of the views of the federal party in the present desperate state of its affrs. It is said they are resolved to prevent the designation by the Ho. of Reps. of the person to be president, and that they mean to commit the power by a legislative act to John Marshall, Saml. A. Otis or some other person till another election. I cannot believe any such project is seriously entertained, because it wod. argue a degree of boldness as well as wickedness in that party wch. I do not think it possessed of. . . . If that party wish to disorganize, *that* is the way to do it. If the union cod. be broken, that wod. do it . . . The Eastern people have no thoughts of breaking the Union, & giving up the hold they have on the valuable productions of the South. They only mean to bully us, thereby preserve the ascendancy, and improve their profits."[17]

In another passage, Monroe considered the various means by which this strategy of the defeated party might be met, and this is the subject of several other letters, which are perhaps some of the most significant written to Jefferson, revealing at his best the man whose devotion to his country and to the political creed which, in his judgment, was in the best interests of his country was the ruling passion of his life.

In this emergency Monroe sprang to immediate action, as he did once before, in the matter of the Negro insurrection. On January 27 he dispatched a terse note to Jefferson, informing him that the Virginia Assembly had adjourned, arrangements being made that "shod. any plan of usurpation be attempted at the federal town, the Execu-

Governor of Virginia

tive wod. convene it without delay. . . ."[18] And to Colonel John Hoomes he wrote, "In a state of things so critical and alarming, it is important that we have daily communication with our Senators and Representatives, to accomplish which it is necessary that a chain of expresses be established between this and the city of Washington, who shall travel day and night with the dispatches intrusted to their care . . . it is expected you have a spare horse at every stage or may immediately place them at such stages as will contribute to the desired dispatch."[19]

To Senators-from-Virginia Mason and Nicholas he wrote peremptorily: "I have not yet received a line from you on the state of affairs at the federal city, nor from any Representative since Thursday last. Three mails are wanting which induces a suspicion they are kept back designedly to withold information we should otherwise receive. On Saturday night I sent an Express to the Bowling Green with letters to you and several of our Representatives, from whence they were forwarded by Mr. Hoomes, who established a line of Expresses to the city of Washington to bring intelligence daily from you of what occurred. We have no answer nor do we know anything of what is done there. We have now sent the bearer Mr. Holton a special messenger who may be confided in & who is instructed to proceed & deliver you this unless he hears on the way that an election is made. By him we request information of the actual state & probable result, as on your answer we shall decide whether it will be proper to convene the assembly or not."[20]

The cudgels were taken up by George Hay, Monroe's future son-in-law, who, under the pseudonym of "Hortensius," penned a bitter attack against the "usurper," Marshall, in the *Richmond Examiner*.[21]

On February 15, Jefferson informed Monroe that the party "thought best to declare openly and firmly, one & all, that the day such an act passed, the middle States would arm, & that no such usurpation, even for a single day should be submitted to."[22]

March 4, 1801, however, saw the happy termination of this period of anxiety for the Republicans, with the inauguration of Thomas Jefferson as third president of the United States. Along the roughly paved footpath that led from Conrad and MacMurin's boarding house to the unfinished North Wing of the Capitol, Jefferson "on foot, in his ordinary dress, escorted by a body of militia artillery . . . and . . .

a number of his political friends" passed to be sworn as the chief executive.[23]

Monroe was not in the procession, for he was unable to attend. But this enforced absence was the only thing that marred his deep satisfaction and happiness over the success of all his plans. Jefferson, his beloved and admired friend and counsellor, now held the highest position in the land. Madison, the other of the triumvirate, was, as Jefferson's Secretary of State, privileged to become the premier, so to speak, of the new administration. As for himself, he was well content with his governorship. Indeed, it was, in the consideration of his fellow Virginians, the second post in the land and was by many of the proud "Lords of the Old Dominion" believed more glorious than the presidency itself. No federal appointment could have so touched Monroe as this token of respect from the men of his own state. Noble traditions enhanced the governorship of Virginia, which, as a heritage from colonial days, enjoyed a distinction equaled only by the governorship of Massachusetts. Moreover, as chief magistrate of Jefferson's own state, Monroe now became, in some respects, the most important official with whom the President was called upon to deal.

The status of the governor with respect to the president, and the status of the state with respect to the federal government was the issue which so agitated the populace in the matter of states' rights. Monroe's high evaluation of his position and the importance he attached to such a trivial question of routine as now arose—whether, in corresponding with a governor, the president should sign his own name to the letters or direct his communications through the Cabinet secretary—were part of his determination that the sovereignty of the states was all-important and must be defended against federal domination. There was nothing of the personal in his championship of a governor's right to such exalted treatment by the federal government. "You will be sensible," he wrote to Jefferson, "that to me personally this is an affr. of the utmost indifference; indeed in the present state of things that it is peculiarly irksome. I had formed my opinion on the subject before I came into this place. . . ." He elaborates as follows: "Before I came into this office I was of opinion that the correspondence between the Executive of the Genl. Govt. and a State shod. be conducted as between parties that were mutually respectful but equally independent of each other. . . . Each govt. is in

Governor of Virginia

its sphere sovereign. . . . If the idea is just, it follows that the communication between the two govts. when carried on by the govr. of a State, shod. be with the President of the U. States."[24]

Jefferson seems to have had different views: "I have ever thought," he replied, "that forms [of address] should yield to whatever should facilitate business. Comparing the two governments together it is observable that in all those cases where the independent or reserved rights of the states are in question, the two executives if they are to act together, must be exactly co-ordinate; . . . the general executive is certainly preordinate—e.g. in a question respecting the militia, and others easily to be recollected. . . . I should say that in the former cases the correspondence should be between the two heads, and that in the latter the governor must be subject to receive orders from the War Department as any other subordinate officer would."[25]

Monroe was willing to bow to Jefferson's decision, as he intimated in a subsequent communication: "I think . . . that the mode of communication ought to be settled on principle. It is not more important to adjust the exterior than the interior policy of our country. . . . If you differ with me in sentiment, . . . it is very far from my wish that you shod. deviate from your opinion. Let it pass in silence. I shall be happy to receive an answer to any publick letter I write you from any head of Department, or any one else authorized by you, . . ."[26]

The marked tone of conciliation in this letter provokes conjecture. Had Monroe, on mature consideration, decided he had been too high-handed in his previous communication and hastened to reassure Jefferson of his desire to follow and not to lead the President? Had he been told by someone, in confidence, that Jefferson had been displeased at the tone of his letter and perhaps complained of his subordinate's presumption?

The letters which Monroe addressed to his council upon his retirement from the governorship, which he had held for three years, summarize the events of his administration, which included numerous important accomplishments for the public weal. With his usual modesty, he expressed himself as not "indifferent to the good opinion of those with whom I have so long acted," and to these citizens he ascribed the principal measure of his success.[27] He made mention of the public improvements that had been made: the almost complete removal of the "obstructions to the navigation of the great rivers the

Potowmack and James" and the completion of communication "between the waters of Elizabeth River and Pasquotank," by which the principal river of Virginia, on which the national capital was situated, had been made navigable for a number of miles "more than 200 above the tide." With unusual eloquence he wrote, "How great the facility which they give to commerce! How vast the amount of produce which they invite to market! How great their ornament to our country!"[28] It was with a peculiarly personal pleasure that he called attention to the progress made in erecting the "publick buildings" in Richmond, which appeared to him to "exhibit an elevation of mind and foresight which become the representative of freemen." Designed in 1785 by Jefferson, the Virginia State House was the first direct adaptation of the classic temple to practical modern use and marked an epoch in architecture. Monroe also called attention to the improvements in the system of education that had taken place under his aegis: "In a government founded on the sovereignty of the people the education of youth is an object of the first importance." Although he recognized that in many ways "the charge of education" was "more burdensome than that of fleets and armies," he made an earnest plea for generosity in this direction. He also recommended revision of the militia system.

The problem, which with Monroe was a recurrent one, of choosing a way of life at the end of a term of public office did not on this occasion trouble him long. On January 10, 1803, Jefferson wrote imploring him to reënter with the least possible delay upon a diplomatic career.

The occasion of this flattering appeal at the most important foreign crisis the country had faced requires a detailed review of the circumstances surrounding the "retrocession" by Spain to France of the vast country that was to be the future empire of the West.

17

Louisiana Purchase, 1803

DURING his years in Congress, Monroe had fought the battles of the new frontier settlements along the Ohio in Kentucky and Tennessee. They were the battles not only of the frontiersmen, but of the Republican party. They were the battles of the South against the northern industrial and shipping interests. The men sending their produce down the Ohio and Mississippi were brothers and sons of the men of Virginia, Carolina, Georgia. They were the political enemies of the men from Boston and New York, whose fortunes were made on the Atlantic seaboard and to whom the navigation of the Mississippi meant less than nothing. Monroe and the other leaders of his party never relinquished the frontier principle that the Mississippi trade was a "natural right"; that the expulsion of the Spaniard, with the termination of the Spanish system of trade monopoly, was a natural duty for "free men."

Louisiana had come under Spanish rule when France, after the signing of the Treaty of Paris in 1763, ceded it to Spain as compensation for her losses sustained in upholding the Bourbon family pact against Chatham's "policy of victory." By the terms of the Treaty of 1763, Florida had been forcibly ceded by Spain to Great Britain, but after the British defeat in the American Revolution it returned to Spanish rule. In 1800, the Floridas, Louisiana, and Texas, with all the waters of the Gulf of Mexico, were indisputably Spanish. And it was only by favor of King Carlos IV that America's western settlements could trade along the river highways of the Mississippi and the other waterways running southward to the Caribbean.

JAMES MONROE

By the Treaty of San Lorenzo el Real in 1795, negotiated by Thomas Pinckney with the Spanish Queen's favorite and Prime Minister, Godoy, the disputed boundary on the Mississippi was settled in America's favor, and the much-coveted "right of deposit" at New Orleans (the object of Jay's long struggle with Gardoqui in 1783-1785) obtained. With the cession of Spanish river posts, and the final settlement of the issue of "occlusion," everything appeared to have reached a happy and permanent conclusion.

Trouble now struck from an altogether unexpected quarter. The first hint of it came to Monroe in a letter from Jefferson, written in May of 1801. "We have great reason to fear," wrote Jefferson, "that Spain is to cede Louisiana and the Floridas to France." And the fear was well-founded. Spain, in return for Tuscany, which was handed over by France to the Duke of Parma, the young husband of the Spanish queen's favorite daughter, transferred to the French the vast empire of the province of Louisiana. The United States suddenly found itself the unwilling neighbor of the aggressive, empire-envisioning Napoleon.

"Spain," lamented Jefferson, "might have retained it quietly for years . . . increase our facilities there, and it would not perhaps be very long before some circumstance might arise which might make the cession of it to us the price of something of more worth to her. Not so can it ever be in the hands of France." He felt it "impossible that France and the U. S. can continue long friends when they meet in so irritable a position."[1]

The new situation demanded, in Jefferson's opinion, a complete reversal of foreign policy. His party had always insisted on a French-American front against Great Britain. But from the moment Napoleon moved into Spain's place on the American continent, the United States must, Jefferson declared, "marry" itself to the "British fleet and nation." A navy must be built and used to keep France out of the American continent. The Americas, both North and South, must be held "in sequestration for the common purposes of the united British and American nations."[2]

Monroe had been wholly preoccupied with his gubernatorial affairs. His correspondence of this period with Jefferson reveals no evidence that he was in close touch with events abroad. Nevertheless, he was the logical person to whom the President might turn for

Louisiana Purchase, 1803

advice, and even assistance, regarding the principal and most immediate cause for uneasiness over the Louisiana situation. This was the unrest and threatened disloyalty of the frontiersmen, whose indignation at the indifference of northern congressmen to such vital matters as the navigation of the Mississippi and the "right of deposit" at New Orleans was rising to dangerous proportions.

On January 10, 1803, Jefferson hurriedly penned a dispatch to Monroe that was to hurl the latter into the very heart of the brewing storm. "I have but a moment to inform you," wrote Jefferson, "that the fever into which the western mind is thrown by the affair at N. Orleans stimulated by the mercantile, and generally the federal interest threatens to overbear our peace. In this situation we are obliged to call on you for a temporary sacrifice of yourself, to prevent this greatest of evils in the present prosperous tide of our affairs. I shall tomorrow nominate you to the Senate for an extraordinary mission to France, and the circumstances are such as to render it impossible to decline; because the whole public hope will be rested on you."[3]

On the very next day, Jefferson presented Monroe's name to the Senate, and on the following, January 12, the new envoy was confirmed.

Immediately after the confirmation, Secretary of State Madison sent for Pichon, the friendly French chargé, and explained the American point of view, emphasizing that it was in the interests of inland communication that the United States wished to possess the Floridas and New Orleans. He added the statement, significant in view of later developments, ". . . that the United States had no interest in seeing circumstances rise which should eventually lead their population to extend itself on the right bank." Such extensions could but "weaken the state" and might lead to dangerous separatist movements.[4]

Both Jefferson and Monroe were convinced that the Louisiana question was largely a party issue, a revival of the old feud between the English-loving Federalists and the Republican Francophiles. The agitation over the suspension of the right of deposit at New Orleans was, Jefferson wrote Monroe, being made use of by the Federalist party, especially by those of its members in Congress, to force a war on the Republican administration, "in order to derange our finances, or if this cannot be done, to attach the western country to them, as their best friends, and thus get again into power."[5]

JAMES MONROE

It is interesting to observe, in the light of this supposition, that whereas a predominantly Republican Congress on January 7 published a resolution expressing complete confidence in "the vigilance and wisdom of the Executive,"[6] a Federalist Senate three weeks later questioned the government's action on the Louisiana situation. Ross, of Pennsylvania, even proposed a motion that the President take immediate military possession of New Orleans. It should be published to the world, declared the Senator, that the balance of power in America was something that the United States would govern, as the dominant power on that continent. He concluded with a proposal to appropriate five million dollars for the war, and to call fifty thousand men to the colors for the purpose of an immediate expedition against Louisiana.[7]

Monroe, writing to Jefferson from New York, pointed to the Ross resolution as proof that "the federal party will stick at nothing to embarrass the admn., and recover its lost power." Free navigation of the Mississippi, he wrote, must be permanently secured for the primary purpose of overwhelming the Federalists completely. Failure to settle the Mississippi question would have as its direct result the restoration of the Federalist party to power.

The strongly partisan feeling is again shown, in another manner, in Monroe's reply to Jefferson. Whether success or failure befell his mission, his motives at least, Monroe felt, would be understood by the administration. "I derive much satisfaction," he wrote, "from a knowledge that I am in the hands of those whose views are sound, are attached to justice, and will view my conduct with candour and liberality; under these circumstances I embark with confidence & am fearless of the result as it respects myself personally."[8]

Monroe's official instructions did not come until nearly seven weeks after his appointment. These, as summarized by Professor Ogg, directed the new envoy as follows: "(1) Should Napoleon be willing to sell New Orleans and the Floridas, any sum not exceeding ten millions might be offered, besides commercial privileges for ten years, a speedy extension of citizenship to the population of the regions acquired, and in case of urgent demand, an absolute guarantee of the west bank of the Mississippi to the French. (2) Should Napoleon refuse to sell any territory whatsoever, even a few square miles on which a post might be built, a renewal of the right of deposit under

Louisiana Purchase, 1803

the most favorable terms possible was to be secured. (3) Should even this be refused, communication of the fact to the President would be followed by special instructions—probably an order for Monroe to cross the Channel to England."

On the basis of these instructions, Ogg points out, it appears that merely by granting the revoked right of deposit at New Orleans or selling a small area for a new entrepôt, Napoleon could have satisfied American demands. "Such a transaction," writes Ogg, "would have involved in no sense the loss of French prestige in America, and indeed such a settlement had already been promised Livingston by Talleyrand."[9]

The acquisition of the Louisiana territory as a whole was not even hinted at. To Claiborne, governor of the Mississippi territory—where the settlements most nearly affected by the Florida Purchase were situated—Jefferson did, indeed, hint at the likelihood of a cession of New Orleans and the Floridas as the price Napoleon might pay for American neutrality in a war between France and Great Britain. But even then, he made mention only of New Orleans, not of Louisiana, except in the words: ". . . taking part in the war, we could so certainly seize and securely hold them *and more.*"[10] It is possible, also, that Jefferson, foreseeing the impending rupture of the Peace of Amiens, might have been expecting the situation respecting Louisiana to be placed on a far more favorable footing for the United States.

In France since 1801, the American minister, Robert Livingston, had become discouraged by repeated failure to negotiate with Napoleon and Talleyrand for the purchase of New Orleans and the Floridas. A month before Monroe's arrival in Paris, Livingston wrote to Rufus King, the American minister at the Court of St. James's, that "Nothing will be listened to in the way of purchase." A fortnight later, he wrote that the negotiations were to be referred to General Bernadotte in America. Further attempts to continue talks on the matter were met by Talleyrand's excuses that the government had "very unhappily received . . . letters from Pichon informing them that the appointment of the Mr. Monroe had tranquillized everything, and that they might safely defer their negotiations in consequence." Later, Livingstone received "a very hasty note full of proposition and arguing the necessity of waiting for Mr. Monroe who may not be here until everything is arranged." Disgruntled, Livingston wrote King he believed Monroe's appointment was "necessary in the United States, but as things have turned out, it greatly embarrassed my operations. . . ."

Livingston finally came to the conclusion that an alliance with England against France, with forcible occupation of the disputed territory was the only answer. He was in favor of the expedition's proceeding at once to Louisiana, where they would "have time to strengthen themselves before they can be attacked."[11]

In the meanwhile, events abroad were approaching the crisis that led to the breaking of the Peace of Amiens. In England, a message of the King to Parliament foretold war and brought in its train a general impress of seamen and the calling of the militia. King, in London, began to speculate on the possible benefits to be derived by the United States from an English occupation of Louisiana and decided that the American expedition to that territory should be delayed until further developments. He nevertheless realized the dangers implicit in a British Louisiana. To Addington, the British prime minister, he took pains to make it clear that though the United States "could not see with indifference that Country in the hands of France . . . it was equally true that it would be contrary to our views, and with much concern that we should see it in the possession of England."[12]

Livingston had already threatened Talleyrand that in case France refused American demands, the United States would be forced "into the scale on the side of England," making the latter mistress of the whole world. In this communication he bade the French take pause at the spectacle of "fifteen or twenty thousand men aided by hordes of Indians" descending the course of the Mississippi to New Orleans while a British fleet blockaded the port.[13] It was not very subtle diplomacy, nor was it a variety calculated to please Napoleon's sensibilities.

In November, 1802, Livingston had written to warn Madison to fortify Natchez and strengthen all the upper posts on the Mississippi. And he threatened Talleyrand that if Monroe agreed, ". . . we shall negotiate no further on the subject but advise our government to take possession."

This was the situation when, with one of those decisive and

Louisiana Purchase, 1803

dramatic changes of policy with which Napoleon loved to astound the nations of the world, the French government suddenly announced that it would cede, not only New Orleans, but all of the Louisiana territory to the United States.

Livingston, finding so much more than he had bargained for suddenly flung into his lap, was completely dumfounded. He had asked for a crumb, and found the whole loaf thrust into his hands. He held it, and did not know what to do with it. Another, a more brilliant statesman might have seized this undreamed-of opportunity for glory and have secured by an immediate acceptance the exclusive credit for the Louisiana Purchase. Instead, he decided to wait for Monroe and consult with him.

Much effort was to be expended by Livingston and his supporters to secure sole credit for the purchase of Louisiana. The tremendous political implications of this diplomatic coup were not lost upon these men. The northerners in the Republican party were looking for a strong candidate to break the "Virginia Succession" to the presidency of the United States. And for a man who could have proved a single-handed conquest of Louisiana, even the presidency was not too high a prize.

Actually, however, the idea of ceding Louisiana to the United States originated with Bonaparte alone. Barbé-Marbois tells that, at a Tuileries conference held just before Monroe's arrival in Paris, Napoleon commented on a passage in a speech made in the English House of Commons, which declared, "France obliges us to recall the injury she did us twenty-five years since by forming an alliance with our revolted colonies." These words, claims Marbois, were the inspiration for the reversal in the First Consul's policy that gave the United States the territory of Louisiana. Napoleon, struck by the reference to the former alliance between America and France, hit on the idea of making the United States a counterpoise to British sea power. He would create a maritime power on the American continent that would one day rival the Empress of the Seas. "That power," he declared, "is the United States. The English aspire to dispose of all the riches of the world. I shall be useful to the entire universe if I can prevent their ruling America as they rule Asia."[14]

Marbois saw in Napoleon's stroke an admission of defeat in his attempts to build a French Empire in the Americas. The keystone of that empire would have been San Domingo, without which Louisiana could not have survived. But the current military campaign on that island had swallowed within a year an army of fifty thousand men, and Rochambeau had written Napoleon that he would need thirty-five thousand fresh troops to hold the island.

"Irresolution and deliberation," declared Napoleon to his ministers at the conference, "are no longer in season. I renounce Louisiana. It is not only New Orleans that I will cede; it is the whole colony, without any reservation. I know the price of what I abandon, and I have sufficiently proved the importance that I attach to this province, since my first diplomatic act with Spain had for its object the recovery of it. I renounce it with the greatest regret. To attempt obstinately to retain it would be folly."

Turning to Marbois, he then said, "I direct you to negotiate this affair with the envoys of the United States. Do not even await the arrival of Mr. Monroe; have an interview this very day with Mr. Livingston."[15]

This, despite the fact, of which Bonaparte must have been aware, that Monroe had already landed at Havre and was actually within a few hours' journey of the gates of Paris. That he declined to await the envoy's arrival may be interpreted as a desire to make his gesture even more grandiose by granting what the United States had wished, as a great and munificent favor. This should not be a cut-and-dried business transaction, but a beautiful renunciation. There is little doubt that in the back of this great showman's mind was the thought that a grateful United States would be a good thing to have on his side in the coming struggle with Great Britain.

As matters turned out, it was Talleyrand, not Marbois, who came to Livingston with the astonishing offer. How the latter received him is recorded in the American's dispatch to the Secretary of State.

"Talleyrand asked me this day," wrote Livingston on the eleventh of April, 1803, "whether we wished to have the whole of Louisiana. I told him no; that our wishes extended only to New Orleans and the Floridas; that the policy of France, however, should dictate (as I had shown in an official note) to give us the country above the River Arkansas, in order to place a barrier between them and Canada. He said that if they gave us New Orleans the rest would be of little value, and that he would wish to know 'what we would give for the whole.'

Louisiana Purchase, 1803

I told him it was a subject I had not thought of, but that I supposed we should not object to twenty millions francs provided our citizens were paid. He told me that this was too low an offer, and that he would be glad if I would reflect upon it and tell him tomorrow. I told him that as Mr. Monroe would be in town in two days, I would delay my further offer until I had the pleasure of introducing him. He added that he did not speak from authority, but that the idea had struck him."[16]

While the two sparred cautiously, Monroe was at Havre, where he had arrived on the eighth and been received, as he wrote his uncle, Joseph Jones, ". . . with more éclat than I expected or wished, being by a salute from the battery, the visit of all the officers of the place, &c. . . ." His arrival, he told his uncle, "was known . . . on the 9th & on the 10th it was decided in the council at St. Cloud to offer us the cession of the whole." After resting a day at Havre, he went to St. Germain to see his daughter and arrived in Paris the twelfth, the day following Talleyrand's interview with Livingston.[17]

Monroe found Livingston much distracted. At the latter's last interview with Talleyrand, he had again been pressed to make an offer, but on his refusal to do so before consulting with Monroe, the Frenchman had only "shrugged up his shoulders and changed the conversation." Talleyrand, indeed, suddenly became entirely elusive, going so far as to assert that Louisiana did not even belong to France.[18] This attitude may have stemmed from a conviction that nothing could come of negotiating with Livingston alone, and that Monroe was the man to deal with.

From Skipwith, who had served as his assistant on his first mission to France, Monroe immediately learned, as he wrote Madison, that "Mr. Livingston, mortified at my appointment, had done everything in his power to turn the occurrences in America, and even my mission to his account, by pressing the Government on every point with a view to show that he had accomplished what was wished without my aid: and perhaps also that my mission had put in hazard what might otherwise have been easily obtained . . . he did not abstain even on hearing that I was on my way, from the topics intrusted to us jointly."

Monroe also told Madison that he suspected his colleague of delaying his official recognition, so that he, Livingston, would remain the only authorized negotiator. Monroe felt himself powerless, since Livingston was also acquainted with the views of the home government and "might speak without my approbation with whom he pleased." Monroe felt he could not withold "confidential communications with him." Under the circumstances, he wrote Madison, he had "been driven by necessity, in private communications with him, signing nothing or authorizing it on his part, to permit him to state to Mr. Marbois that I would assent to the purchase of Louisiana at the price we were willing to give for the territory to the left of the river, France relinquishing all pretensions to the Floridas, & engaging to support with her influence our negotiation with Spain for them."[19]

Two days after Monroe wrote this letter, Livingston sat down in the small hours of the morning to compose a hurried dispatch to Madison, relating the highly intriguing events that had kept him up so late. While dining in company with Monroe, ran the narrative, Livingston saw, strolling in the garden outside the apartment, Barbé-Marbois. A servant was sent to invite the Frenchman inside, and in the course of the next hour Marbois found an opportunity to suggest that, after his guests had left, Livingston should come to his house. As soon as Monroe had taken his leave, his host hastened through the deserted streets to his rendezvous with Marbois. In the midnight conference that followed, claimed Livingston, the purchase of Louisiana was practically settled. No price had been arrived at, however. On this score, wrote Livingston, he had not yet formed an opinion. The transaction was so far beyond his instructions that he could not but take pause. Nevertheless, "the field opened to us is infinitely larger than our instructions contemplated; the revenue increasing, and the land more than adequate to sink the capital"; he reasoned, that his "present sentiment is that we shall buy." On the matter of price, he would consult Monroe, he told Madison, but the reason for his writing immediately, though the matter was still unsettled, was that it was "so very important that you should be apprised that a negotiation is actually opened, even before Mr. Monroe has been presented, in order to calm the tumult which the news of war will renew...."[20]

The question arises, was Livingston's real solicitude on the score of calming the tumult or of assuring to himself the full credit for the negotiation?

Louisiana Purchase, 1803

Marbois's own account of these negotiations establishes that a full exposition of Napoleon's aims was conveyed at an interview at which both Livingston and Monroe were present. At his conference, Marbois relates, "Mr. Monroe, still affected by the distrust of his colleague, did not hear without surprise the first overtures that were frankly made. . . . Instead of the cession of a town and its inconsiderable territory, a vast portion of America was in some sort offered to the United States. They only asked for the mere right of navigating the Mississippi, and their sovereignty was about to be extended over the largest rivers of the world. . . ."[21]

This can only be interpreted as meaning that Monroe was learning for the first time, and from Marbois, not Livingston, the full extent of the proposed transaction. Moreover, it shows that, whatever importance Livingston attached to his midnight interview with the Frenchman, Marbois seems to have looked upon Monroe as the principal American negotiator.

Monroe, soon after his arrival, had fallen ill and, except for the brief interview recorded by Marbois, had to leave the business in hand largely to Livingston. Nearly two weeks now passed without any progress in the affair. Livingston found the French unaccountably evasive. Opposition among those close to Napoleon had arisen. Especially displeased with the First Consul's decision to cede Louisiana were his brothers Joseph and Lucien. Adams describes the scene in Napoleon's private chambers when the hot-headed Joseph, standing over Bonaparte as the latter lay submerged in his bath, and shouting, "You will do well, my dear brother, not to expose your project to parliamentary discussion—for I declare to you that if necessary, I will put myself at the head of the opposition!" was deluged with the soapy, perfumed water. Frightened, presumably by the expected outburst of Napoleon's notorious temper, the First Consul's valet fainted, throwing everyone into a fit of laughter that successfully cleared the thunderous atmosphere.

Unfortunately for Napoleon, however, Joseph had the right of it. As Adams so clearly saw it, "the sale of Louisiana was the turning point in Napoleon's career; no true Frenchman forgave it."[22]

It is ironic that Livingston, completely in the dark about the real situation, was very busy trying to beat down Marbois's price! Not only that, but at one time, he actually appealed to Joseph for help.

JAMES MONROE

On April 23, a "Project of a Secret Convention," relating to the terms of the Louisiana purchase, was drawn up by Napoleon and given to Marbois to present to the American envoys. What had begun as a renunciation and a favor, now began to appear no such thing. Under the terms of the "Project," the territory of Louisiana would have to be divided into "one or more states on the terms of the federal constitution," presumably for the protection of the French people already resident in the territory. There were also provisions for six "perpetual" places of deposit for French commerce along the Mississippi and a much more onerous arrangement regarding debts due American citizens.

Marbois, accompanied by Livingston, brought this paper to Monroe, still abed with his complaint. The Frenchman himself admitted the "Project" to be "hard and unreasonable," and presented at the same time his own project, not yet seen by the French government. Marbois told the Americans that he presumed Napoleon would assent to this second document, though he had not seen it, as he had told the Consul "he would not insist on the terms contained in the first, and would only ask or propose such as he had drawn in the second; but to which . . . the first consul had not assented explicitly."[23]

Monroe and Livingston studied Marbois's project for all of one day. They found it more lenient than Napoleon's where questions of boundaries and entrepôt were concerned. But the price demanded was eighty million, thirty more than Napoleon's fifty million. Putting the paper aside, the Americans set to work on a project of their own, in which they offered fifty million, and twenty more "on account of her debt to citizens of the United States, making seventy in the whole."

The matter of price was one of grave concern to both Monroe and Livingston. The amount mentioned in their instructions, having been arrived at on the basis of the purchase of only a fraction of the territory now offered, was so much smaller than the millions involved in the present transaction. "Our fellow-citizens," Livingston protested, "have an extreme aversion to public debts; how could we, without incurring their displeasure, burden them with the enormous charge of fifteen millions of dollars?"[24]

Monroe, more clearly cognizant of the values involved, was less exercised over the financial obligations.

The University of Virginia

JAMES MONROE'S HOME ON MONROE HILL

Early in 1789 Monroe wrote Jefferson, "It has always been my wish to acquire property near Monticello. I have lately accomplished it." The house is now a part of the University of Virginia.

THE SIGNING OF THE LOUISIANA PURCHASE TREATY

James Monroe, as President Jefferson's special envoy to France, joins Barbé-Marbois (Napoleon's councillor of state) and Robert R. Livingston (American Minister to France), in signing "the largest transaction in real estate which the world has ever known." From a painting by André Castaigne.

L. C. Handy Studios

CELEBRATION OF THE LOUISIANA PURCHASE

On December 20, 1803, a great celebration was held in New Orleans as the French tricolor was hauled down and the Stars and Stripes run up. A similar celebration was held in St. Louis. Copy of a lithograph furnished through the Jefferson Bicentennial Commission.

Brown Brothers

THE DESTRUCTION OF THE CITY OF WASHINGTON BY THE BRITISH

Monroe was Madison's Secretary of State when the British burned Washington. Th last-minute defense of the Capital, under General Winder, was a complete fiasco, an Monroe took the lead in redeploying the badly-led troops. "He did not undress himsel for ten days and nights, and was in the saddle the greater part of the time." After th catastrophe, Madison named Monroe Secretary of War and military commander of th Federal District. From a print by Beale.

Louisiana Purchase, 1803

Marbois persisted in his demand for eighty million and finally wangled it, though the Americans made the condition that twenty millions of this be used for the payment of the claims of their own citizens.

On the first of May, Monroe was at last presented to Napoleon, at the Palace of the Louvre. When the introduction had been made by Livingston, the Consul remarked conversationally, "Je suis bien aise de le voir," and said to Monroe, "You have been here 15 days?"

Monroe replied that he had.

"You speak French?" asked Napoleon.

"A little."

"You had a good voyage?" continued Napoleon.

"Yes."

"You came in a frigate?" persisted the great man.

No, Monroe told him. He had come in a merchant vessel charged for the purpose.

Colonel Mercer was next presented. Napoleon wished to know whether he was the secretary of the legation. Monroe replied that he came merely as a friend of his.

Turning next to Livingston, Bonaparte inquired how his family and that of Livingston's secretary were. "Then," reports Monroe, he "turned to Mr. Livingston & myself & observed that our affairs should be settled."

That one remark was the only one bearing upon Monroe's mission which Napoleon deigned to make. After the company had gone in to dinner, Monroe had no more conversation with his host until everyone retired into the "saloon," where Napoleon again engaged him in conversation, as trivial as that which had gone before. They discussed the size of the national capital, whether it grew much, how many people lived in the city. Napoleon then wanted to know how old Jefferson was, whether he were married or single, had children, lived always in the federal city.

"You, the Americans," he finally remarked, "did brilliant things in your war with England, you will do the same again."

"We shall, I am persuaded," replied Monroe, "always behave well when it shall be our lot to be in war."

"You may probably be in war with them again," probed Bonaparte.

That, replied Monroe, was an important question that would be decided when the occasion arose.[25]

And so the interview, to which Monroe must have looked forward with eager interest, ended.

That evening Monroe and Livingston spent with Marbois over maps. Having been formally presented, Monroe was at last qualified to sign the treaty which would transfer Louisiana to American rule. First, however, it was necessary to determine just how Louisiana must be described in such a treaty. Marbois writes that the three negotiators "made a few historical researches on the first occupation and the first acts of sovereignty," but finally the entire question of boundaries was left quite open. The basis of the first article of cession, describing the extent of the territory to be ceded, was the general description of Louisiana contained in the third article of the Treaty of San Ildefonso. Marbois warned that the vagueness of this description "might give rise to difficulties," but for want of a better, this plan was finally the one adopted.

In the terms of the final draft, the United States was to pay the debts incurred by France through the spoliations of her privateers during the stormy period of '98, damages which had been allowed American citizens by the Treaty of 1800 and afterward cancelled by mutual consent. It was this part of the convention that was to give rise later to charges of carelessness on the part of Livingston and to do much damage to his reputation.

The most extraordinary part of the momentous transaction, however, was perhaps the fact that having by the terms of their instruction been sent to purchase the Floridas, as well as New Orleans, the American negotiators seem to have lost sight of the former. Monroe does state that "he was assured by Marbois that Napoleon had offered "to engage his support to our claim to the Floridas with Spain." But the matter had never been finally settled between the French and the Spanish. When Marbois called Napoleon's attention to the ambiguity of the articles concerning the Louisiana frontiers, the latter contented himself with observing that "If an obscurity did not already exist, it would perhaps be good policy to put one there!"[26]

In the treaty negotiated between France and Spain in 1800, it was agreed that Spain was to "retrocede to the French Republic the colony of Louisiana, with the same extent it actually has in the hands of Spain, and such as it should be according to the treaties subsequently passed between Spain and other States. Spain shall further join to this cession that of the two Floridas, eastern and western, with their actual limits."[27]

But in spite of this, King Carlos demurred at parting with the cherished Floridas, and, the French were told, it was "both useless and impolitic to talk with him about it."[28] And the matter was allowed by the French to remain in nebulous *statu quo*.

All of Napoleon's subsequent attempts to obtain the Floridas from Spain proved futile. Ironically enough, the United States had had a hand in supporting Spanish intransigency on this score. Now that the States themselves desired the Floridas, Napoleon found it vastly diverting to see them disappointed.

Monroe was far more opposed to the vague definition of the Louisiana boundaries than was Livingston. There exists a draft of a protest to his colleague, drawn up by Monroe but endorsed as not sent, on this question. Monroe persisted in his efforts to clear up the matter, but twenty years were to pass before he succeeded.

Monroe considered the moment ripe to initiate the negotiations with Spain for the Floridas outlined in his instructions. He felt that the cession of Louisiana must lessen Florida's value to the Spanish, that the crisis between England and France, which necessarily involved Spain, would make it easier to bring pressure to bear on the latter, and that no interference need be looked for from England. He wished to proceed immediately to Madrid.[29]

Had Monroe's plan of action been adopted, one of the most humiliating chapters in American diplomacy need never have been written.

It was Livingston who insisted on a different course, that of laying claim to West Florida as part of the territory of Louisiana purchased from the French. To Madison he wrote advising that the United States take immediate possession . . . "at all events, to the River Perdido." No doubts assailed him. "I pledge myself," he declared to the Secretary of State, "that your right is good."[30]

Monroe was only with difficulty convinced. And upon him fell the burden of persuading the Spanish of his country's rights to the disputed land.

18

London Mission, 1803-1804

MONROE'S instructions on leaving America had taken into account possible failure of the New Orleans negotiation and had directed a mission to London to arrange all outstanding questions in view of a possible military alliance. But the unexpected purchase of Louisiana, raising boundary questions and making essential an agreement on the Floridas, made an immediate visit to Spain more logical than a journey to the Court of St. James's. Monroe nevertheless went first to England. From London he wrote Madison the reasons for this step.

Dining with the Consul Cambacérès, who had just come from a conference at St. Cloud with Napoleon, Monroe was told by the Frenchman that he "must not go to Spain at present." More than that Cambacérès would not say. A few days later, Monroe saw the Consul Lebrun, who "suggested precisely the same idea" and told the American envoy that he would accomplish his purpose "but that this was not the time for it."[1]

Monroe, still clinging to his faith in Napoleon's support of American hopes of securing the Floridas, did not question the good faith of the Consuls Cambacérès and Lebrun.

Monroe's mission to London was undertaken seemingly under the happiest auspices. Anglo-American relations during the early days of Jefferson's administration had become increasingly cordial. On the eve of Monroe's departure for France, the British minister at Washington had conveyed his government's wishes for the new envoy's success and had even ventured to inquire of the President whether

London Mission, 1803-1804

he intended to have Monroe "pass over to England and hold any conversation with his Majesty's ministers upon the general question of the free navigation of the Mississippi."[2] England, although she had lost a probable ally, nevertheless seemed to be accepting the *fait accompli* in good part.

From London, where he had arrived July 18, 1803, Monroe wrote Madison that from every conversation he had had with those high in the councils of the kingdom, it appeared that the British considered the Louisiana purchase "the most glorious attainment for our country, the effect of a masterly policy in its government." And those of the "most eminent" with whom he was not acquainted, "especially Mr. Pitt," were "reported to have spoken of it in the same light." The acquisition of the vast territory had ". . . unquestionably added greatly to our national character & political importance in Europe," declared Monroe.[3]

But beneath the thin crust of official civility there seethed a deep distrust and hostility which Monroe was characteristically slow to perceive. A few weeks after his arrival in London, a significant incident occurred which brought to the surface the subterranean current of suspicion aroused in the British mind by everything American.

The British government, learning that the English firm of Boulton & Watt had received an order from Robert Fulton for two steam engines designed by the Francophile, Joel Barlow, forbade the company to fill the American's order. Their reason, Gore wrote (August 20, 1803) to Rufus King, was that the engines undoubtedly "were intended for Fulton's diving machines that are to blow up the British Navy, the dockyard, etc., at Portsmouth, of which they have some apprehension."[4]

The protests of Monroe and the explanations of Gore, a member of the American Claims Commission in London, were of no avail.

That same August, Gore was writing to King, "Monroe knows little that passes in London. He has seen Hawkesbury twice; once on his arrival and once on his introduction to the King. . . . He appears to have a sort of creed that it is improper to know what is passing in relation to European Powers, unless the United States are directly interested. He will therefore have a quiet time in England, for you know they do not press their knowledge, no more than their civility, on any man."[5] Gore's prophecy was well made.

JAMES MONROE

Monroe turned to the most serious matter in hand—an attempt to secure for the United States the full rights of peaceful commerce belonging to a neutral nation, rights with which the British policy of impressment was incompatible.

Until the formation of the Grand Coalition, Great Britain was almost wholly dependent for her safety upon her naval strength. Vital to it was her policy of impressment, so abhorrent to the young republic across the Atlantic. With the exception of those who were its victims, every true Britisher rallied to the defense of this practice.

As Rufus King, then American envoy to England had written to the Secretary of State in 1796, ". . . as they [the British] believe that their national safety depends essentially upon their marine, they feel unusual caution relative to a stipulation that by mere possibility can deprive their navy of a single seaman, who is a real British subject, or that may even diminish the chance of obtaining the services of those who are not British subjects, but who by various pretences are detained in service as such. . . .

"I have no reason to doubt the sincere desire of this Government to cultivate our esteem. I believe that the administration, together with the nation throughout, desire to live with us in friendship, and I do not think they would for a slight cause disagree with us. But their colony trade and marine are topics intimately and exclusively connected with their prosperity and security and more deeply with their prejudices. If we cannot agree, we may still remain friends."[6]

The situation had not changed in the intervening seven years. The English were ready to give Monroe, as they had King, a promise of friendship but nothing more. They, too, had their grievances on the score of impressment.

The American naturalization law, which made it possible for any deserting British sailor to obtain American papers by the transfer of "a few dollars from hand to hand," was a thorn in the British lion's side. Whole ships' companies had been known to disappear a few hours after a vessel touched an American port. The British therefore maintained that had the American government been prepared to live up to the obligations of neutrals, it would have enacted stricter naturalization laws, or at least would have shown a willingness to punish this type of fraud.[7]

But the federal government was unable to compel the states to

London Mission, 1803-1804

respect such obligations, determined as Jefferson was to maintain strict American neutrality. The administration was dominated by the men and political philosophies of Virginia, one of the strongest adherents of states' rights. Monroe, for example, had as governor of Virginia helped the passage of legislation protecting deserting and mutinous English sailors, in direct contravention of the terms of the Jay Treaty.

King, while minister at London, had in a letter to John Quincy Adams reported instances in which "some of our people have lent their names to cover enemy goods." And to Pickering he had reported, significantly using cypher, that "Some discoveries unfavourable to the American claims have in one or two of these cases been made and operate against others in the same trade."[8]

Monroe, unlucky man, soon enough perceived how unfounded was the optimism of his first reports home that on the issue of impressment, the British government "was disposed to do everything in its power to satisfy our just claims in that & every other respect."[9]

Meanwhile, the ill luck that inevitably made its appearance on the scenes of Monroe's diplomatic missions was already at work on the other side of the Atlantic, manipulating with malicious skill the strings in a Washington comedy of bad manners that was to give Monroe some bad hours in London.

No more suitable stage for the diplomatic farce enacted at this delicate juncture of world history can be imagined than the Washington of that day. Only a vivid imagination could fashion a city worthy of the term out of the few newly erected government buildings, scattered houses, miserable inns, and poorly stocked shops rising out of the surrounding wilderness of field and swamp and wood. It was, as the aristocratic Gouverneur Morris had acidly remarked, "the best city in the world for a *future* residence. We want nothing here but houses, cellars, kitchens, well-informed men, amiable women, and other little trifles of the kind, to make our city perfect." Even as late as 1809, Jackson, then British Ambassador, found Washington vividly reminiscent of Hampstead Heath. Had he not "started a covey of partridges about three hundred yards from the House of Congress"?[10]

The irritability of one of the chief actors in the drama, the British Minister Merry, was provoked, even before the plot was fairly developed, by its setting. "I cannot describe to you," he wrote to a correspondent not long after his arrival in Washington in November, 1803, "the difficulty and expense which I have to encounter in fixing myself in a habitation. By dint of money I have just secured two small houses on the common which is meant to become in time the city of Washington. They are mere shells of houses, with bare walls, and without fixtures of any kind, even without pump or well, all which I must provide at my own cost. Provisions of any kind, especially vegetables, are frequently hardly to be obtained at any price. So miserable is our situation."[11]

A French diplomat had bewailed his fate even more bitterly, crying, "My God! What have I done, to be condemned to reside in such a city!"[12]

Merry was not alone in his opinion, nor was it an exaggeration of the situation in which he found himself. Oliver Wolcott had experienced similar difficulties. To his wife he complained, "I have made every exertion to secure good lodgings near the office, but shall be compelled to take them at the distance of more than half a mile. There are in fact but few houses at any one place, and most of them small, miserable huts, which present an awful contrast to the public buildings."[13]

In the woods and muddy clearings of the new capital, the courtly practices that had distinguished official life in New York and Philadelphia were rather out of place. Nevertheless, the Spartan John Adams and his Abigail had bravely continued them. This despite such obstacles as a presidential mansion that lacked a main staircase, outer stairs, fences, mantels, bells. There was no other place to hang the wash; so the practical Mrs. Adams pre-empted for this important purpose the windowless East Room.

Jefferson's administration put an end to all pretence at ceremony. It was Jefferson's intention to conduct official Washington life in what according to his lights was the true spirit of democracy.

President George Washington's weekly levees, which John Adams had decided should be conducted with formal ceremoniousness, Jefferson had utterly condemned, hurling at Adams the accusation that "the glare of royalty and nobility, during his mission to England, had made him believe their fascination a necessary ingredient in government."[14] A prophetic Pennsylvania Republican had snorted,

London Mission, 1803-1804

during the 1800 campaign, "Etiquette! Confound the word, it ought not to be admitted into an American dictionary. Ought we to follow the fashions and follies of old corrupt courts? Are we not a young Republic? And ought we not to be plain and honest, and to disdain all their craft, pageantry and grimace? . . . . It is also to be hoped, that the next President will discontinue ridiculous levies [levees], squaring the heel and toe and bowing like a country dancing master . . . aping old worthless sovereigns and courtiers and all . . . for the sake of etiquette. Mr. Jefferson, should he be our next President, will doubtless trample under foot these baubles. . . . He is elevated far above the nonsense of parade—mere adulation and asiatic servility are not to his taste."[15]

And he was quite right. Jefferson would have none of it. And when, one day, to balk his intention of abolishing levees, certain members of Washington society appeared at the White House at the traditional receiving hour, Jefferson, returning from his customary two-hour ride on horseback to find the reception rooms filled with elaborately dressed visitors, strode into their midst as he was, boots and corduroys muddied, his whip in his hand. There were no more levees after that.

State dinners also went almost entirely by the board. The President preferred informal dinners in the plantation style. "You drink as you please and converse at your ease," wrote one of his guests.[16] Excellent food and eccentric etiquette marked Jefferson's dinners.

It was, indeed, one of these dinners which touched off the diplomatic fireworks whose reflected glare across the Atlantic was to cause Monroe such distress. Mr. Anthony Merry should not have been taken entirely unawares by its odd ceremony, or lack of it, for his very first encounter as representative of the Court of St. James's with the eccentric Jefferson had been unconventional in the extreme. Resplendent in the glitter of full diplomatic dress, Merry found himself being received, in a "narrow entry from which his Majesty's representative had to back out in a most undignified manner," by the President of the United States wearing "an old brown coat, red waistcoat, old corduroy small-clothes much soiled, woolen hose, and slippers without heels." Merry did not know that it was Jefferson's customary attire, but it is doubtful if that knowledge would have lessened his ire.

JAMES MONROE

To crown the indignity, Jefferson, at the state dinner tendered the Merrys a few days later, offered his arm not to Mrs. Merry, who was the guest of honor, but to Mrs. Madison. And, as if that were not outrage enough, Mrs. Merry was placed by Madison below the Spanish minister, who had the seat next to Mrs. Madison. "I was proceeding," wrote Merry to a correspondent in a letter describing these shattering events, "to place myself, though without invitation, next to the wife of the Spanish minister, when a member of the House of Representatives passed quickly by me and took the seat, without Mr. Jefferson's using any means to prevent it, or taking any care that I might be otherwise placed...."[17]

When these indignities were repeated at a subsequent dinner given by Madison, Merry frankly took the ground that his treatment was a premeditated insult directed not alone at himself but against his master, the King of England. Demanding official explanation, he was informed about Jefferson's "Canons of Etiquette." These were the new, democratic rules of etiquette formulated by Jefferson for the regulation of the relations between the Executive and the diplomatic corps. But Merry was unsatisfied.

Downing Street was not the only foreign government office to buzz with details of Merry's discomfiture. The French and Spanish ministers were not slow in reporting the incidents to their own governments as the latest tid-bit of diplomatic gossip.

In England, Jefferson's treatment of Merry was interpreted as a studied insult to the whole British nation. Gore wrote to King that in "this silly business, they probably see here a disposition to affront England, and it will, with others, increase a growing discontent with us."[18]

Monroe accordingly found the cordial atmosphere in which he had been received quickly evaporating. It was "at the time the Etiquette story was in circulation" that Monroe thought the Queen passed him in a crowd "intentionally."[19] London daily grew chillier. Dining with Lord and Lady Holland, Monroe mentioned the February "course" at Charlestown and the crowds and fashionable "equipages" gathered there. Whereupon Lord Castlereagh innocently asked "what kind of equipages?" and Monroe, surprised, answered such as he saw in London. And Sir William Scott, less subtle, rather brutally remarked that at a grand fête at the Cape of Good Hope

London Mission, 1803-1804

"all 'the beauty, taste and fashion of Africa were assembled. . . .' "[20]

Such was the treatment accorded the man fresh from a Paris which had given him the *accolade,* where the exquisite Mrs. Monroe, known everywhere as *la belle Américaine,* entering the Monroe box at the theatre was greeted, so the story goes, by "a storm of cheers" and the rendition of "Yankee Doodle" by the orchestra.[21] In London, Mrs. Monroe's calls on ladies of the Court were not returned.[22]

Driven into seclusion by this retaliatory incivility, the Monroes saw almost no one, longed for home. On March 12, 1804, Monroe sat down to write nostalgically to Judge Jones, expressing his passionate desire to be home again, and the eagerness with which he looked forward to his homecoming.[23] One of his little girls was ill at Cheltenham, where he had taken her at a physician's advice.[24] Mrs. Monroe's spirits were not aided by the recurrent attacks of rheumatism suffered since Napoleon's coronation festivities. And the London fog and chill were not more salubrious for Monroe's own persistent and severe complaint of the same nature.[25] Were it not for the diplomatic business rising out of the seizure by the English of American ships, Monroe would have fled home that autumn.[26]

When the law of blockade was extended by the British cruisers in the West Indies, Monroe was instructed to negotiate a new convention on this important matter. But, wrote Monroe to Madison on June 28, 1804, he found it impossible to put himself "on that kind of familiar footing" he once "had the prospect of, and had in some degree effected." He had begun to realize that England, despite her protestations, had been deeply disappointed when Napoleon's cession of Louisiana had put beyond the realm of possibility American cooperation in her war with France.

London merchants were growing jealous of the impetus given to American shipping by the war. And the exploits of the American squadron against the African pirates in the Mediterranean had set on edge the British naval commanders there; the Union Jack resented any other police banner in those waters. American demands, at the time of Britain's hour of peril, began to be irksome. Blockade and impressment were matters of little interest to a nation fighting for survival. Both the press and the government took the view that Monroe's protests were importunities of a selfish and self-centered government, which deserved but little consideration at such a time.

Monroe nevertheless doggedly set about the task Madison had set him. "The conduct of Lord Harrowby," he wrote dejectedly, after his interview with the new foreign minister, "was calculated to wound & to irritate. Not a friendly sentiment toward the U States or their govt. escaped him."[27]

These dark hours were not made happier by the echoes that drifted across from Paris of the strife and bickering attending Livingston's negotiation of the problems raised by his Louisiana claims convention. To the last day of his Paris interlude, Monroe seems to have kept his relations with the difficult Livingston cordial. The controversy over credit for the Louisiana deal was none of Monroe's seeking. In America, the matter began to take on a political aspect of national importance. It began to be apparent that the presidency might well be the reward of the man who could claim sole credit for having added the vast realm of Louisiana to the United States. Behind Livingston were massed the New York members of the Republican party. Any attempt on Monroe's part to claim a part in the transaction was an abomination in their eyes.

Monroe would scarcely have been human had he not taken some notice of the claims which Livingston now advanced to exclusive credit in the Louisiana negotiations. He tried to make his own attitude in the matter clear to Livingston in a letter written October 9, 1803:

"Whether either of us failed in our duties to the public or each other in our late political relation at Paris," he wrote to Livingston, "is a subject which perhaps ought never to be discussed anywhere, especially on this side of the Atlantick. I shall only observe that if such a discussion becomes at any time necessary it will be owing to you & not to me. I have had but one object in view which was to obtain & secure on proper principles the cession of Louisiana to the U. States, & it is in my opinion our duty to think of nothing else till that is accomplished...."[28]

This policy of somewhat self-conscious modesty was materially helped by Livingston's own behavior. Although France and Great Britain were at war, Livingston now decided to visit London. "His visit," Monroe reported to Madison three days after Livingston's arrival in London, "will certainly not be well recd. by the govt.; at

London Mission, 1803-1804

least such is my opinion. It seems to excite a considerable sensation, and in the present state of parties here, may very probably be attributed to some political motive."[29]

All these annoyances served only to distract Monroe in the pursuit of his main objectives in London. It was with distinct relief that he received orders from Washington to leave London immediately for Spain, where a fresh diplomatic disaster, arising from the inept handling of the pressing situation there, required quick action. Before he left London on October 4, he had a "free and full" interview with Lord Harrowby on the subject of impressment. The latter, listening with "apparent candor," expressed regret that Congress had become so exercised over the matter. That was, countered Monroe, "only to be considered as a proof of the great sensibility of the nation to" the subject. But all that Monroe brought away with him from the interview was the impression that Harrowby considered the American demands unreasonable.

19

Spanish Mission

IN PARIS, Monroe found himself faced with a situation which he had long foreseen and had attempted to forestall. A full year before, he had warned Madison against the very eventuality that now made the mission to Spain so urgent. At that time he had advised that, in the event of ratification of the treaty by which Louisiana became American, Jefferson should without fail take "the most prompt and decisive measures" to put its provisions into effect. New Orleans must be immediately occupied by American troops and the Spanish be made to feel that they were expected to give the territory up "without delay or equivocation." Otherwise, he argued, "the favorable moment may pass & everything be lost. If the affair is whiled away by negotiation, France may assume the character of mediation between us, and a year hence a bargain be made up by compromise much to our injury."[1]

This suffered the fate of most good advice and was rejected in favor of the formula of Livingston, whose view of Florida as a part of the territory of Louisiana was based on the article in the treaty of retrocession describing Louisiana as having "the same extent that it now has in the hands of Spain." When France had "possessed" Louisiana, at least until the cession of 1762, the provinces had unquestionably included West Florida. Napoleon, had he seen any advantage in giving offense to Spain, might even have claimed its inclusion. But, unfortunately for the United States, no such claim had ever been put forward. Livingston was reduced to claiming that Spain had retroceded West Florida to France without knowing it,

Spanish Mission

and that France, in ignorance of its involuntary ownership, had transferred her rights to the United States, "that the United States had bought it without paying for it, and that neither France nor Spain . . . were competent to decide the meaning of their own contract."[2]

It was this colossal assumption that Monroe was now instructed to make plausible enough to impose on the Spanish court.

In Paris, Livingston outlined to Monroe his project for the solution of the problem. This was that "Spain should put us in possession of the disputed territory and that we should create a stock of about seventy millions of livres which should be transferred to Spain of which ten millions should be reimbursed annually, and that provision should be made for settling amicably in the interim the question of boundaries between the two countries." So Monroe described the plan to Madison.

To Livingston, Monroe observed that, as he saw it, the United States would be paying twice for the same thing, since it was improbable that any of the money advanced would be returned or that the boundary could be favorably settled without sacrificing the stock thus transferred. Another objection to the plan was that it did not secure for the United States the territory known as East Florida, the only point admitted to be in question, nor did it ensure payment of the sums due American citizens.

Livingston was, on the contrary, convinced that by his plan the United States "should get the country without paying a farthing for it, as the reimbursement might be secured by drafts on Mexico, and that East-Florida might be comprized in it and likewise put in our possession."[3]

As the days went by, it was no easier, Monroe realized, to work with Livingston, whose experience in the Louisiana affair made him determined to keep all the threads of the negotiation in his own hands. Every move of Monroe's was watched; every attempt was made to circumscribe his activities. On presenting him to Talleyrand and, later, to Napoleon, Livingston made no mention of Monroe's proposed journey to Spain, or of the reason for his presence in Paris. All this Monroe noted and reported to Madison.[4]

On November 8, 1804, Monroe, Livingston, and General Armstrong, the man Jefferson had sent to replace Livingston, came to an agreement regarding the terms of a note which, signed by Monroe, was to be sent to Talleyrand. Along with it was to go an explanatory letter written by Livingston. Livingston, who had long tried without success to secure Talleyrand's intervention in the Spanish negotiations, had little faith in this manoeuver, but Monroe was insistent. He had never ceased believing in French sympathy with American ideals and aims.

But French feeling about the present situation was far from idealistic. Three days after Monroe's arrival in Paris, Marbois had suggested a step that was nothing short of a proposal to buy French mediation.[5] France, declared Armstrong in disgust, "was determined to convert the negotiation into a job."[6] The straightforward Monroe found all this distasteful. Besides, his instructions from Madison made such intrigue "altogether out of the question."[7]

By the time the French replied to the American note, Monroe was already across the frontier. He was in Spain when he read the stinging message, which ran, in part: "No one can suppose the United States to be convinced of the justice of their rights; and we are warranted in thinking that the Federal government, as a result of confidence in its own strength, of its ambition, and its ascendency in America, raises pretensions to a part of Florida in order to show itself afterward more exacting toward Spain. The Emperor will feel that justice requires him not to recognize such pretensions. If he should assist by his good offices an arrangement between the United States and Spain, he would wish good faith and impartiality for its base."[8]

The opening of new proposals to Spain was made trebly difficult by this scornful refusal. Most bitter of all to Monroe was the conviction that Jefferson's intentions towards Spain—so different from his actions—required a vindication that he was at a loss to put into words.

Monroe's commission authorized him to act alone in Spain, the American minister at Madrid, Charles Pinckney, having asked for his recall before Monroe's appointment.[9] Pinckney had been a political appointee, the Madrid post a reward for his defection from the Federalist party. At the time it was made, the choice of the aristocratic South Carolinian had appeared a happy one. But his capacities proved disappointing. The same day on which Monroe's instructions on the Spanish matter were written, Madison dispatched a

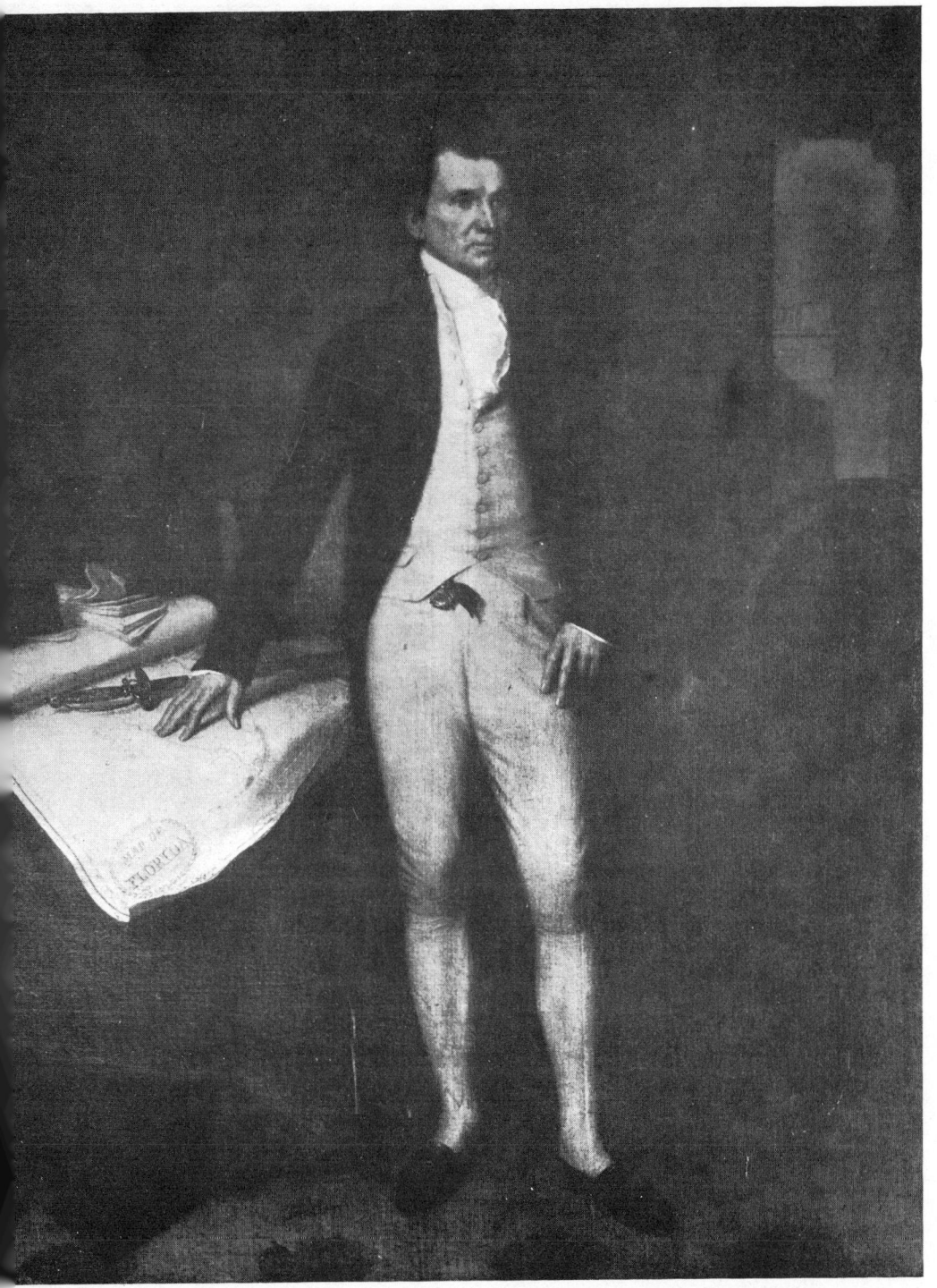

Courtesy of Mr. Laurence Gouverneur Hoes

PRESIDENT JAMES MONROE

From a portrait painted by John Vanderlyn in 1822, now in the City Hall, New York.

MRS. JAMES MONROE

"The most stately, gracious, and regal-looking lady ever to be Queen of the White House." From a portrait by Benjamin West.

L. C. Handy Studios

THE WHITE HOUSE AND ST. JOHN'S CHURCH

The White House, still showing one wing damaged by fire, was not entirely repaired when Monroe became president. St. John's Church, built in the form of a Greek cross, was one of Latrobe's important works. The unpaved street, the swampy fields, and the cows grazing near the church show the extreme youth of the new Capital. From a drawing by Latrobe in 1816.

L. C. Handy Studios

THE WHITE HOUSE DURING MONROE'S ADMINISTRATION

Completely renovated after the fire, the White House was resplendent in a gleaming coat of white paint. For weeks in advance of public functions, it is said, slaves were kept busy making candles under Mrs. Monroe's personal supervision. The lighting costs for each entertainment were $100, paid out of the private purse of the President. From an original lithograph.

Spanish Mission

warning to Pinckney to "refrain from all diplomatic activities." The advice was inspired by the knowledge in Washington that Yrujo, the Spanish minister, was inditing venomous reports to his government that made all friendly negotiation impossible. Pinckney paid no heed to the warning, but kept up an active correspondence, the echoes of which threw Madison into a state of consternation.

A real crisis developed when Pinckney, striking a Napoleonic attitude particularly irritating to Spanish sensibilities, engaged Cevallos in a foolhardy discussion of certain aspects of the West Florida question. Completely impervious to the dangers of such a step, the American minister, bent on a Livingstonian ruse of snatching glory from Monroe, actually proceeded to the point of threatening hostile measures. He would apprize all American consuls in Spain, he warned, of the "critical situation" that existed between the two countries, and would similarly advise the commander of the American squadron cruising in the Mediterranean.[10]

The Spanish, at this dramatic moment, received news of the French refusal to intervene in America's favor. Cevallos proceeded to give the American minister the retort direct, laying aside the customary courtly language in which Spanish diplomacy clothed the most unpalatable statements.

In Washington, the Secretary of State also received the rebuke which took Pinckney by surprise in Madrid. Madison's conciliatory reply informed the Spanish of the imminent arrival of a special envoy to settle the differences between the two countries. To Monroe he hurriedly dispatched advice to make haste.[11]

After an uncomfortable Christmas and New Year's Day spent en route, Monroe reached Madrid on the second day of the year 1805. He found a chastened Pinckney awaiting him in some trepidation and assuring him "he was perfectly willing to withdraw."[12] Monroe might with advantage have accepted the offer. By doing so, he would have emphatically marked off his own negotiations from those which Pinckney had brought to so disastrous a deadlock. But natural courtesy prevailed, and the two men embarked on their hopeless task in perfect harmony.

On January 28 a note was dispatched to Cevallos summarizing the situation. In it the entire budget of American grievances was itemized: the Spanish and French spoliations, suppression of the entrepôt at New Orleans, the American claims in West Florida and the Rio Bravo.

The reply which Cevallos proceeded to frame cleverly picked a fatal flaw in the American note, a single sentence intended by the Americans as a diplomatic flourish. It urged the Spanish minister to "examine, impartially, the several points at issue in each case." That, indeed, accorded only too well with Cevallos' favorite diplomatic trick. He returned the compliment with a proposal to begin the negotiations with consideration of the claims convention of August, 1802, on the score of which Pinckney had already had very sad experience. Monroe was in no haste to make the same mistake. Insisting that his note be considered as a whole, he told Cevallos that it was in the power of the Spanish king without further ado "to fix at once the relations which are to subsist in future between the two nations."[13]

Cevallos dared not appear too adamant. He agreed to ratify the convention of August, 1802, but would offer no satisfaction on any of the other matters under discussion. Monroe reiterated his ultimatum. Cevallos now played his trump card, a note from Talleyrand dated July 27, 1804, in which Napoleon announced that neither Spain nor the United States was further concerned with the French spoliation claims forming part of the Louisiana settlement. And again, the negotiations bogged down.

To break them off entirely, at this juncture, was to risk a far more serious rupture, one between the United States and France. Hesitating to take such a radical step, Monroe pretended to consider Napoleon's stand as merely an expression of opinion.

To Armstrong in Paris, Monroe opened his heart. "It cannot be doubted," he wrote, "that if our government could be prevailed on to give ground, that of France would be very glad of it." He was ready to employ almost any means, and begged Armstrong to go to those French officials who might be willing to listen to "reason" with the news that the Madrid negotiations, entirely owing to Talleyrand's attitude, were about to break up. He still clung to his amazingly naïve faith in Napoleon's sympathy for American aims and built on it part of his conviction that France would discontinue her support of Cevallos in the present emergency. The second and more practical reason for this belief was the conviction that France was too dependent on supplies carried in American vessels to risk American

Spanish Mission

retaliation in the shape of a "good understanding with England."[14]

Armstrong's answer reached Madrid with all the speed proverbially associated with bad news. That diligent gentleman had sounded the French Foreign Office to some purpose and was now able accurately to define for Monroe the French position. Concerning "reparation for spoliations committed on our commerce by the French within the territory of his Catholic Majesty," Armstrong was of the opinion that there was "nothing of solidity in it" and believed it must be abandoned. The French position with respect to boundaries was equally discouraging. And as for Monroe's big stick, "a possible approachment with Great Britain," Armstrong quoted the French as saying that in case of a rupture with the United States, "France would be found aligned on the side of her actual ally."[15]

Up to this point Monroe had kept his irritation in check. But, disappointed in his hopes of France, he allowed a gesture of impatience to escape him in a note asserting that "it did not comport with the object of his mission or its duties to continue the negotiation" unless he could be assured that the Spanish king "cherished the same views." And on April 9, he wrote Cevallos that he considered the negotiations terminated.

If Monroe thought that he had written finis to the Madrid episode he was destined to learn otherwise. King Carlos still considered himself "Emperor of the American Indies," and Cevallos, supported by Talleyrand, now advanced Spanish claims to an important area afterward included in the state of Louisiana.

Monroe made every attempt to bring the matter to a close. There followed undignified interchanges of notes, with Cevallos having the last word in his declaration that the American government's sense of justice would not "permit it to insist on proposals so totally to the disadvantage of Spain."

On May 18, Monroe was forced to arrange for his departure. He had obtained nothing from the display of firmness urged in his instructions. France and Spain were now one, not only in their diplomatic policies but also by virtue of an alliance which might even be used against the United States. Obtaining his papers with a celerity that contrasted ominously with the slow pace of the negotiations, Monroe returned to London.

In West Florida and Texas, where the Spanish garrisons were now reinforced and aggressions were committed against American settlers, the United States could observe at leisure how unsuccessful its diplomacy had been. On August 26, 1805, Secretary of State Madison was informed that since Monroe had left Madrid, the Spanish agent in New Orleans had been duly informed of the desire of the Court of Spain to make "the Mississippi River the boundary, and, in time, it was expected that the object would be attained."[16] As the months passed, Indian outrages against the settlers who were invading the disputed territory were fostered by the Spanish troops, and Spanish spoliations on American commerce in the Gulf were renewed.

Five months after Monroe dejectedly left Madrid, George W. Erving, replacing Pinckney at Madrid, was received by the Spanish with the startling announcement that Spain would no longer abide by the terms of the treaty permitting American vessels to carry English property. Spanish privateers, moreover, were to help enforce the French blockade of the West Indies. "You may choose either peace or war," coolly declared the Spanish minister, Godoy. "It is all the same to me." The moment was "opportune" for war, if the United States thought such a course best.

This, then, was what Jefferson's incoherent "diplomacy of force" had brought matters to. Using, during his own administration, an entirely different approach, Monroe was to write the final solution to the vexatious problem. But for sixteen years the Spanish question was to plague and weaken his party.

20

Return to London

IN ABANDONING his Spanish mission, Monroe at least had the satisfaction of knowing that the step was in full accord with the administration's view of the situation. Jefferson had one aim at this juncture of affairs: to secure a treaty with Great Britain. His one fear was "procrastination till a peace in Europe shall leave us without an ally."[1] He still believed that "the first wish of every Englishman's heart is to see us once more fighting by their sides against France." So eager must the British be for an American alliance, thought he, that they would be only too happy to give the United States "their general guarantee of Louisiana & the Floridas."[2]

Madison saw eye to eye with Jefferson on this score, but realized more clearly than the President that the English would expect some return for the favor of an alliance.

Monroe, sent posthaste back to London, arrived there on July 23. There was every reason to believe that Great Britain, once more facing a military test of the most serious proportions on the continent, would welcome a negotiation in any form dictated by American interests. But Monroe was appalled to discover that during his six months' absence from London relations between the two countries had become deeply embittered. He had been keenly alive to the dangers of leaving Pitt's government unwatched by an American representative, and had so warned Washington.

Monroe's return to the American legation in London coincided with the bringing into port by British cruisers of more than a score of American prizes. The very day he arrived was the one chosen by

JAMES MONROE

Sir William Scott to pronounce his disturbing decision in the case of the American ship *Essex*, a decision which set up a new law of prize, making the English tribunals a part of the governmental program to throttle neutral trade.[3] That decision struck the death-knell of Monroe's latest plans.

Scott's decision, a reversal of one of his previous rulings in the case of the American ship *Polly*, quite understandably aroused suspicion that it had been activated by political rather than legal necessities. To Monroe's protests on this issue, the Foreign Minister, Lord Mulgrave, assured him "in the most explicit terms that nothing was more remote from the views of this government than to take an unfriendly attitude."[4] And with this Monroe had to be satisfied. Finally, even his letters to the ministry remained unanswered, while the channel harbors became crowded with American prizes.

In Washington, Madison, controlling his "natural irritability" with what good grace he could muster, "delivered his sentiments on this subject" to Merry, limiting himself largely to the expression of a hope that at least the vessels and cargoes already captured might be liberated.[5] But no approach, however patient and conciliatory, proved successful.

Hopeless to stem these new aggressions, Monroe fell back on the issue of impressment. His complaint on the score of depredations by the *Cambrian* under the very batteries of New York harbor resulted merely in the recall of the vessel's commander, Captain Bradley, who was soon after promoted to the command of a line-of-battle ship. The only thing that kept Monroe from throwing the whole thing up and going home was fear of an actual conflict growing out of the situation.

It was with a surprised reluctance that Jefferson finally brought himself to abandon hope of an English alliance. Monroe's dispatches of the closing months of 1805, urging a more realistic foreign policy, might have had an effect. He had argued that nothing could be done in England until American claims against France and Spain were firmly pushed. Firmness, "a spirit of independence," protest reinforced if necessary with naval action were needed.[6] In considering Jefferson's subsequent treatment of Monroe, these dispatches must not be lost sight of.

If Austerlitz, fought in December, 1805, gave Napoleon the mastery of the continent, the naval victory won by Nelson in Octo-

Return to London

ber had made Great Britain mistress of the seas. In the ensuing struggle between the "Tiger" and the "Whale," which was to endure until the downfall of Napoleon's Continental System, the real sufferers were the shipowners of New England.

Jefferson now changed his tactics. Napoleon's preoccupation with Europe's conquest, he felt, now left the "Eagle" no time in which to enforce coercive measures against the United States. President Jefferson once more began to talk of a "peaceable settlement" independent of Great Britain. And that settlement could and should be secured at Paris, through Armstrong, or Armstrong and Monroe, with "France as the mediator, and the price of the Floridas as the means." Sure of Napoleon's inability to reinforce policy by force, he grew daily more confident that "should Spain attempt to change the *status quo*, we shall repell force by force." Despite his previous enthusiasm for an English alliance, he was willing to cross the Emperor's palm with some badly needed gold.[7]

Monroe and Madison, the President's favorite counsellors, had steadily rejected the idea of bribery, originally suggested by the French themselves. Armstrong's scruples were less delicate. To him came Talleyrand's memorandum, in that fine gentleman's own hand, hinting that the time was ripe to renew pressure on Madrid. Godoy, it was delicately conveyed, might prove more malleable than the Americans had found him if he were warned that the whole question of the Floridas must be reopened under the auspices of Napoleon and his ministers. If Godoy should be forced to accept, the Emperor would be satisfied with commercial privileges in the American Floridas and a settlement of French spoliation claims through bills on the Spanish colonies. Finally ten million dollars was to be paid by the United States for a boundary settlement that included East Florida and the Rio Colorado on the west, together with a buffer territory between the western boundary of Louisiana and the Spanish settlements.

Armstrong found little difficulty in declining a preliminary offer that so suggestively gave Spain far more than she had demanded in the way of a cash compensation. The negotiations took on a familiar cast. From ten millions, the price quickly fell to seven, with other "adjustment" to make the transaction more attractive.[8] At last, informally, and with certain reservations added by Armstrong, the proposition was laid before the Cabinet in Washington.

21

Politics and Policies

WHEN THE SMOKE had cleared from the council chambers of the Cabinet, the new policy of the administration emerged in definite form. It was decided, first: to ask French mediation, for a monetary consideration, in securing the Floridas; second: to accept cession of the disputed part of Louisiana, extending from the Rio Bravo to the Guadalupe; third, to accept in lieu of money payment of spoliations claims against Spain, the aforementioned territory.

Jefferson's next task was to persuade the Republican majority of Congress of the wisdom of this sudden reversal of policy. Spain was hated and feared, especially in the South, and a war against such an enemy would have had wide popular support. But Napoleon's envoy, Turreau, believed that this new, more pacific policy not only suited the "personal character and philanthropic principles" of the President but would be supported by "all the party leaders, even by those who have most pretensions and well-founded hopes to succeed the actual President,—such as Mr. Madison."[1] But opposition there was to be, of the most sensational and unexpected kind.

Using as his text the concept that "moral duties make no part of the political system of those governments of Europe which are habitually belligerent,"[2] a sure and popular appeal to the accepted sentiment that American foreign policy was guided by "a system of morals wholly apart and superior from those governing European nations," Jefferson went about preparing his message to Congress. It was his intention, admitted only to the inner circle of advisers, to

Politics and Policies

assume a warlike tone in his public message against an unnamed enemy which would satisfy at once the northern states outraged by British depredations and the southern states angered by Spanish hostilities in the Floridas, in Texas, and on the high seas. The real remedy already decided upon in secret council was to be concealed until the legislative debates should begin.

The President's public message, read on the third of December, 1805, breathed war and hostility enough to satisfy the most bellicose hearers. Monroe's failure to conclude a satisfactory agreement at Madrid was reviewed, the shameful story of the rejection of the claims convention told, and recent Spanish aggressions against American commerce reported. A new attitude toward Spain must be adopted, Jefferson declared, for the protection of American citizens and the spirit and honor of their country. But only "to a certain degree" should force be used. How far, was exclusively the task of Congress to decide. To its members Jefferson promised to communicate "the documents necessary to enable them to judge for themselves." The facts upon which they were to determine the course which the country must pursue were to be presented in a special message to be debated behind closed doors.

Except for the initiated few, the country at large received the President's message as tantamount to a declaration of war against Spain. Suspicion did, however, stir darkly in one quarter. John Randolph of Roanoke, one of the most picturesque figures among the Virginia Republicans, smelled a "job." Jefferson disclosed the real situation, saying that Florida would have to be bought for two million dollars. Randolph exploded. Such a step, after the failure of all negotiations, he thundered, would mean the deepest disgrace. For the first time, Jefferson was forced to listen not only to a frank criticism of his policy, but also to what was the first utterance of beginning revolt within his hitherto completely controlled party.

It was at this juncture that a party in the Senate began to talk of a special mission to England to negotiate a commercial arrangement. And around this question of a special mission was to be fought the first battle within the Republican party in the private war over what began with a disagreement on foreign policy and ended in an undignified tussle over the succession to the presidency. In this struggle, Monroe was suddenly to find himself the key figure, playing a role that put to the most severe test those qualities of his character—more ruggedly honest than impressively brilliant—that won him his place in the history of his country. From that fiery crucible he was to emerge with a prestige that made him the central figure in the golden age of his party—the Era of Good Feeling.

In the debates in Congress over Jefferson's new policy, Randolph loosed one of the most vicious attacks on the President, on Madison—who had conducted the "foreign business . . . from first to last . . . in the most imbecile manner," but he spared Monroe. "I do not speak of the negotiator—God forbid!—but of those who drew the instructions of the man who negotiated."[3] Gradually the House became aware of the daring and ingenious plan Randolph had hit upon. With a refinement of malice of which this Lucifer alone was capable, Randolph had settled upon the President's own close friend and favorite envoy, Monroe, as the spearhead of an offensive campaign against the administration.

From Randolph and Jefferson both, Monroe, still in England, soon learned of his thrust into embarrassing prominence. Randolph's letter of March 20 informed him that there was "no longer a doubt but that the principles of our administration have been materially changed . . . everything is made a business of bargain and traffic, the ultimate object of which is to raise Mr. Madison to the presidency. To this the old republican party will never consent, nor can New York be brought into the measure. Between them and the supporters of Mr. Madison there is an open rupture. Need I tell you that they are united in your support? that they look to you, sir, for the example which this nation has yet to receive to demonstrate that the government can be conducted on open upright principles, without intrigue or any species of disingenuous artifice? . . . . Your country requires, nay demands your presence. It is time that a character which has proved invulnerable to every open attack should triumph over insidious enmity."[4]

On March 16, Jefferson had told Monroe, "Some of your new friends are attacking your old ones, out of friendship for you, but in a way to render you great injury."[5]

To Randolph's letter of invitation Monroe wrote a gracious but firm refusal. He was proud of the compliment paid him, he said, but felt that he could not accept the honor. There were older men,

Politics and Policies

whom he had always considered as having first claim to what was being offered him, a claim it would be painful to him to see rejected. His friendship for Madison, he made clear, made it impossible to contest what he felt was due his friend. Besides, questions of political expediency were to be considered. Such a step as Randolph had suggested would put "in opposition, through the whole community men who have been in the habit of dangerous and laborious co-operation."[6]

The loyalty that was one of the strongest traits in his character had dictated a clear answer to a temptation few men in his position could have resisted. It was a final answer. None of the flattering solicitations that he was to receive in the course of the following months was to swerve him from his decision.

The plan now adopted by the administration to offset Randolph's bolt from the party policy was to placate and thus win to its side the Federalist minority. This was to be effected by appointing a Federalist as special agent in the business to be concluded with England. The man chosen was first supposed in London to be John Quincy Adams.[7] But Jefferson's letter of March 16 informed Monroe that his new colleague was to be William Pinkney of Maryland. The collaboration came at a particularly undesirable moment for Monroe, when a change in the British political situation seemed to promise, for the first time, at least partial success of his own mission.

The younger Pitt passed from the scene as Austerlitz was added to Napoleon's brilliant firmament of victories. In the Whig ministry, which now came in, two statesmen friendly to the United States took prominent places, Charles James Fox as Foreign Minister, and Erskine as Lord Chancellor. Fox, Monroe wrote to Madison after his first interview, received him with great kindness and attention. In fact, he rejoiced, Fox had put him more at ease than anyone in office since his English sojourn began. Although the new minister promised nothing, he at least held out hopes that Monroe's protests against the application of the Scott decision and the illegal condemnation of American vessels might at least be accepted as the basis of negotiation when Pinkney should arrive. To the long-suffering Monroe, even so minor a concession held a golden promise.

Unfortunately, the equilibrium of the Grenville ministry proved unstable. Supported as it was by Liberal public opinion, Fox could be relied on only to carry out the popular measures. British trade interests, not recognition of American legal rights in the current controversy, were to determine British policy. With Trafalgar balancing Austerlitz, prize money—and the system of prize law applied to neutrals—became essential to English superiority on the high seas. And rivalry between the United States and Great Britain on the score of colonial trade was at its bitterest.

In addition, resentment at the American non-importation act was growing. And coupled with it was a contemptuous conviction that America was neither able nor willing to support such radical measures as the non-importation and non-intercourse decrees by force of arms except in alliance with France. Assaulted by a howling press demanding that the law of the sea should be administered in the interests of Great Britain to the exclusion of "hostile" interests, Fox could offer Monroe nothing better than irritating half-measures. Without invalidating past judicial decisions or abrogating Orders in Council, the new solution proposed by the Foreign Minister was presented to the neutral powers on the sixteenth of May. This was in the form of a modification in the British Orders of Blockade. The French and German coasts from Brest to the river Elbe were still to be forbidden territory, but the penalties to which Monroe had so strenuously objected were to be applied only between Ostend and the Seine—a region where actual blockade could be enforced.

This measure, it seemed to Monroe, "clearly . . . put to an end further seizures on the principle which heretofore had been in contestation," and so was something he could congratulate himself upon achieving.[8] Perhaps wisely, he ignored the failure to assert or vindicate abstract principles of international law. He knew that this "Fox Blockade," as it was contemptuously called, was a friendly attempt by Fox, backed by Erskine, Lord Holland, and a small group of merchants anxious to conciliate American trade, to placate public opinion across the Atlantic.

It was at this juncture that Monroe learned that the exigencies of the political situation at home had made necessary the sending of Pinkney, a manoeuver by which his powers would be limited and his achievements possibly jeopardized. From Joseph Nicholson he received a disturbing letter declaring that of the "real friends of the present administration" there were not wanting those "who believe

Politics and Policies

that such an appointment was ... intended to take from you the task of settling our difference with England." The move was intended, he wrote, "to have an effect on the next Presidential election," and was "a bait to the Federalists." As to the latter, he insinuated that if they did not "bite at this, something more highly flavored will be offered—Mr. King has well nigh been the man."[9]

Late in May Pinkney arrived, an aloof, overbearing, foppish Baltimorean who had never enjoyed popularity at home. The sparks that might have been expected to fly from the encounter of the two men were never set off, surprisingly enough. So far as their correspondence discloses, the ill-assorted pair not only worked in harmony but seem to have actually felt a certain admiration and respect for each other.[10]

Monroe nevertheless held the opinion that special missions were bad policy. From the point of view of the envoy already present on the scene, such a mission was "never gratifying" and never would be "while men are governed by those useful passions which stimulate them to virtuous actions." He argued that even from the moment it became known that a special mission was contemplated by a home government, the resident envoy was "reduced ... to a cypher."[11] Such were his own feelings in the present situation. They were not eased by the letter from Jefferson which Pinkney had brought with him to be given confidentially to Monroe. In it, the President rather tactlessly offered him his "choice of the two governments of Orleans & Louisiana" in order that he might be "just that much withdrawn from the focus of the ensuing contest, until its event should be known," which he thought would be to Monroe's advantage.[12] Without definitely supporting Madison's candidacy for the presidency, Jefferson was nevertheless making it clear that he meant the logical order of succession in the Virginia dynasty to be kept.

To this offer, which he could hardly have regarded as other than an attempt to eliminate him from the political scene, Monroe replied in a friendly but direct manner. Such an appointment, he wrote, he had indeed at one time thought attractive, and had therefore spoken of it both to his correspondent and to Madison. But he had since abandoned the idea completely. He had much to do in Virginia, where he wished to live, of a private nature, and many interesting duties to perform there. And so he must say no thank you.[13]

JAMES MONROE

The administration, it was undoubtedly true, was beginning to be embarrassed by Randolph's intrigue. The latter's lieutenant, Nicholson, had pronounced, in the House, that Monroe was second to no one in the United States.[14] He was openly supported now by all the *Tertium Quids*, as Randolph's faction came to be known, John Taylor of Caroline, Tazewell, Macon, Clay, Bryan among them. To his standard came forward others who had known him as soldier, member of Congress, governor of Virginia, foreign representative. His probity and firmness of character, good judgment, public spirit, and sympathy with orthodox Virginia Republicanism had won for him prestige and respect in many circles.

Jefferson saw he must take steps. And so he appealed to Monroe by the surest route to the man's susceptibilities. "I see with infinite grief," he wrote eloquently, "a contest arising between yourself and another, who have been very dear to each other, and equally so to me. . . . The object of the contest is . . . equally open to you all, and I have no doubt the personal conduct of all will be so chaste as to offer no ground of dissatisfaction with each other. But . . . I know too well from experience the progress of political controversy . . . not to fear for the continuance of your mutual esteem. One piquing thing said draws on another . . . with increasing acrimony, until . . . it becomes difficult for yourselves to keep clear of the toils in which your friends will endeavor to interlace you. . . . A candid recollection of what you know of each other will be the sure corrective. . . . I have ever viewed Mr. Madison and yourself as two principal pillars of my happiness. Were either to be withdrawn, I should consider it as among the greatest calamities which could assail my future peace of mind. I have great confidence that the candor and high understanding of both will guard me against this misfortune, the bare possibility of which has so far weighed on my mind that I could not be easy without unburdening it."[15]

But Monroe, studying the instructions with which Pinkney had come armed and perusing certain correspondence from Jefferson, was coming to an unavoidable conclusion that Madison had deliberately laid a trap intended to diminish his reputation as a diplomat. He could not but perceive that he was neither desired nor expected to succeed in his task.

Madison, true enough, was unaware that Monroe had been mak-

Politics and Policies

ing progress of late with Fox. And it may have been purely his ignorance of such developments that dictated the tone of the instructions given Pinkney. For the special envoy he had forged an impressive vocabulary of strong language with which to assault British officialdom, and which Pinkney wished immediately to unloose. Not only was he to demand satisfaction of all outstanding grievances on the score of impressment but was also to insist upon British repudiation of the whole principle. And, should these demands not be instantly complied with, the British lion would immediately feel the effect of a lethal non-importation act.

Convenient as it might have been in the days of the Pitt ministry, an ultimatum was a foolish manoeuver considering the "fair prospect" [16] Monroe felt he now had of arranging matters amicably and satisfactorily with Fox. He could not help seeing in it Madison's hand against him. His suspicions were fed by Jefferson's letters, oddly out of accord with Pinkney's instructions. In one of them the President had written, "No two countries upon earth have so many joint interests of friendship, and their rulers must be great bunglers indeed if . . . they break asunder." [17] He still cherished a hope of an alliance between the two English-speaking nations.

From their inception, the negotiations of Monroe and Pinkney were dogged by ill-luck. The very day of the special envoy's arrival saw Fox take to his bed, from which he was never to rise. For two months, the Americans awaited the outcome of what was to prove the Minister's final illness. The interim was not made the happier for Monroe by the constant stream of letters arriving from home confirming his suspicions that the whole affair of the special mission was a political manoeuver. To the letters from Randolph persuading him to accept the highest honors the Old Republicans could give, he nevertheless dispatched circumspect and noncommittal replies. [18] To Bowdoin he wrote, much later, how much these appeals embarrassed him. [19]

Despite the fact that he felt Madison to have turned against him, and believed Jefferson to be championing the Secretary of State in the political struggle taking shape in the nation, Monroe nevertheless made every attempt to facilitate the success of the administration's foreign policy. He was very greatly concerned over what appeared to be the intimate connection between the Claims Convention scandal growing out of the Louisiana treaty and the French mediation in the purchase of West Florida. About this matter he now wrote to Jefferson. "If I was not personally your friend," ran the letter written on the fifteenth of June, 1806, "and did not wish success to your administration, from the interest I take in your welfare, as in that of my country, I should not write you with the freedom I propose to do in this letter. It is my intention to enter fully into some topicks which are of very high importance to your reputation as to the best interest of the U States, & I do it in confidence that you will see in it a proof of the sincerity of the motive which prompts me to it...." He then proceeded to relate how the secretary of Bowdoin, Jefferson's representative in Paris, had come to Monroe only the night before with the story of Armstrong's "personal disrespect and insult" toward Bowdoin. Not only that, but Bowdoin suspected Armstrong's "integrity" and believed him to be "connected with the stock jobbers who hope to derive a profit from any treaty which we may form with Spain." Indeed, "the honor & interest of our govt. & country are ... in jeopardy," declared Bowdoin. Monroe made clear that he had no opinion on the score of Armstrong's honesty. He was concerned only about "the delicate situation in which the important interests of our country" and Jefferson's reputation, both of which were in Armstrong's hands, were placed.[20]

In London, meanwhile, Fox had delegated to represent him in the negotiations with the Americans the liberal-minded Whig, Lord Auckland, and Lord Holland, the nephew of Fox and a personal friend of Monroe. But the advantage of having well-disposed commissioners was soon offset by the death of Fox and the succession to his office of a minister of an entirely different stamp, Lord Howick, the future Earl Grey. The government, moreover, was evidently to be replaced by an unsympathetic group of Tories. It was under the constant apprehension that at any moment the advent of these reactionaries would not put an end to all hope of compromise that the Americans continued on their forlorn task. As a matter of fact, something like a panic seems to have seized them as the Tory majority in Parliament rapidly increased. Aware of the futility of insisting upon the ultimatum he had been directed to present, Pinkney seems to have taken the part of encouraging Monroe to abandon even the slight advantages he had wrenched from Fox. Thus it was that on the last

Politics and Policies

day of December, 1806, Monroe and Pinkney affixed their signatures to a treaty wholly incompatible with the instructions both had received.

To Jefferson, Monroe wrote eleven days later in defense of his unusual diplomatic action that on the whole what had been gained by the treaty was all that "could reasonably have been expected." He argued the importance of standing well with some power—any power. He felt that the United States had at least "sustained the attitude they took with dignity, and that by this arrangement they will terminate a controversy, not in favor of themselves alone, but of neutral rights, with some degree of credit." What they had done would attract the attention of European powers, he advanced, and would make the United States "better known & more respected as a power."[21]

Communicating the general terms of the treaty to Bowdoin, Monroe stressed, interestingly enough, the "strict reciprocity" principles on which tariff matters had been settled, the fact that the India trade had been replaced on the footing of the 1794 treaty, that the West Indies trade question had been left open for further adjustment, and that the treaty had put the "great question of trade with enemy colonies . . . we presume on a good footing."[22]

But the most important aspect of the treaty was that which was to lead in the end to Jefferson's total rejection of the agreement, the failure to come to an arrangement on impressment. Only an "understanding" had been obtained on that subject, which appeared in the treaty only in the form of diplomatic memoranda recalling the points at difference. No abrogation of Scott's decision had been won, and only a measure of compromise was arrived at respecting colonial trade. West Indian produce of enemy origin, property of United States citizens, might still enter Great Britain from American ports if it had actually paid American customs duties before the transshipment required by the ruling of 1756. Respecting the much desired arrangement to regulate trade with Canada, no negotiation had been possible. Perhaps the most objectionable clause in the treaty to Republicans was that requiring the United States to put the seal of approval on English enforcement of the rule of 1756 by furnishing proofs of neutrality in the form of custom house receipts.

Lord Holland, in his *Memoirs*, throws an extremely interesting light on the omission from the treaty of perhaps the most important of the various matters on which the United States had demanded satisfaction: impressment. "My colleague and I," writes Holland, "took credit to ourselves for having convinced [Monroe and Pinkney] of the extreme difficulty of the subject, arising from the impossibility of our allowing seamen to withdraw themselves from our service during war, and from the inefficacy of all the regulations which they had been enabled to propose for preventing their entering into American ships. They, on the other hand, persuaded us that they were themselves sincere in wishing to prevent it; and we saw no reason for suspecting that the government of the United States was less so. But though they professed, and I believe felt, a strong wish to enforce such a provision, they did not convince us that they had the power or means of enforcing it. There was, consequently, no article in the treaty upon the subject."[23]

The news of Napoleon's triumphant campaign in Germany, which was received in London while the negotiations for the Pinkney-Monroe treaty were at their most critical stage, had its part in the extraordinary outcome. To the American envoys, the language of the Berlin Decree may well have foreshadowed the necessity of an English alliance. This extraordinary manifesto of 1806 began with a denunciation of the English Ministry's disregard of the law of nations and proposed to turn against England her own methods of warfare. The British Isles were declared to be in a state of blockade. Every Englishman found within French territory became a prisoner of war; and all British property, private and public, was declared good prize.

Like the British carrying trade, so too the American was paralyzed. Had Fox been alive, his genius might have turned such an event to good account by cementing an alliance between the two carrying nations. To the American negotiators, unaware of Jefferson's final decision on French policy, the situation appeared acute. Nor was their anxiety mitigated by the supplementary British demands that the United States should refuse to recognize the Berlin manifesto, else the British government would not feel bound to honor the treaty.[24]

A week after the signing of the Monroe-Pinkney treaty, England published her answer to Napoleon by the issuance of Orders in Council which came to be known as "Lord Howick's Orders." One of the

Politics and Policies

earliest measures to be enforced was one forbidding all coasting trade between European ports[25] belonging to France or her allies. The effect on American trade was disastrous.

It was upon the heels of these developments that the Monroe-Pinkney treaty arrived in America. Had it not been for Lord Howick's Orders it would have been ratified by the Senate. Even Madison would have found it possible to reconcile himself to a British alliance of such a nature. France was the great villain of the piece. So acute was the indignation over the Berlin Decree that Jefferson attributed to it the failure of his envoys to obtain satisfaction on the score of impressment, and neutral commerce.

But the new Orders in Council were more than America could swallow. When a preliminary copy of the treaty reached Jefferson, he expressed his anger "in strong, very strong terms." He took the view that impressment was a *"sine qua non* of the instructions," and spoke of returning "the treaty without consulting the Senate." But, as one of his Cabinet saw the situation, he could not do that unless he wished to disgrace the envoys, risk Monroe's enmity, alienate the Senate, which had advised the special mission and chosen Pinkney, and be accused of jealousy of Monroe and unreasonable antipathy toward England. He might even by such a step make "Monroe . . . a martyr and the martyr will be President."[26]

Jefferson handled the situation with his usual tact. The Howick Orders were for the time being allowed to pass unnoticed, except for a hint to Erskine that they might be as ruinous to American commerce as contrary to American rights. The envoys were instructed to "back out of the negotiation, letting it die insensibly and substituting some informal agreement." And to Monroe was sent a second offer of the governorship of Louisiana, touted "as the second office in the United States in importance."

22

The "Chesapeake" Incident

MONROE'S London Mission had yet to reach its climax —a dramatic one.

On the eighth of April, 1807, a reactionary Tory administration swept into power. Both George Canning, who took over the portfolio of Foreign Affairs, and Spencer Perceval, the real head of the Cabinet, were without aristocratic connections. Yet in both these commoners the blind reactionary sentiments of the aristocracy and "county" people who made up the majority in Parliament were strong. In the crisis of the struggle with Napoleon, the British electorate had given these men a mandate to revoke the liberal concessions made by the Whigs. The triumphant note of the hour was nationalism.

Such was the keynote when in the early summer of this same year an outrage offered to the national dignity of the United States united every class and party in common indignation against England.

On the afternoon, of June 21, the American ship of war, *Chesapeake*, its crew largely new recruits, left Hampton Roads for her station in the Mediterranean. The next morning, the half-equipped vessel slowly threaded her way through the British fleet lying in Lynnhaven Bay. Signals were fluttering at the mast-head of the Admiral's flagship, which was communicating with the cruiser *Leopard* lying farther out to sea. The *Chesapeake's* Captain Barron paid no particular attention, knowing the British to be mainly on the search for French privateers. At half-past three o'clock, however, the *Leopard* and the American vessel were tacking off Cape Henry,

The "Chesapeake" Incident

when the British ship hailed the other, signalling a desire to send mail on board. Instead of mail, Captain Barron found himself facing a demand for the surrender of certain British sailors "supposed to be now serving" on the *Chesapeake*.

Barron was not slow in recognizing the gravity of his position. The commander of an American ship of war whose crew was being mustered as if she were an ordinary merchantman could do but one thing—resist. After a quick consultation with an American official on board who was on his way to a consular post in the Mediterranean, Barron communicated to Captain Humphries of the *Leopard* his refusal to submit to search. "I know of no such men as you describe," he declared. "The officers that were on the recruiting service for this ship were particularly instructed by the Government, through me, not to enter any deserters from his Britannic Majesty's ships, nor do I know of any being here. I am also instructed never to permit the crew of any ship that I command to be mustered by any other but their own officers. It is my disposition to preserve harmony, and I hope this answer to your despatch will prove satisfactory."[1]

Seventeen minutes later the *Chesapeake* lay a helpless hulk beneath the smoking guns of the *Leopard*. Captain Barron demanded that his surrender be accepted and the vessel taken over as a prize.

The news of this incident reached London after some delay. It was almost the end of July when Monroe received from Canning an ominous note announcing a "transaction which has taken place, off the coast of America, between a ship of war of His Majesty, and a frigate belonging to the United States." The Foreign Minister expressed his "sincere concern and sorrow" and promised that should the British officers prove to have been culpable, "the most prompt and effective reparation shall be afforded."[2]

The press was far from apologetic however. Great Britain, it declared, was supreme on the seas, and what she found necessary to do in that realm was essential to maintenance of her sovereignty. Never, boasted the bellicose *Morning Post*, would "it . . . be permitted to be said that the Royal Sovereign has struck her flag to a Yankee cockboat."

On July 29, a routine interview was granted Monroe at the Foreign Office. Canning suavely protested the government's innocence in the affair. What had occurred was in no way "the result of instructions from the ministry." That same day, Monroe, with Canning's approval, wrote his first formal communication on the subject, in which he drew the government's attention to the "aggression on the sovereignty of the United States of a very extraordinary nature." The conduct of the British officer concerned, he maintained, was but "rendered more reprehensible" because it had occurred "in the waters of the Chesapeake, where ... he enjoyed the rights of hospitality." He scored a point in the statement that Captain Barron had been "relying on the good faith of His Majesty's Government."

In his reply, Canning "permitted" himself to express surprise at the "tone" of Monroe's note, and countered with the excuse that it was difficult to take immediate steps without "any precise knowledge of the facts." Although His Majesty was ready to take into consideration the whole of the "circumstances of the case when fully disclosed," the Foreign Minister declared that for the present he could go no further than the note he had written "in an unofficial form . . . on the first receipt of the intelligence of this unfortunate transaction."[3]

Both Canning and Monroe were being guilty of bad diplomatic strategy. The former was attempting to make a distinction "in case the men were American citizens or British subjects," one Monroe very properly refused to recognize, arguing that "a ship of war protected all the people on board, and could not be entered for search for deserters or for any purpose without violating the sovereignty of the nation."

Monroe made the mistake of bringing into the controversy the general principle of impressment. He did, however, insist that the *Chesapeake* incident was the "more serious cause for complaint." Monroe's error was repeated with even more unfortunate consequences by Madison, who, instead of supporting the envoy, took the stand that the incident should be considered by itself.

Canning was not slow to take advantage of this disagreement within the enemy camp. His note of September 23 insisted that the practice of impressment, as far as American merchant ships were concerned, was founded "on the soundest principles of natural law" and was not "to be explained whenever they might come into contact with the interests or feelings of the American people." Taking advantage of Madison's attitude as an excuse for evading any immediate

The "Chesapeake" Incident

apologies, he told Monroe, "If your instructions leave you no discretion, I cannot press you to act in contradiction to them. . . . I have only to regret that the disposition of His Majesty to terminate amicably and satisfactorily is for the present rendered unavailing." Canning indeed was careful not to leave the negotiators "under the impression that there was any prospect that the government of Great Britain would recede from its declared intention." His excuse was the "nature and mode of the hostility which France was now waging."

On the tenth of October Monroe sent Madison the news that a British envoy would be sent to Washington to attempt settlement of the dispute. He would not, however, be empowered to treat on the general issue of impressment. George Rose, the man chosen for this delicate mission, called on Monroe, who returned the visit and later sent the Englishman a cordial note in which one finds no trace of the chagrin he felt at Canning's high-handed treatment.

The effect of the *Chesapeake* incident upon the general course of the Monroe-Pinkney Mission was to terminate all discussion. In Monroe's opinion, the agreement of November 8, 1806, was the limit of possible British concessions. Every reason for his prolonging his London sojourn, therefore, had been removed. To Bowdoin he wrote on the eleventh of October that he expected to sail for home in about eight days and had already engaged a cabin on a ship sailing for the Chesapeake.[4]

Before Monroe sailed, George Rose embarked on his difficult mission to Washington. But an even more significant event than this occurred as Monroe was leaving England. While he waited at Portsmouth for a fair wind, the newspapers were brought him carrying the announcement of new Orders in Council, frankly designed as reprisals against the Continental System of Napoleon but again making a victim of American trade. As Perceval, who was chiefly responsible for their final form, coldly stated their purpose: ". . . British produce and manufactures, and trade either from a British port or with a British destination, is to be protected as much as possible. For this purpose, all the countries where French influence prevails shall have no trade, but to or from this country, or from its allies."[5] This "paper blockade" effectively denied every principle of neutral rights which Americans had championed since Washington's day. Neutrality became a word without meaning. A *Times* article of November 10, analyzing the combination of commercial and military motives behind the new Orders, declared frankly that ". . . the continent must and will have colonial productions in spite of orders and decrees, and we are to take care that she have no other colonial products than our own." Under such circumstances, the practical effect of Jefferson's embargo and non-importation measures was to facilitate British monopoly of continental trade.[6]

Jefferson's message to the Congress called in extraordinary session to consider these developments declared that America's "love of peace and forbearance under so many wrongs" might "not insure our continuance in the quiet pursuits of industry." Monroe's failure to secure a satisfactory arrangement on impressment was blamed on circumstances, not on lack of ability. But Jefferson was determined to go beyond implications and vague threats. On the eighteenth of December, the President's embargo message was read to the Senate and promptly passed by that body, soon after. The bill hit obstacles in the House but triumphed finally.

The Embargo was the outstanding political experiment of Jefferson's career—and a failure. When he had first proposed substituting non-intercourse for armed coercion and war, the majority of his party had risen as one man to support him. His own enthusiasm and his unequalled personal influence had been enough to make his followers second him in overriding private rights in the interests of the highest of public duties. But human nature could not long withstand the devastation of the purse that enforcement of the embargo wrought. As customs receipts dwindled and disappeared, as ships rotted at the wharves, and ports filled with grumbling, idle seamen, a revulsion of public opinion was inevitable. The New England Federalists, unable to see that what was happening would eventually cause their states to manufacture for themselves the imported commodities under ban and thus attain new prosperity, were furious against the President. They saw only their closed country houses, dismantled ships, the hated patrols enforcing the President's more hated law on the waterfront. The central and western states and settlements watched wheat fall from two dollars to seventy-five cents a barrel and finally become unsalable. River traffic dwindled and then ceased as New Orleans and Mobile wharves became glutted with the produce of the frontiers. Ironically, it was upon Jefferson's

The "Chesapeake" Incident

beloved Virginia that the blow fell heaviest. Tobacco, deprived of a European market, became as worthless as the common weed. Cotton and rice suffered the same fate. Only the whip and musket held the smouldering slave revolt in check. And not the least of the evils in the eyes of the South was the violence done by the Embargo Act to states' rights.

Perhaps the most fatal of the various faults being found with his pet legislation was that Jefferson by his Embargo was but carrying out Napoleon's hated Berlin and Milan decrees. It was this, coupled with the belief that Jefferson's unpopular French policy had been opposed by Monroe, that made the latter the standard-bearer and white-haired boy of the anti-Embargo party and anti-Madison party in the South.

Homecoming of an Envoy

THE NATION was still discussing Jefferson's message to Congress when the *Augustus* docked at Norfolk on a December day. Twenty-four hours later, the Non-Importation Act went into effect, under which much of the *Augustus*' cargo would have been banned. A week was yet to elapse before the Embargo bill was passed on the twenty-first of December, 1807.

On the thirteenth, the day of his arrival at Norfolk, Monroe dispatched a note to Madison telling him of his plans to go immediately to Richmond and from there to Washington, to report on affairs abroad. He was in Richmond on the day the Cabinet met to decide that the Embargo should be enforced. On the twentieth of December, he rode into Washington. In its new home, resplendent with painted ceiling, sandstone columns, and crimson brocade hangings, the House was listening to Randolph, Crowninshield of Salem, and sundry other oratorical gentlemen debate the Embargo. The Senate was equally busy with the crisis on hand. Monroe waited, patiently, to be called into Jefferson's councils. But no word was spoken. He returned, heart-sick, to Virginia, to take up again the threads of his private life. His uncle's death had left him heir to considerable estates whose settlement demanded his immediate attention. Illness in his immediate family added to his cares. And his own affairs had suffered from long neglect.

With these matters Monroe tried to busy himself. But it was not easy to lose himself in these labors with the realization sharp as pain within him that after five years of honest, patient, painstaking work

Homecoming of an Envoy

he had returned to such a welcome. The truth was that Monroe was suspect in the innermost conclave of the party. Not only had Randolph's faction openly come out for Monroe as Jefferson's successor, but a group of Federalists, led by Pickering, had bolted from their party to Monroe's support. It was the object of the latter group to defeat Madison by representing Monroe to the voting public as a victim of Jeffersonian duplicity.

But even the snub delivered him by his beloved Jefferson at this moment could not damage the man's unique loyalty. A month after Madison's nomination for the presidency by a congressional caucus, Monroe was writing Jefferson his intention to remain "an inactive Spectator" during the approaching election. He was also writing to Madison, he said, "in the most amicable terms" about their differences over the treaty. That unfortunate negotiation he begged the President to consider "as little more than a project."[1]

In that same month, Monroe received a letter from William Wirt, whose devotion had many times been proved. Wirt wrote that he had declined an offer to act on the standing committee to promote Monroe's "electoral ticket," because he had thought that his candidacy would have a "permanently ill effect" on his political future.[2] A man less loyal and generous than Monroe would not have replied, as Monroe did, that he was "equally surprised and hurt" that Wirt should think his or any other friend's lack of support would or could affect their friendship.[3]

More and more definitely, Monroe began to withdraw from the embraces of Randolph and his other supporters. In a letter to Tazewell he wrote that his desire was to be neutral. He wished neither to identify himself with the administration nor to oppose it.[4]

Yet he had every reason to take advantage of the situation to declare his independence of Jefferson. The latter was no longer riding the crest of the wave of popularity that had meant so much to him. As time went on and the economic disaster that trailed in the wake of the Embargo became increasingly apparent, friends as well as enemies of the administration were agitating for the withdrawal of commercial sanctions. Privately, and through the press, men as widely different in opinion and political affiliations as Wilson Cary Nicholas, Rufus King, John Marshall, and John Randolph took a stand against Jefferson's cherished law.

Moreover, the development of the Rose negotiation was involving Jefferson in embarrassing difficulties. Rose was proving adamant. He would be satisfied with nothing less than immediate withdrawal of Jefferson's proclamation excluding British warships from American ports. Madison demurred, protested that the move had only been one of "precaution against further affronts to British naval dignity."[5] But Rose insisted that his instructions required withdrawal of the offending proclamation as a preliminary to any further negotiation. His firmness stemmed from a realization that he had Jefferson where he wanted him. The only obstacle to his object, he wrote Canning, was Jefferson's fear of public opinion, already in jeopardy. Only the President's dread of "exposing himself to the charge of inconsistency and disregard of the national honor," the British envoy wrote, kept him from making the desired concession. In the event that the British could not satisfy the United States on the score of the *Chesapeake*, he assured the Foreign Minister, there would be no war, but merely a continuation of the Embargo.

Madison, with amazing confidence in the Englishman's discretion, actually told Rose that he "must be aware how dear to Mr. Jefferson his popularity must be, and especially at the close of his political career." And then, wrote Rose, Madison pressed him "to take such steps as would conciliate the President's wish to give his Majesty satisfaction on the point in question and yet to maintain the possession of what was preeminently valuable to him. . . ."[6]

But Rose could not be softened. On February 5, Madison was informed that express directions had come from Canning to secure "a formal disavowal of Commodore Barron"! And His Majesty had the graciousness not to "require any proceedings of severity" against the *Chesapeake's* commander!

And thus the negotiation had come to an end, leaving Jefferson in an extremely uncomfortable position.

Had malice been native to him, the opportunity for revenge lay ready to Monroe's hand. But he would have none of it. Strong as his belief was that his treaty had been "suppressed" to serve the political ends of Madison's friends, among whom Jefferson was the chief, bitter as was his disappointment at his exclusion from the Rose negotiation and the Embargo deliberations, he nevertheless refused to violate the bonds of friendship.

Homecoming of an Envoy

In September, 1808, he submitted to Jefferson his entire correspondence with Randolph, to prove that there was "nothing in them to sanction what has been by some most ungenerously insinuated."[7]

In March of the following year Monroe wrote to his patron that he was "perfectly satisfied" that Jefferson had never meant to injure him. The details of the campaign of vilification carried on against himself which arose out of the rejection by the administration of the treaty concluded in London would, he was sure, give Jefferson as much pain to read as it would give him to recite.[8]

≽ 24 ≼

Monroe and the New Republicans

IN VIRGINIA, Monroe's political strength, throughout his long career, found continuous refreshment and renewal. Like the hero-wrestler of Greek mythology whose strength renewed itself every time his body touched his mother-soil, so Monroe, returning exhausted and despairing from the diplomatic feats-at-arms abroad, found in his native state a fount of new power.

His very first visit to Washington after his five-year absence abroad had proved that his long labors and devotion to the administration had earned him only the suspicion and distrust of Jefferson and Madison. Madison, after his election, had omitted him from his Cabinet. Heaping insult upon injury, Jefferson had again offered Monroe the governorship of Louisiana. Monroe had not changed in his view that this was a poorly disguised attempt to send him into political exile. He would have liked, he once wrote, to have given Jefferson the "answer given by the King of Prussia to Count Saxe when he offered him the Island of Barbadoes . . . that he must find another Sancho for his Barataria." But, he said, "respect for my old friend prevented it," and instead he told Jefferson that "Mr. Madison had had it in his power" to offer the "one proposition which he could have made" him or which he could have accepted, the secretaryship of state.[1] That was the canker that gnawed at him these dark days. It was one of the most bitter of the disappointments that beat about his head during the months following his return. There were others of the same nature, but less acute. His old enthusiasm for soldiering awoke briefly at some talk of a post along "the military

Monroe and the New Republicans

line," and flickered out with the discovery, acidly enough described, that it was to be "something like the govt. in the neighborhood of the Rocky Mountains." Again, there was the time when Colonel Nicholas's seat in Congress suddenly became vacant, and Monroe learned to his surprise that Randolph, his former supporter, was a candidate. None of his friends pushed Monroe's candidacy.

But the tide was on the turn. Madison in his inaugural speech had held forth little encouragement that what he was pleased to call the "unexceptionable course" followed under the Jeffersonian administration in foreign affairs would give place to any other policy than that of cherishing ". . . peace and friendly intercourse with all nations having corresponding dispositions." In Virginia the growing faction of young Republicans found little satisfaction in this and looked to Monroe and Taylor for leadership in the coming struggle with the new administration.

The issues over which the political battles of the intra- and extra-party war would be fought soon clarified themselves. In the fall of 1810, the return of General Armstrong from France added another name to the list of possible candidates for the headship of the State Department. Armstrong had had no easy time coping with the diplomacy of the volatile, unpredictable Napoleon, who veered from offering the Floridas in return for an American alliance, to a wholesale seizure of American vessels in French ports. When he returned to the United States in September, Armstrong, however, had in his possession a letter dated August 5, 1810, and bearing Napoleon's signature, which announced that the decrees of Berlin and Milan were revoked as of November 1, either conditionally upon the similar revocation of the British Orders in Council, or, failing that, upon the United States' causing "their rights to be respected by the English."

So delighted had Armstrong been with this prize, that he had taken no pains before leaving France to make the Emperor express himself in more precise language than that in which these half-hearted concessions were phrased. Cadore had read the American's mind quite exactly when he reported to Napoleon that the American minister had not desired to raise "difficult questions" because he had not wished to arrive in America without the "glory he attaches to having obtained the Note of August 5th."[2]

JAMES MONROE

Madison was content enough with this somewhat ambiguous document to issue, on the second of November, a proclamation declaring that the edicts of France had been revoked, and instructed Gallatin to issue a circular announcing that all commercial intercourse with Great Britain would cease after February 2, 1811. The issue was now fairly joined between the partisans of an accommodation with England and those who leaned on the slender reed of Napoleon's good faith.

Also occupying the nation's statesmen was the problem posed by the Florida situation. The twenty-sixth of September had brought the electrifying news of a revolt in West Florida led by American settlers. Baton Rouge had been captured, only feebly defended by the Spanish garrison. Immediately, Madison ordered occupation of the area by American troops. In so doing, he won the favor of the frankly expansionist Congress, and particularly of men like the young and ambitious Henry Clay, William Lowndes, and John Calhoun, who wanted action in the Florida affair.

The presence in Washington of men of Clay's temper and ideals was significant for Monroe's political future. Monroe was, in the eyes of the westerners, still the leader who had battled for their right to navigate the Mississippi and who had brought the vast tract of Louisiana under the American flag. Men like Clay were determined to bring western issues to the fore, and where those issues were fought Monroe's name would be heard. And in the debates on the newly acquired territory and on the Florida question, it was indeed heard. In Congress, Clay's brilliant defense of the act of October 31, 1803, by which Jefferson's acceptance of Louisiana was authorized, worsted Monroe's old antagonist, Pickering, of Massachusetts. The Clay-Pickering encounter brought Monroe out of the temporary eclipse in which he had been languishing since his return from London, and catapulted him into the Republican limelight. The final days of the congressional session re-established him with the party at a moment when Republicanism knew again a long-lacking zest and vitality.

The source of this rejuvenating elixir was the new nationalism that was inspiring American political feeling. The younger Republicans were spurred on by the contempt and indignation aroused in them by Federalist pandering to the English. Lost to all patriotic

Monroe and the New Republicans

sense of duty, Federalist shipowners in Salem and Boston asked for and were rarely refused the convoy of British war vessels in the Baltic, around Portugal, and in the West Indies.[3] The British blockade of New York had been lifted temporarily, and impressment was rarely practiced.

The Republican nationalist faction, with whom Monroe had now thrown his lot, found another source of grievance in the Federalist proposal to recharter the United States Bank. The main reason for the opposition was the fact that fully two-thirds of the bank's stock was owned by London bankers; notably the great house of Baring Brothers. Moreover, even though Jefferson had approved the transaction when it was made in 1802, later-day Republicans regarded the bank as a financial institution run for the sole benefit of New England and the overseas trade.[4] The bank issue brought out sharply the dividing line between the old and the new Republicans.

The platform of the dissenting bloc in the Republican party was what concerned Monroe during the autumn months of 1810. Letters flew between him and Taylor, Tazewell, and other prominent Republican separatists. Monroe clung firmly to the thesis that a complete split was suicidal, that ". . . the rival, or federal, party alone would profit by it."[5] On the Republican party, he believed, depended the "safety of free government." If that party were broken, it meant that the Federalists would be in power, and how long, he asked, would the sole republic in the world last under that regime?[6] Tazewell wanted the dissenting Republicans to form a third and distinct party. Monroe assured him that there could never ". . . be more than two efficient parties in the country."[7] The efforts of the group could, within the fold of the party, best be expended in the interests of an understanding with Great Britain and a modification of Jefferson's commercial sanctions policy. This opposition, he advised, should be systematic, prudent, moderate—"or it will fail in its object. . . ."[8]

If his words of wisdom ever reached the eyes and ears of the much harassed Madison, the sudden call that Monroe was later to receive to replace the lazy, tactless Smith as Secretary of State becomes easily understandable.

❧ 25 ❦

Secretary of State

IT WAS INEVITABLE that Monroe should return to public life at this stage of affairs, and fitting that his own state should recall him to it. When the General Assembly of Virginia pressed a nomination to the Senate upon him, however, he refused on the grounds that "the acceptance of such a trust would be ruinous" to him.[1] But he did not refuse the offer of the governorship when that was made. He had first to submit to the state legislature's cross-examination on his party orthodoxy and his stand on the foreign policy being pursued by Madison, but he passed with flying colors and stepped again to the helm of state. From this safe vantage point he could look on with perhaps no little satisfaction at the difficulties with which Madison and the State Department were wrestling.

In December, news of the seizure at Bordeaux of two American vessels then in port struck a blow to the bright hopes entertained by those optimists who had pinned their faith to Napoleon's promises in the letter of August 5, which Armstrong had so triumphantly brought home with him. Madison's pro-French policy appeared in rather a bad light, and the plan he was contemplating of enforcing commercial sanctions against England began to look somewhat absurd. To complicate matters, Madison, like a bull baited by two toreadors, in his uncertainty whether to turn against England or France, surprisingly feinted at Spain. On January 3 he sent a secret message to Congress asking authority to seize East Florida. Congress complied, first specifying that the seizure must have the consent of the local authorities and should be made only in the face of a

Secretary of State

threatened foreign occupation of the territory he wished to seize.

As if these were insufficient troubles for the harassed President, a bitter quarrel was rising between the Secretary of the Treasury, Gallatin, who was the only real statesman in the Cabinet, and Secretary of State Smith. Gallatin finally handed in his resignation. Even then, however, Madison might not have taken the drastic step that was to be so significant for Monroe if he had not reached the end of his patience with the inept and treacherous Smith, whom the President suspected of sabotaging his policy of commercial sanctions.

The logical successor to Smith's post was Monroe. Madison knew that Monroe's influence in the faction of young Republicans was tremendous and was being used to keep the party intact. To have one of the leaders of the potentially dangerous minority in his Cabinet would be a great tactical advantage. Madison was not unaware of the unpopularity of his measures.

But Monroe was no longer in the mood to jump at Madison's call. Not in sympathy with the administration's foreign policy, sure of its failure, and reluctant to identify himself with its consequences, Monroe would have to be carefully courted. He declared, in fact, that he felt it his duty to remain at his post in Richmond, from which only the conviction that it was his greater duty to take over the State Department in his country's interests could lure him.[2]

And that, precisely, was the argument Taylor used to persuade Monroe to accept the offer, when appealed to for advice. "One consideration of great weight," was Taylor's view, "is that the public think you an honest man. If this opinion is true, the acceptance seems to be a duty toward relieving it from the suspicion that there are too many avaricious or ambitious intriguers of apparent influence in the government. I suppose the President and Gallatin . . . to be wholly guided by what they think to be the public good; and should you happen to concur with them, it will abate much of the jealousy (though I hope it will never be smothered) with which Executive designs are viewed; and to moderate it, under the perilous situation of the country, is in my view desirable."[3] Taylor also urged that with Monroe in the State Department, Madison's pro-French policy and commercial sanctions against England, which were apparently leading the United States into a war with Great Britain, would possibly be changed.

JAMES MONROE

Taylor also studied the effect Monroe's acceptance of Madison's offer might have on his political future. Would Monroe be in a more favorable position in the coming presidential contest if he remained the popular governor of the powerful state of Virginia, or if he were guiding his country's fate from the State Department? To become entangled in the web of foreign affairs at such a time might be very dangerous. At the same time, there was no denying the advantage of being so much in the public eye as the Secretary of State must necessarily be.

"Our foreign relations seem to be drawing to a crisis," wrote Taylor to Monroe, "and you ought to be in the public eye when it happens, for your own sake, independently of the services you can render your country. It is probable that this crisis will occur on a full discovery that France will not do our commerce any substantial good without an equivalent which would amount to its destruction. So soon as this discovery is made, the Government, in all its departments, will alter its policy, and your occupancy of a conspicuous station will shed upon you the glory of its having come round to your opinion." Taylor also pointed out that if Monroe didn't accept the offer, someone else would. And, argued Taylor, "Suppose this other should be a competitor for the Presidency, will it not be a decisive advantage over you? General Armstrong is probably taking measures for this object. . . ."[4]

Taylor's astute analysis largely dispelled what doubts were still lingering in Monroe's mind. But when he finally sent his reply to Madison it was not in a letter of unqualified acceptance. Neither did it present "views of policy" that might, in effect, be construed as a refusal. "I have no hesitation in saying," he wrote, "that I have every disposition to accept your invitation to enter into the Department of State. But . . . some considerations occur which claim attention from us both, and which candour requires to be brought into view, and weighed at this time. My views of policy towards the European powers are not unknown. They were adopted on great consideration, and are founded in the utmost devotion to the publick welfare. I was sincerely of opinion, after the failure of the negotiation with Spain, or rather France, that it was for the interest of our country, to make an accommodation with England, the great maritime power, even on moderate terms, rather than hazard war, or any other alter-

Secretary of State

native. On that opinion I acted afterwards, while I remained in office, and I own that I have since seen no cause to doubt its soundness. . . ."[5].

Madison's answer was conciliatory. The administration, he assured Monroe, had not ceased to desire peace and a "cordial accommodation" with Great Britain. Making no direct promise to change his policy, he did, however, intimate that the frank advice of all factions would be welcome. He conceded that there existed differences of opinion on a British understanding, differences which, he said, lay "within the compass of free consultation and mutual concession as subordinate to the unity belonging to the Executive department." Most important of all was Madison's assurance that he saw no "commitments, even in the case of the abortive adjustment with that Power, that could necessarily embarrass deliberations on a renewal of negotiations."[6] And with these words, Madison even raised from the ashes of the past the hope so near Monroe's heart that his rejected treaty might be resurrected and restored to honor.

But Robert Smith was still Secretary of State, and summarily to dismiss him would mean alienating the whole Maryland bloc in the Republican party. Madison, however, was sufficiently convinced of Smith's ineptitude and more serious disloyalty in failing to support the administration's policies to proceed with brutal directness to lop off this rotten branch of the tree of state. Smith, accordingly, heard himself charged with showing "an apparent cordiality, and even a sufficient concurrence of opinion" during Cabinet sessions, while "out-of-doors counteracting what had been understood within to be the course of the administration." But far more damaging to the man's vanity was Madison's accusation ". . . that whatever talents he might possess, he did not, as he must have found by experience, possess those adapted to his station."[7] The President charged him with lack of system, dilatoriness, and a deplorable conduct of the foreign correspondence.

There followed the usual difficulties and unpleasantness attendant upon the dismissal of an influential and articulate gentleman, but on the fifth of April Monroe was able to assume the duties of his new office. Relations with Madison were established on an amicable and completely satisfactory basis.

"The conduct of the P. since my arrival," Monroe wrote to his old comrade, Dr. Charles Everett, "has corresponded with our antient relation, which I am happy to have restor'd. On publick affairs we confer without reserve, each party expressing his own sentiments, and viewing dispassionately the existing state, animated by a sincere desire to promote the public welfare. I have full confidence that this relation will be always preserved in future. . . ."[8]

Madison and his new secretary, nevertheless, differed from the beginning on the most basic issue confronting them: whether to adhere to Great Britain or France. American trade was neatly caught between the millstones of both countries' aggressions. Monroe favored making peace with the English, arguing that the Napoleonic decrees had never in actual practice been repealed. Madison still insisted that the only way to make the British repeal their oppressive Orders in Council was by a French understanding. Despite every evidence to the contrary he repeated to the nation that the Napoleonic decrees had been rescinded.

Monroe found his position made even more difficult by an unexpected development in London, where Pinkney, just before Monroe became head of the State Department, had suddenly abandoned his post. Occurring at a time when all New England was fearful of a break with Great Britain, Pinkney's action—tantamount to a diplomatic rupture between the two countries—was doubly difficult to fathom, since it struck a blow to his own party's dearest hopes of a British understanding.

Events in England had, true enough, been of a nature to exasperate the most patient diplomat. The legal recognition of the King's madness on the sixth of February had placed the reins of government in the hands of the Prince Regent, the friend of Fox and his successors Wellesley, Grenville, Grey, and Holland—all well-disposed toward the United States. Those who had anticipated as the result of such a development that Perceval's Tory ministry would fall and the whole obnoxious policy of the Orders in Council be reversed were doomed to disappointment. Two days before he took over the government, the Prince, sheltering himself behind the "King's wishes," deserted his Whig friends and asked the old ministry to remain in office. Pinkney's reaction was that his long struggle with the Foreign Office having reached an impasse, the only course left open to him was to break the deadlock by making a forceful move. Accordingly

Secretary of State

he suddenly announced his intention of taking an "immediate leave" of England. Refusing to accept an invitation to the Prince's first diplomatic levee, he asked instead when he could be granted his audience of leave.[9] Wellesley's reply was in the shape of a private letter of apology announcing that a British minister, Augustus Foster, would immediately be sent to the United States. He suggested, at the same time, that Pinkney withdraw his request for a final audience. But the American persisted in his intention and sailed soon after for Washington.

Already sufficiently strained, Anglo-American relations were now brought almost to the breaking-point by the dramatic encounter between the United States' frigate *President* and the British schooner *Little Belt*. It was the *Chesapeake* incident reversed, Commodore Rodgers of the *President* having overhauled the *Little Belt*. When the British envoy, Foster, arrived in Norfolk, with instructions in his portfolio designed to conciliate American feeling on the *Chesapeake* outrage, he was greeted by a jubilant American press celebrating the *President*'s feat of wiping out the *Chesapeake* insult.

The ruffled Englishman opened the negotiations with a strong protest against "American aggressions" in the disputed Spanish territory, not realizing that he was treading on the toes of the Secretary of State. Monroe was still the champion of Western interests and very sensitive about his part in laying claim to West Florida as a part of the Louisiana Purchase.

The question of Spanish sovereignty, moreover, was claiming especial attention in Washington. In the correspondence carried on during the last months of Smith's incumbency of the State Department, South American affairs had already begun to take an important place. And the significance of the instructions issued by Monroe to Poinsett, whom he had appointed to the post of consul-general to the revolted provinces of Buenos Aires, cannot be too strongly emphasized. He wrote:

"The disposition shewn by most of the Spanish provinces to separate from Europe and to erect themselves into independent States excites great interest here. As Inhabitants of the same Hemisphere, as Neighbors, the United States cannot be unfeeling Spectators of so important a moment. The destiny of those provinces must depend on themselves. Should such a revolution however take place, it cannot be doubted that our relation with them will be more intimate, and our friendship stronger than it can be while they are colonies of any European power."[10]

The question, then, was not only whether Spain should be eased out of the United States but embraced also the larger issue of Spanish rule in the whole western hemisphere. And the larger issue involved Great Britain, whose ally Spain was and who had her own reasons for wanting the Spanish flag to remain flying across the Atlantic. In Brazil, too, where the refugee Portuguese court was established at Rio de Janeiro, the English were giving every support to the Royalists against the republican movement.[11] It was not a question of ideology, but of economics. A Spanish or Portuguese government meant new trade possibilities for English merchant ships, shut out from every port on the European continent by Napoleon. A native republican government meant American ships in those same ports.

When Foster added to his protests against American activity in Spain's North American settlements the threat of "further measures of retaliation for the Non-Importation Act . . .,"[12] and expressed himself in no uncertain terms, challenging Madison's contention that the Berlin and Milan decrees had been rescinded, all possibility of coming to an understanding disappeared.

From the frontier settlements echoed the cry for war insistently sounded in Congress by Clay and his "war-hawks." In December, 1811, came the Army Bill, bringing nearer the threat of war. And in the same month the House adopted the resolution allowing merchant vessels to arm and to resist the aggressions of foreign ships of war—a measure tantamount to a declaration of war.

During the trying weeks which preceded the formal declaration of hostilities, Monroe appears to have succeeded in maintaining his cordial relations with both British and French envoys. Private correspondence, friendly interviews, and unofficial negotiations of too delicate a nature to be entrusted to paper and ink filled these troubled days. Foster actually turned to Monroe for advice and assistance, finding in the sober-mannered, honest secretary ". . . a very mild, moderate man" who was willing to listen to reason if impregnable to persuasion.[13]

Monroe's intercourse with Sérurier, the French minister, was less amicable. Monroe was not in a mood to comfort the Frenchman

Secretary of State

when he protested against the serious popular outbreak which occurred against French privateers at Savannah. And he took pains to caution Sérurier that Barlow's departure for France "must not mislead Napoleon."

Napoleon's brand of diplomacy, in fact, was a constant source of trouble to the Secretary of State, who was faced with the onerous task of interpreting to Congress and the American public the Emperor's offensive and presumptuous manner of expressing himself on international issues. Napoleon wrote and spoke as though he were the head of a league of neutrals whose policy was embodied in his Continental System. But by this system, the United States was put on the same footing as the vassal states of the Napoleonic empire. The imperial tirades, moreover, were generally framed with an assumption of legality out of all proportion to the actions of his cruisers and his broken promises to the President of the United States.

Monroe was hampered by the absence from both Paris and London of American ministers. Jonathan Russell, the American representative in Paris, was fortunately a man of undoubted diplomatic courage, however, and possessed a considerable aptitude for negotiation. He fully realized the hollowness of the pretext by which American ships were relieved from the working of the Berlin and Milan decrees only to be sequestrated under custom house regulations craftily designed to secure the same end. His dispatches did not cease to urge that any obligation to enforce the Non-Intercourse Law against Great Britain "is certainly weakened, if not destroyed, by the conduct of the government here."[14]

Russell's private accounts of the rages in which Napoleon was indulging were both frank and revealing. Only illusions of grandeur could explain the language used by the Emperor respecting the United States. "The decrees of Milan and Berlin are the fundamental laws of my empire," he declared in the tones the ruler of the civilized world might have suitably used. "The lot of American commerce will be soon decided. I will favor it if the United States conforms to these decrees." Russell complained that the Custom House was now instructed to make "no reports on American cases," while the Duke of Bassano, the new French Foreign Minister, whose appointment had coincided with Monroe's, advanced his "unfamiliarity with the situation" as an excuse to avoid either information or apology.

JAMES MONROE

The only ray of hope on the continental horizon was the gradual weakening of the Tilsit Alliance between France and Russia under the strain which its terms imposed upon Russian commerce. Russian merchants, in fact, had never accepted the part assigned them by Napoleon in his Continental System. English merchants were still considered their nearest friends and allies. A large share of English trade in the Baltic was carried on by American shipowners, and when the license issued by Napoleon to American vessels allowing them to trade on the Baltic was subsequently revoked by his orders, the Tsar was prevailed upon by the American ambassador, John Quincy Adams, to allow the ships into remote ports like Archangel. "Our attachment to the United States," Adams delightedly heard Tsar Alexander declare, "is obstinate, more obstinate than you are aware of."

Monroe, indeed, had cause to hope that his struggle with Napoleon might be made more successful by Alexander's intervention. By August, 1811, Napoleon reached a decision in regard to the Tsar's intransigency which foreshadowed the beginning of hostilities between them in the spring of 1812.

As the situation moved inevitably towards a Franco-Russian war, Monroe continued to press Napoleon for some definite recognition of the promises made to the Madison administration, and formally demanded French confirmation of the engagement assumed by Cadore in his correspondence with Armstrong.

Until the autumn of 1811, Monroe's conduct of the State Department was in accord with the views of the faction of Republicans he had joined after Jefferson's rejection of his London treaty. This dominant Virginia group—if inclined to war at all—insisted that the offenses of which France was guilty against the United States far outweighed those offered by Great Britain. Their implied promise to Monroe of support of his candidacy for the presidency when he entered Madison's Cabinet obligated him to correct the President's supposed leanings towards a French alliance.

"War, dreadful as the alternative is," wrote Monroe to an English correspondent in the fall of 1811, "could not do us more injury than the present state of things, and it would certainly be more honorable to the nation, and gratifying to the publick feelings. . . . Pressure from G. Britain, and even the injuries she might do us, would produce

Secretary of State

results not less injurious to her, without taking into the estimation those injuries of a positive kind which she would receive in return. War would give activity to our infant manufactories, which would soon be able to shut the door on British industry." Monroe's earnest wish for a British understanding was made even more manifest in the next lines. ". . . Shew respect for our rights," he appealed to the Englishman, "repeal your orders, institute & maintain lawful blockade only, & what may not this lead to? Friendship with America; free trade with this whole Western hemisphere; security to your trade, from us, in the Eastern hemisphere; good wishes to your general commerce with the Continent. . . ."[15]

Madison had offered no objections to Monroe's plans of conciliating Great Britain. He allowed his Secretary of State to continue this course in which he himself had lost all confidence, but insisted that his own policy of commercial sanctions inherited from Jefferson be respected at least in form, and that the decrees of Berlin and Milan be considered as revoked.

Therefore, when the Twelfth Congress, to which fell the momentous decision of choosing between the two aggressor nations, met in November, 1811, the door was still open to an accommodation with either.

26

Declaration of War

THE CURIOUS diplomatic prelude to the outbreak of hostilities between the United States and Great Britain shows clearly how much a matter of pure chance it was that war was declared against England rather than against France or both England and France.

When the Twelfth Congress met in Washington on the fourth of November, 1811, British frigates were once more blockading New York Harbor and seizing American ships in sight of land. The halls of the House and Senate reverberated with the cry of the Republican majority (Randolph's faction excepted) for a "protest in arms." And the House Committee of Foreign Relations was prompt to recommend "open and decided war" against the English. When on the twenty-sixth of the following March, a profoundly excited Washington heard that the instructions Foster had that day received from England declared that the British were determined not to repeal their Orders until Napoleon had in truth repealed his decrees, the administration considered the situation beyond remedy.

Dramatically at this moment of decision to act against Great Britain came the utterly astounding news that American ships were being burned and sunk by a French squadron acting under Napoleon's orders. Captain Samuel Chew of the brig *Thomas* deposed before a magistrate that on the second of February his vessel had been stopped in mid-Atlantic by a French squadron whose officers boasted that they had burned the American ship *Asia* and the brig *Gersham*. The French commander had also declared "that he had

Declaration of War

orders to burn all American vessels sailing to or from an enemy's port."[1]

The news spread abroad. The press sent up a howl for a war against both nations. "The Devil himself," wrote Macon to Nicholson, giving expression to the national state of mind, "could not tell which government, England or France, is the most wicked."[2]

The administration found itself in an embarrassing dilemma. Monroe vented his anger and vexation at poor Sérurier. "You know," he accused the Frenchman bitterly, "what warlike measures have been taken for three months past . . . within a week we were going to propose the embargo, and the declaration of war was the immediate consequence of it. . . . It is at such a moment that your frigates come and burn our ships, destroy all our work, and put the Administration in the falsest and most terrible position in which a government can find itself placed."[3]

To add to their troubles, Madison and Monroe at this point became involved in an incident that further embarrassed the administration. A French adventurer calling himself Count Edward de Crillon, and later proved to be an agent of Napoleon's secret police, found means to win the President's confidence, then offered to sell certain "secret papers" belonging to one John Henry, supposedly a spy in the pay of the Governor-General of Canada. Crillon was persuaded by Monroe to part with the documents for less than half of the hundred and twenty-five thousand dollars first asked for them, and on March 9 Madison sent the papers to Congress. He charged the English government with employing a secret agent to "foment disaffection to the constituted authorities," since the papers purported to show an intrigue between the English and the Federalist party aimed at destroying the Union. The disloyal opposition party, it was charged, had designs of "forming the eastern part" of the country "into a political connection with Great Britain." Unfortunately for the accusers, the papers offered very little actual evidence of such an intrigue. When the Senate moved a resolution calling on the President for the names of the persons involved in the project, the embarrassed Madison and Monroe had to admit they could give no further information. The names had all been carefully deleted from the papers. The Federalists abandoned themselves to unholy jubilation.

JAMES MONROE

With Foster and Sérurier, Monroe continued to play his game of cat and mouse. When Foster learned of Madison's "secret" message to Congress of April 1, 1812, recommending "a general embargo . . . on all vessels now in port, and hereafter arriving for a period of sixty days," he came to Monroe with a demand for explanations. Monroe was cautious, conciliatory, "deprecated" the message "being considered as a war measure," suggested Foster consider it an effort to comply with the British demand that no preferences be shown between the English and French. To Sérurier, however, Monroe declared that the embargo was a ruse to gain time in which to complete the necessary preparations for "the imminent war with England" which was "inevitable if the news expected from France answered to the hopes they had formed." At the same time, he threatened the French envoy that the administration might yet "be obliged to propose war against both Powers."[4]

On the tenth of April, the President was authorized by Congress to call up one hundred thousand militia. Throwing the responsibility for future action upon Madison, Congress then adjourned, with ill-concealed relief. Gallatin was left with the difficult and embarrassing task of raising money for equipping the army. Obliged to appeal to private and state banks, the Secretary of the Treasury addressed himself to the center of the country's financial power, New England, and was met with almost general refusal. The Federalist capitalists of New York and Philadelphia could provide him with only three million dollars. In the South and West, the war spirit was high, but resources low, and Gallatin could obtain but seven hundred thousand dollars.

Madison, in the meanwhile, put the business of war aside for the more pressing demands of the coming election. April thus passed into May, and the war party began to suspect the President of not having meant "his late hostile measures." Even the weeks following Madison's nomination by the Washington caucus saw little preparations for actual hostilities. National sentiment on the war was still divided. Only Clay and the "war-hawks" of the South and West showed enthusiasm.

The nineteenth of May saw the arrival of the sloop-of-war, *Hornet*, with the first official communication from the new British Foreign Minister, Lord Castlereagh. It was a logical, temperate argu-

Declaration of War

ment for peace, a clear attempt at friendly discussion of American grievances. Again it was pointed out that the French decrees were still in force, and that the British could not therefore rescind their Orders. When the country learned that France, on the other hand, was not willing to withdraw the decrees, feeling again was fanned into hostility towards the French.

Madison, bent on keeping American public opinion anti-British, now had recourse to the old grievance of impressment. Congress was convened in secret session on the first of June to listen to the presidential message, a martial piece built around the resurrected theme of England's "continued practice of violating the American flag on the great highway of nations and of seizing and carrying off persons sailing under it." The outrages perpetrated by France against American shipping were passed over almost in silence. The President recommended no measures against Napoleon's government.[5]

On June 18, both the House and the Senate completed formalities required by the Constitution for declaring war. And two days previously, on the other side of the Atlantic, an equally momentous event had taken place in the British Parliament. On that day, Brougham brought his motion for a repeal of the Orders in Council before the House, and Lord Castlereagh rose to announce that the new government had determined to suspend the Orders immediately. Since January there had been a movement afoot to prevent war with the United States. Perceval and Brougham, Holland, Wellesley, and Canning had all come to the conclusion that such a war would be fatal to British prosperity. Unfortunately, Monroe was almost completely ignorant of this change of front, because of the ineptitude of the young and inexperienced chargé d'affaires in London. Furthermore, communication was a slow and painful process. And thus it came to pass that England's historic and complete capitulation to American demands came to the knowledge of the United States only after war had been irrevocably declared and hostilities already begun on the Canadian frontier.

One key to the puzzle of the beginnings of the War of 1812 can be found in the impulse to empire which was stirring to life during the years of Madison's administration. When Monroe took over the Department of State, he found in his predecessor's files an extremely intriguing correspondence between Smith and one Mathews, a former Revolutionary officer and one-time governor of Georgia. Mathews, as one of the War Department's secret agents and, later, as a commissioner under the Act of January, 1811, empowering the President to occupy East Florida under certain given conditions, had been busy nourishing the beginnings of an infant, American-manufactured revolution in East Florida which would bring that territory under the American flag.

Monroe, when he took over Smith's post, authorized Mathews to continue his questionable activities, "especially if you entertain any reasonable hope of success there," he wrote. The matter eventually attracting too much public attention for the comfort of the administration, Monroe had been forced to abandon the adventure and adventurer both, primly informing Mathews by letter that his activities in Florida were "not authorized by the law of the United States, or the instructions founded on it" sent by the government.[6]

And not only Florida, but Canada also, tempted the more ambitious nationalists. In a letter to Jackson, Grundy of Tennessee was writing of his anxiety "not only to add the Floridas to the South but the Canadas to the North of this empire," that in the coming war with England these two territories would be "the Theatres of our offensive operations."[7] Even Monroe, neither by nature nor by party-philosophy an imperialist, was calmly discussing a possible invasion of Canada, "not as an object of war," true enough, "but as a means to bring it to a satisfactory conclusion."[8]

Monroe was now completely committed to the purposes of the Clay faction in Congress, which constituted the heart and soul of both the war party and the imperialist party. And it was fundamentally the nationalism of this group and not the interests of American trade on the high seas that dictated the war against England, from whom an empire might be wrested in the hour of victory.

General Hull had already invaded Canada and was facing the English under Brock when Monroe, deciding to accept the olive branch proffered by London, dispatched instructions to Jonathan Russell to negotiate an armistice. Immediately afterwards, a communication from General Dearborn in Albany reached the State Department stating that the Governor of Canada was also asking for a cessation of hostilities. Nothing could have been more unfortunate than the concatenation of circumstances which kept Hull ignorant

Declaration of War

of these developments, with the consequence that he had already engaged in battle with the English and surrendered all his forces as the peace move began.

Monroe received the news of the disaster with what he described to Clay as "equal astonishment and concern."[9] Both he and Clay placed the whole blame on Hull, but public opinion more fairly laid emphasis on the culpability of Congress and the administration. The pending negotiations for an armistice were immediately broken off, Monroe telling Sérurier that never was the United States "more determined on war." What had happened, he insisted, made it imperative to carry on hostilities until the nation's honor had been restored. "For myself," Monroe declaimed, "Secretary of State as I am, if tomorrow a British minister should arrive in Washington to negotiate peace, I would say to him, 'No; I will not treat with you now! wait till we have given you a better opinion of us! When our honor shall be avenged, when you shall have recrossed the rivers, when our generals shall occupy the best part of your Canada, then I shall be disposed to listen, and to treat of peace.'" Sérurier listened, admiring, and thought Monroe's indignation "altogether military and worthy one of the founders of Independence."[10]

To Jefferson, Monroe expressed himself with more despair than indignation. "Our military operations," he wrote, "have been unsuccessful. One army has been surrendered under circumstances which impeached the integrity of the commander; and to the north, in the whole extent of the country, so important and delicately circumstanced as it was, the management had been most wretched."[11]

Both the War and Navy departments were without competent leadership. Monroe recognized that fact. But the approaching elections made any changes in the Cabinet too risky, politically. It was Madison who hinted that Monroe himself should take over the War Department. Monroe was the only member of the administration with any military experience, and Madison had been relying on him for advice during the period of hasty military preparation that had kept Madison burning candles till daylight in the offices of the Departments of War and the Navy. Monroe, however, whose lifelong weakness was an ambition to see himself in a leading military role, wished to take a more active part in the war than even the highest post in the War Department would afford him. Indeed, im-

[259]

mediately after receiving the news of Hull's surrender, he had written to Madison, offering to take a volunteer commission and to assume command of the forces gathering in Kentucky and Ohio to recapture Detroit.[12] Madison doubted that he could legally give such a commission but was willing to risk it.

In the meanwhile, Secretary of War Eustis, aware of the general dissatisfaction with his direction of the war, sent in his resignation. And when, at the moment Monroe was on the point of starting for the West, there arrived letters containing news of the commission of Major-General just given by Kentucky's governor to Harrison, the popular idol of the moment in that state and in Ohio, Monroe could do nothing but gracefully comply with the President's request that he take Eustis's place immediately, if only *pro tempore*. It was understood that this left "the ultimate decision on the other question open to further consideration."[13]

27

The British in Washington

MADISON could hardly have hoped that the war would not figure as an issue in the presidential campaign of 1812. It was a foregone conclusion that the Federalists would make the most of the ignominious defeats suffered on the Canadian border by the government forces and themselves take full credit for the astounding successes which had distinguished the little navy's performance. The glorious naval victories of the summer of 1812—the *Constitution's* capture of the *Guerrière*, Decatur's *Macedonian* exploit, the *Wasp's* capture of the *Frolic*, Admiral Bainbridge's capture of the *Java*—all were claimed as Federalist successes. Were they not due entirely to the initiative of Federalist commanders in pursuing a strategy directly opposed to that laid down by the Republican Secretary of the Navy, Hamilton, who had directed that the navy be gathered in squadrons and limited to defense of the ports of New York and Boston? It was Decatur who had proposed the plan of sending out American ships "with as large a supply of provisions as they can carry, not more than two frigates in company, without giving them any specific instructions as to place of cruising, but to rely on the enterprise of the officers." Sailing far beyond Hamilton's puny horizons, these ships had triumphed against British might again and again, each triumph an indictment of the Republican Secretary of the Navy and the Republican Congress that had refused every Federalist appeal for a navy.

Neither the Federalist attack on the administration's conduct of the war, however, nor the bitter offensive launched against Madison from within the party, especially by the rival candidate for the Republican nomination, De Witt Clinton, proved effective enough. Re-elected, Madison turned to the problems of reorganization within the Cabinet. Monroe was given to understand that he could, if he wished, remain permanently in the War Department. Sérurier, having heard the rumor, was inclined to believe it, on the score of Monroe's "zeal in organizing his department." His comments, impersonal, unprejudiced, the evaluation of a contemporary, have unique value. "Mr. Monroe," he writes, "is not a brilliant man, and no one expects to find a great captain in him; but he served through the War of Independence with much bravery under the orders and by the side of Washington. He is a man of great good sense, of the most austere honor, the purest patriotism and the most universally admitted integrity. He is loved and respected by all parties."[1]

But Monroe still longed for a military role, and, as he wrote Jefferson, "the question remaining undecided relative to the command of the army," he decided against the War Department post.

The appointment went, instead, to General Armstrong, a choice Madison was bitterly to regret. The antagonism between Armstrong and Monroe was of long standing. Gallatin thought the new secretary a "devil." And the fatal dissension within the Cabinet bred by the friction between its most important members was to come dangerously near wrecking the already fragile Madisonian structure.

Monroe was not slow in perceiving Armstrong's own ambition to assume command of the armies in the field, and soon warned Madison, cautioning him against the danger of allowing one man to combine the duties of head of the War Department and of the Army. In Armstrong, Monroe saw an infant Napoleon plotting his way to the country's highest office through its battlefields.[2] Madison, as usual, temporized, and paid the awful price of the fall of Washington.

It was Armstrong who, in his role of generalissimo of the American forces, instituted in Canada a policy of ruthlessness that provoked the British to the series of reprisals culminating in the capture and burning of the American capital.

On the eighteenth of August, Monroe had received the British manifesto declaring that "in carrying into effect measures of retaliation . . . for the wanton destruction . . . committed in upper Canada . . ." orders had gone out to the British fleet in American

The British in Washington

waters "to destroy and lay waste such towns and districts upon the coast as may be found assailable."[3] America had been expecting something of the sort for many months. In July, 1813, indeed, a British reconnaissance cruise up the Chesapeake had spurred Congress to thoughts of placing arms "in the hands of all able-bodied men . . . willing to be embodied to perform military duty" to defend Washington.[4] But the suggestion had been opposed with all the energy characteristic of the Committee of Military Affairs when fighting any useful expenditure of the public funds. The committee was supported in its stand by Madison himself, who still cherished the delusion that the enemy would take no action that might imperil the valuable contraband trade humming along the Atlantic coast. As Dolly Madison fretfully exclaimed, ". . . all the city and Georgetown (except the Cabinet) have expected a visit from the enemy. . . ."[5]

On the twentieth of July, 1813, Mrs. Samuel Harrison Smith was writing to her sister Jane that despite the fact that "the British are such near neighbours and continue to menace us" there was "so little apprehension of danger in the city, that not a single removal of person or goods has taken place,—a number of our friends have desired leave to send their trunks here and a number have determined to come themselves, should the British effect a passage by the fort, so you see we are esteemed quite out of danger. . . . At present all the members and citizens say it is impossible for the enemy to ascend the river. . . ." And, adds the writer, "The presence of Genl. Armstrong and Col. Monroe animates and invigorates our soldiers."[6]

The war seemed to Washingtonians as remote as some martial passage in one of Scott's current best sellers. Weddings, dinners, assemblies, and Navy Yard balls at which the newly introduced waltz was the season's sensation, glittering embassy functions kept society from brooding too much upon the British menace. Washington was never more gaily populous. Describing the ball given in November, 1813, in honor of Captains Hull, Morris, and Stewart, Mrs. William Seaton remarked, "The assembly was crowded with a more than usual proportion of the youth and beauty of the city." The city was full of the nation's most personable young men, their attractiveness enhanced by uniforms. And Washington belles had never enjoyed a more crowded social program. When they were not dining or dancing with the young beaux, they gathered to discuss them at "fringe parties," ostensibly arranged for the making of cotton epaulets for the soldiers' uniforms.[7]

The New Year's reception in January, 1814, was no less brilliant than that of other years. But already, beneath the surface glitter, was gathering a dark current of apprehension. "You will see by the *Federal Republican,*" wrote Mrs. Seaton to her mother only a few months before the final catastrophe to the city, "that the plan might be carried into execution without a miracle, of seizing the President and Secretaries with fifty or a hundred men, and rendering this nation a laughing stock to every other in the world. I did not think much of these possibilities until hearing them discussed by General Van Ness and others, who, far from wishing a parade of guards or ridiculous apprehension to be entertained, were yet anxious that the city should not be unprepared for a contingency the danger of which did certainly exist."[8]

And when August, 1814, brought to the shores of the Chesapeake Admiral Cockburn and several thousand redcoats, the federal city was plunged into frenzy. The treasury was empty. The available troops were pitiably few. The city itself, hill-encircled, though in General Washington's opinion admirably situated for defense, was unprotected. Only the still uncompleted Fort Washington just below Alexandria and the hastily erected earthworks dating from the defense of Havre de Grace in 1813 could be classed as fortifications. The citizens' committee formed at that time to reorganize the District militia had since suspended its activities.

The first fine burst of activity dissipated itself in abuse of Madison. Then it flowered in a revival of the defunct committee above mentioned, and a call came from the mayor's office summoning all able-bodied men to the task of raising earthworks at the bridge across the Eastern Branch. Almost continuous drilling filled the open square facing the White House with noise and color, and from her windows Mrs. Madison discovered one morning an overnight flowering of tents on Meridian Hill.

Washington and Georgetown emptied quickly. "Very few women or children remained in the city," wrote Mrs. Smith. Mrs. Monroe was among the refugees, taking with her Maria and Eliza home to Virginia.[9] "Our troops," continues Mrs. Smith, "were eager for an attack and such was the cheerful alacrity display'd, that a

The British in Washington

universal confidence reign'd among the citizens and people. Few doubted our conquering."[10]

Madison had roused himself sufficiently to formulate a plan for mobilizing the militia in the Federal District and neighboring states for the city's defense, and the Cabinet had distinguished itself by agreeing to the measure. But Armstrong unfortunately found little difficulty in convincing the President, despite the dissenting opinions of Generals Van Ness, Wilkinson, and other experienced officers, that not Washington, but Baltimore was the goal of the invaders. The capital's defense was then placed in the hands of Brigadier General Winder, and Armstrong immediately withdrew from further preparation for Washington's defense, becoming, as Madison afterwards accused, "merely passive."

Winder, a Baltimore lawyer with a regular's commission, had but recently returned from Canada, where he had been held as a prisoner of war since June, 1813. Even an experienced, able general would have found the task facing him difficult: no ammunition, no trained troops, interference from the White House, all freedom of action strangled by a formidable array of superior officers. Hampered by lack of material, and the poor quality of what forces were given him—farmer-tradesmen militia for the most part—even a skilled soldier would have found himself in a quandary. But Winder had neither skill nor experience. His ineptitude reached unbelievable heights. From the very beginning, his conduct spelled disaster. Instead of remaining at headquarters to establish and organize the defensive force, he fluttered in every direction on scouting expeditions. Six precious weeks were wasted in this eccentric activity. Finally, Winder came to rest at Bladensburg, where he stationed one company of Maryland militia—two hundred and fifty men. The remaining Maryland militiamen and those of Virginia were hastening to the capital, which still was unfortified.

Two days after Monroe had received the British warning, the enemy troops, convoyed by the fleet, had landed at the little town of Benedict.

What happened then is vividly etched in the letters of fifteen-year-old Miss Brown describing to her family the hectic hours that followed in Washington:

"The news soon came that the British had landed at Benedict. . . .

JAMES MONROE

Then we hear of fifty-one British ships in Chesapeake Bay. The military are ordered out, those of Pennsylvania, Maryland, and Virginia, by order of General Armstrong, Secretary of War, commanded to be in readiness in case an attack should be made. The publick officials began packing up their valuable papers to be removed to places of safety. Now all is hurry and panic, armies gathering, troops moving in all directions, the citizens trying to secure such things as were most valuable and most easily transported, and flying from their homes to the country, Mr. Homans, in whose family I was a visitor, among the number.

"What became of the Secretary of State I do not remember, but much of his household furniture, together with the books and papers of the Department, were put on board of sundry flour boats and committed to the guardianship of Mr. Homans, who sent them up the Potomac."[11]

Monroe himself tells us "what became of the Secretary of State." In a letter of much later date he tells the story: "Calling on the President on the morning of the 18th of August, he informed me that the enemy had entered the Patuxent in considerable force, and were landing at Benedict. I remarked that this city (Washington) was their object. He concurred in the opinion, I offered to proceed immediately to Benedict with a troop of horse to observe their force, report it, with my opinion of their objects, and, should they advance on this city, to retire before them, communicating regularly their movements to the government. This proposal was acceded to. Captain Thornton, of Alexandria, was ordered to accompany me with a detachment of twenty-five or thirty of the dragoons of the District. I set out about one o'clock P. M. on the 19th, and arrived at ten next morning in sight of the enemy's squadron lying before Benedict, and continued to be a spectator of their movements until after the action at Bladensburg on the 24th."

The British commander camped, in a thunderstorm, only four miles above Benedict. Next morning, Monroe arrived and "took a view . . . from a commanding height below Benedict creek, of all the enemy's shipping near the town, and down the river to the distance at least of 8 or 10 miles. I counted 23 sq: rigged vessels. Few others were to be seen, & very few barges. I inferred from the latter circumstance that the enemy had moved up the river, either against

The British in Washington

Com: Barney's flotilla at Nottingham, confining their views to that object, or taking that in their way & aiming at the city, in combination with the force on Powtowmac, of which I have correct information. I had, when I left Aquosco Mills last night, intended to have passed over to the Powtowmac, after giving you an account of the vessels from the height below Benedict: but on observing the very tranquil scene which I have mentioned, I was led by the inference I draw from it to hasten back to take a view of the enemy's movements in this quarter, which it might be more important to the govt. to be made acquainted with." [12]

The guess Monroe had hazarded about an attack on Barney's flotilla at Nottingham proved correct. But his next attempt at anticipating the enemy's actions proved less fortunate, and he found himself "on the main road from Washington to Benedict" with Ross's redcoats nowhere in sight. The enemy had taken the road to Nottingham, marching from there to Marlboro. Winder himself, with an "observation force" spent the twenty-second of August watching their progress from Nottingham, with no attempt to hinder the advance. This bewildered general still held back from engaging the enemy for the reason that he was undecided as to their objective. And it was this indecision that bred his fatal plan of scattering his available forces along every possible road giving access to the capital, instead of assembling them in one body for the defense of the capital.

While Winder was making up his mind, the citizens of Washington had themselves taken the only step for the city's adequate defense, the erection of fortifications (and for this they themselves paid) in the village of Bladensburg.[13] It was toward Bladensburg that the British made their way. Eight miles from the village they struck camp for the night.

That same night, Winder, camped at Oldfields, was suddenly seized by a fear that the British, whose destination he was still uncertain of, might approach Washington by the river, and withdrew eight miles into the city, leaving a small defensive force at the bridge across the Eastern Branch, near the capital's Navy Yard. Apparently, his move had the consent of his numerous military advisers. The following morning, Winder sent a hurried message to Armstrong, expressing his doubts about the enemy's destination and asking for the "assistance of counsel from yourself and the Government." [14]

JAMES MONROE

With the reading of this incredible missive, there finally dawned upon Madison the imbecility of Winder's whole conduct and, doubtless, an inkling of the magnitude of his own folly in appointing Winder to the capital's defense. It was an unhappy and anxious President, who, accompanied by his Cabinet, followed Winder to the battlefield when the latter finally realized where the enemy lay.

The news of the British advance on Bladensburg had reached Washington at ten o'clock on the morning of August 24. Monroe, who happened to be with Madison at the moment, immediately offered to join General Stansbury and the Maryland militia, who were facing the British. Both the President and Winder urged him to do so, and Monroe left immediately. In something more than an hour he reached Stansbury's main forces, already deployed on open high ground commanding "the pass into Bladensburg and the bridge southwesterly of the town."[15]

Monroe's first move was to bring up into the front line of battle Lieutenant-Colonel Sterett's Fifth Regiment of Baltimore volunteers, who had been stationed fifty yards in the rear, as a reserve force. It was this change that gave rise to the criticism directed at Monroe on the score of Bladensburg. Armstrong, in particular, seized upon it in a deliberate attempt to throw a share of the responsibility for the disaster that followed on his old enemy's shoulders, referring to Monroe in the reports and inquiries that followed the battle as an "amateur, blundering tactician."[16] General Stansbury confined himself to the criticism that Monroe's action had caused the reserve regiment to leave the concealment of some orchards and thus be exposed to the enemy. Otherwise, he reported, "Colonel Monroe ... appeared extremely active in his efforts to aid the officers in the discharge of their duties, and exposed himself to much danger."[17]

Most interesting of all is the report of Lieutenant-Colonel Sterett, who records Monroe's own words to him as the debated change was being made: "Although you see I am active, you will please bear in mind that this is not my fault."[18] Monroe, obviously, was only too painfully aware of the shortcomings of the American command.

Winder did not arrive on the scene until the change in Stansbury's formation had been made. Asked by Monroe to view and approve what he had done, Winder was on the point of inspecting the new line when a column of British was made out about a mile

The British in Washington

away moving up along the eastern branch of the river. Whether Monroe would have at least received Winder's approval, whatever that was worth, will never be known. But the ensuing engagement certainly confirmed the wisdom of his action.

The eastern branch of the river being everywhere fordable, some of Stansbury's men had been deployed to cover the bridge and the river banks on either side. Numbering not more than six hundred men,[19] the American force was entirely too weak to act as more than an outpost to absorb the first shock of attack. Stansbury's remaining forces, despite Monroe's well-calculated attempt at reinforcement, were still too far in the rear to support the foremost ranks. These advance troops, moreover, were entirely ignorant of the fact that they were to bear the whole brunt of the imminent attack. Their first inkling of the real situation was the sudden arrival on the scene of a few breathless units of the main army of twenty-seven hundred men from Washington, and the far more astonishing appearance on horseback of Madison himself, accompanied by his Cabinet. And only the warning of a volunteer scout prevented the President and the highest officers of his government from riding right across the bridge into the arms of the enemy.[20]

The British, surging steadily forward, were not a little surprised to find the enemy a puny assemblage of "a few companies only, perhaps two or at the most three battalions." And, in the words of one of His Majesty's officers, "the rest seemed country-people."[21] Therefore the Light Brigade did not wait for its supports, but dashed across the bridge, sweeping it clear of its few defenders. Another body of redcoats was fording the river. Once on the opposite bank, the British were beyond reach of the battery in the half-completed fortifications, and the day's work was practically over for them. What remained of the American forces melted into a disorganized mob choking the road leading to Washington. Commodore Barney's few hundred bluejackets, who, refusing to obey the order to retreat persisted in facing the enemy, delayed the British at the capital's boundary line for only a brief half-hour.

"Ah, their commanders, Armstrong and Winder," laments Mrs. Smith. "On their shoulders lies the blame of our disastrous flight and defeat. Our men were all eager to fight and were marching on with a certainty of victory. More than 2000 had not fired their muskets, when Armstrong and Winder gave the order for a retreat, and to enforce that order added terror to authority! The English officers have told some of our citizens that they could not have stood more than 10 minutes longer, that they were exhausted with thirst, heat and fatigue."[22]

It was eight o'clock that evening before the silent, deserted streets of Washington filled with several British patrols, who lost no time in setting fire to the chief government buildings. The arsenal, the navy yard, the president's house, some private residences, and the great bridge across the Potomac also went up in flames. Admiral Cockburn, in his report, explains the slow progress of the British by admitting that "the victors were too weary . . ." for greater despatch.[23]

On her return to the city a few days later, Mrs. Smith wrote thus to a correspondent:

"The poor capitol! nothing but its blacken'd walls remained! 4 or 5 houses in the neighbourhood were likewise in ruins. Some men had got within these houses and fired on the English as they were quietly marching into the city, they killed 4 men and Genl. Ross's horse. . . . It was on account of this outrage that these houses were burnt. We afterwards look'd at the other public buildings, but none was so thoroughly destroy'd as the House of Representatives and the President's House. Those beautiful pillars in that Representatives Hall were crack'd and broken, the roof, that noble dome, painted and carved with such beauty and skill, lay in ashes in the cellars beneath the smouldering ruins.[24]

Mrs. Madison had remained in her house until a few hours before the enemy's arrival. She was so certain of an American victory, she told Mrs. Smith, that "she was calmly listening to the roar of cannon, and watching the rockets in the air, when she perceived our troops rushing into the city, with the haste and dismay of a routed force. The friends with her then hurried her away."[25]

Miss Brown related how her mother and sister saw "Mrs. Madison in her carriage flying full speed through Georgetown, accompanied by an officer carrying a drawn sword."[26]

The First Lady's place of refuge was apparently Mr. Richard Love's country house, Rokeby. Here, the story is told, the old colored cook, told by Mrs. Love to make some fresh coffee for the exhausted

The British in Washington

refugee, exclaimed, "I make a cup of coffee for you, Mis' Matilda, but I'm not gwine to hurry for Mis' Madison, for I done heerd Mr. Madison and Mr. Armstrong done sold the country to the British."[27]

Three days after Bladensburg, Madison emerged from his refuge in a private house some miles down the Potomac and reëntered the smoke-blackened capital to find himself reviled by the public, whose frame of mind was almost that described by the cook. Armstrong was at Fredericksburg, Winder absent also. Madison alone had to bear the brunt of the insults hurled by a bewildered, disappointed, blindly resentful city. The President, "miserably shattered and wo-begone,"[28] as a contemporary describes him at this moment of his career, was powerless to exercise the authority of his high office. His ineffectual activities before and during Bladensburg made him the butt of caricaturists and writers of doggerel, who gleefully created such gems as:

> Fly, Monroe, fly!
> Run, Armstrong, run
> Were the last words of Madison![29]

In another literary commemoration of current events, he is made to say:

> *Armstrong* and *Rush*, stay here in camp,
>   I'm sure you're not afraid.
> Ourself will now return; and you,
>   *Monroe*, shall be our aid.
> And *Winder*, do not fire your guns,
>   Nor let your trumpets play,
> 'Till we are out of sight—forsooth,
>   My horse will run away![30]

And so Madison, in his dilemma, turned to Monroe, whose popularity throughout these trying hours, remained undiminished, and asked him to take at least temporary charge of the War Department and to assume the military command of the Federal District. Monroe found no difficulty in establishing and maintaining his authority with both the citizenry and the army.

The errant Armstrong, equally culpable with Madison in the

JAMES MONROE

public eye, returned to Washington on the very day formal resolutions were passed by the First Brigade of militia stating their intention to serve no longer under his orders. Sulkily, Armstrong tendered his resignation. Winder, when his turn came, was even more reluctant to yield his command. But he had no choice.

Monroe remained alone in the field, a virtual dictator.

28

Secretary of War

AFTER THREE WEEKS as acting Secretary of War, Monroe came to a decision to take permanent charge of that department. Having twice accepted the post, he told Madison that twice to resign from it might give rise to the damning charge that he shrank from the responsibility. His permanent acceptance of the post—one which he declared he had "not sought, never wished"—would also, he felt, be the best answer to Armstrong's accusation that his removal from office had been "an affair of intrigue."[1]

Now, as Secretary both of War and of State, Monroe was given the greatest opportunity of his long career, in the critical period following the fall of Washington, to prove his ability. Hitherto, the chief events and accomplishments of his public life had been clouded by misunderstanding, untoward circumstance, and partial failure. As a diplomat he had been twice recalled and disavowed, first by the Federalists, then by Jefferson himself. This despite the important part he played in preventing an imminent war with the French Jacobin Republic and delaying another with Great Britain. The credit for his share in negotiating the Louisiana Purchase had been withheld from him by the northern members of his own party and by the supporters of Livingston. And, as for his military reputation, Bladensburg would not easily be forgotten.

In the long hours he was spending with Madison attempting to restore the prestige of the country and the administration, Monroe could not but be keenly aware that he was mending the warp and woof of his own battered past and gathering up the threads that would fashion the design of his own future.

JAMES MONROE

The gloom pervading the Octagon House, which was serving as the temporary capitol, was somewhat lightened by news that the British raid on Baltimore had failed and that the British fleet had come off badly in the engagement. And it was comforting to Madison's bruised pride and Monroe's dashed hopes to know that even Bladensburg had not diminished their personal popularity in the South, at least. Jefferson, voicing the sentiment of southerners, attributed that shameful episode solely to "the insubordinate temper of Armstrong" and "the indecision of Winder."[2]

The two men at the Octagon House needed all the encouragement the country could give them in the face of the desperate emergencies demanding immediate action. The British threatened from every side. Invasion "from Detroit, along the lakes Erie & Ontario, along the St. Lawrence, & Lake Champlain, & from Maine to the Mississippi, thro' the whole extent of the coast,"[3] as Monroe envisioned the danger, appeared imminent. A naval attack on New Orleans was to be expected. In the Chesapeake, British ships and men kept Washington in constant terror of a new attack. The lion, finished with its victim in Europe, would soon be on the hunt again on this side of the Atlantic, its claws completely free for the new prey.

The gravity of the situation within the country was no less disturbing. The most immediate danger facing the administration was the imminent collapse of the Treasury. The skillful Gallatin was absent, attempting to negotiate a peace at Ghent. His successors had been dismal failures. Just before the fall of Washington, the Philadelphia and Baltimore banks had been obliged to suspend specie payment. On the first of September, the banks of New York followed suit. New England was still sound financially, thanks to the influx of British gold. But a New England that was celebrating the English victory on the Continent by festal banquets and the singing of a *Te Deum* in King's Chapel, a New England that, in the words of its own illustrious John Quincy Adams, was in this dark hour guilty of "faction for patriotism, a whining hypocrisy for political morals, dismemberment for union, and prostitution to the enemy for state sovereignty,"[4] this New England controlled by a fanatically anti-administration, pro-British Federalist party would certainly be of less than no assistance to a Republican administration.

The United States was tacitly admitted to be bankrupt. Monroe,

Secretary of War

in September, 1814, not only found a "large amount of drafts which had been accepted by the late Secretary of war" to be lying over under protest, but also made the alarming discovery that "drafts for immense amounts were hourly appearing."[5] Grumblingly, the officers and men of the army defending the country accepted the depreciated notes with which the government had to pay them. The bounties provided by Congress for recruits could not be paid at all. And the ranks must be filled—immediately.

Congress, summoned in extra session on the nineteenth of September to cope with the urgent problems of national finance and the need for strengthening the military force, failed miserably of reaching a solution.

Monroe met the crisis with typical courage and sacrifice of self. For a month, he later related, he "never went to bed." "I had a couch in a room in my house on which I occasionally reposed, but from which even in the night, I was called every two hours, when the expresses arrived, to receive the intelligence which they brought, & to act on it." He had established a "chain of expresses" linking Washington with Baltimore, Philadelphia, Richmond, and the mouth of the Potomac.[6] Leaving Congress to its futile devices, Monroe wrested from District of Columbia banks their consent to advance funds, on his bare word of honor that they would be repaid. And endless future embarrassment was to be his reward for his generosity in personally guaranteeing the payment of drafts.

In his capacity as head of the War Department, he struggled frantically to recruit the strength of the regular army. The opposition he encountered was formidable. Not only was there Federalist championship of a state militia policy to overcome, but the unexpected opposition of the West, and Jefferson's own unshaken belief in the country's dependence on militia.

"It is nonsense," wrote the Republican party head to Monroe on October 16, "to talk of regulars. They are not to be had among a people so easy and happy at home as ours. We might as well rely on calling down an army of angels from heaven."[7]

But Monroe pleaded the necessity of a draft before a hostile Congress. Randolph sneeringly reminded the Secretary of his earlier distrust of such a measure. Miller of New York, voicing the sentiment not only of his own state but of the state legislatures of New

JAMES MONROE

England and the western communities, declared that the "States must and will take care of themselves: and they will preserve the resources of the States for the defense of the States."[8] The coalition formed to defeat the bill embodying the carefully studied propositions for increasing the regular army—dubbed "Monroe's conscription"—was too powerful. And all consideration of this vitally important issue was effectively postponed by a Senate vote on the twenty-eighth of December.

But from the ruins of his plans, Monroe was at least able to salvage such minor objectives as a doubling of the land bounty given for regular enlistments, authorization to enlist minors, and exemption from militia duty for persons who could furnish recruits for the regular army.

In lieu of a draft to create a large regular army, Monroe was forced to support the principle of individual state armies. By the Act of January 27, 1815, the President was authorized to incorporate state troops in the national army, the state forces to be raised locally but paid by the federal government.

The problems facing Monroe as Secretary of State were fully as serious as those posed by the War Department.

When Alexander I of Russia, desiring for private reasons a cessation of Anglo-American hostilities, communicated to the United States Minister to Russia, John Quincy Adams, a desire to mediate, Washington responded with alacrity. The situation at home—an empty Treasury, a weak army, a war-weary people, in New England a strong move towards secession—was one to urge a quick peace. The administration lost no time in sending envoys post-haste to St. Petersburg. But when Albert Gallatin and Senator James A. Bayard arrived in the Russian capital, it was to learn that Britain had refused Russian mediation.

The winter passed. Rumor told Washington that the English might be willing to treat directly, and an eager State Department quickly sent new instructions to the St. Petersburg embassy. When Great Britain confirmed the report by a clear offer to negotiate directly with the Americans, Henry Clay and Jonathan Russell quickly left to join the American commission.

July, 1814, saw Clay, Russell, Bayard, Gallatin, and Adams together for the first time, in Ghent, Belgium. Admiral Lord Gambier,

Secretary of War

Mr. Goulburn, under-secretary of state, and William Adams arrived to speak for England—an England victorious and proportionately arrogant. She had finished with Europe, for the time being, and could take her leisure in finishing off her opponent across the Atlantic. That this was her state of mind was immediately apparent from the tenor of the terms laid before the Americans. They were the demands of a victor dictating to a defeated enemy—despite the fact that British land victories had been offset by American exploits on the high seas, and neither side could claim a decisive triumph.

In October, 1814, Monroe sat studying the initial terms on which England would make peace: a neutral, Indian-occupied territory under British hegemony between the English and American frontiers in the north and west, American withdrawal from their fortified Great Lakes areas, curtailment or abolition of New England rights to the Canadian fisheries, the cession of a substantial area in northern Maine, and the granting to the British of the right to navigate the Mississippi.

The American commissioners, realizing their country's plight, decided to swallow their pride and play for time. It was an honorable stand. But across the Atlantic, the government was faced with a shameless New England eager enough to accept the galling terms. Two counties of Massachusetts were in the hands of the British; yet Pickering heaped abuse on the government for refusing terms that would make the loss permanent.[9] (This Federalist die-hard, when the rumor of a British naval expedition against New Orleans winged its way from Ghent, wrote to Lowell, gloating over the prospect of its probable success and the consequent severance of the Union.) [10] Peace with Great Britain was, to the Federalist party in the East, worth the dissolution of the United States of America.

The administration, no less than the negotiators in Ghent, however, would have none of it. The British suggested that the Americans offer a counter proposal. But the commission showed as little ability to reach a satisfactory agreement among its own members as had the opposing representatives of England and the United States. This internecine warfare was carried on chiefly between John Quincy Adams and Henry Clay, the first refusing to yield on the fisheries issue that concerned the East, the other remaining adamant in a determination to keep Britain out of the Mississippi by which the

West set such store. Each judged the other unreasonable, and what Adams described to his wife as "the most animated mutual oppositions" between the two men promised to keep the interminable negotiations going for another four months. Meanwhile hostilities continued across the Atlantic.

Less than a fortnight before the initial peace proposals reached him, Monroe had sent a warning message to General Jackson: "There is great cause to believe that the invasion menaced would take effect, in the expectation that while so strong a pressure was made from Canada & in this quarter, whereby the force of the country, & the attention of the government would be much engaged, a favorable opportunity would be afforded them to take possession of the lower parts of Louisiana, & of all the country along the Mobile."[11] The same post carried a letter from Monroe to the governor of Tennessee, asking for five thousand troops to be sent to Jackson. And a few days later a similar request went to Kentucky's governor, asking that twenty-five hundred men be dispatched to the General. Positive news had been received by the State Department, wrote Monroe, that "twelve or fifteen thousand men sailed from Ireland early in September." The expected raid on New Orleans was in motion. The frontier states lost no time in sending their best fighting material down the Mississippi to New Orleans' defense.

But the inimitable and provoking Jackson was very busy at the moment with plans for the capture of Pensacola. New Orleans would have to wait. Monroe must have been very near frenzy. He pleaded with the eccentric soldier to "take no measures that would involve this government in a contest with Spain," tried to persuade him that the defense of New Orleans was the prime military objective, wrote in December that it was "hoped" he would have "long since taken a suitable position on the river to afford complete protection to that city."[12]

Jackson was not the man to be easily perturbed. He lingered on in Mobile until the twenty-second of November, only four days before the British expedition under Sir Edward Pakenham sailed from Jamaica. His reason was a fear, he later said, that the fall of Mobile might leave the left bank of the Mississippi in the hands of the enemy, with the result that New Orleans would be lost.[13] To Monroe he dispatched a letter holding out the hope that "if his health permitted"

Secretary of War

the journey to New Orleans would take him but twelve days. He would go by land, "to have a view of the points at which the enemy might effect a landing."[14]

Only his characteristic good luck brought the imperturable General to New Orleans in advance of the enemy. Once arrived, his preparations proceeded in rather casual fashion. The first scene of the drama ended in the defeat and capture of the little flotilla defending the approach to the city. But a foggy night gave Jackson the advantage in the first land engagement. The advance British column had been checked. Back to a strategic vantage ground between a river and a thick tangle of swamp the astute Jackson marched his troops. All day his soldiers, together with Negroes of neighboring plantations, worked throwing up a breastwork. Before the hastily erected defenses curved a canal.

Pakenham, when he arrived at the place with the main army was, as one of his officers admits, taken completely by surprise and withdrew for a week of meditation. His attack, when it came, developed with surprising suddenness and met with complete failure. Before the mercilessly accurate fire of Jackson's frontiersmen Pakenham himself fell, like so many of his men. Once the British rallied, and the tide of battle almost turned. But General Lambert, the only British officer of high rank to have escaped injury or death, had lost the courage to face once again the terrible marksmanship of the enemy. He withdrew, and the Battle of New Orleans passed into history.

The news of New Orleans reached Washington almost simultaneously with the arrival in New York of a British sloop of war flying a flag of truce and bringing the news that the war was over. Britain had signed and ratified a peace satisfactory to the American commission.

Jackson's victory was no greater than that of the five gentlemen in Ghent, though more spectacular. Those five had fought a completely defensive battle, and a waiting game, and won. At the moment the first proposals had been made by England, she had had the Continent under her heel, and therefore acted as though the United States were there too. But certain events had, in the interval, worked a change. Stormy scenes between Alexander of Russia and Frederick Wilhelm, on the one hand, and Britain's Lord Castlereagh, on the other, had enlivened the early sessions of the Congress of Vienna.

JAMES MONROE

Castlereagh, up to then the chief obstacle to peace with the United States, began to see a possible need in the near future for all the military and naval resources England could muster. And the arguments of the all-powerful Duke of Wellington, who had bluntly told him that he had "no right, from the state of the war, to demand any concession of territory,"[15] no longer fell on deaf ears.

Thus the patience of the American negotiators was rewarded. When the new British proposals were studied, they were found innocent of any claim to the northwest territory or to sole possession of the Great Lakes and the *uti possidetis*. Gallatin's tactful suggestion to postpone the fisheries and Mississippi questions for future consideration was accepted, and the treaty signed.

True, the British still refused to treat on impressment and blockade or to consider the chief issues contained in Monroe's instructions to his envoys. But only Clay insisted on refusing the English offer on this account. The others, weighing more carefully the desperate situation at home, stood their ground, and December twenty-fourth, 1814, saw peace signed.

The wave of joyous relief which swept over the nation when news of the peace reached Washington washed away all the bitterness fomented by the disastrous events of the war. The coach and four that thundered down Pennsylvania Avenue on a February afternoon on its way to the Octagon House was sped on by the cheers of a wildly happy citizenry who knew that its passengers carried in their port-manteaux the Treaty of Ghent. And the graceful doors that looked out on New York Avenue and Eighteenth Street were thrown wide open in an orgy of entertaining and merrymaking that extended, the story goes, even to the servant quarters.[16]

"So general and heartfelt was the joy at being at peace again," wrote William Sullivan reminiscently some years later, "that celebrations were had in all the cities, in which both sexes, all ages, and all parties united, with the strongest enthusiasm. There were splendid processions, bonfires, and illuminations, as though the independence of the country had been a second time achieved."[17]

29

President James Monroe

IN THE PRESENCE of the Senate and House of Representatives, on February 12, 1816, Monroe and Tompkins, having received the electoral votes of all the states except Massachusetts, Connecticut, and Delaware, were declared President and Vice-President of the United States. On March 4, in a ceremony on which the "mildness and radiance of the day cast a brilliant hue,"[1] Monroe, who had been elected with "less bustle and *national* confusion than belongs to a Westminster election for a member of Parliament in England,"[2] took the oath of office as fifth president of the United States. *Niles' Register*, quoting from the *National Intelligencer*, described the ceremonies, which were performed in the open air for the first time since 1789, as "simple, but grand, animating, and impressive."[3]

Monroe had previously informed the President of the Senate that he would follow the usual custom of taking the oath of office in the chamber of the House of Representatives.[4] The Senate committee had accordingly drawn up an elaborate order of exercises. The Senate committee of arrangements was to have met Monroe, accompanied by the heads of the departments, the marshal of the District, and various other officials, at the door of the House, and to have escorted him to the Speaker's chair. The President of the Senate was to sit on the right, and the retiring President and Speaker on either hand. Definite places had been assigned to the foreign ministers and their suites, the justices of the Supreme Court, senators, and members of the House, while a limited section had been reserved for ladies. The gallery was to be open to the public. Unfortunately, however, the committee became embroiled in a quarrel with Clay, the Speaker of the House, already chagrined and deeply disappointed over Monroe's failure to appoint him to the coveted position of Secretary of State, and he refused the use of the House chamber, on the grounds that he did not believe the floor of the room was strong enough to support so great a crowd. The truth of the matter was that a disagreement existed concerning the use of the furniture belonging to the House, and Clay refused to yield. Consequently the committee erected an elevated portico in front of the hall of Congress, to accommodate the ceremonies.[5]

At eleven-thirty in the morning Monroe and Vice-President-elect Tompkins left Monroe's private residence,[6] attended by a large cavalcade of citizens on horseback and marshalled along the muddy, uneven streets of the designated route by the special deputies appointed for the occasion. Contemporary reporters were unable accurately to compute the number of carriages, horses, and persons present, but in estimating that between five and eight thousand people had turned out for the event, they were unanimous in declaring that "such a concourse was never before seen in Washington."

As Monroe, "the last of the Virginians," rose to deliver his inaugural address, his resemblance to Washington was striking. Broad shouldered and raw-boned, although shorter of stature than his illustrious predecessor, the calm and almost serene expression of his face, combined with features so heavily lined and regular as to have been chiselled from rock, and the grayish blue eye "which invited confidence,"[7] were very similar to the lineaments of the founder of the "Virginia Dynasty." Monroe, following the custom by which the inaugural address had become a statement of administrative policy, outlined the course he intended to pursue. Passing over in discreet silence such unorthodoxies as the establishment of the second national bank—the necessary outcome of the War of 1812—he assured the nation that the government once again lay "in the hands of the people," to whom all credit was due; that the states, respectively protected by the government under a "mild parental system," still "enjoyed their separate spheres." "From the commencement of our Revolution to the present day, almost forty years have elapsed, and from the establishment of this Constitution, twenty-eight. Through

President James Monroe

this whole term the Government has been what may emphatically be called self-government. And what has been the effect? To whatever object we turn our attention, whether it relates to our foreign or our domestic concerns, we find abundant cause to felicitate ourselves in the excellence of our institutions. During a period fraught with difficulties and marked by very extraordinary events the United States have flourished beyond example. Their citizens individually have been happy and the nation prosperous."[8]

But the Federalists found comfort in the promise to build roads and canals, with a "constitutional sanction," to give manufacturing "the systematic and fostering care of the Government." Industry and finance were to be encouraged: "Possessing as we do all the raw materials, the fruit of our own soil and industry, we ought not to depend in the degree we have done on supplies from other countries. While we are thus dependent the sudden event of war, unsought and unexpected, can not fail to plunge us into the most serious difficulties. It is important, too, that the capital which nourishes our manufactures should be domestic, as its influence in that case instead of exhausting, as it may do in foreign hands, would be felt advantageously on agriculture and every other branch of industry. Equally important is it to provide at home a market for our raw materials, as by extending the competition it will enhance the price and protect the cultivator against the casualties incident to foreign markets."[9]

Foreign policy would take a course based on preparedness at home and a firm intention to cherish and preserve the national honor, which Monroe deemed "national property of the highest value." Speaking of "dangers from abroad," he said: "We must support our rights or lose our character, and with it, perhaps, our liberties. A people who fail to do it can scarcely be said to hold a place among independent nations. National honor is national property of the highest value. The sentiment in the mind of every citizen is national strength. It ought therefore to be cherished."[10]

The failure of Jefferson's policy of embargoes and commercial sanctions had taught a lesson which the War of 1812 had confirmed. To protect citizens engaged in commerce and navigation, as well as in the fisheries, the country must have an army and a navy. ". . . our coast and inland frontiers should be fortified, our Army and Navy, regulated upon just principles as to the force of each, be kept in perfect order, and our militia be placed on the best practicable footing. To put our extensive coast in such a state of defense, as to secure our cities and interior from invasion, will be attended with expense, but the work when finished will be permanent, and it is fair to presume that a single campaign of invasion, by a naval force, superior to our own, aided by a few thousand land troops, would expose us to a greater expense, without taking into the estimate the loss of property and distress of our citizens, than would be sufficient for this great work. Our land and naval forces should be moderate, but adequate to the necessary purposes—the former to garrison and preserve our fortifications and to meet the first invasions of a foreign foe, and, . . . the latter, retained within the limits proper in a state of peace, might aid in maintaining the neutrality of the United States with dignity in the wars of other powers and in saving the property of their citizens from spoliation."[11]

The black-robed Chief Justice Marshall administered the oath to the man who as a boy had shared with him a hard bench in Parson Campbell's wilderness schoolroom. The report of a single gun, followed by salutes from the navy yard, the battery, and Fort Warburton, and from several pieces of ground artillery, announced the accession of the last "revolutionary" Executive.[12]

Monroe and his wife returned to their home to receive the congratulations of their friends, the heads of the departments, and the foreign ministers as well as the members of Congress and the great throng of citizens and strangers who had come to Washington for the occasion. The ceremonies were fittingly concluded at a brilliant ball that evening at Davis' Hotel.

When the Madisons were forced to flee from the blazing presidential residence by Ross's troops, they transferred their menage to the Tayloe house. Here they remained until the end of Madison's term, for their former home had been badly damaged and was undergoing extensive repairs. Because of the numerous details involved in the winding up of their affairs in Washington, the Madisons lingered on at the Tayloe house until April 8, when they quietly set out for their rural Virginia home at Montpellier. Mr. Crowninshield, who was at that time Secretary of the Navy, has left among his papers a rather sad picture of this departure. "They came on board the steamboat about 8 o'clock," he wrote, "no people no friends to accompany them just as I expected it would be, so Commander Rodgers, Paulding and myself agreed to go down the river as far as Acquia Creek . . . & saw them started, I hope not forever for I love them dearly. . . ."[13]

The Monroes continued to stay on in the residence they had lately occupied, for Mrs. Monroe refused to live in the former President's house, and intended to have the drawing room "with a little more distinction."[14] About the middle of May she left Washington to spend the summer with her children on the Monroe estate, in Loudoun County, Virginia, while her husband, pending his reoccupation of the "President's Palace," also prepared to leave Washington.

Even before he had announced his Cabinet appointments, Monroe had declared his intention of visiting all the forts and posts along the seaboard from Baltimore to Portland, and from Portland to proceed westward, by way of the lower lakes, to Detroit. He contended that inasmuch as Congress had voted large sums of money for the coastal fortifications and the frontier outposts, for the building of ships and naval dockyards,[15] and had placed the responsibility for seeing that the construction was faithfully carried out upon the executive, it was up to him to make a personal inspection of the work while it was in the process of building. He also intended to inspect the various manufacturing establishments. Daniel Webster himself had called upon Monroe, and as a representative from a Federalist section had urged a New England tour as a means of strengthening patriotism, placating the disaffected Federalist groups, and restoring political harmony.[16] Many members of his own party grumbled about the considerable expense entailed and the loss of valuable time that should have been devoted to the pressing problems confronting the new administration.

This criticism notwithstanding, Monroe left Washington May 31 on a journey of three and one-half months, which was to take him through thirteen states in a triumphal tour such as had not been seen since the days of Washington.[17] In accordance with his desire to "assume no style in regard" to his countrymen other than that of a fellow citizen, he travelled as privately as he could, his dress and manners giving him more the appearance of a plain, substantial, but well-informed farmer, than the distinguished personage he was.[18]

Monroe arrived in Baltimore about two o'clock on the first Sunday in June. After inspecting Fort McHenry and the militia, and addressing the citizens of the city, he left by steamboat for Philadelphia. Here, and at Trenton (where he himself had been wounded) and New Brunswick, he received the same thunderous welcome. Municipal authorities, militia, and crowds of townspeople, eager to see a president, met him on the outskirts of each town, and amid the firing of the cannon and the ringing of bells escorted him to the appointed reception point, where addresses were exchanged. By the time the President had reached New York, on June 9, what had started as a tour of duty had become a triumphal progress. In New York he remained with Vice-President Tompkins, at his home on Staten Island, visiting the military works in the vicinity. Landing at the Battery under a salute,[19] he delivered an address, visited Harlem Heights, the forts in the lower bay and the state arsenal, and later was conveyed in a steam frigate manned by "the brave tars of the navy yard"[20] up the palisaded Hudson to make a minute inspection of the frowning fortress at West Point.

Having won the hearts of the people of New York by his republican plainness, ease, and simplicity, he left on the twentieth for New Haven. Throughout New England, in every town along the route, the remnants of the old trained bands of '76, together with the 1812 vintage of heroes, turned out to greet their comrade-in-arms. In recalling the glories of the two wars which the nation had suffered, the feuds and divisions so long separating Republicans and Federalists faded into the background. They vied with one another in doing honor to this "last of the revolutionary farmers." To the music of fife and drum the new civic accord was ratified, and an Americanism was reborn that submerged the old Anglo-Gallic factions.

The editor of the New Haven *Herald* adequately described the feeling prevalent throughout New England:

"The dress of the President has been deservedly noticed in other papers for its neatness and republican simplicity. He wore a plain blue coat, a buff under dress, and a hat and cockade of the revolutionary fashion. It comported with his rank, was adapted to the occasion, well calculated to excite in the minds of the people, the remembrance of the day which 'tried men's souls.' It was not the sound of artillery, the ringing of bells, nor the splendid processions alone, from which we are to judge of the feelings and sentiments

President James Monroe

of the people on this occasion — It was the general spirit of hilarity which appeared to manifest itself in every countenance, that evinced the pride and satisfaction with which the Americans paid the voluntary tribute of respect to the ruler of their own choice—to the magistrate of their own creation. The demon of party for a time departed, and gave place for a general burst of National Feeling."[21] And so the President proceeded—from New Haven to Hartford, to New London, and thence to Newport. Arriving at Bristol, he stopped at the splendid mansion of George DeWolf and "partook of refreshments."[22] The approach to the house had been strewn with roses, and the large crowds of women lining the pathway showered him with blossoms.[23] A reception was held at Providence, to which he had come by steamboat. While viewing the cotton mills at Pawtucket, he was shown "the first frame upon the Arkwright plan put in operation in this country."[24]

Monroe's prospective visit to the worthy commonwealth of Massachusetts, the stronghold of Federalism, had been a subject of legislative discussion and provision, and the manner of his entry had been laid down at a town meeting with the greatest nicety and precision. On his arrival at Dedham he was welcomed by one of the Governor's aides and escorted to Boston-neck. Here the municipal authorities, the reception committee, and squadrons of cavalry met him, while thousands of citizens on horseback and in carriages thronged the narrow streets. Approximately forty thousand people, including four thousand school children, participated in the opening reception in which "the representative of eight millions of people was received as kings never can be."[25]

The strain of the subsequent six days must have told on Monroe. It was a constant round of festivities, excursions, inspections, and addresses, which took him through the harbor, to Bunker Hill, and to Cambridge, and opened to him the portals of many a Beacon Hill home. Among numerous others, Mrs. William Gray gave a magnificent reception, where Monroe captivated the female portion of the social élite. The *Patriot* observed: "The easy and affable manners of the president charm all hearts; and make him as great a favorite with the ladies, for his urbanity and politeness, as he is with the other sex for those high and commanding powers of mind, which have produced for him his present exalted situation."[26]

JAMES MONROE

In connection with his trip out to Cambridge, where Dr. Kirkland, the venerable President of Harvard College, conferred upon him the degree of Doctor of Laws, Edward Everett Hale has recounted an amusing Harvard tradition. At a meeting of the college faculty in 1817 it was announced that a certain senior, who was commander of the Harvard Washington Corps, the military establishment of the college boys, was to be suspended for a misdemeanor. Dr. Kirkland, "dear and courteous, dozing in his chair," was roused to life and activity. "Send away Mr. ―― when Mr. Monroe is coming? Who will command my Harvard Washington Corps when the President visits the college?" The student remained, presented arms to Mr. Monroe, and fifty years later "donated a very important and expensive building" to the college.[27]

In spite of the tremendous ovations accorded him in Boston, Monroe found that some of the people, still moved by party feeling, were "unwilling to amalgamate with their former opponents."[28] In an address to the minority of the legislature of Massachusetts he expressed a hope that these recalcitrants would "all unite in the future in the measures necessary to secure ... the success" of the government, and pointed out that "the circumstances of the present epoch" were "peculiarly favorable" to such a course.[29]

The *Chronicle and Patriot*, a local paper, observed: "The visit of the President seems wholly to have allayed the storms of party. People now meet in the same room who would before scarcely pass the same street—and move in concert, where before the most jarring discord was the consequence of an accidental rencounter.... If no other effect is produced by the president's visit, this alone will be an ample remuneration to him for his journey."[30]

Another contemporary publication, the *Centinel*, characterized Monroe's visit "as an event which has a more direct tendency than any other, without any violation of principles, to remove the prejudices, and harmonize feelings, annihilate dissentions, and make us *one people:* for we have the sweet consolation ... to rest assured that the president will be president, not of a party, but of a great and powerful nation."[31] And it was this same newspaper which coined the expression, the "Era of Good Feeling," used ever since, perhaps somewhat erroneously in the light of later developments, to characterize the administration of Monroe.

President James Monroe

Monroe proceeded eastward through Lynn, Salem, Beverly, Dover, Kennebunk, and Saco to Portland (where a year-old calf weighing 1300 pounds was exhibited to him),[32] the same ovations greeting him everywhere. The Salem *Register* reported that "the president engaged all hearts. The most brilliant circles were formed around him, and the rising generation received every token of his friendship with sure records on their hearts of that affection he displayed before them. The President, in the constant attention he paid to the importunate wishes of the citizens, discovered no symptom of fatigue, and gave no notice of the hours which were to limit our pleasures. The same cheerfulness, freedom, and presence of mind, appeared through all the services which each day required of him. . . ."[33]

The President turned westward, crossed New Hampshire and Vermont, and steamed down Lake Champlain to Plattsburg, where he paused to write to Jefferson:

"I have been, eastward, as far as Portland, and after returning to Dover in N. Hampshire, have come here, by Concord & Hanover in that State, & Windsor, Montpelier, & Burlington, in Vermont. Yesterday I visited Rouse's Point, within two hundred yards of the boundary line, where we are engaged in erecting a work of some importance; as it is supposed to command the entrance into the lake from Canada.

"When I undertook this tour, I expected to have executed it, as I might have done, in an inferior station, and even of a private citizen, but I found, at Baltimore that it would be impracticable for me to do it. I had, therefore, the alternative, of either returning home or complying with the opinion of the public, & immediately I took the latter course, relying on them to put me forward as fast as possible, which has been done. I have been exposed to excessive fatigue & labour in my tour, by the pressure of a very crowded population, which has sought to manifest its respect, for our Union, & republican institutions, in every step I took, and in modes wh. made a trial of my strength, as well physically as mentally."[34]

Late in July he reached Ogdensburg and thence proceeded to Sacketts Harbor. From this, the finest harbor on the lake and the site of Fort Pike, a naval vessel carried him to Fort Niagara, Niagara Falls, and Buffalo, where he was entertained by Peter B. Porter. Before turning homeward he went as far westward as Detroit, preferring the storms of Lake Erie to the hazards of the wilderness road through northern Ohio.

Reëntering Washington in September, Monroe was happy in the thought that the old prejudices against him as a Southerner, a Virginian, and a President opposed to the interests of the North and the East, had disappeared.

By this time the presidential mansion had been made habitable; a heavy coat of white paint had been applied to obliterate the marks of the fire that had permanently disfigured the stone work of the house, and soon it was known as "The White House." Monroe, however, was very apprehensive of the effects of the fresh painting and plastering, and as he also wished to visit his family and recuperate from his arduous journey, he spent only two or three days in Washington, during which he greeted his new Secretary of State, John Quincy Adams, and then he set out for Virginia.[35]

During the previous fall and early spring, Monroe had devoted a great deal of thought to the selection of his Cabinet. This was to be not only an advisory body in every sense of the word, rather than a collection of "mere appendages and creatures" of the President, but it must be a representative and congenial group. He originally intended to bestow the four most important Cabinet positions on men from the four principal sections of the Union: the East, Middle, South, and West. Not only would this preserve harmony among the sections, but the knowledge of local details which each man would bring him would be of inestimable value in Cabinet discussions.

Such was his original intention, but he found it impracticable to carry it out completely.[36] Rising above sectional predilections and recognizing capacity, he did not hesitate to appoint John Quincy Adams as his Secretary of State. Adams' long experience and eminent success in the foreign service, and the fact that he represented the more or less disgruntled North, made him the logical choice. In a letter to Thomas Jefferson, on February 23, 1817, Monroe explained his motives for the selection:

"On full consideration of all circumstances, I have thought that it would produce a bad effect, to place anyone from this quarter of the Union, South in the dept. of State, or from the south or west. You

President James Monroe

know how much has been said to impress a belief, on the country, north & east of this, that the citizens from Virga., holding the Presidency, have made appointments to that dept., to secure the succession, from it, to the Presidency, of the person who happens to be from that State. . . . It is, however, not sufficient that this allegation is unfounded. . . . With this view, I have thought it advisable to select a person for the dept. of State, from the Eastern States, in consequence of which my attention has been turned to Mr. Adams, who by his age, long experience in our foreign affairs, and adoption into the republican party, seems to have superior pretentions to any there." [37]

Henry Clay, burning with presidential ambitions, had long coveted the secretaryship as the "stepping stone" to the presidency. Furious at the selection of Adams, he coldly turned down Monroe's offer of the Department of War. To William Crawford, the Georgian, Monroe's only serious rival for the presidency, fell the Treasury Department. Unable, after Shelby's and Jackson's refusal, to find a western candidate to take over the War Department, Monroe appointed John C. Calhoun, a rising congressman from South Carolina. To William Wirt of Virginia, a close personal friend of Monroe's and one of the ablest lawyers of his day, went the attorney-generalship, while Crowninshield of Massachusetts, a hold-over from the previous administration, continued as the Secretary of the Navy. Thus, although his plan had not completely succeeded, for the West failed to secure representation, and although Virginia and the South had gained a preponderance of weight, he anticipated some protest from his fellow Virginians on his selections: "I can hardly hope," he wrote, "that our Southern gentlemen, who have good pretentions, will enter fully into this view of the subject, but having form'd my opinion on great consideration, I shall probably adhere to it." [38]

Nor was Monroe able, in dealing with such diverse personalities and with men so fundamentally jealous of one another, each so seriously intent on pushing his own individual cause, to achieve complete harmony in his Cabinet. Adams, Calhoun, and Wirt remained true to their chief, but Crawford was a different matter. His disappointment over failure to capture the presidency for himself was too acute to allow gratitude to Monroe for the magnanimity of offering him a Cabinet seat. He continually prepared wily pitfalls for the new Executive and in general exacerbated the underlying personal rivalries and ambitions in the Cabinet. But, as Adams' invaluable *Diary* attests, Monroe, by proceeding carefully and slowly and allowing crises to subside of their own accord, did succeed admirably in keeping the peace and restraining the rival personalities: "These Cabinet councils," wrote Adams, "open upon me a new scene and new views of the political world. Here is a play of passions, opinions, and characters different in many respects from those in which I have been accustomed heretofore to move. There is slowness, want of decision, and a spirit of procrastination in the President, which perhaps arises more from his situation than his personal character."[39]

Other important appointments to which Monroe turned his attention were those in the diplomatic corps. Richard Rush, the former attorney-general, replaced Adams at the Court of St. James's, while Albert Gallatin remained on at the French capital. William Pinkney, who was serving in St. Petersburg but who wished to return home to attend to professional duties, was succeeded by George Campbell of Tennessee.

In addition to this capable group of official advisers and representatives, both at home and abroad, Monroe had in Jefferson and Madison two of the ablest living statesmen. A voluminous correspondence, at times of flood-like proportions, was carried on by this illustrious triumvirate; Monroe usually sought the advice of both upon every important question. And even on many points upon which no opinion had been sought, Jefferson poured forth advice. On every conceivable subject, from the "different kind of wines to be procured in France and Italy" for the denuded cellars of the White House to the latest military escapades of that irrepressible Republican, General Jackson, the old party leader had his say. Often it would appear that his correspondent had difficulty in keeping pace with him, for on April 23, 1817, Monroe wrote apologetically: "I have to acknowledge three letters from you of the 8th, 13th, and 16th of this month."[40]

Thus with a new feeling of national solidarity ushering in an era of peace and prosperity, with domestic breaches healed for the time being, Monroe turned his attention to the foreign breaches which "gaped with threatening jaws."[41] Almost immediately he plunged into the pressing problems in the field of foreign affairs created by the vexatious relations existing between Spain and the United States. In the early years of the nineteenth century the Spanish Empire in the western hemisphere had split into states which were now proclaiming their independence of the mother country. Their clamorous pleas for recognition and aid from the United States had been a constant menace to American neutrality and amicable relations with Spain all during Madison's administration, and had already been under discussion during Monroe's term as Secretary of State. This issue proved to be one of Monroe's gravest presidential concerns.

Spain's South American subjects, along with those in Central America and Mexico, had never lacked for general grievances against Spain. They had long suffered under the tyrannous rule of Castilian viceroys intent only on extorting the maximum profits from their hapless colonists. While Spain had been master of her own domain in Europe, she had pursued a narrow and selfish economic policy, treating her colonies as her own private trading monopoly and excluding all foreign commerce and intercourse. As her influence in Europe waned toward the latter part of the eighteenth century, adventurers from various European countries mysteriously appeared in the many provinces, stirring up trouble and seeking to break down the commercial monopoly by promoting illicit trade with Europe. Added to these fundamental causes of disaffection was the leaven of philosophical doctrines, springing from the American and French revolutions, eagerly accepted and glibly discussed by the alert young creoles.[42]

Aside from an unsuccessful attempt, made by the Indians of Upper Peru in 1780, to throw off the yoke of Spain, the first intelligent attempt at independence—the real forerunner of the nineteenth-century disturbances—was made by one Francisco de Miranda. He was a soldier of fortune born in Caracas, Venezuela, who had served with the French forces in the Revolutionary War. His plots for establishing the independence of South America were discovered, and after fleeing to the United States he sailed for Europe, where, during the late 1780's he wandered from one capital to another seeking material support for his schemes. In 1806, at his own expense, and with the aid of two American citizens, he equipped a vessel and sailed from New York for Venezuela on a filibustering expedition. Landing near Caracas, he proclaimed the Colombian Republic but was shortly put to flight. A second attempt in 1810, after a hasty proclamation of republics in Venezuela and New Granada, was defeated and resulted in his capture and imprisonment.[43]

Goaded on by their grievances and fired by this example, the Spanish vice-royalties rose in a general revolt about 1808. Napoleon had invaded Spain, deposed the reigning monarch, Charles IV, and established his brother Joseph upon the Spanish throne. Immediately juntas sprang up both in Spain and in the colonies, pledging allegiance to Charles's son, Ferdinand VII. During the European struggles of the ensuing six years, while Spain became the football of European power politics and her relations with her colonies became daily more tenuous, a change was occurring in those South American dependencies. To thinking people who realized that Ferdinand might never be restored and who abhorred the idea of an alien rule, the idea of independence grew daily more attractive. New ideas of liberty, fresh from Europe, were flooding the continent and were quickly propagated by the printing presses and the radical societies which sprang up.

Open rebellion flared first in Miranda's own province, under Bolívar. After Napoleon's defeat and the restoration of the Bourbons in the person of Ferdinand, the latter attempted a reactionary program. Setting aside the liberal constitution adopted by the Cortes of Cadiz in 1812, which recognized the colonies as an integral part of the nation, the restored king attempted to reduce Buenos Aires, Cartagena, and Mexico by force. Buenos Aires sent a deputation to Madrid, offering a conditional allegiance. The offer was refused, and revolt flared throughout South America: in the mountain fastnesses of Chile and in Paraguay, under Bolívar in the North, and under San Martín in the southern provinces. Only in Brazil, where an hereditary empire had been established in 1808, was there comparative quiet.

It was obvious from the very beginning of the struggle that although the United States of necessity must insist upon a policy of strict neutrality, a rigid pursuance of the principles of international law would be impossible, considering the intensity of the feelings provoked by the revolutions. To the idealistic American citizens, the South American patriots were kindred souls fighting for liberty and, as such, deserved all aid and assistance which could be given. And

President James Monroe

from the very outset of the struggle the South Americans earnestly and actively sought English and particularly American aid and sympathy for their cause, hoping for early recognition of their independence. Thus, while the United States government sought to maintain a strict neutrality, sending only unofficial observers to South America to report on the progress of events, the entire situation was clouded by the clamoring of South American agents for aid and recognition and by the over-zealous attitude of various American citizens who insisted upon active participation in the cause.

In 1811 the Junta of Venezuela sent Orea as a special agent to the United States. His unofficial conference with Monroe, who was then Secretary of State, brought forth expressions of friendliness and sympathy for the struggling colonies; but news of Miranda's surrender and the apparent failure of the movement made recognition impossible. While Monroe was cautious, he was nevertheless in ardent sympathy with the cause. It occurred to him that the question of recognition might be raised in Congress, and that through the American ministers abroad influence could be exerted in Europe to secure like action there.[44] And on May 14, 1812, Secretary Monroe issued the following instructions to Alexander Scott, who had recently been appointed American agent to Venezuela:

"The United States are disposed to render to the Government of Venezuela, in its relations with Foreign Powers, all the good offices that they may be able. Instructions have been already given to their Ministers at Paris, St. Petersburg, and London, to make known to these Courts that the United States take an interest in the independence of the Spanish Provinces."[45]

From the moment that Joseph Bonaparte was placed on the Spanish throne in 1808, diplomatic relations between Spain and the United States had ceased to exist. In spite of the fact that the Supreme Central Junta in Spain, which claimed to act in the name of the deposed Ferdinand VII, had sent out in 1809 Don Luis de Onis as envoy extraordinary and minister plenipotentiary to the United States, Onis was accorded no official recognition. Madison assured him of the desire of the United States to maintain a good understanding with Spain, and said that as long as the crown was in dispute the United States, in accordance with the laws of 1794 and 1797, would follow a policy of strict neutrality. She would be neutral not only in the struggle between the Spanish factions but in that between Spain and her revolted colonies. It would be regarded in the light of a civil war, the public vessels of both belligerents being received on the same footing, and both might purchase or export articles not appearing on the enumerated list of contraband.

Such were the intentions of the United States government, but the loopholes in the neutrality legislation were gaping, and the President had no power to interfere to prevent the commission of offenses. All that had to be done to sidestep the law was to have an American construct and equip a vessel in any American port, and sell it to a foreigner, who in turn utilized it to plunder the shipping of friendly nations. This practice was followed extensively. Ship after ship cleared from the Baltimore and New Orleans customs houses as merchantmen, and after touching at an adjacent "foreign" port would hoist the flag of some South American republic and start depredations on Spanish commerce. There were instances, too, of ships from the South American provinces entering American ports, openly purchasing contraband, and even enlisting United States citizens to serve in the rebel forces. Meanwhile, all that Don Onis could do was to protest these outrages in public notices.

By 1815 the contest in Spain was no longer in doubt. Don Onis was received as minister and immediately began action to secure prosecution and conviction of the men involved in the breaches of neutrality. The ensuing investigation yielded the Neutrality Act of 1817, which extended the laws so that violators of the act would be subject to fine, imprisonment, and forfeiture of their vessels.[46]

Thus affairs stood at Monroe's accession to the presidency. Along with the majority of American people he warmly sympathized with the South American cause but he hesitated to recognize at once the independence of the revolting provinces. Not only did he realize that such an act on the part of the United States might very well involve that country in serious difficulties with Europe, but before committing the country to such a change of attitude he felt it important to ascertain, at first hand, just what were the prospects for the colonies' maintaining their independence. To the average outsider a disunited population, lately released from centuries of ignorance and poverty, and now under the leadership of rival generals, presented no great promise of maintaining that precarious independence.

President James Monroe

Accordingly, in May, 1817, acting on his own responsibility, Monroe publicly announced in the press his appointment of three commissioners to study at first hand the South American situation.[47] Caesar A. Rodney, Theodore Bland, and John Graham were the men selected to coast among the South American ports in a ship of war. There were innumerable delays of a personal nature, and these commissioners did not set sail until December. Meanwhile, other events occurred which caused Monroe to think that actual recognition might be advisable.

During the first summer of Monroe's administration a swarm of pirates and vagabonds, adventurers and filibusters, under the leadership of a Scotsman, Gregor MacGregor, descended upon Amelia Island. A semitropical island off the Florida coast at the mouth of the St. Marys River near the Georgia boundary line, Amelia Island had long been a place of rendezvous for pirates and smugglers and held nothing to tempt either the United States or Spain. In 1810 it had been seized by the Georgians and, very soon after, returned to Spain by the federal government. On June 29, 1817, the piratical MacGregor, pretending to be commissioned by the revolutionary forces of South America, "annexed" Amelia Island, which became the headquarters of his sordid enterprises. He made of his pirate band a "Congress," whose decrees were supported by an "army" of some twenty men, and who issued commissions to citizens of the United States. The Georgians soon had reason to complain that MacGregor's republic had become a place of refuge for runaway Negroes, many of whom he promptly sold back into slavery. Late that year another filibusterer of even more lawless nature and habits, one Louis Aury, arrived at the island with approximately one hundred and fifty followers. Fresh from provoking irresponsible insurrectionary schemes in Mexico and the Southwest they arrived in MacGregor's absence. Declaring the island a part of the Republic of Mexico, on October 4 Aury set up his rule.[48]

Just as affairs reached this critical juncture, Monroe returned to Washington from Virginia. His newly appointed Cabinet assembled for the first time, and he prepared to plunge into the problems posed by the South American affairs. On October 25, and again on the 28th and the 30th, he held a series of Cabinet meetings in which Crawford, Rush, Graham (the acting Secretary of War), and Adams participated. Following out his intention of dealing with his Cabinet as an advisory body in the fullest sense of the word, Monroe submitted for consideration a detailed list of written "questions," "relating to South American affairs, to our relations with Spain, and to a piratical assemblage at Amelia Island and at Galveston."[49]

Perhaps it was because it was a new Cabinet and the members not yet well enough acquainted with one another to express their opinions that Mr. Adams found that "all the gentlemen were backward in giving their opinions"[50] upon almost every question. Monroe, for his own part, was forthright in favoring a strong policy. Adams agreed that the "marauding parties at Amelia Island and Galveston ought to be broken up immediately."[51] Adams felt, with Monroe, that the commissioners whom the latter had appointed earlier in the summer ought to be dispatched immediately to Buenos Aires. But while Adams was very definite in his conviction that the Executive was "competent," the suggested recognition was "not now expedient." Monroe, not fully convinced, decided to postpone a decision. Adams was directed to prepare instructions for the South American commissioners and to draft a letter to the Spanish Government relative to the proposed action in Amelia Island. The Executive gave orders that this irregular establishment, including the one near Galveston, should be suppressed immediately. General Gaines was instructed to occupy the Island, and several naval vessels were dispatched to execute the order.

The policy of the new administration regarding Spain and the colonies, then, was one of watchful waiting. The Executive would follow a line of strict neutrality, and independence was not yet to be recognized. The message which Monroe sent to the Fifteenth Congress, assembled to approve or disapprove of the proceedings of the administration, had already been read, criticized, and revised, paragraph by paragraph, by the Cabinet.[52] Recognizing the fact that a preponderance of sympathy for immediate recognition prevailed, Monroe skillfully posed the facts: "It was anticipated at an early stage that the contest between Spain and the colonies would become highly interesting to the United States. It was natural that our citizens should sympathize in events which affected their neighbors. . . . These anticipations have been realized." He went on to justify the neutral conduct of the United States, at the same time hinting that the coun-

President James Monroe

try would welcome the South American republics as independent states:

"Through every stage of the conflict the United States have maintained an impartial neutrality, giving aid to neither of the parties in men, money, ships, or munitions of war. They have regarded the contest ... as a civil war between parties nearly equal, having as to neutral powers equal rights. Our ports have been open to both. ... Should the colonies establish their independence, it is proper now to state that this Government neither seeks nor would accept from them any advantage in commerce or otherwise which will not be equally open to all other nations. The colonies will in that event become independent states, free from any obligation to or connection with us which it may not then be their interest to form on the basis of a fair reciprocity."

In closing his remarks on the Spanish situation, the President officially announced the appointment and expedition of the commissioners to South America, for purposes of observation only, as being in conformity with the policy of neutrality. "To obtain correct information on every subject in which the United States are interested; to inspire just sentiments in all persons in authority, on either side, of our friendly disposition so far as it may comport with an impartial neutrality, and to secure proper respect to our commerce in every port and from every flag, it has been thought proper to send a ship of war with three distinguished citizens along the southern coast with instruction to touch at such ports as they may find most expedient for these purposes."[53]

Commenting upon the other important foreign question, Monroe characterized the activities of the Amelia Island filibusters as converting the island into "a channel for the illicit introduction of slaves from Africa into the United States, an asylum for fugitive slaves from the neighboring States, and a port for smuggling of every kind." A similar indictment of the activities in Galveston was concluded with the forceful assertion that "A just regard for the rights and interests of the United States required that they should be suppressed, and orders have been accordingly issued to that effect."[54]

No sooner had the message been concluded than Henry Clay, the Speaker of the House, jumped to his feet and with the assistance of his western supporters clamored for documents and papers, challenging the "callousness" of the administration toward the deserving republics. As Adams confided to his journal on December 6, 1817, Mr. Clay had "mounted his South American great horse" with the fixed purpose of accomplishing that in which John Randolph had failed, "to overthrow the Executive by swaying the House of Representatives."[55] From the moment he realized the State Department post was to be given to Adams instead of himself, Clay was bent on revenge. To guide foreign affairs to the discomfiture of his rival in the State Department was his main object. As Speaker he was in a strategic position for his battle with the administration, and he used his advantage to put every obstacle in Monroe's way. Like his Executive, Clay had long been sympathetic with the South American rebels, but the means he chose for serving them were designed primarily to embarrass the administration. Rather than share with it the credit for achieving the ends desired both by himself and the President, he refused all Monroe's proposals for coöperation and persisted in a course of action which was seriously to menace the success of what he professed so eagerly to desire.

Monroe's request for an appropriation of $30,000, to assist in defraying the expenses of the mission to South America was Clay's first object of attack. Late in March, 1818, he charged Monroe's action in appointing the commissioners as "unconstitutional and impolitic," as it had been done without the advice or consent of the Senate. As a substitute, Clay moved the appropriation of $18,000 for an outfit and a year's salary for a minister to Buenos Aires, and "in that mingled strain of passionate appeal and invective in which he surpassed all his American contemporaries,"[56] he demanded the formal recognition of South American independence. In substance he insisted upon the abrogation of the Neutrality Law of 1817 in order to make United States neutrality as advantageous as possible to the insurgent colonists. Forsyth, of Georgia, came to the defense of the administration in the impassioned debate which followed, defending Monroe on all points, but it was not so much Forsyth's efforts as Clay's own tactics which settled the issue. Adams observes in his *Diary:* "Forsyth is a man of mild, amiable disposition and good talents, but neither by weight of character, force of genius, nor keenness of spirit at all able to cope with Clay."[57]

President James Monroe

Clay's contemptuous flings at the President and at Adams, his "sneering hints and innuendoes," and his ill-concealed factiousness displeased the House and his motion was defeated, 115 to 45.[58] The original $30,000 was granted in the form of a contingent fund.

Although bitterly disappointed at this rebuff, Clay managed to a certain extent to restrain his unfavorable remarks in public, but in private "he came out with great violence against the course pursued by the Executive upon South American affairs and especially in relation to Amelia Island."[59] This incident of Clay's defection and violent opposition to his administration seemed to obsess Monroe to the exclusion of all other matters. In a private conversation with Adams, after Clay's motion had failed, Monroe confided his deep concern: "There might have been perfect harmony if Mr. Clay had taken the ground that the Executive had gone as far as he could go with propriety towards the acknowledgement of the South Americas, that he was well disposed to go further if such were the feeling of the nation and of Congress, and had made his motion with that view, to ascertain the real sentiments of Congress."[60]

Meanwhile, the Amelia Island affair was arousing repercussions. A series of Cabinet meetings in January had been devoted to formulating a policy with regard to this region. It was then in the hands of American forces, but the complete inability of Spain to enforce law and order there brought up the question of continued occupation by the United States. Crawford, Crowninshield, and Wirt supported Monroe's policy of immediate withdrawal, while Adams and Calhoun took the ground that to retain the island might prove an advantage in later diplomatic bargaining with Spain. In spite of Adams' urging, the President decided to retain Amelia Island "for the present" only, and on January 13, 1818, sent a special message to Congress announcing the suppression of Amelia Island "without the effusion of blood." He justified the action of the American interference on the basis of the law of 1811.[61]

While the President thus strove for unanimity in his councils and sought to take a course whereby the safety of the southern states would be assured with the least affront to Spain, trouble was brewing in another quarter, which put in motion a train of events leading eventually to the solution of the problem of defending the southern borders against Indian encroachment and Spanish impotency.

30

The Seminole War and the Florida Treaty

WHEN in 1814 Jackson had succeeded in conquering the Creeks, those Indians dwelling in the regions of disputed borderlands in southern Georgia and the Spanish provinces of Florida, he had imposed upon them the Treaty of Fort Jackson. By this treaty the Indians ceded to the United States several million acres of land and it was hoped that quiet would reign on that turbulent front. Many of the Creeks promptly fled across the border into Florida and joined their brothers, the Seminoles, a renegade tribe which inhabited the Everglades and was very susceptible to English and Spanish influence.[1]

There appeared here, in the summer of 1814, to exploit the grievances of this border population in imitation of the policy of British colonial officials among the Indian tribes of the Canadian border, one Colonel Edward Nicholls and Captain George Woodbine. With the avowed purpose of organizing, training, and leading the red men, they concluded a treaty of offensive and defensive alliance between Great Britain and the Seminoles. To the Indians they promised to restore the lands lost by the Treaty of Fort Jackson. To intrench his position Nicholls rebuilt on the Apalachicola River a stockade which had served him as headquarters for his own buccaneering raids. Stocking the fortress with cannon and gunpowder, muskets, carbines, and swords, he departed early in the summer of 1815 for London.

There were, at the time, dwelling on farms along this river, about a thousand fugitive Negroes who hated the Seminoles as well as their

Seminole War and Florida Treaty

former masters in Georgia. Upon the abandonment of Nicholls' fort these Negroes promptly seized it and in alliance with the Creeks started plundering expeditions across the border, driving off cattle, firing on river boats, luring Negroes into running away, and generally menacing slave property in Georgia. It was an alarming state of affairs, and in March, 1816, Crawford, in charge of the War Department, ordered Jackson, in command of the Southern Division, to demand that the Spanish government reduce the fort. Should they refuse, the United States would take steps to do so.[2]

Meanwhile, the previous autumn, the United States government commissioners had been sent to the border to draw the demarcation lines of the recent cession and to survey township lines. General Gaines, on the spot with the Georgia troops, had succeeded in intimidating the Indians. Fearful of the menace of the Negro fort, he had secured Jackson's permission to build a new fort, later christened Fort Scott, on the Apalachicola, just north of the Florida line. To secure requisite supplies it was necessary to bring them up the river, past the Negro fort. Gaines accordingly dispatched a gun-boat convoy with the express order not to attack the Negroes. Meeting a band of Seminoles and learning that the Negroes had already attacked and slain a boat-crew, they pushed forward and invested the fort. On July 27 the Negro fort was blown up, killing 270 men and wounding sixty more.

For a while quiet reigned. The Negro menace had been annihilated and the Seminoles subdued by the display of force on the part of the federal government. This situation was soon altered, for the Seminoles were far indeed from being pacified. But no general outbreaks occurred until November, 1817, when General Gaines, in command of the government forces in Georgia, opened the Seminole War by attacking and burning Fowltown, the town of an Indian chief who was in league with the filibusters on Amelia Island. The Indians retaliated by massacring a party of American soldiers, who with their wives and children were proceeding to Fort Scott.

A report of these outrages was duly sent to Washington by Gaines, and upon its receipt Monroe called a Cabinet meeting, at which it was determined to order Gaines to assemble all the regular forces available, with the addition of one thousand militia from the state of Georgia, and to reduce the Indians by force. Should they flee into East Florida for refuge, the General was to pursue them over the border, and pacify the entire Georgia frontier.[3] On no account was he to molest or threaten a Spanish post, and if the enemy sought refuge within a Spanish fortress he was to relinquish the pursuit and take no further steps without new orders from the War Department.[4] Since conditions on Amelia Island demanded immediate attention, Gaines had already taken command there. Consequently, in his official orders of December 26, Calhoun, Secretary of War, gave to Andrew Jackson the command at Fort Scott, subject to the restrictions already imposed upon Gaines. Jackson was to concentrate his forces, "and to adopt the necessary measures to terminate a conflict which it has ever been the desire of the President, from considerations of humanity, to avoid, but which is now made necessary by their settled hostilities."[5]

At this moment Jackson was at the Hermitage, his Tennessee home, where he had been enjoying a brief retirement. As an inveterate don-hater and a man of rapid and decisive action, he had for years advocated the seizure of Pensacola and the occupation of the Floridas to indemnify the United States for claims against Spain. Learning of the President's determination to seize Amelia Island, Jackson, on January 6, 1818, wrote confidentially to Monroe, approving the plan, but urging that a mere pursuit or raid into Spanish territory was not enough. East Florida should be seized and held as an indemnity for Spanish outrages on United States property: "This can be done," wrote Jackson, "without implicating the government. Let it be signified to me through any channel (say Mr. J. Rhea) that the possession of the Floridas would be desirable to the United States, and in sixty days it will be accomplished."[6]

This amazing letter, later to become famous as the "Rhea Letter," crossing the official orders of December 26, arrived at the White House while Monroe was ill in bed. Concerning what then happened, two completely irreconcilable versions are extant. Monroe claimed that when the letter arrived he did not read it; seeing it was from Jackson, he had turned it over to Calhoun, who happened to come in at that point. The latter read it, remarked it was "confidential and relating to Florida," and required an answer. "Have you forwarded to General Jackson the orders of Gaines on that subject?" asked Monroe. Calhoun replied that he had and Monroe, believing

Seminole War and Florida Treaty

the matter to be fully covered by the instructions already forwarded to govern Jackson's conduct, showed the letter to Crawford, who in like manner read and returned it without comment. Monroe then laid it aside and forgot it until its serious consequences had led the country to the brink of war.[7]

Jackson, on the other hand, later claimed[8] that Monroe did read the letter, that he did send the required permission through John Rhea, and that this letter reached him before his arrival at Fort Scott. This letter he saved until April 12, 1819, when he burned it at Rhea's request, who said Monroe wished it that way. This story was to be the source of great embarrassment and grief to Monroe in his declining years. If Monroe had read the letter and had secretly replied to Jackson, thereby fulfilling John Rhea's back-stairs mission, there would certainly have been some allusion to it in the prolonged correspondence which Monroe and Jackson carried on from July to December, 1818. Not once in all those letters was even so much as a suggestion of complicity hinted at; and it was not until the final letter of the series, on December 21, 1818, that Monroe gave a full explanation as to the receipt of the January letter, which was apparently satisfactory to Jackson.[9] It is reasonably safe to assume, then, in the light of this evidence and of Monroe's personal integrity, that he never had any dealings with John Rhea.

On the other hand, if Monroe had actually read the January letter, it is a question of conjecture as to what active course he would have pursued in regard to stopping Jackson, other than the one he did take in complete ignorance of the details of that letter. The President had been receiving free advice from Jackson ever since his election, and while respecting the General's originality and forcefulness and encouraging him to offer suggestions, Monroe had nevertheless guided his administration according to his own convictions. He doubtless would have felt that Jackson was bound to follow out the official military orders, which explicitly stated the limits to which he might go.

However, Monroe apparently never read the letter or thought of it again until after the fall of Pensacola; for, according to John Quincy Adams' scrupulous *Diary*, never overly indulgent toward the administration, this event came as a complete surprise not only to the President, but to the entire Cabinet, Calhoun and Crawford included, both of whom had actually read the letter but had said nothing to the President. Any censure, therefore, which must fall on the administration for failing to restrain Jackson's headlong course must be placed upon these two Cabinet members for failing to acquaint Monroe with the gravity and tenor of Jackson's letter. The preponderance of evidence clearly exonerates Monroe. As an educated man, an individual of proved integrity, and as a trained official his word can be relied upon, for no responsible executive could possibly have thus lawlessly provoked the hostility of three leading European countries by such an act of duplicity.

What Monroe actually aimed at was the establishment and maintenance of peace on the southern border. He seems to have contemplated nothing more than "taking the Indians under our protection, compelling them to cultivate the earth."[10] The official orders permitted the crossing of the border line. Under no circumstances was a Spanish post to be molested or threatened, however, and should the Seminoles retreat to a fortress, Jackson was to abandon the pursuit and await further orders. These original orders reached Jackson in Tennessee on January 11, 1818. With characteristic initiative he wasted no time in raising Tennessee militia, but, setting forth from Nashville, reached Fort Scott, in command of two thousand men, on March 9. Proceeding southward to meet Lieutenant Isaac McKeever's armed naval force escorting the provision ships, he began to construct a new fortification, named Fort Gadsden, on the site of the old Negro fort.

Rumors began seeping through to Jackson that Francis and Peter McQueen, the "prophets" who had done much to inflame Indian wrath against the United States, were then near St. Marks, inciting the Seminoles to hostility; that Woodbine, Ambrister, and some equally shady associates had assembled a group of fugitive slaves and enraged Seminoles near the town and were planning to seize the fort from the Spanish garrison. Accordingly, Jackson and McKeever, then in Spanish territory, proceeded toward St. Marks. As they approached it, a third person was converging on the same place.

In 1817, one Alexander Arbuthnot, a seventy-year-old intelligent and benevolent Scots trader, had appeared in Florida. Pronounced by Gaines as "one of those *self-styled philanthropists* who have long infested our neighboring Indian villages in the character of

Seminole War and Florida Treaty

British agents,"[11] he won the confidence of the Seminoles and the Creeks. These Indians, long oppressed by the sharp trading practices of Woodbine and Forbes & Company, who held a monopoly on the Florida trade, granted to him a power of attorney. This he promptly exercised in British interests, urging that government to send out an agent who should keep the British minister informed of what the Americans were doing in Florida. Thus trading with the redskins, by a mere chance he reached St. Marks in April, 1818. There, hearing for the first time of the approach of Jackson and the arrival of McKeever's fleet, he dispatched a letter to his son, warning him to sail his goods and vessel, which was lying in the Suwanee River, to a place of safety. Arbuthnot was found within the fort, preparing to leave, and was promptly taken prisoner when Jackson took the town and invested it with American troops.

Resuming the march toward Chief Bowlegs' town of Suwanee, Jackson found it abandoned by the Seminoles and Negroes, who had received warning from the letter Arbuthnot had sent to his son urging evacuation. He did capture Robert C. Ambrister, a former lieutenant under Nicholls and an accomplice of Arbuthnot, who accidentally stumbled upon the American camp. The purpose of his long overland march having been thwarted by the abandonment of the town and the retreat of the Indians into their inaccessable swamps, Jackson returned to St. Marks.

The war against the Seminoles was ended, but there remained one more act of imperial authority to complete the picture of Jackson's amazing conduct. The fate of Arbuthnot and Ambrister having to be decided, the General turned the prisoners over to a court-martial of fourteen officers, presided over by General Gaines. The members of this court were taken from a population that had long resented the intrigues of these English agents. Arbuthnot, a British citizen, charged with inciting the Indians to war, acting as a spy, and furnishing arms to the savages, was found guilty and sentenced to be hanged. The hapless Ambrister, on a charge of inciting and leading the Indians, was at first sentenced to be shot but on reconsideration was to receive fifty lashes and serve one year at hard labor. Jackson, with typical ruthlessness, invoked the original penalty and Ambrister, too, was executed on April 29.

Having crushed the Indians, the real purpose of Jackson's mission had been fulfilled. There was no reason why he should not return to American territory. But he had his own plans. Pensacola was the key to West Florida, and hearing that the Governor was assembling and outfitting five hundred Indians at that point, he marched and captured the city, forcing the Spanish Governor to flee to Barrancas. Thus, with Florida completely within his grasp, the victorious General left the American garrisons to enforce the revenue laws he had imposed, and set out for Tennessee.

Jackson's official dispatches announcing the capture of Pensacola, following closely upon the heels of the circumstantial newspaper accounts, reached Washington early in July, the first set having been lost en route. They thrust themselves into the midst of a long and delicate negotiation for the purchase of Florida, threatened momentarily to defeat it, but eventually hastened a favorable conclusion.

After years of negotiation for Florida, a change of ministry in Madrid in 1817 renewed American hopes that some sort of agreement could be reached. Don José Pizarro, who had succeeded Cevallos in the Spanish Foreign Office, proposed that the negotiations be transferred to Madrid and carried on by the American Minister, George W. Erving. After a month's exchange of notes Pizarro submitted a proposition whereby Spain would cede the two Floridas in exchange for all of the Louisiana territory west of the Mississippi, from its source to its mouth.[12] It was impossible for the United States to accept such an offer, and it was promptly and unequivocally rejected. At least it was an indication that haughty Spain was yielding. With the transfer of the negotiations back to Washington, Monroe redoubled his efforts. The acquisition of the Floridas by diplomacy rather than by conquest was absolutely necessary to preserve peace in that area and to stamp out the Indian depredations. Spain's inability to maintain order had been clearly demonstrated to the world at large; but to make that country, its council of state, its bigoted and narrow-minded grandees and priests, still living amidst the glories of the days of Charles V, realize the present decrepit condition of the kingdom, was a difficult and arduous task.

Meanwhile, John Quincy Adams on December 19, 1817, three days after Calhoun first gave Gaines permission to pursue the Indians into Florida, renewed the discussions with Don Onis. With the

Seminole War and Florida Treaty

Spanish minister in Washington, Adams had his troubles. As he confided to his *Diary*, Don Onis, "a finished scholar in the Spanish procrastinating school of diplomacy"[13] was "cold, calculating, wily, always commanding his own temper, proud because he is a Spaniard, but supple and cunning, accommodating the tone of his pretensions precisely to the degree of endurance of his opponents, bold and overbearing to the utmost extent to which it is tolerated, careless of what he asserts or how grossly it is proved to be unfounded."[14] Like Spain herself, he found it difficult to cast aside the attitude of haughty arrogance and assume a mien more commensurate with her new lowly condition. There followed a thirteen-months discussion and exchange of notes, studded with many a tedious and alarming pause, during which time Hyde de Neuville, the French minister, who took a warm interest in the negotiations, frequently served as a channel of communication and carried propositions and counter-propositions, arguments and denials, between Adams and Don Onis.

Early in January, Monroe, who had learned something which made him believe Spain might be willing to discuss practical terms, advised Adams to see Don Onis personally: "Mr. Biddle had told him [Monroe]," Adams noted, "that some person of the family of Mr. Onis had in the most positive terms affirmed that Spain was in a desperate and desponding condition, and Onis had very lately received a dispatch ordering him to dispose, as soon as possible, of the Floridas to the United States upon the best terms he can obtain. The President therefore wished me to see Onis this day and ask him simply what Spain would take for East Florida, that is to say, for all Spain's possessions east of the Mississippi."[15]

Adams did so, but, as predicted, Onis insisted that it was the turn of the United States to make a proposition. By the middle of January, 1818, as Jackson was preparing to go to Florida, Adams offered to accept the two Floridas in satisfaction of the claims of the United States against Spain for damages, and suggested as the western boundary the Colorado River.[16] This demand Don Onis considered so preposterous that on March 23 he transferred the negotiations back to Madrid, where Erving and Pizarro took them up.[17]

Two days later, on March 25, 1818, as Jackson was approaching St. Marks, Monroe sent a message to Congress, outlining the state of affairs in Florida and justifying the entrance of United States troops into Spanish territory on the ground that Spain had failed to restrain Indian attacks as she was bound to do by treaty.[18]

In the meanwhile Adams had heard from Hyde de Neuville of "a convention about South American affairs on foot in Europe"[19] while Great Britain and France, Monroe knew, were discussing the possibility of arbitrating Spanish-American differences. On January 27 Great Britain made a definite offer "to settle the differences between the United States and Spain."[20] Bagot, the British minister, professed the friendly disposition of his country toward the United States. Sweetening the diplomatic pill he was directed to administer with reference to the "preservation of universal peace," he implied that Great Britain had reason to complain of "certain restrictions upon the British commerce in Spain, and that if Great Britain alone, or the allied powers jointly, should interpose between Spain and the South American Provinces, the system recommended and urged by Great Britain would be one of perfect liberality to the provinces." He claimed that Pizarro, in a letter to Sir Henry Wellesley the previous summer, had suggested to Britain this offer of an impartial mediation.[21]

Upon submission of these letters to the President and his advisers, Adams found Monroe and Crawford "evidently averse to the acceptance of the mediation," and the rest of the Cabinet no less so. There was a positive determination to decline the offer, but the real question was upon what grounds to base the refusal. After considerable discussion, and with the assistance of Monroe, Adams formulated the principle which was to govern the reply to Bagot: "I suggested the idea of answering, with thanks for the friendly manifestation of Great Britain, and the strongest assurances of their being reciprocated, that we were obliged to accommodate our measures to the public feelings of the country; that our controversies with Spain, though not of the first rank in importance, had a strong hold upon the popular sentiments; that to refer them to any interposition of a third party would certainly be disapproved by all parties in this country, and have the tendency to create ill will between this country and England, which we were very desirous of avoiding."[22] Bagot professed to be very well satisfied with the reasons and declared that if "there should occur any occasion upon which Great Britain could do any good by throwing in a word, his Government would be happy to do it."[23]

Seminole War and Florida Treaty

Thus, when Jackson's official dispatches arrived on July 6,[24] the peaceful acquisition of the Floridas had reached an "interesting stage of development"[25] for, according to Adams, Don Onis had just "received new instructions from Spain, which would have enabled him to conclude a treaty with me [Adams] satisfactory to both parties if it had not been for this unfortunate incident."[26]

At the same time it was a moment fraught with danger, for not only had Don Onis sent a note of invective against General Jackson[27] and entered a formal remonstrance on the part of the Spanish government against the capture of the Florida towns as an overt act of war, but Jackson had caused to be executed two British citizens. Although Great Britain's offer of mediation had been turned down, the administration was well aware that England and France both were keenly interested in the Florida situation; and it was not at all likely that England would pass lightly over this bold affront to her sovereignty.

Monroe and his Cabinet received the news of the capture of the three towns and the details of the court-martial with amazement and perplexity, for explicit orders had been given to Jackson forbidding the capture of Spanish posts without express permission. From noon until five o'clock on July 15, 1818, the Cabinet deliberated. "The Administration were placed in a dilemma from which it is impossible for them to escape censure by some, and factious crimination by many."[28] It was an embarrassing and complicated situation for Monroe, for not only did it involve an actual war with Spain, but the question of the executive power to authorize hostilities without a declaration of war by Congress was also concerned. Adams wrote after the meeting: "The President and all the members of the Cabinet except myself are of the opinion that Jackson acted not only without, but against, instructions: that he has committed war upon Spain . . . in which, if not disavowed by the administration, they [the Cabinet] will be abandoned by the country."[29]

The theme of discussion throughout the course of the turbulent Cabinet sessions was not whether or not to punish Jackson, but simply whether to approve or disapprove of his military proceedings, and what course to take in relation to Spain. Nevertheless, various members of that Cabinet did express in very outspoken terms personal dissatisfaction with the General's conduct, and although what was said at the time remained a closed secret for ten years, Crawford later, out of malice for Calhoun and to strengthen himself with Jackson, disclosed these remarks. Calhoun, already nettled by Jackson's insubordinate conduct in a private affair involving the War Department and believing that Jackson's object was to produce a war for the sake of commanding an expedition against Mexico [30] and that the General was interested in Florida land speculation,[31] went so far as to propose that Jackson be court-martialed. This utterance Crawford later betrayed, and Jackson, who for years had believed that Calhoun alone supported him, at this juncture turned against the man who so needed his support to secure the coveted presidency. This remark "cost Calhoun what in the vicissitudes of politics had become by 1829 the most essential friendship of his national career, and he fell like one climbing a precipice who receives a stab in the back just as he stretches a hand to grasp the summit."[32]

Crawford, too, opposed the proceeding, saying that "if the Administration did not immediately declare itself and restore Pensacola, it would be held responsible for Jackson's having taken it, and for having commenced a war in violation of the Constitution; that the people would not support the Administration in such a war; that our shipping, navigation, and commerce would be destroyed by privateers from all parts of the world, under the Spanish flag, and that the Administration would sink under it."[33]

Adams, on the other hand, went to the opposite extreme. Knowing nothing of Jackson's predilections for conquest, completely disgusted with Spanish insolence and the humiliating delays he had been forced to endure in the Florida negotiations, he thought "that the whole conduct of General Jackson was justifiable under his orders, although he certainly had none to take any Spanish fort. My principle is that everything he did was *defensive;* that as such it was neither war against Spain nor violation of the Constitution."[34] The grim Puritan even went so far as to contend that the United States keep Pensacola, upon the principle on which Jackson had taken it, until Spain could guarantee to restrain the Indian hostilities.[35]

The entry in Adams' diary under date of July 20 indicates the struggle which took place in the Cabinet. Having presented a new

Seminole War and Florida Treaty

point upon which to justify Jackson, Adams commented on the ensuing arguments:

"It appeared to make some impression upon Mr. Wirt, but the President and Mr. Calhoun were inflexible.

"My reasoning was that Jackson took Pensacola only because the Governor threatened to drive him out of the province by force if he did not withdraw; that Jackson was only executing his orders when he received this threat; that he could not withdraw his troops from the province consistently with his orders, and that his only alternative was to prevent the execution of the threat. . . .

"Mr. Calhoun principally bore the argument against me, insisting that the capture of Pensacola was not necessary upon principles of self-defense, and therefore was both an act of war against Spain and a violation of the Constitution; that it was not the menace of the Governor of Pensacola that had determined Jackson to take that place; that he had really resolved to take it before; that he had violated his orders, and upon his own arbitrary will set all authority at defiance."[36]

As the responsible guide of the deliberations and as the individual upon whom all censure and any praise would ultimately fall, Monroe had to choose his position carefully. He received all the suggestions "with candor and good humor,"[37] but, confident that Jackson had acted not only without, but against, his orders, and had waged a war on Spain, felt he ought to be disavowed immediately. "I think," he said, "that the public will not entirely justify the general; and the true course for ourselves is to shield and support him as much as possible, but not commit the administration on points where the public will be against us."[38]

The final outcome of these Cabinet sessions was, first, the preparation of an article by William Wirt, to appear in the *National Intelligencer*, explaining to the American people just what had happened and defending the administration; second, an explanation to England; and, third, the framing of a reply to Don Onis surrendering the captured forts and at the same time justifying the conduct of the United States.

Adams undertook to calm ruffled British opinion by describing the activities of Nicholls, Arbuthnot, Woodbine, and Ambrister, as justifiable cause for court-martial and execution. In England the executions had become the subject of parliamentary inquiry, and excitement everywhere was at fever heat. The newspapers were particularly bitter in their denunciation of the United States. General Jackson was referred to in their columns by the opprobrious names of "tyrant," "ruffian," and "murderer." After a full deliberation the Cabinet, however, declared that the conduct of Arbuthnot and Ambrister had been unjustifiable and did not therefore call for interference on the part of Great Britain. England, isolated from the rest of the continental powers ever since the Second Treaty of Paris, was anxious for United States support against the reactionary doctrines promulgated by the Holy Alliance and in the furtherance of British interests in South America. In the ensuing days of mounting popular passion, when war would have been certain "if the ministry had but held up a finger," the Cabinet stood firm for peace. Throwing to the winds the traditional jealousy with which England ever guarded the lives and interests of her subjects, she dropped the matter without a threat of retaliation.

To Adams also fell the task of composing the defense of the American conduct to Spain. In this document, destined to become famous, he proceeded in a narrative form. Spain, by her failure to keep peace along the frontier as she was bound to do by the treaty of 1795, and apparently unable to restrain the Indians, had forced the United States to undertake that work as a defensive measure. The seizures of Pensacola and St. Marks were Jackson's own acts made necessary by Spanish impotency. The reproof was placed upon the Spanish commandants instead of Jackson, while at the same time any acts of the latter which appeared to encroach upon Spanish sovereignty were repudiated. Adams discussed in no uncertain terms of indignation and wrath the affair of Amelia Island and MacGregor, and embodied in the note a demand for the punishment of the Spanish officers for their misconduct, and a further demand for a just and reasonable indemnity to the United States for the expenses the latter had incurred. He wound up the document with a threat that "if the necessities of self-defense should again compel the United States to take possession of the Spanish forts and places in Florida" Spain could not expect another unconditional restoration of them.[39]

It was a highly ingenious paper, and though no reference was made to the defenseless and pitiable condition of the Seminoles nor

Seminole War and Florida Treaty

to the articles of capitulation of Pensacola, it averted war. The document cleared the air so heavily charged with war rumors by silencing the English government on the subject of the execution of its subjects, by convincing Pizarro of the legality of the American action, and by giving ground to the European powers for refusing to aid Spain in a war against the United States.

There remained only the delicate task of pacifying Jackson, whose temper was well known, and reconciling him to the Cabinet disavowal of his actions. It was a task for which Monroe with his patience and tact, his pliant and smooth disposition, was eminently fitted, but a task which not only worried and caused him much anxiety, but occupied his mind to the exclusion of all other matters. Adams was worried about Monroe. He wrote, "He is still so much absorbed in this subject that he relucts at thinking of any other—so that when I am talking to him about the proposed negotiation in England, the instructions for Everett, or even South America, he stops in the midst of the discourse and says something about Jackson and Pensacola."[40]

By July 19, 1818, Monroe had his letter to Jackson ready: "I shall withhold nothing in regard to your attack of the Spanish posts, and occupancy of them, particularly Pensacola, which you ought to know; it being an occurrence of the most delicate and interesting nature, and which without a circumspect and cautious policy, looking to all the objects which claim attention, may produce the most serious and unfavorable consequences.

"In calling you into active service against the Seminoles, and communicating to you the orders which had been given just before to General Gaines, the views and intentions of the Government were fully disclosed in respect to the operations in Florida. In transcending the limit prescribed by those orders you acted on your own responsibility, on facts and circumstances which were unknown to the Government when the orders were given, many of which, indeed, occurred afterward, and which you thought imposed on you the measure, as an act of patriotism, essential to the honor and interests of your country."

Patiently Monroe explained to the General that Adams had been instructed to make ample amends to the Spanish minister, and that the conquered posts had been handed back to their rightful owners:

"If the Executive refused to evacuate the posts, especially Pensacola, it would amount to a declaration of war, to which it is incompetent. It would be accused of usurping the authority of Congress, and giving a deep and fatal wound to the Constitution. By charging the offense on the officers of Spain, we take the ground which you have presented, and we look to you to support it. You must aid in procuring the documents necessary for this purpose. Those which you sent by Mr. Hambly were prepared in too much haste, and do not I am satisfied, do justice to the cause. This must be attended to without delay."

Skillfully he sought to soothe Jackson by intimating that Jackson's campaign might lead to the ultimate acquisition of Florida by diplomacy: "The events which have occurred in both the Floridas show the incompetency of Spain to maintain her authority; and the progress of the revolutions in South America will require all her forces there.

"There is much reason to presume that this act will furnish a strong inducement to Spain to cede the territory, provided we do not wound too deeply her pride by holding it."[41]

This letter was the first in a prolonged and dreary series extending from July to December; Jackson, deeply wounded in pride, was not easily appeased. He confined his immediate reply to Monroe's statement that he had transcended the limits of his orders and had acted on his own responsibility. With no reference to any "Rhea Letter," Jackson defended himself by his orders of December 26, 1817, which authorized him to "adopt the necessary measures to terminate a conflict which it has ever been the desire of the President, from motives of humanity, to avoid."[42]

Monroe, admitting the possibility that Jackson had misconstrued his orders, then advised him to explain himself to Calhoun and the War Department.[43] Jackson, however, refused and upon a repetition of his claim that he had not transcended his instructions, Monroe good-humoredly let the matter drop.

As already noted, in none of this extensive correspondence is there any allusion to a private understanding with Monroe, nor is there any reference to the Rhea Letter. Yet in December, 1818, the whole matter was brought up in a new light. In an anonymous contribution to the Philadelphia *Aurora*, it was hinted that the administration was

Seminole War and Florida Treaty

fully aware of Jackson's intentions before he marched into Florida. Adams visited Monroe at the time Monroe and Crawford were reading the article and recorded the fact that both men agreed it had been written at Jackson's instigation.[44]

Monroe, determined to clear up the misunderstanding, wrote to Jackson on December 21, 1818, fully explaining, as told above, the circumstances attendant upon the reception of Jackson's letter of January 6.[45] This explanation, was apparently satisfactory to Jackson for no further reference was made to the affair and the harmony of their personal relations was restored. But many years later the matter was resurrected by Jackson in his bitter feud with Crawford and Calhoun, blighting and plaguing Monroe's last years.

The Seminole controversy, however, was not thus allowed to sink into oblivion. Another phase, one with more momentous consequences, was unfolding against the backdrop of Florida affairs. To the Fifteenth Congress in session in December, 1818, Andrew Jackson was the man of the hour. An experienced politician, a man of unquestioned physical and intellectual boldness, he had, by his audacious conduct, captured the imagination of his fellow Tennesseeans. His brilliant feat at New Orleans had already given him a firm hold upon the hearts of all Americans. Sweeping eastward, the wave of enthusiasm in the West reënforced his popularity gained in the late war, and almost overnight cast him into the arena of presidential possibilities. Already candidates were being discussed for the next election. In the absence of larger national issues, vigorous personal campaigns were being conducted by Clay, Calhoun, and Crawford also. Of them all Clay was the most outspoken in his opposition to the administration. He had already tried unsuccessfully to embarrass Monroe on the South American question. The sting of defeat there, plus the sudden appearance of Jackson as a possible threat to his presidential hopes, was the signal for even more hostile attacks on his part. As Adams noted, "All the restless and uneasy spirits naturally fall into the ranks of the opposition, and Clay, who has seen all this, has, from the time of Mr. Monroe's election, squared his conduct accordingly. He has been constantly looking out for positions upon which to erect his batteries against the Administration, and this Florida affair appears so favorable to him."[46]

JAMES MONROE

Seeking public sanction of his conduct as Chief Executive, Monroe determined to place before Congress a full explanation of all that had occurred, together with all papers relevant to the affair. With this avowed purpose he sent to the legislative body his Second Annual Message, which he devoted almost exclusively to Spanish affairs. Describing the situation in the Floridas as one where Spanish authority was practically extinct, he classified the inhabitants as adventurers, fugitive slaves, and ferocious Indians.[47] Approving Jackson's conduct on the ground of necessity, he threw the responsibility upon the Spanish officials.[48] But in spite of this approval of Jackson's activities there was no hesitation as to what course the government would pursue: "As there was reason to believe that the commanders of these posts had violated their instructions, there was no disposition to impute to their government a conduct so unprovoked and hostile. An order was in consequence issued to the general in command there to deliver the posts—Pensacola unconditionally to any person duly authorized to receive it, and St. Marks, ... on the arrival of a competent force to defend it against those savages and their associates."[49]

Both in the House and in the Senate this message was sent to committees on military affairs, while Clay prepared openly for a general inquiry into the Florida invasion. Meanwhile Jackson, knowing that trouble was brewing, and against the advice of his friends, arrived in Washington, paid his respects to Monroe, and even had the consummate audacity to appear in the halls of Congress as his fate was being debated. All questionable points having already been settled with Spain, the inquiry centered around the condemnation of the execution of Arbuthnot and Ambrister. Inasmuch as England had already expressed herself as satisfied with Adams' explanation of the executions and had agreed to let the matter drop, what subsequently took place in Congress was nothing more or less than a personal attack by Clay and his followers on a man who seriously threatened Clay's chances in the coming presidential election.

The majority report from the House Military Committee was taken up in the Committee of the Whole. The resolution "That the House of Representatives of the United States disapproves the proceedings in the trial and execution of Alexander Arbuthnot and Robert Ambrister" was debated for twenty-seven days without inter-

Seminole War and Florida Treaty

ruption and to the exclusion of all other business, attracting the finest orators and cleverest politicians and statesmen of the generation.

It was before a House filled to capacity that Clay rose to his feet to conclude the bitter attack against Jackson. Beginning with a disclaimer of all hostility to either Jackson or to the administration, he launched into a most impressive speech replete with vivid imagery. Not only did he strongly affect the House, but he earned the undying hatred of Jackson.

Throughout the country the debates were followed eagerly, for Jackson's followers were legion. Monroe, unwilling to launch himself into the arena and maintaining his customary impartiality, nevertheless privately sympathized with his unruly general. In a letter to Madison, written the day before the final vote was taken he wrote: "With respect to General Jackson's conduct I considered it a question of merit or demerit in him, & seeing sufficient justification of him, in the injuries received from the criminal aggressors in Florida, & nothing to palliate their conduct in any claims of Spain on us, there seemed to be no reason for censoring him, & much for giving just weight, and turning to the best account all the circumstances which operated against them and her."[50]

In the House, Jackson's supporters, among them Johnson, Tallmadge, and Poindexter, though less spectacular in the field of verbal warfare, ably met the onslaught of detraction. They tore Clay's speech to shreds with so much success that when the votes were taken on February 8, 1819, Jackson was found to be vindicated both by the House and by the Committee of the Whole. The Senate, where the Tennesseean's popularity was less pronounced, returned a condemnation of his conduct upon every point. The report was tabled, and so remained when Congress adjourned on March 4.

Early in 1819 Jackson embarked upon a hero's tour. He visited New York, Philadelphia, and Baltimore, everywhere fêted and greeted with almost hysterical enthusiasm. Thus ended the Seminole controversy. Clay's efforts to scotch the rising ambitions and popularity of Jackson by prolonging that controversy in Congress, and thereby converting it into a personal and national campaign of detraction, had only resulted in elevating Jackson into a prominence so great as to make him really dangerous to Clay's own cherished presidential ambitions.

JAMES MONROE

Adams' letter to the Spanish Court, justifying Jackson's conduct in Florida, had the desired effect. Spain appeared to be appeased and the Spanish authorities, realizing it was hopeless to continue to hold the provinces and that Florida must ultimately come under the sovereignty of the United States, sent to Adams on October 24, 1818, a proposition to cede the Floridas under certain conditions. When these conditions were rejected by Adams, and Spain had reciprocated to a set of American conditions, belligerent measures seemed imminent. Adams wrote to Onis: "The President is deeply penetrated with the conviction that further protracted discussion cannot terminate in a manner satisfactory to our governments. From your answer to this letter he must conclude whether a final adjustment of all our differences is now to be accomplished, or whether all hope of such a desirable result is, on the part of the United States, to be abandoned."[51]

By January 11, 1819, after several exchanges of letters, Onis indicated Spain's willingness to dispose of the provinces on terms more favorable to the United States than she had heretofore granted. The entire difficulty in the matter lay not so much with the disposal of the Floridas themselves, as with the definition of the western boundary of the Louisiana Purchase. Ever since its acquisition in 1803 the line of demarcation had been in dispute, the United States claiming the Rio Grande as the boundary of the purchased territory, including Texas, while Spain insisted that the Mississippi was the western boundary. By the time Onis announced his new instructions, early in 1819, however, the United States had capitulated to the extent of being willing to recognize the Sabine River, while Spain was yielding in her stand on the Mississippi. This was the beginning of the end, and in the ensuing weeks Onis gradually yielded, though bitterly and constantly protesting. In thus making his final stand at the Sabine, compelling Spain to meet his terms, and sacrificing the right of the United States to Texas, Adams fully expected trouble from the West. He himself was anxious to procure for the United States the lucrative southwestern province, and had he held out for the Rio del Norte as the western boundary he could undoubtedly have procured it from Spain. But the Secretary of State could find no support from Monroe, from the rest of the Cabinet, or from General Jackson. On February 1, 1819, Adams reported the following interview with Monroe:

Seminole War and Florida Treaty

"Called upon the President, and had a conversation with him upon this renewal of negotiations with the Spanish Minister. There are various symptoms that if we do come to an arrangement there will be a large party in the country dissatisfied with our concessions from the Rio del Norte to the Sabine on the Gulf of Mexico. Clay has taken the alarm at hearing that Onis was again treating with us, and is already taking ground to censure the treaty, if one should be made. . . . I received a long and impertinent letter from Lexington making many objections to the line which we have proposed; and I mentioned all this to the President for his consideration. He desired me to see and converse with General Jackson upon the subject, and to ask his confidential opinion."[52]

In accordance with Monroe's instructions Adams called upon Jackson the following two days and acquainted him with the state of the negotiations. The latter agreed that there would be considerable opposition but felt that since the people were acquiring Florida, they would not persist, for the time being, in their demand for Texas. "He said," Adams continued, that "there were many individuals who would take exception to our receding so far from the boundary of the Rio del Norte, which we claim, as the Sabine, and the enemies of the Administration would certainly make a handle of it to assail them; but the possession of the Floridas was of so great importance to the southern frontier of the United States, and so essential even to their safety, that the vast majority of the nation would be satisfied with the western boundary as we propose, if we obtain the Floridas."[53]

An alarming pause occurred in the deliberations early in February, and Monroe, anxious for the treaty and fearful lest Onis absolutely refuse to yield another inch, urged, on February 11, that the United States give up all the territory remaining in contest and accept the one-hundredth degree of longitude and the forty-third parallel of latitude.[54] Such a concession was unnecessary, for the two sparring diplomats defined the boundary in a "Treaty of Amity, Settlements, and Limits," signed on Washington's birthday, 1819, and thereby consummated almost a quarter of a century of diplomatic effort on the part of the United States.

The message and documents had already been prepared and, with the treaty, were sent to the Senate. By the Senate ratification and the formal presidential proclamation of February 25, the United States

JAMES MONROE

received the Floridas in return for an agreement to settle the disputed claims of certain of her citizens against Spain to an amount not to exceed $5,000,000, while the Spanish claims against the United States, provided for in the Convention of 1802, were expunged. The western boundary was defined by the Sabine, Red, and Arkansas Rivers, up to the forty-second degree of north latitude, and along that degree to the Pacific.[55] Congress, expecting a like ratification by the Cortes, passed on March 3, 1819 an act authorizing Monroe to take possession of the ceded territory and to establish local governments over the acquired domain.

The President proposed to carry through the Florida treaty with Spain and, once having secured the province, guide American public opinion, already clamoring for recognition of the South American Republics, toward the realization of that object. John Forsyth of Georgia, the new minister to Spain replacing Erving, was dispatched with the treaty to secure ratification by the Cortes. The United States felt that a speedy conclusion was at hand, but a new difficulty arose which thwarted the President's purposes and delayed Spanish ratification for almost two years.

In February, 1818, while the Florida negotiations were under way, Erving had written that the Spanish king had made, to three Spanish noblemen, large grants of land in the American provinces, which he (the king) believed contained all the land in Florida and the adjacent islands not already ceded. The bad faith of the Spanish king, and his ulterior motive—to deprive the United States of ownership in case of cession, were apparent, and by the eighth article of the final treaty Onis declared these specific grants, whatever their dates, to be null and void. To avoid further ambiguity on this particular point Forsyth was specially instructed to deliver a written declaration to this effect when exchanging ratifications.[56]

Forsyth, however, was by no means accorded a cordial reception, his attempts to appoint a day for formal ratification were evaded, and the Cortes delayed action on the document. In response to his letter emphasizing the importance of immediate acceptance, in view of the fact that the *Hornet*, the sloop of war designated to carry the treaty back to the United States, was soon to sail, he was told that the great interest and importance attaching to the treaty made it necessary for the King to deliberate, and that a high Spanish official

Seminole War and Florida Treaty

would be dispatched to the United States to secure certain explanations from that government.

Thus, while most of the principal powers of Europe were urging Spain to conclude the affair, the obstinate King held back at the last stage of ratification of a solemn obligation and sought to extort some new guarantee from the United States. What really blocked the normal proceedings was Ferdinand's dread of the very advantage for which Monroe hoped—that of dealing with the South American problem unhampered by the Florida dispute. Rumors that Spain was withholding ratification because of a misunderstanding on the land grants and was desirous of extracting a pledge from the United States not to recognize South American independence reached the United States in midsummer. The Cabinet, sensitive to the delicacy of the international aspects of the situation, informed the Spanish government in August that if the treaty should be ratified and transmitted at any time before Congress met, it would be treated as if ratified according to stipulation.

Spain's reply was the arrival in November of a vessel confirming earlier reports that Ferdinand had delayed acceptance of the treaty but intended sending a minister to seek and give certain explanations. This news arrived in the midst of a long series of Cabinet discussions, which dealt with the annual message whereby Monroe intended to seek congressional permission to take summary possession of the disputed provinces. Pending the arrival of the minister, Monroe, with the aid and suggestions of Adams, toned down his originally impetuous message and recommended the occupation of the Floridas, not immediately and absolutely, but in such a way as to permit of the explanations desired by Spain: "From a full view of all circumstances," the message began, "it is submitted to the consideration of Congress whether it will not be proper for the United States to carry the conditions of the treaty into effect in the same manner as if it had been ratified by Spain. . . . By pursuing this course we shall rest on the sacred ground of right, sanctioned in the most solemn manner by Spain herself by a treaty which she was bound to ratify, for refusing to do which she must incur the censure of other nations. . . ."[57]

This message, so painstakingly prepared by Monroe, so cautiously phrased, and so thoroughly discussed in Cabinet meetings, was handed to Congress on the second day of the session, read, and promptly tossed aside in the rising agitation on the Missouri question. It slumbered in the anteroom until the following March, when, in a lull in the slavery discussion, the House Committee on Foreign Relations proposed authorizing and requiring Monroe to take possession of Florida, rather than conferring upon him a discretionary power. Monroe, counselled by the European powers, and appreciating that delay rather than action was the prudent course, addressed a special message to Congress on March 27, 1820. He mentioned the friendly interest taken in the matter by the great powers of Europe—England, Russia, and France, expressed the hope that in response to their solicitations the King of Spain would soon ratify the treaty, and suggested that Congress defer action until the Spanish representative should arrive.[58]

This was the opportunity for which Clay had been waiting. As a champion of the expanding West he had been furious when it became known that Adams had sacrificed Texas and set the western boundary at the Sabine River. Reasoning that the Transcontinental Treaty with Spain had fallen because that party had failed to ratify within the stipulated six-month period, Clay introduced into the House resolutions that the treaty not be renewed.

By this time a notable change in attitude on the Florida question had taken place. Already the halls of Congress had rocked to the great slavery controversy over the Missouri admission, in which sectional jealousy had been brought out in bold relief. Whereas prior to 1819 all sections were interested in expansion to natural and "manifest" boundaries and apparently satisfied with the provisions of the Florida treaty, by 1820 the North and the East were jealous of and violently opposed to aggrandizement of the West and the South, for that ultimately meant expansion of the slaveholding interests. The South and the West, greedy for land, anxious to lay hands on Florida and upon as far-reaching an area as possible in the direction of Mexico, were demanding with Clay the framing of a new treaty including both Floridas and Texas.

With remarkable clarity Monroe had foreseen and anticipated this state of affairs, which threatened the very Union itself. Early in 1819 he had restrained Adams' hand and insisted, in the interests of national solidarity and to allay sectional irritation, that he accept the Sabine boundary. In the height of Clay's attack on the treaty in

Seminole War and Florida Treaty

1820, in two discerning letters, one to Jackson and the other to his mentor Jefferson, he recapitulated the state of affairs and justified the action taken. To Jefferson on May 3, 1820, he wrote:

"If the occurrence involv'd in it [Treaty with Spain] nothing more, than a question between the U States & Spain or between them & the Colonies, I should entirely concur in your view of the subject. I am satisfied, that we might, regulate it, in every circumstance, as we thought just, & without war, that we might take Florida as an indemnity, and Texas for some trifle as an equivalent. Spain must soon be expelled from this Continent, & with any new govt. which may be formed in Mexico, it would be easy to arrange the boundary in the wilderness, so as to include as much territory on our side as we might desire.... But the difficulty does not proceed from these sources. It is altogether internal, and of the most distressing nature and dangerous tendency.

"From this view it is evident that the further acquisition of territory, to the West & South, involves difficulties, of an internal nature, which menace the Union itself. We ought therefore to be cautious in making the attempt."[59]

In a similar letter to Jackson, toward the end of the month, he expressed a disinclination to expose the administration to a charge of subserviency to southern ambition and advocated postponement of the Texas acquisition: "Having long known the repugnance with which the eastern portion of our Union, or rather some of those who have enjoyed its confidence (for I do not think that the people themselves have any interest or wish of that kind), have seen its aggrandizement to the west and south, I have been decidedly of opinion that we ought to be content with Florida for the present, and until the public opinion in that quarter shall be reconciled to any further change."[60]

Clay's resolutions failed. Early in April, 1820, after what amounted to practically a grand tour of Europe in the interests of killing time, the long-promised Spanish envoy, Don Francisco Dionisio Vives, arrived in Washington. But he brought no authority to execute a treaty or to deliver the Floridas. In fact, he admitted "that there was no reason for his government, to decline the ratification of the treaty, but insists that it shall be made dependent, not on the conditions contain'd in it, but a stipulation, that the U. States will form no relations with the So. A: Colonies, especially of recognition, untill they be recognized by other Colonies."[61]

Vives and Adams entered into a lengthy discussion of demands and refusals, the former seeking to extort new pledges and the latter firmly holding his ground. Agreement seemed almost hopeless. Adams, "so wearied out with the discussion that it had become nauseous," became completely indifferent to Vives. He flatly told the Spanish envoy that Spain must either ratify the present treaty, make one on the basis of the United States' demands, or take the consequences. The outbreak of a new revolution in Spain forced Monroe to place before Congress, on May 9, the new facts. While professing himself ready to seize Florida as an indemnity, unless Spain should yield, he advised postponing action for the present session.[62] The House consented and shortly adjourned until November 13, while Vives was asked to secure from Spain a final decision before Congress should meet again. On October 5 the Cortes advised the King to ratify the treaty. This he did almost three weeks later.

Four months later, Vives delivered the long-delayed document to Monroe, who resubmitted it to the Senate, where it was ratified with only four dissenting votes.[63] On February 22, 1821, the President announced a full reacceptance of the treaty and asked for legislation to carry it into effect.

Thus was Jefferson's desire for the Floridas achieved. An acquisition long sought for, essential to internal peace and to preserve the country from the danger of foreign strife and conspiracies, was consummated. For almost twenty-five years, negotiations had been pursued in Spain or Washington, interrupted frequently by periods of suspension of diplomatic intercourse. Europe's internal dissensions, Spain's impotency, and the refusal of England, France, or any other European power to help her had compelled capitulation. The patience, dignity, forbearance, and diplomatic skill of Madison, Monroe, Pinckney, Erving, and Adams had at last achieved the desired end.

❧ 31 ❧

The Banking Crisis

REËCHOING the confident tone of his inaugural address, Monroe's first message to Congress, on December 2, 1817, had voiced the buoyant spirit of his northern tour. The establishment of peace, leaving the United States free for the first time in twenty-two years to turn its attention to its own domestic affairs, projected the country at once into a career of rapid development. Along with the bonfires and cannonading which welcomed the peace treaty went the practical disappearance of party lines and an intense national feeling, in every rank of society. The enthusiasm and fraternal affection with which the old Federalist strongholds had received the President had been manifestations of this widespread sentiment. Agriculture, manufacturing, and trade were flourishing, and the messages from the governors of the various states corroborated the President's report on the gratifying state of the national finances.

Freed from an intense concentration upon war, the population and resources of the republic increased hourly. Mountain and wilderness trails were replaced by roads, as the wagons of pioneers rolled westward, toward new lands and greater opportunities. Towns and cities sprang up west of the Alleghenies, giving political weight and aggressiveness to the West in its rivalry with the two older sections of the Union. New England mill towns, attracting thousands of European immigrants, stimulated by the wartime demand for woolen and cotton goods, hummed with activity. The obvious prosperity and national well-being caused Monroe to state exuberantly, "At no period of our political existence had we so much cause to felicitate ourselves at the prosperous and happy condition of our country. The abundant fruits of the earth have filled it with plenty. An extensive and profitable commerce has greatly augmented our revenue. The public credit has attained an extraordinary elevation. . . . Our free Government, founded on the interest and affections of the people, has gained and is daily gaining strength. Local jealousies are rapidly yielding to more generous, enlarged, and enlightened views of national policy. . . ."[1]

And in view of this prosperity, he continued: "It appearing in a satisfactory manner that the revenue arising from imposts and tonnage and from the sale of the public lands will be fully adequate to the support of the civil Government, of the present military and naval establishments, including the annual augmentation of the latter to the extent provided for, to the payment of the interest of the public debt, and to the extinguishment of it at the times authorized, without the aid of the internal taxes, I consider it my duty to recommend to Congress their repeal. . . ."[2]

Monroe had ample justification for his optimistic outlook; the country as a whole was prospering; and his message struck a responsive chord in his fellow countrymen. *Niles' Register* editorialized: "This message has received almost unqualified approbation. There never was a better time, for a *good* president to make an *agreeable* message. We have peace and plenty—an overflowing treasury has prompted a recommendation of the reduction of the taxes, and the national credit is so high as to interrupt the operations of the committee for the sinking fund in paying off the public debt; party, too, has lost its fervor—never since the political divisions of the people first began were there so few points to elicit passion as at the present calm and happy period.

". . . The message, in the whole, shews a sound intelligence faithfully devoted to the best interests of the republic and will do much to rivet Mr. Monroe to the affection of his fellow citizens, and exalt his character, with that of his country, abroad."[3]

In accordance with the President's recommendation Congress, early in the session on December 23, 1817, repealed the internal taxes and made provision for winding up the direct taxes. This act greatly increased the popularity of the administration, but subsequent events

The Banking Crisis

were to prove only too forcibly, that its repeal was premature. The financial prosperity upon which the repeal of the internal taxes was based proved delusive.

The era of feverish prosperity upon which the country embarked was based upon an economic derangement consequent upon the war itself and typified by the psychology of all postwar periods.

As usual after a war, there followed a period of sharp speculative reaction. The people, released from the economic and psychological pressure of the war, plunged. Long-withheld crops of cotton found markets at the fabulous price of nearly thirty cents a pound, while $78 an acre was bid for government land in the Southwest.[4] Men to whom the aspect of quick and substantial profits appealed, purchased vast tracts of land, hoping to resell at a higher price before their own loans were due. But this feverish prosperity contained within it the germ of its own disintegration. Disaster was not long delayed.

The great British manufacturing centers, freed from the commercial restrictions of the period of 1810 to 1812 and the second war with the United States, flooded the markets of the new republic, with the express purpose of throttling their young and dangerous rivals. In the seaboard cities, where extravagance abounded as a reaction from the economies of wartime, imported manufactures found a ready market. The effect of this direct dumping of British goods, unimpeded by a protective tariff, on the new industries which had sprung up since the beginning of the war and on the older established industries was disastrous. Thousands of mill operatives in the North and the East, to whom a new means of earning a livelihood had been opened, were thrown out of work. Suffering and misery were widespread, since the American mills, unable to compete with the English, were forced to work at half speed or to close down entirely.

Coupled with this policy of dumping, increasing the general disorder, were Great Britain's renewed restrictions on American commerce. Gone were the profits of the blockade-running war trade. Europe was rapidly usurping the ocean carrying trade which the United States had arrogated to itself during the Napoleonic struggles. There was no longer any great demand for American ships or sailors. Great Britain promptly closed her West Indian ports to American ships, thereby cutting off a large market for the produce of American

JAMES MONROE

farms and effecting a precipitate drop in the prices of crops in the middle states and the West. With shipping prostrate, manufactures languishing, and crops spoiling, there arose a definite demand for protection against European competition in general and British restrictions in particular.

The first years of Monroe's administration marked a new era for American manufactures, for they witnessed the first organized national effort among manufacturers for the protection of industry. In 1816 several influential New York capitalists organized the American Society for the Encouragement of American Manufactures, electing to membership such eminent citizens as Vice-President Tompkins, ex-President Jefferson, retiring President Madison, and President-elect Monroe. The organization maintained that the protection of home industries was a measure indispensable to the attainment and maintenance of industrial independence while its express purpose was to act in the role of a pressure group, to force Congress to raise the tariff, thereby excluding goods of foreign manufacture, and promoting the infant American industries. Before the war the tariff acts had been only incidentally protective. Henceforth protection was to be a distinct national object.

In spite of all the agitation and urgent need for a higher tariff, the Act of 1816 resulted in only a very slight revision upward and the friends of national industry believed the measures to be ample. But as events moved toward 1818 and 1819, with increasing economic stress, general dissatisfaction took a new form. The flood of English products added to the immense accumulation of goods in consequence of the use of labor-saving devices, the ruin of the banks and the farmers, the decline in land values and the presence of idle workmen in the great cities, revived the arguments and increased the demand for a higher tariff. Throughout the North and the East people were meeting, organizing, complaining and petitioning Congress and the state legislatures. It became impossible for any body of men to assemble for any purpose without issuing an appeal for the exclusion of English goods.

By the spring of 1820,[5] with manufacturers in distress, thousands of operatives unemployed, and the western crops falling in price, an organized appeal to Congress to raise the duties established by the Tariff of 1816 was inevitable. Accordingly, a tariff bill, not merely

The Banking Crisis

for restoring a Treasury deficit, but for protection, was introduced and passed by the House. This bill, which raised the *ad valorem* duties from 7½ to 15 per cent and provided for a tax on imported woolens and cottons, failed of passage in the Senate and went down to the people on the eve of a presidential election. It was clearly too early to make the tariff a national issue, and it was not until after 1824 that a definite swing to protection occurred. Monroe's administration, however, saw the beginning of the intersectional tariff struggle, for in the 1820 failure the declining shipping industry and maritime interests of New England united with slaveholding cotton growers and tobacco planters of the South in opposing the measure so vigorously supported by the manufacturing areas of New England and the middle states and the grain and wool raisers of the West.

Not the least important of the many factors contributing to the panic of 1819 was the disordered currency and the thoroughly unsound financial and credit condition of the country. Not only had the ravages of the war drained the country of specie circulation, but the unusual demand for precious metals in Europe, the gravitation of gold and silver to the East Indies, and the inundation of the South and the West by floods of bank paper at anywhere from 50 to 75 per cent discount, made the reëstablishment of specie payments in America very difficult.

Until 1811 the Bank of the United States had exercised a powerful steadying influence over the currency. Its bills, which were good the country over, assured prompt transmission of funds from one part of the United States to another. In the case of lack of medium of exchange in one locality, by equalizing the financial pressure, it could alleviate the situation, minimize the danger of a panic, and greatly facilitate government as well as private business. In 1811, however, Congress refused to recharter the Bank and an epidemic of careless banking set in. Since the doors of the National Bank had been opened, on July 4, 1791, an era of more or less wild speculation had been in progress. Stock-issuing corporations had sprung up on every side. Among them were projectors of state banks, and within a year eight had been chartered. By 1811, when the charter of the United States Bank expired, eighty-eight of these institutions were in business, stretching as far west as Orleans territory, into Kentucky and Ohio. Two years later the number had jumped to 208.

JAMES MONROE

Each bank, under a more or less standard form of charter, could issue bills to an amount equal to three times its capital. Nominally the notes of such institutions, limited by law to denominations of two and five dollars, were redeemable on demand in gold or silver, but no penalty was imposed for refusal to redeem and no check existed to prevent an issue of notes beyond the legal limit. Consequently, with some two hundred institutions issuing notes, far in excess of their ability to redeem them, with specie steadily flowing into New England and as a consequence with the probability of redemption outside that section remote, the suspension of specie payment was inevitable. Boston notes stood at a nine or ten per cent premium in Philadelphia, while bills on banks in the South and West were not receivable at all.

The final plunge into irresponsibility came when the news of the burning of Washington reached the banking centers. By 1814 every bank outside New England had been forced to suspend specie payment. The chief sufferer in the predicament was the government, which lost outright at least five million dollars. Unable to secure a dollar in specie or move a cent from one city to another, near the end of 1814 the Secretary of the Treasury was forced to admit that the Treasury was empty.

In the midst of so debased a paper currency, arising from more than four hundred sources of issue, among them chartered and unchartered banks, factories, individuals, cities and towns, the movement for a Second United States Bank gained headway. The first bill, passed by both Houses and submitted to Madison shortly after he had appointed A. J. Dallas of Pennsylvania to the Treasury, was vetoed by the President. Turning the problem over to the next Congress Calhoun submitted a bill on January 8, 1816. This bill, calling for a capital of $35,000,000, seven million of which was to be subscribed by the United States, ably defended by Clay and Calhoun and violently opposed by Webster, was signed by Madison on April 10, 1816.

The situation which the new Bank had to face was grim. Not only was it to force the state banks to resume specie payments, but it must provide a paper medium which would circulate and be redeemable everywhere. The United States Treasury had agreed to accept the notes of the state banks in payment for lands, on condition that these

The Banking Crisis

banks should resume specie payment. Then the banks, while taking only nominal steps toward resumption, loaned their paper freely to the individuals who wished to invest in the public domain. Even the newly established United States Bank, whose aim it was to achieve some semblance of financial order, under the mismanagement of the inefficient President William Jones, aided and abetted the land speculation by granting liberal loans in the West and South. Facing ruin in the summer of 1818, and with the situation of the whole country thoroughly unsound, the Bank of the United States, which held much of the state bank paper, precipitated the financial crisis by instructing all its branches to accept no notes but its own, to demand immediate payment of all state bank notes, and to renew no personal loans.

As the branches of the National Bank began to stop discounts and press the local banks to redeem their paper, they in turn began to press the people, who were engrossed in reckless land speculation. Disaster ensued. State bank after state bank crashed; merchants, farmers, and planters were ruined over night. To Adams, Secretary of the Treasury Crawford echoed the disastrous state of affairs: "The banking bubbles are breaking. The staple productions of the soil, constituting our principal articles of export, are falling to half and less than half the prices which they have lately borne, the merchants are crumbling to ruin, the manufactures perishing, agriculture stagnating, and distress universal in every part of the country."[6]

That the Bank of the United States should escape the storm which was overwhelming the state institutions was impossible. The debtors, in their distress, turned in fury upon the Bank and its branches, charged them with a large share of responsibility for the financial conditions, and threatened to destroy them. Even in the days of laxity there had been bitter enemies of the Bank and many states had already passed acts taxing it. In his *Register* the ever-vigilant Niles suggested that every candidate for Congress or the state legislature be required to pledge himself to oppose the establishment of any bank during his term.[7] Early in 1819 a desperate attempt was made in Congress to secure the repeal of its charter while the state legislatures, who lacked the power, were swamped with demands to tax the Bank out of existence. In Maryland, Ohio, Kentucky, and Tennessee heavy taxes were laid by the respective legislatures, on all banks doing business under charters which the state had not granted, and in each case resisted. In Maryland the Baltimore branch refused to comply. In the case of *McCulloch v. Maryland*, as it came before the Supreme Court of the United States, the questions at issue were—Has Congress the power to incorporate a Bank? Has such a Bank the right to open branches in the several states? and Have the States the power to tax such branches? On March 6, 1819, John Marshall, reversing the judgment of the Maryland Court of Appeals, handed down the historic opinion of the Court that Congress did have the power under the Constitution to incorporate the Bank; that the Bank had the power to establish branches in the states; and that the state tax was unconstitutional.

As a result of the congressional Bank investigation demanded by the public and made by the House Committee, the Fifteenth Congress at mid-session resolved to reform rather than destroy the institution. The examination of the Baltimore branch brought to light the fact that an institution, recently chartered to aid the whole Union, had been prostituted to the interests of a ring of favored stockholders at Baltimore. The criminally lax President Jones and the board of directors were forced to resign. With the Bank on the brink of irretrievable ruin, Monroe prevailed upon Langdon Cheves of South Carolina, a man noted for his financial ability, to take over the management of the Bank affairs.

In the midst of the financial panic which ensued in Baltimore and the epidemic of runs on banks throughout the South, Monroe decided to make a tour through the southern states like that which he had taken through New England at the beginning of his administration. Not only was the man in great need of diversion, oppressed as he was by the financial ills of the country, but other reasons dictated his course. There were several fortifications and harbors on Chesapeake Bay which required his attention, as did the entire coast. The rising tide of sectionalism which the Missouri debates* and the financial depression had caused, made such a tour imperative for the purpose of allaying sectional jealousy. On March 30, 1819, with the Florida and Spanish affairs temporarily in abeyance, with Spain's ratification of the annexation treaty pending, and with the Missouri question referred to the next session, Monroe sent his family to their Loudoun estate and left Washington.

*Described in the next chapter.

The Banking Crisis

Accompanied by his Secretary of War and South Carolina's favorite son, John C. Calhoun with Mrs. Calhoun and family, his nephew Lieutenant Monroe, Major-General Thomas Pinckney, and his private secretary, Samuel L. Gouverneur,[8] the President set out for Norfolk along the same route which Washington had travelled nearly thirty years earlier. Arriving in Norfolk, where the citizens vied with one another in tendering him "their best respects," he officiated at the laying of the cornerstone of the new customs house and carefully inspected the shipyards and arsenals in the harbor. Although he was fêted at the customary public dinners and was received everywhere with great attention and respect, there was "much less pomp and parade than took place on his eastern journey."[9]

After several days of travel, with Charleston as the next objective, the party spent the night at a plantation on the Cooper River, about ten miles from the city. Early the next morning the group drove to Clement's Ferry, opposite the navy yard, whence they were rowed to the city on an immense barge, "rowed by twenty-five members of the Mariner's Society, steered by their President, Thomas Jervey; the style very fine."[10] Reaching Charleston Monroe was honored by much the same program of speeches, salutes, dinners, and balls which had been accorded George Washington. On Washington's visit the mayor had forbidden fireworks for fear of starting another conflagration, a common occurrence in Charleston, but on Monroe's visit there were fireworks, without disaster. During his week's stay he was accorded the honor of a special St. Cecilia Ball, the only occasion in the history of that exalted society when a special ball honored a visitor. Mrs. Ravenel said, "It was the only occasion a St. Cecilia was ever given 'to any one man'. Its times and seasons are as fixed as if ordered by the heavenly bodies. Lent alone disturbs its dates! Saturday is unheard of! That would hardly be a real St. Cecilia which did not begin on a Thursday 9 P. M."[11]

The President's unfailing charm and gracious manners had captivated the people, and as his cavalcade passed up Meeting Street, on the way out of town, the way was lined with "ladies on each side who crowded the doors and windows to take a farewell view."[12] At Ashley River Bridge, where the President declined to take a salute from his escort, he bade farewell to the city and turned toward Savannah.

JAMES MONROE

Monroe's arrival in the Georgia city coincided with a momentous occasion in its history. Earlier in the spring the steamship *Savannah*, a vessel of 380 tons burden, had been launched in New York. A group of Charleston merchants, among them a Mr. Scarborough, at whose home Monroe was a guest, had arranged that the boat sail from Savannah on her first trans-Atlantic trip. Commanded by Captain Moses Rogers, the vessel reached Savannah on March 28 and was enthusiastically received. As part of the entertainment planned for the visiting Executive, a round trip to Tybee, on board the steamship, was scheduled. The President was so impressed with the advantages of the steam vessel over the old sailing variety that he advised his host, Mr. Scarborough, to bring her to Washington after the Atlantic trip, as there was a possibility that the government might purchase the ship to be used as a cruiser on the China coast.[13] After a pleasant stay in the massive brick and stucco residence of Mr. Scarborough and an outdoor reception in Johnson Square, the presidential party pushed on to Augusta and Athens, and then swung over toward Tennessee.

Aside from the usual public receptions and banquets, Monroe's visit at Athens was marked by two significant toasts, significant in that they indicated that even in the deep South in 1819, the slavery question was still regarded as a social issue and had not as yet assumed political importance. One of these toasts was made to the Colonization Society, "Planned by the wisest heads and purest hearts. May it eventuate in the happiness of millions"; while the other was drunk in condemnation of the slave trade, "The scourge of Africa; the disgrace of humanity. May it cease forever, and may the voice of peace, of christianity, and of civilization, be heard on the savage shores."[14]

On the long journey from Georgia to Nashville Monroe passed through the territory of the Cherokee nation and visited a missionary school where sixty Indian children were being instructed on the Lancastrian plan.[15] Early in June the President and his party reached Nashville and later in the month proceded to Louisville and Lexington in Kentucky. In Lexington Monroe was accorded what was perhaps the warmest reception of his southern tour. A committee of leading townsmen met him fifteen miles from the city and escorted him to the city hall. John Quincy Adams attributed the

The Banking Crisis

heartiness of the demonstration to a desire to counteract an attempt by Clay's friends to slight the President by showing him little attention.[16]

After a visit with General Jackson and a speech on internal improvements, in which he expressed his anxiety for a constitutional amendment to empower Congress to provide for canals, roads, and bridges, Monroe turned toward Washington. He reached the Capital on August 7, in good health, although exhausted by the rigors of his journey of several thousand miles made in the height of the summer heat and over the rough mountain roads of the interior. Monroe was now the man of the hour. The last of the Revolutionary fathers was no longer a vague figure presiding in Washington, but a man of flesh and blood, personally interested in the welfare of the people.

In the late summer, when Monroe returned to Washington, financial conditions were still in a state of chaos, and Langdon Cheves was heroically struggling to reorganize the Bank and to save the institution for the fulfillment of its proper mission. The President did not remain in Washington. He sought relaxation and seclusion with his family at Loudoun, in preparation for the opening of the first session of the Sixteenth Congress in December.

Monroe was not deceived by the lavishness of the entertainment accorded him on his recent tour. He saw the distress of his fellow countrymen and he understood the underlying causes of that misery. In his third annual message to Congress, Monroe outlined the discouraging state of affairs:

"The great reduction in the price of the principal articles of domestic growth which has occurred during the present year and the consequent fall in the price of labor, apparently so favorable to the success of domestic manufactures, have not shielded them against other causes adverse to their prosperity. The pecuniary embarrassments which have so deeply affected the commercial interests of the nation have been no less adverse to our manufacturing establishments in several sections of the Union.

"The great reduction of the currency which the banks have been constrained to make in order to continue specie payments, and the vitiated character of it where such reductions have not been attempted, instead of placing within the reach of these establishments the pecuniary aid necessary to avail themselves of the advantages resulting from the reduction in the prices of the raw materials and of labor, have compelled the banks to withdraw from them a portion of the capital heretofore advanced to them. That aid which has been refused by the banks has not been obtained from other sources, owing to the loss of individual confidence from the frequent failures which have recently occurred in some of our principal commercial cities."[17]

Condemning the policy pursued by England of unloading her goods on the already over-stocked American market, and voicing the sentiment of the American people, the Executive pleaded the cause of protection for American manufacturers and charged Congress with the responsibility for raising the tariff: "It is deemed of great importance," he said, "to give encouragement to our domestic manufacturers. In what manner the evils which have been adverted to may be remedied, and how far it may be practicable in other respects to afford to them further encouragement, paying due regard to the other great interests of the nation, is submitted to the wisdom of Congress."[18]

But the Congress to which Monroe submitted his recommendation had already been presented with a far more momentous problem than that of the tariff; a problem involving the very existence of the Union. For in the dark period of the commercial crisis of 1819, while the expiring Fifteenth Congress was considering the application of Missouri for statehood, the slavery issue had flared up into high political significance. To the Sixteenth Congress had been turned over the immediate issue of Missouri's admission, with all the ramifications of the slavery question, fateful and ominous, transcending in significance the economic ills which beset the nation.

32

The Missouri Compromise

WHILE the Colonies were under the British Crown slavery as an institution and the slave trade to support it existed in each. But in those sections, chiefly in the North and the East, where no great staple crops, such as cotton or rice were grown, where climatic or economic factors made slavery an unprofitable form of labor, and where the demand for all types of labor, both skilled and unskilled, was fully supplied by bondservants, menials, apprentices, and free workers, the moral prejudices against slavery were strongly aroused.

Realizing that the most effective way of combating the evil was to stop the source of supply, repeated attempts were made by the colonists to cut off the slave trade. The Revolution absorbed all attention for a few years, but after the Treaty of Paris the old attacks were renewed. Pennsylvania, Rhode Island, and Connecticut enacted gradual emancipation laws, soon followed by similar legislation in New York State. In 1787, with the exclusion of slavery forever from the states which would one day be carved from the Northwest Territory, the southern boundary of Pennsylvania and the Ohio River formed the dividing line between the free and the slave states.

Aside from the abolition of the slave trade, the racial problem which really most concerned both North and South was the condition of the free Negro, the former slave to whom freedom had been granted. How to incorporate him was the problem of the philanthropic spirit of the age. In the South the people lived in daily dread of a great slave insurrection, while in the North the freedman, suffer-

JAMES MONROE

ing from the ravages of disease, cold, and crowded factory conditions, was a burden and menace to each community.

The policy favored by most humanitarians, and given especial emphasis by the southerners, was that of deportation. In 1800 the General Assembly of Virginia passed a resolution requesting Monroe, who was then Governor, to communicate with the President of the United States with the view of purchasing lands beyond the limits of Virginia for colonization purposes. Although Monroe and Jefferson had carried on a considerable correspondence on this subject, nothing practical resulted from the negotiations.[1] In January of 1805 the legislature passed another resolution requesting Virginia's representatives in Congress to use every effort to secure a portion of the territory of Louisiana for the colonization of such Negroes as had already been or were to be emancipated in Virginia. The difficulties with France and England at the time prevented further prosecution of the subject, but after the termination of the war between the United States and England, a resolution was passed by the General Assembly of Virginia, in December, 1816, requesting the Governor to correspond with the President with the view of acquiring upon the coast of Africa, or at some point in the United States, an asylum for freed Negroes, who desired to emigrate, and a haven for all those who should in the future be emancipated.[2]

Monroe, although a slaveholder himself, heartily approved of the subsequent formation of the American Colonization Society and watched its progress with interest. He also approved the legislation of 1819 providing for the return to Africa of Negroes illegally captured, and was zealous in enforcing the provisions of the law. Although his constitutionality scruples caused him to disclaim any exercise of a colonizing power, and he declined to purchase African territory in the name of the United States, he appointed two agents and sent a public ship to the territory acquired in Africa in the name of the Society. In 1824, in recognition of Monroe's services, the inhabitants of Liberia named their capital Monrovia.

The Constitution had attempted to counterbalance the numerical advantage presented by the North's growing population by permitting the southern states to count three-fifths of their slaves in representation, while at the same time maintaining absolute political

The Missouri Compromise

equality in the Senate by providing for the selection of two men from each state. Up until the assembling of the Fifteenth Congress this political equality had remained undisturbed in the North-South race for the admission of free and slave states. The prohibition of slavery in any state created out of the Northwest Territory had given an advantage to the North, but a slave state had been admitted each time a free state had been granted statehood. At the time of the assembling of the second session of the Fifteenth Congress there were twenty-two states, eleven free and eleven slave, maintaining the political equilibrium.

By 1819, however, the various northern states, under favorable conditions of climate and industrial life, had extinguished slavery or were in the process of emancipation, and were rapidly increasing in population, thereby establishing a superiority in representation over the South. In the southern tier of states, united by common traditions, blood, and the pursuit of staple agriculture, the population remained practically stationary. Southern leaders were drawn together not only to protect a system which to them meant property, stability, life itself, but were united by the instinct for self-preservation, to seek some means of protecting the interests of their minority section.

This, then, was the situation when in 1819 the legislature of Missouri applied to Congress for admission into the Union as a slave state. The section of the country included within the proposed boundaries of Missouri was a part of the Louisiana Purchase. No one had expected settlement in this territory for one hundred years and consequently nothing had been said in the debate on its purchase as to the existence of slavery. However, the treaty with France obliged the United States to protect all the inhabitants of the ceded territory in their rights of person and property. Since Missouri had been settled largely by slaveholders from the southern states, the question whether slavery should or should not exist there was directly involved.

The bill to enable the people of Missouri to form a state government, preliminary to admission into the Union, came before the House of Representatives on February 13, 1819. Transcending the question of whether or not slavery was to be permitted in Missouri was a question of even greater magnitude—should the Louisiana

Purchase be free or slave? Were Missouri to be admitted with permissive slavery, Congress would abdicate all constitutional control over territory purchased by the United States. The Free Soilers in Congress were determined to prohibit the introduction of slavery into Missouri. Just as determined were the southerners in their fight for the right to extend slavery beyond the Mississippi, for not only would the limitation of the slave area diminish the value of their slaves and leave the South to support a redundant population, on land which already showed signs of soil exhaustion, but the concentration of an ever-increasing supply of slaves in a restricted area would increase the dangers of a slave uprising.

The undoubted purpose of the North found a complete political expression in the ensuing first debate. James Tallmadge, of New York, proposed to amend the bill of admission to the effect that the further introduction of slavery be prohibited, and that all children of slaves born within the state after its admission should be free after reaching the age of twenty-five. The first Missouri debate was brief but it kindled a conflagration. It presented arguments to which the later voluminous discussions added but little. Clay, leading the opposition to restriction was so vigorously opposed by Tallmadge and John W. Taylor, of New York, that Cobb of Georgia prophetically commented, "You have kindled a fire which all the waters of the ocean cannot put out, which seas of blood can only extinguish,"[3] while Adams made the following entry in his Diary: "A motion for excluding slavery from it [Missouri] has set the two sides of the House, slaveholders and non-slaveholders, into a violent flame against each other, and Middleton told me Clay had seized the opportunity of pushing himself forward as the champion of the Southern interest."[4] Passing the House with the Tallmadge amendment, the anti-slavery provision was struck out by the Senate, on February 27, and returned to the Chamber. With its failure in the Fifteenth Congress, when the House voted to adhere to its amendment, the bill went over to the next session and the dispute which Congress adjourned without settling was transferred to the people, to the voters, and to the state legislatures.

During the summer and fall of 1819 popular excitement steadily increased. Anxious and restless in the throes of increasing financial panic and frightened that an illegal traffic had been secretly revived

The Missouri Compromise

to restock the labor sources of the South, people all over the North gathered at public meetings and organized committees of correspondence to forbid the further extension of slavery into the national domain and to pass resolutions against the admission of new slave states.

South of the Mason and Dixon's line the tone changed. Just as the previously listless attitude in the North had been succeeded by violent and aggressive excitement, just so an angry spirit now pervaded the South. Southerners feeling that the efforts to restrict slavery were leveled at an institution inextricably interwoven with their very existence, violently declared that Congress had no authority to dictate to the people of Missouri. They believed that if the anti-slavery party were successful at that point the next inevitable step would be in the direction of general emancipation, which would impoverish them and create a new problem, even more difficult of solution than slavery itself.

It was in this mood that the Sixteenth Congress assembled. Its membership, too, reflected the changed attitude in the nation at large, for there were eighty-six newly elected members who had never before been in Congress, and fifty-six of these represented the free states. Thus the North entered the pending congressional battle with a considerable numerical advantage over the South.

For the first time since the pillage of Washington by the British five years earlier, each house of Congress assembled in its proper wing of the rebuilt and repainted Capitol building. The annual presidential message, almost exclusively devoted to the pending Florida treaty and relations with Spain, to which Monroe had devoted so much thought and so many anxious hours, was thrust aside for the Missouri question.

At the opening of this Congress one of the first problems with which Monroe was called upon to deal involved frank, suave, and emotional Henry Clay, who had so ardently espoused the southern cause in the opening Missouri debates, and had conspicuously embarrassed and opposed the administration on its policies pertaining to the recognition of South America and the Florida situation. Several members of the House approached the President to consult him as to whether it would be advisable to displace Clay as speaker, because of his general hostility to the administration. Monroe, as usual declining any active interference in congressional affairs, refused to replace Clay on the grounds that it would give the fiery Kentuckian more "consequence than belonged to him," and because it was important to have a westerner in the Chair. "In all this," wrote Adams, "I think the President has acted and spoken wisely."[5] Upon the reelection of Clay as speaker, the House turned immediately to the question which had caused the first violent outbreak of sectional passion since the establishment of the Republic.

On the day following the President's message the country moved one step nearer to the settlement of the Missouri question, for a new free state was ready to enter the Union. On that day, having secured permission from Massachusetts to petition for a separate existence, Maine, along with Missouri, asked for admission, the former with a free and the latter with a slave constitution. When the bill was introduced to the House, John W. Taylor, of New York, offered a new amendment providing that, as a condition of admission, Missouri should be required to adopt a constitution forever prohibiting slavery within its limits. This provoked a long and vigorous debate on the power of Congress to impose conditions upon the admission of a state to the Union. The situation was greatly complicated by the petition of Maine. In spite of Clay's vehement threat that he would never give his assent to the admission of Maine while a restriction of any sort was imposed on Missouri, the House passed upon the Maine admission on January 3, 1820. The question of a restriction upon Missouri remained to be dealt with, and in the prolonged and acrid House debates the angry sentiments of the country at large were reflected. The two most brilliant protagonists in the verbal warfare in the House were Rufus King of New York and William Pinkney of Maryland. The latter championed the cause of slavery while the former so bitterly and eloquently attacked the system that "the great slave-holders in the House gnawed their lips and clenched their fists as they heard him."[6]

Meanwhile the Senate, the scene of more rational discussion and less high-flown oratory, was proceeding toward a solution. When the Maine bill had come up for consideration in January, 1820, the Senate had coupled it with that of the unrestricted admission of Missouri, and refused to consider the two bills separately. Before the bill was returned to the House, Senator Thomas of Illinois moved a

The Missouri Compromise

compromise amendment, providing that Missouri should be admitted with a constitution permitting slavery but that in all the rest of the Louisiana territory, north of 36° 30′ north latitude, slavery should be forever prohibited.

This amended Senate bill was passed on to the House while the latter was still engaged in its own debates. Here, as well as in the Senate, as the arguments day after day aggravated the hostility between the rival forces, and as the struggle waxed hotter and more bitter, threats of disunion were freely exchanged: "In the hottest paroxysm of the Missouri question in the Senate, James Barbour, one of the Virginia Senators, was going around to all the free-State members and proposing to them to call a convention of the States to dissolve the Union, and agree upon the terms of separation and the mode of disposing of the public debt and of the lands and make other necessary arrangements of disunion."[7]

Although there was no discussion of actual civil warfare, and although dissolution was generally regarded as merely a threat, farseeing statesmen were appalled. About three weeks before the Compromise was adopted John Quincy Adams had a conversation with Henry Clay, while the two were walking over to the home of Chief Justice Marshall, after having heard an address by Edward Everett, of Massachusetts, at the Capitol. Clay expressed his belief that the Union had not long to live:

"Clay started . . . immediately to the Missouri question, . . . and, alluding to a strange scene at Richmond, Virginia, last Wednesday evening, said it was a shocking thing to think of, but he had not a doubt that within five years from this time the Union would be divided into three distinct confederacies. I did not incline to discuss the subject with him."[8]

The Secretary of State, too, was fearful of the consequences of the slavery discussion and disagreed with Monroe's opinion that the entire question would be amicably settled by a compromise: "The Missouri question," he said, "has taken such hold of my feelings and imagination. . . . I take it for granted that the present question is a mere preamble—a title page to a great tragic volume. . . . The President thinks this question will be winked away by a compromise. But so do not I. Much am I mistaken if it is not destined to survive his political and individual life and mine."[9]

JAMES MONROE

Again on February 24, 1820, in a conversation with Calhoun, Adams decried the existence of slavery in the Union and reiterated his belief that no compromise would permanently settle the issue. Slavery must be exorcised from the Union, and to accomplish this he even contemplated a temporary dissolution and reorganization of the Union based upon the fundamental principle of emancipation. "This object," he said, "is vast in its compass, awful in its prospects, and sublime and beautiful in its issue." [10]

Monroe was fully aware of the dangers of the situation, and in his intense devotion to the interests of the Union as a whole, sought advice from his most loyal guide and counsellor. In a letter to Jefferson, February 7, 1820, he expressed his anxiety, but at the same time reiterated his faith in the ultimate triumph of the bonds of Union:

"The Missouri question, absorbs by its importance, & the excit'ment it has produc'd, every other & there is little prospect, from present appearances of its being soon settled. The object of those, who brought it forward, was undoubtedly to acquire power, & the expedient well adapted to the end, as it enlisted in their service, the best feelings, of all that portion of our Union, in which slavery does not exist, & who are unacquainted with the condition of their Southern brethren. . . . I am satisfied that the bond of Union, is too strong for them, and that the better their views are understood, throughout the whole Union, the more certain will be their defeat in every part. It requires, however, great moderation, firmness, & wisdom, on the part of those opposed to the restriction, to secure a just result. These great & good qualities, will I trust, not be wanting." [11]

In succeeding letters to Jefferson, as the congressional struggle increased in bitterness, Monroe's apprehension mounted. On February 19 he wrote:

"I have never known a question so menacing to the tranquility and even the continuance of our Union as the present one. All other subjects have given way to it, & appear to be almost forgotten. As however there is a vast portion of intelligence & virtue in the body of the people, & the bond of Union has heretofore prov'd sufficiently strong to triumph over all attempts against it, I have great confidence that this effort will not be less unavailing." [12]

And again, in May, 1820:

"Certain however it is, that since 1786, I have not seen, so violent

The Missouri Compromise

& persevering a struggle, and on the part of some of the leaders in the project, for a purpose so unmasked and dangerous."[13]

As a southerner and a slaveholder his sympathies were naturally with the South on the issue, but his conception of his presidential duties led him to abstain from all interference in the struggle and to assume an impartial attitude during the wrangle in Congress, until the bill should come to him for signature. It was known, however, that he would have refused to sign any bill admitting Missouri subject to restraint.[14] Possessing a greater breadth of vision than the majority of his southern contemporaries Monroe, in a private letter of February 15, 1820, declared his belief that "the majority of States, of physical force, & eventually of votes in both houses, would be on the side of the non-slaveholding States."[15]

He thought it probable that the non-slaveholders would succeed in their purpose or the Union be dissolved. But while he apprehended great danger from the struggle, "he believed a compromise would be found and agreed to, which would be satisfactory to all parties."[16]

Unlike most of the southern leaders, Monroe carefully reserved judgment on the issue. In his studied attempt to interpret the question on purely constitutional lines he exhibited that love for his country and devotion to national rather than sectional ideals which transcended party schemes and sectional jealousies and which marked him as the man preëminently qualified to guide his country through that difficult era of transition.

On March 3 the bill was presented to Monroe for his signature—its fate still uncertain. Monroe was, after all, a southerner and a slaveholder, and many of his southern friends had strongly urged him to veto. The election of 1820 was pending, and a party caucus was assembling, whose support of Monroe as the presidential candidate might be switched elsewhere, were he to pass the measure. Others besides Monroe appreciated the ticklish position in which he found himself. William Plumer, Jr., a representative from New Hampshire, decidedly unfriendly to Monroe wrote the following to his father, on February 12, 1820:

"This Missouri question has given rise to some movements in Virginia which show in how little estimation the President is held in his native state—They are about to select candidates for electors; & it is there, & here, distinctly announced, that, if Mr. Monroe con-

JAMES MONROE

sents to the bill which, it is thought, will pass both Houses, restricting slavery in the territories, they will look out for a new president. Should the bill pass, it will place the President in a sad dilemma. If he rejects it, acting under his threat he loses all the north, where his best friends now are—if he approves it, he is at open war with Virginia and the South."[17]

On February 17, 1820, Monroe had been the recipient of a strongly worded letter from his son-in-law, George Hay, a Richmond attorney: "I have never said how you would act, but simply that you would do your duty. The members have gone up to the caucus under the conviction that you will put your veto on this infamous cabal and intrigue, in all its forms and shapes; this I would certainly and promptly do. You may be injured in the Northern and Eastern States, but you will be amply repaid by the gratitude and affection of the South....

"The whole affair is regarded as a base and hypocritical scheme to get power under the mask of humanity, and it excites the most unqualified indignation and resentment...."[18]

That this letter had any effect upon Monroe is purely a matter of conjecture. He did prepare the draft of a veto message to Congress which he never submitted for fear of causing a civil war. In this veto, based not on promoting a selfish interest but upon an early and sincere belief that the compromise was unconstitutional, he used this language: "That the proposed restriction to territories which are to be admitted into the Union, if not in direct violation of the Constitution, is repugnant to its principles."[19]

Determining at length not to veto the bill, but by no means sure that Congress had the constitutional power to exclude slavery from the states formed in the future within the Louisiana territory, the President followed his usual custom of submitting all important issues to his Cabinet for discussion and opinions, and asked for written responses to two questions:

1. Did Congress have the constitutional right to prohibit slavery in the territories?

2. Did the compromise section, which interdicted slavery "forever" north of 36° 30′, apply only to the territorial condition of the tract, or did it extend the prohibition to the states erected therein?

Several stormy sessions followed, as a result of which the Cabinet

The Missouri Compromise

members "unanimously agreed that Congress had the power to prohibit slavery in the Territories," but neither Crawford, nor Calhoun, nor Wirt could find any express powers to that effect.[20] At the suggestion of Calhoun, who was averse to a written view, Monroe modified his second question so that all would be able to answer that the act was constitutional, leaving each member to construe the section to suit himself.

The bill was approved by Monroe on March 6, 1820, thus setting the first precedent for Congress to exclude slavery from a public territory acquired since the adoption of the Constitution, and also thus clearly recognizing that Congress had no right to impose upon a state asking for admission into the Union conditions which did not apply to those states already in it.

John Quincy Adams, a strong anti-slaveryite, had voted for the Compromise, but only after expressing his indignation at the methods to which Clay had resorted in the end to secure its passage, and after an expression of his misgivings.

The Compromise was destined to last twenty-eight years, but two more episodes occurred, threatening the Union, before the Missouri Compromise and the slavery question were "laid to sleep." When the constitution of Missouri, including a paragraph making it the duty of the legislature to prevent the immigration of free Negroes into the state, was presented to Congress for approval at the next session, a new and even more heated debate occurred concerning the duty of the federal government to protect the citizens of each state in the exercise of their civil rights of citizenship in every other state, and it was only after a protracted negotiation, again led by Clay, that a bill was finally introduced providing that Missouri should be considered admitted as a state only after its legislature had declared that no law would ever be passed, nor any construction placed upon the obnoxious paragraph which could justify any law in Missouri abridging the rights guaranteed all citizens by the federal Constitution.[21]

An anxiously interested spectator of the new turn the discussion of the Missouri question had taken in Congress was the aging Jefferson. Late in 1820, when it had become apparent that Missouri would be refused admission unless some compromise solution were worked out, he wrote to Monroe: "Nothing has ever presented so threatening an aspect as the Missouri question. The Federalists, completely put down, and despairing of ever rising again under the old division of Whig and Tory, devised a new one, of slave-holding and non-slave States, which, whilst it had a semblance of being moral, was, at the same time, geographical and calculated to give them ascendancy by debauching their old opponents to a coalition with them...."[22]

As far as legislation was concerned, not much else of importance occurred during the waning months of Monroe's first administration. An act, known as Crawford's Act, was passed at the last session, introducing a definite term of office for minor civil officers. When the First Congress had asserted the right of the President to remove such officials, it was thought a dangerous power. In practice that power had been little used and rarely for political purposes. Then Crawford, Monroe's Secretary of the Treasury, was infected with presidential aspirations. It was with the purpose of building up his own patronage that he initiated and fought for the passage of the law of May 5, 1820, which came to bear his name, and which, years later, gave rise to the spoils system. The provisions of the law limited to four years the term of district attorneys, collectors, and various other inferior officers, who had formerly served under good behavior. Madison was very unfavorably impressed. He wrote to Monroe, inquiring whether to vacate these offices periodically was not an encroachment upon the constitutional powers of the executive. Although Monroe, who according to Adams had signed the bill "unwittingly," failed to answer the letter, he expressed his disapproval of the act by renewing the appointment of all officers against whom no charges had been brought.

With the approach of fall in 1820, the country had reached the depths of the depression, but on the horizon was a glimmer of financial improvement. The people as a whole were rallying to the aid of the government and the United States Bank to assist in the restoration of specie payment. While a safer foundation for business was gradually being reached in the North and the East, through the collapsing of fictitious credit, nevertheless failures were still common in the West and the South. Confidence had not yet been restored, and vast sums of money were accumulating in the vaults of the sound banks, since safe investments were returning very small percentages.

The principal effect upon the general government had been a

The Missouri Compromise

sharp general reduction of the revenue. Imports, customs receipts, and public land receipts had dropped precipitately, followed by stringent economy and retrenchment in all departments, particularly in the Army. Perhaps it was irritability caused by having to operate on reduced funds which caused its chief, Calhoun, to paint such a gloomy picture of vague but widespread discontent to Adams in the spring of 1820:

"The primary cause is that which has been the scourge of this country from its colonial infancy—speculation in paper currency, now appearing in the shape of banks; the great multiplication, followed by the sudden and severe reduction, of fictitious capital; then the great falling off in the prices of all our principal articles of exportation, the competition of foreign manufactures carried on by starving workmen, with ours loaded with high wages, the diminution of commerce and the carrying trade, and the accumulation of debt as long as credit could be strained—all this, with ambitious and crafty and disappointed men on the watch for every mischief, and welcoming every disaster, together with the ... mortifying reverses of the Florida treaty, accounts too well for the loss of popularity by the Administration within the last year."[23]

Nor was Adams more cheerful:

"The bank, the national currency, the stagnation of commerce, the depression of manufactures, the restless turbulence and jealousies and insubordination of the State Legislatures, the Missouri slave question, the deficiencies of the revenue to be supplied, the rankling passions and ambitious projects of individuals, mingling with everything, presented a prospect of the future which I freely acknowledged was to me appalling."[24]

However, in spite of these dire predictions, and in spite of the fact that Congress had provided for two loans, one in 1820 and one in 1821, business, if still slack, was again on a firm footing, and it was only a matter of time before financial conditions would be returning to a normal level.

In an era of transition and comparative calm Monroe had made an excellent president. His high ideals and sympathy with all that promoted the general good and the national welfare, his temporizing disposition and ability to rise above petty personal intrigue, and his tremendous personal popularity, which had been stimulated by his

JAMES MONROE

two good-will tours, all recommended him for reëlection. Although an anti-slavery party was crystallizing in the North, nothing approaching a nation-wide party was yet in evidence. Aside from the slavery issue, which was highly sectional, politics was still on a personal basis. Early in April, 1820, several congressmen became uneasy because no candidate had been formally named for the presidency. The Constitution had made no provision for nomination of candidates for the offices of president and vice-president, and previously the candidates had been nominated either by state legislatures or by a committee in Congress known as the Congressional Caucus.

Several congressmen approached Samuel Smith, who had been chairman of the caucus of 1816, with a view to having him name the time and the place for the new caucus. On the appointed Saturday evening only about forty members appeared at the Capitol, too few to act, and after resolving that it was unnecessary to name a candidate, adjourned. The Federalist party was dead, and since Clinton, of New York, the choice of the anti-slaveryites, was the only candidate who had been put into the field, it was up to the presidential electors to make the decision. Monroe received the electoral vote of every state in the Union and seemed about to share with Washington the honor of unanimous reëlection. But when the Electoral College met on December 5, 1820, William Plumer, of New Hampshire, cast his ballot for Adams and Rush, thereby marring Monroe's perfect record. Plumer publicly justified his action by explaining that he wished no one to share with Washington the honor of unanimous reëlection. Both Plumer and his son were known to be hostile to Monroe, on personal grounds, and letters of both reveal their dislike. Plumer's vote against Monroe caused Adams much "surprise and mortification."[25]

Surveying the record of his first four years Monroe could regard his efforts and actions with satisfaction. It is true that in the realm of domestic concerns the country had passed through its worst financial crisis, and was still far from the prosperity of wartime and prewar days, but in the successful conclusion of the Missouri Compromise an exceedingly dangerous and highly explosive issue, which had frequently threatened the existence of the Union itself, had been temporarily settled in what was the most momentous document of Monroe's political life to date. In the field of foreign affairs con-

The Missouri Compromise

siderable progress had been made and the outlook was bright. While the United States, under Monroe's restraining hand, had refused official recognition to the newly established South American Republics, their progress was being carefully watched and judiciously applauded. Without recourse to an actual declaration of war, though only after a long, tedious, and nerve-wracking negotiation with Spain, the province of Florida had been acquired, thus removing from the national boundary a neighbor which had proved a source of long-standing irritation. It was with his own house in a state of comparative good order, and with the knowledge that the people of the nation as a whole were behind him, that Monroe could turn to his next administration and to a subject of even more vital concern than those which had engrossed him during the last four years—that of the United States' relations with Europe.

～ 33 ～

The Monroes and Washington Society

INAUGURATION Day in 1821 fell on Sunday, for the first time since the establishment of the Constitution. Monroe, uncertain whether to defer the ceremonies until the fifth, consulted Chief Justice Marshall and the Supreme Court on the subject, and they advised postponing the affair until Monday.[1]

Shortly before twelve noon, on a day of driving sleet, and with the Washington thoroughfares deep in mud, the members of Monroe's Cabinet gathered at his home, preparatory to proceeding to the chamber of the House of Representatives at the Capitol. The President, "attired in a full suit of black broadcloth of somewhat antiquated fashion,"[2] with shoe- and knee-buckles, headed the procession in an unostentatious carriage, drawn by four horses, and manned by a single colored footman. Closely followed by the heads of the various departments, each in "a carriage and pair," the procession splashed toward the Capitol. In contrast to Monroe's first inaugural, when vast throngs of people, enjoying an unseasonably mild day, had crowded the streets all along the way, the thoroughfares, churned into almost impassable morasses by the driving rain, were practically deserted. However, when he reached the Capitol, such crowds of people had gathered outside the building and had choked the passages to the hall of the House, that it was only with the greatest difficulty that Monroe could enter. Stratford Canning, the English minister resident in Washington at the time, who left some very entertaining comment upon Washington and the American way of life, described the inaugural in a letter to his friend Planta:

The Monroes and Washington Society

"Monday, when we all attended the President's inauguration, in lace coats and silk stockings, was a most wretched day of snow and mud and cold: and though we had acquired an invitation in form from the Secretary of State, we had a tremendous crowd of sturdy and ragged citizens to squeeze through on our way into the House of Representatives. As for Antrobus and myself, we stuck about ten paces from the door and were utterly unable to get in until the arrival of the President, who to our great concern and satisfaction was squeezed as handsomely and detained as long as ourselves. This adventure made some stir. The President and almost everyone who had heard of it expressed his regret, always with the exception of Adams, and Commodore ———— assured me that he had attempted to sally forth to our succour, but had not been able to force his way through the sovereigns assembled round the door.... In addition to the squeezing and shoving which the poor *Prezzy* experienced at the door, his speech, which was indeed rather long, was occasionally interrupted by queer sounds from the gallery; and although the citizens had been duly invited to meet him at his house and attend him on his way to ... the Capitol—the devil a citizen, except the four secretaries of state and Attorney General, was to be seen. To say the truth the weather was a little too severe for any extraordinary demonstrations of attachment."[3]

Taking a seat upon the platform, just in front of the Speaker's chair, the Executive found himself surrounded by his Cabinet associates, the members of the Supreme Court, the foreign missions, the President of the Senate, and the Speaker of the House. Chief Justice Marshall solemnly administered the oath of office and the President stepped forward to address the thronged galleries of the House.

The address was a summary of the main points of his policy, a résumé of events which had occurred during his first term of office, and an optimistic view of the future. In his customarily modest fashion the President opened with the remark that "Having no pretension to the high and commanding claims of my predecessors, ... I consider myself rather as the instrument than the cause of the union which has prevailed in the late election."[4]

He dwelt upon the ravages of the War of 1812 and described the precautions the government had taken against a recurrence of such an invasion. He stressed his policy of peace and good will, reënforced by preparedness. "It need scarcely be remarked," he said, "that these measures have not been resorted to in a spirit of hostility to other powers.... They have been dictated by a love of peace, of economy, and an earnest desire to save the lives of our fellow-citizens from that devastation, which is inseparable from war, when it finds us unprepared for it. It is believed, and experience has shown, that such a preparation is the best expedient that can be resorted to, to prevent war."[5]

The only false note in the speech lay in the exuberance with which Monroe described the state of the material resources of the country. His assertion of "extraordinary prosperity" combined with the repeal of "the direct tax and excise"[6] could scarcely be appreciated by the hundreds of eastern and western farmers who were still being dispossessed by relentless foreclosure, or the manufacturers and laborers who were working at half speed and capacity. Although the depths of depression had been plumbed, and although conditions were on the up-grade, a general prosperity was still on the horizon. However, in closing, the President qualified his extravagant phrases, almost to the point of contradiction, in touching upon the two loans which Congress had been forced to make to meet a deficiency in the general revenue.[7]

The conclusion of his speech was greeted with a "cheering shout" from the galleries, and by the stirring music of the Marine Band, which was making its first public appearance at an official ceremony. The crowd dispersed and the dignitaries adjourned to the White House, where Mr. and Mrs. Monroe received the congratulations of hundreds of friends. "All the world was there," wrote Justice Joseph Story to his wife. "Hackney coaches, private carriages, foreign ministers and their suites were immediately in motion, and the very ground seemed beaten into powder or paste under the trampling of horses and the rolling of wheels. The scene lasted until 3 o'clock, and then all things resumed their wonted tranquility."[8]

The day's festivities were concluded with the customary inaugural ball, held that year at Brown's Hotel. Monroe and his wife left the ball at an early hour, "even before supper was served."

In 1817 the President and his wife had been forced to remain in their house on I Street, where they had lived when Monroe was

The Monroes and Washington Society

Secretary of State. In 1821 they went directly to the White House, which had been their Washington residence for the past three and a half years. The original presidential mansion, from which the Madisons made their historic flight in 1814, with Washington's portrait tucked under Dolly Madison's arm, had been renovated and redecorated and set in order to receive Monroe, in the fall of 1817. Located on a promontory and surrounded by large trees, the house commanded an excellent view of the Potomac. Baron Axel Klinkowström, of Sweden, in the United States for a two-year study during 1818-1820, described the White House to a friend: "The Residence is situated on a charming high place from which one has an unobstructed view towards the Potomac River. On the raid which the British made during the past year to the City of Washington [date is confused] the President's home was burned; but the United States has now rebuilt it in a very handsome Ionic style. Otherwise the Residence is neither large nor impressive. I once said to one of the members of Congress that the highest official of the United States was none too luxuriously housed. He answered that the building was quite practical for its purposes, adding that if it were larger and handsomer some President might find himself disposed to be its continuing inhabitant, against which one must guard."[9]

Resplendent in a gleaming coat of white paint, the executive mansion was nevertheless devoid of furnishings worthy of the President's home. A frugal Congress had assigned to Monroe the task of purchasing the requisite furniture.

During their continental travels and residences abroad, the Monroes had acquired a great deal of French furniture. This, together with their personal silverware, bearing their initials, was purchased by the government and used in the White House down to Van Buren's time.[10] The vast rooms were still far from being filled, however; so Monroe ordered more equipment from Russell and La Forge in Paris. Anticipating trouble with Congress over the outlay involved, and realizing that Congress had failed to grant enough money to furnish the place in a style befitting an executive mansion, he prepared a special message to that body, explaining that each article had been selected with the idea of fitness for the President's home, and even though the bills were high, the purchases were wise. He advocated the appointment of a superintendent of buildings whose task it would be to keep a complete inventory, supervise the buildings, and officially hand them over to the successive occupants of the White House.[11]

In 1817, the Monroes had spent their first spring in their Loudoun County home in Virginia, and that summer the President was away on his New England tour. Although they took up their official residence in the White House late in the fall, the rebuilt mansion was not formally thrown open to the public until January 1, 1818. As the day approached for this important annual affair, which officially launched the Washington social season, Monroe was troubled about what procedure to follow, for presidential receptions and functions were governed by stringent rules. Failure to receive guests in the order of their social and diplomatic precedence would create an incalculable furore and might cause irreparable damage to the President's social prestige. In view of the importance of the subject Monroe consulted his Cabinet and learned that up to that time the members of the diplomatic corps had had no fixed place in the annual reception: "He told me," said Adams, "that his house would be opened on New Year's Day at noon to receive company. I enquired if a short time sooner should be appointed for the foreign Ministers. He at first objected, but afterwards said he would have a Cabinet consultation upon it tomorrow between eleven and twelve."[12]

The President, accordingly, determined to receive the diplomatic corps at eleven-thirty in the morning, and to hold a reception of the general public from noon until three o'clock.[13] The unusually mild weather and the natural curiosity of the public to greet their newly elected President and First Lady and to view the interior of the remodelled dwelling, made the Monroes' first reception an unqualified success. The *National Intelligencer* of the following day was enthusiastic in its praise:

"The charming weather of yesterday contributed to enliven the reciprocal salutations of kindness and good wishes which are customary at every return of New Year's Day. The President's House, for the first time since its re-aerification, was thrown open for the general reception of visitors. It was thronged from 12 to 3 o'clock by an unusually large concourse of ladies and gentlemen, among whom were to be found the Senators, Representatives, Heads of Departments, Foreign Ministers, and many of our distinguished citizens,

The Monroes and Washington Society

residents, and strangers. It was gratifying once more to be able to salute the President of the United States with the compliments of the season in his appropriate residence; and the continuance of this truly Republican custom has given, as far as we have heard, very general satisfaction. The Marine Corps turned out on the occasion and made a very fine appearance."[14]

Anyone following directly in the footsteps of the lovable and popular Dolly Madison, probably the most society-loving mistress who ever graced the White House, would have found it difficult to maintain her standards of lavish and spontaneous large-scale entertainment. The Monroes were no exception. The President, dignified and courteous always, was so modest and shy that he made no attempt to dominate a social gathering, even in his own home. He was fifty-nine years old at his first inauguration and was still a handsome man and strongly built. He was devoted to those dear to him and was too much absorbed in politics to be greatly concerned over a successful social season. He studied alone, far into the night, the problems confronting his administration. His conservative temperament was reflected in the dark suit, with light knee-length pantaloons, the dark beaver hat, and the white-topped boots which he elected as his customary day-time attire, and in his old-fashioned headdress, with hair cut short in front and powdered and gathered into a cue behind.[15] He was much happier riding through the countryside, attended only by a colored groom, stopping to speak to men along the way and learning of their problems, than he was when engaged in the more superficial chit-chat of the formal drawing room of his own home. "Mr. Monroe's exterior was grave and mild," wrote Mrs. Ellet. "Few persons ever knew him intimately who did not love him. There was a downrightness, a manliness, a crystal-like integrity in his conduct, which constantly grew upon his associates."[16]

The President's wife, beautiful and gracious Elizabeth Kortright Monroe, who in her girlhood had figured prominently in the social life of New York and was accustomed to the brilliant pageantry of the continental capitals and versed in the elaborate amenities of European courts, was admirably fitted to do the honors of the White House with grace and dignity. Said to be the most stately, gracious, and regal-looking lady ever to be Queen of the White House, she might easily have succeeded to and surpassed Dolly Madison's popularity. But she was a chronic invalid and was forced to delegate much of the responsibility of entertainment to her older daughter, Eliza Hay, an extremely capable, but a far less charming and diplomatic woman than her mother.

Eliza was many years older than her younger sister, Maria Hester. She had married Judge George Hay, an influential Virginian, the son of the keeper of the Raleigh Tavern at Williamsburg.[17] He was the United States District Attorney from Virginia and had been the prosecuting officer at the trial of Aaron Burr.[18] Added to the prestige she enjoyed as the President's daughter and as the wife of a prominent man, was Eliza's knowledge that during her early school days in France, in Madame Campan's Seminary at St. Germain, she had sat on the same bench with duchesses and queens and had formed a fast friendship with Hortense Beauharnais, the daughter of Josephine Bonaparte. Thus, feeling that she had been born to the purple, and realizing that her mother was far too frail to manage the many arduous presidential functions, she willingly gave up her home in Richmond and installed herself at the White House as undisputed mistress of the establishment and everyone in it.

Mrs. Monroe, shortly after assuming the duties of First Lady of the Land, felt obliged to limit some of the civilities with which her predecessor, Mrs. Madison, had worn herself out. Dolly Madison's retirement had been sincerely regretted, for she entertained frequently and lavishly. She had called upon all visiting notables, had always been ready to receive callers when at home, and had presided at each of the many state dinner parties given by her husband. But her popularity had been gained at the cost of her health. Meanwhile, the social etiquette of Washington was undergoing distinct changes. The population of the city was growing rapidly. New states were being admitted to the Union and the population of those already in was increasing at a tremendous rate. With the consequent increase in the number of congressmen in Washington, and the influx of visitors from other cities, the social duties of the higher government officials, and especially of the President, if conducted upon the generous lines established by Mrs. Madison, would have proved too arduous. For anyone in Mrs. Monroe's delicate state of health it would have been disastrous.

Before the Monroes entered the White House, the President's

The Monroes and Washington Society

wife had customarily paid the first call upon the wives of visiting foreign dignitaries and ministers, and even upon the wives of new congressmen. When Mrs. Monroe's intention of paying no first calls at all became known, she became immediately and definitely unpopular. Feeling she was perfectly justified in her stand, yet desiring some official approbation, she asked Mrs. Adams to call upon her shortly after the New Year's Reception of 1818. Mrs. Adams counselled her to adhere to her decision, but to base it upon her physical disability rather than on any question of etiquette.[19]

Mrs. Monroe further increased her unpopularity by establishing certain visiting hours when she would be available, instead of holding a continuous open house as had her predecessor. She delegated to her daughter Eliza the duty of returning all calls, explaining that she would be happy to receive visitors, although her own ill health prevented her from visiting. Eliza, however, in refusing to call on the ladies of the diplomatic corps, because they had failed to call in the first place, did not pay all the visits which Washington expected of her. She influenced her father to keep all the foreign ministers "at a cold and cautious" distance, and so injected her own private jealousies and feuds into the conduct of the White House that in a short time social Washington was in a furore.[20]

Just at the point when this "obstinate little firebrand" was perpetually interrupting Mr. Adams to render a decision on a weighty matter of "etiquette visiting" in her "senseless war," when he was harassed with the intricacies of the Florida negotiations and sparring with the British minister, the diplomatic corps took a hand. Mr. Hyde de Neuville, the French minister, gave a ball in celebration of the evacuation of France by the Allies and wished Mr. and Mrs. Monroe to attend. When the President refused on the ground that it was contrary to precedent, and Mrs. Monroe refused to go without him, it was decided that Mrs. Hay attend. The latter made it very clear that her attendance was unofficial and attached so many conditions to her acceptance, that poor Mr. Adams, who carried all the messages, was sorely tried to maintain amicable relations with the French embassy.[21] Whether Mrs. Hay enjoyed herself at the brilliant ball, attended by three hundred persons, is unknown.

The "whole senseless war," which Mrs. Hay had precipitated, had its repercussions in the senatorial field, casting its reflections on

JAMES MONROE

the Secretary of State and his wife. Not only were the ladies of Washington boycotting Mrs. Monroe, so that her drawing rooms opened "to a beggarly row of empty chairs,"[22] but Mrs. Adams, too, was being snubbed by the elect. Several of the senators had spoken to Monroe, complaining that the Secretary of State had refused to pay them the first visit. The President mentioned the fact to Adams with much delicacy and suggested that in view of the "uneasiness, heart-burnings, and severe criticisms,"[23] which had been evoked, a Cabinet meeting should be held with the purpose of agreeing upon some rule of procedure. Mr. Tompkins, the Vice-President, substantiated Monroe's statement of complaint by telling Adams that some of the southern senators were "peculiarly tenacious of their claim to a first visit and the principle on which they rested their claim was, that the Senate being by their concurrence to appointments a component part of the Supreme Executive, and therefore the Senators ought to be first visited by heads of Departments."[24]

Adams' reply was that the claim was highly illogical, as it carried with it the obligation for senators at home to visit every member of the legislature by which they were chosen.[25]

A Cabinet meeting was accordingly scheduled for December 20, 1819. After it was decided that each member was to follow his own course in the question of first calls, Adams was requested to prepare for the President a statement of his attitude and that of Mrs. Adams. During the course of the discussions it became apparent that Monroe was "inclined to think it would be well for the heads of Departments to indulge this humor of the Senators, and then, to avoid an invidious discrimination between the two Houses, to do the same thing by the members of the House, and at the commencement of every session of Congress."[26]

In accordance with the Cabinet request, on Christmas Day Adams sent to Monroe a voluminous exposition of etiquette which was characteristic of the earnestness and clearness with which he treated even the apparently trivial details of this "paltry passion for precedent."

"It has, I understand from you, been made a subject of complaint to you, as a neglect of duty on the part of the Secretary of State, that he omits paying at every session of Congress a first visit of form to every member of the Senate, and that his wife is equally negligent of her supposed duty, in omitting similar attention to the ladies of every

The Monroes and Washington Society

member of either House, who visit the city during the session. . . . I must premise, that having been five years a member of the Senate, and having during four of the five sessions been accompanied at the seat of government by my wife, I have never received a first visit from any one of the heads of department nor did Mrs. Adams ever receive a first visit from any of their ladies. . . . Visiting of form was considered as not forming a part either of official right, or official duty."[27] This letter, transmitted to Vice-President Tompkins on December 29, which was to be relayed by him to the senators, gave an excellent argument for the policy which Adams adopted. He realized that if he were to visit the senators, the members of the House would expect and demand the same favor. This would entail not only a "very useless waste of time" but would seriously interfere with his more pressing and infinitely more important State Department duties. Nor did the custom appear to him "altogether congenial to the republican simplicity of our institutions."[28] "The only principle of Mrs. Adams," he continued, "has been to avoid invidious discrimination; and the only way of avoiding them is to visit no lady as a stranger. She first visits her acquaintances, under the usual rules of private life, and receives or returns visits of all ladies, strangers, who pay visits to her."[29]

Upon the assurance of Vice-President Tompkins that the senators disclaimed any pretention to claim the first visit, Adams commented in his characteristically acid style that "those Senators who have set up the pretension are ashamed of avowing it, and yet are too proud to renounce it."[30] This code of social etiquette, which in its salient features was similar to that of President Washington, now decreed, as in the days of Washington, Adams, and Jefferson, that the President and his wife should not be expected to make and return visits.

Having settled the difficulty with the senators, President Monroe found himself in trouble over his diplomatic dinners, for he had made an innovation in their character. Since the members of the diplomatic corps were not ambassadors, but ministers of the second order, it had been customary to invite the Secretary of State. He took precedence over the ministers. Monroe learned that the other secertaries desired to be placed on an equal footing with the Secretary of State, and were thoroughly offended at being omitted from the guest list. On the other hand, the ministers were frankly hostile to the idea that four or five department heads and their wives should take precedence

JAMES MONROE

over them and refused to be superseded. Monroe was indeed between two fires. Here in the capital of the Republic, in the very citadel of democratic virtues, where Jeffersonian principles of *pêle-mêle* and *en masse* had ruled supreme, he found the question of aristocratic precedence assuming vital and menacing proportions. Once again trouble was averted. Monroe, the soother of outraged egos, calmed the tempest by inviting Mr. Adams to each dinner, taking one other secretary and his wife in rotation.

According to the report of a New York representative, dinner parties at the Monroe's, which Mrs. Monroe seldom attended and to which, as a consequence, the wives of the guests were rarely invited, were exceptionally dull. The guests seated themselves in a row in the drawing room after their arrival, awaiting the summons to the dining room. As soon as the introductions had been completed absolute silence reigned, "and everyone looked as if the next moment would be his last."[31] Although the White House dinners were rather gloomy functions in the French style, devoid of anything approaching hilarity, and with a cloud of servants handing the dishes around, James Fenimore Cooper, in his *Notions of the Americans*, published in 1828, has left a not too bleak account of a formal dinner: "The table was large and rather handsome, the service was in china, as is uniformly the case, plate being exceedingly rare, if used at all. There was, however, a rich plateau and a great abundance of the smaller articles of tableplate. The cloth, napkins, etc., etc., were fine and beautiful. The dinner was served in the French style a little Americanized. . . . In the drawing room coffee was served and everyone left the house before nine."[32]

White House dinners were not exactly hilarious affairs but they were not completely devoid of drama. At one ministerial dinner, given to the diplomats by the President, Sir Charles Vaughan, the British minister, found himself seated opposite the Count de Sérurier, the French representative. Several times Vaughan noticed that the French minister bit his thumb when he made a remark. At length he could conceal his irritation no longer, and asked, "Do you bite your thumb at me, Sir?" "I do," came the Count's reply. Both men instantly left the table, withdrew into an adjoining hall, and had their swords crossed when Monroe, who had followed them from the table, arrived upon the scene and threw up their swords with his own. After

The Monroes and Washington Society

calling his servants and ordering the two gentlemen into separate apartments, he sent for their carriages. The dinner was resumed and both miscreants sent their apologies the following morning.[33]

The Washington of Monroe's day was hardly the city of marble and endless, beautifully shaded vistas envisioned by L'Enfant. Having ceased to be an object of enthusiasm to the average visitor, it was in actuality a rural neighborhood in the painful process of changing into a city. It was a waste of woods and bogs. Blocks of cheap and hideous brick buildings squatted in the shadows of the recently completed Capitol; scattered throughout the city were the slave blocks and their squalid quarters. In the absence of paved streets and an adequate drainage system the annual rains changed the streets into rivers of mud and cesspools of vermin. The result was periodic epidemics of fever and disease, which twice ravaged the city during Monroe's administration. In 1820, during the course of the first epidemic, Mrs. Calhoun lost her five-months-old daughter, and her second was to die in the same manner. "Ladies of the first and gayest fashion," wrote a friend to Mrs. Kirkpatrick, "as well as particular friends, pressed their attendance, in a way not to be denied. The President called every day, and his daughter, Mrs. Hay . . . came three evenings successively to beg to sit up and was denied as other ladies were already engaged.[34]

The second epidemic, even more disastrous than the first, left scarcely a family untouched: "Disease and death, are making sad havoc in many parts of our country. . . . Our city is very sickly. . . . Not a family on Capitol Hill have escaped disease."[35] But at the same time it was considered to be of a milder character than that which raged in adjoining counties. S. L. Gouverneur wrote from Washington in October, 1821, "It is true that this city is unusually sickly at this period, but we think the fevers prevalent, of a much milder character, than those which have afflicted the adjoining country. Innumerable cases of fever have occurred but few deaths have resulted from them. In some families, four or five have been prostrate at the same moment."[36]

Even the President's family failed to escape the current malady. In a letter to Madison in the spring of 1821 Monroe expressed his concern over the condition of the various members of his family: "Mrs. Monroe and Mrs. Hay have been sick since Congress left us &

JAMES MONROE

recently our g^rd. daughter, Hortensia, has been dangerously ill with a sore throat & fever which had nearly carried her off. The complaint is atmospheric, & has taken off several children in this part of the city. The fever has left her & her throat getting well, but she is reduced to a skeleton. I shall move them to Loudoun (where Mrs. Gouverneur was sent with her child for safety) as soon as she can travel."[37]

It was said to be a common occurrence for snakes two feet long to invade stately drawing rooms, for cattle to graze within a stone's throw of the White House, and for state carriages to upset their regally-clad inhabitants into an impassable quagmire at the very door of a foreign minister's residence. Baron Axel Klinkowström wrote in 1819: "Very few of the streets have been built up in this lovely tract, and one comes upon only a few houses here and there. The region around the wharf, Greenleaf Point, Pennsylvania Avenue, and the vicinity of the Capitol are built up to some extent, but only with difficulty can one find in the whole city any stretch of houses that extends for 800 yards without seeing empty lots between. . . .

"The most frequented street is Pennsylvania Avenue; but it is not paved, and so in dry weather and wind one is choked by the dust that is raised by the numerous carriages that daily pass to and from the Capitol and that usually follow this street; in rainy weather again the mud is frightful, and one sinks down above the ankles; the sidewalks left on the sides of the road are not entirely paved. The distances between the houses are very long, one reckons them in miles."[38]

Mr. George Ticknor, the most celebrated globe-trotter of his era, felt that Washington suffered by comparison with the other capitals of the world:

"The first time we were in Washington we passed a little less than a fortnight; the last time between three and four weeks. It is altogether a very curious residence; very different from anything I have seen in any part of the World. The regular inhabitants of the city from the President downwards lead a hard and troublesome life. It is their business to entertain strangers, and they do it, each one according to his means, but all in a very laborious way. . . . The President gives a dinner, once a week, to 30 or 40 people—no ladies present—in a vast, cold hall. He invited me to one, but I did not go.

The Monroes and Washington Society

I was, however, at a very pleasant dinner of only a dozen that he gave to Lafayette, when the old gentleman made himself very agreeable; but this was quite out of the common course. . . . Mr. Adams gives a great dinner once a week, and Mrs. Adams a great ball once a fortnight; it keeps her ill half the time, but she is a woman of great spirit, and carries it through with a high hand."[39]

Nor was Mr. Mills, a Representative from Massachusetts, more agreeably impressed: "It is impossible for me to describe to you my feelings on entering this miserable desert, this scene of desolation and horror. . . . My anticipations were almost infinitely short of the reality, and I can truly say that the first appearance of this seat of the national government has produced in me nothing but absolute loathing and disgust."[40]

The arrival of Congress was the signal for commencing the round of social activities, although the season was officially launched by the President's New Year's reception. Aside from the weekly drawing rooms, levees, and state dinners at the White House during the session, the foreign embassies, distinguished citizens of Washington, and the heads of the departments gave a series of balls and entertainments which livened up the winter months. The southern senators and representatives, particularly, accompanied by their beautiful wives, were noted for their hospitality. Their sumptuous dinners and suppers, replete with rich wines and seasonal delicacies, their ornate carriages and liveried servants, gave an unmistakably southern flavor to Washington society.

In a society which exhibited such tremendous concern over the precedence accorded to foreign ministers at state dinners and over the intricacies of "etiquette visiting" between the ladies of Congress, the attempts made by the members of the French embassy, to raise the *ton* of diplomatic society, were heartily applauded. Mrs. Seaton describes how, at a formal function, the attention of the assembled company "was attracted through the window towards what we conceived to be a rolling ball of burnished gold, carried with swiftness through the air by two gilt wings. Our anxiety increased the nearer it approached, until it actually stopped before the door, and from it alighted, weighted with gold lace, the French Minister and suite. We now also perceived that what we had supposed to be wings, were nothing more than gorgeous footmen with *chapeaux bras,* gilt-braided skirts and splendid swords. Nothing ever was witnessed in Washington so brilliant and dazzling."[41]

Mrs. Monroe outlived the spasm of unpopularity which greeted her early social restrictions. The members of the Old Washington Families, "just then beginning to lay claims to antiquity," had been offended by her exclusiveness. However, her charm and beauty, and the sincerity of the manner in which she welcomed her daily visitors and the guests at her weekly drawing rooms and fortnightly receptions won the admiration and esteem of all, including her formerly most severe critics. Washington society accepted her doctrine, and her White House successors were in time duly grateful.

In opening her home every Wednesday evening and receiving her guests at a formal reception, Elizabeth Monroe sought to restore the formality of the Washington régime. As the guests arrived, about nine o'clock, they were received gravely and simply at the entrance by the President and then were presented to Mrs. Monroe and her two daughters. They received their visitors in the spacious and attractive rotunda, from which opened up two or three large reception rooms, prepared for the occasion. The warmth and glow emanating from the hickory-wood fires in the many fireplaces, the gleam of the massive silver trays in the candlelight,[42] and the solemn demeanor of the liveried colored servants who passed the wine, created an atmosphere of fastidious elegance which characterized the serene and aristocratic First Lady. About ten o'clock in the evening coffee, tea, and iced cakes were served, amidst political debate and idle gossip, and by midnight everyone had departed. Baron Klinkowström has given a charming description of Elizabeth Monroe:

"Mrs. Monroe's courts, or as they are called here, levees, are very interesting for one who to some degree can make a comparison with the court etiquette of the Old World. From the entrance hall below one comes *á plein pied* into a large and attractive rotunda; a little to the left of the center of this room stood Mrs. Monroe. On arriving, all go up to her and bow, and she answers the greeting with a little nod of the head. Mrs. Monroe was very elegantly dressed at the first court; her costume consisted of a white gown of India mull, embroidered with gold, her hair was braided with pearls and adorned with a lovely diadem of gold set with pearls, and ornaments of pearls adorned her throat, arms, and ears. She seemed to be between thirty

The Monroes and Washington Society

and forty years old, medium sized, her face set off to advantage by her beautiful hair."[43]

Although Mrs. Monroe issued no formal invitations to her drawing rooms and levees, a strict line of demarcation was recognized and strictly observed. However, it was a period of flux in the social strata. The well-defined gentry of the Revolutionary period was rapidly disappearing, and the higher average of dress and manners, developed in the later years of rising fortunes and large newspaper circulation, had not yet begun to show itself. Prominent westerners, born and tested on a savage frontier and recognizing the triumph over adversity as their only badge of social distinction, thronged Washington in rough, coarse hunting coats, leggings, and boots. They mingled freely with the richly clad southern plantation owners and the more conservatively, yet expensively dressed northern manufacturers and merchants. Consequently, Mrs. Monroe's drawing rooms afforded a curious social medley, crowded with "secretaries, senators, foreign ministers, consuls, auditors, accountants, officers . . . farmers, merchants, parsons, priests, lawyers, judges, auctioneers, and nothingarians . . . —all with their wives and some with their gawky offspring . . . some in shoes, most in boots and many in spurs; some snuffing others chewing and many longing for their cigars and whiskey waiting at home, some with powdered heads, others frizzled and oiled, whose heads a comb has never touched, and which are half hid by dirty collars (reaching far above their ears) as stiff as pasteboard."[44]

The extremely cosmopolitan gathering was a source of amazement to the European-bred Baron Klinkowström:

"At the Court was a large gathering of all classes and ranks of the community; and, as I judge, every free American that owns ground or carries on his business has the right to appear at the courts of the President's wife. Foreign ministers, consuls, travellers, American officers and officials were quietly dressed, partly in uniforms, partly in plain clothes; but there were also others, badly and slouchily dressed, who seemed to want to display themselves in a costume less tidy and less suitable to the occasion. I noticed some farmers or other men in stained clothes, uncombed hair, unbrushed and muddy boots, just as they had come from the street, whose figures contrasted sharply with the rest of the gathering. At one of the courts I attended there was also a chief of the Creek tribe, together with some of his Indians, dressed according to the custom of their people."[45]

Amidst all the pomp and ceremony with which receptions and entertainments were carried on, and in spite of the importance attached to rank and precedence in all walks of society, Monroe maintained his direct simplicity, his easily approachable mien, which had endeared him to the country at large on his tours. Justice Joseph Story wrote, "There is a great deal of gayety, splendor, and as I think, extravagance in the manners and habits of the city. The old notions of republican simplicity are fast wearing away, and the public taste becomes more and more gratified with public amusements and parades. Mr. Monroe, however, still retains his plain and gentle manners; and is in every respect a very estimable man."[46]

Baron Klinkowström, accustomed to the inaccessibility of the European monarchs, expressed great surprise at the informality and geniality of his reception by Monroe: "I passed no guards or sentinels in the avenue to the President's house; . . . a servant in livery showed us up one flight and went in to announce us. In a little while we were admitted; the President, dressed in a plain brown coat, came very courteously towards us and asked us to sit before the fire. Two other persons were there and talked in a rather confidential tone; one of them, dressed in a surtout, sat in a very unceremonious position. . . .

"I handed the President the letter that the American Minister residing in Stockholm, Mr. Russell, had given me; and asked for the privilege of visiting the naval docks of the United States, which the President very graciously granted me, adding with a smile that it would please him if a stranger could find anything new and instructive in so young a country as the United States; to which I answered that I thought the time was very near when Europeans would visit America not to bring over new inventions but to fetch information and instruction about new things regarding which in the old world one had either incomplete ideas or none."[47]

By the end of the first administration Mrs. Monroe, whom Mrs. Edward Livingston termed the "Ninon of the day" and the "most beautiful woman of her age she had ever seen,"[48] was on cordial terms with most of the Washington hostesses. Not so with her daughter, Eliza Hay. In 1820, when the younger daughter, Maria Hester, was married, Mrs. Hay was still carrying on her feud.

The Monroes and Washington Society

Maria Hester, who was only twelve when her father was elected to the presidency, had always been an attractive and vivacious youngster, winning the hearts of all. The family had taken great pains with her education, and Mrs. Monroe had made the most of her beauty by dressing the child in the latest Parisian creations. In fact, Judge Tucker, of Virginia, who visited the Monroes shortly after their arrival in Washington in 1807, was so captivated by the little girl and the costume she wore, that he wrote a letter to his daughter, describing the dress in detail, so that she might copy it for her own little girl: "Your mama has refer'd you to me for an account of little Maria Monroe, who is I believe a few months older than our darling Francilea. She was dress'd in a short frock, that reach'd about half-way between her knees and ancles—under which she display'd a pair of loose pantaloons, wide enough for the foot to pass through with ease, frill'd round with the same stuff as her frock and pantaloons. . . . The little monkey did not fail to evince the advantage of her dress. She had a small Spaniel dog with whom she was continually engaged in a trial of skill—and the general opinion seemed to be that she turned and twisted about more than the Spaniel. . . . I must recommend her dress for my dear Brats."[49]

In 1818 Mr. Monroe secured the services of Samuel L. Gouverneur, a nephew of Mrs. Monroe's, as his private secretary. Those were not the days of official stenographers, typewriters, and innumerable secretaries. Economy was the watchword, and one private secretary was all that was allotted to the President, who painstakingly wrote and copied in longhand all his messages. The official status of the President's private secretary, in addition to his blood relationship, made Mr. Gouverneur practically a member of the family.

A handsome and brilliant young man, he later, like many another gentleman of his day, went through an inherited fortune, via wagers, horse racing, and champagne. At one time he owned the famous horse, "Post Boy." A man of decidedly social tastes, after his marriage he owned and occupied the DeMenou Buildings on H Street in Washington and entertained brilliantly with his charming young wife.[50] It is slight wonder that this dashing young man-about-town soon captured the heart of his beautiful young cousin. The attraction was mutual and two years later he asked for her hand in marriage.

JAMES MONROE

Although Maria Hester was only sixteen, her father's favorite daughter, and several years younger than her prospective husband, she was a precocious child and her father, highly satisfied with the arrangement, willingly gave his consent.

Mrs. Monroe was in very poor health at the time, and the preparations for the wedding fell upon the shoulders of Mrs. Hay. That worthy young matron determined to extend the policy of exclusiveness, which marked the social side of the Monroe administration, to her sister's wedding. Invitations were issued only to relatives and close personal friends. The members of the Cabinet were not even included and Mrs. Hay informed the diplomatic corps that they were not expected to take any notice of the event, a suggestion which they followed with considerable alacrity.[51]

In spite of the exclusiveness of the affair, Maria's approaching marriage became the absorbing topic of social interest of the day, for she would have the honor of being the first daughter of a president ever to be married in the White House. Miss Albertina Van Ness, a school friend of Maria's, one of her bridesmaids and soon herself to become the bride of Arthur C. Middleton, wrote to another mutual friend in Philadelphia, Miss Ann Chew, "I suppose the news of our old school-mate's engagement has reached you, long since; The ninth of this month is the day fixed on for the wedding. I can scarcely realize it; to think that last winter, we were at school together, and now she is about to become Mrs. Gouverneur.... I have laughed at little Rias (as we used to call her) more than once about it."[52]

On March 9, 1820, the members of Maria's immediate family and a few intimate friends, gathered in the East Room of the White House. Formerly used by Mrs. Adams as a place in which to dry her washing, this largest and now most famous room of the executive mansion had been furnished by Monroe, and was opened on that day to the public for the first time. The Reverend Dr. William Hawley, a gentleman of the old school and rector of old St. John's Church in Washington, performed the ceremony, while the gallant General Thomas S. Jesup, one of the heroes of the War of 1812, acted as groomsman to Mr. Gouverneur. Maria Hester was a lovely bride, gowned in a light blue stiff silk dress, with intricate embroidery of real wheat stalks. After the ceremony a grand reception was held,

The Monroes and Washington Society

at which the new Mrs. Gouverneur presided, taking over her mother's customary position. Mrs. Seaton, one of the favored few to secure an invitation, has left an account: "The New York style was adopted at Maria Monroe's wedding. Only the attendants, the relations and a few old friends of the bride and groom witnessed the ceremony, and the bridesmaids were told that their company and services would be dispensed with until the following Tuesday, when the bride would receive visitors."[53]

Mr. and Mrs. Gouverneur left for a week's bridal tour, and when they returned to Washington, the social world had an opportunity to pay its respects at a formal White House drawing-room. All guests were received by Mrs. Gouverneur, who presided in her mother's place on that evening, while Mrs. Monroe mingled with her guests. This reception inaugurated a series of brilliant festivities, including invitations for balls and informal parties in honor of the popular couple.

On March 20 Commodore and Mrs. Stephen Decatur gave the bride her first grand ball, in their home on Lafayette Square. Two mornings later social and official Washington was stunned to receive the news that the popular Commodore had been killed at Bladensburg, as the result of a duel with Barron. Both men had fallen wounded at the first exchange of shots. The latter eventually recovered, but Decatur died within a few hours. Death came as a personal grief to the entire official group. Never had the city been so stunned and wrought up. Sermons were preached and addresses given against the senseless custom of "affairs of honor." The untimely and shocking death of the popular officer put a check upon all social functions. The wedding gaieties and many invitations were cancelled. The city went into mourning.[54]

The next few months Maria Gouverneur and her husband spent in Washington, preparatory to establishing their permanent residence in New York City. Maria's impending departure weighed heavily on the family, for it was to be the first real break in their closely-knit circle. Both the girls and their father were extremely devoted to Mrs. Monroe and rarely spent much time away from one another. Aside from the President's two long trips and an occasional visit to Madison or Jefferson in Albemarle, the family invariably accompanied him and spent frequent weekends at their Loudoun

County estate. Even Eliza's marriage had caused no real break, for while she was living in Baltimore, she was near enough to see her family at frequent intervals. And then, since 1817 she, too, had taken up her residence, with her daughter Hortensia, at the White House.

The two sisters, though widely separated in age, had always been rather close, coöperating in waiting on their invalid mother, but as the day approached for Maria to leave, a cloud hung over their friendship. Mrs. Hay cherished some secret dislike for her new brother-in-law,[55] and made no effort to conceal or forget it. She even treated her sister with marked coolness. Both Mr. and Mrs. Monroe were grieved at this first appearance of discord in the family, and Maria and Sam Gouverneur tried to clear up the situation, to no avail. At length, late in the fall, the young couple left for New York with the promise that Maria would return to Washington early in the spring to spend the summer with her mother and sister.

Apparently the failure to appease the ill-will which Eliza bore Sam Gouverneur, combined with lonesomeness for her younger daughter, lay heavily upon Mrs. Monroe. Her letters revealed her unhappiness, and at length young Gouverneur made one final attempt to settle the matter. In a letter of December 6, 1822, he wrote to the President:

"Maria has received your letter of which I have also read—I regret extremely to hear, that Maria's absence, should continue to be a subject of affliction to her mother—I had hoped that our promise to be with you early in the Spring, would have reconciled her to the necessary separation during the winter. I regret the more that any recollection of ———— that are past, should be permitted to affect the health of any of the family, or that you, in the midst of your present laborious and responsible duties, should experience any distress therefrom. It was my sincere hope, and ardent wish that every recollection of unpleasant occurrences had been obliterated from the memories of all, and that they had been succeeded by an anxious desire to promote the common felicity of the family. Such are the feelings which I have not ceased to indulge since we left you. I am conscious of the painful emotions, with which both Aunt M and yourself have witnessed the existence of sentiments of a different character, and I feel it to be an object sincerely to be wished, that by an unqualified renewal of the same affectionate feelings, which formerly existed,

The Monroes and Washington Society

you may both find consolation in a family again effectionately united to each other. For my own part I can sincerely say that feelings in unison with such hopes, have taken complete possession of my heart and eradicated therefrom every recollection of an opposite character.[56]

That winter Eliza, never robustly healthy, spent much of her time in bed and sincerely hoped that Maria would come in the early spring to supervise the house. The arrival of a son, James, at the Gouverneur home precluded such a visit, and Sam patiently and tactfully explained the situation to the President: "Maria evinces so much anxiety on account of James, fearing lest a change of climate and the fatigues of travelling, at this precarious moment, may injure his health, that I think it better to remain stationary for the moment. She regrets very much the longer separation, which this determination must occasion, from her family, and particularly considering, the state of her sister's health—Should however at any moment, her situation be such as may render her sister's services useful to her, she will most readily join her."[57]

When James was a little older and stronger, Maria spent much time with her mother and sister, taking him along to be cared for by Hortensia Hay, whose godmother was Eliza's former schoolmate, Hortense de Beauharnais, the former Queen of Holland.

Occasionally Monroe would take a trip to New York to visit his daughter, but both he and his wife were tiring of the gaudy White House, with its profusion of French bric-a-brac and its demanding formality. They eagerly anticipated the day when they could retire to the quiet Virginia countryside. The last year Monroe was in office, both his wife and Eliza were so indisposed that upon the advice of Maria and Sam, they did not even open their house for entertainment. Sam wrote, "I sincerely hope that you will not think of opening your house for entertainments this winter. The state of Aunt M's. health, will furnish the most ample apology to all, for such a course, and in fact at your period of life, and at the close of a laborious term of years in office, it is not, and it ought not to be expected."[58]

Aside from the formal reception at the White House when the result of the next presidential election was announced, the last gala affair of the Monroe administration was the New Year's reception in 1825. The same procedure as at all former drawing-rooms was followed. A guest has left an excellent description of the family, once again gathered together:

"Mr. Monroe was standing near the door, and as we were introduced we had the honor of shaking hands with him and passing the usual congratulations of the season. My impressions of Mr. Monroe are very pleasing. He is tall and well formed. His dress plain and in the old style, small clothes, silk hose, knee-buckles, and pumps fastened with buckles. His manner was quiet and dignified. From the frank, honest expression of his eye, which is said to be 'the window of the soul', I think he well deserves the encomium passed upon him by the great Jefferson, who said, 'Monroe was so honest that if you turned his soul inside out there would not be a spot on it.'

"We passed on and were presented to Mrs. Monroe and her two daughters, Mrs. Judge Hay and Mrs. Gouverneur, who stood by their mother and assisted her in receiving. Mrs. Monroe's manner is very gracious and she is a regal-looking lady. Her dress was superb black velvet; neck and arms bare and beautifully formed; her hair in puffs and dressed high on the head and ornamented with white ostrich plumes; around her neck an elegant pearl necklace. Though no longer young, she is still a very handsome woman. . . . Mrs. Judge Hay's dress was crimson velvet, gold cord and tassel round the waist, white plumes in the hair, handsome jewelry, bare neck and arms. The other daughter, Mrs. Gouverneur, is also very handsome—dress, rich white satin, trimmed with a great deal of blonde lace, embroidered with silver thread, bare neck and arms, pearl jewelry and white plumes in the hair.

"The rooms were warmed by great fires of hickory wood in the large open fireplaces, and with the handsome brass andirons and fenders quite remind me of our grand old wood fires in Virginia. Wine was handed about in wine-glasses on large silver salvers by colored waiters, dressed in dark livery, gilt buttons, etc. I suppose some of them must have come from Mr. Monroe's old family seat, 'Oak Hill,' Virginia."[59]

Socially Monroe's era had been one of transition, just as it had been in the political and economic sphere. Like all eras of transition, it had been painful. When Mrs. Monroe left the White House, however, she had outlived her unpopularity and had endeared herself to all who knew her.

❧ 34 ❧

Jackson and the Governorship of Florida

IN FEBRUARY, 1821, just before Monroe's second inauguration and after two years of delay, the Florida Treaty of 1819, now ratified by the Spanish Cortes and its arrogant monarch, was re-ratified by the Senate. There was not time, in the remaining ten days of the congressional session, to legislate a detailed and properly matured program for the organization of the territory. Under the temporary government which Congress created for the new province, large discretionary powers of a vague and temporary nature were granted to the President. Monroe was authorized to appoint a governor, who should exercise all the powers and functions permitted to the Spanish Captain-General of Cuba and the sub-governors of East and West Florida. With the exception of not being able to levy new taxes or to make land grants, this governor was to have a free hand. The territory was to be governed along the same lines as formerly, except that the United States revenue laws and the regulations prohibiting the importaton of slaves were to be rigidly enforced. To assist the governor in his task of carrying the treaty into effect, the President was to appoint as many sub-officials as he deemed necessary.

The man to whom Monroe turned as the most logical person to receive Florida from Spain and to inaugurate the American rule was Andrew Jackson, the general who had wrested the province from Spanish grasp. Soon after the Seminole War and the humiliation he had suffered in the House debates, Jackson had expressed to Monroe his desire to resign from the army. The President had succeeded to a certain extent in assuaging his wrath and, by pointing out to him the possibility of war if Spain failed to ratify the treaty, had induced the General to remain in the service. "Such being the state of affairs," Monroe wrote, "I leave it entirely to yourself to decide whether to remain in the service, or to retire at this time. I well know that wherever you may be you will always be ready to obey the call of your country in an extremity. But whether your being in service may not have a tendency to prevent such extremity, and have a happy effect on other important interests of your country, especially in preserving order along our frontiers, is to be decided. Whatever your decision may be, be assured that my entire confidence & affectionate regards will always attend you."[1]

Shortly after the beginning of 1821, when it became apparent that Spain would sign the treaty, Monroe sounded out Jackson in regard to the Florida situation. Jackson was ready to accept, but shortly thereafter wrote to Monroe, declining the offer on the grounds that Mrs. Jackson refused to live in Florida.[2]

Meanwhile, another factor had entered the situation, which not only caused Monroe to renew his efforts to obtain the services of Jackson but also influenced Jackson to accept the President's overtures. Following the suggestion of rigid economy and drastic retrenchment necessitated by the depression and sharp drop in government revenue, which Monroe had made in his annual message to congress, that body had reduced the military peace establishment of the army. By the Act of March 2, 1821, Brown was designated the sole Major General, and provision was made for two brigadier generals. Gaines, Scott, and Jackson were the logical candidates, but since the rules of seniority governed, Jackson would have to be either eliminated entirely or degraded in rank.[3] Neither action would have been tolerated or merited by the irascible Tennesseean. Not only was the country indebted to him for brilliant services rendered at crucial moments in its history, but he had captured the popular fancy of thousands of citizens, while his unjust treatment in the House during the Seminole debate warranted some compensation. Monroe avoided the awkward dilemma on the following day[4] by appointing him Governor of East and West Florida, authorizing him to execute the new treaty with Spain. Jackson accepted the appointment and left Nashville in April.

Jackson and Florida

In the interim Monroe was beset with difficulties in his task of organization in Florida. Not only was he responsible for appointing officers for the region, but it was up to him to institute a Board of Commissioners to settle the claims against Spain, which the United States had promised to assume up to the amount of $5,000,000. As was his custom he sought the advice of Madison, and in a letter of March 31, 1821, his concern and reasons for it were evident: "The law for executing the Florida treaty has subjected me to great trouble and embarrassment. The organizing a government in Florida & appointing of officers there, is in itself a serious duty. I have as yet appointed the governor only, who is Genl. Jackson. The institution of a board of Commissioners for the settlement of claims on Spain, is attended with still greater difficulty. In general the persons best qualified live in the great towns, especially to the Eastward. In those towns also the claimants live. If I appoint a Commissioner in one only, & not in the others, all the latter will complain; and it is impossible to appoint them in all, the number not admitting of it. I have therefore thought it best to avoid the great towns, & propose to appoint Govr. King of Maine, Judge Green of Fredericksburg, & Judge White of Knoxville, Tenn.; 2 lawyers and 1 merchant."[5]

For some reasons Judge Green refused the appointment, and L. W. Tazewell, of Virginia, completed the triumvirate.[6]

Having settled this problem satisfactorily, Monroe proceeded to create three revenue districts, with a collector in charge of each, and two judicial districts, each with a judge. Jackson, of course, was to govern over the whole, but to obviate any difficulties that might result from the remoteness of some of the districts, a sub-governor was appointed to reside at Pensacola, and another for St. Augustine, the former to be in charge of West Florida, and the latter, of East Florida. Monroe explained this organization to Madison in a letter of May 19, 1821. "The territory from St. Marys to Cape Florida makes one collection district for the revenue; from the Cape to Apalachicola, a second; & thence to the Perdido, the third. At the last I have appointed Mr. Alexander Scott collector, Steuben Smith naval officer, who will appoint John Martin Baker, Inspector. At St. Augustine Mr. Hackley is appointed surveyor and Inspector. The salaries to these offices will be small, but I shall endeavour to send them to their stations in a public vessel, & have them quartered in the

JAMES MONROE

public buildings. The territory ceded having been divided under Spain into two provinces, & St. Augustine being so very distant from Pensacola & separated by a wilderness, it was thought advisable to retain in some circumstances that form. The appointment of the Governor extends, of course, over the whole; but as he will probably reside at Pensacola, a second is appointed for St. Augustine, and another for Pensacola. Two judicial districts are also formed, & one judge appointed for each. Mr. Fromentin to the one, and Mr. Duvall, formerly a member of Congress from Kentucky, for the other. Judge Anderson's son is appointed district attorney for Pensacola."[7]

From the moment Jackson left Nashville in April, with his wife, until he abandoned Florida that November, he was in a bad temper. He hated and detested the Spanish and it was only by force of circumstances and through no desire of his own that he had gone to Florida in the first place.[8] Proceeding to Pensacola by way of New Orleans, he became enraged at an official of the branch of the United States Bank for refusing to honor his draft on the State Department for an advance on his salary.[9] No sooner had he entered on Spanish soil than he was at cross-purposes with Callava, the Spanish Governor at Pensacola. A don of the old school, and as such particularly hateful to Jackson, he found it impossible to assume a mien suitable for the function of surrender which he was about to perform. He intended to play the role of the Spanish Governor until the proper authority for transferal arrived. The failure of Forbes caused two full months of delay while Jackson fretted, growing daily more irate as his suspicions of Spanish treachery and hatred of their attitude increased.

In the midst of his wrath there came a long letter from Monroe, couched in the phrases of well-moderated praise and encouragement so typical of the Executive, which served partially to soothe the General's wrath:

"In executing that portion of the trust relating to the Floridas, I have gratified in a high degree my feelings in committing the chief power to you, who have rendered such important services, and have such just claims to the gratitude of your country. It must be agreeable to you, for many considerations which will occur, to take possession of the Floridas, and cause the Spanish authorities and troops to be removed to Cuba. It must be equally so to establish the government of the United States, and to administer it in their behalf, in those territories. I have every reason to believe that the nation generally have beheld with profound interest and satisfaction your appointment, considering it a just tribute of respect to your extraordinary services and merit, and having the fullest confidence that its duties will be discharged with the utmost ability and integrity."[10]

Jackson's indignation flared again when he read the list of offices and the names of the incumbents. Not only had he not been consulted, but there was not a single friend of his in the lot.[11]

Monroe closed with an expression of gratitude for his services and a friendly warning to guard his movements against the possibility of criticism by personal enemies: "I have full confidence that your appointment will be immediately and most beneficially felt. Smugglers & slave traders will hide their heads, pirates will disappear, & the Seminoles cease to give us trouble. So effectual will the impression be that I think the recollection of your past services will smooth your way as to the future. Past experience shows that neither of us are without enemies. If you still have any, as may be presumed, they will watch your movements, hoping to find some inadvertent circumstance to turn against you. Be therefore on your guard. Your country indulges no such feelings. From it you will find a liberal confidence, and a generous support."[12]

At length after tedious delay the formalities were completed. On July 10 flags were exchanged at St. Augustine, and on the seventeenth in West Florida and in Pensacola. Of those officers whom Monroe had appointed, not one was in Florida on that date. Jackson, in an ill humor over this state of affairs, received in person the province of West Florida on July 17, and on August 4 his deputy commissioner took over the eastern province. At Pensacola Governor Callava handed over the keys and the Spanish garrison embarked. No sooner had this been accomplished than Jackson quarreled with the former Governor over some inaccuracies in an inventory of the fort supplies. This high feeling was fanned during the ensuing months by the fact that Callava stayed on in Pensacola on the plea of finishing his work as a commissioner and refused to surrender the public archives. In September came the explosion.

Eligius Fromentin, no Jackson enthusiast, had been appointed one of the two new federal judges. He had already run himself into debt during his brief tenure and was working hand and glove with Callava and with one John Innerarity, the Pensacola representative of Forbes & Company, a trading concern. Jackson, suspecting trickery and subterfuge, exasperated at the federal civilians and at Callava for the trouble over the inventory, feared the latter would attempt to carry off with him the public documents.

For sixteen years Forbes & Co. had been handling a law suit for the heirs of one Vidal, but had apparently done nothing. In September, 1821, a poor woman, one of the heirs, came to Jackson claiming that Callava held in his possession papers which would protect her against the other claimants but that he refused to surrender them to her. The infuriated General dispatched an officer to the ex-Governor, demanding the papers, and when the latter demurred Jackson had him imprisoned and seized the papers. The following morning Callava sought the aid of his friend Fromentin, who issued, and in the absence of the marshal served, as a private citizen, a writ of habeus corpus. Jackson, feeling this to be an act of contempt and arrogating to himself the powers of high judge, summoned Callava to an interview. As a result, all three appealed to the President, violently assaulting one another's conduct and motives.[13]

On the question at issue, whether the scope of Jackson's discretionary powers included that of judge, Adams, who supported Jackson, sent an aggressive dispatch to Pensacola. This third public embarrassment at the hands of Jackson strained even Monroe's good nature. Yet so great was his admiration of the General and so deep his understanding of the man's disposition and character and of the irritating and procrastinating personalities with whom he had been forced to deal, that in letters to his friends he exonerated the Governor and assumed all blame for sending to Florida a man with powers so ill-defined. He wrote to Daniel Brent: "The dilatory proceedings of the Spanish authorities, which excited so much surprise and anxiety with us, were more sensibly felt by him, owing to his exposed situation with his family in the interior, at a season which became daily more unhealthy, and when he personally was much indisposed. . . .

"From the view which I have of his conduct, I entirely approve it, both with respect to his efforts to obtain possession of the territory & the organization of the internal government, on which, however, I should be glad to receive Mr. Adams' opinion."[14]

Jackson and Florida

The President called a Cabinet meeting on October 23, to consider the questions of privilege and implied authority involved in the dispute. In the course of the heated discussions, which continued for several days, Adams was the only Cabinet member who strongly upheld Jackson. The President, Calhoun, and Wirt, while approving, in general, Jackson's conduct in trying to safeguard the documents, were of the opinion that "Fromentin, having issued the writ, tho' erroneously, in his judicial capacity, was not amenable for it to Jackson, and that Jackson had no right to summon him before him to answer for it."[15] So great was Jackson's popularity that when the public discovered that the administration might find cause to reprimand him, the press "was full of inflammatory hate,"[16] and even Monroe received several threatening letters which he burned.[17]

Once again the normal course of events eased the course of duty for Monroe, obviating the danger of having to rebuke a national favorite. Jackson, disgusted because his own friends had been excluded from the Florida patronage, in poor health and high temper, went home to Nashville in October, and tendered his resignation.

To an originally warm friendship, already slightly chilled by the executive disavowal of Jackson's acts in the Seminole War, this governorship brought an increased coolness. In his annual message on December 3, to a Congress in which Jackson's bitter rivals, Crawford and Clay, had many supporters, Monroe stated the case mildly.[18] While he praised Jackson he repeated his confidence in Fromentin, and this stung Jackson deeply.

There remained only the President's personal acceptance of the General's resignation. On the last day of the year Monroe wrote: "I received some time since your resignation, and should have answered it sooner had I not wished to retain you in the service of your country until a temporary government should be organized over the Floridas, and an opportunity to be afforded me to appoint your successor. On great consideration, especially as I know that it is your fixed purpose to withdraw, I have at length determined to accept it, in which light you will view this letter. The same sentiments which I have heretofore entertained of your integrity, ability, & eminently useful services are still cherished towards you. That you may live long in health & in the affections of your country is my most earnest desire."[19]

JAMES MONROE

During the ensuing months Monroe was the recipient of several disgruntled letters from Jackson, accusing him of failing to stand by him and of injustice in the statement of his views. When Jackson learned that his conduct had been discussed in Congress he remonstrated with Monroe, saying, "I have adopted as a rule through life, never to abandon my friend, unless he first abandons me."[20]

Concluding a series of letters in which the President reiterated his faith in the General and assured him of his friendship, Monroe rather wearily wrote: "I have been much hurt to find complaints in your late letters that I had not done you justice in the views which I presented to Congress of proceedings in Florida. . . . I am utterly incapable of doing injustice to anyone intentionally, and certainly, if it were otherwise, an injury to you would be among the last acts of which I could be capable, in any form whatever."[21]

Here the correspondence on the subject somewhat abruptly ended, to be continued at a later date, for Jackson was now launched on his own presidential campaign and Monroe was too closely identified with the Virginia faction, whose candidate was Crawford, to permit the complete restoration of their formerly cordial relations.

While Florida continued to be governed under strict federal oversight, little more was heard of the territory until almost twenty-five years later, when it applied for statehood.

≽ 35 ≼

Roads, Bridges, Canals

WITH THE new territory of Florida formally integrated into the American system of government, the President took stock of the situation of the country. Externally, a hazardous source of long-standing controversy had been removed from the southern border, and the western boundary had been specifically defined by treaty. The problem of the recognition of South American independence had still to be dealt with, but there were no pressing European diplomatic problems or threatening situations. Internally, the nation was on the up-grade. The depths of the depression had been passed late in the year 1820, and business was on a much sounder basis than it had been at any time since the Embargo. It was true that the government still felt the effects of the diminished revenue, for the customs receipts, which were almost the only source of public supply, had shown slight deficiencies, but Congress had provided for two loans by which to tide over the government. The National Bank itself, under the capable management of Langdon Cheves, had retrieved its losses and reputation by regaining its capital early in 1820. Nicholas Biddle, who succeeded Cheves upon the latter's retirement, carried on the constructive work, and by midsummer of that year the United States Bank declared a dividend.[1] Everywhere were signs of general prosperity, as the financial problem seemed to solve itself. With increasing prosperity the national revenue rose so steadily that in Monroe's last three messages he was able to announce an annual revenue equal and more than equal to all current demands upon it.

JAMES MONROE

When Monroe returned from his tours he was convinced that, more truly than any of his predecessors, he was the president, not of a political party, but of a great united people, extending from the Atlantic seaboard to the ridge of the Appalachians and beyond. Yet, in the space of a few short years, the national picture had changed—almost radically. Long hard years of war and its attendant miseries and deprivations had driven thousands of refugees to the American shores. It was estimated that about twenty-two thousand immigrants, mostly Irish, had arrived during 1817 alone.[2] Finding employment difficult to obtain, and attracted by the excellent prospects of cheap and productive land in the West, these "agricultural" immigrants were moved across the mountains into the West by various organizations which sprang up for the purpose. The tide of westward expansion was augmented by economic conditions at home. The depression, which had left so many mills and factories idle, forced hundreds of thousands of people from the Atlantic seaboard into the Mississippi Valley. The exodus made a marked impression on the East, for some towns and cities ceased growing while many others were depopulated. This movement was by no means confined to the Northeast; it was almost as noticeable in the South. Simultaneously the southern soil was becoming exhausted. Uninterrupted cultivation of cotton, with no crop rotation and little fertilizer had starved the land. Southern planters, led by the uplanders were moving westward, seeking larger plantations in the virgin lands of Alabama, Mississippi, and Missouri, where the extinction of Indian titles had opened up a vast acreage.

This tremendous dislocation of population was accompanied by an equally important reallocation of political power. The scepter of this power was inevitably passing from the hands of Virginia, whose aristocratic statesmen had controlled nine successive presidential terms, into the control of the rising West across the mountains. Already its influence had been felt on a national scale. Under the aegis of the Young War Hawks, led by Henry Clay, who voiced the chauvinism of the West, harassed by the presence of a foreign power in its backyard, the United States had entered a costly war with England. It entered a war (when it was apparent that staying out of it was going to succeed) to fight for national honor—a cause the country failed to defend. Clay and Calhoun, young exponents of the rising school of nationalism, representatives of a solid West from the Great

Roads, Bridges, Canals

Lakes to the Gulf, were pushing and popularizing the American System. This scheme aimed to promote national ends by creating a self-sufficient nation and conducting a three-cornered trade for mutual profit. A high protective tariff was to exclude European competition and promote New England manufactures. These were to be shipped to the West in return for food and raw materials, and to the South in return for raw cotton. The keystone of the system, which was to evolve an immense and self-sufficient ocean-bound Republic, was an efficient communication system. The revenue from the protective tariff was to defray the expenses of the canals, highways, and river and harbor improvements requisite for the great project.

Monroe's administration witnessed the height of the turnpike era and saw the beginning of the canal epoch. Private enterprise, combined with state aid, covered the Atlantic seaboard with a network of turnpike roads and bridges: the Lancaster Pike between Philadelphia and Gettysburg; the Boston Post Road uniting Worcester and Springfield, and Boston and Providence; the National Road between Cumberland, Maryland, and Wheeling, West Virginia. Simultaneously came the canal era. Pennsylvania had an extensive system, as did Ohio and Indiana, while in New York State the Erie Canal, the imperial undertaking of the Clinton machine, was getting under way. Throughout America new roads and new canals were being projected at a feverish pace. To meet the enormous outlay entailed, state and public, and soon national aid were solicited.

During the early months of his first administration and after his northern tour of inspection of the fortifications and harbors, it was brought home to Monroe that the question of internal improvements was rapidly resolving itself into a national issue. As such it was imperative that he consider what was to be his policy in relation to it. After great thought he determined to adopt the conservative course of his predecessor, favoring all such works, but requiring a better sanction than the existing Constitution afforded, and at the same time he determined to receive Madison's sanction. Accordingly, late in the fall of 1817, Monroe wrote to the former President, informing him of his decision:

"The question respecting canals and roads is full of difficulty, growing out of what has passed on it. After all the consideration I have given it, I am fixed in the opinion, that the right is not in Congress and that it would be improper in me, after your negative, to allow them to discuss the subject & bring a bill for me to sign, in the expectation that I would do it. I have therefore decided to communicate my opinion in the message & to recommend the procuring an amendment from the States, so as to vest the right in Congress in a manner to compromise in it a power also to institute seminaries of learning."[3]

In the light of his inaugural address, the proponents of internal improvements felt sure that the Executive would give his sanction. When the first message was read to Congress, their hopes rose as he emphasized the importance of these works: "When we consider the vast extent of territory within the United States, . . . we can not fail to entertain a high sense of the advantage to be derived from the facility which may be afforded in the intercourse between them by means of good roads and canals. Never did a country of such vast extent offer equal inducements to improvements of this kind, nor ever were consequences of such magnitude involved in them. As this subject was acted on by Congress at the last session, and there may be a disposition to revive it at the present, I have brought it into view for the purpose of communicating my sentiments on a very important circumstance connected with it. . . . A difference of opinion has existed from the first formation of our Constitution to the present time . . . respecting the right of Congress to establish such a system of improvement."[4]

But high hopes were dashed when, in conclusion, displaying a tenderness for the letter of the Constitution which infuriated Clay, Calhoun, and the younger men, the President expressed his belief in the desirability of internal improvements, but declared he did not believe Congress had a right to use public money for internal improvement. No such power had been expressly granted, nor was it incidental to the use of any power so granted. He therefore advised that Congress should recommend to the states a constitutional amendment, empowering that body to establish them.[5]

To Clay and his followers these constitutional scruples, although accompanied by presidential approval of a system of federal expense, came as a challenge. The response of the House to this suggestion was prompt, clearly drawing the issue as to the constitutional power

Roads, Bridges, Canals

between the House and the President. The committee to which the message was referred declared that internal improvements were necessary and that, under the power to establish post offices and post roads, Congress, with the consent of the states concerned, had ample power to appropriate money for the construction of military roads and of other roads and canals, and for the improvement of water courses. These principles were embodied in four resolutions, submitted to the House by William Lowndes of South Carolina.[6] The House, however, in spite of the brilliant persuasion of Calhoun and Clay, was not ready to support the committee and override the veto. After a vigorous debate, which was marred by Clay's vindictive diatribes against Monroe for attempting to influence legislation, and a debate which turned upon the practical distinction between the right of the national authority to originate and the right to appropriate in aid of state construction, the vote taken was 89 in favor of the resolutions, and 75 against,[7] an insufficient majority to override the inevitable presidential veto of any bill which Congress might pass.

The course of the debate had revealed a sharp degree of sectionalism. Throughout the West the demand for internal improvements was unified. Those states, too poor to undertake the financial burden of improving streams and constructing new roads, looked to the federal government as the only source of those improvements essential to their prosperity and general welfare. To this western demand for improved transportation was allied the desire of the seacoast cities of the Middle Atlantic States. New York, Baltimore, and Philadelphia were the eastern termini of the transmontane routes from the interior and stood to reap vast profits from improved facilities. In opposition were the New England states and the states of the southern seaboard, which had nothing to gain by such legislation and which, having provided for such improvements from their own treasuries, were loathe to see the federal government build up the western states. The efforts apparently were stalled indefinitely, for Clay and his followers were unwilling to hazard the rights which they claimed to possess, by appealing for an amendment to the states.[8] There remained, then, nothing to be done but to study the question further.

In compliance with a congressional resolution Calhoun, the Secretary of War, submitted on January 7, 1819, a lengthy report outlining a comprehensive system of internal improvements requisite for military purposes. At the same time Crawford was invited to present a report on roads and canals not designed particularly for military purposes, and a list of buildings meriting congressional aid. Calhoun evaded presenting an opinion on the question of constitutionality. By 1819 the panic threatened to deplete the Treasury and as a result the reports were tabled by the House until returning prosperity again caused the question to be taken up vigorously in 1822.

Meanwhile, the popularity of the Erie Canal, which had captured the fancy of the people, and the state demands for improvements, forced the subject to the attention of the House, in spite of the depression. The committee appointed to present a bill combined Gallatin's report of 1808 and Calhoun's of 1819 and recommended a line of canals from Boston to Savannah and a highway extending from Washington to New Orleans. The bill provided for the appropriation of a sum of money "to procure the necessary surveys, plans, etc."[9] This radical bill was never passed, and in view of Monroe's veto of a much more conservative proposition, later in the session, it would have been an idle gesture.

The Cumberland Road assumed a monumental importance in American history, for "on its lengthy line was fought out one of the severest political issues of the next twenty years."[10] Projected in 1806, actual construction was begun in 1811, and the road had been completed as far as Wheeling, West Virginia, on the Ohio, when the panic of 1819 temporarily suspended activity. So useful was it found to be that from time to time Congress had appropriated sums for its extension, without drawing attention to the importance of the precedent established, as Madison pointed out in a letter to Monroe in 1818:

"The Cumberland Road having been a measure taken during the administration of Mr. Jefferson, and, as far as I recollect, then not brought to my particular attention, I cannot assign the grounds assumed for it by Congress, or which produced his sanction. I suspect that the question of Constitutionality was but slightly if at all examined by the former. And that the Executive consent was doubtingly or hastily given. Having once become a law, and being a measure of singular utility, additional appropriations took place, of

Roads, Bridges, Canals

course under the same Administration, and, with the accumulated impulse thence derived, were continued under the succeeding one, with less of critical investigation perhaps than was due to the case."[11]

Before the extension of the road to Wheeling, most of the traffic of the Middle States had gone by way of Philadelphia or Baltimore to Pittsburgh and thence to Ohio. Being the only route, and therefore having no competitors, the Pittsburgh road had fallen into disrepair. The West saw in the Cumberland Road and its extension westward the solution of its difficulties. Their appeal to Congress was irresistible and by the Act of May 15, 1820, commissioners were appointed to examine the country west of Wheeling, with the plan in mind to extend the road to the Mississippi.[12] Adams noted in his Memoirs:

"This road is to be continued by an Act of the last session of Congress, and appears to have introduced sufficient for practical purposes, the principle of expending public monies upon internal improvements. The reason assigned for laying out this road is to make the public lands more valuable, and, as the Land Office is an appendage to the Treasury Department, the road and all operations concerning it are also under its management. Mr. Crawford had a plan of the road at the President's the day that he left the city, and told me that although the law required the road to be run as nearly straight as possible he should see to make it run so as to pass through the seats of government of the three states of Ohio, Indiana, and Illinois."[13]

The Seventeenth Congress assembled as the country was emerging from the gloom of the depression years. Every state and community was submerged in enterprises involving physical improvements, most of which could never be financed on local revenues. In this Congress, deeply infected with the presidential fever, where all leaders were bidding for popularity, it was only natural that these leaders should attempt to shift the financial burden to the nation, and favor liberal expenditures from the national treasury to assist local internal improvements. If left to itself Congress would have sunk the national credit in the quicksands of local enterprise. One of the most eloquent in the cause of internal improvements was gifted Henry Clay, who espoused the cause of the Cumberland Road. The idea of constructing the road from Wheeling, through the Northwest, and probably to the Pacific, was one of the most stupendous products of his creative mind.

Although several appropriations for extensions and repairs had been made for the road, and a survey authorized with a view to its extension to the Mississippi, further repairs were necessary. On April 29, 1822, Congress passed a bill appropriating $9,000 for the repair of the Cumberland Road. To facilitate payment of future repair bills, the President was authorized to cause the erection of toll gates along the road, and to appoint toll gatherers. By fixing toll charges and penalties for non-payment in the bill itself, it assumed for the general government not only the power of appropriating and expending money for road construction, but the power of operating the road and jurisdiction over it. The vote on the bill, which passed the House by a margin of 87-68, was interestingly distributed along sectional lines. New England, on the whole indifferent, was equally divided. New York, fearing competition for its own Erie Canal then almost completed, opposed it. Pennsylvania, also jealous, was divided, while Virginia, South Carolina, and Georgia were against it. Maryland stood solidly with the Northwest and Kentucky for the measure.[14] The Senate passed the bill 29-7.

It was presented to Monroe on March 4, 1822. In an attempt to recall the people from their feverish expenditures on internal improvements, to constitutional views, Monroe vetoed the bill on the grounds that since violators of the regulations would have to be dealt with, the measure was an infringement on the police power of the states. He contended that the practical execution of works of internal improvement by the federal government was not specifically granted by the Constitution, or "incidental to some power specifically granted." "A power to establish turnpikes with gates and tolls," he said, "and to enforce the collection of tolls by penalties, implies a power to adopt and execute a complete system of internal improvement. . . .

"I am of opinion that Congress do not possess this power; that the States individually cannot grant it, for although they may assent to the appropriation of money within their limits for such purposes, they can grant no power of jurisdiction or sovereignty by special compacts with the United States. This power can be granted only by an amendment to the Constitution and in the mode prescribed by it."[15]

Roads, Bridges, Canals

Monroe had long been pondering the problem. In a letter to Spencer Roane, July 9, 1821, he wrote: "You may recollect, that soon after I came into this office, I considered it my duty to take my stand against the power of the General Government, in regard to Internal Improvements; that I declared, in a message to Congress, that I did not think it possessed that power, and that I should be compelled to refuse my assent to any bill, founded on that principle. Expecting to be called on to perform that duty, I turned my attention immediately to the subject, with a view to be prepared to acquit myself in the best manner in my power to the just claims of my country, . . . I have written much on the subject, . . . It is possible, that I may publish this paper, even while I am in office, . . .

"I do not know, that on every point, I shall concur with any one, but I shall advance no opinion on any point, which I shall not give the ground of, . . .

"If I shall be so fortunate, as to enjoy a short leisure, in the country, I shall finish this paper and soon afterwards I shall decide, in what manner to dispose of it."[16]

Embodied in the veto message was the promise of a detailed exposition of his views on the subject. On the same day that he announced his veto, he submitted to Congress this lengthiest of his state papers, a document which he had thought of submitting to the legislature in 1819, but which he had withheld at the request of his Cabinet. Knowing that Adams, Crawford, and Calhoun stood on the popular side of the question and that he could expect no support from them, he determined to act upon his own responsibility and sent in the message without his customary Cabinet conference. The circumstances are described by Adams:

"He read to us a message which he had prepared to send to the House of Representatives with his negative upon a bill appropriating nine thousand dollars for repairs upon the Cumberland Road, and authorizing the erection of toll-gates upon it, and a toll for keeping it in repair. He said he had been suddenly called to take this measure, and had not time to consult the members of the Administration upon it. He promised with this message, and afterwards sent in the course of the day, his long dissertation against the Constitutional power of Congress to make internal improvements."[17]

There is nothing of Monroe's which better illustrates the thorough and conscientious research with which he examined all the great problems of his administration than the elaborate disquisition on internal improvements. It was a confused and confusing paper, the longest and most formidable ever communicated to Congress, but upon the question at issue, the propositions he advanced were forceful and intelligible. While reaffirming the ground he had taken in his first annual message, he reviewed the entire argument for and against the constitutional right, expounding his conception of the construction of the Constitution and of the relation of the states and the nation under the theory of divided sovereignty: "There were two separate and independent governments established over our Union, one for local purposes over each State by the people of the State, the other for national purposes over all the States by the people of the United States."[18]

He minutely examined the powers of the general government as specifically granted in the Constitution, in an attempt to find a constitutional sanction.[19] The examination proved to him that while no specific grant had been given to Congress, he was now willing, in contrast to his earlier beliefs, to allow elasticity in the constitutional interpretation. "On further reflection," he said, "my mind has undergone a change, for reasons which I will frankly unfold."[20]

Monroe had come to the conclusion that the power of Congress to legislate on internal improvements was to be found only by implication, implied in the powers to appropriate money, and, therefore, its character and limitations were to be drawn from the nature of the power to appropriate money. He maintained that the power of Congress to appropriate money was not limited to an enumerated list in the Constitution, but was limited to national purposes by the spirit of the Constitution. He concluded, accordingly—and thereby yielded to the opinion of the House in 1818—that while Congress was empowered to appropriate money for internal improvements which were on a national scale, at the same time Congress could not, under this power of appropriating money, establish jurisdiction over these improvements, or authorize the Executive to administer them.[21] Although he denied to the federal government the right of jurisdiction and construction, he asserted that Congress had unlimited power to raise money and that "in its appropriation, they have a discretionary power, restricted only by their duty to appropriate it to pur-

Roads, Bridges, Canals

poses of common defense and of general, not local, national, not state, benefit."[22]

In brief, while the Constitution as it stood did not warrant the practical execution of works of internal improvement by the general government, Monroe admitted the power of Congress to grant and appropriate money in aid of internal improvements, executed by other agencies. In consequence of the vital importance which internal improvements had assumed in relation to the national welfare, he thought it advisable that an amendment to the Constitution be recommended to the states. The amendment should be worded so as to confine federal legislation to great national works, leaving all minor improvements to the separate states.

Apparently the views which Monroe had stated so elaborately in his paper were convincing to many who had voted for the measure, for when the vetoed bill was presented to the House it failed of passage over the veto by a vote of 68-72. The President himself was proud of his veto and "confident of the ground he had chosen."[23] He had copies of the message prepared and sent to the members of the Supreme Court, his Cabinet advisers, and close friends. The responses which he received, on the whole, approved of his course of action with varying degrees of enthusiasm. Andrew Jackson, who was to clash so violently in the years to come with Clay and Adams on the subject of internal improvements, decisively defended the states rights theory in his reply: "My opinion has always been that the Federal Government did not possess the constitutional right; that it is retained to the states; and that in time of war the national authority may repair roads and control them but must surrender them when peace returns."[24]

William Wirt, one of Monroe's closest friends, expressed his approval in a letter written shortly after the appearance of the message: "The argument is, to me, conclusive—yet I doubt whether it will change the opinion of a majority of Congress. But it may convince the Nation—and thereby lead to an amendment of the Constitution. . . . I consider the question as having an important effect on the union, itself, of the States."[25]

Joseph Story was more non-committal: "It is a subject on which many divide in opinion, but all will admit that your views are profound and that you have thought much on the subject."[26]

JAMES MONROE

While his Cabinet and friends still proclaimed him as a friend of the popular national policy, Monroe was subjected to severe criticism in the West. He had stretched the implied powers of the Constitution to the limit in acquiring Florida, and yet he insisted upon so restricting those powers, with regard to internal improvements, that the great bulk of future development was left dependent upon the states alone. To the new western states, in no condition to be taxed even for improvements absolutely necessary for local purposes, these rules of constitutional interpretation were incomprehensible in view of the Florida acquisition. They felt that if the federal government could acquire land or exercise ownership over public domain within a state, it possessed also the incidental power to make interstate improvements to attract immigration and increase the value of that land.

In the face of the President's veto and state paper, all hopes of a national system of internal improvements during his term faded. Maryland made an attempt to introduce a constitutional amendment by giving her senators and representatives special instructions, but this came to naught,[27] and even Monroe's subsequent pleas for an amendment failed to bring the desired results.

In the meantime the Cumberland Road was in urgent need of repairs. In his sixth annual message the President again pleaded for an amendment, but in the case of failure to secure it he maintained that since the road had been constructed by congressional appropriation, Congress had the right to provide for its repairs. "Surely," he said, "if they had the right to appropriate money to make the road they have a right to appropriate it to preserve the road from ruin. From the exercise of this power no danger is to be apprehended."[28]

Acting on his intimation of power to appropriate money, an act was passed on February 28, 1823, providing for a simple appropriation to repair the Cumberland Road.

Again, the following year, Monroe advocated in his message an executive agreement with each state through which the road passed, to establish toll gates and bridges, each within state limits, to assist in defraying the costs of maintenance.[29]

In the absence of a constitutional amendment, the next great difficulty in the way of the realization of Monroe's principle of the appropriation of national money for internal improvements of a national character, was the definition as to what improvements were

Roads, Bridges, Canals

of such a character. The irresistibility of the demand for better internal communication and the immense popularity of the multitudes of local projects had a strong hold on the people, and each state was furiously promoting its own enterprises in the hope of federal assistance. Chief among these projects was a plan for uniting Chesapeake Bay with the Ohio by a canal along the Potomac. Monroe was so impressed with the idea that he recommended its consideration by Congress in his seventh annual message:

"Many patriotic and enlightened citizens who have made the subject an object of particular investigation have suggested an improvement of still greater importance. They are of opinion that the waters of the Chesapeake and Ohio may be connected together by one continued canal, and at an expense far short of the value and importance of the object to be obtained. If this could be accomplished it is impossible to calculate the beneficial consequences which would result from it.... Connecting the Atlantic with the Western country in a line passing through the seat of the National Government, it would contribute essentially to strengthen the bond of union itself. Believing as I do that Congress possess the right to appropriate money for such a national object (the jurisdiction remaining to the states through which the canal would pass) I submit it to your consideration whether it may not be advisable to authorize ... the examination of the unexplored ground during the next session."[30]

The issue of internal improvements appealed to the many presidential candidates, for their promises to obtain federal grants in aid of state enterprises would secure for them much-needed votes. The danger that the appropriation bills would become log-rolling measures to obtain national money for local enterprises was imminent. It was this danger which Congress attempted to meet by the act of April 30, 1824, introduced as the General Survey Bill. A $30,000 appropriation was proposed to defray the expenses which would be incurred by authorizing the President to employ the engineering corps of the army in making the "necessary surveys, plans, and estimates ... for such a system of roads and canals as he might deem of national importance from a postal, commercial, or military point of view."[31] This bill, phrased so as to involve no constitutional difficulties, was laid before Congress.

The debate which preceded its passage was stormy, and once again Clay threw down the gauge of battle to the administration.

JAMES MONROE

Ever since 1816 he had been trying to realize some rational system to multiply roads and canals and to facilitate inland commerce and communication. The debates turned on the point of constitutional power, and in his efforts to convince the House that the power "to establish" post roads implied the power to build and repair roads, and that the power to "regulate commerce among the several states" implied the power to promote inter-state canals, Clay savagely assailed and ridiculed Monroe's constitutional principles. By directing the attention of Congress to the number of public buildings, light houses, harbor improvements, and fortifications which had been erected on the Atlantic seaboard—"everything on the margin of the ocean, but nothing for domestic trade; nothing for the great interior of the country"—[32] he attempted to convince Congress that it possessed the power to construct roads and canals for the benefit of circulation and trade in the interior as much as it did to promote coastwise traffic. Clay voiced the united opinion of the West when he tried to commit Congress to the construction of interstate roads and canals which were too expensive to be borne by the states alone, but he revived, also, the memory of his old opposition to the Monroe administration, thereby hindering his presidential cause.

Clay's foremost opponent in the verbal struggle was vitriolic Randolph of Roanoke, who voiced the opposition of the southern seaboard. Threatening "every other means short of actual insurrection" to defeat the bill, he warned his fellow-slaveholders that if Congress possessed the powers stipulated by the provisions of the bill, it could emancipate every slave in the Union.[33] The bill easily passed the House and the Senate, however, and was presented to Monroe for his signature. He signed it on the ground that it merely provided for the collection of information and appointed a Board to carry the act into effect.[34]

Clay's eloquence in supporting his vast schemes for a transcontinental highway succeeded in bringing before Monroe an act for extending the Cumberland Road from Canton, Ohio, to Zanesville, and providing for a survey for a future extension to the capital of Missouri. The act was so framed as not to interfere with Monroe's constitutional scruples, and, since there was a treasury surplus, he signed the bill on March 3, 1825, in the closing hours of his administration.[35]

❧ 36 ❦

Recognition of South American Republics

THE CHRISTMAS present which the American people received in December, 1814, was a period of almost one hundred years during which they were cut off from actual participation in the wars and struggles of Europe and could further their own national development and expansion. In accordance with the new spirit prevalent upon the release of the country from the wartime restrictions, Monroe had guided the nation along the pathway to what was later to be known as its "manifest destiny." The borders in the South and the West had been defined and extended as a result of the acquisition of Florida. The slavery question had caused alarm, "like a firebell in the night," but had been temporarily resolved in the Compromise of 1821; and the issue of internal improvements had been successfully dealt with. But while internal issues were thus successfully being met and handled, the foreign situation was a continuing menace to America's newly won independence from the European scheme of politics. During eight years of threatening interference the country had been piloted safely through the shoals of foreign diplomacy to emerge at the end of Monroe's administration with a clear-cut policy of American isolation and independence from Europe, destined to be respected by all nations for years to come.

The most pressing and threatening of the foreign problems which Monroe was called upon to handle was that of the recognition of the South American republics.[1] Involving as it did the danger of European intervention and war, the independence of the entire New World and the destiny of the United States in North America, as well as complicating the negotiations for the purchase of Florida, Monroe had to proceed cautiously. An ardent sympathizer with their cause, he was forced to restrain the enthusiasm of Clay and the nation as a whole for immediate recognition.

Following the opening of the second phase of the revolutions in 1817, an increasing volume of books and pamphlets, popularizing the cause and advocating immediate recognition, flooded the country and aroused public interest in the struggle. H. M. Brackenridge composed a bitter denunciation of Spanish rule entitled "A Letter to James Monroe . . . upon the Present State of South America," in which he called upon the President to jettison some of his scruples and to recognize the rebel governments. William Duane, editor of the Philadelphia *Aurora*, an intimate friend of Manuel Torres the Colombian agent, did much to popularize the cause, while Niles devoted an unusually large amount of space to Spanish-American affairs. Everywhere was a new enthusiasm for the rebellious South Americans in their struggle for liberty and progress.

In spite of this wide acclaim of the South American cause, the numerous rebel agents which the newly created governments sent to the United States to secure munitions, loans, and recognition, did not get an impression of whole-hearted support. Chile and Buenos Aires sent Aguirre to secure a loan for a fleet, authorizing him to issue letters of marque to Americans willing to enlist their ships for privateer duty. The stringency of the neutrality legislation of 1817 was a severe blow to his hopes, and although Washington society lionized him, his money ran out and he was imprisoned.[2] In 1818 Juan Martín de Pueyrredón, Supreme Director of the United Provinces, made another attempt to enlist American money and aid, and commissioned General William Winder, a Baltimore lawyer and friend of Monroe's, to act as an agent for Buenos Aires. Winder, wishing to act only with the approbation of the President, sent a copy of the letter from Martín to Monroe, along with an exposition of his views.[3]

Monroe gave the matter very careful consideration, pointing out to Winder in elaborate detail the considerations on both sides of the question, and while he did not forbid his accepting the commission he succeeded in dissuading the General from any official participation in the cause. Among other things, he wrote: "I have

The South American Republics

no hesitation to state to you, that the sincere desire of this government, is, that the Spanish Colonies may achieve their independence, and that we shall promote it, . . . by honourable & impartial measure, which we can adopt, . . . I am satisfied that the true interest of the Colonies, consists, in leaving us perfectly free, to pursue, such course in regard to them, as we think proper, & that on the ground of interest there can be no disagreement much less collision between us. It is a miserably shortsighted, & contracted, policy, in those who represent the colonies, . . . to pursue a different course, since its tendency is to deprive them of the friendship, of the only power on earth, sincerely friendly to them, & of the immense advantages, which they derive, by the supplies, which they receive from us, & from the countenance which we give them and for what purpose encounter this danger? Equally satisfied I am, that were we ever to engage in the war, in their favour, they would be losers by it. . . ."[4]

Although the United States never concealed its sympathy, there was great reluctance on the part of the administration to act alone, in opposition to Europe. On May 13, 1818, Adams noted that President Monroe suggested at a Cabinet meeting on that date the possibility of joint action with England to promote independence.[5]

Calhoun supported the President, feeling that such a step would assist the administration to withstand the pressure in Congress for immediate recognition. The French minister, likewise, approached Adams with proposals for combined French and American intervention. Adams was at first opposed,[6] but late in 1818 he told Bagot and the French minister that he desired joint and harmonious action, but by that time his chief had had a change of heart.

Although Monroe had at first been favorable to the idea of American participation in joint intervention he soon rejected the idea. The European powers, with the possible exception of Great Britain, favored a compromise settlement, whereby the colonies would remain in a dependent state, whereas the United States was morally committed to a policy of complete independence for the new states.[7]

A still more important deterrent, and the one which most influenced Adams, was the information he received from Bagot of the projected European intervention in South America.[8] Ferdinand VII, having been so successful in enlisting the aid of his brethren of the purple in his internal affairs, determined to secure their services in the restoration and resubjugation of his rebellious colonies. Accordingly, a congress of the powers was arranged to gather at Aix-la-Chapelle in September of 1818 to consider, among other matters, the question of the restoration of the colonies. Both France and Russia attempted to lure the United States into sending delegates, but Adams and Monroe, following the dictates of Washington, refused the invitation. Largely because of the aloofness of England, too vitally interested in the South American trade to see it return to the Spanish monopoly, nothing was arranged by the congress in regard to the colonies. However, France and Russia, as well as Great Britain, expressed disapproval of the possibility of the United States' recognizing the rebels. In a "Sketch of Instruction for Agents for South America," Monroe wrote: "When the sentiments of the United States in favor of the independence of the Colonies, with their intention to recognize it at some earlier period, were made known to the Congress at Aix-la-Chapelle, we were assured . . . that all the allies, especially France and Russia, expressed great disapprobation of the proposed recognition, and that the Minister of Great Britain, declared he should consider it rash."[9]

Monroe had at first been greatly agitated over the prospect of such a congress. In a letter to Madison in April, 1818, he expressed his concern: "We have lately obtained from Madrid, by Mr. Erving, a copy of the instructions of the Emperor, at Moscow, to his minister at the allied courts, designating the manner in which he wishes the dispute between Portugal and Spain to be settled, & with their concert afterwards, with the other allies, that existing between Spain and her Colonies. Portugal must give up the territory she has occupied and the Colonies restored to Spain on the footing of the proposed mediation by Great Britain, of a free trade, with something like colonial government."[10]

Yet, even before the results of the congress became known in this country Monroe, unwilling to believe that force would be used, urged in his second annual message, a continued policy of watchful waiting and delayed recognition.[11]

None of these considerations could rival in importance the restraining influence of the Florida negotiations.* Monroe, in his special

---

*Described in Chapter XXX.

The South American Republics

message to Congress on Spanish affairs, May 9, 1820, wrote a stinging paragraph on the arrogance and perfidy of Spain:

"In regard to the stipulation proposed as the condition of the ratification of the treaty, that the United States shall abandon the right to recognize the revolutionary Colonies in South America, or to form other relations with them when in their judgment it may be just and expedient so to do, it is manifestly so repugnant to the honor and even to the independence of the United States that it has been impossible to discuss it."[12]

The two-year period of waiting to which the United States settled down before Spain ratified the treaty was a trying one. Monroe's official attitude and that of the government are best illustrated in his "Sketch of Instructions for Agents for South America—Notes for the Department of State":

"The best mode of promoting this object was to take no part in the contest ourselves. . . . Had we recognized them there is much reason to believe that we should have given offense to every other power, and excited in them a disposition to counteract its probable effect.

"The United States have given to the colonies all the advantages of a recognition, without any of its evils. The mission to Buenos Ayres was particularly calculated to produce that effect."[13]

He amplified this policy in a letter of May 26, 1820, to Gallatin, in which he said, "With respect to the Colonies, the object has been to throw into their scale, in a moral sense, the weight of the United States, without so deep a compromitment as to make us a party to the contest. . . . By taking this ground openly and frankly, we acquit ourselves to our own consciences; . . . I am satisfied that had we even joined them in the war, we should have done them more harm than good, as we might have drawn all Europe on them, not to speak of the injury we should have done to ourselves."[14]

The annual messages all contained references to the current progress of the struggle, coupled with hopes for the continued successes of the South American Republics.

In his third annual message, Monroe said, "The progress of the war, . . . has operated in favor of the Colonies. Buenos Ayres still maintains unshaken the independence which it declared in 1816, and has enjoyed since 1810. Like success has also lately attended

JAMES MONROE

Chili and the Provinces north of the La Plata bordering on it, and likewise Venezuela."[15]

And again in 1820: "There is little to say about South America except to note the continued success of the rebels and the conclusion of an armistice between Bolívar and Morillo which, it was hoped, might soon lead to a peace and a general recognition of the new status of Spanish America by all powers."[16]

Another factor which enabled the President to hold down enthusiasm of the country as a whole, was the discouraging tone of the reports which his commissioners sent in from South America. The complete disillusionment which they revealed moderated public enthusiasm; and, while the bulk of sympathy was still with Spanish America, the waiting policy of the administration met with greater approbation than at any time theretofore.[17] Fortunately the Washington officials had to deal with very few direct agents from the colonies during these two years. Most of them, like Aguirre, became discouraged by the official American attitude, and running short of money were forced to return home. Torres, the Colombian agent, was the only one of any importance who remained. Working quietly and legally for recognition and for munitions, he held a respectable position in the eyes of government officials and was cordially received by Washington society.

The President refused consistently to be driven by Clay, and even the final ratification of the treaty by Spain in February, 1821, failed to bring any immediate change in the attitude of the administration. Early in March, 1821, Clay hazarded a personal interview with Adams, in an attempt to discover what could then be holding up the course of events. Amazingly enough, the interview was a calm and friendly one. Adams continued to maintain that the provinces were not yet ready for independence, although hinting that recognition on the part of the United States was not far in the offing.[18] He reiterated similar sentiments to Stratford Canning later in the month. Canning wrote Planta: "Government and citizens, one and all, are very proud of the pending measure for acknowledging the independence of South America, though it is quite clear that they are not disposed to incur any real risk for the sake of this favorite object. Adams confessed to me that he regarded Spain as a man under the pressure of a nightmare, longing to raise his arms, but unable to stir

The South American Republics

a muscle. I had previously accosted him by saying, 'So, Mr. Adams, you are going to make honest people of them?' 'Yes, Sir,' was his answer; 'we proposed to your Government to join us some time ago, but they would not, and now we shall see whether you will be content to *follow* us'."[19]

To Torres, the Colombian agent, the situation looked hopeful later that fall, and he again approached Adams requesting formal recognition and munitions. His statement presaged one of the principles which Monroe was to enunciate in his message of 1823. Said Torres:

"The glory and satisfaction of being the first to recognize the independence of a new republic in the south of this continent belongs, in all respects and considerations, to the Government of the United States. The present political state of New Spain requires the most earnest attention of the government of the United States. There has occurred a project, long since formed, to establish a Monarchy in Mexico, on purpose to favor the views of the Holy Alliance in the New World; this is a new reason which ought to determine the President of the United States no longer to delay a measure which will naturally establish an American Alliance, capable of counteracting the projects of the European Powers, and of protecting our republican institutions. My government has entire confidence in the prudence of the President, in his disposition to favor the cause of the liberty and of the independence of South America, and his great experience in the management of public business."[20]

Adams put him off with an evasive reply. Monroe's annual message of 1821 followed the pattern of those of previous years in its allusions to Spanish America.[21]

With the new year, however, news of recent events in South America which had radically altered the political geography of the continent, reached Washington. During the summer and fall San Martín in the South and Bolívar in the North had been winning decisive victories. With the evacuation of Lima, last citadel of royalism, and with the final liberation of Venezuela, recognition, in accordance with Adams' definition, was no longer a matter of right, but an established fact. It was patent to the world that Spain had lost her colonies. By 1822 the European situation was more favorable to an independent declaration on the part of the United States.

JAMES MONROE

Great Britain's disapproval of the congress system and her aloofness at Troppau made the European royalist front less ominous. The long-threatened European intervention in South America had not yet materialized, nor did there appear to be any serious likelihood of it.

On January 30, 1822, Representative Nelson, of Virginia, asked Monroe for information concerning "the political condition" of the revolted colonies of Spain and "the state of war between them and Spain."[22] The following day Trimble of Kentucky undertook to spur on the President by moving before the House that Monroe be requested to recognize Colombia and to exchange ministers with the new republic. The same action was recommended in relation to any other republics which were actually independent. There was no debate and the resolutions were never voted upon. On March 8, 1822, more than a year after the formal exchange of ratifications with Madrid, Monroe sent a special message to Congress, recommending recognition of the independent South American governments and asking for an appropriation for ministers to South America.[23] He reviewed at great length the history of the revolutions and the declarations of independence by Mexico, Chile, Peru, Argentina, and Colombia, and stated that since Spain, after so many years of attempt had failed to subdue them, they were actually in a state of independence and ought to be recognized: "It is manifest," he said, "that all those Provinces are not only in the full enjoyment of their independence, but, considering the state of the war and other circumstances, that there is not the most remote prospect of their being deprived of it."[24]

Even at this stage Monroe proceeded cautiously. Fearing to arouse European antipathies, he not only avoided giving any publicity to the affair while Congress was considering the message, but he contemplated soft-pedalling the measure even after it had passed. "A doubt arises in my mind," he wrote to Jonathan Russell, "whether it will be politic to give any *distinguished* eclat to the recognition until we see its effect on the powers of Europe, who will, I have great cause to presume, be much excited by the measure, from its bearing on *legitimacy*."[25]

As usual he turned to Jefferson, seeking approbation of the course he had pursued: "You have I doubt not read the message respecting

The South American Republics

the independent governments to the South of the U. States. There was *danger* in standing *still* or moving *forward*, of a nature, in both instances, which will readily occur to you. I thought that it was the wisest policy, to risk that, which was incident to the latter course, as it comported more with the liberal & magnanimous spirit of our own country than the other. I hope that you will concur in the opinion that the time has arriv'd, beyond which it ought not to have been longer delayed."[26]

On March 19, 1822, the House, hoping that Europe would follow the American example, reported two resolutions. It concurred with the President in his opinion that the American colonies who had declared and were enjoying their independence ought to be recognized, and it authorized the Ways and Means Committee to report an appropriation bill.[27] After a spirited discussion a bill was framed and signed on May 4, providing for $100,000 to defray the expense of "such Missions to the independent nations on the American continent" as the President might deem proper.[28] This bill had been passed with but one dissenting vote. So eager was Monroe to achieve complete unanimity on that particular question, that he wrote a special letter to Robert S. Garnett, the lone nay, in an attempt to persuade him to reverse his vote:

"Your vote of yesterday against recognition of our Southern neighbors has given many of your friends, and among them myself, much concern, partly as it affects the public, it being the only vote against it, but more especially, the great unanimity accomplishing every public object, as it respects yourself.

". . . The question being carried, it is important, as relates to the character of the measure and the public feeling, that it be unanimous. The incident, in my opinion, affords you an excellent opportunity of conciliating the public opinion, as well as of Congress toward you, which may be done by stating in your place that you had thought, on great reflection, that the measure was hazardous, but seeing that your country had taken its step you were resolved to go with it, & therefore changed your vote."[29] But Garnett refused to be budged in his decision.

Spain and Europe in general branded the act as one of "bad faith." However, Monroe had never given an implied or a formal pledge not to accord recognition and had delayed more than a year after the ratification of the Florida treaty before taking action. Subsequent events gave overwhelming proof that Spain was incapable of subduing her former subjects. Manuel Torres, the official Colombian agent, was rewarded for his long years of patient service by being the first chargé d'affaires to receive official United States recognition of his country—in May of 1822. During the course of the ensuing four years, diplomatic relations were established with all the stronger republics, including the constitutional monarchy of Brazil.

The Cuban question, like that of the independence of the South American provinces, originated in the Napoleonic conquest of Spain and the subsequent inability of that country to retain possession of her far-flung empire. Cuba and Porto Rico were all that remained to Spain of a three-century-old imperial domain, when the United States formally accorded recognition to the mainland South American colonies. Because of Cuba's strategic position, commanding both the Gulf of Mexico, with the Central American and Mississippi Valley trade, and the Caribbean Sea, it was of the highest importance to the United States, as well as to the West Indian powers, England and France. The greedy eyes of the commercial world were fixed upon the island, in an estimate of Spain's ability to retain it.

President Madison had formulated a Cuban policy to which the United States had consistently adhered, as early as October 30, 1810, in a letter to William Pinkney: "The position of Cuba gives the United States so deep an interest in the destiny, even, of that Island, that although they might be an inactive, they could not be a satisfied spectator at its falling under any European government, which might make a fulcrum of that position against the commerce and security of the United States."[30]

The United States was peculiarly susceptible to fear regarding the fate of Cuba. As early as 1817 a wave of newspaper propaganda spread the report that England had proposed relinquishing the claims she held against Spain for the maintenance of British troops during Wellington's peninsular campaign, amounting to £15,000,000, in return for the cession of the island.[31] These reports were given widespread credence but the question failed to concern the administration until 1819, when Adams was negotiating with Onis for the cession of the Floridas. The British press, backed by the trading interests,

The South American Republics

then threatened that acquisition of the Floridas by the United States would give that country such a trading advantage in the West Indies that England must of necessity seize Cuba, to equalize the effect.[32] Although Rush secured from Castlereagh adequate assurance that England had no intention of annexing the island, the administration still felt concerned. There still remained the fear that Spain might cede the island to Great Britain.

While all eyes were thus turned anxiously on the "Pearl of the Antilles," an unexpected move was made by a portion of the inhabitants of the island. From a party in Cuba itself, in September, 1822, advances were made to the United States, requesting annexation. Adams described the situation:

"The President sent me a letter from P. S. Duponceau, of Philadelphia, to General John Mason, of Georgetown, informing him of a certain Mr. Sanchez . . . [who] comes as a secret Agent from a number of the principal inhabitants of the place, who have formed the plan of declaring the island independent of Spain and are desirous of being admitted as a State into the American Union. The object of the mission of Mr. Sanchez is, to inquire if the government of the United States will concur with them in that object. The plan is represented as being so far matured that they want nothing but the assurance of being seconded from this country to act immediately."[33]

Monroe sent an agent to investigate, meanwhile refraining from lending any official encouragement to the movement. In a series of Cabinet meetings devoted to a discussion of the United States' attitude toward the Cuban solicitations, it became apparent that the administration was tempted by it. Calhoun went so far as to state that it would be "worth a war with England."[34] Adams and Monroe, however, favored a policy of watchful waiting and it was concluded that the answer to Mr. Sanchez must be a refusal to give any encouragement to the revolutionary movement.

George Canning, who was convinced that no questions relating to Continental Europe could be more vitally or immediately important to Great Britain than those which related to America, became Prime Minister of England in September, 1822. Alarmed that the United States might occupy Cuba, now that the independence of the rest of South America had been recognized, he submitted to his Cabinet in November the question whether any blow that could be struck by any foreign power anywhere would more affect the interests of England.*35*

Meanwhile, at the Congress of Verona it had been determined that France conduct an armed invasion of Spain to restore the hapless Ferdinand. As these preparations progressed in 1823, the Americans maintained little hope that the island would remain in the possession of Spain. Rumor had it that England was to secure Cuba from Spain in return for financial assistance in her pending war with France. The naval force which Canning had dispatched to the islands, for the ostensible purpose of checking piracy, bore out the suspicions. Although Canning denied all allegations of such a bargain, the American government was by no means reassured, and the ministers abroad were warned to keep a close watch upon all negotiations between Spain and England. Adams was so suspicious that on April 28, 1823, when he issued instructions to Mr. Nelson, Forsyth's successor at Madrid, he exceeded his customary length and declared:

"In looking forward to the probable course of events for the short period of half a century, it seems scarcely possible to resist the conviction that the annexation of Cuba to our Federal Republic will be indispensable to the continuance and integrity of the Union itself....

"We were not then prepared for annexation but there are laws of political as well as physical gravitation; and if an apple, severed by the tempest from its native tree, cannot choose but fall to the ground, Cuba, forcibly disjoined from its own unnatural connection with Spain, and incapable of self-support, can gravitate only toward the North American Union, which, by the same law of nature, cannot cast her off from its bosom." *36*

Adams' immediate policy favored the retention of Cuba and Porto Rico by Spain, but he refused to commit the United States to a guarantee of Cuban independence against all the world except that power.

The mutual jealousies of the nations as reflected in the Cuban issue raised the greater question of the possible entanglements with Europe likely to derive from it. Jefferson expressed the view that "Cuba alone seems at present to hold up a speck of war to us. Its possession by Great Britain would indeed be a great calamity to us. Could we induce her to join us in guaranteeing its independence against all the world, except Spain, it would be nearly as valuable as

The South American Republics

if it were our own. But should she take it, I would not immediately go to war for it; because the first war on other accounts will give it to us, or the island will give itself to us when able to do so."[37]

Monroe concurred with Jefferson in the importance of securing the island, but of awaiting a propitious moment for the act. "I have always concurr'd with you in sentiment," he wrote, "that too much importance could not be attached to that Island, and that we ought, if possible, to incorporate it into our Union, availing ourselves of the most favorable moment for it, hoping also that one would arrive, when it might be done, without a rupture with Spain or any other power.

"I consider Cape Florida & Cuba, as forming the mouth of the Mississippi; & other rivers, emptying into the Gulph of Mexico, within our limits, as of the Gulph itself, & in consequence that the acquisition of it to our Union, was of the highest importance to our internal tranquility, as well as to our prosperity and aggrandizement."[38]

The intriguing and meddlesome Seventeenth Congress witnessed only two acts of any importance—the President's veto of the Cumberland Road bill and the recognition of the South American republics. But with the achievement of the latter the United States entered upon a new era. The festering sore that had been Florida had been healed by incorporation into the American system of government; the constant quarrelings with Spain had ceased; the boundaries of the nation had been specifically defined; the Mississippi ran untrammeled through United States territory to the Gulf. The cautious but firm diplomacy of Monroe had been finely tempered in preparation for the bold stand he was to take the following year.

❧ 37 ❦

Relations with Russia

SOUTH AMERICA and the Spanish province of Florida were not the only sections of the Western Hemisphere which proved a thorny problem to Monroe and his Cabinet. As Spain's South American empire broke away, its possessions in North America on the Pacific coast were exposed to seizure by rival powers. The United States and Great Britain had deferred for ten years the question of ultimate ownership of the Oregon territory, that land lying between the Rockies and the Pacific coast, extending roughly from the Columbia River to 54° north latitude. To the south, extending through Lower California and Mexico, lay Spanish territory, the bequest of the conquistadores. To the northward, Alaska and the Bering Strait country were the property of the Russian government. Encroachment upon the Spanish domain threatened from two sources—England and Russia.

The importance of trading posts and the presence of actual settlers in determining the question of ownership of a territory had not been lost upon the Americans in their negotiations with England over the joint occupation following the Treaty of Ghent. Priority of discovery was seriously rivalled by exploration, settlement, and the establishment of posts. Accordingly, in 1820 a motion was carried in the House of Representatives authorizing the United States to form an establishment on the Columbia River. Although the Convention of 1818 permitted joint occupation and trade and travel within the territory, England was much averse to immigration into the region and objected to the 1820 resolution.

Relations with Russia

Great Britain at that time was represented in the United States by Stratford Canning. Having learned through several experiences that it required very little to fan the flames of American animosity, the British were to follow a policy in which conciliation was to be the dominating note. It was Canning's task to show the American people that the English meant well by them. He was a proud and high-tempered Briton and it was inevitable that he and the aggressive, uncompromising Puritan, John Quincy Adams, should quarrel. When Canning recorded England's protest against the proposed Columbia River settlement a brisk dispute ensued. Although Castlereagh eventually decided to let the matter drop, Adams, feeling the American continent to be the special preserve of the United States, challenged any claim of England to the shores of the Pacific. "Keep what is yours," he said, "but leave the rest of this continent to us."[1]

In a similar abrupt and brusque fashion Adams met the encroaching claims of Russia. In 1727 Bering discovered the straits which bear his name and subsequently trading posts were established on the islands off the coast and along the Alaskan mainland. At the close of the eighteenth century exclusive fishing, whaling, and sealing rights had been granted by the Imperial government to the Russian American Company to 55° north latitude. By 1811 the Russians had extended their activities and established a trading post at Bodega Bay, near San Francisco. The Americans, attracted by the lucrative trade, gradually infringed upon the Russian domain. Trading was carried on among the fur posts in a friendly enough fashion, and since the Russian interests were considered to be commercial rather than territorial, there was no complaint from the American State Department.

Early in 1822 the question of the relationship of the United States to the North American continent and to Russia in particular, was brought conspicuously to the front. On February 28 of that year Adams was notified by the Chevalier du Poletica, the Russian minister at Washington, that the Czar, annoyed by the foreign contraband trade, had issued an important ukase the previous September. This imperial decree announced the claim of Russia to the Pacific Coast from Bering Straits to the fifty-first parallel of north latitude, and interdicted to the commercial vessels of other powers the approach on the high seas within one hundred Italian miles of this claim. Not only was this an untoward assertion of sovereignty over the high seas, but indicated that Russia was prepared to push the southern boundary of Alaska deep into Oregon country, the territory which England and the United States claimed jointly as far north as 54°.

Curiously, the news of this decree failed to cause widespread alarm in the United States. Oregon was a remote and far-away country; there was an abundance of land much nearer home; and the American trading interests on the west coast had not as yet assumed vital proportions. American public opinion was therefore apathetic. *Niles' Register,* December 29, 1821, reflected the common sentiment: "Even if the Emperor of Russia should make good his claim to the 51st degree, we *guess* that there will be a region of the country large enough left for us."[2]

Far more energetic was Monroe. The President was thoroughly alarmed and instructed Adams to demand the grounds upon which the claim was based.[3] The Russian minister informed him that the Russians had long maintained a settlement at Novo-Archangelsk, located on the fifty-seventh parallel of north latitude. The fifty-first parallel, referred to in the decree, lay about half way between that and the Columbia River. The restriction, forbidding the approach to the coast had been inserted to prevent foreigners from carrying on an illicit trade with the natives, to the detriment of the Russian American Fur Company. This assertion, which would have closed Bering Sea, met with a vigorous protest by Adams and a blunt warning to the Russian minister at Washington. By July Baron de Tuyll had displaced Poletica, and Adams, having in mind Russia's posts in California, informed the minister: ". . . that we should contest the right of Russia to *any* territorial establishment on this continent, and that we should assume distinctly the principle that the American continents are no longer subjects for *any* new European colonial establishments."[4]

On August 8, 1822, Mr. Middleton, the United States representative in St. Petersburg, reporting to Adams, stated: "For some time past I began to perceive that the provisions of the ukase would not be persisted in. It appears to have been signed by the Emperor without sufficient examination, and may be fairly considered as having been surreptitiously obtained. There can be little doubt, therefore, that with a little patience and management it will be molded into a less objectionable shape."[5]

Relations with Russia

That year Monroe suggested to Congress that the time had come to think seriously of taking up the question of the occupation of the Oregon territory. When Congress refused to consider the question, Baron de Tuyll suggested that the issue be settled by negotiation at St. Petersburg.[6] Adams and Monroe acquiesced, and in acknowledging the communication from Baron de Tuyll Adams observed:

"Penetrated with these sentiments, and anxiously seeking to promote their perpetuation, the President readily accedes to the proposal that the minister of the United States at the court of His Imperial Majesty, should be furnished with powers for negotiating, upon principles adapted to those sentiments, the adjustment of the interests and rights which have been brought into collision upon the northwest coast of America, and which have heretofore formed a subject of correspondence between the two Governments, as well at Washington, as at St. Petersburg."[7]

Adams followed this up on July 22, 1822, with a dispatch to Middleton, declaring that no Russian territorial right could be admitted on the North American continent, as the Russians had made no settlements upon it except in California: "There can, perhaps, be no better time for saying, frankly and explicitly, to the Russian government, that the future peace of the world, and the interest of Russia herself, cannot be promoted by Russian settlements upon any part of the American Continent."[8]

After prolonged negotiations Russia concluded a treaty on April 17, 1824, by which she agreed to form no establishment on the northwest coast south of 54° 40'. The United States reciprocally agreed to make no establishment north of that line. At the same time Russia abandoned her extreme claim of maritime jurisdiction. That summer Madison wrote to Monroe, congratulating him on the convention with Russia. "The Convention with Russia," he wrote, "is a propitious event as substituting amicable adjustment for the risks of hostile collision. But I give the Emperor however little credit for his assent to the principle of 'Mare liberator' in the North Pacific. His pretensions were so absurd, & so disgusting to the Maritime world that he could not do better than retreat from them thro' the forms of negotiation. It is well that the cautious, if not courteous policy of England towards Russia has had the effect of making us, in the public eye, the leading Power in arresting her expansive ambition. . . . It

JAMES MONROE

favors the hope that bold as the Allies, with Russia at their head, have shewn themselves in their enmity to free Govt. everywhere, the maritime capacities of the United States, with the naval and pecuniary resources of Great Britain, have a benumbing influence on all their wicked enterprises."[9]

38

European Background of the Monroe Doctrine

BY THE FALL of 1823 the American people were more disturbed by the Holy Alliance than by any other foreign problem. Said *Niles' Register* on September 6, "Though separated by a wide ocean from the old world, we are deeply interested in its concerns.... In the perfection of the schemes of the 'holy alliance' we must anticipate the extinction of civil and religious liberty...."[1]

This concern over the intentions of the Holy Alliance spread to the administration. After a gloomy Cabinet meeting of November 13, 1823, Adams wrote that Calhoun, the Secretary of War, was "perfectly moonstruck" by the success of the French invasion of Spain. As for Monroe: "I find him... alarmed, far beyond anything that I could have conceived possible, with the fear that the Holy Allies are about to restore immediately all South America to Spain. Calhoun stimulates the panic, and the news that Cadiz has surrendered to the French has so affected the President that he appeared entirely to despair of the cause of South America."[2]

To understand this American preoccupation with European diplomacy, which led to the formulation of the Monroe Doctrine, one must glance back over the preceding decade.

When, after Waterloo, Napoleon was shipped to St. Helena, the curtain fell upon a world shaken and broken by a war which, with one brief interlude, had lasted for twenty-three years. It had involved the British Empire and all Europe, eventually drawing into its vortex the United States. The complete wreck of economic conditions, which involved the destruction of capital and savings to an unprecedented extent, had seriously diminished the world's purchasing power. Beneath the glitter and elegance which remained lay poverty and bitter disappointment mixed with discontent, the spoils of war for both the victors and the vanquished. Those individuals upon whose shoulders lay the burden of reconstruction, were determined that such a war must never come again. Those militant seekers of democracy, liberty, and popular governments, responsible for the convulsive upheaval, must never again be allowed to raise their standards. To mitigate the danger of such a recurrence, those in control of the political peace-making machinery knew the correct formula. The boundaries must be rearranged, old dynasties reëstablished and maintained, kings and emperors supported, and such a balance of power preserved as might not easily be again disturbed.

By the Second Treaty of Paris of November 20, 1815, Austria, Russia, Prussia, and England committed themselves to a solemn pact whereby the status quo was to be preserved, Napoleon excluded from France, and the restored French monarchy maintained. Representatives of the four powers were to meet at stated intervals to consult concerning problems of common interest and to take such measures as might best serve the peace and happiness of Europe: "In order to consolidate the intimate ties which unite the four sovereigns for the happiness of the world, the high contracting parties have agreed to renew at fixed intervals, either under their own auspices or by their respective ministers, meetings consecrated to great common objects and the examination of such measures as shall be judged most salutary for the peace and prosperity of Europe."[3]

This sixth article of the Second Peace of Paris was the epitome of what Metternich called the "System of 1815." This system for reconstructing Europe in reality had resulted from a long series of debated agreements which, beginning with the politico-military pacts of Toeplitz, Reichenbach, and Chaumont had been continued by the two Treaties of Paris and the Acts of the Congress of Vienna. Built upon the shattered foundations of Napoleonic world empire, it assumed the form of a European Confederation[4] complete with the diplomatic machinery of international congresses and councils.

The European Background

Distinct from this four-power police regimentation of Europe there was evoked in 1815, by the idealist Tsar, Alexander of Russia, a "League of Peace," or Holy Alliance, to which Russia, Austria, and Prussia adhered, but from which Great Britain shrank. The germ of this fantastic coalition had been generated in September, 1804, while Monroe was most deeply concerned with the negotiation which grew out of the Louisiana Purchase, for at that moment Pitt and Alexander were preparing their coalition against Napoleon. Monroe was in London when the Tsar's envoy and friend, Novosiltzov, arrived to explain Alexander's views regarding the diplomatic arrangement which should complement the military alliance against the French. These instructions to Novosiltzov[5] laid the foundations upon which, ten years later, rested the program of intervention and reconstruction contained in the Treaties of Kalisch and Chaumont. The opening paragraph contained an eloquent recognition of the growing force of public opinion in international affairs: "The most effectual weapon which France now wields—one with which the French continue to menace their neighbors—is their ability to persuade public opinion that their cause is that of the liberty and prosperity of all nations."

As a condition precedent to the "moral union" Alexander sought with Great Britain, he requested the latter's acceptance of a "new order," a highly practical program of "self-determination," the outlines of a reconstruction of Europe along "national" lines. The King of Sardinia, who had been deprived by Napoleon of his throne, was to be re-established, but not until he had promised to give his people the benefits of a "wise and free constitution." The importance of maintaining Swiss neutrality was also recognized "as an essential factor in the peace of Europe." In restoring Holland to national existence the modern theory of self-determination was recognized—"the character of the *national* desires must be considered before deciding upon the form of government to be established."

There was no suggestion in the Tsar's plan of a superstate, the favorite remedy of the eighteenth-century philosophers for all international ills, nor any hint of the doctrine of intervention in the internal affairs of neighboring states, the policy which was later to render the pretensions of the Holy Alliance most hateful in the eyes of the constitutional powers. Alexander envisioned a Europe whose guiding principles would be those of international law, a league of nations, where mediation was to be substituted for war.[6]

This constructive plan for the government of Europe which Alexander had conceived in 1804, he revived to put into practice in 1815. But in this ten-year period the idealist Tsar, the pupil of Laharpe, one of Rousseau's most ardent followers, had been subjected to severe disillusionment. The agreement into which he was forced to enter at Tilsit with Napoleon was the negation of every policy and principle he had ever professed. The curious blending of international idealism and practical advantage to Russia was still there, but distorted by the mystical and religious influence exerted over him by the Baroness von Krüdener, and the conservative teachings of the reactionary philosopher, Bergasse. The Baroness von Krüdener was "The daughter of a wealthy Livonian noble and widow of a Russian ambassador, and after a youth spent in frivolity, she had in 1806 'found salvation' through the agency of a pious cobbler of Riga."[7] She had first apparently met the Emperor on June 4, 1815, at his headquarters at Heilbronn, where she sought an interview.[8]

In the first days of September, 1815, not without intention of restoring the prestige which the Russian armies had lost by their absence from Waterloo, a great review of the entire Russian force which had invaded France was held upon the Plain of Vertus, near Chalons. This spectacle the Tsar also determined was to be the dramatic prelude to what he now considered the most important political act of his career, the manifesto of a Holy Alliance of Justice, Christian Charity, and Peace.

On September 10, the magnificent troops of Alexander's guard and line, drilled even in war to a state of precision for which the Emperor Paul's "paradomania" was largely responsible, passed before the Russian sovereign and his guests, the Emperor of Austria and the King of Prussia. The religious ceremony was perhaps the most remarkable part of the spectacle. On the broad plain seven altars had been erected, where the imposing ritual of the Greek service was celebrated in the presence of this reverent host. Their thundering responses to the chanting of the priests showed them ready to die with fanatical zeal at the word of their Emperor.

Still under the powerful influence of this significant military pageant, the sovereigns present at the review were invited by Alex-

The European Background

ander to affix their signatures to the famous document subsequently known to history as the Holy Alliance.[9] The Tsar, the Emperor of Austria, and the King of Prussia formally declared that henceforth their united policy had but a single object:

"To manifest before the whole universe their unshakable determination to take as their sole guide, both in the administration of their respective states and in their political relations with other governments, the precepts of religion, namely, the rules of Justice, Christian Charity, and Peace.

"These precepts, far from being applicable only to private life, should, on the contrary, govern the decisions of Princes, and direct them in all their negotiations, forming, as they must, the only means of giving permanence to human institutions and remedying their imperfections."[10]

Following this unusual preamble came the terms of a diplomatic agreement, no less extraordinary in the eyes of contemporary statesmen:

"Conformably to the words of the Holy Scriptures, which command all men to consider each other as brethren, the three contracting Monarchs will remain united by the bonds of a true and indissoluble fraternity. Considering each other as fellow countrymen, they will on all occasions and in all places lend each other aid and assistance; towards their subjects and armies, they will extend a fatherly care and protection, leading them (in the same spirit of fraternity with which they are themselves animated) to protect Religion, Peace, and Justice."[11]

The language of the pact thus suddenly presented by the Tsar to the Emperor of Austria and the King of Prussia for their signatures had no parallel in the archives of diplomacy. In adhering to the Holy Alliance these sovereigns bound themselves to nothing more than a promise to observe in their foreign and domestic policy "the duties which the Divine Saviour has taught to mankind"; yet they were "amazed and terrified" by the possible consequences of their act. Reliance upon moral principles so general and wide-sweeping was indeed to lead to policies and events unforeseen at the time by their author. If the mystical language of the Holy Alliance contained practical meaning, this lay in its affirmation that the sovereigns of Europe should "on all occasions and in all places lend each other aid and assistance." Nor was this to be a "partial and exclusive alliance." All powers who should choose solemnly to avow its sacred principles were to be received in its bonds "with equal ardor and affection." It was the bond of undeviating solidarity, believed by Alexander to be the essence of the Holy Alliance, which Metternich at a later date turned to his own devious and complicated purposes and to the aims of Austrian diplomacy. Although the Austrian diplomat declared the Holy Alliance to have "no other value or sense except considered as a philanthropic aspiration cloaked in religious phraseology,"[12] he identified those principles of indiscriminate solidarity with his own separate system of 1815, for the reorganization of Europe.

Great Britain at the time was, under the leadership of Castlereagh, devoted to the idea of the government of Europe through congresses, to meet at stated intervals. As such, England was a party to the Second Peace of Paris, the Articles of the Congress of Vienna, and the Quadruple Alliance. Liberal opinion in Great Britain, however, had shown itself immediately suspicious of the Brotherhood of Sovereigns, and of the whole language and tone of the "Holy Pact," and furious speeches in Parliament and denunciations in the papers of the day were heaped upon the Alliance by the liberals. The Prince Regent, too, had refused to join because English constitutional law provided that the signatures of the ministers and not of the sovereign governed in treaties.

During the period of reconstruction between the formation of his Alliance and the Congress of Aix-la-Chapelle, Alexander became convinced that in order to obtain the universality which he desired for his system, the Holy League must include not only the Christian powers of the Continent, but also Great Britain and the United States. His efforts to persuade the two Anglo-Saxon nations to adhere to his pact of "Justice, Christian Charity, and Peace" form an interesting chapter in the development of internationalism. It soon became evident that, in spite of the duties laid upon her by the Treaties of Chaumont, Paris, and Vienna, England was determined to return as quickly as possible to her policy of independent action.

From the beginning Alexander was suspicious of the spirit shown by the opposition in Parliament towards his League and sought to exploit the differences between Great Britain and the United States

The European Background

in a sense favorable to his own policies of an "unalterable" union among the Great Powers. The expansionist movement which had characterized the War of 1812 had not passed unnoticed in Europe. The close of Madison's administration and the early months of Monroe's were to be marked by a curious Russian negotiation, the details of which are merely hinted at in Monroe's *Writings*. When the repeated appeals of the Tsar's envoys failed to obtain the results which their master so ardently desired, Alexander's sensitive pride caused him to bury among his secret official *dossiers* all traces of these negotiations. But in the archives of the Russian Foreign Office, and in the pages of Adams' *Diary*, proofs are not lacking of the long and patient efforts made between 1816 and 1819 to induce the young American Republic to abandon her policy of isolation and to play a part in an international system.[13] In a letter to Middleton in Russia, on July 5, 1820, Adams alluded to the Russian attempts and explained Monroe's attitude:

"The Russian government has not only manifested an inclination that the United States should concur in the general principles of the European league, but a direct though inofficial application has been made by the present Russian minister here, that the United States should become formal parties to the Holy Alliance.

". . . No direct refusal has been signified to Mr. Poletica. . . . The President, approving its general principles and thoroughly convinced of the benevolent and virtuous motives which led to the conception and presided at the formation of this system by the Emperor Alexander, believes that the United States will more effectually contribute to the great and sublime objects for which it was concluded by abstaining from a formal participation in it; than they could as stipulated members of it."[14]

The Holy Alliance was formally made public by an imperial ukase ordering a summary of the treaty to be read in all the churches of the Empire, and caused a stir all over Europe. Several months elapsed, however, before the matter was noticed in the American newspapers of the day. On August 26, 1816, the New York *Evening Post* announced that "the King of the Netherlands has acceded to the Holy League, considering that it will have a beneficial effect on the state of society and the reciprocal relations between nations." On September 4 of the same year a meeting of the sovereigns of the

Holy Alliance is reported by the same paper "as likely to take place at Carlsbad." To this notice was added the following comment, certainly far from hostile in tone: "No doubt matters of great importance will be discussed at this assembly, and if discussions run upon the means of consolidating the peace of the world . . . and removing the burden of taxes and unwieldly military establishments which press at this moment upon every country, the members of the Holy League will establish an imperishable claim on the gratitude of mankind."[15]

In *Niles' Register* of April 6, 1816, appeared a definite expression of the generous approval which public opinion in America is always ready to accord to schemes promising an increment of international solidarity and good will. The Massachusetts Peace Society, addressing the Emperor Alexander, "recalls to the attention of His Imperial Majesty that the Society was founded in the very week in which the Holy League of the three sovereigns was announced in Russia" and has as its object "to disseminate the very principles avowed in the wonderful Alliance."[16] The absurdity of being treated as "brothers" by the three most reactionary sovereigns of Europe, apparently escaped the founders of the League. Uninformed public opinion could hardly foresee that the future policy of the Holy Alliance, as applied during the reactionary phase, was destined to become an unqualified support of "legitimist principles" abhorrent to American ideals.

Following the Congress of Vienna the particularist views and traditional interests of the Great Powers had postponed the consideration of many European issues such as the Turkish question and the affairs of the German Confederation. All questions of purely European origin were to be relegated to a secondary position, for American affairs became the first matter with which the newly constituted Confederation concerned itself during the three years preceding the Congress of Aix-la-Chapelle and throughout the succeeding era of international conferences.

Spain, Russia, and Great Britain were all great American powers. The King of Spain was the nominal ruler of all of South and Central America, where revolutions had been recently proclaimed and sustained with varying degrees of success, and of the province of Florida which threatened to fall shortly into the hands of the United States.

The European Background

On the northern continent of America the Tsar of Russia was the ruler of vast possessions whose vague frontiers stretched from Alaska far down the coast to California. England was the owner of Canada and held jointly with the United States the Oregon territory. Not only had intervention been suggested between Spain and the South American revolutionaries, but Spain had applied to the principal powers of Europe to mediate between the United States and herself in the Florida dispute, and England had intimated her willingness to do so.[17] Monroe was aware that some sort of mediation was pending at this time for early in September, 1817, Pinkney had written from St. Petersburg that South American affairs would be discussed at Aix-la-Chapelle, and later in the same month he wrote to Adams to the effect that: "There is no doubt a Russian fleet will very soon proceed to Cadiz,"[18] for ships to transport troops to South America had been sold to Spain.[19] Niles elaborated on the rumor by publishing a report that Russia had engaged to help suppress the South American revolts with "a squadron of 6 ships of the line, and several smaller vessels, and an army of 15 or 20,000 men, for which Spain cedes to Russia Old and New California in America."[20]

The Tsar, at the time, was torn between his desire to secure the support of the United States for his schemes of international concert, and his fear that both with respect to Florida and the South American insurgents the American government might act in a fashion to controvert a monarchical "mediation." The power of the moral example which America exercised over the South American colonies and the assistance which the privateers lent, did not escape Alexander and his European brethren. By the time Jackson had invaded Florida, the mediation by the Great Powers with respect to Ferdinand's differences with his revolted subjects in South America, was actually taking place. Ferdinand VII had formally sought the aid of the Council of Ministers of the Allied Powers in Paris in bringing about a forced reconciliation. In proposing this arbitration the King of Spain also demanded that military measures be taken against Portugal which was supporting the revolutionaries in the Banda Oriental. Ferdinand also begged to be present at the Congress, a request which the French government strongly seconded. After three weeks of debate England finally pronounced an absolute negative with respect to Spanish intervention and it was determined that the subject of mediation between

JAMES MONROE

Spain and Portugal and of the pacification of the revolted colonies was to be pursued at Aix-la-Chapelle. Alexander was determined that his great idea of concerted action, which had been thrust aside at Vienna, should receive consideration. The organization of Europe was to be the first step toward securing the reign of Justice, Christian Charity, and Peace.

By the end of September, 1818, when the Congress of Aix-la-Chapelle convened, Alexander's conversion from republican liberalism to a philosophy of monarchical paternalism was complete. In his wish to secure an international peace, based on the status quo, he was willing to put his army, and himself, at the disposal of Europe.[21]

It was largely through the influence of Richelieu, who proposed a plan for the establishment of Bourbon princes in the revolted Spanish American provinces, that the subject had been brought up for debate. Because of the opposition of Castlereagh this plan broke down, and it was determined that force was not to be used. The whole question of mediation or armed intervention was shelved, because Spain proudly refused to accept the results of a conference from which she had been excluded.

Before the Congress disbanded, however, the debates took an important turn. There was a proposal advanced by France and Russia to invite the United States to participate in a conference to be held at Madrid on the subject of the relation between Spain and her colonies. In a verbal communication, which the Tsar felt more suitable than a written note, he pointed out that while the United States was at that time no menace to Europe, should a large portion of South America emulate its institutions, a "complete republican world, young and full of ardour," would be set up in opposition to overpopulated and revolution-ridden Europe.[22] These secret *dossiers* in the Russian archives prove with what care Europe strove to prevent or retard growing relations between North and South America, and demonstrate the wisdom of Monroe and Adams in clinging to the policy of isolation and abstaining from adherence to the European League. Had the United States accepted the Russian overtures, they would have found themselves in a minority with England, or supporting Russia. The latter would have ended in limiting the action of the United States in America, while the powers of the Holy Alliance imposed their own policy through "concerted action."

The European Background

The threat of Aix-la-Chapelle had been more apparent than real, and the outcome had been to range the United States more nearly in line with British policy. At home Congress and Clay were clamoring for an independent course of recognition, while Adams and Monroe, in an effort to complete ratification of the Florida Treaty, were councilling a policy of watchful waiting, free from both Russian and English commitments. Adams wrote to Middleton in July, 1820: "Should renewed overtures on this subject be made, Russia would be answered that the organization of our government is such as not to admit of our acceding formally to that compact. But it may be added that the President, while approving of its final principles and thoroughly convinced of the benevolent and virtuous motives which led to the conception and presided at the formation of this system, by the Emperor Alexander, believes that the United States will more effectually contribute to the great and sublime objects for which it was concluded by abstaining from formal participation in it. As a general declaration of principles, the United States not only give their hearty assent to the articles of the Holy Alliance, but they will be among the most earnest and conscientious in observing them."[23]

A few months later the Holy Alliance entered on its career of reactionary repression. The years 1819 and 1820 were such as to give cause for apprehension to all European monarchs, including Alexander. In spite of Metternich's Carlsbad Decrees and propaganda campaign for crushing liberalism everywhere, thus making of all Europe a vast prison camp, there were signs of revolutionary unrest in almost every country on the continent. Although Alexander still clung to the illusion that he was the champion of "international rights," he could not tolerate insurrection and revolution against kings. The year 1820 saw a series of revolutions following the Riegos uprising in Spain. In July a military revolt, followed by flagrant disorder, occurred in Naples, which compelled the King of the Two Sicilies to accept the Spanish Constitution of 1812. The repression of this constitutional movement became the chief concern of the powers, and on October 29, 1820, a conference opened at Troppau. On the twenty-fourth Metternich had an interview with Alexander in which the latter, disillusioned, is reported to have stated that in everything he had done from 1814 to 1818 he had been mistaken. On the day prior to the opening of the conference, word arrived that his own

Russian regiment had mutinied in St. Petersburg. Believing it was part of a vast Carbonari plot he refused to be convinced otherwise. Thus by 1820 the Tsar was finally ranged on the side of reaction, under the domination of Metternich, to whose services he had committed his "firm and unalterable resolution."[24] Declaring it to be the sacred duty of the great states of Europe to put down pernicious uprisings by force of arms, the plenipotentiaries drafted the preliminary Protocol of Troppau, from which France and England dissociated themselves.

"States which have undergone a change of government due to revolution, the results of which threaten other states, *ipso facto* cease to be members of the European Alliance, and remain excluded from it until their situation gives guarantees for legal order and stability. If, owing to such alterations, immediate danger threatens other states, the Powers bind themselves, by peaceful means, or if need be by arms, to bring back the guilty state into the bosom of the Great Alliance."[25]

The conference was adjourned to Laibach the following year, only Russia, Austria, and Prussia participating. As Metternich carefully continued to respect the Tsar's illusion that these gatherings were an administrative directorate of Europe, the Monroe Cabinet became more strongly confirmed than ever in their determination to remain aloof from the Holy Alliance. The revolutions in Greece, Naples, and Spain, and the liberal constitutions for which they fought, had struck a responsive chord in America. As Europe's repressive attitude became more apparent with the Austrian suppression of Italy, the demand for recognition of South American independence rose to a clamor, and with the ratification of the Florida Treaty by Spain, Monroe was forced to employ double caution in delaying recognition.

The conference which met at Verona in October, 1822, was the last of the conferences held pursuant to the treaty of November 20, 1815. At this conference Alexander, weaned from his democratic altruism, renewed the offer he had made at Aix-la-Chapelle, to place his army at the disposal of Europe. He proposed to march 150,000 men through Germany to be used against France or to assist the hapless Ferdinand in regaining his throne. England, France, and Austria were definitely opposed to the plan, and Wellington left the

The European Background

Congress altogether, after stating that his government had adopted as a basic principle of foreign policy, the principle of non-intervention in the internal affairs of other states. His memorandum on colonial problems hinted at recognition of the colonies by Great Britain and invited the opinions of the Allies on the subject. The French reply, which committed that country to coöperation with the Allies, was a declaration that "a general measure taken in common by the cabinets of Europe would be the most desirable."[26]

Left to their own devices and lacking England's restraining influence, Austria, France, Russia, and Prussia signed a revision of the treaty of the Holy Alliance, the purpose of which was to promote the doctrine of legitimacy in support of the divine right of rulers, and to promote the doctrine of intervention, to restore to their rightful thrones those members of the purple who had been deposed by revolution or whose powers had been circumscribed by written constitutions. A united effort was to be made on the part of these allies to eradicate all forms of representative government in Europe and to prevent its further introduction.

With the record of a cruel suppression of popular uprisings in Piedmont and Naples behind them, the Holy Allies empowered a French force, under the duc d'Angoulême to invade the Spanish peninsula, replace Ferdinand upon his throne, and to destroy the Constitution of 1820.

Louis XVIII had selected Montmorency and Chateaubriand to represent France at the Congress of Verona, the latter in the hope that his "liberal principles" would counterbalance the vagaries of the ultra royalist Montmorency. Both, however, had fallen under the spell of the Tsar, and become converts to his "Sublime Idea" of intervention in Spain by an allied expeditionary force. Chateaubriand, the diplomatic impresario, carried away by his enthusiasm, forgot the instructions of his monarch, and pictured himself as the principal figure in a grandiose scheme. With the success of the French invasion assured and the restoration of Ferdinand complete on April 7, 1823, Chateaubriand broached to the Spanish King the idea which had obsessed him for months. By the terms of his proposed compromise he aimed to extend the scope of Royalist adventure by transforming the South American colonies into a confederation of American kingdoms and principalities. At the head of each of them he

[429]

dreamed of placing a prince of the Bourbon House, chosen from the French, Spanish, and Italian branches, and underwritten and guaranteed by the Holy Alliance. Chateaubriand's plan as such was probably the product of his own highly imaginative mind, although Richelieu had previously favored a similar scheme; yet it voiced a fundamental French interest at the time. The merchant classes had been in power for several years in France, and as early as 1821 there had been a strong demand that the Spanish American markets be opened to French enterprise. Such a system as Chateaubriand proposed, under French tutelage, would therefore have appesed both the Royalists and the practical reactionaries.

It was at this moment that George Canning made his first overtures for a coördination of the liberal policies of England and the United States. Great Britain was definitely isolated from the concert of Europe, for Castlereagh, the ardent exponent of the congress system, had committed suicide in August of 1822 and had been succeeded by Canning, a bitter foe to the concert of Europe, an advocate of a purely British policy and America's *bête-noire* of pre-1812 days. British Cabinet policy might condone intervention in Spain and even applaud the preservation of the monarchical system in South America, but it could never accept the Family Pact. Disturbed by the possibility of French domination of Spain and the resultant upset in the balance of power, Canning had made known the fact that Great Britain would under no circumstances tolerate the subjection of the Spanish colonies by foreign force. His instructions to Wellington of September 27, 1822, went so far as to suggest the possibility of tacit recognition of the *de facto* governments of South America.[27]

These instructions were motivated by commercial as well as political considerations. English merchants had been enjoying a lively and lucrative trade since the revolting colonies had broken away from the Spanish commercial system. These great English mercantile interests would never tolerate any radical change in a situation that without expense or effort on their part was rendering obsolete the Spanish trade monopoly. In addition to the commercial aspects of the case, there was a large party in the English Parliament in sympathy with the constitutional pretensions of the South American republics. British statesmen, deriving their power from Parliament, could not approve war on representative government.

The European Background

Alarmed by the prospect of French hegemony in Spain and the proposed extension to the New World, and unwilling to risk the rupture with the European alliance which outright recognition would involve, Canning determined to act. On March 31, 1823, just before the invasion of Spain, Canning addressed a dispatch, amounting to an ultimatum, to the British minister in Paris, to inform the French Foreign Office that while Great Britain disclaimed all intention of appropriating to herself the smallest portion of Ferdinand's former dominion, she "confidently expected" that no attempt would be made by France to bring under her dominion any of those possessions, either by conquest or by cession from Spain.[28] Having thus broken with Europe, and having been unsuccessful in his attempt to secure a self-denying pledge from France, Canning concentrated his efforts on securing coöperation from the United States.

On March 31, 1823, Richard Rush, the American minister in London, had an interview with Canning. Referring to Canning's instructions to Wellington prior to the invasion of Spain, in which he had suggested the possibility of a *de facto* recognition of the South American governments, Rush asked whether England would remain passive under any attempt by France to cause the resubjugation of the American colonies.[29] Canning replied that while concert of action probably wouldn't be necessary, he would like to know the attitude of the United States on a policy of proceeding "hand in hand with England."[30] This query on Canning's part had been influenced by the dispatches of the British minister in Washington who, reporting on a series of conversations he had had with Adams, felt that the Secretary of State had suggested an alliance. Adams had told Canning that England had divorced herself from the repressive measures of the Holy Allies, and definitely avowed the same principles as the United States. This coincidence of principle, in view of the momentous changes occurring in the world, seemed to Adams an opportune time for England and the United States "to compare their ideas and purposes together," and settle a few points upon which they had previously differed.[31] It was a misconstruction on the part of the British minister, for while Adams had stated that he believed England and the United States had much in common, and that England ought to recognize the independence of the revolting provinces, he was referring specifically to joint negotiation with England in the ques-

JAMES MONROE

tion of Russian occupation of the Northwest territory. Inveterate isolationist that he was, he suggested not an alliance but diplomatic rapprochement. Rush informed Canning that he had received no instructions along those lines and asked for time to communicate the proposition to his government.

By early fall, when news of the wholesale suppression of revolutionary movements in Europe and of the defeat of the Spanish effort by French troops reached the United States, the people became really concerned. There was a widespread fear that South America would be the next field for revolutionary suppression, followed by an attack on the United States, or the seizure from Spain of enormous tracts of land upon which would be erected powerful monarchical establishments.

39

Formulation of the Monroe Doctrine

AS THE INVASION of Spain drew near to a successful close, the moment of decision for America approached. During August of 1823 Canning and Rush in London were discussing the possibility of joint action on the question of the Spanish American colonies, while in Washington Monroe and Adams were preparing for the autumn meetings of the Cabinet. Early in the month Canning had sounded out Rush, the United States minister at the Court of St. James's, as to an understanding with England to stop all repressive designs on the South American republics. Rush, unable to give a definite answer, had pleaded for an opportunity to secure instructions.

On August 22 Rush was the recipient of a "private and confidential" communication from Canning which read as follows:

"Before leaving town I am desirous of bringing before you in a more distinct, but still in an unofficial and confidential shape, the question which we shortly discussed the last time that I had the pleasure of seeing you.

"Is not the moment come when our Governments might understand each other as to the Spanish American colonies? And if we can arrive at such an understanding, would it not be expedient for ourselves, and beneficial for all the world, that the principles of it should be clearly settled and plainly avowed?"[1]

Included in the note was a résumé of the British position, which recognized the recovery of the colonies by Spain as a hopeless cause; that although the question of their recognition was one of time and circumstances, still England was in no way desirous of impeding an amicable negotiation between the colonies and the mother country; and that while England desired no portion of the colonies for herself, she "could not see the transfer of any portion of them to any other Power with indifference." At the same time Canning declared: "Nothing could be more gratifying to me than to join with you in such a work, and I am persuaded there has seldom, in the history of the world, occurred an opportunity when so small an effort of two friendly governments might produce so unequivocal a good, and prevent such extensive calamities."[2]

Three days later Rush replied confidentially and categorically to Canning, agreeing with everything, except with regard to recognition, which of course had already been made by the United States: "I would regard as unjust," he wrote, "and fruitful of disastrous consequences any attempt on the part of any European power to take possession of them by conquest, or by cession, or on any ground or pretext whatever."[3]

Rush then dispatched Canning's notes and his own replies thereto, to Adams and Monroe, seeking their approbation and further instructions. He informed them that while he had met the spirit of the British proposals, he had avoided any act or commitment which might "implicate it [the United States] in the federative system of Europe."[4] These were received in Washington on October 9.

On the twenty-sixth Rush was the recipient of a further communication from Canning, informing him that France's impending triumph in Spain was to be followed by a European congress on Spanish American affairs. The rapid development of events and the lack of instructions from home placed Rush in a quandary. He made a declaration to Canning that the United States would not remain inactive should the Holy Alliance make an attack on the South American colonies:

"The United States would regard as objectionable any interference whatever in the affairs of Spanish America, unsolicited by the late provinces themselves and against their will. It would regard the convening of a Congress to deliberate upon their affairs, as a measure uncalled for, and indicative of a policy highly unfriendly to the tranquility of the world. It could never look with insensibility upon such an exercise of European jurisdiction over communities now of

Formulation of the Monroe Doctrine

right exempt from it, and entitled to regulate their own concerns unmolested from abroad."[5]

This declaration, however, was made contingent upon England's immediate recognition of the republics. Thus Rush, without explicit instructions to the contrary, would have proceeded to a joint declaration with England, had that nation been ready to accord the recognition which it announced the following year.

On September 7 Canning again made an overture to Rush, regretting the fact that Rush felt it necessary to secure instructions from his government. Rush continued to insist upon British recognition as his *sine qua non* and declared that unless it were granted, he would attend no conference on South America. The following day Rush forwarded to Adams Canning's note, together with the information that the British minister was unwilling to pledge immediate recognition. This communication reached Washington November 5. Rush followed this up on September 15 with a letter to Monroe in which, reviewing England's foreign policy for the past fifty years, he saw in the overtures to secure American coöperation, some secret and selfish design of gain by England: "I shall therefore find it hard to keep from my mind the suspicion that the approaches of her ministers to me at this portentous juncture for a concert of policy which they have not heretofore courted with the United States, are bottomed on their own calculations."[6]

Once more, on September 26, Canning approached Rush, emphasizing the fact that England's continental commitments placed her in an embarrassing position as regarded immediate recognition, and solicited American assent to his proposals, on the basis of a promise by England of *future* recognition. Hard-headed Rush, unwilling to be trapped, refused for the fourth time.[7] He clearly saw that without prior recognition of independence by Great Britain that country would gain a distinct advantage by securing a self-denying pledge from the United States. Early in October there were discussed general negotiations between Great Britain and the United States, and on the eighth Canning informed Rush that British commercial agents were ready to leave for South America, but with the offer of September 26, Rush's communications to Monroe and Adams ceased to influence directly the formation of the President's message, for this date marked an abrupt termination in the conversations between

Rush and Canning, which were not renewed until November 24.

Meanwhile Canning, realizing that coöperative action with the United States was impossible because of the latter's insistence regarding recognition, decided to proceed alone and to turn to France. On October 9, the day Rush's first communications reached Washington, Canning had an interview with Prince Polignac, the French ambassador in London. Informing him that any attack on Spanish America would be followed by war with England, Canning secured French acquiescence in the principal points of his policy, which was similar to the memorandum he had submitted to Rush, and secured the renunciation by France of any intention to appropriate Spanish possessions in America, to assist Spain against the colonies, or to get any exclusive commercial advantages. Polignac, however, declared that future relations between Spain and her colonies ought to form the subject of discussion at a special European congress.

Acting upon this suggestion Ferdinand, in December, made a last attempt to obtain the intervention of the Three Powers. After Great Britain had appointed consuls in South America, Spain invited Russia, France, and Austria to a conference to help the Spanish government adjust the affairs of the revolted colonies. In the midst of preparations for this congress, the President's message, containing what came to be known as the Monroe Doctrine, was issued.

No details of the Polignac conference reached Rush before his interview with Canning on November 24, and it is therefore improbable that it could have reached Monroe in time to influence the Cabinet, whose councils ended on the twenty-sixth. In America the real danger of intervention was felt to lie in France. Therefore, had the details of the Polignac interview been known to Monroe, he would have made some mention of it in his message and would not have suffered the state of dejection which Adams recorded he did in November. The balance of probability would seem to indicate that Monroe and Adams shared with Rush the ignorance of the conference and that it had no influence on the formation of the Doctrine.

Meanwhile, in Washington, the Monroe Doctrine was being slowly forged out in a series of stormy Cabinet sessions. Rush's dispatches had arrived at the White House on October 9, just before the end of the summer recess, and had created an entirely new atmosphere at the capital. Adams was still in Quincy, and in his

Formulation of the Monroe Doctrine

absence Monroe determined to consult his two predecessors. His own first reaction was favorable to a joint policy and in his letter to Jefferson, explaining the enclosed communication from Rush, he clearly intimated his own belief that the case in point might prove to be an exception to the general principle of abstention from European entanglements.[8] He asked Jefferson to forward the communication to Madison, and sought an opinion from each.

On October 24, 1823, Jefferson replied to Monroe, with a creative suggestion of a permanent system of American foreign policy: "The question presented by the letters you have sent me, is the most momentous which has been ever offered to my contemplation since that of Independence, That made us a nation, this sets our compass and points the course which we are to steer thro' the ocean of time opening on us."

Jefferson advocated a bilateral pronouncement with England, on the ground that it would eliminate the opposition of Great Britain, the one nation which could disturb America in its efforts to have an independent system. He felt that by acceding to her proposals her mighty weight would be brought into the "scale of free government," and it would be possible "to emancipate a continent at one stroke." He even went so far as to state that he was ready to yield his keen desire for the annexation of Cuba, to secure English cooperation. Yet behind it all was a clear-cut delineation of an American system, with the United States insisting upon an exclusion of all European influence from the new world and an abstention from all participation in the affairs of the old world.[9]

Madison, likewise, was prepared to accept England's overtures, at the same time inviting her to join with the United States in a statement of disapproval of the French campaign in Spain. Infected by the fever of Greek sympathy which came to a climax late in 1823, with a profusion of sermons, orations, and balls, Madison desired also a bold declaration in behalf of the Greek revolutionists. More canny than Jefferson on this occasion, however, he inclined to Adams' and Monroe's opinion that English "casuistry" was guided more by interest than by a principle of general liberty.[10] It thus became clear that the Virginia dynasty, the traditional antagonists of England, were willing to surrender their right of sole leadership in American affairs and to mingle in European concerns, in close association with a European power in matters in which the interests of the United States might be promoted by such an association.

While Monroe had been consulting Jefferson and Madison concerning Rush's dispatches, Adams, returned from Quincy, was carrying on a diplomatic duel with Baron de Tuyll. On October 16 the Russian minister called upon Adams to inform him that Alexander refused to receive ministers from the new states:

"His Imperial Majesty . . . can not in any case receive near him any agent whatever, either of the administration of Colombia, or of any of the other Governments, *de facto*, which owe their existence to events, of which the new world has been for some years the theatre."[11]

The minister's declaration of Russian satisfaction at American neutrality, took Adams completely by surprise, for the language of the Russian minister encouraged the hypothesis that the Continental Powers were contemplating the reconquest of Spain's former colonies and their restitution to the mother country. These incidents convinced Adams that there was immediate need for setting forth explicitly the opposition of the United States to intervention and European interference.

In the long Cabinet debates which followed, from November 7 to the end of the month, the discussion devolved upon three distinct issues: the framing of a reply to the Russian minister, the preparation of instructions for Rush and an answer to Canning's proposals, as well as the consideration of the statement of the American government relative to the South American republics. In preparation of a mode of procedure on the subjects Adams suggested to Monroe that the reply to Russia and the instructions to Rush must be part of a combined system of policy. He explained to Monroe:

"The ground that I wish to take is that of earnest remonstrance against interference of European powers by force with South America, but to disclaim all interference on our part with Europe; to make an American cause and adhere inflexibly to that.[12]

"My purpose would be in a moderate and conciliatory manner, but with a firm and determined spirit to declare our dissent from the principles avowed in those communications; to assert those upon which our own Government is founded, and, while disclaiming all

Formulation of the Monroe Doctrine

intention of attempt to propagate them by force, and all interference with the political affairs of Europe, to declare our expectation and hope that the European powers will equally abstain from the attempt to spread their principles in the American hemisphere, or to subjugate by force any part of these continents to their will."[13]

Monroe's Cabinet was composed at this time of Crawford, S. L. Southard, Calhoun, Wirt, and Adams. Throughout the long days of discussion Adams played an undeniably influential and important part, but Monroe was emphatically the head of the administration, and while he was vigorous and determined to preserve the Western Hemisphere from European control, he strove to preserve the peace of the world. It was without a doubt Monroe who thought of dealing with the Spanish colonial question in his forthcoming message to Congress, and he who drafted the famous paragraph dealing with the problem.

In spite of the fact that the entire Cabinet believed in bold action, the atmosphere of the first weeks of discussion was pervaded by fear. Monroe and Calhoun were convinced that the danger of intervention was imminent, whereas Adams, figuring that the lack of a concrete program of active procedure on the part of the Allies made the danger of intervention rather slight, scoffed at Calhoun's fears. "I no more believe," he declared, "that the Holy Alliance will restore the Spanish dominion upon the American continent than that the Chimborazo will sink beneath the ocean."[14]

The Secretary of State was sure that even if Europe attempted intervention, England's control of the high seas would be an effective block, for England would see to it that her own trading interests were protected by keeping open the Spanish markets. The arrival of the news that Cadiz had fallen into the hands of the French invaders only served to increase Monroe's fears and to deepen his anxiety. This atmosphere of alarm and impending disaster and the effect it had upon the various members of the Cabinet were reflected in their respective attitudes toward the extent of coöperation advisable with England, in the discussion of the Canning proposals.

The first week or two of meetings was devoted to a discussion of the Canning proposals, and the danger of actual intervention in South America by the Holy Allies. While Monroe was at first inclined to meet Canning's advances, and Calhoun favored giving discretionary powers to Rush to join in a declaration against the Holy Alliance, if necessary, even if the United States would have to pledge itself not to take Cuba or Texas, both Monroe and Adams spurned taking a position in any way subordinate to England. Monroe "was averse to any course which should have the position of taking any position subordinate to that of Great Britain, and suggested the idea of sending a special minister to protest against the interposition of the Holy Alliance."[15]

It was Adams' opinion that the United States should pursue a nationalistic and individualistic course and issue an aggressive declaration to both Russia and France separately: "It would be more candid as well as more dignified, to avow our principles explicitly to Russia and France, than to come in as a cock-boat in the wake of the British man-of-war."[16]

However, in the question of what answer should be given to Canning, a more pressing consideration for an immediate decision became apparent. Canning's proposal contemplated a public pledge from the United States, not only against the forcible intervention of the Holy Alliance in South America, but a pledge especially against the acquisition by the United States of any portion of South America. At that moment the administration was particularly interested in Cuba while large portions of the North American continent, such as Texas and California, lay open to settlement and acquisition by the United States. Adams, who realized that Canning had inserted this proviso because he was nervous about Cuba, suspected a self-denying trap, and urged this upon the Cabinet members as another reason for turning down Canning's proposals. Thus Monroe and Calhoun, who were most fearful of active intervention, favored a mode of coöperation with England, while Adams, who doubted the ability of the Holy Alliance to intervene forcibly, and who was distrustful of Canning's objectives, urged a go-it-alone policy, or if common action were decided upon, British recognition of the colonies as an antecedent condition.

After a number of consultations as to the nature of the reply Adams, on November 17, submitted to Monroe the first draft of his answer to Canning. The draft was returned, three days later, with Monroe's amendments appended: "I send you the sketch which you left with me, of a letter to Mr. Rush, with amendments, which are

Formulation of the Monroe Doctrine

intended for your consideration and which, if you approve, I wish, when a copy is made, that we submit to a meeting of all the members of the administration. . . ."[17]

Adams' first draft was in its essentials a categorical reply to the five principles set forth by Canning, and these principles were accepted by Monroe and the entire Cabinet. Further than that, the communication stated that because the United States had recognized the independence of the colonies, coöperation with Great Britain on any other basis than recognition was utterly impossible.

Monroe's amendments, which were discussed in the Cabinet and incorporated into the final draft, exercised an important influence on the tone of the note. While he abandoned his own inclinations toward the granting of discretionary powers to Rush, he modified Adams' flat refusal to coöperate. He was reluctant thus to close the door on every avenue of rapprochement; so he proceeded to revise the wording. The final message made coöperation between England and the United States conditional on recognition and provided that if an emergency arose where a joint declaration of opinion by the two governments could influence the Allies, the United States would cheerfully so act.[18] The statement was explicit: "That for the most effectual accomplishment of the object, common to both Governments, a perfect understanding with regard to it being established between them, it will be most advisable that they should act separately. . . . Should an emergency occur, in which a joint manifestation of opinion; by the two governments, may tend to influence the Councils of the European Allies . . . we shall cheerfully join in any Act."[19]

Adams had thus prevented a bilateral declaration, but his draft of a reply contained none of the broad principles of foreign policy found in the actual Doctrine. The nearest approach to the principles of the presidential message was found in the substitution made by Monroe in Adams' first draft, which was deleted from the final note: "Much less could we behold with indifference the transfer of those new governments, or of any portion of the Spanish possessions, to other powers, especially of the territories, bordering on, or nearest to the U. States."[20]

In spite of the eventual omission of this paragraph from the draft to Rush, the final reply shows that Monroe's amendments formed an important part of the letter at that crucial juncture and indicated

JAMES MONROE

the painstaking care which Monroe always exercised in the control of his diplomatic affairs, to avoid provocative utterances and to steer a middle course through the tortuous channels of European diplomacy.

The question of framing a reply to Baron de Tuyll was likewise taken up in the Cabinet, concurrently with the reply to the Canning proposals. The customary procedure in Monroe's Cabinet meetings which preceded the issuance of the annual messages, was to have each secretary submit to him a sketch of the topics falling within his particular jurisdiction, which might interest the President and be appropriate to include in the message. It was in this fashion that the principle of non-colonization, in the language of Monroe's message, was first stated in a draft of minutes made by Adams to be considered by the President in his annual address. The diplomatic negotiations in connection with which it arose were those concerning the conflicting Anglo-Russian claims on the northwest coast, and its development of the non-colonization principle was due almost exclusively to Adams. Monroe, more concerned with the South American question and the threat of the Holy Alliance, had given Adams a free hand in dealing with Russia and the Ukase of 1821.

Almost contemporaneously with Adams' interview with Baron de Tuyll in July, 1823, the Secretary of State had framed a set of instructions to Rush in London, in which the whole theory of the doctrine of non-colonization found careful expression. After declaring that the American continents were henceforth no longer to be subjects for colonization he had stated: ". . . occupied by civilized independent nations, they will be accessible to Europeans and to each other on that footing alone, and the Pacific Ocean in every part of it will remain open to the navigation of all nations, in like manner with the Atlantic. . . . The application of colonial principles of exclusion, therefore, cannot be admitted by the United States as lawful upon any part of the northwest coast of America, or as belonging to any European nation."[21]

When, in November, Adams drew up the customary sketch of topics of foreign policy for Monroe's message, he included a reference to the non-colonization doctrine, which was taken over almost unchanged by Monroe. The Holy Alliance was the chief concern of the moment, not Russia; and consequently there was no considera-

Formulation of the Monroe Doctrine

tion of the principle in the Cabinet discussions preceding the declaration. Calhoun, referring to the principle in a speech twenty-five years later stated:

"My impression is, that it never became a subject of deliberation in the Cabinet.... It originated entirely with Mr. Adams, without being submitted to the Cabinet, and it is, in my opinion, owing to this fact that it is not made with the precision and clearness with which the two former are.... I will venture to say that if that declaration had come before that cautious cabinet—for Mr. Monroe was among the wisest and most cautious men I have ever known—it would have been modified, and expressed with a far greater degree of precision."[22]

What in reality occurred was that Adams privately read to Monroe, on November 13, his draft of foreign policy topics, and Monroe jotted these points down on a scrap of paper.[23] Adams' draft furnished the basis for the points discussed by Monroe in the first portion of his message, and was the source of the principle which Monroe incorporated without verbal change, in the seventh paragraph of his message: "... That the American continents by the free and independent condition which they have assumed and maintain, are henceforth not to be considered as subjects for future colonization by European powers."[24]

As for the reply to the Russian communication of November 16, it was discussed in the Cabinet between November 7 and the 21. The Russian Emperor had sent to Adams two long communications, airing his views on the South American colonies. In setting forth his conclusion not to receive representatives from the new states, the Russian ruler presented his opinions of the monarchical and republican forms of government. After many Cabinet discussions and conferences with Monroe, Adams submitted a paper which drew up an exposition of the republican principles of the United States, contrasting them and showing their superiority to the monarchical principles of Europe.

From November 25 to the 27 the primary question for discussion was whether certain paragraphs of Adams draft be deleted before sending it to the Russian government.[25] Calhoun felt that the paper should not be sent to the Russian minister, but merely a copy of Monroe's projected message, which contained certain paragraphs enunciating the American principles. Monroe, with his customary tactfulness, prevailed upon Adams to delete those paragraphs in his draft which might prove objectionable to Russia. The President's efforts were exerted to maintain the rights of the United States and of the colonies, but at the same time to prevent a criticism of the Emperor which might lead to an open breach between the two governments. Adams, always confident of his own good judgment, had been particularly scornful of Calhoun's criticism of his draft, but he accepted and respected Monroe's point of view, in modifying his statement to Baron de Tuyll. In this dispatch to Russia, Adams' principle of non-colonization found no place, indicating that he did not associate it with his exposition of republicanism.

Thus, aside from the principle of non-colonization growing out of a specific emergency, Adams failed completely to suggest an enunciation of an American system of policy in the annual message. With the exception of this courageous verbal ultimatum to De Tuyll, the principle of which was incorporated in the Doctrine, revision rather than authorship was Adams' role.

The third problem with which the Cabinet was concerned during those feverish November days, involved the treatment of the colonial question in the annual message. The experience of the first four years of Monroe's presidency had enabled Adams to write in 1820:

"The composition of these messages is upon a uniform plan. They begin with general remarks upon the condition of the country, noticing recent occurrences of material importance; passing encomiums upon our form of government, paying due homage to the sovereign power of the people, and turning to account every topic which can afford a paragraph of public gratulation; then pass in review the foreign affairs; the circumstances of our relations with the principal powers of Europe; then, looking inwards, adverting to the state of the finances, the revenues, public expenditures, debts, and land sales, the progress of fortification and naval armaments, with a few words about the Indians, and a few about the slave trade."[26]

Nor had this practice changed. Every message had held some reference to the progress of the revolutions in South America, even after official recognition had been accorded them by the United States. Indeed, as the European wave of reaction overcame one revolution after another in central Europe, suppressing liberalism and freedom everywhere, and as it threatened to spread even to the New World, Monroe had determined to preserve the liberties of

Formulation of the Monroe Doctrine

South America and to give a firm declaration of his nation's attitude toward the South American neighbors. Early in 1823, before the Canning-Rush interviews and the Russian problem became critical, it seemed to Monroe that the logical method of referring to the matter was to include it in his annual message to Congress.

His grasp of the seriousness of the situation and determination to take some positive action better to insure the safety of the American position, was clearly set forth in a letter to Jefferson of June 2, 1823. After reviewing the progress of reaction in Europe and that of the revolutions in South America, he sought Jefferson's advice on two questions:

"Such is the state of Europe, & our relation to it is pretty much the same, as it was, in the commencement of the French revolution. Can we, in any form, take a bolder attitude in regard to it, in favor of liberty, than we then did? Can we afford greater aid to that cause, by assuming any such attitude, than we now do, by the form of our example? These are subjects on which I should be glad to have your sentiments."[27]

When Rush's dispatches arrived on October 9, Monroe was on the verge of leaving Washington on a short vacation before returning to the fall Cabinet meetings in preparation for the annual message. He took the dispatches along and gave them careful study. On October 17 he wrote to Jefferson the letter already mentioned, seeking his advice on the critical issue which Canning's proposals had presented. He wrote, "My own impression is that we ought to meet the proposal of the British govt., to make it known, that we would view an interference on the part of the European powers, and especially an attack on the Colonies, by them, as an attack on ourselves, presuming that if they succeeded with them, they would extend to us."[28]

Although Jefferson, in his reply of October 24, advised coöperation with Great Britain, feeling that a joint prohibition would effectually prevent a European invasion of the continent, at the same time he added to the policy of non-intervention in European affairs the doctrine of the prohibition of all European intervention in American affairs, and principles of liberty and freedom: "Our first and fundamental maxim should be," he replied, "never to entangle ourselves in the broils of Europe. Our second never to suffer Europe to

JAMES MONROE

intermeddle with cis-Atlantic affairs. America, North and South has a set of interests distinct from those of Europe and peculiarly her own. She should therefore have a system of her own, separate and apart from that of Europe."[29]

When Monroe returned to Washington, feeling that the "auspicious" circumstances in which to "introduce and establish" Jefferson's and his own American system had arrived, he was determined in the course he would pursue. He had favored coöperation with England before hearing from Jefferson and Madison; their opinions but strengthened his resolve. Further than that he was prepared to make a vigorous stand against the aggression of the Holy Alliance in his annual message, combined with his enunciation of the new corollary to the doctrine of non-intervention in the affairs of Europe.

Cabinet discussions, during the first few weeks, of the reply to Canning's proposals, served to modify his stand as to coöperation with England, but he remained firm in his purpose to handle the question of the South American colonies in the annual message. In preparation of this message the reports of the heads of the departments were considered in full Cabinet meetings and thus the subject of the American colonies was gone over in every possible shape and detail. On November 21 the President presented his first draft for Cabinet criticism. Far from being a timid utterance, it was couched in a tone of "deep solemnity and of high alarm." After a scathing denunciation of the French invasion of Spain and the motives behind it, Monroe made a ringing declaration of recognition of Greek independence and recommended that Congress appropriate sums to defray the expenses of a minister to the republic.[30]

Then it was the turn of the usually aggressive Adams to apply the soft pedal. Although he was willing to defy the Old World nations, even to condemn them, he did not approve of such a provocative declaration, wishing to avoid anything which might be construed as hostility to the Allies.[31] In Cabinet meetings and in private he pressed these considerations upon Monroe. As it stood, "the message would at once buckle on the harness, and throw down the gauntlet."[32] At length he persuaded the President to subdue the vigor of his statements and on November 24, when Monroe read his last four paragraphs, which dealt with Greece, Spain, Portugal, and South America, Adams declared them "quite unexceptionable."[33]

Formulation of the Monroe Doctrine

Throughout the discussions, and particularly during the last few days, there was great debate over the proposition as to how the statement of the position of the United States would be announced. Some of the Cabinet members, feeling that a positive and unequivocal statement of United States policy was not desirable, advised that it should be announced by the various ministers, privately, to the European governments. Monroe, who took the crisis seriously, believed in vigorous action and refused to be swayed in his determination that the message to Congress should take a clear and decisive tone on the Spanish colonial question. On December 2, 1823, his seventh annual message was presented to Congress. It contained the following widely separated paragraphs, which came to be known as the Monroe Doctrine. The first, near the beginning of the message, related to Russia's encroachment on the northwest coast and asserted that the American continents were no longer open to European colonization. The second paragraph, occurring toward the end of the message, and relating to Spanish America, was a declaration against the extension of the repressive principles of the Holy Alliance to the New World:

"At the proposal of the Russian Imperial Government, made through the minister of the emperor residing here, a full power and instructions have been transmitted to the minister of the United States at St. Petersburg to arrange by amicable negotiation the respective rights and interests of the two nations on the northwest coast of this continent. A similar proposal had been made by His Imperial Majesty to the government of Great Britain, which has likewise been acceded to. The government of the United States has been desirous by this friendly proceeding of manifesting the great value which has invariably attached to the friendship of the emperor and their solicitude to cultivate the best understanding with his government. In the discussions to which this interest has given rise and in the arrangements by which they may terminate, the occasion has been judged proper for asserting, as a principle in which the rights and interests of the United States are involved, that the American continents, by the free and independent condition which they have assumed and maintain, are henceforth not to be considered as subjects for future colonization by any European powers.[34]

. . . .

"In the wars of the European powers in matters relating to themselves we have never taken any part, nor does it comport with our policy so to do. It is only when our rights are invaded or seriously menaced that we resent injuries or make preparation for our defense. With the movements in this hemisphere we are of necessity more immediately connected, and by causes which must be obvious to all enlightened and impartial observers. The political system of the allied powers is essentially different in this respect from that of America. This difference proceeds from that which exists in their respective governments; and to the defense of our own, which has been achieved by the loss of so much blood and treasure, and matured by the wisdom of their most enlightened citizens, and under which we have enjoyed unexampled felicity, this whole nation is devoted. We owe it, therefore, to candor and to the amicable relations existing between the United States and those powers to declare that we should consider any attempt on their part to extend their system to any portion of this hemisphere as dangerous to our peace and safety. With the existing colonies or dependencies of any European power we have not interfered and shall not interfere. But with the governments who have declared their independence and maintained it, and whose independence we have, on great consideration and on just principles, acknowledged, we could not view any interposition for the purpose of oppressing them, or controlling in any other manner their destiny, by any European power in any other light than as the manifestation of an unfriendly disposition toward the United States. In the war between those new governments and Spain we declared our neutrality at the time of their recognition, and to this we have adhered, and shall continue to adhere, provided no change shall occur which, in the judgment of the competent authorities of this government, shall make a corresponding change on the part of the United States indispensable to their security."[35]

It can thus be seen that the Monroe Doctrine was an expression of a faith rather than a carefully reasoned exposition of American opposition to European intervention in the New World. It was a sincere expression of the belief in the superiority of American institutions and ideals, and of the right of self-preservation, grounded in the conviction that the extension of European principles was dangerous to the peace and safety of the American system.

In the literal and verbal sense, there can be no doubt that the

Formulation of the Monroe Doctrine

Doctrine was the President's, for it was on his initiative alone that it was decided to deal with the South American question in his message to Congress. Yet the influences and formative factors were manifold. Canning's interviews with Rush and his unwillingness to grant immediate recognition to the South American states had great influence, but he certainly suggested no presidential declaration and was not overjoyed at its publication. Adams had been directly responsible for the elaboration of the non-colonization principle, and while in the message itself he had no direct influence in the statement of an all-embracing foreign policy or the declaration of the doctrine of the two spheres, nevertheless, the statement of this doctrine is found again and again in his writings. Yet Adams had always regarded the South American countries with an air of pessimism and scorned the idea that their system, republican though it might be, could ever approximate that of the United States. "As to an American system," he declared, "we have it; we constitute the whole of it; there is no community of interests or of principles between North and South America."[36]

It was Monroe, on the other hand, who had expressed again and again his profound sympathy with the cause of the South American countries and his faith in their republican institutions.

Long before the message was written, its two cardinal principles had been formulated by Henry Clay, in specific application to South America. Yet, as far as the language is concerned, it most nearly approximated the various utterances of Jefferson. As early as 1808, in a discussion of the incipient South American revolts, he stated: "We consider their interests the same as ours, and the object of both must be to exclude all European influence in this hemisphere."[37] And on August 4, 1820, he wrote to William Short, outlining his American system, in reply to approaches made by the Portuguese minister: "The day is not distant, when we may formally require a meridian of partition through the ocean which separates the two hemispheres, on the hither side of which no European gun shall ever be heard, nor an American on the other; ... and I hope no American patriot will ever lose sight of the essential policy of interdicting in the seas and territories of both Americas, the ferocious and sanguinary contests of Europe."[38]

Jefferson sent a copy of this letter to Monroe, who replied on

JAMES MONROE

August 23, 1820: "The sentiments expressed in favor of an American interest and policy, extended in the first instance to the preservation of order, along our coast, & in our Seas, are sound, and will in all probability ripen into a system, at no distant period. The destiny however of this western world depends on the continued prosperity & success of this portion of it."[39] The most explicit statement of the doctrine of the two spheres appeared in Jefferson's advice to Monroe, just before the November Cabinet meetings.

Thus, the fundamental ideas were neither new nor original. They were not the sudden creation of individual thought, but rather the result of slow, constructive processes of thought, developed during the formative years of the nation. They stemmed from the colonial period and from Washington's Farewell Address, and had been repeatedly foreshadowed, gradually formulated, and given conviction by Washington, John Adams, and Thomas Jefferson. Whoever drafted the particular clauses, the primary responsibility belonged to Monroe. It was he who determined to treat the South American question boldly in his message; it was he who penned the words in which it was discussed and who assumed complete responsibility for their effect. The Doctrine has never, in any acceptation, received a legislative confirmation, nor does it derive its power and authority from Monroe or from Adams. A codification of the ideas which were in the air, its power lay in the fact that it epitomized what thousands of people everywhere had thought, and were thinking, and would continue to think. The genius of creating must be denied to Monroe, but the genius of apprehending the opportune moment for enunciation is his. He boldly and permanently formulated a sentiment which previously had been simply a matter of American public opinion and aspiration alone.

L. C. Handy Studios

Throughout November, 1823, President Monroe (standing, with hand on globe) discussed with his Cabinet, paragraph by paragraph, the Message to Congress which was to contain the Monroe Doctrine. In his Cabinet were J. Q. Adams, Secretary of State; John C. Calhoun, Secretary of War; W. H. Crawford, Secretary of the Treasury; Samuel L. Southard, Secretary of the Navy; and William Wirt, Attorney General. *Left to right*, Adams, Crawford, Wirt, Monroe, Calhoun, Tompkins (Vice-President), and one unidentified. Note that Monroe is the only one wearing long silk stockings and smallclothes. From a painting by Clyde Osmer De Land.

most enlightened Citizens, and under which we have enjoyed unexampled felicity, this whole nation is devoted. We owe it therefore to candor and to the amicable Relations existing between the united States and those powers, to declare that we should consider any attempts on their part to extend their system to any portion of this Hemisphere, as dangerous to our peace and safety. With the existing Colonies or dependencies of any European power, we have not interfered, and shall not interfere. But with the Governments who have declared their Independence, and maintained it, and whose Independence we have, on great consideration, and on just principles, acknowledged, we could not view any interposition for the purpose of oppressing them, or controuling in any other manner, their destiny, by any European power in any other light, than as the manifestation of an unfriendly disposition towards the United States. In the war between those new Governments and Spain, we declared our neutrality at the time of their recognition, and to this we have

Brown Brothers

THE FIRST STATEMENT OF THE MONROE DOCTRINE

A page from Monroe's message to Congress, December 2, 1823. The original is in the Library of Congress.

40

The End of a Dynasty

IN AMERICA the interest aroused by the promulgation of the Monroe Doctrine was soon overshadowed by the hotly contested presidential election. The method of electing the president, as prescribed in the Constitution had never given much popular satisfaction, for upon several occasions the popular will had appeared to be thwarted. As provided in the Constitution, each state was to appoint, according to laws made by the state legislature, as many electors as there were senators and representatives from that state. These electors were to meet in their respective states, and to write upon their ballot the names of two persons. A copy of this list was then to be sent to the President of the Senate who would tabulate the returns and announce, if a majority existed, the election of the president. The person receiving the second highest number of votes was declared to be the vice-president.

The national convention method for the nomination of candidates had not yet been invented. The party caucus method, whereby the party with a majority in Congress nominated its candidates, had been in use since Adams' day, but its exclusiveness and remoteness from popular control had earned it the opprobrious title of "King·Caucus." Used in the elections of 1808, 1812, 1816, and 1820, it passed out of existence in 1824. Meanwhile, presidential recommendations by state legislatures or meetings of citizens gained in importance and popularity.

During Monroe's first administration the Federalist party disappeared as a national organization, continuing to maintain only a scattered, ineffective, local existence. From 1816 on there was but one national political party, the Republican. Among the Republicans there existed varying degrees of opinion on such matters as the tariff, the United States Bank, and internal improvements necessary to national development, but there were no lasting or irreconcilable divisions. Even the slavery controversy, which had burst forth with such fury and caused such violent debate, subsided like a thunderstorm.

As the years passed, however, and the old issues became less popular and sectional interests became paramount, the Republican party began to divide. On the day Monroe was a second time inaugurated, the "Era of Good Feeling" ended, and the once-omnipotent Republican party began to fall to pieces. The old leaders of the Revolutionary Era were dead or in retirement, and among the active party leaders there was none whose accomplishments so surpassed those of others as to entitle him to complete party support. The campaign for the 1824 election made it apparent that the period of Monroe's administration had been, politically, one of slack water. When the storm broke, the flood swept the country with a bitterness that was to endure for a generation.

The election became a contest of individuals rather than of issues and, as such, was one of the most bitter ever staged. Rival and sectional leaders, each supported by his personal coterie and popular following, struggled for the mastery. In the absence of important public questions to absorb the energies of the men in public life, this petty game of personal politics was played zealously. It indicated a revolt against the outmoded methods of King Caucus and meant the assertion by the people of a right to have a direct voice in the nomination and election of a president, a right never contemplated and little desired by the constitutional fathers.

Although the campaign of 1824 was officially launched in 1822, it had in reality begun as early as 1816.[1] By 1818 Adams observed that the government was assuming daily more and more the character of cabal "and preparation, not for the next presidential election, but for the one after."[2] In January, 1819, he recorded in his *Diary*, which is a study of the dark side of the political society of the age, the fact that "all public business in Congress now connects itself with intrigues, and there is a great danger that the whole Government will degenerate into a struggle of cabals."[3]

The End of a Dynasty

By 1820 not only Congress but the country at large was engaged in bitter factional fights among the friends of the rival candidates. From the details of the personal struggles one can see the growing tendency toward the reappearance of political parties. In the election of 1824 personal traits and qualifications carried greater weight than in any similar contest before or since.

Thus, one year after Monroe's second inauguration, there were some sixteen aspirants for the office, "preening themselves more or less conspicuously in the public view."[4] By the end of the year, however, the ranks had been considerably thinned, and Adams, Crawford, Calhoun, Clay, Jackson, and Clinton remained as serious contenders.

New England's favorite son, John Quincy Adams, the Secretary of State, was the only available northern candidate. The cold, austere, and forbidding Puritan had been richly schooled in matters of statecraft and the art of diplomacy. He accompanied his father to Paris at the age of eleven, and he had himself seen service in almost every branch of the diplomatic corps, to say nothing of having served as Senator from Massachusetts. The broad culture and wide learning he had acquired were augmented by a tirelessness in work and a meticulousness of detail which were unsurpassed. He was, in many ways, an ideal person to succeed to the presidency; yet his harsh and vindictive judgments, his inability to attract a personal following, and his indifference to popular prejudices had cut him off from public favor. Although as secretary of state he occupied the logical "stepping stone to the Presidency," and northern jealousy of Virginia's monopoly of the presidency gave him an advantage over the other aspirants, widespread popularity had been denied to him. He found himself competing in the struggle against some of the most engaging personalities in American history.

In opposition to the northern candidate, the South presented two other members of Monroe's Cabinet as likely successors to his office —Calhoun and Crawford. William Crawford, Secretary of the Treasury, and Virginia-born, had migrated with his parents to South Carolina and eventually to Georgia, but had become the leader of the Virginia slave-holding element against the interior democracy. An ardent states rightist, he demanded a return to strict constructionist principles. In the congressional caucus of 1816 he had been Monroe's

JAMES MONROE

only serious rival, polling 54 votes to Monroe's 65, but while he had built up a considerable following in Congress, he was not popular with the country at large. His strength lay with the old-line Republicans of the South and to the extent that the old regime had a machine, it was with Crawford. In 1820 he had secured the passage of the four-years-tenure-of-office act, which did so much to develop the spoils system, and he had filled the Treasury Department with his personal following. The patronage he had thus built up was augmented by the newspaper support he received. A selfish and scheming politician in every sense of the word, he was characterized by Adams as "a worm preying upon the vitals of the Administration in its own body." With his large following of political and personal friends, no one seemed to have a better chance than he. Yet he had been too long in the field and his advancing years told on his strength.

John C. Calhoun, the other southern candidate, likewise held a Cabinet position, serving Monroe as Secretary of the War Department. He was a descendant of frontier Indian fighters, and his branch of the family had remained in the Carolina uplands and had grown up with the section, instead of crossing the Appalachians into Kentucky as so many others did. A friend of Clay's, he was in 1822 an ardent young Republican. Clamoring for internal improvements and voicing the sentiments of the nationalistic West, he was at the same time the chief leader of the South.

Out of the West, as favorite sons, came Henry Clay and Andrew Jackson. Clay, the Kentuckian, was the epitome of all that state represented—sporting blood, whiskey, honor, and poker, and to Adams was "in politics, as in private life, essentially a gamester."[5] Frank, suave, courteous, and emotional, he charmed his followers with his magnetic personality and qualities of leadership. His ready mastery in debate and the fact that his best work was done with the inspiration of an audience had caused him to make of the speakership, one of the most important of American offices, one from which the occupant might aspire to the presidency. Ever since his War Hawk days in Congress, when he had been so influential in promoting war with England, he had been a bold champion of constructive legislation. In his almost factious opposition to Monroe, he had forged a new set of American political issues, in ardently preaching the gospel of western expansion and internal improvements at federal expense,

The End of a Dynasty

and in advocating the United States Bank, the tariff, and the recognition of the South American republics. More than any other candidate, he was precisely the man around whom would crystallize the elements of a new political party.

While Clay represented and appealed to the progressive business and property interests, Andrew Jackson was the embodiment of the rough and rampant West, the coonskin-capped frontiersman. Comparatively unknown outside his native Tennessee, this gaunt, lantern-jawed, choleric soldier had sprung into overnight fame with his heroic and opportune defeat of the British at New Orleans in 1815. Sinking into oblivion for a few years, his name suddenly flashed across the public consciousness in 1818, when the undue zeal of this reckless military hero brought Monroe's administration to the brink of war with Spain over the capture of the Florida posts. His subsequent conduct in Florida, involving the imprisonment of the Governor, accorded with the secret inclination of the country. Without training and experience in statecraft, he sat, uninfluential and unnoticed, in the Senate when, in January, 1822, the newspapers, at the behest of William B. Lewis, began urging his candidacy. Lewis, the clever and unscrupulous master of the art of winning the support of the unthinking and the impressionable, determined to become the Tennesseean's campaign manager. Typical of a rude and turbulent democracy, Jackson became the political idol of a popular movement, national in its sweep. Two years before the election there were before the public five candidates for the presidency, representing four sections of the Union and nominated by members of state legislatures, mass meetings, and the congressional caucus.

The Seventeenth Congress, which held session from December, 1821, until the spring of 1823, was one of the most ineffective legislative bodies in the nation's history. In the absence of Clay, who had returned to private practice in Kentucky, there was no discipline. Congress deteriorated into a battleground of personal conflicts, an arena for mud-slinging and the destruction of personal reputations. With three of the potential candidates members of his Cabinet, Monroe found himself in the midst of the abuse and quarreling. Seeking a lofty detachment, he declared at an early date his complete disinterest and neutrality in the approaching election. It was said of him that "During the pendency of this contest, Mr. Monroe observed a most scrupulous resolve against all interference with the freest expression of the public sentiment in regard to the candidates. In this he was fully seconded and sustained by his Cabinet, by none more than by those whose names were on the list for suffrage. For, at that time, *it was not considered decorous in the Executive to make itself a partisan in a presidential or any other* election. Indeed there was a most wholesome fastidiousness exhibited on this point, which would have interrupted the attempt of a cabinet officer, or any other functionary of the government, to influence the popular vote by speech, by writing, by favor, fear, or affection, as a great political misdemeanor worthy of sharp rebuke. These were opinions of that day derived from an elder age. They are obsolete opinions now."[6]

In spite of his firm intention to abstain from politics, Monroe was sorely perplexed and disturbed over the picayune bickering and petty quarreling in Congress. In a letter to Madison in the spring of 1822 he disclosed his misgivings:

"I have never known such a state of things as has existed here during the last Session, nor have I personally ever experienced so much embarrassment and mortification. While there is an open contest with a foreign enemy, or with an internal party, in which you are supported by just principles, the course is plain, and you have something to cheer and animate you to action, but we are now blessed with peace, and the success of the late war has overwhelmed the federal party, so that there is no division of that kind to rally any persons together in support of the administration. The approaching election, 'tho distant, is a circumstance that excites greatest interest in both houses, and whose effect, already sensibly felt, is still much to be dreaded. There being three avowed candidates in the administration is a circumstance which increases the embarrassment."[7]

Even in his Cabinet, where, in view of the integrity of the candidates, he should have expected tranquillity, he met with jangling animosities. Monroe had always been the recipient of the confidence and affection of his Cabinet members, and their personal rivalries had heretofore never disturbed the harmony. However, a man wiser than Monroe in the field of psychology would have deferred his announcement of neutrality. Had he withheld the announcement of his decision to abstain from the canvass, he would in all probability have preserved a better harmony among the group, as each would

The End of a Dynasty

have tried to outdo the other in competing for his indorsement. As it was, Crawford was the disturbing element. His chagrin that Monroe did not prefer him for the presidency caused him openly to oppose the President.

No sooner had Calhoun's candidacy been announced in 1821 than Crawford's satellites in Congress attacked Calhoun's record as the War Secretary. There were several military appointments to be made, which Monroe executed upon Calhoun's recommendation. When they appeared in the Senate, awaiting the necessary ratification, that august body refused to ratify on the ground that they were not in accordance with the law for the reduction of the army, a measure of retrenchment which Crawford had advocated because of the depletion of the Treasury. In the ensuing Cabinet discussions Crawford openly supported the Senate refusal, and his relations with Monroe became exceedingly strained. In the spring of 1822 rumors were thick that the President would demand his resignation.[8] Monroe's friends urged him to remove Crawford. Although among the President's papers there were found several undated drafts which would have disrupted the Cabinet, he never demanded Crawford's resignation. That summer the matter was brought to a head—Crawford heard the rumor and opened the subject. In a bitter correspondence Monroe accused him of having agreed openly with accusations that his (Monroe's) principles and policies were diametrically opposed to the early Jeffersonian system of economy and states rights. In his fear that Crawford aimed at the creation of a new party, the existence of which he regarded as the "curse of the country,"[9] Monroe emphasized that it was the duty of a Cabinet officer, once the policy of an Executive had been determined, to support and defend that policy.[10] Crawford denied the charge that he had been antagonistic toward the administration, and his explanations evidently convinced Monroe, for he was requested to remain in the Cabinet. However, the relations between the two men were permanently strained, and after Crawford, late in the administration, in a fit of rage cursed the President and was on the verge of assaulting him bodily, their personal intercourse ceased. Monroe wrote to Wirt: "My own opinion has been, taking the whole subject in view, that it comported better with the principles of our government and with my own character to permit him to remain than to remove him, and

I have so acted. Had I taken a different view of the subject I should not have hesitated to remove him; in that event I would have gone directly to the object."[11]

As early as 1821 Adams had realized that the number of candidates in the field made it almost a certainty that the election would be decided by the vote of the states in the House of Representatives. Nor did he change his opinion as the eve of the election drew near. In 1823 Crawford suffered a paralytic stroke, which removed him from his position of preëlection favorite, but there still remained four powerful and determined candidates. For the first time in campaign history, the power of the press and the profusion of stump orators were turned upon personalities, and even Clay, accustomed to the flinging of invective, was forced to admit: "The bitterness and violence of presidential electioneering increase as the time advances. It seems as if every liar and calumniator in the country was at work day and night to destroy my character.... It distracts my attention from public business and consumes precious time."[12] For the first time campaign badges became popular, and *Niles' Register* commented upon the introduction of fancy vests and sporting pictures of the various candidates.

In the midst of this lively and yet degrading political campaign came the news that the venerable Marquis de Lafayette contemplated making a final visit to the country he had helped to create. On February 4, 1824, Congress authorized Monroe to tender him a national ship for his voyage. This Lafayette graciously declined, alleging that as he came as a private citizen he preferred to embark in a merchant packet ship. However, it was "with feelings of respectful, affectionate, and patriotic gratitude" that he accepted the invitation of Congress and promised to visit "the beloved land" of which it had been his "happy lot to become an early soldier and an adopted son."[13] His plans for an unobtrusive leave-taking were interfered with by Louis XVIII's objections; so he embarked in an American packet ship, the *Cadmus*. After a thirty-one-day voyage he arrived in New York City, and was received at Staten Island by Vice-President Tompkins on Sunday, August 14, 1824, just forty years after he had taken his leave of Washington. After an unprecedentedly warm reception in New York and a triumphal tour to Boston and

The End of a Dynasty

through the New England states, in which the people determined to regard him as a national guest for the duration of his stay, he turned toward Washington.

The personal relations between Monroe and Lafayette were cordial and intimate. By his efforts, during his sojourn in France, to secure the Frenchman's release from the dungeons of Olmütz, Monroe had won the grateful friendship of Lafayette. It was an imposing and cordial welcome which was accorded the distinguished visitor in Washington in October, and one fraught with drama when Monroe, the last of the Revolutionary Presidents greeted Lafayette, the sole surviving general officer of Washington's army. The General remained in the Capital only a short time, planning to return in December for a longer sojourn.

Early in October, after Lafayette's arrival, there was some diversity of opinion in the Cabinet as to the etiquette which the authorities were to observe at the official reception. Calhoun, especially, was overcautious in his hesitancy. He sent an eight-page letter to Monroe, saying that he thought it would be "hazardous for the administration to follow too sympathetically the General's movements," but at the same time he admitted that it would be "ungracious to run counter to the enthusiasm which the American people were showing in anticipation of Lafayette's journey through their respective communities." He eventually concluded that it would be better to endure the criticism of the English than to be condemned by the American people for coldness to a national benefactor.[14] A few days later Monroe, answering inquiries from Lafayette in regard to certain routes, told the General that his arrival ". . . has given rise to a great political movement which has so far taken the direction and had the effect among us, and I presume in Europe, which the best friends to you and to sound principles could desire. It is of great importance that it should terminate in like manner."[15]

In December Lafayette returned to Washington as the guest of the White House. On the tenth he was received by both Houses of Congress, becoming the only person, up to that time, to have a public reception in the Senate. As a Christmas present the American people generously granted to the impoverished Lafayette "200,000 in money and a township of public land," as a tangible proof of the public gratitude. Monroe selected a tract in the vicinity of Tallahassee,

JAMES MONROE

Florida, and personally presented the land warrant thereto—"Be it enacted, That in consideration of the services and sacrifices of Gen. Lafayette in the war of the revolution, the secretary of the treasury be, and is hereby, authorized to pay to him the sum of two hundred thousand dollars; out of any money in the treasury not otherwise appropriated:

"sec. 2: That there be granted to the said gen. Lafayette and his heirs, one township of land; to be laid out, and located, under the authority of the president, on any of the unappropriated lands of the United States." [16]

It is an interesting commentary on the motives and emotions of men that while Congress so unhesitatingly granted this lavish bequest, Thomas Jefferson was in great financial need, and Monroe spent the six years of his retirement in a protracted struggle to secure fulfillment of his just claims upon Congress to the amount of $30,000. On New Year's Day, 1825, Congress gave Lafayette a public dinner, following the White House reception, at which Monroe officiated. It was held in "the front rooms of Williamson's range of buildings" [17] and about two hundred distinguished guests were assembled, to pay tribute not only to Lafayette but to the retiring President: "When the health of Mr. Monroe was proposed," *Niles' Register* recorded, "the company rose, with one accord, and seemed to pay him the homage, not merely of their lips, but of devoted hearts. . . . The presence of the chief magistrate of the nation, on this grateful occasion, was an incident which seemed to spread satisfaction through the whole assembly." [18]

Lafayette stayed on in the United States until September, 1825, when he took formal leave of President Adams at Washington. His triumphant tour through all the states had evoked an unprecedented national enthusiasm and unanimity, ably expressed in the following editorial from *Niles' Register:*

"The volumes of history furnished no parallel. No one like Lafayette has ever reappeared in any country. To us he is like a venerated father, returned from the grave, to bless and receive the blessings of a mightily increased and joyous posterity.

"The king and priest-ridden population of the European continent—the white slaves of Russia, Prussia, and Austria—the degraded people of France, and the miserable wretches who make up the races

The End of a Dynasty

that inhabit Spain, Portugal, Italy, cannot have anything more like a just conception of our feelings, as associated with the arrival of gen. Lafayette, than a Hottentot possesses of Algebra."[19]

Lafayette's arrival upon the American scene had acted like oil upon troubled waters, while his presence at Washington, the heart of the political strife, had its influence in preventing untoward political demonstrations. Wherever the General had gone the bitter quarrel of the presidential struggle had been silenced by the enthusiasm that greeted him.

In December it became generally known that there had been no election by the people. When the electoral vote was counted it was discovered that, while Calhoun had been elected vice-president, no president had been chosen. Jackson led the field with 99 votes, far from the 131 necessary for a majority and election. Adams was second with 54, while Crawford had secured 41. To his deep chagrin, Clay trailed with 37. As predicted, Jackson had carried Pennsylvania and New Jersey, large sections of the South and the New West, with the exception of Ohio. Adams' strength lay in the practical unanimity of New York and New England, augmented by a scattering in the South, while Clay carried Ohio, Missouri, and his native Kentucky, along with a few New York votes. Crawford secured the support of Georgia and Virginia, in addition to a few scattered votes.

For the second time in the history of the office, the election was to be determined by the House of Representatives. Here Clay's followers were legion and his mighty influence could easily have carried the result for himself. However, not being among the three highest he was barred from consideration. Although he could not claim the prize, his influence could easily obtain it for another. That winter the friends of Crawford, Jackson, and Adams sedulously cultivated Clay, wining and dining him, and showering him with favors. Each candidate, including Adams, who remained rigidly aloof from such connivance, had a group of managers, practical politicians who were determined to get votes by any means.

"I am sometimes touched gently on the shoulder by a friend, for example, of General Jackson," wrote Clay, "who will thus address me: 'My dear sir, all my dependence is upon you; don't disappoint us, you know our partiality was for you next to the hero, and how much we want a Western President.' Immediately after, a friend of

JAMES MONROE

Mr. Crawford will accost me: 'The hopes of our Republican party are concentrated on you; for God's sake preserve it. If you had been returned instead of Mr. Crawford, every man of us would have supported you to the last hour. We consider him and you as the only genuine Republican candidates.' Next a friend of Mr. Adams comes with tears in his eyes: 'Sir, Mr. Adams has always had the greatest respect for you, and admiration of your talents. There is no station to which you are not equal. Most undoubtedly, you are the second choice of New England and I pray you to consider seriously whether the public good and your own future interests do not point most distinctly to the choice which ought to be made?' How can one withstand all this disinterested homage and kindness?"[20]

As far as Clay was concerned Crawford, as a paralytic, was out of the running, in spite of the fact that he most nearly represented the things for which Clay stood. Clay had vigorously opposed Jackson in the Seminole War controversy and little love was lost between them, while at the same time Clay had no predilection for Adams and many of his policies. As a choice between the two candidates, however, Adams, with his wealth of experience, marked ability, and integrity was the logical choice over the untutored and turbulent Jackson. Although Clay made no formal announcement of his selection, the rumor that he favored Adams got around in January. On the twenty-eighth of that month an unsigned letter, purporting to come from an anonymous member of the House, appeared in the *Columbian Observer* of Philadelphia,[21] charging that in spite of the fact that Jackson had corralled the most votes, a corrupt bargain had been entered into by which Clay was to throw the election to Adams, in return for being appointed secretary of state. Clay was furious and in his anger published not only a denial but intimated that, if the assailant would reveal himself, there would be a duel. Lewis and Eaton, Jackson's campaign managers who were at the bottom of the affair, trotted out one George Kremer, of Pennsylvania, who acknowledged the letter and with bravado said he would prove his statements. When Clay demanded an investigation, Lewis and Eaton wrote a letter for Kremer, asserting rights and freedom of speech and of the press, and declined to appear before the committee. The investigation collapsed, and on the day the letter was brought before the House, February 9, Adams was elected.

The End of a Dynasty

Jackson showed no resentment, for that evening at a presidential reception Jackson and Adams met face to face. Each man hesitated and then the General, who was with a lady, stepped forward. "How do you do, Mr. Adams? I give you my left hand, for the right, as you see, is devoted to the fair. I hope you are very well, Sir." Adams replied coolly, "Very well, Sir. I hope General Jackson is well."[22] An observer of the scene said, "It was curious to see the western planter, the Indian fighter, the stern soldier who had written his country's glory in the blood of the enemy at New Orleans genial and gracious in the midst of a court, while the old courtier and diplomat was stiff, rigid, cold as a statue. It was all the more remarkable from the fact that, four hours before, the former had been defeated, and the latter was the victor, in a struggle for one of the highest objects of human ambition. The personal character of these two individuals was in fact well expressed in that chance meeting: the gallantry, the frankness, and the heartiness of the one, the self-concentration of the other, which repelled all."[23]

When the news became known on February 14 that Adams had appointed Clay as secretary of state, Jackson's suspicions of conspiracy were confirmed and he turned against Adams and Clay.[24] Although there was no canard in the history of politics more tenaciously believed, there was no basis of fact for Randolph's charges, denouncing the "coalition of Blifil and Black George—the combination unheard of till now, of the Puritan with the Blackleg."[25] Clay had told various people, among them Benton, that he would vote for Adams even before he had had any interview with the latter. Adams, on his part, did what in any circumstance would have been fitting and proper. Jackson would have been no man to have in the State Department, as Adams with his experience knew. Clay was upset over the effect of his acceptance on public opinion. Acceptance would seem to indicate the truth of the charges of a bargain, while failure to accept would be pointed to as cowardly hesitancy to accept the fruits of a bargain. In determining to stand by Adams, Clay accepted and made a lengthy statement which to thinking men was a complete vindication of his action.

And now the last months of Monroe's administration were running out. His interests and efforts did not flag. From the very start

JAMES MONROE

he had been emphatic in his determination that the unpreparedness of the coast defenses, which had so exposed the country to the English depredations during the War of 1812, should be repaired.[26] With a view to inspecting the harbors, fortifications and defenses he had taken two extensive tours, through every state of the Union. Practically every annual message referred to the progress of the operations for improvement which had been made, and he was tireless in his recommendation of a large and effective navy. On December 15, 1823, the House moved a resolution that the President "communicate a plan for the peace establishment of the Navy of the United States." It was no surprise, therefore, to learn in his message of January 30, 1824, that he advocated a peace-time establishment which was strange reading to Jefferson, the father of his party:

"The Navy is the arm from which our Government will always derive most aid and support of our neutral rights. Every power engaged in war will know the strength of our naval force, and the number of our ships of each class, their condition and the promptitude with which we may bring them into service, and will pay due consideration to that argument. . . . The great object in event of war is to stop the enemy at the coast. If this is done our cities, and whole interior will be secure. . . .

"It is to the execution of these works, both land and naval, and under a thorough conviction that by hastening their completion I should render the best service to my country and give the most effectual support to our free representative system of government that my humble faculties would admit of, that I have devoted so much of my time and labor to this great system of national policy since I came into this office, and shall continue to do it until my retirement from it at the end of your next session."[27]

One further problem in which Monroe took a kindly and spirited, though little-remembered, humanitarian interest was that of the alleviation of the conditions of the Indians. Crowded to the frontiers, their land seized, and their tribes decimated by slaughter and disease, the Indians were becoming a source of grave concern to the nation. By a treaty of 1802 the United States had undertaken to purchase tracts of land from the Indians in Georgia, thereby extinguishing their title. This policy had been pursued, although little systematic provision had been made for the disposition of the Indians. In his

The End of a Dynasty

first annual message to Congress Monroe reported the recent progress made in acquiring lands, and at the same time took up the cudgel for the Indians by suggesting to Congress that it enact some program for the further amelioration of their condition:

"From the several of the Indian tribes inhabiting the country bordering on Lake Erie, purchases have been made of lands on conditions very favorable to the United States, and . . . to the tribes themselves.

"By these purchases the Indian title, with moderate reservations, has been extinguished to the whole of the land within the limits of the State of Ohio, and to a part of that in the Michigan Territory and of the State of Indiana. From the Cherokee tribe a tract has been purchased in the State of Georgia and an arrangement made by which, in exchange for lands by the Mississippi, a great part, if not the whole, of the land belonging to that tribe eastward of that river in the states of North Carolina, Georgia, and Tennessee, and in Alabama Territory will soon be acquired. . . . A similar and equally advantageous effect will soon be produced to the South. . . . In this progress, which the rights of nature demand and nothing can prevent, marking a growth rapid and gigantic, it is our duty to make new efforts for the preservation, improvement and civilization of the native inhabitants. . . . It will merit the consideration of Congress whether other provisions not stipulated by treaty ought to be made for these tribes and for the advancement of the liberal and humane policy of the United States toward all the tribes within our limits, and more particularly for their improvement in the arts of civilized life."[28]

This urge that the Indians be secured in their lands by definite grants to them immediately aroused the hostility of the frontier. Congress did make an appropriation in 1818 for the education of the Indians, but the meagre and completely inadequate sum of $10,000 then provided underwent no annual increase for many years.

During the remainder of his term of office Monroe continued to plead for recognition of his doctrine of a national political guardianship over the Indians, with reciprocal powers and obligations over the wards and their property. In his second inaugural address, pointing out that the Indian tribes succumbed when they came in direct contact with white civilization, he suggested incorporating them in tribes under jurisdiction of the United States.[29]

JAMES MONROE

By the end of his administration Monroe was able to secure for the Indians the establishment of the Indian territory, open to those tribes which might be induced by treaties to accept land there in lieu of their holdings in the East, where certain destruction was threatening them. His plan for the division of this territory into districts with civil government and special schools and churches would promote their welfare and happiness and shield them from impending ruin. His final message contained a thought for their welfare:

"The condition of the aborigines within our limits, and especially those who are within the limits of any of the states, merits particular attention. . . . Difficulties of the most serious character present themselves. . . . To remove them from it, the territory on which they now reside, by force, even with a view to their own security and happiness would be revolting to humanity and utterly unjustifiable. Between the limits of our present States and Territories and the Rocky Mountains and Mexico there is a vast territory, to which they might be invited with inducements which might be successful."[30]

As Monroe pondered his last message to Congress, he could view with satisfaction the accomplishments of his administration. His untiring application and indomitable perseverance, united with his all-embracing love for the Union, had enabled him to guide the country through the first dangerous currents of the sectional quarrel, postponing for a time the inevitable conflict. By his ability to secure the loyal support of his friends and to effect a compromise among the diverse personalities in his own Cabinet he had allayed the storm of menacing partisanship. With deep sincerity and conviction he could state:

"The situation of the United States is in the highest degree prosperous and happy. There is no object which as a people we can desire which we do not possess, or which is not within our reach. . . .

"Against foreign aggression the policy of the government seems to be already settled. The events of the last war admonished us to make our maritime frontier impregnable by a well-digested chain of fortifications, and to give efficient protection to our commerce by augmenting our Navy to a certain extent, which has been steadily pursued. . . . To give full effect to this policy great improvements will be indispensable. Access to those works by every practicable communication should be made easy and in every direction. The

The End of a Dynasty

intercourse between every part of our Union should also be promoted and facilitated by the exercise of those principles which may comport with a faithful regard to the great principles of the Constitution. . . . In pursuit of these great objects let a generous spirit and national views and feelings be indulged, and let every part recollect that by cherishing that spirit of improving the condition of the others in what relates to their welfare the general interest will not only be promoted, but the local advantage be reciprocated by all. . . .

"From the present prosperous and happy state I derive a gratification which I can not express."[31]

The *London Times*, commenting upon the message, presented an acutely keen interpretation of the position in which the country found itself:

"It is not merely as the last message Mr. Monroe will ever communicate in his character of president, that we consider this an interesting production. To a lover of humanity and of public liberty, it possesses the valuable qualifications of describing an amount of national prosperity, enjoyed by a people who speak our language and are cemented to Englishmen by a common blood and lineage, superior to all that has been recorded of any community on earth. Towards foreign states, the president indulges a spirit of uniform and impartial good will. Aloof from the anxieties and heart burnings of the old world, he disclaims all share in those systems of policy which engage, combine or distract the European powers. The balance of power in Europe is declared to be a thing indifferent to America. The growth of the new republics, near neighbors to the United States, the sympathy between their respective institutions, are dwelt upon with natural exaltation by Mr. Monroe; and we are happy to see, he reiterates the maxim that no enemy from Europe ought to be permitted by the United States, to molest or disturb the independence of South America with impunity. . . . England is spoken of in terms of cordial respect and amity. The abolition of the slave trade is pronounced to be an object 'near to the heart' of both nations."[32]

Monroe was by no means loath to turn over the responsibilities of his office to his successor. Beset by financial difficulties and wearied by the great problems he had been called upon to face, he eagerly sought the seclusion of his Virginia home, to set his own house in order. From the various states he received, as he retired from office,

[467]

JAMES MONROE

innumerable testimonials of satisfaction at his conduct, but, of all these, Monroe treasured most the letter from his schoolmate of long ago—the great John Marshall, who wrote, "In the momentous and then unlooked for events which have since taken place, you have filled a large space in the public mind, and have been conspicuously instrumental in effecting objects of great interest to our common country. Believe me when I congratulate you on the circumstances under which your political course terminates, and that I feel sincere pleasure in the persuasion that your administration may be viewed with real approval by our wisest statesmen."

41

Last Years of a Great American

AN ADMINISTRATION of eight years, one of the most dignified and successful in history, stood behind Monroe. The accomplishments of that era are probably best described in the words of John Quincy Adams, the man who was to succeed him:

"There behold him for a term of eight years, strengthening his country for defense by a system of combined fortifications, military and naval, sustaining her rights, her dignity and honor abroad; soothing her dissensions, and conciliating her acerbities at home; controlling by a firm though peaceful policy the hostile spirit of the European Alliance against Republican Southern America; extorting by the mild compulsion of reason, the shores of the Pacific from the stipulated acknowledgement of Spain; and leading back the imperial autocrat of the North, to his lawful boundaries, from his hastily asserted dominion over the Southern Ocean. Thus strengthening and consolidating the federative edifice of his country's Union, till he was entitled to say, like Augustus Caesar of his imperial city, that he had found her built of brick and left her constructed of marble."[1]

At the close of his term of office, Monroe almost eagerly surrendered the helm of government to his former Secretary of State, John Quincy Adams. At the age of sixty-seven, his face deeply marked with lines of anxiety and care, although still stalwart of frame, Monroe looked forward to spending the rest of his life on his estate in Loudoun County, Virginia. His letters to Jefferson and Madison during the winter of 1824-1825 indicate how eagerly he anticipated the day when he could hand to another the responsibility which the presidency entailed, and return to rustic life to enjoy the companionship of former associates and his beloved family. "I shall be heartily rejoiced," he wrote to Jefferson, "when the term of my service expires, and I may return home in peace with my family, on whom, and especially on Mrs. Monroe, the burdens & cares of my long public service, have borne too heavily."[2]

Monroe retired under most favorable auspices. Already several states, among them South Carolina, Alabama, Maine, and Massachusetts, had communicated to him through their governors the sincere wish of their respective legislatures that "the evening of a life, so honorably devoted to the public service, may be as tranquil and happy as its noon and meridian have been illustrious and useful."[3] Nor were these isolated sentiments. Monroe was held in high esteem by a nation of devoted people who wished him complete happiness in his retirement.

In contrast to the rather quiet ceremonies which had ushered in Monroe's second term, Washington presented a scene of unusual bustle on the morning of Inauguration Day, 1825. There had been a great influx of strangers all day Thursday. But despite the feeling of suppressed excitement which usually accompanied the inauguration of a new president, the atmosphere of almost hysterical pageantry with which the city had recently greeted Lafayette was wholly lacking. Indeed, the *National Journal* commented: "The entire grandeur [of the occasion] consists in its simplicity, and the variety of associations to which it naturally gives birth. Whatever of splendor belongs to it is entirely intrinsic; there is no external show, no borrowed grandeur, none of the tingling, nor glitter, nor circumstances of artificial pomp; yet its effect throws into the deepest shade the most magnificent spectacles which are dependent only on their gorgeousness for the interest which they create."[4]

The inaugural ceremonies were preceded by the customary parade of marshals, followed by the officers of Congress, the President-elect, Mr. Monroe and his family, the Justices of the Supreme Court in their official robes, and lastly, the senators and members of the House of Representatives. Chief Justice Marshall administered the oath of office to Mr. Adams, who, "after two successive sleepless nights"[5]

Last Years of a Great American

and clad in a "complete suit of domestic manufactures," had acquitted himself in the inaugural address so as to command the respect of all. *Niles' Register* commented, "His appearance was such as the imagination would conceive of the chief magistrate of a republic, just beginning to feel the extent of its own resources, and the importance of its own character. In the delivery of his address he was visibly and considerably agitated; while the emphatic distinctness and propriety of his manner, produced a powerful effect upon his auditors. His compliment to the wise administration of Mr. Monroe was as just as it was eloquent. That virtuous citizen retires from his high office followed by the love and gratitude of a nation, to whose prosperity he has so greatly contributed. The mantle of his wisdom will fall on his successor: and may he also fulfill the high duties of this important station so as, like him, to promote the public good; and, like him, to merit and receive the public gratitude."[6] The customary inaugural ball that evening, at Carusi's Hall, closed the ceremonies and launched the new administration.

There were numerous details attendant upon evacuating the White House which demanded Monroe's attention and, to add to the difficulty, Mrs. Monroe was suffering from the recurrence of a chronic disorder. It was therefore not until March 23 that they bade farewell to Washington and turned toward their Loudoun County home. Those last few days the house was thronged with visitors taking affectionate leave, and when the family finally set forth they were escorted to the line of the District by a troop of horse.

Oak Hill, the home Monroe had planned for his retirement, had been built during his presidency to replace a dormer-windowed cottage which had been in the family for years. Thomas Jefferson drew the plans, and James Hoban, builder of the White House, executed them.[7] Oak Hill was a spacious edifice of colonial architecture, constructed of bricks burned on the place, with a wide portico fronting south and massive, thirty-foot Doric columns. From a commanding eminence its deep-set windows looked across rolling farm lands, toward the Blue Ridge in one direction and the Catoctin Hills in another, while a lofty mountain, named Sugar-Loaf, dominated the southeastern skyline. Surrounded by a sloping, velvety lawn, the house was set in a grove of locusts, poplars, and oaks. Monroe himself had planted the oaks—a tree from each state in the Union, presented to him for the purpose by the congressmen from the respective states.[8] The interior was handsomely furnished, with hand-carved woodwork throughout, and the many rooms afforded ample accommodation for the Hays and Gouverneurs and their children, who spent much time with the Monroes.

The family was well acquainted in the neighborhood, for they had spent many of the congressional recesses there, and during the course of the next few months they entertained extensively. The most distinguished visitor that summer was General Lafayette, who, accompanied by his private secretary and his son, John Quincy Adams and his son, as well as Mr. Tench Ringgold, the Marshal of the District, spent several days at Oak Hill, to bid farewell to his "earliest and best" friend, before returning to France. The party set forth from Washington about four in the afternoon of August 6, and proceeded as far as Fairfax Courthouse. Here they spent the night, and Lafayette reminisced with several of the Revolutionary veterans who gathered from the surrounding countryside. The following noon, after a slight mishap to one of the carriages, and on the "hottest day of the season," the party arrived at Oak Hill. They found Monroe in good health and spirits, and Mrs. Hay and her daughter Hortensia acting as hostesses in the absence of Mrs. Monroe in New York.

The next day was spent "in desultory conversation with Mr. Monroe, Mr. Hay, General LaFayette, Dr. Wallace, Mrs. Hay, and the visitors at the house,"[9] for the extreme heat precluded any more active recreation. On the ninth, two troops of horse and a carriage arrived to escort Lafayette to Leesburg, where the General was to review several troops of militia and attend a public dinner in his honor.[10] Monroe was toasted publicly and the following day said good-bye to the sole surviving officer of Washington's general staff, his last link with the Revolutionary age.

As he rode back to Oak Hill his thoughts naturally turned to that subject which had been ever on his mind and which was to add to the burdens of his last years—finances. During the many years he had spent in England, France, and Spain on special missions for his government, his affairs at home had fallen sadly into neglect, and several pieces of land had had to be sold to stave off the more pressing of his creditors. In addition, not only had he spent much of his private fortune to augment the necessarily niggardly congressional grants,

Last Years of a Great American

but as President the lavish entertainment and profuse hospitality requisite for the proper fulfillment of the duties of that office had depleted his private reserves.

Before entering Madison's Cabinet as Secretary of State, Monroe had taken up with him the matter of the expenses of his recent mission. Madison assured him that everything would be settled satisfactorily, but evidently no action was taken. Once having entered public life, Monroe had deemed it unadvisable to allude to his accounts, and it was not until late in 1824 that he decided to consult Madison and Jefferson on the subject, and to send a formal message to Congress requesting an investigation of the accounts and an equitable settlement.

On December 11, 1824, he wrote to Jefferson. "In the settlement of the accounts of both my missions to Europe, that commencing in 1794 under Genl. Washington, and that of 1803 under you, I have thought that injustice was done me.... The period of my retirement approaching, I intend to invite the attention of Congress to both subjects, ...It would be gratifying to me to be permitted by you to show to the Committee to whom the subject will probably be referred the first paragraph of your letter of the thirteenth of January, 1803, announcing to me my appointment.... The sole object ... would be to shew the haste with which I hurried from home; & from the country, leaving my private concerns in consequence unsettled."[11]

In similar vein he wrote to Madison, on December 13: "You may recollect that one of the items in my acct. for compensation in my last mission to Europe, the 8th, involving the expenses incurred in England after my return from Spain, by various causes, and particularly the special mission in which I was associated with Mr. Pinkney, was suspended by your order for further consideration when the account was settled. In that state it has remain'd since.... In my absence my tract of land above Charlottesville, of 950 acres, was sold, to pay neighborhood debts, which, if the outfit had been allowed me, might have been avoided.... It is my intention to bring the subject before Congress, with a view to give the explanations necessary before my retirement, to leave them to be recurr'd to, at another Session, when decided on."[12]

That year the gaiety of the Capitol holiday season was marred for Monroe by the necessity of collecting the many papers and other data pertinent to his earlier missions, preparing a detailed financial statement, and writing a special message to Congress. On January 5, one draft of his message, asking for the appointment of a committee to examine his accounts and claims, was presented to the Senate and another to the House of Representatives. In it Monroe said, "It is my wish that all matters of account and claim between my country and myself be settled with that strict regard to justice which is observed in settlements between individuals in private life."[13] The message continued with an elaborate discussion of his reasons for not previously having taken up the matter, and concluded by saying that, "A citizen who has long served his country in its highest trusts has a right, if he has served with fidelity, to enjoy undisturbed tranquility and peace in his retirement."[14] This memorial announced all too modestly the financial need in which he stood upon his retirement. Congress adjourned, however, without taking action.

In April, 1825, Monroe advertised in the leading eastern papers that he would offer at public sale on the first Monday of June his 3500-acre Albemarle establishment in Virginia, as well as another tract of land of 700 acres near Milton.[15] The applicants were instructed to address themselves directly to him. But late summer of that year found him harassed by his insolvent circumstances, even though he had found a purchaser. In August he wrote McLean, "My land and slaves have all been sold in Albemarle, as has been the tract of 20,000 acres in Clay county, Ken., in satisfaction of debts contracted in the public service, and large balances are still due."[16]

Creditors, too, became more importunate. In April, 1826, he was the recipient of the following letter from John Jacob Astor:

"Permit me to congratulate you on your Honourable retirement [from public life] for which I most sincerely wish you may enjoy that Peace and Tranquility to which you are so justly entitled.

"Without wishing to cause you any Inconveniency [sic] on account of the loan which I so long since made to you I would be glad if you would put it in a train of sittlement [sic] if not the whole let it be a part with the interest Due.

"I hope Dear Sir that you and Mrs. Monroe enjoy the best of health and that you may live many years to wittness [sic] the Prosperity of the country to which you have so generously contributed."[17]

Last Years of a Great American

Monroe was reaping the bitter fruits of a life devoted to the best interests of his country, at the expense of his own. "Poverty was the badge of all his public honors." His correspondence of the next four years, particularly with Madison, Jefferson, and McLean is filled with references to his embarrassed condition and with melancholy reiteration of the justice of his claims which Congress continued to ignore. It was in mid-winter of 1826, that he chanced to read an article which gave him the first inkling that Jefferson, too, was in a similar situation. He had just finished writing to Jefferson that his hopes of an independent existence for the rest of his life had been defeated by his "public employments, and especially those abroad." "Such is actually my situation," he wrote, "that I do not think that the grant of my claims will nearly relieve me, by which I mean, will leave me enough to exist in tolerable comfort with my family. My debts abroad were great, and my plantations in Albemarle & here, [Oak Hill] have added considerably to them every year, so that with accumulated loans and interest, compound added to simple, they have become immense. This is a true, tho' a melancholy picture of the actual state of my affairs."[18]

At this juncture he heard that Jefferson had applied to the Virginia legislature for a grant of a lottery for the sale of his estate. From that time forward he bent all his efforts toward soliciting aid for Jefferson from his own friends and pushed his own financial affairs into the background. Only twice more in letters to Madison, one from Albemarle in 1826, and again in 1828, when he informed Madison of the sale of some of his slaves to Colonel White of Florida[19] did he refer to them—"I have failed in the sale of my lands in this county, or any part thereof, and in consequence, being informed that there were several persons desirous of purchasing, tho' not willing to give the price I asked, I have advertised both tracts for sale, to the highest bidder, on the 18th & 20th of the next month."[20]

Jefferson died poor, on July 4, 1826, so poor that a national subscription was started for his relief on the day he died.[21]

Monroe grew apathetic toward the question of his claims in Congress. The weary history of the actions of that body is indeed disgraceful. Those worthy dignitaries, who recently without a murmur had granted LaFayette a gift of $200,000 and a landed estate, now stalled over granting a perfectly honest and well-substantiated claim, to a man who, according to Buchanan, "was the very last person against whom the charge of an avaricious love of money, and base collusion with a subordinate officer would ever be brought, or could ever be substantiated."[22] At times Jackson, whom Monroe had so often befriended and championed, vindictively blocked proceedings. The accounts were read, tabled, re-read and examined, reported to committees and referred interminably, with no final action being taken.

In 1828 Lafayette, again in comfortable circumstances by virtue of the generosity of Congress, heard of Monroe's predicament and with a delicacy and generosity which did him honor, proffered his assistance:

"In the meanwhile, my dear Monroe, permit your earliest, your best, and your most obliged friend to be plain with you. It is probable that, to give you time and facilities for your arrangements, a mortgage might be of some use.

"The sale of ½ of my Florida property is full enough to meet my family settlement and the wishes of my neighbors. . . . You remember that in similar embarrassment I have formerly accepted your intervention. It gives me right to reciprocity. My friend Mr. Graham has my full powers (of attorney). Be pleased to peruse the enclosed letter, seal it and put it in the post office. I durst not send it before I have obtained your approbation."[23]

Monroe's sensitive disposition caused him to decline this generous offer and also a subsequent one which LaFayette made the following year. "My dear friend," he replied, "I can never take anything from you, nor from your family."[24] Even here Monroe again went into a detailed justification of his actions in Europe in 1803.

The citizens of Albemarle County presented a memorial to Congress early in 1829, praying for that body to reconsider the claims of Mr. Monroe upon the government, and to remunerate him for his losses and sacrifices in the service of his country.[25] A similar meeting of citizens was held in New York City, in January, 1831, which adopted a like memorial, inviting attention to his claims.[26] But still Congress reached no settlement. Not only had Monroe given up hope of a decision, but he had become irritated to the point of anger over the petty quibblings of Congress and offended at their questioning of his integrity. On December 5, 1827, he wrote to McLean, "I shall

Last Years of a Great American

never apply again to Congress, let my situation be what it may."[27] As late as April 11, 1831, after he had been forced to give up Oak Hill and when the shadow of death was already upon him, he wrote to Madison, almost pathetically: "The accounting officers have made no decision in my claims, & have given me much trouble. I have told them that I would make out no account adapted to the act, which fell far short of making me a just reparation, and that I had rather lose the whole sum than give it any sanction, be the consequences what they may. I never recover'd from the losses of the first mission, to which those of the second added considerably."[28]

Shortly after this, Congress, in far from a generous mood, granted him $30,000 in partial fulfillment of his claims.[29] There is reason to believe that this amount, augmented by monies brought in through additional land sales, satisfied the debts outstanding against him, but if Monroe had lived longer than he did, he would have been entirely dependent upon the generosity of his son-in-law, Mr. Gouverneur.

While in public office Monroe had strictly adhered to the principle that the First Magistrate should stand aloof from party politics. The President should neither by deed nor word demonstrate his preference for one candidate or another to succeed him. This policy he carried on into retirement, maintaining a dignified impartiality in affairs, and accepting only those appointments and honors befitting a former President. In 1826 he accepted the appointment as regent of the University of Virginia, as being not inconsistent with his views of the entire retirement from public life becoming an ex-President. He took an active interest in the affairs of his own neighborhood and discharged the duties of a local magistrate.

In 1826, Governor Tyler of Virginia was elected to serve in the United States Senate. This left the office of chief magistrate open. Since the governor in Virginia was elected by the legislature, Mr. James McIlhany, on the advice of that body, wrote to Monroe, asking if he would consent to serve again as governor. In refusing, Monroe wrote that the situation had aroused his "sensibility" in a high degree:

"Having commenced my public service in very early life, under the good opinion & suffrage of my fellow citizens of my native State, and been plac'd in many important trusts by the General Assembly, nothing could be more gratifying to me, after so long a service in other trusts, than to return to the station which I formerly held, & to the society of those who are now members of that body, & of the descendents of others with whose good opinion & confidence I was first honored, nor should I hesitate one moment to accept the appointment, should it be conferr'd on me under other circumstances than those which now exist. Such has become the state of my private affairs as to render it impossible for me to withdraw my attention from them, even for a short period, without being involved in absolute ruin."[30]

Probably the most important public service which Monroe rendered in retirement was that to his native state of Virginia. Here the privileged class was fortified behind property qualifications and an allotment of legislative seats by which the small slaveholding counties of the East outvoted the large and populous counties of the West. Large numbers of western men became so discouraged in the futile fight for equality that there was a notable exodus to the Northwest Territory. For fifty years a convention for the purpose of amending the Constitution had been petitioned and fought for. At length the project had been carried by popular vote, a few weeks before the presidential election of 1828. Both Madison and Monroe were nominated as candidates and, although Monroe, at least, was in favor of such a convention,[31] both at first apparently refused. In March, 1829, Monroe wrote to Madison: "I understand that you have been nominated as a candidate for the approaching convention, & have declined serving. A like nomination has been made of me, as I am informed, and I think that I shall follow your example."[32] Sometime during that summer both men reversed their decisions, for when the convention met on October 5, 1829, both were among the ninety-six members, which included some of the most brilliant personages of the day—Marshall, Upshur, Doddridge, Tazewell, and Randolph of Roanoke.[33] Madison nominated Monroe to preside, and, in the absence of any other nominations, Marshall conducted him to the chair.

Monroe's patience, tolerance, and complete understanding of the seriousness of the fundamental issues involved were of inestimable value in presiding over the stormy debates of the next two and one-half months. Ostensibly it was a question of representation, but in

Last Years of a Great American

reality it was the slavery issue in another guise, and men whose passions were aroused in a struggle over this as yet only smouldering issue, were difficult to handle. It was essentially a contest between the eastern and the western counties. The former, represented by the large slaveowners, demanded a representation based on both property and numbers, while the latter, who saw no reason to give slaveholders a voice in the government out of proportion to their numerical strength, when at the same time white men with no property were denied the ballot, sought white manhood suffrage. Under the old system of representation the West, in urgent need of roads, canals, and bridges to facilitate the exportation of their produce, was unable to secure these because outvoted by the East. The eastern counties, at the same time, being taxed for their slaves and therefore paying the greatest amount of revenue, situated as their cities were on the navigable rivers near to the sea, had no need of internal improvements. They saw no need for pouring state revenues across the mountains. In reality, slavery was the stumbling block. Although the western counties wanted to gain numbers to get approriations for public works and disclaimed the idea of any attack on slavery, nevertheless the East was apprehensive.

When Lafayette, an antislavery enthusiast, had heard of the proposed convention, he wrote to Monroe: "Oh! how proud and elated I should feel if something could be contrived in your Convention whereby Virginia, who was the first to petition against the slave trade and afterwards forbid it, who has published the first declaration of rights, would take an exalted station among the promoters of measures tending first to meliorate, then gradually to abolish the slave mode of labor."[34] Monroe, too, appreciated the underlying difficulty. In an address to the convention in November, he said, "I am satisfied, if no such thing as slavery existed, that the people of the Atlantic border would meet their brethren of the west upon the basis of a majority of the free white population."[35]

But Virginia was not destined to lead the way. The elderly statesmen assembled at Richmond, most of them strict constructionists, slaveholders, and fearful of the increasing power and prominence of the West, were unequal to the task. The result was a virtual victory for the eastern counties. There was an extension of the suffrage, with the retention of the moderate property basis. The reallotment

JAMES MONROE

of the seats in the Assembly had gained 41 per cent of the legislature for the West, which had formerly held but 33 per cent.

Late in January, 1830, with the work of the convention finished, Monroe turned homeward. Being in bad health, he preferred steamboat conveyance homeward as far as possible. Disembarking at Norfolk he went to Washington for a visit at the home of Mr. Ringgold. John Quincy Adams, who also happened to be in the city at the time, came to see him and was struck by his emaciated appearance.[36] The occasion was memorable, for it was the first instance of two former presidents' having been in Washington at the same time.[37]

By the end of his second term Monroe had well earned a quiet and untroubled retirement, and probably no president had greater cause to believe that the evening of life might be spent in tranquillity and repose. Not without reason were his eight years of office termed the Era of Good Feeling, and there seemed to be not a spot on the public record to indicate that a peaceful retirement should not be his.

He knew Adams to be a strong individualist, with ideas of his own, and therefore very unlikely to consult him frequently for advice, and he knew that no faction of the rising parties hung upon his favor. Yet, not only were his last years harassed with the humiliating struggles of pride and poverty and constant illnesses, but he was dragged unnecessarily into the bitter intrigues, the furious rivalries, and the jostling ambitions engendered by the stagnation of national issues. Again and again he was called upon to make involved written defenses of his conduct and policies while in office. Only death freed him from the unwelcome and uncalled-for publicity which transformed his later life into a nightmare.

The idea was slowly forming which was to burst forth as a practical policy in the next administration—the spoils system. Appointments to public office were to be won not by merit, but as rewards for having assisted in electing the successful candidate. Adams was sharply criticized for retaining in office men held over from the previous administration. John McLean had been appointed postmaster general by Monroe, during his second term, to replace Meigs, at the latter's death. Adams, feeling that McLean had performed excellent service in revamping the department, and not anticipating any personal hostility on his part, reappointed him to his own Cabinet. But McLean, a follower of Calhoun, who was now in the Jackson

Last Years of a Great American

camp, thoroughly disapproved of the manner in which Clay had been brought into the Cabinet and, in addition, criticized the administration in general. Clay, on his part, besought Adams to remove this hostile Cabinet member. Adams was probably well aware of McLean's activity [38] and his use of his large patronage for the opposition, for in a *Diary* entry in the spring of 1827, he states: "There is an opinion abroad that McLean is hostile to the Administration, which he, however, very earnestly disclaims. His conduct is ambiguous, and he is much devoted to Calhoun, bearing also no friendship to Mr. Clay. This position and these dealings have prompted him to acts adverse in their effects to the Administration, and give countenance to the prevailing opinion of his hostility to it. As he is an able and efficient officer, I have made every allowance for the peculiarity of his situation, and have not believed him wilfully treacherous." [39] Adams refused to violate his principles and at the expense of his own popularity retained McLean.

McLean had always been attached to Monroe, and kept up a filial correspondence with him. In these letters of 1826 and 1827 McLean echoed Monroe's sentiments in outlining the type of conduct he intended to follow in the public strife and party proscription. He would be absolutely impartial in carrying out his official duties and would decline to take an active partisan course of any kind. And yet, his letters to Monroe constantly referred to the poor methods of the administration, cast aspersions on Clay, and in a veiled manner tried to enlist the former President's sympathies on the side of Calhoun and Jackson. He even went so far as to suggest that he visit Monroe to discuss in private those affairs relating to the future candidates which ought not to be entrusted to correspondence. Monroe replied that he deemed it unwise for a visit at that time in view of the "state of the public mind," and refused to be committed to one side or the other. "It has been my object since I left office," he explained, "as it was before, to take no part in the election between the competitors, & in which I have been guided equally by feeling & principle. I had given to each, while in office, strong proofs of confidence & regard, which I have wished to preserve. To be made a partizan of either against the other, in the pending contest, would be very distressing to me." [40]

On the whole, McLean's covert thrusts at the administration

JAMES MONROE

escaped Monroe, who was probably pleased to hear his own views echoed so patly. Schouler suggests that Monroe found in McLean ready sympathy for his pecuniary distress which others had denied.[41] Be that as it may, Monroe approved of McLean's course in general, and praised his management of the Postoffice Department.[42]

Men high in the administration made a strong bid to bring Monroe out on the side of Adams. It was through their intervention that he came once again to sword's point with hot-tempered Jackson. In the summer of 1826 Southard, Secretary of War, and personal enemy of Jackson, in a private dinner party conversation at Fredericksburg, Virginia, criticized the defense of New Orleans in the War of 1812 and praised Monroe's activity as Secretary of War. He attributed to the latter much of the merit of saving the city. An exaggerated account of the incident was immediately relayed to Jackson. He was furious and, regarding the charge as officially made by the administration against him, dispatched a severe letter through Samuel Houston to Southard, demanding an explanation. Southard denied he had intended a reflection on the General's military conduct.

Meanwhile, Jackson's followers were preparing revenge on the Adamsites. At the annual banquet celebrating the anniversary of the victory at New Orleans, friends of Jackson charged Monroe with neglect during the siege and asserted that Jackson was the real hero. A Tennessee newspaper then took up this counter-charge and publicly declared that Monroe, then Secretary of War, did not support Jackson fairly in that military expedition.[43]

Monroe, already annoyed at the way Jackson's followers were slighting his claims in Congress, was thoroughly aroused. He undertook to refute the editor of the Tennessee paper. Writing to Senator White of Tennessee he offered to submit documents in substantiation of his claim that he had given all possible aid to the operations in Louisiana.[44] The letter contained an account of the intricate details of the campaign and the provisions for implements of war, and quoted all letters and orders pertinent thereto. Monroe closed with the assertion that his object in writing was "to remove erroneous impressions, by making you acquainted with all the facts belonging to the case."[45] While the reply reassured White, it failed to placate Jackson, who froze toward Monroe. Thus, though sincerely wishing to refrain from any participation in the political turmoil, Monroe

Brown Brothers

OAK HILL, MONROE'S HOME IN LOUDOUN COUNTY

With the exception of the piazza on the right, this view of the mansion is much the same as in Monroe's day. It was built by Monroe from plans drawn by Thomas Jefferson and executed by James Hoban, architect and builder of the White House. The Monroes first occupied it in April, 1823.

OAK HILL TODAY

This façade, the same as the one above, shows additions made in the remodeling of the mansion.

Courtesy of Mr. Frank C. Littleton

Upper left, the entrance hall of Oak Hill. The walls, the floor, the fan-light, and the lock are the same as in Monroe's day. *Upper right*, one of the two marble mantels sent to Monroe by Lafayette.

Below, a view of Oak Hill from the northeast. The driveway was laid out by Monroe. These views used by courtesy of Mr. Frank C. Littleton.

Last Years of a Great American

was drawn in by the necessity of defending his own honor.

Southard and the Adams leaders, having succeeded in embroiling Monroe with Jackson, now made further overtures to lure him into the 1828 presidential struggle on the side of Adams. They wished to have Madison and Monroe head the electoral ticket in Virginia. This request was sent to Monroe informally through his son-in-law, Mr. Hay, of Richmond. Upon receipt of it he wrote to Madison, enclosing the request. In declaring his intention of refusing the offer, he assumed that Madison likewise would decline.[46] In his letter to Colonel Hugh Mercer, refusing the honor on the grounds of his near relationship to both candidates and his desire to preserve friendly relations with them in the future, he stated: "Persons who have so long served their country in its highest offices, especially in the late one, as Mr. Madison and I have done, should take no part in contests of this kind. No questions excite more feeling, or, notwithstanding their importance, are more of a personal nature, than those relating to election to office.

"Believing, as I do, that the public interest might be injured, and could not be benefited by my service, in the instance referred to, and feeling that I should be subjected to great pain should I be called on, I repeat my earnest hope that such call may not be made."[47]

Meanwhile the gazettes and newspapers had got hold of and printed the information that Monroe and Madison had been approached. The official nomination did not arrive until February 21, 1828, the lapse of time placing both men in an equivocal position. Monroe immediately wrote a formal refusal to Brooke, stating it was his earnest desire to cherish tranquillity in his retirement, and urging Brooke to publish his refusal immediately. "Having held, in the office from which I lately retired, a very friendly relation with both the candidates," he explained, "& given to each strong proofs of confidence & regard, it would be very repugnant to my feelings to take the part of either, against the other. . . . Those who have held the office of Chief Magistrate, should abstain, after their retirement, from becoming partisans in subsequent elections to that office."[48] Both Monroe and Madison were highly displeased when early in March the officers of the convention had not yet published their intentions of remaining neutral. Another stiff note to Brooke secured the requested action.

JAMES MONROE

Fully to appreciate the futility, bitterness, and rancour of the public quarrel into which Monroe was drawn, it is necessary to understand the relations existing between the leading candidates for the presidential chair and the tactics which each pursued to further his own cause.

Almost before Adams completed delivering his inaugural address, the factions were planning their campaigns and grooming their candidates for the next election. Crawford, though not fully recovered from his paralytic stroke of the year before, was back in the active political conspiracy to prevent Calhoun's alignment with Jackson. Calhoun, the South Carolinian, college bred, socially prominent, and long experienced, strongly nationalistic at this point, was veering toward Jackson, in the hope that by deferring his own burning presidential ambitions for one term and throwing his support to Jackson, he might secure Jackson's aid in elevating himself to the presidency in 1832. The Tennessee faction supporting Jackson found in Martin Van Buren, the astute political adviser, of New York, a welcome ally in resisting the threatened domination of the party by Calhoun. The Adams-Clay following, though small, was well organized and, in addition to the tactics we have already noted, bitterly attacked Jackson. They brought up all the early squabbles of his life, the Florida executions, his quarrel with Callava, and the irregularity of his marriage ceremony.

Jackson's friendship with Calhoun dated from the Seminole War, which began late in 1817. Jackson, stimulated by his intense hatred for Clay, who steered the charges against him in the House on his Florida activities, turned to Calhoun, believing him to be the one man in the administration who had supported him. In reality, Calhoun had stated that he believed Jackson ought to be court-martialed, while Adams had staunchly supported the warhorse.[49] Calhoun, coldly calculating, never corrected this misunderstanding and, after the 1824 election, offered his support to Jackson for the reason already mentioned. By 1828 the *Daily Telegraph*, the official newspaper of the party, run by Duff Green, a Calhoun supporter, announced Jackson and Calhoun as the Democratic-Republican ticket.

In the meanwhile, however, a dangerous rift had appeared in this friendship. About the time Monroe wrote to Senator White defending his actions at New Orleans, the anti-Calhoun faction, jealous of

Last Years of a Great American

the ascendancy Calhoun was acquiring in the party, started its work. Sam Houston got hold of a letter written September 9, 1818, by Monroe to Calhoun. This letter pointed out that while the blame for the Florida upheaval should be placed upon Spain for failure to enforce the Treaty of 1795, and while Jackson should be shielded and supported as much as possible, nevertheless the administration did not approve of the insubordination of the Florida invader.[50] This was something new to Jackson, for he had always understood that the administration had tacitly approved and that Calhoun had warmly defended him. When this purloined letter arrived at the Hermitage, Jackson was furious, and declared, "It smelled so much of deception that my hair stood on end for one hour."[51] Although Calhoun realized that a letter had been taken from him he did not know its identity until a year later. Meanwhile Jackson's wrath waxed warmer against Monroe, for he felt Calhoun had been instrumental in acquainting him with the letter in an attempt to show Monroe's falsity.

Early in 1827 the plot thickened, with the entrance upon the scene of another band of mischief-makers. Crawford, too ill to be in politics but intent upon keeping Calhoun from the vice-presidency, used the services of his henchmen to charge Calhoun with duplicity in the Seminole affair. Charges and counter charges flew thick and fast, both Calhoun and Crawford nervously appealing to their late Cabinet associates, and particularly to Monroe, for information to substantiate their accusations and defenses. Once again Monroe was aroused to defend himself, for this battle involved more than veiled insinuations that he had misused Jackson, more than an attempt to bring him out in favor of one candidate or another. It was a direct attack upon his honor. For among the issues of veracity raised between the two was Crawford's challenge of the receipt and use made by Calhoun of Jackson's January letter.

As noted elsewhere in this narrative, Monroe had been the recipient in January, 1818, of a letter from Jackson, written just before the General received his orders to march into Florida. This letter, in which Jackson stated that if Monroe were to signify to him, unofficially, through John Rhea, the desire of the United States to gain immediate possession of the Floridas, it would be accomplished in sixty days, was received at the White House while Monroe was ill. He gave it to Calhoun to read, who did so and who informed

JAMES MONROE

Monroe that it was marked "Confidential" and related to Florida.[52] When Calhoun told Monroe that Jackson's orders had already gone forward, the President laid aside the letter and forgot about it until Calhoun reminded him of it in connection with Jackson's explanation of his conduct in Florida.*

Monroe's explanation contemporaneous with the event seemed to satisfy Jackson, for he made no reply.[53] And so the matter rested until 1827, when Calhoun and Crawford resurrected it in their feud.

That Monroe sensed an attack upon himself is obvious from the letter he wrote to Calhoun in December, 1827, in which he said, "It would be very gratifying to me to know by whom, and from what quarter, this attack on me has been meditated.... I have been much annoyed in this way ever since my retirement, which is the more extraordinary because I am satisfied that I have not given just cause for it to anyone."[54]

Monroe generously placed all his correspondence on the affair at the disposal of Calhoun to enable him to meet Crawford's fraudulent charges and to reinstate himself in Jackson's esteem. To clear himself of the charge of having injured Jackson, he detailed at great length the four occasions when he had sustained Jackson, largely on his own responsibility—in his resistance to the order of the War Department, in the Pensacola episode, in Jackson's trouble with Fromentin while Governor of Florida, and in the proof of his good intentions indicated by his appointment of Jackson as minister to Mexico. To Calhoun he wrote, "In regard to Genl. Jackson, I am not only free from this charge of injuring him, but have done him, in many instances, the most essential services, have sustained him in measures, on my own responsibility, and at great hazard, and much abuse, which, without such support, would have fallen heavy on him, if they had not had a more serious effect....

"I am no partisan between the candidates, and wish not, by persecution on one, to be thrown, apparently, before the public into the opposite scale."[55]

He solemnly reiterated the explanation of Jackson's letter, which he had given to Jackson in 1818. Not only that, but he amplified his explanation with a statement which proved to be of great value in the light of subsequent events:

---

*The account of Monroe's receipt of this letter is given above in Chapter XXX.

Last Years of a Great American

"I asked Mr. Rhea, in a conversation, whether he had ever intimated to Genl. Jackson his opinion that the administration had no objection to his making an attack on Pensacola, and he declared that he never had. I did not know, if the Genl. had written to him to the same effect that he had to me, as I had not read his letter . . . that he might have led me innocently into a conversation in which, wishing to obtain Florida, I might have expressed a sentiment from which he might have drawn that inference. But he assured me that no such conversation ever passed between us. I did not apprize him of the letter which I had received from the General on the subject, being able to ascertain my object without doing it."[56]

During 1828 the bitterness of the feud appeared to wane. The election was approaching, and while there was a marked coolness between Calhoun and Jackson, they were both running on the same ticket and apparently headed for success. Calhoun continued to communicate with Monroe, and although the Jackson affair was discussed time and again, a new theme gradually crept into the correspondence. The presidential fever which burned in Calhoun's blood and shaped and colored every idea and movement, was gradually transforming the man. Early in his career, a national of nationals and a fervent protectionist, advocating a national policy of internal improvements, by 1828 he was the leading exponent of states rights. In opposing the high protective tariff of 1828, he enunciated the later doctrine with which he has become forever identified—the doctrine of nullification: the right of a state to deny coercion by the federal government, the right of a state to secede from the Union.

While in his 1828 correspondence with Monroe there is nothing to indicate that he actually championed so radical a doctrine as secession, nevertheless in discussing the unfavorable reaction of the southerners to the tariff, he considered it perfectly within the realm of possibility. He wrote Monroe, "I feel confident that the attachment to the Union remains unbroken with the great body of our citizens. Yet it cannot be disguised that the system pushed to the present extreme acts most unequally in its pressure on the several parts, which has of necessity a most pernicious tendency on the feelings of the oppressed portions."[57]

It was perfectly possible to discern, in his brilliant dogmas of the evil wrought by unequal tariff laws and the proper remedy for that evil, a parallel in resisting federal coercion on the slave problem. Certainly the South soon buttressed itself with his theories, and Monroe, being a southerner, readily understood. But being a southerner with comprehensive views of public policy above narrow sectionalism and petty partisanship, he foresaw with amazing clarity the dire results of such a procedure—disunion and death on many bloody battlefields. Assuming the rôle of fatherly adviser, with unerring accuracy he sought to point out to Calhoun the fallacies in his reasoning and to urge him, in the interest of his country, to return to less radical ways. He wrote:

"As to the Union, all movements which menace, or even suggest the least danger to it, cannot fail to have an ill effect. None of the States are so deeply interested, according to my best judgment, in its preservation, as the Southern. Rivalry, restraints on intercourse, would immediately ensue, under partial confederacies, or any other arrangements, which could be formed, the pernicious consequences of which may easily be conceived. Hostility and wars would be inevitable, whereby our free system of government would be overwhelmed. The Southern States would soon become a scene of the most frightful calamities, because their slaves would be incited to insurrection. It is my candid opinion, if there is any portion of the Union which ought to feel peculiar solicitude for its preservation, it is those States, as it likewise is that they should promote the connection and dependence of the several states on each other, by intercourse, commerce, & every practicable means tending to obliterate local distinctions, diffuse a common feeling, and bind the Union by the strongest ties of interest & affection, more closely together."[58]

And again, in January of 1829, he pointedly joined the slave and tariff issues:

"My own views are founded in experience and a particular consideration of the state of the southern country, and especially when the slaves exceed in number the white population. We should provoke no issue to shake the system. The best way is to let the experiment operate, and appeal to other motives in case the result should correspond with anticipations. To appeal to disunion may have a different effect; and if the power to regulate trade is to have no internal operation whatever, may not eastern and western States find it for their interest to break off?"[59]

Last Years of a Great American

Calhoun, however, was not to be dissuaded. In his doctrine of nullification he saw the flaming banner beneath which the South would rally under his leadership. Realizing that Jackson's friendship grew daily more tenuous and his support in 1832 accordingly less probable, Calhoun clutched at this as his last means of securing the coveted presidency.

Meanwhile, his implacable foes, unable to prevent his becoming vice-president but intent on scotching his hopes of election to the presidency, had set on foot another plot, which once again involved Monroe and further wearied his already over-burdened shoulders. The spring of 1830 was decided upon to deliver the *coup de grâce* to Calhoun's hopes—to disclose to Jackson the secrets of Monroe's Cabinet debates of 1818.

Although Calhoun was the vice-president, he and his friends in the Cabinet were practically excluded from the confidence of Jackson. That worthy Democrat trusted Van Buren, his Secretary of State, and sought advice from his now famous Kitchen Cabinet, an unofficial group comprised of William B. Lewis, Blair, J. Hamilton, and Donelson. The President and his running mate became even more estranged as the result of the furor over Mrs. Eaton. Eaton, a Cabinet member, had chosen to marry a Mrs. Timberlake, a lady of questionable character and totally unacceptable to Washington society. Mrs. Calhoun led the social boycott in which every worthy matron participated. Jackson regarded this combination to discredit Eaton as a personal affront and charged Calhoun with fomenting the conspiracy. Added to this was the fact that by 1830 Calhoun was thoroughly committed to states' rights, whereas Jackson was more national in his point of view. The time was ripe for the blow which the Kitchen Cabinet members, Lewis and Hamilton, with the connivance of Governor Forsyth, of Georgia, and Crawford, had been preparing.

In 1828, James Hamilton, son of Alexander Hamilton and an old Crawfordite, got in touch with Crawford through Governor Forsyth. Through him he learned that it was really Calhoun and not Crawford who had opposed Jackson in the Cabinet of 1818 and had proposed a court-martial. This information was immediately relayed to Major Lewis, Jackson's unofficial campaign manager.

The following month Monroe was Jackson's dinner guest, along with Lewis, Eaton, and Tench Ringgold, the marshal of the District.

JAMES MONROE

There was a great appearance of cordiality between the two Presidents as they sat side by side at the table in earnest conversation. During dinner Ringgold, in his enthusiasm for his close friend Monroe, innocently remarked that in 1818 Monroe had been the only member of the government who favored Jackson in the Seminole affair. Lewis then made the assertion that Calhoun, too, had been on his side. After the guests left, Lewis and Eaton passed a few side remarks on the subject, and when pressed for an explanation by Jackson they informed him of the existence of the Forsyth letter and its accusation of Calhoun. He insisted upon getting a statement to that effect directly from Crawford.

The following April 15, at the Jefferson birthday dinner, Jackson threw down the gauntlet with his famous toast to Calhoun, "Our Federal Union, it must be preserved." The next month Crawford's letter arrived and on the thirteenth of May, Jackson furiously sent the whole correspondence to the surprised and dismayed Calhoun. As Schouler states, this was to Calhoun like a fatal stab in the back just as he had the presidency practically within his grasp. He acknowledged Jackson's letter and promised to reply fully. His twenty-two-page response, more closely resembling a legal brief, betrayed the tenacity and depth of his national aspirations. Instead of answering the charges or refusing to discuss Cabinet confidences, he admitted the charge in substance, and spent the greater part of the letter in vilifying Crawford and denouncing the whole thing as a plot of enemies.

Immediately both Calhoun and Crawford again appealed to Monroe and other members of his Cabinet. A curious issue then arose regarding Jackson's January letter. Crawford charged Calhoun with suppressing the knowledge it contained, while the latter thrust back with the accusation that Crawford had stolen the letter from the files of the War Department. Crawford, in turn, maintained that the letter was read in the Cabinet after the fall of Pensacola, while Calhoun denied it had been.

In a letter to Calhoun, Monroe reviewed the already threadbare tale of the circumstances attendant upon the reception of the letter and added, "Mr. Crawford came in soon afterwards, (just after the letter had arrived) and I handed it also to him, for perusal. He read it, and returned it, in like manner, without making any comment on its contents, further than it related to the Seminole War, or something to that effect. I never shewed it to any other person. . . . You ask whether that letter was before the Cabinet, in the deliberation on the despatches received from the General communicating the result of that war, or alluded to by any member of the administration. My impression decidedly is that it was not before the Cabinet, nor do I recollect, or think that it was alluded to in the deliberation on the subject. Had it been I could not, I presume, have forgotten it."[60]

In short, both Calhoun and Crawford knew of the existence of that letter, and what it contained. Calhoun insisted that it had never been read in the Cabinet, and therefore Crawford must have stolen it from the files. The latter, on the other hand, maintained it had been read in Cabinet meeting by Monroe, at the insistence of Calhoun. The preponderance of evidence seems to uphold Monroe's assertion that it was not brought into consideration in 1818 at all, and that shortly after its reception, and without having been read by him, he handed the letter to each of them separately. "Had I read the Genl.'s letter when I recd. it," reiterated Monroe, "I should never have shewn it to anyone. . . . Coming from the commanding general I concluded that it must relate either to men or money, & therefore handed it to the heads of each department, as he entered, but as neither suggested anything of the kind, the subject being disposed of, the letter was deposited with other papers, & forgotten when I arose from my sick bed."[61] To the other members of that Cabinet, Adams and Wirt, the knowledge of the letter came as a complete surprise, and both furnished Calhoun with testimony which upheld his contention that the letter had never been brought up before the Cabinet.

In May Calhoun journeyed to Oak Hill to visit Monroe, for the first time since his retirement, and to thank him for his generous and disinterested offices. Again the whole matter was discussed, and Monroe evidently sought to convince Calhoun that in the best interests of his country he ought to drop the matter and cease trying to injure Jackson, for the day after his visit he wrote to Calhoun: "Any step which might be considered as an attack on him [J], at the present time, might have an ill effect on the individual, and likewise on public concerns. The period is eminently delicate & interesting for our country, & its system of govt., and therefore great caution, in every political movement, or which may have that bearing, especially by those in high public trusts, is peculiarly proper."[62] At this point there came a lull in the hostilities which was not renewed until early the following spring.

Beset on all sides with financial difficulties, embroiled in the personal wranglings of presidential aspirants, and forced to defend his conduct against base calumnies, Monroe sought solace in the company of his family and friends, in long rides and conversations, in laboring personally on his farm, and even in the unwonted task of writing a treatise on free government. This work, entitled *A Comparison of the American Republic with the Republics of Greece and Rome*, was privately printed and circulated among his closer friends.

It was his habit, each morning and evening, to ride over the countryside, alone or accompanied by whichever of his numerous friends happened to be visiting at Oak Hill. The humblest slave he chanced to pass was addressed as respectfully and as courteously questioned as to the state of his health and that of his family as though he were a member of the gentry. And then there were the numerous Visitors' meetings and faculty reports to be made in connection with the University of Virginia. After Jefferson's death in 1826, he and Madison drew closer and frequently made their inspection tours together.

Primarily Monroe was a family man, and certainly what happiness he found these last few years was in his immediate family circle. In June of 1829, in keeping with the family tradition of privacy, a small and rather quiet wedding ceremony took place when Monroe's granddaughter, Hortensia Hay, became the bride of Mr. Rogers, of Baltimore. Both Mrs. Hay and Mrs. Gouverneur, with their husbands and children, spent much time at Oak Hill, and the Monroes paid several visits a year, usually in the summer, to the Gouverneurs. The latter had an attractive summer home on the water near Fort Washington, and Mrs. Monroe, always in delicate health, seemed to be invigorated by the refreshing sea breezes. In spite of her recurring illnesses her personal attraction and accomplishments still commanded the affection of many and the respect of all. She possessed that rare trait of personality which enabled her successfully to complement rather than overshadow her less socially gifted husband. For almost half a century, in this country and abroad, in bleak or prosperous times, she had shared all his hopes and fears, his successes and reverses.

Last Years of a Great American

When in the fall of 1828 Monroe suffered a serious fall from his horse and lay motionless on the ground for about twenty minutes before a neighbor, Mr. Lucket, found him and took him home, Mrs. Monroe herself nursed him through the fever and shock.[63] Again the following spring, when he was incapacitated by an injury to his wrist, she did much of his writing for him.

There came a day when this comfort, too, was denied to Monroe, for on September 23, 1830, his wife died. He was grief-stricken and, unable to realize that the ultimate had arrived, deferred her burial several days. He had designed a vault on the property for her remains as well as his, and the work was not yet quite complete. Judge E. R. Watson of Charlottesville was a house guest at the time death occurred, and he has left a vivid description of Monroe's loss: "I shall never forget the touching grief manifested by the old man on the morning after Mrs. Monroe's death, when he sent for me to go to his room and with trembling frame and streaming eyes spoke of the long years they had spent happily together, and expressed in strong terms his conviction that he would soon follow her."[64]

Monroe was right. With her sudden loss, all of his hopes faded rapidly. Mr. Hay, his son-in-law, died soon after Mrs. Monroe, and after their departure the elderly statesman found his lonely farm life insupportable. The kindly condolences and visits of friends and neighbors could not fill the void, nor could the affectionately sympathetic letter from Lafayette, who wrote, "The papers have confirmed my fears of your pecuniary situation being still worse than I had for a long time apprehended. Under those circumstances, there is great need of her and your fortitude. My feelings on every account it were superfluous to express. The settlement of your claims has been left open. May the actual session finish what the last one has begun!"[65]

It was just about the time of this most personal of all his misfortunes that Monroe abandoned all hope of aid from Congress. Accordingly, he made provisions for a caretaker to look after his property, and in November he went up to New York to make his home with Mr. and Mrs. Gouverneur. Monroe's son-in-law had been appointed postmaster of New York City by John Quincy Adams. The Gouverneurs owned a modest little dutch-roofed dwelling at Prince and Marion Streets, near the Bowery, and here Monroe made his last home. Their proximity to the water front enabled him to spend much

JAMES MONROE

time inspecting the shipping and harbor defenses. To the small boys in the neighborhood he was a familiar and kindly figure in his black velvet or satin knee breeches and buckled shoes.[66]

On the whole, however, Monroe led the life of a recluse. Most people had no idea that he was residing in New York until they heard of his death. His recent bereavement, his pecuniary distress, and his illness all prompted him to seek seclusion. One exception, however, he did make, and that was to preside over a great meeting in Tammany Hall, November 26, 1830, to celebrate the dethronement of Charles X, of France.[67] It was his last public appearance. The recurring illnesses which had hindered so much of his activity during his retirement and to which he constantly alluded in his correspondence had developed into a racking cough, which confined him to his bed for days at a time. Accurate diagnosis was a rare thing in those days and nowhere does Monroe mention anything more specific than a cough, but the fact that his physician prescribed a Saratoga rest would seem to indicate a tubercular condition. In March he wrote to Dr. Charles Everett, "I am free from pain, but my cough annoys me much, both night and day. I take no medicine but to moderate it, such as syrup of horehound, horehound candy & my physician, Dr. Bibby, thinks that I am too much reduced to take any medicine which should operate on the liver, & that, when the season permits, exercise, and the Saratoga waters will relieve me."[68]

The same letter sadly announced the offer of his Loudoun estate for sale. This was a melancholy day for Monroe—to be forced to part with the home so intimately connected with his beloved wife, for they had planned it together and spent so much of their time there. He unburdened his heart to Madison: "It is very distressing to me to sell my property in Loudoun, for besides parting with all I have in the State, I indulged a hope, if I could retain it, that I might be able occasionally to visit it, and meet my friends, or many of them, there. But ill health and advanced years prescribe a course which we must pursue."[69] He concluded by bidding Madison a final farewell, feeling that the possibility of ever seeing him again was rather remote. Shortly after this Adams, on his way through New York to Massachusetts, stopped off for a visit. He found Monroe confined to his bed, very feeble and emaciated. Although Adams realized it would be the last time he would see Monroe alive, he dared

Last Years of a Great American

not stay long, for even the slightest exertion of speaking left Monroe completely exhausted.[70]

The old Virginian grew daily weaker, and yet once again his privacy was destined to be invaded by events on the national stage. Calhoun and Jackson were almost reconciled when, in the spring of 1831, Calhoun's advisers felt he should publish the entire Seminole correspondence, in an attempt to ruin Van Buren, whom they believed to be the author of the whole disturbance. He did so in February, using Duff Green's *Telegraph* as a vehicle. It carried an explanatory address to the people, and for the first time the public became aware of the breach which existed among Calhoun, Jackson, and Crawford. Even Monroe had not fully appreciated the intensity of the hatred smouldering among the members of this triumvirate. He wrote to Adams, "With the origin of Genl. Jackson's variance with Mr. Crawford, & of that between the latter and Mr. Calhoun, I am ignorant. I knew at an early period that much hostility existed between the two former, and that the two latter had no friendly communication with each other."[71]

Once again the issues of the Seminole War burned brightly, while both Calhoun and Crawford, in their rancorous feud, turned again to Monroe, to Adams, and to Crowninshield, former Secretary of the Navy, seeking additional information with which to implement the additional pamphlets they planned to publish in the *Globe* and the *Telegraph*.

In this controversy Jackson took no open part, but his political staff was investigating the military conduct of 1818-1819 and concocting a fantastic plan. John Rhea, the man through whom, in 1818, Monroe was to have given to Jackson the sly hint to capture the Floridas, and who had already assured Monroe that he had never communicated such a wish to Jackson,[72] was drawn into the plot. He wrote an amazing letter to Monroe in an attempt to trap him into a correspondence which would admit that he had connived at a treacherous seizure of the Floridas and had actually dropped the desired hint to Rhea to transmit to Jackson. Sixteen days before Monroe died this strange letter, demanding to know whether Monroe had "received a confidential letter from Andrew Jackson, dated January 6th, 1818," was delivered to 66 Prince Street. It read, in part: "I had many confidential conversations with you respecting General

Jackson at that period. You communicated to me that confidential letter, or its substance, approved the opinion of Jackson therein expressed and did authorize me to write to him. He says he received my letter on his way to Fort Scott, and acted accordingly. After that War a question was raised in your Cabinet as to General Jackson's authority and that question was got over. I know that General Jackson was in Washington in January, 1819, and my confidential letter was probably in his possession. You requested me to request General Jackson to burn that letter, in consequence of which I asked General Jackson, and he promised to do so. He has since informed me that, April 12, 1819, he did burn it."[73]

Mr. Gouverneur, who acted as Monroe's private secretary, was considerably upset. He realized the gravity of the charge, especially since it was made at a time when Monroe was very ill, but he hesitated to act alone and sent the letter to William Wirt, former attorney general, and close friend of Monroe's. Of the letter he said, "It is a singular production and seems to have some singular object in view. The lapse of time since the subject of it became a matter of discussion and the most extraordinary statement of the burning of a letter of the most vital consequence to the possessor strike me with singular effect. All the statements respecting conversations with Mr. Monroe I know from his own lips to be false and unfounded. It is really important that Mr. Monroe should be made acquainted with the contents. I know it would create considerable excitement in his mind and might have an injurious effect. Again, would I be justified in assuming the responsibility of keeping it from him?"[74]

Wirt agreed that a formal statement was absolutely essential and, accordingly, on June 19, 1831, sensitive to the honor of his acts, in the presence of witnesses, Monroe made a deposition to the effect that the statements of Rhea's letter to him, then read for the first time, were utterly false. The deposition read as follows:

"A letter of John Rhea of Tennessee is shown to me this 19th day of June, 1831, for the first time, nor have I previously had any intimation of the receipt of such a letter or its contents. It was received by Mr. Gouverneur, as I am told by him, and after having been read, kept from me, for reasons which he will explain, until this time. Had it been communicated to me before, I should have made, as I do now, the following declaration and reply thereto, which I wish to be filed with the said letter as my reply to its contents.

Last Years of a Great American

"1st. It is utterly unfounded and untrue that I ever authorized John Rhea to write any letter whatever to General Jackson, authorizing or encouraging him to disobey, or deviate from the orders, which had been communicated to him from the Department of War.

"2nd. That it is utterly unfounded and untrue that I ever desired the said John Rhea to request General Jackson to destroy any letter written by him, the said John Rhea, to General Jackson, nor did I at any time wish or desire that any letter, document or memorandum, in the possession of General Jackson, in respect to the Seminole War, or any other public matter should be destroyed.

"A note applicable to this subject will be found among my papers at Oak Hill, in Virginia, to which, as well as to my whole correspondence with General Jackson, as well as others, I refer for the truth of this statement."75

This statement was signed by Monroe and declared to be true in the presence of two witnesses, a Mr. Gelston and Mr. Edward M. Greenway.

That the entire affair was purely a trumped up scheme was very obvious. A dispassionate consideration of the evidence indicates that as early as 1818 Monroe satisfied Jackson that he had never read his January letter. At a later date Rhea assured Monroe that Monroe had neither inadvertently dropped a remark alluding to the desirability of obtaining the Floridas nor had he, Rhea, transmitted any such hint to Jackson.

Adams knew that Monroe had made a statement *in extremis*, and his indignant and vituperative *Diary* entry was characteristic: "There is a depth of depravity in this transaction at which the heart sickens."76

"The working up of a circumstantial fabrication," Adams continued, "by practicing upon the drivelling dotage of a political parasite, is beyond the comprehension of an honest man. Jackson's excessive anxiety to rest the justification of his invasion of Florida upon a secret, collusive, and unconstitutional correspondence with Mr. Monroe can be explained only by an effort to quiet the stings of his conscience for the baseness of his ingratitude to me. Writhing under the consciousness of the return which he has made to me for saving him from public indignation and defending him triumphantly against the vengeance of Britain and Spain, the impeachment of Congress, the disavowal of Mr. Monroe, and the Court-martial of Calhoun and

Crawford, he struggles to bring his cause before the world and before posterity upon another basis. This basis is itself as rotten as his own heart. It is, that his conquest of Florida was undertaken and accomplished, not, as I had successfully contended for him, upon principles warranted by the law of nations and consistent with the Constitution of the United States, but by a secret fraudulent concert between him and Mr. Monroe. . . . It is fortunate that Mr. Monroe lived and retained his faculties to make a solemn and authentic declaration of the total falsehood of John Rhea's abominable statement."[77]

Here the matter ended, for Rhea kept silence, dying the following year, and the public was undoubtedly sick of the prolonged Seminole War controversy.

Monroe's deposition was his last state paper. He lingered for about two weeks more, and although he retained his faculties to the last, his death was momentarily expected. At half past three in the afternoon of July 4, 1831, five years to the day after the death of Adams and Jefferson, James Monroe's earthly struggles ceased, ending a life marked with vicissitudes as great as had befallen any citizen of the United States since the beginning of its national existence. He was seventy-three years of age.

New York City immediately went into mourning, as it prepared a public funeral for its most distinguished resident. On Thursday afternoon at two o'clock, a squadron of cavalry assembled at the late residence to escort the cortège to the City Hall. Here Monroe's body was deposited on a platform, behind which a temporary stage covered with black cloth had been erected. President Duer, of Columbia, delivered the eulogy, and later, at St. Paul's Episcopal Church, the Reverend Bishop Onderdonk and the Reverend Dr. Wainright officiated at the religious rites. Thousands of people followed the black-and-gold-draped hearse up Broadway to the Marble Cemetery on Second Street, while the detonations of the guns from the battery, firing seventy-three salutes at minute intervals, mingled with the solemn tolling of bells in all sections of the city.[78]

Here Monroe rested in the Gouverneur vault until July of 1858. The previous April, on the centenary of his birth, the legislature of Virginia, desiring that every native president should rest in Virginia soil, made an appropriation for removing the remains to Hollywood Cemetery, in Richmond. With much ceremony the remains were

Last Years of a Great American

placed on board the steamer *Jamestown* and, under the escort of Colonel Duryee and the Seventh New York Regiment, conveyed to Richmond.[79] Occurring as it did, on the eve of the Civil War, the removal excited warm interest throughout the country and momentarily quieted the storm of menacing partisanship.

APPENDIX

APPENDIX

JAMES MONROE'S ANCESTRY

THE APPEARANCE of the first Monroe on the American scene is veiled in obscurity and contradiction. The controversy over the identity of James Monroe's earliest ancestor on this side of the Atlantic has divided scholars into two schools of thought, which the most recent research promises to conciliate.

According to the celebrated student of genealogy, Alexander Mackenzie[1], and to family tradition[2], James Monroe stems from an officer in King Charles's army who was made a prisoner of war after the Battle of Preston on the seventeenth of August, 1648, and banished to Virginia. This Scottish soldier is thought to be the son of David and Agnes Munro of Scotland, of the Munros of Fowlis. Mackenzie describes him as having the rank of major in the Scottish army; Samuel Laurence Gouverneur merely as an "officer"; and Lund Washington, who married the granddaughter of Captain Benjamin Grayson and Susannah Monroe, says "he belonged to an ancient highland clan and was Captain in the service of Charles I."[3]

The version of Andrew Monroe's earliest activities in America given by the other authorities differs in several respects.

In 1644, two years after the struggles between King and Parliament had blazed out into civil strife, reflected on this side of the Atlantic by mounting disquiet in Protestant Virginia and Catholic Maryland, one Richard Ingle, a trouble-making commander of a merchantman, armed a ship and invaded royalist Maryland. For two years, during which he exacted tribute, pillaged plantations, stripped mills of machinery and houses of their locks and hinges—shipping the booty to England—his insurgent government lasted, then collapsed, Ingle fleeing to the mother country. Certain of his supporters made their escape across the border into Virginia.

"It is likely, if not certain," writes James D. Evans, a student of Monroe genealogy, "that Andrew Monroe went to Virginia from Maryland in 1647, with Thomas Youell and Thomas Sturman . . .

JAMES MONROE

[who] originally settled in Kent Isle in the Chesapeake . . . In 1645 Sturman, his son John, and Thomas Youell joined Richard Ingle in a revolt against Leonard Calvert, deputy-governor, and were condemned as rebels . . . They fled to Virginia . . . In 1647/8 Thomas Sturman and Andrew Monroe left St. Mary's and settled near Youell in Westmoreland County." James Evans traces the Andrew Monroe who came to Virginia from St. Mary's county, Maryland back to 1642 in that county.[4]

To complicate the picture still further, the records still preserved in the Virginia State Land Office in Richmond evince that Andrew Munrow (Monroe) had an order for 200 acres of land in the county of Northumberland (later Westmoreland) on 8 June, 1650, due to him for the transportation of four persons into the Colony of Virginia.[5] Andrew Monroe had paid for the transportation of these persons and in return was entitled under the laws of the colony to fifty acres for each person so imported into the colony. On 29 November, 1652, Andrew Monroe was granted 440 acres of land for the transportation of nine persons into the Colony and this further grant is described as "upon a Creek issueing out of Potomack River and South East upon his own plantation." This creek later was called Monroe Creek or Monroe Bay by which names it is yet identified.

According to Lund Washington, who married a descendant of Major Andrew Monroe and interested himself with the family history, Andrew Monroe "in the time of Charles II . . . returned to Scotland and induced others of his family to emigrate and another extensive grant of land . . . was made to him by the crown."

Andrew Monroe was a vestryman in Appamattocks [sic] Parish Westmoreland county in 1661. That he was a gentleman of social standing is certain as he is described in an early Westmoreland county Court Order Book as "Andrew Monroe, Seignior." He died at his plantation on Monroe Creek in 1668.[6]

One way of solving the riddle is suggested by Colonel Brooke Payne and George Harrison Sanford King, who, using the Westmoreland and King George County Records as a basis of study, consider the evidence sufficient for the theory that the Andrew Munro who was the third son of David Munro of Katewell, Scotland, and Agnes Munro, and fought in the Battle of Preston, and the Andrew Munro who fought with Ingle in Maryland are one and the same. Payne

Appendix

and King present the thesis that Andrew Monroe ". . . came first to America about 1642 and settled in St. Mary's County, Maryland, where he lived and we find record of him, moving about 1647 to Virginia and living at Appomattox, Westmoreland county, until about April 1648, when (as intimated in the quotation from Lund Washington) he returned to Scotland, fought in the Battle of Preston with the rank of Major on the 17th of August, 1648, where he was taken prisoner and banished to Virginia—again settling in Westmoreland county where he died in 1668."[7]

The researches of Colonel Payne and Mr. King have also brought to light records which correct an error in the Monroe genealogy as it appears in the Morgan *Life of Monroe*. Andrew Monroe, according to all authorities, married Elizabeth, thought to have been a daughter of a Colonel John Alexander but never proved so. Of this marriage six children were born. A son, Andrew, married Eleanor Spence, and by her had a son, Andrew, and another, Spence. It is this Spence who is described by Lyon G. Tyler as the father of James Monroe, and whose death is dated by him 1774. But the researches of Colonel Payne and Mr. King into the old Court Order Books of Westmoreland County prove this Spence to have died in 1749, nine years before James was born. He married Margaret, daughter of Nathaniel Gray.

The Spence Monroe who was James's father was not descended from the second Andrew Monroe and Eleanor Spence, but from Andrew's brother William Monroe (1666-1737), who married Margaret, daughter of Mr. Thomas Bowcock. Among the seven children of this marriage was the Andrew Monroe who was James's grandfather. This Andrew, called "Sheriff Andrew," as he held that much desired position in Westmoreland County, died in November, 1735. He married Mrs. Christian (Tyler) Monroe, widow of his first cousin Spence Monroe (who died in 1726) and daughter of Charles Tyler, Gentleman, of Westmoreland County. The children of Sheriff Andrew and Christian (Tyler) Monroe were: (1) Andrew (who died in Caroline County, Va. 1775); (2) Spence (who died at the ancestral plantation on Monroe Creek in 1774), and (3) Jane Monroe, who married Mr. John Chancellor (1726-1815).

The above Spence Monroe married, in 1752, Elizabeth Jones, daughter of James Jones, a considerable land holder of King George

JAMES MONROE

County, Virginia, and his wife nee Hester Davis, daughter of Joshua Davis, Gentleman, of Richmond County, Va., a distinguished colonial lawyer of the Northern Neck of Virginia. The issue of Spence and Elizabeth (Jones) Monroe were: Elizabeth, James, Spence, Andrew and Joseph Jones Monroe.

Spence Monroe was one of those bold Virginians who met at Leedstown, Westmoreland County, on 27 February 1766 and grafted a set of resolutions asserting in bold language the rights essential to Civil Liberty. In speaking of these Resolutions of the Westmoreland Association of 1766, Bancroft, noted historian says: "Thus Virginia rang the alarm bell for the Continent."

President James Monroe thus had one sister, Elizabeth Monroe, who married Captain William Buckner, of "Mill Hill," Caroline County, Virginia; and three brothers: Spence Monroe, who is said to have died in young manhood; Andrew Monroe, who married Frances Garnett, of Essex County, Virginia, and died in 1826; and Joseph Jones Monroe, namesake of Judge Joseph Jones, who was married three times (to Elizabeth Kerr, Sally Gordon, of Northumberland County, Virginia, and Elizabeth Glasscock). From 1804 to 1810 he was clerk of the District Court of Northumberland County, Virginia. He moved to Missouri, and died in Franklin, Missouri, on August 5, 1824.

NOTES
LIST OF REFERENCES
INDEX

NOTES

CHAPTER I

1. For colonial Williamsburg, the following sources have been used: Rutherfoord Goodwin, *A Brief & True Report concerning Williamsburg in Virginia*; J. A. Osborne, *Williamsburg in Colonial Times*; Louis Morton, *Robert Carter of Nomini Hall*.

2. Journals of the House of Burgesses, 1773–1776, p. 124.

3. Goodwin, *A Brief & True Report*, p. 67, quoting George Washington's Diary.

4. Journals of the House of Burgesses, 1773–1776, p. xiv.

5. H. J. Eckenrode, *The Revolution in Virginia*, p. 35.

6. Ibid., pp. 25-26, citing *Journals of the House of Burgesses, 1761–1765*.

7. H. D. Farish, ed., *Journal & Letters of Philip Vickers Fithian, 1773–1774: A Plantation Tutor of the Old Dominion*, pp. 226–27. Hereafter cited as Fithian.

8. For a discussion of James Monroe's ancestry, see Appendix.

9. Lyon G. Tyler, "James Monroe," *William and Mary College Quarterly Historical Magazine*, First Series, IV (April, 1896), 272–75.

10. Rose Gouverneur Hoes, "James Monroe's Childhood and Youth," MS Collection in the James Monroe Law Office, Fredericksburg, Virginia. The immediately following account of Monroe's boyhood also comes from this source.

11. Albert J. Beveridge, *The Life of John Marshall*, I, 44 ff.

12. Rose Gouverneur Hoes, *op. cit.*

13. Thomas Jefferson, *Notes on the State of Virginia*, p. 275.

14. Fithian, pp. 106-7.

15. Lyon G. Tyler, "Early Presidents of William and Mary," *William and Mary College Quarterly*, First Series, I (October, 1892), 73.

16. William and Mary College Quarterly, First Series, XV (July, 1906), 1–4.

[509]

CHAPTER 2

1. Goodwin, *A Brief & True Report*, p. 70.
2. *Ibid.*, p. 71.
3. Rose Gouverneur Hoes, "James Monroe, Soldier: His Part in the War of the American Revolution," *Daughters of the American Revolution Magazine*, LVII (December, 1923), 724.
4. Deposition made in Richmond, Va., in 1832, by Robert Greenhow. MS in possession of James D. Evans, Esq., of Philadelphia. For details concerning the Williamsburg Companies and for the Greenhow document, the author is indebted to Mr. Evans. See also "The Williamsburg Companies," *Tyler's Quarterly Historical and Genealogical Magazine*, IX (July, 1927), 46–47.
5. Robert Leroy Hilldrup, *The Life and Times of Edmund Pendleton*, p. 121.
6. Charles Ramsdell Lingley, *The Transition in Virginia from Colony to Commonwealth*, pp. 68–69.
7. Eckenrode, *Revolution in Virginia*, pp. 51–52.
8. Lingley, p. 69.
9. *Ibid.*, p. 73.
10. Hoes, "James Monroe, Soldier," *loc. cit.*, p. 724.
11. Rev. Philip Slaughter, *A History of St. Mark's Parish*, pp. 107 f.
12. Allen French, *The First Year of the American Revolution*, p. 458.
13. Lingley, pp. 158–59.
14. Monroe's participation in this adventure is stated in Charles Campbell's *Introduction to the History of the Colony and Ancient Dominion of Virginia*, p. 151, where the *Bland Papers*, I, xxiii, are cited as authority.
15. Campbell, p. 151.
15-a. Francis B. Heitman, *Historical Register of the Officers of the Continental Army during the War of the Revolution, April, 1775, to December, 1783*.
16. Eckenrode, p. 83. For a firsthand account of this episode see "The Letters of Woodford, Howe, and Lee," *Richmond College Historical Papers*, I (June, 1915), 96–163.
17. Eckenrode, p. 75.
18. Campbell, p. 154.
19. Hilldrup, p. 155.
20. French, p. 466.
21. *Ibid.*
22. Eckenrode, p. 90, citing the *Virginia Gazette*, May 24, 1776.
23. *Dictionary of American Biography*, XI, 98-99.
24. Lingley, pp. 158–59.
25. Hilldrup, p. 163.
26. Lingley, pp. 175–77.

CHAPTER 3

1. W. C. Abbott, *New York in the American Revolution*, pp. 190–91, 195–96.

1-a. Claude Halstead Van Tyne, *The American Revolution, 1776-1783*, pp. 102 ff.

2. Ibid., p. 107.

3. John C. Fitzpatrick, "George Washington," *Dictionary of American Biography*, XIX, 515: Abbott, p. 197.

4. Ibid., p. 199.

5. George H. S. King, "General George Weedon," *William and Mary College Quarterly*, Second Series, XX (April, 1940), 246.

6. Monroe Johnson, "James Monroe, Soldier," *William and Mary College Quarterly*, Second Series, IX (January, 1929), 110–17. It has been suggested that his uncle's influence may have accounted for Monroe's early rank as an officer in the Continental Line, but it is quite as likely that in the organization of new regiments there was a shortage of officers, and that young Monroe was, as he later proved, excellent officer material.

7. Heitman, *Historical Register of the Officers of the Continental Army during the War of the Revolution, April, 1775, to December, 1783*.

8. Campbell, p. 161.

9. Henry P. Johnston, *The Campaign of 1776 around New York and Brooklyn*, p. 251.

10. Campbell, p. 161.

10-a. Abbott, pp. 201–2.

11. William S. Stryker, *The Battles of Trenton and Princeton*, p. 2. The following account is based mainly upon this important book.

12. Ibid., p. 308.

13. Ibid., p. 27.

14. Ibid., p. 18 n.

15. Ibid., pp. 106 f.

16. W. W. H. Davis, "Washington on the West Bank of the Delaware, 1776," *The Pennsylvania Magazine of History and Biography*, IV (No. 2, 1880), 148.

17. Ibid., p. 141.

18. Moncure Daniel Conway, *The Life of Thomas Paine*, pp. 84–85.

19. Stryker, pp. 340–41.

20. Ibid., p. 342.

21. Conway, p. 85.

22. Ibid., p. 86; Stryker, p. 81.

23. Stryker, p. 130.

24. Davis, p. 148.

25. Ibid., p. 152; Stryker, pp. 136–37.

26. Davis, p. 153. This was told by President Monroe to Lewis S. Coryell, of New Hope, Bucks County, Pennsylvania, at dinner in the White House. Monroe also asked Mr. Coryell to try to find some of the doctor's descendants for him, but no trace of the family could be found.

27. Stryker, p. 362. The vivid details of the weather are taken from the account of one of Washington's staff officers, as reprinted in Stryker.
28. Davis, p. 150.
29. Stryker, p. 142.
30. *Ibid.*, p. 363.
31. James Wilkinson, *Memoirs of My Own Times*, I, 128.
32. Davis, p. 153.
33. Stryker, p. 364.
34. Letter in the Gouverneur-Hoes MSS, quoted in Rose Gouverneur Hoes, "James Monroe, Soldier: His Part in the War of the American Revolution," in *Daughters of the American Revolution Magazine*, LVII (December, 1923), 726. This account was written by Monroe six months before his death in New York and is dated January 9, 1830. It is owned by one of his descendants.

CHAPTER 4

1. Letter in the Gouverneur-Hoes MSS, quoted in Rose Gouverneur Hoes, "James Monroe, Soldier," *Daughters of the American Revolution Magazine*, LVII (December, 1923), 726. See Chap. III, n. 34, above.
2. George Morgan, *The Life of James Monroe*, p. 61, n. 2. The statement here is based upon Dr. Julian T. Hammond, Jr.'s *Vredens-Hof*, a monograph privately printed in Philadelphia in 1909. "Vredens-Hof" is the name of Judge Wyncoop's home.
3. Washington's letter to Archibald Cary, quoted in Daniel C. Gilman, *James Monroe*, p. 11.
4. Worthington C. Ford, ed., *Letters of Joseph Jones, 1777-1787*, p. 1. A letter written by Monroe to Major John Thornton from Fredericksburg on July 3, 1777, tells of his fruitless attempts to raise a company in Virginia during the summer of 1777.—*Tyler's Quarterly Magazine*, IX (April, 1928), 246-47.
5. William Alexander Duer, *The Life of William Alexander, Earl of Stirling*, p. 76.
6. Henry Lee, *Memoirs of the War in the Southern Department of the United States*, p. 89. Hereafter cited as Lee, *Memoirs*.
7. Charles Francis Adams, ed., *Familiar Letters of John Adams and His Wife Abigail Adams, during the Revolution*, p. 302.
8. Sir George Otto Trevelyan, *The American Revolution*, IV, 230; Lee, *Memoirs*, pp. 95-97.
9. Moncure Daniel Conway, *The Life of Thomas Paine*, pp. 107-8.
10. Lee, *Memoirs*, pp. 94, 102 ff.
11. Stanislaus Murray Hamilton, ed., *The Writings of James Monroe*, I, xxvii. Hereafter cited as *Writings of Monroe*.
12. Duer, pp. 181-82.
13. *Ibid.*, pp. 182 f.
14. Benson J. Lossing, *The Pic-*

[512]

torial *Field-Book of the Revolution*, II, 352, n. Here is given a facsimile of Stirling's oath.

15. *Writings of Monroe*, I, xxvii. There is a facsimile of this oath on p. lxxv of this same volume. It contains the signatures of both Monroe and Stirling. The originals of these oaths of allegiance are in the National Archives.

16. Monroe Johnson, "James Monroe, Soldier," *William and Mary College Quarterly*, Second Series, IX (January, 1929), 113; Matthew L. Davis, *Memoirs of Aaron Burr*, II, 434.

17. Worthington Chauncey Ford, ed., *The Writings of George Washington*, VI, 260.

18. Albert J. Beveridge, *The Life of John Marshall*, I, 112, n.3.

19. Conway, pp. 111–12.

20. William Starr Myers, ed., *The Battle of Monmouth*, by William S. Stryker, pp. 3–4. Hereafter cited as Stryker, *Monmouth*.

21. John Hyde Preston, *Revolution, 1776*, p. 218.

22. Beveridge, I, 111 ff.

23. Lee, *Memoirs*, p. 93.

24. Preston, pp. 223–24.

25. Stryker, *Monmouth*, pp. 38–39.

26. *Ibid.*, p. 45.

27. *Ibid.*

28. Van Tyne, pp. 236 ff.

29. *Ibid.*, p. 245.

30. Stryker, *Monmouth*, pp. 48–49.

31. The account of the events leading up to the battle of Monmouth and of the battle itself is based upon Stryker's *Monmouth*, previously cited. Like the author's account of the battles of Trenton and Princeton, it is the prime authority on the subject.

32. Stryker, *Monmouth*, p. 82.

33. *Ibid.*, p. 71.

34. *Writings of Monroe*, I, 1. It is not indicated in Monroe's note whether "4 o'clock" refers to morning or afternoon, but all the probabilities are that it is in the early morning. As is told later, Monroe was actively in the battle in the afternoon of June 28, and during the latter part of it was Stirling's adjutant general. As such, it hardly seems likely that he would be sent out on a separate scouting mission reporting to Washington, even granting that the fighting was over for Stirling's wing by four o'clock, which does not seem likely.

35. Stryker, *Monmouth*, p. 172.

36. Samuel H. Wandell and Meade Minnigerode, *Aaron Burr*, I, 74.

37. Stryker, *Monmouth*, p. 209.

38. *Ibid.*, pp. 244–45. The case of Charles Lee appears to need careful reëxamination. Stryker, who is said to have given the best account of the closing days of Lee's military career, accepts (as do most historians), the verdict of G. H. Moore's *Treason of General Lee* (New York, 1860), but Stryker's own careful account of events would warrant a different conclusion, and some recent historians hint at doubts. Maude H. Woodfin, who wrote the sketch of Lee in the *DAB*, suggests several possibilities other than treasonable intention, and John Hyde Preston, in his *Revolution, 1776* (1933), espouses Lee's cause with warmth and points to Clinton's judgment of Lee's acts

Notes to Pages 44-50

at Monmouth, as seen in "some recently discovered papers."

39. For Henry Lee's opinion of General Charles Lee and of the court-martial, see the *Memoirs*, pp. 115-16. Lee's account of the battle of Monmouth, told on pp. 111 ff. of the *Memoirs*, also interprets Lee's conduct sympathetically.

40. Beveridge, p. 137.

41. Washington's letter to Archibald Cary, May 30, 1779, quoted in Gilman, p. 11.

CHAPTER 5

1. Stryker, *Monmouth*, p. 272.

2. W. C. Ford, ed., *The Writings of George Washington*, II, 761.

3 Duer, pp. 199 ff., 201 ff.

4. Mrs. Prevost is herself a figure of no little interest. She was the wife of Colonel Prevost, of the British army, who was with his regiment in the West Indies, where he died some time after Monroe's letter was written. Mrs. Prevost's home "was the resort of the most accomplished officers in the American army when they were in the vicinity of it. She was highly respected by her neighbors, and visited by the most genteel people of the surrounding country. Her situation was one of great delicacy and constant apprehension."—Davis, *Memoirs of Aaron Burr*, I, 183.

5. The young lady is said to have been Miss Nannie Brown, a relative of the Duers and hence closely connected, through Lady Kitty's marriage, with Lord Stirling's family. See note *8* below.

6. Monroe's efforts were here directed toward saving Mrs. Prevost, as the wife of a British officer, from being compelled to withdraw into the British lines, in accordance with the laws of the state concerning British adherents. Her friends, including Governor Livingston, seem to have been powerful enough to prevent it.—Davis, *Memoirs of Aaron Burr*, I, 183.

7. Ibid., I, 184-86.

8. Gouverneur-Hoes MSS. See Mrs. John King Van Rensselaer's version of the incident in the *Ladies Home Journal*, February, 1923, and the refutation of the charge that Monroe "cruelly jilted a relative of Lord Stirling's," by Rose Gouverneur Hoes in the *Washington Post*, April 1, 1923. This incident is without bearing on the story of Monroe's development and career except that it did subsequently become part of the campaign of detraction carried on against him by Hamilton's supporters after the rift between the two men occurred.

8-a. December 20, 1778, is the date given for Monroe's resignation in "Revolutionary Letters," *Tyler's Quarterly Magazine*, IX (April, 1928), 246.

9. Writings of Monroe, I, 9 f.

10. Washburn Papers (Massachusetts Historical Society), IV.

The letter was written from Headquarters at Middle Brook.

11. D. D. Wallace, *The History of South Carolina*, II, 186–87, 294.

12. A reorganization of the army in 1779 gave an excess of officers, in which case the younger officers were retired, and Monroe was one of these, as was also John Marshall.

13. *Writings of Monroe*, I, 20–21 n.

14. Lee, *Memoirs*, p. 121.

15. *Ibid.*, p. 134.

16. *Dictionary of American Biography*, XX, 588.

17. Roy J. Honeywell, *The Educational Work of Thomas Jefferson*. Appendix D, pp. 217–21.

18. *Writings of Monroe*, I, 8–9.

19. Van Tyne, p. 297.

20. Colonial Williamsburg, Inc., *The Capitol*, p. 17.

21. Daniel C. Gilman, *James Monroe*, pp. 13–15.

22. Morgan, p. 76.

23. Henry S. Muhlenberg, *The Life of Major-General Peter Muhlenberg of the Revolutionary Army*, pp. 179, 191.

24. R. D. W. Connor, *North Carolina: Rebuilding an Ancient Commonwealth, 1584–1925*, I, 352.

25. Gouverneur-Hoes MSS.

25-a. Clinton sailed for New York on June 5.—Connor, I, 349–50.

26. *Writings of Monroe*, I, 3–8.

27. Van Tyne, p. 300; Connor, I, 352.

28. Connor, I, 352, 359.

29. Eckenrode, p. 264.

30. Muhlenberg, p. 205.

31. In the Records Division of the Adjutant General's Office appears a receipt for "11 kettles issued to Captain [sic] Monroe."—Document .034369. This is the only record of Monroe's Virginia service that a diligent search has revealed among the papers of the War Department.

32. Muhlenberg to Washington, Muhlenberg, p. 208.

33. *Ibid.*, p. 210.

34. Eckenrode, p. 264.

35. *Ibid.*, p. 270.

36. *Ibid.*, p. 268.

37. Saul K. Padover, *Jefferson*, pp. 95–97; *DAB*, X, 222.

38. *Writings of Monroe*, I, 11–12.

39. *Ibid.*, p. 13.

40. *Ibid.*

41. George H. S. King, "General George Weedon," *William and Mary College Quarterly*, Second Series, XX (April, 1940), 246.

CHAPTER 6

1. *Writings of Monroe*, I, 14.
2. *Ibid.*, pp. 15–16.
3. H. A. Washington, ed., *The Writings of Jefferson*, III, 56.
4. Duer, pp. 250–51.
5. *Writings of Monroe*, I, 19.
6. Albert J. Beveridge, *The Life of John Marshall*, I, 202.
7. "Journal of Alexander Macaulay," *William and Mary College*

Quarterly, First Series, XI (January, 1903), 188.

8. Beveridge, *Marshall*, I, 211.
9. *Ibid.*, II, 55.
10. *Writings of Monroe*, I, 23.
11. *Ibid.*, p. 24.
12. *Ibid.*, p. 29.
13. Gouverneur-Hoes MSS.
14. *Writings of Monroe*, I, 72.
15. *Ibid.*, p. 71 n. Alexander Hamilton aided Jefferson in securing congressional approval of a site on the Potomac, in return for Jefferson's assistance in passing a bill for the assumption of the state war debts by the Federal government.—John Spencer Bassett, *A Short History of the United States*, p. 260.
16. *Journals of Congress*, January 13, 14, 1784.
17. Gouverneur-Hoes MSS.
18. *Writings of Monroe*, I, 23.
19. F. J. Turner, "Western State-making in the Revolutionary Era," *The American Historical Review*, I (October, 1895), pp. 81 ff. This is a highly important article with a valuable map.
20. *Ibid.*, p. 20.
21. *Ibid.*, p. 72.
22. Jay to Jefferson, December 14, 1786. Quoted in Beveridge, *Marshall*, I, 237.
23. Turner, "Western State-making," *loc. cit.*, p. 77.
24. Washington, ed., *Writings of Jefferson*, III, 401.
25. "George Rogers Clark Papers," *Collections of the Illinois State Historical Library*, Virginia Series, XIX (1926), 250.

CHAPTER 7

1. *Dictionary of American Biography*, X, 192.
2. Worthington C. Ford, ed., *Letters of Joseph Jones, 1777–1787*, p. 16.
3. "George Rogers Clark Papers," *Collections of the Illinois State Historical Library*, Virginia Series, XIX (1926), 250.
4. Frederic L. Paxson, *History of the American Frontier, 1763–1893*, p. 60.
5. "Next to the Declaration of Independence (if indeed standing second to that), this document ranks in historical importance of all those drawn by Jefferson."—Ford, ed., *The Writings of Thomas Jefferson*, III, 430 n.
6. *Ibid.*, pp. 429 ff.
7. *Writings of Monroe*, I, 38.
8. *Ibid.*, p. 39.
9. *Ibid.*, pp. 40–41.
10. *Ibid.*, pp. 39–40.
11. *Ibid.*, pp. 42, 44.
12. Beveridge, *Marshall*, I, 179.
13. Gouverneur-Hoes MSS.
14. A document (undated) in the Old Records Division of the War Department shows that Monroe was granted 5,333 acres of western land, the share of a Major in the Militia.—Document 17449.
15. Beveridge, *Marshall*, I, 168–69.

16. *Writings of Monroe*, I, 49.
17. *Ibid.*, p. xxxiv.
18. Arthur Preston Whitaker, *The Spanish American Frontier: 1783–1795*, p. 10.
19. *Ibid.*, p. 11.
20. *Writings of Monroe*, I, 137, 141, 145, 148.
21. *Ibid.*, I, 150.
22. George Pellew, *John Jay*, pp. 139 ff. See also Adolphe de Circourt's translation of George Bancroft's work, *Histoire de l'action Commune de la France et de l'Amérique pour l'Indépendance des Etats-Unis; Traduit et Annoté Par le comte Adolphe de Circourt; Accompagné de Documents Inedits.* One of the letters published at the end of the history, from Vergennes to Luzerne, contains the following instructions: "Sa Majesté vous autorise en outre à continuer les donatifs que M. Gérard a donnés ou promis à différent auteurs Américains, et dont ce dernier vous aura sûrement remis la note." De Circourt gives this note for *donatifs:* "Secours temporaires en argent. Ce sujet délicat a été, même de nos jours, l'objet de critiques et de controverses lesquelles nous n'avons point à entrer."
23. Pellew, *John Jay*, p. 140.
24. Charles Francis Adams, ed., *The Works of John Adams*, I, 340 f.; W. P. Cresson, *Francis Dana*, pp. 39 ff.
25. Frederic L. Paxson, *History of the American Frontier*, p. 60.
26. S. F. Bemis, *Jay's Treaty: A Study in Commerce and Diplomacy*, p. 17.
27. W. C. Rives, *History of the Life and Times of James Madison*, II, 20.
28. *Writings of Monroe*, I, 50–51.
29. *Ibid.*, p. 69.
30. *Ibid.*, I, 94.
31. *Ibid.*, p. 61. Jay's demands were acquiesced in by a congressional resolution of February 11, 1785.—*Ibid.*, I, 62 n.
32. *Ibid.*, I, xlvii.
33. *Ibid.*, I, 131–35.
34. *Ibid.*, I, 144–50.
35. *Ibid.*, I, 151–52.
36. *Ibid.*, I, 120.
37. Thomas Boyd, *Light-horse Harry Lee*, p. 154.
38. Charles H. Ambler, *Washington and the West*, pp. 183–85.
39. *Writings of Monroe*, I, xlviii.
40. *Ibid.*, pp. lviii–lxxii.
41. *Ibid.*, p. 112.
42. *Ibid.*, p. li.
43. John Fiske, *The Critical Period of American History*, p. 148.
44. *Writings of Monroe*, I, 80 n.
45. *Ibid.*, pp. 84 f.
46. *Ibid.*, p. 85.
47. Gouverneur-Hoes MSS.
48. *Writings of Monroe*, I, xlii–xliii.

CHAPTER 8

1. Gouverneur-Hoes MSS.
2. Ibid.
3. Ibid.
4. Monroe Papers, New York Public Library.
5. Harriet Taylor Upton, *Our Early Presidents*, p. 243.
6. William Sullivan, *Familiar Letters on Public Characters*, p. 357.
7. Gouverneur-Hoes MSS.
8. Upton, *Our Early Presidents*, p. 243.
9. Gouverneur-Hoes MSS.
10. Upton, *Our Early Presidents*, p. 245.
11. Gouverneur-Hoes MSS.
12. *Writings of Monroe*, I, 128 f.
13. Ibid., p. 169.
14. Gouverneur-Hoes MSS.
15. *Writings of Monroe*, I, 158.
16. Now a national shrine.
17. *Writings of Monroe*, I, 171.
18. Ibid., p. 173.
19. Monroe Papers, New York Public Library.

CHAPTER 9

1. *Writings of Monroe*, I, 174.
2. The dissenters were Edmund Randolph and George Mason.
3. *Writings of Monroe*, I, 176.
4. "Some Observations on the Constitution, & C . . . ," *Writings of Monroe*, Appendix I, I, 307. One of the rarest of printed Americana; this exists only as a single copy of the printed proof, which was returned to Monroe and suppressed by him.
5. Ibid., p. 349.
6. "Observations on the Federal Government. . . ."—*Ibid.* It is now among the Madison Papers in the Department of State.
7. Worthington Chauncey Ford, ed., *The Writings of George Washington*, XI, 255.
8. Edward S. Corwin, *National Supremacy*, p. 69.
9. *Writings of Monroe*, I, 190.
10. Quoted in Beveridge, *Marshall*.
11. Alan B. Magruder, *John Marshall*, pp. 72 ff.
12. Ibid., p. 444.
13. *Writings of Monroe*, I, 184 ff.

14. Ford, ed., *Writings of Washington*, XI, 335 n.
15. Moses Coit Tyler, *Patrick Henry*, p. 304.
16. *Ibid.*, p. 306.
17. *Writings of Monroe*, I, 199.
18. Short MS. William and Mary College.
19. Jefferson MSS. New York Public Library.
20. Monroe Papers, New York Public Library.
21. *Writings of Monroe*, I, 199 f.
22. *Ibid.*, p. 205.
23. *Ibid.*, p. 281; *Virginia: A Guide to the Old Dominion*, p. 626.
24. *Writings of Monroe*, II, 411.
25. *Ibid.*, pp. 444 f.
26. Ford, ed., *Writings of Jefferson*, V, 143.
27. *Ibid.*, p. 143.
28. *Ibid.*, pp. 187 ff.
29. *Writings of Monroe*, I, 209.
30. *Ibid.*, p. 211.
31. *Ibid.*
32. Claude G. Bowers, *Jefferson and Hamilton*, p. 54.
33. *Writings of Monroe*, I, 215 f.
34. Madison, *Letters and Other Writings*, I, 517.
35. *Writings of Monroe*, I, 217 f.
36. See Bowers, *Jefferson and Hamilton*, pp. 58–68.

CHAPTER 10

1. William C. Rives, *History of the Life and Times of James Madison*, III, 155 ff. This measure was especially obnoxious to the Virginians of the inaccessible western settlements, whose grain could be marketed in its only portable form—whiskey.
2. *History of the United States of America under the Constitution*, I, 185. James Schouler is one of the earliest American historians to treat Monroe objectively and with a fairness that barely avoids partiality. The New England school of writing, imbued with neo-Federalist prejudices, invariably considers the Virginia statesman a blind opponent of Washington and the ideal of "National Unity," which it believes a monopoly of the Federalists.
3. Schouler, *History of the United States*, I, 186.
4. *Ibid.*, p. 188.
5. *Writings of Monroe*, I, lxxiii.
6. *Ibid.*, p. 223.
7. *Ibid.*
8. A. A. Lipscomb, ed., *Writings of Jefferson*, VIII, 245.
9. *Writings of Monroe*, I, 221 f.
10. Bowers, *Jefferson and Hamilton*, p. 80.
11. Schouler, *History of the United States*, I, 186.
12. *Writings of Monroe*, I, 230 f.
13. *Ibid.*, pp. 231 ff.
14. *Ibid.*, p. 238.
15. Ford, ed., *Writings of Jefferson*, V, 351 f.

16. Bowers, *Jefferson and Hamilton*, p. 86.

17. *Writings of Monroe*, I, 240 f.

18. *Ibid.*, pp. 243 f.

CHAPTER 11

1. *Writings of Monroe*, I, 252.
2. *Ibid.*, p. 256.
3. Hamilton MSS. # 2582. Library of Congress.
4. *Ibid.*
5. He had taken care to bring to Washington's attention "the unexceptional conduct of the British Government towards the vessels of the United States."—Hamilton MSS. # 2561.
6. Washington, ed., *Writings of Jefferson*, pp. 548 ff.
7. John Bassett Moore, *International Law Digest*, VII (1906) 1022 ff.
8. Schouler, *History of the United States*, I, 244 ff; also, Bowers, *Jefferson and Hamilton*, pp. 214 ff.
9. Ford, ed., *Writings of Jefferson*, VI, 346.
10. Washington, ed., *Writings of Jefferson*, III, 557.
11. *Ibid.*, p. 562.
12. Ford, ed., *Writings of Jefferson*, VI, 238 f.
13. Hamilton MSS, Library of Congress.
14. *Writings of Monroe*, I, 258.
15. *Ibid.*, p. 261.
16. Ford, ed., *Writings of Jefferson*, VI, 277.
17. *Writings of Monroe*, I, 265.
18. Hamilton MSS, Library of Congress.
19. *Ibid.*
20. *Writings of Monroe*, I, 273, n. 1.
21. *Ibid.*, pp. 272 f.
22. *Ibid.*, pp. 263 ff.
23. *Ibid.*
24. *Ibid.*, pp. 281 f.
25. *Ibid.*
26. *Ibid.*, pp. 282 f.
27. *Ibid.*, p. 284, n. 1.
28. Schouler, *History of the United States*, I, 255 f.
29. *Writings of Monroe*, I, 285 ff.
30. *Ibid.*, p. 290.
31. *Ibid.*, p. 291.
32. Gratz MSS, Philadelphia Historical Society.
33. *Writings of Monroe*, I, 292, n.
34. *Ibid.*, pp. 294 f.

CHAPTER 12

1. *Writings of Monroe*, I, 294 f.
2. *Ibid.*, p. 298.
3. *Ibid.*, pp. 299 f.
4. *Ibid.*, p. 299.
5. *Ibid.*, II, 37.
6. *Ibid.*, pp. 3 ff.
7. *Ibid.*, pp. 37 ff.
8. A letter of Washington's to Morris, dated June 19, 1787, contains these compromising words: "The difficulties under existing circumstances of knowing what to write you has determined me to write nothing, but to let the matter rest altogether upon the public communication of the secretary of state. Coming to this plan, however, on a flying visit to Mt. Vernon, and finding the vessel on which Mr. Monroe is on board, I have so far departed from my determination to assure you that my confidence and fond regard for you remains undiminished." (Washburn Papers, Massachusetts Historical Society). Monroe suggests (*Writings*, III, 409) that Randolph's letter of recall, written in a similar vein (see Sparks, *Life of Gouverneur Morris*, II, 441), was intercepted by the French. It was the opinion of Dr. Edwards, a Paris associate of Monroe's, that Washington's letter to Morris was read aloud by Morris at a dinner at which several officials of the French government were present. See Charles King, ed., *Life and Correspondence of Rufus King*, II, 82.
9. *Writings of Monroe*, II, 39.
10. *Ibid.*, p. 31.
11. *Ibid.*, p. 196.
12. *Ibid.*, III, 390.
13. *Ibid.*, II, 11.
14. *Ibid.*, p. 32.
15. See Morgan, *Life of James Monroe*, p. 183.
16. *American State Papers, Foreign Relations*, I, 447.
17. *Writings of Monroe*, II, 15 n.
18. *Ibid.*, p. 13.
19. *Ibid.*, p. 34.
20. *Ibid.*
21. Henry P. Johnston, ed., *The Correspondence and Public Papers of John Jay*, IV, 58.
22. A later comment of Washington's was that it "was as unnecessary, as it was impolitic to make a parade of . . . the Secretary's letter and Monroe's speech." See Ford, *Writings of Washington*, XIII, 475.
23. *Writings of Monroe*, II, 193 f.; 193 n.
24. *Ibid.*, p. 40.
25. *Ibid.*, pp. 193 ff.
26. Gouverneur-Hoes MSS.
27. *Writings of Monroe*, II, 212.
28. *Ibid.*, p. 209.
29. B. W. Bond, *The Monroe Mission to France, 1794–1796*, Johns Hopkins University Studies, Series XXV, p. 17.

30. *Writings of Monroe*, II, 41 ff.
31. *Ibid.*, p. 102.
32. Randolph again sent a reprimand by mail.
33. The president contended that "no circumstances warrant his relinquishment of our rights." See Ford, *Writings of Washington*, XIII, 455.
34. *Writings of Monroe*, II, 6.
35. *Ibid.*, pp. 117 f.

CHAPTER 13

1. *Writings of Monroe*, II, 136.
2. *Ibid.*, III, 395 f.; 395 n.
3. *Ibid.*, II, 157 f.
4. *Ibid.*, p. 169, n. 1.
5. *Ibid.*, p. 169, n. 2.
6. *Ibid.*, III, 403.
7. *Ibid.*, II, 163.
8. *Ibid.*, p. 180, n. 1.
9. *Ibid.*, p. 181.
10. William Jay, *The Life of John Jay*, I, 336 f.
11. *Writings of Monroe*, II, 229 ff.
12. *Ibid.*, p. 238.
13. *Ibid.*, pp. 238 ff.
14. Bond, *Monroe Mission to France*, p. 34.
15. *Writings of Monroe*, II, 243, n. 1.
16. Bond, *Monroe Mission to France*, p. 34.
17. H. P. Johnston, *Correspondence and Public Papers of John Jay*, IV, 179.
18. *Writings of Monroe*, II, 244.
19. See *ibid.*, pp. 257, 301, 303.
20. *American State Papers, Foreign Relations*, I, 696.
21. *Writings of Monroe*, II, 415.
22. *Ibid.*, p. 303.
23. *Ibid.*, p. 311.
24. Bond, *Monroe Mission to France*, pp. 46 f. Again, says this author, Monroe "put himself in the position of openly supporting the policy of the administration by continuing in its service, and of privately not hesitating to express his decided disapproval of its acts."
25. See *Writings of Monroe*, II, 339.
26. *Ibid.*, pp. 247 ff.
27. Bond, *Monroe Mission to France*, p. 49.
28. *American State Papers, Foreign Relations*, I, 705.
29. *Ibid.*, p. 719.
30. *Writings of Monroe*, II, 439.
31. *Ibid.*, p. 228.
32. *Ibid.*, p. 206.
33. *Ibid.*, p. 283.
34. *American State Papers, Foreign Relations*, I, 535.
35. Bond says (in *Monroe Mission to France*, pp. 40 f.), "The importance of Monroe's work in bringing about this final adjustment is readily apparent."
36. *American State Papers, Foreign Relations*, I, 670.
37. *Writings of Monroe*, II, 316.
38. *Ibid.*, III, 418.
39. *Ibid.*
40. *Ibid.*
41. *Ibid.*, II, 357.

Notes to Pages 145-153

42. *Ibid.*, pp. 368, 374.
43. *Ibid.*, p. 455. The French envoy was Governor Vincent of Santo Domingo.
44. *Ibid.*, pp. 456 ff.
45. *Ibid.*, p. 463.
46. *Ibid.*, p. 464.
47. *Ibid.*, p. 484.
48. *American State Papers, Foreign Relations*, I, 732.
49. *Ibid.*, p. 733.
50. *Writings of Monroe*, II, 348.
51. *Ibid.*, p. 480.
52. *Ibid.*, III, 1, 4.
53. *Ibid.*, p. 8.
54. *Ibid.*, p. 28. When Monroe denied that a few nations may by treaty change an old established rule so as to bind non-signatory powers, he raised the whole question of the proof necessary to establish the existence of a rule of international law.
55. *American State Papers, Foreign Relations*, I, 745.
56. *Writings of Monroe*, III, 49 ff. See notes.

CHAPTER 14

1. Moncure D. Conway, *The Life of Thomas Paine*, II, 111 ff.
2. Born in 1787.
3. Gouverneur-Hoes MSS.
4. *Writings of Monroe*, II, 441.
5. *Ibid.*, III, 20.
6. *Ibid.*, p. 27.
7. Gouverneur-Hoes MSS.
8. *Ibid.*
9. *Ibid.*
10. *Writings of Monroe*, III, 24. Washington's caustic comment (Ford, ed., *Writings of Washington*, XIII, 460): "Curious and laughable to hear a man under his circumstances talking seriously in this stile, when his recall was a second death to him."
11. *Writings of Monroe*, III, 53.
12. Notes of May 12, 1796. Pickering MSS, VI, Massachusetts Historical Society.
13. Rives, *James Madison*, III, 576.
14. H. C. Lodge, ed., *The Works of Alexander Hamilton*, VIII, 403.
15. Ford, ed., *Writings of Washington*, XIII, 218 f. Washington also asked Hamilton "what should be done with Mr. M[onroe]?"
16. *Ibid*, p. 214.
17. Pickering MSS, VI.
18. *Ibid.*
19. H. C. Lodge, ed., *The Works of Hamilton*, VIII, 408.
20. Ford, ed., *Writings of Washington*, XIII, 235 f.
21. *Writings of Monroe*, II, 482, n.
22. Ford, ed., *Writings of Washington*, XIII, 250 f.
23. *Ibid.*, p. 461.
24. To Rufus King, American minister of Great Britain, Pickering wrote (*Life and Correspond-*

ence of Rufus King, II, 84): "Mr. Monroe's own communications in February and March laid the foundation of his recall."

25. *American State Papers, Foreign Relations*, I, 747.
26. *Ibid.*
27. *Writings of Monroe*, III, 63.

CHAPTER 15

1. Henry Adams, *The Life of Albert Gallatin*, p. 187.
2. *Ibid.*
3. H. C. Lodge, ed., *Works of Hamilton*, VI, 482 f.
4. *Ibid.*, p. 507.
5. *Ibid.*, pp. 463 ff.
6. *Ibid.*, pp. 507 ff.
7. *Ibid.*, pp. 495 ff.
8. Schouler, *History of the United States*, I, 200.
9. H. C. Lodge, ed., *Works of Hamilton*, VI, 508.
10. James Gordon Bennett MSS.
11. H. C. Lodge, ed., *Works of Hamilton*, VI, 451.
12. James Gordon Bennett MSS.
13. Charles King, ed., *Life of Rufus King*, II, 193.
14. See Henry Stephens Randall, *Life of Thomas Jefferson*, III, 16. In the Jefferson MSS at the Library of Congress, however, we find a note from Callender to Jefferson dated Philadelphia, September 28, 1797, saying: "I expect that your remaining numbers of the History of 1796 have come duly to hand." The letter also refers to "some assistance in a pecuniary way that you intend to make me." This evidence scarcely corroborates Jefferson's statement to Monroe. On March 21, 1798, the same correspondent reports that "in less than five weeks 700 have gone off." This may refer to the History of 1796 and lends color to the surmise of Hildreth that there was a connection between Jefferson and the "respectable Party." On the other hand, Schouler (in his *History of the United States*, I, 363) writes: "Callender says that Jefferson advised a suppression of this publication, but that his interposition came too late." A letter from Monroe to Jefferson (*Writings of Monroe*, III, 355) shows that the former did not have his friend's confidence in this matter.
15. Schouler, *History of the United States*, I, 363.
16. Gelston's account is preserved in the Gratz MSS, Philadelphia Historical Society.
17. H. C. Lodge, ed., *Works of Hamilton*, VI, 517 f.
18. The other was an explanation of the attitude he had assumed in the *Gazette* connecting Reynolds and Clingman with "a party hostile to his conduct and administration." See H. C. Lodge, ed., *Works of Hamilton*, VI, 518.
19. *Ibid.*, pp. 520 f.
20. *Ibid.*, p. 521.
21. *Ibid.*
22. *Ibid.*, p. 524. The publication referred to is his pamphlet,

Observations on Certain Documents contained in Nos. V. and VI of "The History of the United States for the Year 1796," in which the Charge of Speculation against Alexander Hamilton, late Secretary of the Treasury, is fully refuted. Written by himself, Philadelphia, 1797.

23. *Ibid.*, pp. 529 f.
24. *Ibid.*, pp. 530 f.
25. *Ibid.*, p. 533.
26. *Ibid.*
27. James Gordon Bennett MSS.
28. H. C. Lodge, ed., *Works of Hamilton*, VI, 534. There is extant an interesting memorandum in Burr's papers under date of August, 1797, the very month this affair was terminated, and bearing his signature, stating that "we certify that, in consequence of Information which we received in December 1792 of a concern in speculation between A. H. then Sec. of the T. and one J. Reynolds, we had an explanation on the subject with said A. H. who by that explanation supported by written documents satisfied us that the above charge was ill founded as we declared to him at the time: That the impression under which we left him of our being so satisfied was reciprocal and is still the same." Wandell and Minnigerode comment (in *Aaron Burr*, I, 283 f.): "... this was presumably the draft of an agreement between the principals, and Mr. Muhlenburgh and Mr. Venable" and that "this agreement was never ratified, or else one is at a loss to understand why Mr. Hamilton should not have published it, rather than the confession he subsequently promulgated."

29. *Ibid.*

CHAPTER 16

1. *Writings of Monroe*, III, 70 f.
2. *Ibid.*, p. 75, n.
3. Washington's own elaboration of the cryptic phrase, "other concurring circumstances," which appears in the note of recall, can be found in his comments on Monroe's self-vindicating *View* (Ford, XIII, 470): "He was promoting the views of a party in his own country that were obstructing every measure of the administration, and by their attachment to France, were hurrying it (if not with the design, at least in its consequence), into a war with Great Britain in order to favor France."
4. *Writings of Monroe*, III, 73 ff.
5. *Reflections on Monroe's View* ... etc.
6. See Ford, ed., *Writings of Washington*, XIII, 452–90.
7. *Virginia Gazette.* See *Writings of Monroe*, III, 134.
8. See *Writings of Monroe*, III, 222 n.
9. Ford, ed., *Writings of Washington*, XIV, 246 ff.
10. *Writings of Monroe*, III, 216.

11. *Ibid.*, pp. 292 f.
12. *John Marshall*, II, 488.
13. *Ibid.*, p. 515.
14. *Ibid.*
15. *Ibid.*
16. Wandell and Minnigerode, *Aaron Burr*, I, 101.
17. *Writings of Monroe*, III, 253 ff.
18. *Ibid.*, p. 257.
19. *Ibid.*, p. 258.
20. *Ibid.*, pp. 260 f.
21. See Beveridge, *Marshall*, II, 542.
22. Ford, ed., *Writings of Jefferson*, VII, 491.
23. Henry Adams, *History of the United States*, I, 198.
24. *Writings of Monroe*, III, 282 f.
25. Ford, ed., *Writings of Jefferson*, VIII, 59 f.
26. *Writings of Monroe*, III, 287.
27. *Ibid.*, p. 377.
28. *Ibid.*, p. 303.

CHAPTER 17

1. Ford, ed., *Writings of Jefferson*, VIII, 144.
2. *Ibid.*, pp. 144 f.
3. *Ibid.*, pp. 187 f.
4. Henry Adams, *History of the United States*, I, 438.
5. Ford, ed., *Writings of Jefferson*, VIII, 190 ff.
6. *Annals of Congress*, 1802–1803, p. 339.
7. F. Barbé-Marbois, *Our Revolutionary Forefathers* (tr. and ed., Eugene Parker Chase), p. 241.
8. *Writings of Monroe*, IV, 5 ff.
9. Frederic Austin Ogg, *The Opening of the Mississippi*, p. 508.
10. Randall, *Life of Thomas Jefferson*, III, 62, n.
11. Grundlach MSS.
12. Charles King, ed., *Life and Correspondence of Rufus King*, p. 241.
13. Barbé-Marbois, *The History of Louisiana*, p. 417.
14. *Ibid.*, p. 260.
15. *Ibid.*, pp. 259 ff.
16. Adams, *History of the United States*, II, 27 f.
17. Gouverneur-Hoes MSS.
18. Adams, *History of the United States*, II, 29.
19. *Writings of Monroe*, IV, 9 ff.
20. *American State Papers, Foreign Relations*, II, 552 ff.
21. Barbé-Marbois, *The History of Louisiana*, pp. 280 ff.
22. Adams, *History of the United States*, II, p. 39.
23. *Writings of Monroe*, IV, 12.
24. Barbé-Marbois, *History of Louisiana*, p. 302.
25. *Writings of Monroe*, IV, 15 f.
26. Adams, *History of the United States*, II, 43.
27. *Ibid.*, I, 367.
28. *Ibid.*, p. 369.

29. *Writings of Monroe*, IV, 26 f.

30. *American State Papers, Foreign Relations*, II, 561.

CHAPTER 18

1. *Writings of Monroe*, IV, 45 f.
2. Adams, *History of the United States*, II, 351.
3. *Writings of Monroe*, IV, 101.
4. Quoted by Beckles Willson, *America's Ambassadors to England*, p. 78.
5. *Ibid.*, p. 77.
6. *Ibid.*, p. 59.
7. Adams, *History of the United States*, II, 337.
8. Willson, *America's Ambassadors to England*, p. 60.
9. *Writings of Monroe*, IV, 97 f.
10. Anne Hollingsworth Wharton, *Salons, Colonial and Republican*, p. 179.
11. Adams, *History of the United States*, II, 362.
12. Helen Nicolay, *Our Capital on the Potomac*, p. 70.
13. Wharton, *Salons, Colonial and Republican*, pp. 179 f.
14. *Ibid.*, p. 37.
15. Meade Minnigerode, *Presidential Years, 1787–1860*, pp. 66 f.
16. Nicolay, *Our Capital on the Potomac*, p. 75.
17. Adams, *History of the United States*, II, 369 f; see also Wharton, *Salons, Colonial and Republican*, pp. 190 f.
18. See Morgan, *James Monroe*, p. 264.
19. *Writings of Monroe*, IV, 150.
20. See Morgan, *James Monroe*, p. 265.
21. Harriet Taylor Upton, *Our Early Presidents*, p. 259.
22. Willson, *America's Ambassadors to England*, p. 79.
23. Gouverneur-Hoes MSS.
24. Willson, *America's Ambassadors to England*, p. 86.
25. His letters to the Judge are full of references to this illness.—Gouverneur-Hoes MSS.
26. Willson, *America's Ambassadors to England*, pp. 86 f.
27. *Writings of Monroe*, IV, 196.
28. *Ibid.*, pp. 79 f.
29. *Ibid.*, pp. 189 f.

CHAPTER 19

1. *Writings of Monroe*, IV, 62.
2. Adams, *History of the United States*, II, 246 f.
3. *Writings of Monroe*, IV, 278 f.
4. *Ibid.*, p. 279.
5. *Ibid.*, p. 281.
6. A manuscript letter in the State Department Archives.
7. *Ibid.*
8. Adams, *History of the United States*, II, 211 f.
9. *Writings of Monroe*, IV, 299.
10. *American State Papers, Foreign Relations*, II, 626.
11. Adams, *History of the United States*, II, 286.
12. *Writings of Monroe*, IV, 300.
13. *American State Papers, Foreign Relations*, II, 541–667.
14. Monroe Papers, Library of Congress.
15. *American State Papers, Foreign Relations*, II, 636.
16. *Ibid.*, p. 682.

CHAPTER 20

1. Ford, ed., *Writings of Jefferson*, VIII, 375, n.
2. *Ibid.*, p. 378.
3. The *Essex* decision asserted that neutral trade between the French and Spanish colonies and their mother countries was prohibited, even when the goods were actually landed in the United States.
4. *Writings of Monroe*, IV, 310.
5. Adams, *History of the United States*, III, 98.
6. *Writings of Monroe*, IV, 336 f.
7. Jefferson to Madison, October 25, 1805, Jefferson MSS, State Department Archives.
8. Adams, *History of the United States*, III, 104 f.

CHAPTER 21

1. Adams, *History of the United States*, III, 84.
2. *Ibid.*, p. 111.
3. *Ibid.*, p. 163.
4. Henry Adams, *John Randolph*, pp. 187 f.
5. Adams, *History of the United States*, III, 165.
6. *Writings of Monroe*, IV, 466.
7. *Ibid.*, p. 398.
8. *American State Papers, Foreign Affairs*, III, 124.
9. Gouverneur-Hoes MSS.
10. *Writings of Monroe*, IV, 480, 494.
11. *Ibid.*, V, 30.
12. Ford, ed., *Writings of Jefferson*, VIII, 448.
13. *Writings of Monroe*, IV, 477.
14. King, *Life of Rufus King*, IV, 509.
15. Ford, ed., *Writings of Jefferson*, II, 443.
16. *Writings of Monroe*, IV, 492.
17. Adams, *History of the United States*, III, 404.
18. *Writings of Monroe*, IV, 460.
19. Bowdoin MSS, Massachusetts Historical Society.
20. *Writings of Monroe*, IV, 451.
21. *Ibid.*, V, 2.
22. Bowdoin MSS, Massachusetts Historical Society.
23. Quoted in Daniel C. Gilman, *James Monroe*, p. 103.
24. Adams, *History of the United States*, III, 412.
25. *Ibid.*, pp. 416 f.
26. *Ibid.*, pp. 432 f.

CHAPTER 22

1. Adams, *History of the United States*, IV, 13 f.
2. *American State Papers, Foreign Relations*, III, 187.
3. *Ibid.*
4. Bowdoin-Temple MSS, Massachusetts Historical Society.
5. Adams, *History of the United States*, IV, 98.
6. *Ibid.*, p. 32.

CHAPTER 23

1. *Writings of Monroe*, V, 26.
2. John P. Kennedy, *Memoirs of the Life of William Wirt*, I, 229.
3. *Writings of Monroe*, V, 84.
4. *Ibid.*, pp. 70 f.
5. Adams, *History of the United States*, IV, 187.
6. *Ibid.*, pp. 187 f.
7. *Writings of Monroe*, V, 64.
8. *Ibid.*, p. 33.

CHAPTER 24

1. *Writings of Monroe*, V, 109.
2. Adams, *History of the United States*, V, 260.
3. *Ibid.*, p. 292.
4. *Ibid.*, p. 328.
5. *Writings of Monroe*, V, 142.
6. *Ibid.*, p. 155.
7. *Ibid.*, p. 176.
8. *Ibid.*, p. 151.

CHAPTER 25

1. Washburn MSS, IX, Massachusetts Historical Society.
2. See *Writings of Monroe*, V, 168, 178, 180.
3. Adams, *History of the United States*, V, 369.
4. *Ibid.*
5. *Writings of Monroe*, V, 182.
6. Adams, *History of the United States*, V, 373.
7. James Madison, *Letters and Other Writings*, II, 495 ff.
8. *Writings of Monroe*, V, 186.
9. Adams, *History of the United States*, VI, 15.
10. William Ray Manning, *Diplomatic Correspondence of the United States Concerning the Independence of the Latin-American Nations*, II, 11.
11. *Ibid.*, pp. 672 ff.
12. Adams, *History of the United States*, VI, 44.
13. *Ibid.*, p. 190.
14. *Ibid.*, V, 396.
15. *Writings of Monroe*, V, 192 f.

CHAPTER 26

1. Adams, *History of the United States*, VI, 193.
2. *Ibid.*, p. 196.
3. *Ibid.*, pp. 194 f.
4. *Ibid.*, p. 200.
5. *Ibid.*, p. 221.
6. J. W. Pratt, *Expansionists of 1812*, p. 112.
7. *Ibid.*
8. Samuel F. Bemis, ed., *The American Secretaries of State and Their Diplomacy*, III, 223.
9. *Writings of Monroe*, V, 217.
10. Adams, *History of the United States*, VI, 415.
11. Jefferson MSS, State Department Archives.
12. Adams, *History of the United States*, VI, 395.
13. Jefferson MSS, State Department Archives.

CHAPTER 27

1. Adams, *History of the United States*, VII, 37.
2. *Writings of Monroe*, V, 245 ff.
3. Adams, *History of the United States*, VIII, 128.
4. For a full account of the British in Washington, see John S. Williams, *History of the Invasion and Capture of Washington*.
5. L. B. Cutts, *Memoirs and Letters of Dolly Madison*, p. 90.
6. Mrs. Samuel Harrison Smith, *First Forty Years of Washington Society*, pp. 89 f.
7. Nicolay, *Our Capital on the Potomac*, p. 105.
8. Anne Hollingsworth Wharton, *Social Life in the Early Republic*, pp. 160 f.
9. Upton, *Our Early Presidents*, p. 261.
10. Smith, *First Forty Years of Washington Society*, p. 98.
11. Wharton, *Social Life in the Early Republic*, p. 164.
12. *Writings of Monroe*, V, 289 f.
13. Adams, *History of the United States*, VIII, 132.
14. *Ibid.*, p. 137.
15. Williams, *Invasion and Capture of Washington*, Appendix, p. 337.
16. *Ibid.*, p. 217.
17. *Ibid.*, p. 341.
18. *Ibid.*, p. 219.
19. *Ibid.*, p. 218.
20. Adams, *History of the*

United States, VIII, 3.
21. *Ibid.*, p. 141.
22. Smith, *First Forty Years of Washington Society*, p. 113.
23. Nicolay, *Our Capital on the Potomac*, p. 110.
24. Wharton, *Social Life in the Early Republic*, p. 171.
25. *Ibid.*
26. *Ibid.*, p. 172.
27. *Ibid.*, p. 172.
28. Kennedy, *William Wirt*, p. 339.
29. Wharton, *Salons, Colonial and Republican*, p. 205.
30. Wharton, *Social Life in the Early Republic*, p. 166.

CHAPTER 28

1. *Writings of Monroe*, V, 294 f.
2. Washington, ed., *Writings of Jefferson*, V, 408.
3. *Writings of Monroe*, VII, 102 f.
4. Dorothie Bobbé, *Mr. and Mrs. John Quincy Adams*, p. 148.
5. *The Memoir of James Monroe, Esq., Relating to His Unsettled Claims upon the People and Government of the United States*, p. 58.
6. *Writings of Monroe*, VII, 102 f.
7. Washington, ed., *Writings of Jefferson*, VI, 395.
8. Adams, *History of the United States*, VIII, 276.
9. *Ibid.*, p. 288.
10. H. C. Lodge, *Studies in History*, p. 210.
11. *Writings of Monroe*, VII, 102 f.
12. War Department Records, MS.
13. See John Henry Eaton, *Life of Andrew Jackson*, pp. 219–82.
14. Adams, *History of the United States*, VIII, 333 ff.
15. *Ibid.*, IX, 41.
16. Wharton, *Social Life in the Early Republic*, pp. 179 f.
17. Sullivan, *Familiar Letters on Public Characters*, pp. 341 f.

CHAPTER 29

1. *Niles' Register*, XII (March 5, 1817), 20.
2. *Ibid.*
3. *Ibid.*
4. James D. Richardson, *A Compilation of the Messages and Papers of the Presidents, 1789–1902*, II, 4.
5. John B. McMaster, *A History of the People of the United States from the Revolution to the Civil War*, IV, 376–77.
6. Successfully restored to its former state, the house still stands on Pennsylvania Avenue and is

now the home of the Washington Art Club.

7. James Schouler, *History of the United States of America*, III, 7. Also, T. W. Higginson, "The Era of Good Feeling," *Harpers Magazine*, LX (1883), 936.

8. Richardson, *Messages and Papers of the Presidents*, II, 5.

9. *Ibid.*, p. 9.

10. *Ibid.*, p. 7.

11. *Niles' Register*, XII (March 8, 1817), 19.

12. *Ibid.*, p. 20.

13. Crowninshield MSS.

14. *Ibid.*

15. Act of 1813, authorizing the construction of a navy.

16. Claude M. Fuess, *Daniel Webster*, I, 269.

17. For a detailed description of the trip, by the official contemporary chronicler, see Samuel P. Waldo, *A Narrative of a Tour of Observation made during the summer of 1817 ... through the North Eastern and North Western departments of the Union: with a view to the examination of their several military defenses.*

18. *Niles' Register*, XII (June 7, 1817), 238.

19. *Ibid.* (June 28, 1817), p. 280.

20. *Ibid.* (June 21, 1817), p. 272.

21. *Ibid.* (July 12, 1817), p. 314.

22. *Ibid.*, p. 315.

23. *Ibid.*, p. 315.

24. *Ibid.*

25. *Ibid.* (July 12, 1817), pp. 316-17.

26. Quoted in *Niles' Register*, XII (July 19, 1817), 327.

27. Edward E. Hale, "Memories of a Hundred Years," *Outlook*, LXX (March 1, 1902), 549-52.

28. *Writings of James Monroe*, VI, 26.

29. *Ibid.*, p. 28 n. Also quoted in *Niles' Register*, XII (July 26, 1817), 343.

30. Quoted in *Niles' Register*, XII (July 19, 1817), 329.

31. *Ibid.*

32. *Ibid.* (August 2, 1817), p. 362.

33. *Ibid.* (July 26, 1817), p. 342.

34. *Writings of Monroe*, VI, 26.

35. J. Q. Adams, *Memoirs* (ed., Charles Francis Adams), IV, 7.

36. Allan Nevins, ed., *The Diary of John Quincy Adams, 1794-1845; American Political, Social, and Intellectual Life from Washington to Polk*, p. 187.

37. *Writings of Monroe*, VI, 2 ff.

38. *Ibid.*

39. J. Q. Adams, *Memoirs*, IV, 37.

40. *Writings of Monroe*, VI, 2 ff.

41. J. T. Morse, *John Quincy Adams*, p. 109.

42. A good general account of the South American colonial background is found in Mary W. Williams, *The People and Politics of Latin America*.

43. For the best account of Miranda's life and activities see W. S. Robertson, *The Life of Miranda*.

44. *Writings of Monroe*, V, 364.

45. Charles Lyon Chandler, "The Pan-American Origin of the Monroe Doctrine," *The American Journal of International Law*, VIII (July, 1914), 515-19.

46. For details of neutrality violation, see Schouler, *History of the*

United States, III, 27–29, and also McMaster, *History of the People of the United States*, IV, 372–76.
47. *Writings of Monroe*, VI, 31.
48. McMaster, *History of the United States*, IV, 434–36.
49. J. Q. Adams, *Memoirs*, IV, 14–15. List of "questions" appears in *Writings of Monroe*, VI, 31.
50. J. Q. Adams, *Memoirs*, IV, 15.
51. *Ibid.*
52. *Ibid.*, p. 25.
53. Richardson, *Messages and Papers of the Presidents*, II, 13-14.
54. *Ibid.*, p. 14.
55. J. Q. Adams, *Memoirs*, IV, 28.
56. Schouler, *History of the United States*, III, 33.
57. J. Q. Adams, *Memoirs*, IV, 66.
58. *Niles' Register*, XIV, 121, 136.
59. J. Q. Adams, *Memoirs*, IV, 30–31.
60. *Ibid.*, p. 71.
61. A secret act which, in an emergency, empowered the Executive to take possession of East and West Florida. These acts had only recently been published.

CHAPTER 30

1. The material in this chapter has been drawn, to a large extent, from Schouler, *History of the United States*, III, 57–97; J. Bassett, *Andrew Jackson*, pp. 233–89; McMaster, *History of the United States*, IV, 430–56; and J. Q. Adams, *Memoirs*, Vol. IV.
2. This demand was based on the provisions of the Treaty of 1795 with Spain which bound her to restrain forcibly all hostilities against the United States on the part of the Indians. Failure to do so implied permission, almost the obligation of the United States to drive over the border against the Indians.
3. J. Q. Adams, *Memoirs*, IV, 31.
4. Bassett, *A Short History of the United States*, p. 370.
5. *Ibid.*
6. Letter of January 6, 1818, quoted and entire controversy discussed in Schouler, "Monroe and the Rhea Letter," *Magazine of American History*, XII (October, 1884), 308–22. J. Rhea, a member of Congress from Tennessee, was a parasite of Jackson's and more familiarly known as Johnny Rhea; quoted in Parton, *The Life of Andrew Jackson*, II, 434.
7. *Writings of Monroe*, VI, 84–87.
8. Thomas H. Benton, "Jackson's Exposition," *Thirty Years' View*. Found among Jackson's papers and posthumously published.
9. *Writings of Monroe*, VI, 85–87. For a well balanced discussion of the "Rhea letter," see Marquis James, *The Life of Andrew Jackson* (one-volume ed.), pp. 527–29.
10. *Writings of Monroe*, VI, 46.

11. Quoted in Bassett, *Andrew Jackson*, p. 241.
12. *American State Papers, Foreign Relations*, IV, 445.
13. Hubert B. Fuller, *The Purchase of Florida*, p. 277.
14. *Ibid.*, p. 299.
15. J. Q. Adams, *Memoirs*, IV, 37.
16. McMaster, *History of the United States*, IV, 476.
17. J. Q. Adams, *Memoirs*, IV, 78.
18. Richardson, *Messages and Papers of the Presidents*, II, 31–32.
19. J. Q. Adams, *Memoirs*, IV, 40.
20. *Ibid.*, p. 48.
21. *Ibid.*, p. 49.
22. *Ibid.*, p. 51.
23. *Ibid.*, p. 52.
24. *Ibid.*, p. 105.
25. Schouler, *History of the United States*, III, 75.
26. J. Q. Adams, *Memoirs*, IV, 105.
27. *Ibid.*, p. 106.
28. *Ibid.*, p. 115.
29. *Ibid.*, p. 108.
30. *Ibid.*, p. 107.
31. *Ibid.*, p. 115.
32. Schouler, *History of the United States*, III, 77.
33. J. Q. Adams, *Memoirs*, IV, 109.
34. *Ibid.*, p. 111.
35. *Ibid.*
36. *Ibid.*, pp. 113–14.
37. *Ibid.*, p. 114.
38. Quoted in Schouler, *History of the United States*, III, 78.
39. Fuller, *The Purchase of Florida*, Appendix C, pp. 340–58.
40. J. Q. Adams, *Memoirs*, IV, 117.
41. *Writings of Monroe*, VI, 55 ff.
42. Quoted in Bassett, *Andrew Jackson*, p. 276.
43. *Writings of Monroe*, VI, 75.
44. J. Q. Adams, *Memoirs*, IV, 194.
45. *Writings of Monroe*, VI, 85–87; Also quoted by Schouler, "Monroe and the Rhea Letter," *Magazine of American History*, XII, 308–22.
46. J. Q. Adams, *Memoirs*, IV, 119.
47. Richardson, *Messages and Papers of the Presidents*, I, 609.
48. *Ibid.*, pp. 610–11.
49. *Ibid.*, p. 612.
50. *Writings of Monroe*, VI, 88.
51. J. L. M. Curry, "The Acquisition of Florida," *Magazine of American History*, XIX (April, 1888), 287 ff. quotes this letter.
52. J. Q. Adams, *Memoirs*, IV, 237–38.
53. *Ibid.*, p. 239.
54. *Ibid.*, p. 250.
55. Schouler, *History of the United States*, III, 95.
56. McMaster, *History of the United States*, IV, 478–88.
57. *Writings of Monroe*, VI, 106–13.
58. *Ibid.*, pp. 117–18.
59. *Ibid.*, pp. 118–23.
60. *Ibid.*, pp. 127–28.
61. *Ibid.*, p. 119.
62. Richardson, *History of the United States*, I, 640–41.
63. Schouler, *History of the United States*, III, 189.

CHAPTER 31

1. Richardson, *Messages and Papers of the Presidents*, II, 11, 12.
2. *Ibid.*, pp. 19–20.
3. *Niles' Register*, (December 20, 1817), 257.
4. *Annals of Congress*, 16th Congress, 1st Session, p. 446.
5. April 29, 1820.
6. J. Q. Adams, *Memoirs*, IV, 375.
7. McMaster, *History of the United States*, IV, 488.
8. Mrs. St. Julien Ravenel, *Charleston, the Place and the People*, p. 425.
9. *Niles' Register*, XVI (May 8, 1819), 192.
10. Mrs. St. J. Ravenel, *Charleston*, p. 425.
11. *Ibid.*, p. 246.
12. *Niles' Register*, XVI (May 15, 1819), 208.
13. Federal Writers' Project, American Guide Series, *Savannah*, p. 39.
14. *Niles' Register*, XVI (June 19, 1819), 287.
15. *Ibid.* (June 26, 1819), p. 298.
16. J. Q. Adams, *Memoirs*, IV, 468.
17. Richardson, *Messages and Papers of the Presidents*, II, 61.
18. *Ibid.*

CHAPTER 32

1. Philip Slaughter, *The Virginian History of African Colonization*, pp. 1–6.
2. Information found in a MS, dealing with Virginians, by Jennings Wise.
3. *Annals of Congress*, 15th Congress, 2nd Session, I, 1204.
4. J. Q. Adams, *Memoirs*, IV, 262.
5. *Ibid.*, p. 471.
6. *Ibid.*, p. 522.
7. *Ibid.*, V, 41.
8. *Ibid.*, IV (February 13, 1820), 525–26.
9. *Ibid.* (February 10, 1820), pp. 502–3.
10. *Ibid.* (February 24, 1820), p. 531.
11. *Writings of Monroe*, VI 114.
12. *Ibid.*, p. 116.
13. *Ibid.*, p. 122.
14. *Congressional Globe*, 30th Congress, 2nd Session, Appendix, p. 67.

15. Quoted in D. C. Gilman, *James Monroe*, p. 148.
16. J. Q. Adams, *Memoirs*, IV, 499.
17. Everett Sommerville Brown, ed., *The Missouri Compromises and Presidential Politics, 1820–1825*, p. 10.
18. Letter quoted in Mrs. Archibald Dixon, *The True History of the Missouri Compromise and Its Repeal*, p. 88.
19. *Congressional Globe*, 30th Congress, 1st Session, XX, 67.
20. J. Q. Adams, *Memoirs*, V, 5.
21. Bassett, *A Short History of the United States*, p. 374.
22. Dixon, *Missouri Compromise*, p. 89.
23. J. Q. Adams, *Memoirs*, V, 128.
24. *Ibid.*, IV, 498.
25. *Ibid.*, V, 279.

CHAPTER 33

1. J. Q. Adams, *Memoirs*, V, 302.
2. *Ibid.*, pp. 317–18.
3. Letter to Planta of March 8, 1821. Stanley Lane-Poole, *The Life of the Right Honorable Stratford Canning*, I, 318.
4. *Niles' Register*, XX (March 10, 1821), 18.
5. *Ibid.*
6. *Ibid.*, p. 20.
7. *Ibid.*
8. W. W. Story, ed., *The Life and Letters of Joseph Story*, I, 401.
9. Letter written by Baron Axel Klinkowström, a Lt. Col. in the Swedish Navy, to Rear Admiral Count Clais Cronstedt, on February 12, 1819, on the occasion of a two-year study trip in the United States, 1818–1820.—"In Monroe's Administration," *American Scandanavian Review*, XIX (July, 1931), 394 ff.
10. Mrs. E. F. Ellet, *The Court Circles of the Republic*, p. 105.
11. Richardson, *Messages and Papers of the Presidents*, II, 26–27.
12. J. Q. Adams, *Memoirs*, IV, 32.
13. *Ibid.*, p. 32.
14. From the *National Intelligencer*, January 2, 1818, quoted in Gilson Willets, *The Inside History of the White House*, p. 47.
15. Schouler, *History of the United States*, p. 206.
16. Ellet, *The Court Circles of the Republic*, pp. 98–99.
17. Monroe Johnson, "Mrs. Monroe—Her Doctrine," *National Republic*, XVIII (December, 1930), 22–23.
18. Marian Gouverneur, *As I Remember*, p. 257.
19. J. Q. Adams, *Memoirs*, IV, 45–46.
20. William Winston Seaton, *A Biographical Sketch with Passing Notes of his Associates and Friends*, p. 136.
21. J. Q. Adams, *Memoirs*, IV, 188–89.

22. Words are Mrs. Seaton's quoted by Meade Minnigerode, "Elizabeth Monroe and Louisa Adams." *Some American Ladies.*
23. J. Q. Adams, *Memoirs,* IV, 479.
24. *Ibid.,* p. 493
25. *Ibid.*
26. *Ibid.,* pp. 480–81.
27. Quoted in Seaton, *A Biographical Sketch,* pp. 137 ff.
28. J. Q. Adams, *Memoirs,* IV, 483-85.
29. *Ibid.*
30. *Ibid.,* V, 511.
31. Francis Leupp, *Walks About Washington,* pp. 149–50.
32. *Notions of the Americans,* II, 70.
33. Ellet, *The Court Circles of the Republic,* p. 104.
34. Margaret Bayard Smith, *The First Forty Years of White House Society* (ed., Gaillard Hunt), p. 150.
35. *Ibid.,* p. 151.
36. Letter written by S. L. Gouverneur from Washington on October 9, 1821. Among the collection of letters in the James Monroe Law Office, Fredericksburg, Virginia.
37. *Writings of Monroe,* VI, 179.
38. Letter of Baron Axel Klinkowström to Count Clais Cronstedt, February 12, 1819, *American Scandanavian Review,* XIX, (July, 1931), 394 ff.
39. G. S. Hilliard, comp., *Life, Letters and Journals of George Ticknor.*
40. Letter quoted in J. T. Morse, *John Quincy Adams,* p. 102.
41. Seaton, *A Biographical Sketch,* pp. 113 ff.
42. For weeks in advance of a public function slaves were kept busy making candles under Mrs. Monroe's personal supervision. It is estimated that lighting costs amounted to almost $100 per entertainment, paid out of the private purse of the President.
43. Letter of Baron Axel Klinkowström, *loc. cit.,* pp. 394 ff.
44. Gilson Willets, *The Inside History of the White House,* p. 302.
45. Letter of Baron Klinkowström, *loc. cit.*
46. Story, ed., *The Life and Letters of Joseph Story,* I, 310–311.
47. Letter of Baron Klinkowström, *loc. cit.*
48. Quoted in Wharton, *Social Life in the Early Republic,* p. 189.
49. Quoted in *Ibid.,* p. 136.
50. Marian Gouverneur, *As I Remember,* p. 257.
51. J. Q. Adams, *Memoirs,* V, 15–16.
52. Quoted in Wharton, *Salons, Colonial and Republican,* pp. 207–8.
53. Quoted in Willetts, *The Inside History of the White House,* pp. 269–70.
54. Wharton, *Salons, Colonial and Republican,* p. 208.
55. Can find no allusion by outsiders to the existence or nature of the quarrel. However, in letters written by Mr. Gouverneur to the President, in Mr. Hoes' collection, now in the James Monroe Law Office in Fredericksburg, there are several allusions to the misunderstanding and a sincere wish on his part to clear it up.

56. MS Collection in the James Monroe Law Office in Fredericksburg.
57. *Ibid.*, April 13, 1823.
58. MS Collection in the James Monroe Law Office.
59. Letter quoted in Gilman, *James Monroe*, pp. 215–16.

CHAPTER 34

1. *Writings of Monroe*, VI, 129–30.
2. Letter quoted in J. Bassett, *Andrew Jackson*, p. 294.
3. Schouler, *History of the United States*, III, 239.
4. March 3, 1821.
5. *Writings of Monroe*, VI, 175.
6. *Ibid.*, pp. 177–78.
7. *Ibid.* For complete list of appointees see Monroe's letter to Jackson of May 23, 1821 (*ibid.*, VI, 182–84).
8. See Marquis James, *The Life of Andrew Jackson*, p. 315.
9. Schouler, *History of the United States*, III, 240.
10. *Writings of Monroe*, VI, 180–85.
11. Bassett, *Andrew Jackson*, p. 295.
12. *Writings of Monroe*, VI, 185.
13. J. Q. Adams, *Memoirs*, V, 359.
14. *Writings of Monroe*, VI, 197–98.
15. J. Q. Adams, *Memoirs*, V, 368.
16. Schouler, *History of the United States*, III, 243
17. J. Q. Adams, *Memoirs*, V, 368.
18. Richardson, *Messages and Papers of the Presidents*, II, 103, 105.
19. *Writings of Monroe*, VI, 207.
20. *Ibid.*, p. 291.

CHAPTER 35

1. Schouler, *History of the United States*, III, 247.
2. *Niles' Register*, XXI, 336, 359, 400.
3. *Writings of Monroe*, VI, 32.
4. Richardson, *Messages and Papers of the Presidents*, II, 17–18.
5. *Ibid.*
6. *Annals of Congress*, 15th Congress, 1st Session, I, 1249.
7. F. J. Turner, *The Rise of the New West, 1819–1829*, p. 229.
8. Quoted in Homer Hockett, *Political and Social History of the United States, 1492–1828*, p. 340.

9. McMaster, *History of the United States*, V, 249.
10. Schouler, *History of the United States*, p. 249.
11. *Writings of Madison* (ed., Gaillard Hunt) VIII, 404–5.
12. Seymour Dunbar, *A History of Travel in America*, p. 700.
13. J. Q. Adams, *Memoirs*, V, 155–56.
14. J. W. Burgess, *The Middle Period, 1817–1858*, pp. 118–19.
15. Richardson, *Messages and Papers of the Presidents*, II, 142–43.
16. Printed in *Bulletin of the New York Public Library*, VI (July, 1902), 249–50.
17. J. Q. Adams, *Memoirs*, V, 516–17.
18. *Writings of Monroe*, VI, 217.
19. *Ibid.*, pp. 223–26.
20. Quoted in R. W. Thompson, *Recollections of Sixteen Presidents*, pp. 87–106.
21. For entire message see *Writings of Monroe*, VI, 216–84; or Richardson, *Messages and Papers of the Presidents*, II, 144–83.
22. *Writings of Monroe*, VI, 265–66.
23. Schouler, *History of the United States*, III, 294.
24. Quoted in Bassett, *Andrew Jackson*, p. 403.
25. *Writings of Monroe*, VI, 284 n.
26. Quoted in Schouler, *History of the United States*, III, 294.
27. McMaster, *History of the United States*, V, 249.
28. Richardson, *Messages and Papers of the Presidents*, II, 190–91.
29. *Ibid.*, p. 217.
30. *Ibid.*, pp. 216–17.
31. Carl Schurz, *The Life of Henry Clay*, I, 206.
32. Quoted in Turner, *The Rise of the New West*, p. 233.
33. *Ibid.*, p. 234.
34. Richardson, *Messages and Papers of the Presidents*, II, 255.
35. Schouler, *History of the United States*, III, 295.

CHAPTER 36

1. For background of revolutions and early attempt at recognition in this country see Chapter XXIX, above.
2. C. C. Griffin, *The United States and the Disruption of the Spanish Empire, 1810–1822*, p. 145.
3. "Correspondence between General William Winder and President Monroe with Reference to Proposals Made by the United Provinces of South America," *Hispanic American Historical Review*, XII (November, 1932), 457–61.
4. *Ibid.*
5. J. Q. Adams, *Memoirs*, IV, 92.
6. *Ibid.*
7. *Ibid.*, p. 72.
8. *Ibid.*, p. 49.
9. Sketch of Instruction for Agents for South America, *Writings of Monroe*, VI, 96.
10. *Ibid.*, pp. 49–51.

11. Richardson, *Messages and Papers of the Presidents*, II, 44.
12. *Writings of Monroe*, VI, 124–26.
13. *Ibid.*, pp. 92–102.
14. *Ibid.*, pp. 132, 128–29.
15. *Ibid.*, p. 112.
16. Richardson, *Messages and Papers of the Presidents*, II, 77.
17. J. Q. Adams, *Memoirs*, IV, 472.
18. Griffin, *The United States and the Disruption of the Spanish Empire*, p. 267.
19. Stanley Lane-Poole, *Life of Canning*, pp. 309–10.
20. Quoted in Charles Lyon Chandler, "The Pan-American Origin of the Monroe Doctrine," *American Journal of International Law*, VIII (July, 1914), 515–19.
21. Richardson, *Messages and Papers of the Presidents*, II, 105.
22. *Annals of Congress*, 17th Congress, 1st Session, I, 825–826.
23. *Writings of Monroe*, VI, 207, 209.
24. *Ibid.*, p. 209.
25. *Ibid.*, p. 211.
26. *Ibid.*, p. 213.
27. W. S. Robertson, "The United States and Spain in 1822," *American Historical Review*, XX (July, 1915), 781–800.
28. *Annals of Congress*, 17th Congress, 1st Session, II, 2603–2604.
29. *Writings of Monroe*, VI, 214.
30. *Ibid.*, VIII, 121–22.
31. *Niles' Register*, XIII, (November 9, 1817), 174.
32. Latané, *A History of American Foreign Policy*, p. 286.
33. J. Q. Adams, *Memoirs*, VI, 69, 72.
34. *Ibid.*, p. 73.
35. E. J. Stapleton, ed., *Some Official Correspondence of George Canning*, I, 52.
36. Quoted in Latané, *A History of American Foreign Policy*, p. 287.
37. Washington, ed., *Writings of Jefferson*, VII, 288.
38. *Writings of Monroe*, VI, 312–13.

CHAPTER 37

1. J. Q. Adams, *Memoirs*, V, 252 ff.
2. *Niles' Register*, XXI (December 29, 1821), 279.
3. February 25, 1822.
4. J. Q. Adams, *Memoirs*, VI, 163.
5. Quoted in J. Reuben Clark, *Memorandum on the Monroe Doctrine*, p. 84.
6. April 12, 1823.
7. Clark, *Memorandum on the Monroe Doctrine*, p. 85.
8. Quoted in Dexter Perkins, *The Monroe Doctrine, 1823–1826*, p. 7.
9. *Writings of James Madison*, IX (ed., Gaillard Hunt), pp. 197–98.

CHAPTER 38

1. *Niles' Register* XXV (September 6, 1823).
2. J. Q. Adams, *Memoirs*, VI, 185.
3. Sixth article. Quoted by H. C. Lodge, "International Events Which Precipitated the Monroe Doctrine," *Congresional Digest*, VI (April, 1927), 115–16.
4. W. P. Cresson, *The Holy Alliance; The European Background of the Monroe Doctrine*, p. 28.
5. Given in full in Czartoryski, *Mémoires*, II, 27, and Appendix. Long buried in the archives of the Russian Foreign Office, these were first made public in their complete form through the publication of the *Mémoires*. They had previously been known only through a partial quotation by Tatistcheff and notably through Pitt's carefully veiled reply.
6. Cresson, *The Holy Alliance*, Introduction, pp. 1–37.
7. W. A. Phillips, *The Confederation of Europe*, p. 129.
8. *Ibid.*, p. 131.
9. While detailed to the French Fourth Army in 1917, William Penn Cresson came across a monument—shattered by German shell fire—which was erected near Chalons to commemorate the Tsar Alexander's dream of perpetual peace.
10. Cresson, *The Holy Alliance*, p. 31.
11. *Ibid.*
12. Metternich, *Mémoires*, I, 209–10.
13. For details of this attempt by Alexander, Dashkov, and de Tuyll, see Cresson, *The Holy Alliance*, pp. 37–53.
14. Quoted in *Writings of Monroe*, VI, 349–50.
15. Files of the New York Public Library.
16. *Niles' Register*, X (April 6, 1816).
17. *Writings of Monroe*, VI, 48.
18. *Cambridge Modern History*, X, 210.
19. *Ibid.*
20. *Niles' Register*, XIII (September 13, 1817), 46.
21. Phillips, *The Confederation of Europe*, p. 168.
22. *Ibid.*, pp. 254–58.
23. Quoted in Cresson, *The Holy Alliance*, p. 95.
24. Phillips, *The Confederation of Europe*, p. 219.
25. *Ibid.*, p. 222.
26. François, Vicomte de Chateaubriand, *Congrès de Vérone*, I, 94.
27. Phillips, *The Confederation of Europe*, p. 262.
28. Stapleton, *The Political Life of Canning*, I, 19.

29. Rush, *Residence at the Court of London*, p. 400.
30. *Ibid.*
31. J. Q. Adams, *Memoirs*, VI, 152.

CHAPTER 39

1. Rush, *Residence at the Court of London*, p. 412. Quoted in *Writings of Monroe*, VI, 365–66.
2. Quoted in *Writings of Monroe*, VI, 366.
3. Rush, *Residence at the Court of London*, p. 415.
4. *Ibid.*, p. 416.
5. Quoted in *Writings of Monroe*, VI, 369.
6. *Ibid.*, pp. 376–77.
7. *Ibid.*, pp. 386–87.
8. *Ibid.*, pp. 324–25.
9. *Ibid.*, pp. 391–92.
10. *Ibid.*, pp. 394–95.
11. *Ibid.*, p. 390.
12. J. Q. Adams, *Memoirs*, VI, 178, 194, 199–212.
13. *Ibid.*, p. 194.
14. *Ibid.*, p. 186.
15. Allan Nevins, ed., *The Diary of John Quincy Adams*, p. 302.
16. J. Q. Adams, *Memoirs*, VI, 179.
17. Quoted in MacCorkle, *The Personal Genesis of the Monroe Doctrine*, p. 44.
18. Complete text of Adams' original draft, Monroe's amendments, and final message contained in MacCorkle, *The Personal Genesis of the Monroe Doctrine*, pp. 44–56.
19. *Ibid.*, pp. 55–56.
20. *Ibid.*, p. 49.
21. Quoted in Dexter Perkins, *The Monroe Doctrine, 1823–1826*, Chapter I.
22. Calhoun, *Works*, IV, 462 ff.
23. J. Q. Adams, *Memoirs*, VI, 185.
24. Richardson, *Messages and Papers of the Presidents*, II, 209.
25. J. Q. Adams, *Memoirs*, VI, 199–216.
26. Extract from Adams, *Memoirs*. Quoted in Raddaway, *The Monroe Doctrine*, Chapter V.
27. Quoted in MacCorkle, *The Personal Genesis of the Monroe Doctrine*, p. 64.
28. *Writings of Monroe*, VI, 324–25.
29. *Ibid.*, pp. 391–92.
30. J. Q. Adams, *Memoirs*, VI, 194.
31. *Ibid.*, pp. 197 ff.
32. *Ibid.*, p. 195.
33. *Ibid.*, p. 199.
34. Richardson, *Messages and Papers of the Presidents*, II, 209.
35. *Ibid.*, p. 218.
36. J. Q. Adams, *Memoirs*, V, 176.
37. A. A. Lipscomb, ed., *The Writings of Thomas Jefferson*, XII, 187.
38. *Ibid.*, XV, 263.
39. *Writings of Monroe*, VI, 151–52.

CHAPTER 40

1. J. Q. Adams, *Memoirs*, V, 89.
2. *Ibid.*, IV, 193.
3. *Ibid.*, p. 212.
4. Meade Minnigerode, *Presidential Years, 1787–1890*, p. 128.
5. J. Q. Adams, *Memoirs*, V. 59.
6. Kennedy, *Life of William Wirt*, II, 168.
7. *Writings of Monroe*, VI, 286.
8. J. Q. Adams, *Memoirs*, V, 525.
9. *Writings of Monroe*, VI, 287.
10. *Ibid.*, pp. 286–91.
11. Quoted in Schouler, *History of the United States*, III, 329 n.
12. Schurz, *Henry Clay*, I, 231.
13. Gilman, *James Monroe*, pp. 153–54.
14. P. A. Bruce, *The Virginia Plutarch*, II, 110–11.
15. Quoted in Gilman, *James Monroe*, p. 154.
16. *Niles' Register*, XXVIII (December 28, 1824), 292.
17. *Ibid.* (January 8, 1825), p. 291.
18. *Ibid.*
19. *Ibid.* (November 6, 1824), p. 145.
20. Calvin Colton, *Private Correspondence of Henry Clay*, p. 109.
21. Bassett, *Andrew Jackson*, p. 359.
22. *Ibid.*, p. 365.
23. S. G. Goodrich, *Recollections of a Lifetime*, I, 403–4.
24. Schouler, *History of the United States*, III, 329.
25. Sherwin L. Cook, *Torchlight Parade: Our Presidential Pageant*, p. 25.
26. *Niles' Register*, XII, 19.
27. *Writings of Monroe*, VII, 6.
28. Richardson, *Messages and Papers of the Presidents*, II, 16.
29. *Ibid.*, p. 92.
30. *Ibid.*, p. 261.
31. *Ibid.*, pp. 262–64.
32. Quoted in *Niles' Register*, XXX (March 5, 1825), 1.

CHAPTER 41

1. J. Q. Adams, *The Lives of James Madison and James Monroe*, p. 293.
2. *Writings of Monroe*, VII, 42–43.
3. *Niles' Register*, XXX (January 29, 1825), 339.
4. From the *National Journal*, quoted in *Niles' Register*, XXX (March 12, 1825), 20.

5. J. Q. Adams, *Memoirs*, VI, 518.
6. *Niles' Register*, XXX (March 12, 1825), 20.
7. Notes supplied by Mr. Laurence Gouverneur Hoes.
8. Robert A. Lancaster, Jr., *Historic Virginia Homes and Churches*, pp. 373-74.
9. J. Q. Adams, *Memoirs*, VII, 41.
10. *Ibid.*, p. 42.
11. *Writings of Monroe*, VII, 50-51.
12. *Ibid.*
13. *Ibid.*, p. 54.
14. *Ibid.*
15. *Niles' Register* (April 23, 1825), 128.
16. *Writings of Monroe*, VII, 61.
17. Quoted in Marian Gouverneur, *As I Remember*, p. 77.
18. *Writings of Monroe*, VII, 67-68.
19. *Ibid.*, p. 163.
20. *Ibid.*, p. 85.
21. Schouler, *History of the United States*, III, 387.
22. James Buchanan, *Works* (ed., Moore), I, 117.
23. Quoted in Gilman, *James Monroe*, p. 157.
24. *Writings of Monroe*, VII, 199.
25. *Niles' Register*, XXXV (January 31, 1829), 376.
26. *Ibid.* (January 8, 1831), p. 333.
27. Quoted in Gilman, *James Monroe*, p. 234.
28. *Writings of Monroe*, VII, 233.
29. *Niles' Register* (May 7, 1831), 168.
30. *Writings of Monroe*, VII, 90-91.
31. In February 1828, in canceling a public dinner engagement at Leesburg because of Mrs. Monroe's illness, Monroe expressed his opinion on the proposed Convention: "In the propriety of holding a convention, to recommend an amendment of its defects, should a majority of that body think that such existed, I fully concur, having perfect confidence that experience is the best test of human institutions, and that an enlightened and free people cannot fail, should a change be made, to improve the system."—Letter quoted in *Niles' Register* (March 1, 1828), 6.
32. *Writings of Monroe*, VII, 193-94.
33. Barton H. Wise, *Life of Henry A. Wise*, p. 131.
34. Quoted in Schouler, *History of the United States*, III, 465; *Niles' Register*, XXXVII.
35. Speech quoted in Wise, *Life of Henry A. Wise*, p. 132.
36. *Niles' Register* (January 23, 1830), 358.
37. J. Q. Adams, *Memoirs*, VIII, 173.
38. "McLean is a double-dealer. His words are smoother than butter, but war is in his heart."—*Memoirs*, VIII, 25.
39. J. Q. Adams, *Memoirs*, VII, 275.
40. *Writings of Monroe*, VII, 122-23.
41. Schouler, *History of the United States*, III, 430.
42. *Writings of Monroe*, VII, 128-29.

43. Bassett, *Andrew Jackson*, p. 495.
44. *Writings of Monroe*, VII, 94.
45. Ibid., p. 111.
46. Ibid., p. 125.
47. Ibid., pp. 134-35.
48. Ibid., pp. 153-54.
49. J. Q. Adams, *Diary* (ed., Nevins), pp. 199 ff.
50. Monroe MSS.
51. Bassett, *Andrew Jackson*, pp. 500-1.
52. Ibid.
53. Schouler, "Monroe and the Rhea Letter," *Magazine of American History*, XII (October, 1884), 315.
54. *Writings of Monroe*, VII, 138.
55. Ibid., pp. 140-43.
56. Ibid., p. 139.
57. Schouler, *History of the United States*, III, 443.
58. *Writings of Monroe*, VII, 175-76.
59. Schouler, *History of the United States*, III, 443.
60. *Writings of Monroe*, VII, 209-10.
61. Ibid., p. 219.
62. Ibid., pp. 211-12.
63. Ibid., p. 185.
64. Quoted in Gilman, *James Monroe*, pp. 218-26.
65. Ellet, *The Court Circles of the Republic*, p. 113.
66. Frank Allaben, *John Watts DePeyster*, I, 95, 99.
67. Morgan, *Life of James Monroe*, p. 441.
68. *Writings of Monroe*, VII, 231.
69. Quoted in James W. Head, *History of Loudoun County*, p. 142.
70. J. Q. Adams, *Memoirs*, VIII, 360.
71. *Writings of Monroe*, VII, 229.
72. *Supra*, pp. 304-5; 316-17.
73. Quoted in Schouler, "Monroe and the Rhea Letter," *Magazine of American History*, XII (October, 1884), 315.
74. *Writings of Monroe*, VII, p. 234.
75. Ibid., pp. 234-36.
76. J. Q. Adams, *Memoirs*, VIII, 404.
77. Ibid., pp. 404-5.
78. *Niles' Register* (July 23, 1831), 369 ff.
79. Marian Gouverneur, *As I Remember*, pp. 108-10.

APPENDIX: GENEALOGY

1. Alexander Mackenzie, *History of the Munros of Fowlis*.
2. See Edward S. Lewis, "Ancestry of James Monroe," *William and Mary College Quarterly* (Second Series) III, No. 3 (July, 1923), 173 ff.; Monroe Johnson, "The Maryland Ancestry of James Monroe," *Maryland Historical Magazine*, XXIII, No. 2 (June, 1928) 193-95; Lyon G. Tyler, "James Monroe," *William and Mary Col-

lege Quarterly (First Series) IV, No. 4 (April, 1896), 272–75.

3. Lewis, *op. cit.*

4. "The Monroe Family," *William and Mary College Quarterly* (Second Series) XIII, No. 4 (October, 1933) 231 ff.; *The History and Register of the Colonial Dames of Virginia* (p. 497) also lists an "... Andrew Monroe of Maryland born in Scotland in ... and died in Virginia, 1668. Resided in Virginia and Maryland 1642–1668."

5. Virginia State Land Office, Patent Book No. 2, p. 225.

6. Information supplied by Mr. George H. S. King, of Fredericksburg, Virginia, who has made an exhaustive study of Monroe genealogy.

7. "The Monroe Family," *William and Mary College Quarterly*, (Second Series) XIII, No. 4 (October, 1933), 231–41.

LIST OF REFERENCES
(This list is confined to works actually cited in the notes.)

I. Published Works

Abbott, W. C. *New York in the American Revolution.* New York, 1929.

Adams, Charles Francis, ed. *See* Adams, John, and Adams, John Quincy.

Adams, Henry. *History of the United States.* New York, 1889–91. Vols. I–IX.

────── *John Randolph.* Boston, 1883.

────── *The Life of Albert Gallatin.* Philadelphia, 1879.

Adams, John. *Familiar Letters of John Adams and His Wife Abigail Adams, during the Revolution.* Ed., Charles Francis Adams. Boston, 1876.

────── *The Works of John Adams.* Ed., Charles Francis Adams. Boston, 1850–56. Vol. I.

Adams, John Quincy. *The Diary of . . . , 1794–1845.* Ed., Allan Nevins. New York, 1928.

────── "Letters of, to Alexander Hill Everett, 1811–1837," *American Historical Review,* XI (October, 1905; January, 1906), 88–116, 332–54.

────── *Memoirs, comprising portions of his Diary from 1795–1848, by J. Q. Adams.* Ed., Charles Francis Adams. Philadelphia, 1874–77. Vols. IV, V, VII, VIII.

────── *The Lives of James Madison and James Monroe.* Buffalo, 1850.

Allaben, Frank. *John Watts de Peyster.* New York, 1908. Vol. I.

Alvarez, Alejandro. *The Monroe Doctrine.* Publications of the Carnegie Endowment for International Peace. New York, 1924.

Ambler, Charles H. *George Washington and the West.* Chapel Hill, 1936.

American State Papers, Foreign Relations. Vols. I–IV.

Annals of Congress, for the period.

Babcock, K. C. *The Rise of American Nationality.* New York, 1906.

Bancroft, George. *Histoire de l'action Commune de la France et de l'Amérique pour l'Indépendance des États-Unis; Traduit et Annoté par le comte Adolphe de Circourt; Accompagné de Documents Inedits.* Ed., Adolphe de Circourt. Paris, 1876.

Barbé-Marbois, F. *Our Revolutionary Forefathers.* Tr. and ed., Eugene Parker Chase. New York, 1929.

────── *The History of Louisiana. . . .* "Translated from the French by an American Citizen." [William Beach Lawrence.] Philadelphia, 1830.

List of References

Bassett, J. S. *The Life of Andrew Jackson.* New York, 1911.
——— *A Short History of the United States, 1492–1920.* New York, 1921.
Battle of Long Island, The. Memoirs of the Long Island Historical Society, Vol. II. Brooklyn, 1869.
Bemis, Samuel F. *Jay's Treaty: A Study in Commerce and Diplomacy.* New York, 1923.
——— ed. *The American Secretaries of State and Their Diplomacy.* New York, 1927–29. Vol. III.
Benton, Thomas H. "Jackson's Exposition," *Thirty Years' View.* New York, 1854–56.
Beveridge, Albert J. *The Life of John Marshall,* Boston, 1916. Vols. I, II.
Bobbé, Dorothie. *Mr. and Mrs. John Quincy Adams.* New York, 1930.
Bond, B. W. *The Monroe Mission to France, 1794–1796.* Johns Hopkins Studies in History and Political Science (Series XXV) Nos. 2–3, 1907.
Bowers, Claude G. *Jefferson and Hamilton.* Boston, 1925.
Boyd, Thomas. *Light-horse Harry Lee.* New York, 1931.
Brown, Everett Sommerville, ed. *The Missouri Compromises and Presidential Politics, 1820–1825.* St. Louis, 1926.
Bruce, Philip A. *The Virginian Plutarch.* Chapel Hill, 1929. Vol. II.
Buchanan, James. *Works.* Ed., J. B. Moore. Philadelphia, 1908–1911. Vol. I.
Burgess, John W. *The Middle Period.* New York, 1897.
Calhoun, John C. *Works.* Ed., R. K. Crallé. New York, 1895. Vol. IV.
Campbell, Charles. *Introduction to the History of the Colony and Ancient Dominion of Virginia.* Richmond, 1847.
Canning, George. *Some Official Correspondence of* . . . . Ed., E. J. Stapleton. London, 1887. Vol. I.
Chandler, Charles Lyon. "The Pan-American Origin of the Monroe Doctrine," *The American Journal of International Law,* VIII (July, 1914).
——— "United States Commerce with Latin America at the Promulgation of the Monroe Doctrine," *Quarterly Journal of Economics,* XXXVIII (May, 1924), 466–86.
Chateaubriand, François Auguste René, Vicomte de. *Congrès de Vérone.* Paris, 1838. Vol. I.
Chase, Eugene Parker, tr. and ed. *Our Revolutionary Forefathers,* by F. Barbé-Marbois. New York, 1929.
Chinard, Gilbert. *Thomas Jefferson, The Apostle of Americanism.* Boston, 1929.
Circourt, Adolphe de. *See* Bancroft, George.

List of References

Clark, George Rogers. "George Rogers Clark Papers," *Collections of the Illinois State Historical Library*, Virginia Series, XIX (1926), 250.

Clark, J. Reuben. *Memorandum on the Monroe Doctrine*. Publications of the Department of State, No. 37. Washington, 1930.

Colonial Williamsburg, Inc. *The Capitol*. Richmond, 1936.

Colton, Calvin, ed. *Private Correspondence of Henry Clay*. New York, 1855–56.

Congressional Globe, 30th Cong., Second Sess.

Connor, R. D. W. *North Carolina: Rebuilding an Ancient Commonwealth, 1584–1925*. Chicago, 1929. Vol. I.

Conway, Moncure Daniel. *The Life of Thomas Paine*. New York, 1892. Vol. II.

Cook, Sherwin L. *Torchlight Parade: Our Presidential Pageant*. New York, 1929.

"Correspondence between General William Winder and President Monroe with Reference to Proposals Made by the United Provinces of South America," *Hispanic American Historical Review*, XII (November, 1932), 457–61.

Corwin, Edward S. *National Supremacy*. New York, 1913.

Crallé, R. K., ed. *See* Calhoun, John C.

Cresson, W. P. *Francis Dana*. New York, 1930.

———— *The Holy Alliance: The European Background of the Monroe Doctrine*. Publications of the Carnegie Endowment for International Peace. New York, 1922.

Curry, J. L. M. "The Acquisition of Florida," *Magazine of American History*, XIX (April, 1888), 286–301.

Cutts, L. B. *Memoirs and Letters of Dolly Madison*. Boston, 1886.

Czartoryski, Adam Jerzy. *Mémoires du Prince Adam Czartoryski, et correspondance avec l'Empereur Alexandre Ier*. Paris, 1887. Vol. II.

Davis, Matthew L. *Memoirs of Aaron Burr, with Miscellaneous Selections from his Correspondence*. New York, 1837. Vol. I.

Davis, W. W. H. "Washington on the West Bank of the Delaware, 1776," *The Pennsylvania Magazine of History and Biography*, IV, No. 2 (June 1880), 133–63, 148.

Dixon, Mrs. Archibald. *The True History of the Missouri Compromise and Its Repeal*. Cincinnati, 1890.

Duer, William Alexander. *The Life of William Alexander, Earl of Stirling*. Publication of the New Jersey Historical Society. New York, 1847.

Dunbar, Seymour. *A History of Travel in America*. Indianapolis, 1915. One-volume edition. New York, 1937.

List of References

Eaton, John Henry. *Life of Andrew Jackson.* Cincinnati, 1827.

Eckenrode, H. J. "The Letters of Woodford, Howe and Lee," *Richmond College Historical Papers,* I (July, 1915).

———— *The Revolution in Virginia.* Boston, 1916.

Ellet, Mrs. E. F. *The Court Circles of the Republic.* Hartford, 1869.

Farish, H. D. *See* Fithian, Philip Vickers.

Federal Writers' Project. *Savannah.* Savannah, 1937.

Fiske, John. *The Critical Period of American History.* Boston, 1899.

Fithian, Philip Vickers. *Journal and Letters of Philip Vickers Fithian, 1773–1774: A Plantation Tutor of the Old Dominion.* Ed., H. D. Farish. Williamsburg, 1943.

Fitzpatrick, John C. "George Washington," *Dictionary of American Biography,* XI, 98–99.

Ford, Paul Leicester, ed. *See* Jefferson, Thomas.

Ford, Worthington C., ed. *See* Jones, Joseph.

———— ed. *See* Washington, George.

French, Allen. *The First Year of the American Revolution.* Boston, 1934.

Fuess, Claude M. *Daniel Webster.* Boston, 1930. Vol I.

Fuller, Hubert B. *The Purchase of Florida.* Cleveland, 1906.

Gilman, Daniel C. *James Monroe.* Boston, 1883; 1898.

Goodrich, S. G. *Recollections of a Lifetime.* New York, 1857. Vol. I.

Goodwin, Rutherfoord. *A Brief & True Report concerning Williamsburg in Virginia. . . .* Williamsburg, 1941. ("Fourth and abridged Edition.")

Gouverneur, Marian. *As I Remember.* New York, 1911.

Griffin, C. C. *The United States and the Disruption of the Spanish Empire, 1810–1822.* New York, 1937.

Hale, Edward E. "Memories of a Hundred Years," *Outlook,* LXX (March 1, 1902), 549–61.

Hamilton, Alexander. *The Works of. . . .* Ed., H. C. Lodge, Boston, 1882. Vols. IV, VI, VII.

Hamilton, Stanislaus Murray, ed. *See* Monroe, James.

Head, James W. *History of Loudoun County, Virginia.* Washington, 1890.

Heitman, Francis B. *Historical Register of the Officers of the Continental Army during the War of the Revolution, April, 1775, to December, 1783.* Washington, 1914.

Higginson, Thomas Wentworth. "The Era of Good Feeling," *Harper's Magazine,* LXVIII (1883), 936.

Hilldrup, Robert Leroy. *The Life and Times of Edmund Pendleton.* Chapel Hill, 1939.

List of References

Hilliard, G. S., comp. *Life, Letters and Journals of George Ticknor.* Boston, 1876.

History and Register of the Colonial Dames of Virginia, 1892–1930. Richmond, 1930.

Hockett, Homer. *Political and Social History of the United States, 1492–1828.* New York, 1925.

Hoes, Rose Gouverneur. Article in the *Washington Post*, April 1, 1923.

——— "James Monroe, Soldier: His Part in the War of the American Revolution," *Daughters of the American Revolution Magazine*, LVII (December, 1923), 721–27.

Honeywell, Roy J. *The Educational Work of Thomas Jefferson*, Cambridge, 1931.

Howe, Henry. *Historical Collections of Virginia.* Charleston, 1856.

Hunt, Gaillard, ed. *See* Madison, James.

James, Marquis. *The Life of Andrew Jackson.* Indianapolis, 1938. One-volume edition.

Jay, John. *The Correspondence and Public Papers of* .... Ed., Henry P. Johnston. New York, 1890–93. Vol. IV.

Jay, William. *The Life of John Jay.* New York, 1833. Vol. I.

Jefferson, Thomas. *Notes on the State of Virginia.* France, 1784–85. Edition used here, Philadelphia, 1801.

——— *Writings of* .... Ed., Paul Leicester Ford. Philadelphia, 1895. Vols. V–VIII.

——— *The Writings of* .... Memorial Edition, ed., A. A. Lipscomb. Washington, 1903–04. Vols. I, II, XII.

——— *Writings of* .... Ed., H. A. Washington, New York, 1853–54. Vols. III, VI, VII.

Johnson, Monroe. "James Monroe, Soldier," *William and Mary College Quarterly* (Second Series) IX (January, 1929), 110–17.

———"Mrs. Monroe—Her Doctrine," *National Republic*, XVIII (December, 1930), 22–23, 32, 38.

———"The Maryland Ancestry of James Monroe," *Maryland Historical Magazine*, XXIII (June, 1928), 193–95.

Johnston, Henry Phelps. *The Campaign of 1776 around New York and Brooklyn.* Brooklyn, 1878.

———*The Correspondence and Public Papers of John Jay.* New York, 1890–93. Vol. IV.

Jones, Joseph. *The Letters of* .... Ed., W. C. Ford. Washington, 1889.

Kennedy, John Pendleton, ed. *Journals of the House of Burgesses, 1773–1776.* Richmond, 1905–15.

——— *Memoirs of the Life of William Wirt.* Philadelphia, 1860. Vols. I, II.

List of References

King, Charles R., ed. *Life and Correspondence of Rufus King.* New York, 1894–1899. Vols. II, IV.

King, George H. S. "General George Weedon," *William and Mary College Quarterly* (Second Series) XX (April, 1940), 246.

King Rufus. *Life and Correspondence of* .... Ed., Charles R. King. New York, 1894–99. Vols. II, IV.

Klinkowström, Baron Axel. "In Monroe's Administration," *American Scandanavian Review*, XIX (July, 1931), 393–402.

Lancaster, Robert A., Jr. *Historic Virginia Homes and Churches.* Philadelphia, 1915.

Lane-Poole, Stanley. *The Right Honorable Stratford Canning.* New York, 1888. Vol. I.

Latané, John A. *A History of American Foreign Policy.* New York, 1929.

Lee, Henry. *Memoirs of the War in the Southern Department of the United States.* Ed., Robert E. Lee. New York, 1870.

Leupp, Francis E. *Walks About Washington.* Boston, 1915.

Lewis, Edward S. "Ancestry of James Monroe," *William and Mary College Quarterly* (Second Series) III, No. 3 (July, 1923), 173–79.

Lingley, Charles Ramsdell. *The Transition in Virginia from Colony to Commonwealth.* New York, 1910.

Lipscomb, A. A., ed. *See* Jefferson, Thomas.

Lodge, Henry Cabot. "International Events Which Precipitated the Monroe Doctrine," *Congressional Digest*, VI (April, 1927), 115–16.

——— *Studies in History.* Boston, 1884.

———, ed. *The Works of Alexander Hamilton.* Boston, 1882. Vols. IV, VI.

Lossing, Benson J. *The Pictorial Field-Book of the Revolution.* New York, 1851–52. Vols. I, II.

"Macaulay, Alexander. Journal of," *William and Mary College Quarterly* (First Series) XI (January, 1903), 180–91.

MacCorkle, William A. *The Personal Genesis of the Monroe Doctrine.* New York, 1923.

Mackenzie, Alexander. *History of the Munros of Fowlis.* Inverness, 1898.

McMaster, John B. *The History of the People of the United States from the Revolution to the Civil War.* New York, 1883–1913. Vols. IV, V.

Madison, Dolly. *Memoirs and Letters of* .... Ed., L. B. Cutts. Boston, 1886.

Madison, James. *Letters and Other Writings.* Philadelphia, 1865. Vols. I, II.

——— *The Writings of* .... Ed., Gaillard Hunt. New York, 1900–10. Vols. VIII, IX.

List of References

Magruder, Alan B. *John Marshall.* Boston, 1898.

Manning, William Ray, ed. *Diplomatic Correspondence of the United States Concerning the Independence of the Latin-American Nations.* Publications of the Carnegie Endowment for International Peace. New York, 1925. Vol. II.

Metternich, Prince von. *Mémoires.* Paris, 1881–86. Vol. I.

Minnigerode, Meade. "Elizabeth Monroe and Louisa Adams," *Some American Ladies.* New York, 1926.

———— *Presidential Years, 1787–1860.* New York, 1928.

———— and Samuel H. Wandell. *Aaron Burr.* New York, 1925. Vol. I.

Monroe, James. "Letters of . . . ." *Bulletin of the New York Public Library,* February, 1900; September, November, 1901; June, July, 1902.

———— *Memoir of James Monroe, Esq. Relating to His Unsettled Claims upon The People and Government of the United States.* Charlottesville, 1828.

———— *The Writings of . . . .* Ed., S. M. Hamilton. New York, 1898–1903. Vols I–VIII. (Invaluable for Monroe and his times.)

———— *Observations on Certain Documents contained in Nos. V and VI of "The History of the United States for the year 1796." in which the Charge of Speculation against Alexander Hamilton, late Secretary of the Treasury, is fully refuted.* Philadelphia, 1797.

"Monroe Family, The," *William and Mary College Quarterly* (Second Series), XIII (October, 1933), 231–41.

"Monroe's View, Reflections on . . . ." Boston, 1798.

Moore, G. H. *The Treason of Charles Lee, Major General.* New York, 1860.

Moore, John Bassett. *A Digest of International Law.* Washington, 1906. Vol. VII.

———— ed. *See* Buchanan, James.

Morgan, George. *The Life of James Monroe.* Boston, 1921.

Morrison, Alfred J. *See* Schoepf, Johann David.

Morse, John T. *John Quincy Adams.* Boston, 1882.

Morton, Louis. *Robert Carter of Nomini Hall.* Williamsburg, 1941.

Muhlenberg, Henry S. *The Life of Major-General Peter Muhlenberg of the Revolutionary Army.* Philadelphia, 1849.

Myers, W. S. *See* Stryker, William Scudder.

Nevins, Allan, ed. *See* Adams, John Quincy.

Nicolay, Helen. *Our Capital on the Potomac.* New York, 1924.

Niles, H. ed. *Niles' Weekly Register.* Baltimore, 1816–1831.

Ogg, Frederic Austin. *The Opening of the Mississippi.* New York, 1904.

List of References

Osborne, J. A. *Williamsburg in Colonial Times.* Richmond, 1935.

Padover, Saul K. *Jefferson.* New York, 1942.

Parton, James. *The Life of Andrew Jackson.* New York, 1860. Vol. II.

Paxson, Frederic L. *History of the American Frontier, 1763–1893.* Boston, 1924.

Pellew, George. *John Jay.* New York, 1890.

Perkins, Dexter. *The Monroe Doctrine, 1823–1826.* Harvard Historical Studies, Vol. XXIX. Cambridge, 1927.

Phillips, Walter A. *The Confederation of Europe.* London, 1914.

Pratt, J. W. *Expansionists of 1812.* New York, 1925.

Preston, John Hyde. *Revolution, 1776.* New York, 1933.

Randall, Henry Stephens. *Life of Thomas Jefferson.* New York, 1858. Vol. III.

Ravenel, Mrs. St. Julien. *Charleston, the Place and the People.* New York, 1907.

Reddaway, William F. *The Monroe Doctrine.* Cambridge, 1898.

"Revolutionary Letters," *Tyler's Quarterly . . . Magazine,* IX (April, 1928), 246–47.

Richardson, James D. *A Compilation of the Messages and Papers of the Presidents, 1789–1902.* Washington, 1907. Vols. I, II.

Rives, William C. *History of the Life and Times of James Madison.* Boston, 1859–68. Vols. II, III.

Robertson, W. S. *The Life of Miranda,* Chapel Hill, 1929. Vol. I.

——— "The United States and Spain in 1822," *American Historical Review,* XX (July, 1915), 781–800.

Rush, Richard. *Memoranda of a Residence at the Court of London, 1819–1825.* Philadelphia, 1845.

Schoepf, Johann David. *Travels in the Confederation.* Tr. and ed., Alfred J. Morrison. Philadelphia, 1911.

Schouler, James. *History of the United States of America under the Constitution,* New York, 1880–1913. Vols. I, III. (Schouler made use of previously unused manuscript papers of James Monroe.)

——— "Monroe and the Rhea Letter," *Magazine of American History,* XII (October, 1884), 308–22.

Schurz, Carl. *The Life of Henry Clay.* Boston, 1887. Vol. I.

Seaton, William Winston. *A Biographical Sketch With Passing Notices of his Associates and Friends.* Boston, 1871.

Slaughter, Reverend Philip. *A History of St. Mark's Parish.* Baltimore, 1877.

——— *The Virginian History of African Colonization.* Richmond, 1855.

List of References

Smith, Margaret Bayard. *The First Forty Years of Washington Society.* New York, 1906.

Sparks, Jared. *The Life of Gouverneur Morris.* Boston, 1832. Vol. II.

Stapleton, Augustus G. *The Political Life of the Right Honorable George Canning.* London, 1831. Vol. I.

Stapleton, E. J., ed. *See* Canning, George.

Story, Joseph. *Life and Letters of* .... Ed., W. W. Story. Boston, 1851.

Story, W. W., ed. *See* Story, Joseph.

Stryker, William Scudder. *The Battle of Monmouth.* Rev. and ed., W. S. Myers. Princeton, 1927.

———— *The Battles of Trenton and Princeton.* Boston, 1898.

Sullivan, William. *Familiar Letters on Public Characters.* Boston, 1834.

Ticknor, George. *Life, Letters and Journals of* .... Comp., G. S. Hilliard. Boston, 1876.

Thompson, R. W. *Recollections of Sixteen Presidents.* Indianapolis, 1894.

Trevelyan, Sir George Otto. *The American Revolution.* New York, 1899–1907. Vol. IV.

Turner, Frederick Jackson. *The Rise of the New West, 1819–1829.* New York, 1906.

———— "Western State-Making in the Revolutionary Era," *The American Historical Review,* I (October, 1895), 70–87.

Tyler, Lyon G. "Early Presidents of William and Mary," *William and Mary College Quarterly* (First Series) I (October, 1892), 73.

———— "James Monroe," *William and Mary College Quarterly* (First Series) IV, No. 4 (April, 1896), 272–75.

Tyler, Moses Coit. *Patrick Henry.* Boston, 1887.

Upton, Harriet Taylor. *Our Early Presidents.* Boston, 1891.

Van Rensselear, Mrs. John King. Article in *Ladies Home Journal,* February, 1923.

Van Tyne, Claude Halstead. *The American Revolution, 1776–1783.* New York, 1905.

Waldo, Samuel P. *A Narrative of a Tour of Observation made during the summer of 1817 ... through the North Eastern and North Western departments of the Union; with a view to the examination of their several military defenses.* Hartford, 1820.

Wallace, David D. *The History of South Carolina.* New York, 1934. Vol. II.

Wandell, Samuel H., and Meade Minnigerode. *Aaron Burr.* New York, 1925. Vol I.

Washington, George. *The Writings of* .... Ed., W. C. Ford. New York, 1891. Vols. II, VI, XI, XIII, XIV.

List of References

Washington, H. A., ed. *See* Jefferson, Thomas.
Wharton, Anne Hollingsworth. *Social Life in the Early Republic.* Philadelphia, 1902.
——— *Salons, Colonial and Republican.* Philadelphia, 1900.
Whitaker, Arthur Preston. *The Spanish-American Frontier: 1783–1795.* Boston, 1927.
Wilkinson, General James. *Memoirs of My Own Times.* Philadelphia, 1816. Vol. I.
Willets, Gilson. *The Inside Story of the White House.* New York, 1908.
Williams, John S. *History of the Invasion and Capture of Washington.* New York, 1857.
"Williamsburg Companies, The," *Tyler's Quarterly . . . Magazine*, IX (July, 1927), 46–47.
Williams, Mary W. *The People and Politics of Latin America.* Boston, 1930.
Willson, Beckles. *America's Ambassadors to England, 1785–1928.* New York, 1929.
Wilstach, Paul. *Jefferson and Monticello.* New York, 1925.
Winsor, Justin. *The Western Movement.* Boston, 1897.
Wise, Barton H. *Life of Henry A. Wise of Virginia, 1806–1876.* New York, 1899.

II. Manuscripts

Bennett, James Gordon, MSS. Owned by Gabriel Wells, Esq.
Bowdoin MSS. Massachusetts Historical Society.
Crowninshield MSS. Massachusetts Historical Society.
Gouverneur-Hoes MSS. James Monroe Law Office, Fredericksburg, Virginia.
Gratz MSS. Philadelphia Historical Society.
Greenhow, Robert. MS in possession of James D. Evans, Esq., Philadelphia.
Hamilton MSS. Library of Congress.
Jefferson MSS. New York Public Library.
Jefferson MSS. Library of Congress.
Madison Papers. Library of Congress.
Monroe Papers. New York Public Library.

List of References

Monroe Papers. Library of Congress.
Pickering Papers. Massachusetts Historical Society.
Short MS. William and Mary College.
War Department Records.
Washburn Papers. Massachusetts Historical Society.

Index

ADAMS, Abigail (Mrs. John), and Washington social life, 202

Adams, John, quoted on British in Philadelphia, 33; in London protests against Navigation Acts, 88; author of *Discourses on Davila*, 116; struggle of with Hamilton for Federalist control, 175-76; and Washington social life, 202; mentioned, 67

Adams, John Quincy, on Napoleon's sale of Louisiana territory, 193; U. S. minister to Russia, 276; member of commission to negotiate peace, 276 ff. *passim;* Monroe's secretary of state, 290; *Diary* of quoted on Monroe's Cabinet, 292; on Monroe's Cabinet meetings, 297 ff. *passim; Diary* of on Rhea letter, 305-6; discussions of with Onis, 308-9; justified Jackson's course in Florida, 312-13; on Clay's opposition to Monroe, 317; and Florida negotiations with Spain, 320 ff. *passim;* and Vives, 325-26; *Diary* of on Missouri question, 342; praises Monroe for handling of Clay, 344; tells of Clay's prophecy that Union would not last, 345; on danger of slavery to Union, 346; voted for Missouri Compromise, 349; on gloomy situation in 1820, 351; mortified at Plumer's vote against Monroe, 352; makes statement on protocol, 362-63; supports Jackson as governor of Florida, 382; *Memoirs* of quoted on Cumberland Road, 391; and recognition of South American republics, 401 ff. *passim;* hears of proposed European intervention in South America, 401-2; supports Monroe in delaying recognition of South American republics, 404; on Cuba's request for annexation, 409; and Oregon, 413 ff. *passim;* and the Holy Alliance, 417 ff. *passim;* on Russian overtures to U. S., 432; diplomatic duel of with Baron de Tuyll, 437; and the Monroe Doctrine, 438 ff. *passim,* 442 ff. *passim,* 449; replies to Canning on coöperation against Holy Alliance, 440-41; sketch of, 453; candidate for president, 453; eulogy of on Monroe, 469; inauguration of, 470-71; visits Monroe at Oak Hill, 472; in 1830 shocked at Monroe's appearance, 480; visits Monroe in New York, 494-95; on the "depth of depravity" which troubled Monroe's last illness with the Rhea letter, 497; mentioned, 151, 201, 221, 408, 417, 480

Adams, Mrs. John Quincy, and Washington society, 361, 363, 367

Adams, William, English representative at Ghent, 277

Adet, M., French minister to U. S., 147

Aguirre, Manuel H., 400, 404

Alexander, Lady Catharine, 47

Alexander I, Tsar of Russia, on "attachment to the U. S.," 251; offers mediation between England and U. S., 276; and the Holy Alliance, 419 ff.; attempts to win America from policy of isolation, 425

Algiers, U. S. trouble with, 124, 144-45

Ambrister, Robert C., executed by Jackson, 307; British reaction to execution of, 313-14, 318

Amelia Island, headquarters of pirates, 297 ff. *passim*

American Colonization Society, 336, 340

American Society for Encouragement of American Manufactures, 330

American System, the, 386-87

Ames, Fisher, on the increase of "faction," 111

Arbuthnot, Alexander, and Seminole

[561]

Index

War, 306-7; executed by Jackson, 307; British reaction to execution of, 313-14, 318
Armand, Colonel, 57
Armstrong, John, succeeds Livingston in France, 209-10; on French attitude toward Spanish negotiations, 210; and Monroe's Spanish mission, 212-13; and Napoleon's note of August 5, 241-42; and Bowdoin, in Paris, 226; as secretary of war in War of 1812, 262 ff. *passim;* mentioned, 217, 252
Army bill, of 1811, 250
Arnold, Benedict, invades Virginia, 59 ff.
Ash Lawn, 105
Assumption, traded for national capital, 111. *See also* Public debt
Astor, John Jacob, duns Monroe, 474
Auckland, Lord, 226
Aury, Louis, and Amelia Island, 297 ff. *passim*

BACK COUNTRY, Monroe's early interest in, 70 ff. *See also* West, the
Bagot, Sir Charles, and Florida negotiations, 310; tells Adams of proposed European intervention in South America, 401
Bainbridge, William, 261
Baker, John Martin, 379
Banking crisis, the, 331 ff.
Bank of U. S., sketch of, 331-32
Banks, forced to suspend specie payments, 332 ff.
Barbé-Marbois, Francois, and the Louisiana Purchase, 189 ff. *passim;* and Spanish negotiations, 210
Barber, Francis, 43-44
Barbour, James, and the Missouri debates, 345
Barlow, Joel, and the Algerian trouble, 144; "Francophile," 199; mentioned, 251
Barney, Commodore, 266-67, 269
Barras, President-Director, replies to Monroe, 153-54
Barron, James, and the *Chesapeake* incident, 230 ff. *passim*
Bassano, Duke of, 251
Bayard, James A., member of commission to negotiate peace, 276 ff. *passim*

Beauharnais, Hortense, school friend of Eliza Monroe, 360, 375
Beaumarchais, P. A. C., 38
Beckley, John, and the Reynolds affair, 162; mentioned, 142
Bee, the, 177
Berlin Decree, 228
Bernadotte, J. B. L., 187
Beveridge, Albert J., on Virginia's opposition to centralized government, 97
"Black scheme," 50-51
Bladensburg, battle of, 267 ff.
Blair, Francis Preston, 489
Bland, Richard, 4
Bland, Theodoric, 14
Blount, Thomas, 152
Bolívar, Simón, 294
Bonaparte, Joseph, 193, 295
Bonaparte, Josephine, 260
Bonaparte, Lucien, 193
Bond, B. W., cited, 134, 140
Boston Post Road, 387
Botetourt, Lord, governor of Virginia, 5
Bowdoin, James, and Armstrong in Paris, 226; mentioned, 93, 225
Bowler, Jack, Negro slave who planned revolt, 174
Brackenridge, H. M., writes Monroe on South American republics, 400
Brackenridge, John, 122
Brandywine, battle of the, 33
Brent, Daniel, 382
Brie, Jean de, Monroe calls on, 143
Brougham, Lord, 257
Burke, Edmund, approved by Federalists, 116
Burr, Aaron, at battle of Monmouth, 43; colleague of Monroe in Senate in 1791, 111; as possible presidential candidate, 117; Monroe asks to handle prospective duel with Hamilton, 167 ff.; captures Hamilton's confidential pamphlet, 177; rising popularity of in 1799, 178; mentioned, 127, 128, 142
Byrd, William, on slavery, 71

CADORE, M., 242, 252
Calhoun, John C., wanted action in Florida affair, 242; represents rising nationalism, 186-87; Monroe's secretary of war, 291; and Rhea letter, 304 ff. *passim;* and the Seminole

[562]

Index

War, 304 ff. *passim;* suggests that Jackson be court-martialed, 312; opposed to administration in 1818, 317; accompanies Monroe on southern tour, 334 ff. *passim;* on constitutionality of Missouri bill, 349; on gloomy situation in 1820, 351; opposes Monroe on internal improvements, 388 ff. *passim;* submits report on internal improvements, 389-90; in Cabinet during Monroe Doctrine discussions, 439; on formulation of non-colonization doctrine, 443; candidate for president, 453; sketch of, 454; attacked by Crawford's satellites, 457; elected vice-president, 461; relations of with Jackson, 484 ff.; change in views of, 487; plot against, 489 ff.; and Jackson's letter, 490-91; visits Monroe at Oak Hill, 491-92; mentioned, 417

Calhoun, Mrs. John C., lost daughter in Washington epidemic, 365; led social boycott against Mrs. Eaton, 489; mentioned, 335

Calhoun-Crawford-Jackson feud, intensity of, 495 ff.

Callava, José María, and Jackson, 380 ff. *passim*

Callender, James Thomson, the Reynolds affair, 161 ff. *passim*

Cambacérès, J. J. R. de, 198

Camden, battle of, 58

Camm, John, president of William and Mary, 6, 19

Campbell, Parson Archibald, teacher of Monroe and Marshall, 7-8, 13

Campbell, Sir Archibald, 51

Campbell, George, Monroe appoints minister to Russia, 292

Canal building, 387

Canning, George, and the *Chesapeake* incident, 230 ff. *passim;* tries to prevent war with U. S., 257; and Cuba, 409-10; and Spanish American colonies, 431, 433 ff. *passim*, 436, 439-40

Canning, Stratford, on Monroe's second inaugural, 354-55; on U. S. delay in recognizing South American republics, 404-5; and J. Q. Adams on Columbia River settlements, 413

Carter, Robert, on professors at William and Mary, 9

Capital, difficulty in locating, 106, 109

Carrying trade, American, paralyzed by Berlin Decree, 228. *See also* Commerce

Cary, Archibald, 45, 51

Castlereagh, Lord, rude to Monroe in London, 204; tries to prevent war with U. S., 257; yields to American demands, 279-80; opposes Richlieu's plan for South America, 416; mentioned, 409

Caswell, Richard, 56, 57

Centinel, on Monroe's northern tour, uses expression "Era of Good Feeling," 288

Cevallos, Pedro, and Monroe's Spanish mission, 211 ff. *passim;* mentioned, 308

Chateaubriand, plan of for South America, 429-30

Chesapeake incident, 230 ff.

Cheves, Langdon, Monroe appoints president of U. S. Bank, 334; as president of bank, 337, 385

Chew, Ann, 372

Chew, Samuel, 254-55

Chew House, fight at, 34

Chronicle and Patriot, on Monroe's northern tour, 288

Cincinnati, Society of the, 74

Clark, George Rogers, 71, 73

Clay, Henry, allied with Randolph, 224; a "War Hawk" urging war with Great Britain, 250, 256; member of commission to negotiate peace, 276 ff. *passim;* speaker of House, 282; angered at Monroe for not appointing him secretary of state, 291; opposes Monroe on South America, 299 ff.; opposes administration in 1818, 317 ff. *passim;* attacks Monroe for delaying occupation of Florida, 324; shows antagonism to Monroe on southern tour, 336-37; in Missouri debates, 342, 343 ff. *passim;* prophesies speedy dissolution of Union, 345; and the Missouri Compromise, 349; represents nationalism of rising West, 386; opposes Monroe on internal improvements, 388 ff. *passim*, 391-92; opposed to Monroe on delay in recognizing South American republics, 404; contribution of to Monroe Doctrine, 449; candidate for president, 453; sketch of, 454-55;

[563]

Index

quoted on presidential campaign, 461-62; advocated J. Q. Adams for president, 462; and Jackson, 462; appointed secretary of state, 463; and McLean, 481

Clingman, Jacob, and Reynolds affair, 156 ff.

Clinton, De Witt, 453, 262

Clinton, Sir Henry, in American Revolution, 16, 19 ff., 39-40, 42 ff. *passim*, 52, 56

Cobb, Mr., of Georgia, on Missouri debates, 342

Cockburn, Admiral, 264

College of William and Mary, 3; faculty and students of in 1774, 5-6; affected by war spirit, 11-12

Collier, Sir George, 52

Collins, Lieutenant, robbed Powder Horn, 10

Columbian Observer, prints canard on Clay, 462

Commerce, American, Monroe interested in right of Confederation to regulate, 88 ff.; state of in the Confederation, 88-89; ruined by Great Britain after War of 1812, 329 ff.

Congress of Verona, 410

Congress of Vienna, 279

Conway, Thomas, and so-called Conway Cabal, 35-37

Cooper, James Fenimore, quoted on White House dinners, 364

Cornwallis, Lord, at battle of the Brandywine, 33; at battle of Monmouth, 42 ff. *passim*; at Camden, 58; in Virginia, 59 ff.; in Yorktown, 61

Corwin, Edward S., 99

Coryell, Mr., host to wounded Monroe, 30

Couthon, Georges, 129

Crawford, William, Monroe's secretary of the Treasury, 291; in Cabinet meetings, 297 ff. *passim*; and Seminole War, 303; and Rhea letter, 305-6; betrays Calhoun's suggestion to court-martial Jackson, 312; opposed to administration in 1818, 317; on bank failures, 333; on constitutionality of Missouri bill, 349; in Cabinet during Monroe Doctrine discussion, 439; candidate for president, 453; sketch of, 453-54; attacks Calhoun, 457, 489; and Jackson's letter, 490-91

Crawford-Calhoun-Jackson feud, intensity of, 495 ff.

Crawford's Act, 350

Crillon, Count Edward de, and his "secret papers," 255

Crowninshield, Jacob, on the Madisons' departure from Washington, 284-85; Monroe's secretary of the Navy, 291; mentioned, 236

Cuba, question of, 408 ff.; requests annexation to U. S., 409

Culpeper Minute Men, enter Williamsburg, 13; at Great Bridge, 14

Cumberland Road (National Road), 387; importance of, 390-91; J. Q. Adams quoted on, 391; Clay espouses cause of, 391-92; in need of repairs, 396

Currency, disordered after War of 1812, 331

DALLAS, A. J., 332

Dana, Judge Francis, 108

Dawson, Mr., 92

Deane, Silas, 38

Dearborn, Henry, 258

Decatur, Stephen, Macedonian exploit of, 261; and Mrs. Decatur give ball for Maria Hester Monroe, 373

Democratic-Republican party, 79

D'Estaing. *See* Estaing, Count d'

Deux Pont, Count, 62

De Wolf, George, Monroe stops at home of, 287

Doddridge, Philip, 478

Donelson, Andrew Jackson, 489

Drayton, John, 175

Duane, William, 400

Duer, Lady Kitty, 47

Duer, William, accused by Reynolds, 159, 160

Duers, the, social life of in New York, 92

Dunlap, John, published Monroe's pamphlet, 116

Dunmore, Lord, Governor of Virginia, dissolves the Assembly, 4; prestige of wanes, 5; and Powder Horn incident, 10 ff.; fled from Williamsburg, 11, 13; charged Henry with outlawry, 12

Duponceau, P. S., 409

Duvall, William P., 380

[564]

Index

EATON, J. H., and canard on Clay, 462
Eaton, Mrs., and Washington society, 489
Ellet, Mrs., describes Monroe, 359
Embargo, Jefferson's, 234-35, 236; effects of, 237
Era of Good Feeling, 220, 288, 452, 480
Erie Canal, 390
Erskine, Thomas, friendly to U. S., 221, 222
Erving, George W., succeeds Pinckney in Spain, 214; and Florida negotiations, 308, 309
Essex, case of, 216
Estaing, Charles Hector Count d', off Delaware Capes, withdrew to West Indies, 46; mentioned, 51, 54, 62
Eustis, William, resigned as secretary of war, 260
Evans, James D., on Monroe genealogy, 503
Everett, Dr. Charles, 248, 494

FAUQUIER, Governor Francis, 5
Federal control over states, opposing attitudes toward, 97
Federal government, Republicans fight centralization of power in, 112
Federalism, versus Republicanism, 115
Federalist, 99
Federalist party, attitude of toward the West contrasted with that of Republican party, 79 ff.; comes out openly in favor of Great Britain, 124, 242-43; versus Republicans, 177 ff., 185 ff.; claims credit for naval victories in War of 1812, 261; end of, 451-52
Fenno, John, Federalist propagandist, 115
Ferdinand VII of Spain, and South America, 295; blocked Florida treaty, 322 ff. *passim;* tries to get Three Powers to intervene, 436
Fisheries, in peace negotiations at Ghent, 277-78, 280
Fithian, Philip, on revolutionary sentiment, 5
Florida, and the Seminole War, 302 ff.; acquired by U. S., 320 ff., 326
Florida, West, revolt in, 242
Floridas, the, as involved in the Louisiana Purchase, 184 ff. *passim;* 208 ff.; a deal proposed for purchase of, 217
Florida Treaty signed by Spain, 326
Forbes & Company, 307, 382
Ford, Paul Leicester, on Jefferson's plan for frontier lands, 74
Forsyth, John, defends Monroe against Clay, 300; and the Florida Treaty, 322 ff. *passim;* in plot against Calhoun, 489
Foster, Augustus, British minister to U. S., 248, 249, 250, 254, 256
Fox, Charles James, friendly to U. S., 221 ff. *passim;* death of, affects Monroe's negotiations in England, 226
France, announced alliance with America, 39; attitude of U. S. toward in 1793, 119; strong declaration against intervention in South America by urged in Cabinet, 440
Franklin, Benjamin, 34, 38, 67
Fredericksburg, Peace Ball in, 61-62; Monroe lives in, 93 ff.
Free Soilers, and admission of Missouri, 342
Freneau, Philip, in *National Gazette* counteracts Fenno's propaganda, 115
Fromentin, Judge Eligius, 380, 381-82
Frontier, eighteenth-century, characterized, 70-71. See also West, the
Fulton, Robert, 199

GAINES, Edmund Pendleton, and Seminole War, 303 ff. *passim*
Gallatin, Albert, at dinner for Monroe, 156; resigns from Madison's Cabinet, 245; in Ghent, 274; member of commission to negotiate peace, 276 ff. *passim;* mentioned, 124, 292
Gambier, Lord, English representative at Ghent, 276
Gardoqui, Diego de, Spanish envoy to discuss Mississippi question, 82 ff. *passim;* and Monroe's first mission to France, 136; and "right of deposit" at New Orleans, 184
Garnett, Robert S., 407
Gates, Horatio, and so-called Conway Cabal, 35-36; sent by Washington to Carolinas, 57-58; defeated at Camden, 58
Gazette of the United States, 165
Gelston, David, gives account of

[565]

Index

Monroe's and Hamilton's meeting and threatened duel, 163 ff.
General Survey bill, 397-98
Genêt, Edmond, as envoy to U. S., 119 ff. *passim*
Georgetown, advocated for national capital, 68; in War of 1812, 263, 264
Germantown, battle of, 33 ff.
Gerry, Elbridge, 83, 103
Giles, William B., 111, 118
Godoy, Manuel de, and Thomas Pinckney, 144; mentioned, 184, 214, 217
Gore, Christopher, on Monroe in London, 199; on Jefferson's treatment of Merry, 204
Gouverneur, James, grandson of James Monroe, 375
Gouverneur, Samuel L., Monroe's secretary, accompanies Monroe on southern tour, 335; on sickness in Washington, 365; marries Maria Hester Monroe, 371 ff.; writes Mr. Monroe of Eliza's dislike for him, 374-75; and the Rhea letter, 496 ff.
Gouverneur, Mrs. Samuel L. (Maria Hester Monroe), at New Year's reception in 1825, 376
Gouverneur-Hoes MSS, Judge Jones's letters in, 69
Gouverneurs, the, visit Oak Hill, 472, 492
Graham, John, commissioner to study South American conditions, 297; in Cabinet meetings, 297 ff. *passim*
Grasse, F. J. P., Count de, 61, 62
Gray, Mrs. William, 287
Grayson, William, 85, 103
Great Bridge, battle of, 14
Great Britain, sends peace commissioner, 39; obstructs American commerce, 88, 124, 205-6; reaction of to *Chesapeake* incident, 231 ff. *passim*; ally of Spain in South American affairs, 250; attempts to prevent War of 1812, 257; offers to treat directly with U. S. to end War of 1812, 276; dumps products on American market after War of 1812, 329, 338; attitude of toward Cuba, 409, 410; and the Holy Alliance, 422
Green, Duff, editor of *Telegraph*, published Seminole correspondence, 495; mentioned, 484
Greene, Nathanael, at crossing of Delaware, 26; led column at Trenton, 28-29; at battle of Monmouth, 43 f. *passim*; advocated "black scheme," 50; took command of southern army, 58; mentioned, 22, 24, 38, 44, 57
Grenville, George Nugent Temple, 248
Grey, Charles, 248
Grundy, Felix, on annexing Canada, 258
Guavain, Mr., Monroe's secretary in France, 141
Gwatkin, Professor, of William and Mary, 6

HALE, Edward Everett, and anecdote of Monroe's visit to Harvard, 288
Hale, Nathan, 21
Hambly, Mr., 316
Hamilton, Alexander, at battle of Trenton, 29; at battle of Monmouth, 41 ff. *passim*; writes letter of recommendation for Monroe, 50; and the *Federalist*, 98; *Report* by on the public debt, 107-8; excise measure of, 110; defends course, 118; and Genêt, 120; and the *Little Sarah*, 122; advises Monroe's recall, 151, 152; feud of with Monroe, 156 ff.; and the Reynolds affair, 156 ff.; struggle of with John Adams for Federalist control, 175-76, 177; as secretary of navy in War of 1812, 261
Hamilton, James, 489
Hand, Edward, 24
Hardy, S., 74
Harlem Heights, battle of, 21
Harrison, Benjamin, 4
Harrowby, Lord, 207
Hawley, William, 372
Hay, Eliza Monroe (Mrs. George Hay), daughter of Monroe, acts as White House hostess, 360 ff., 370 ff.; nurses sick in Washington epidemic, 365-66; and her brother-in-law, 374; at New Year's reception in 1825, 376; at Oak Hill, 472
Hay, George, Monroe's son-in-law, 179, 483; writes Monroe on Missouri bill, 348; marries Monroe's daughter Eliza, 360; death of, 493
Hay, Hortensia, granddaughter of Monroe, suffers from Washington

Index

epidemic, 366; at Oak Hill, 472; marries Mr. Rogers, 492; mentioned, 375

Hays, the, visit Oak Hill, 472, 492

Henley, Professor, of William and Mary, 6

Henry, John, spy, 255

Henry, Patrick, speech of in 1765, 5, 6; marches on Williamsburg, after the Powder Horn incident, 12; organizes minute men and cadets in Williamsburg, 14-15; resigns his commission, 15; elected Governor of Virginia, 17; Monroe urges to act in interests of free navigation on Mississippi, 84-85; at Virginia Ratifying Convention, 98 ff. *passim;* continues to oppose Constitution, 102-3; mentioned, 4, 11, 97

Hichborn, Benjamin, and the Jay Treaty, 140-41

Hoban, James, built Oak Hill, 471

Holland, Lord, personal friend of Monroe, 226; *Memoirs* of quoted, 227-28; mentioned, 222, 248, 257

Holy Alliance, feared in America, 417 ff.; formation and nature of, 419 ff.; made public by ukase, 423; danger of intervention by in South America, 439-40

Hoomes, John, 179

"Hortensius," 179

Houston, Samuel, 482

Howe, Lord Richard, 19 ff., 40

Howe, Robert, 51

Howe, Sir William, 16, 19 ff., 33, 39

Howick, Lord, 226, 228-29

Hull, William, invaded Canada and precipitated War of 1812, 258-59; mentioned, 263

Humphreys, Colonel, envoy to the Dey of Algiers, 144-45

Humphries, Captain, of the *Leopard,* and the *Chesapeake* incident, 231 ff. *passim*

Hunt, Abraham, 28

IMPERIALISM, stirring to life in Madison's administration, 257-58

Impressment, Britain's policy of, Monroe's efforts to modify, 200 ff.; in connection with *Chesapeake* incident, 232; Madison raises issue again for political reasons, 257

Indians, Monroe's interest in, 87, 464 ff.

Innerarity, John, 382

Innis, James, captain of Williamsburg Volunteers, 12

Internal improvements, in Monroe's administration, 385 ff.; and sectional differences, 389 ff.

JACKSON, Andrew, and defense of New Orleans, 278 ff.; refused Monroe's invitation to be secretary of war, 291; and the Seminole War, 302 ff.; and the Rhea letter, 304 ff. *passim;* Monroe attempts to pacify, 314-15; rising popularity of in 1818, 317; and the investigation of his conduct in Florida, 318 ff.; embarks on hero's tour, 319; advice of on accepting Spanish offer of Florida, 321; Monroe visits, on southern tour, 338; and the governorship of Florida, 377 ff.; resigns as governor of Florida, 383; sides with Monroe on internal improvements, 395; candidate for president, 453; sketch of, 455; and Clay, 462; angered by Southard's claims for Monroe, 482; friendship of for Calhoun, 484; informed of Monroe's and Calhoun's disapproval of his Florida invasion, 485, 490; and his Kitchen Cabinet, 489

Jackson-Calhoun-Crawford feud, intensity of, 495 ff.; mentioned, 258, 292

Jackson, F. J., on Washington, D. C., 201

Jay, John, Monroe's distrust of on the Mississippi question, 80-81; spokesman for the East as opposed to the South, 81; and the Mississippi question, 82 ff. *passim;* as envoy to Great Britain, 125, 128-29; negotiations of in England and Monroe's first mission to France, 132-33, 137 ff. *passim;* and Gardoqui, 184

Jay Treaty, signed in London, 138; effect of on Monroe's first mission to France, 138 ff.; Monroe's attitude toward, 142-43; French objections to, 146; mentioned, 155, 201

Jefferson, Thomas, as governor, tutors Monroe in law, 53; as governor during the war, 55; sends troops to aid Muhlenberg, 58; escapes capture by Tarleton, 60; Monroe deplores with-

[567]

Index

drawal of from public office, 64; quoted on his withdrawal from public office, 64; intimacy of with Monroe during Fourth Congress of the Confederation, 67-68; interest of in back country, 70 ff.; characterizes Monroe, 95; aided Monroe's career, 97; from Paris, writes on the Constitution, 103; expresses wish for Monroe to settle near Monticello, 104; supervises building of Monroe's house while latter is in France, 105; becomes Washington's secretary of state, 106; on the "fixing of a central residence" for Congress, 106; on the funding of the public debt, 106; bargained with Hamilton for location of capital, 109; at odds with Hamilton, 111; intimacy of with Madison, 113; cultivates Philip Freneau, to offset Fenno's Federalist press, 115; welcomes Tom Paine for same reason, 115-16; corresponds with Madison and Monroe on party strategy, 117; and Genêt, 120 ff. *passim;* on Washington's proclamation of neutrality, 120-21; resigns from Cabinet, 123; and Callender's *History,* 162; as party leader, 177-78; inaugurated third president of the U. S., 179-80; fears prospect of French ownership of Louisiana, 184 ff. *passim;* and the Louisiana Purchase, 184 ff. *passim;* and Washington social life, 202 ff.; and the Spanish negotiations, 210; effect of "diplomacy of force" of, 214; works for a British alliance, 215, 216; turns to France, 217 ff.; Randolph attacks, 220 ff.; offers Monroe governorship of Louisiana, 223, 229; embarrassed by Randolph's intrigue, 224; decline in prosperity of after Embargo, 237; opposed to regular army, 275; voluminous correspondence of with Madison and Monroe, 292; on Missouri question, 349-50; on Cuba, 410-11; advises Monroe on his forthcoming statement concerning South America, 437; contribution of to the Monroe Doctrine, 449-50; in financial need, 460; drew plans for Oak Hill, 471; applied unsuccessfully to Virginia legislature for financial aid, 475; mentioned, 4, 7, 9, 88, 330, 406, and *passim*

Jervey, Thomas, 335

Jesup, Thomas S., 372

Johnson, Richard Mentor, 319

Johnson, William Samuel, 83, 89

Jones, James, grandfather of James Monroe, 6-7

Jones, Judge Joseph, uncle of James Monroe, 7; financed Monroe at College, 9; writes Washington about Monroe, 31-32; advises Monroe to study law with Jefferson, 54-55; on location of national capital, 68; belief of in session of western lands, 73; on federal control of commerce, 90; advises Monroe on his career and marriage, 92-93; aided Monroe's career, 97; mentioned, 33, 50, 133, 149, 191, and *passim*

Jones, William, as president of Second U. S. Bank, 333, 334

Jouett, John, warns Jefferson of approach of British, 60

KALB, Johann de, sent south to defend Carolina, 56; mentioned, 57

King, George H. S., on Monroe genealogy, 504

King, Rufus, and the Louisiana Purchase, 187 ff. *passim;* on Britain's attitude toward impressment, 200, 201; opposed to Embargo, 237; and the Missouri debates, 344; mentioned, 89, 199, 379

King's Mountain, battle of, 58, 71

Kirkland, John Thornton, of Harvard, confers Doctor of Laws degree on Monroe, 288

Kirkpatrick, Mrs., on Washington epidemic, 365

Klinkowström, Baron Axel, quoted on Washington, D. C., 366, 369, 370

Knox, Henry, at crossing of Delaware, 27; and the *Little Sarah,* 122; mentioned, 24, 44

Knyphauser, Wilhelm, Baron von, at battle of Brandywine, 33

Kortright, Elizabeth, 92. *See also* Monroe, Mrs. James

Kremer, George, and Clay canard, 462

LAFAYETTE, Marquis de, wounded at Brandywine, 33; at battle of Mon-

[568]

Index

mouth, 41 ff. *passim;* in defense of Virginia, 59 ff.; intimate with Monroe, 459; receives grant of land and money from Congress, 458-60; visits U. S., 458 ff.; visits Monroe at Oak Hill, 472; offers to help Monroe, 476; on Virginia's constitutional convention of 1829, 479

Laurens, Henry, suggests "black scheme," 50

Laurens, John, in attempt to take Chew House, 34; at battle of Monmouth, 43; and the "black scheme," 50; mentioned, 62

Lebrun, Charles François, 198

Lee, Arthur, 74

Lee, Charles, in Williamsburg, 16; sketch of, 16-17; delayed in joining Washington, 22; in hands of British, 24; at Valley Forge, 38-39; at battle of Monmouth, 41 ff. *passim;* court-martial of, 44; case of needs reexamination, 513-14

Lee, Henry (Light-horse Harry), on Congress, 38; attacks Paulus Hook, 54; opposed to free navigation of Mississippi, 85-86; at Virginia Ratifying Convention, 99-100; mentioned, 44, 56, 61

Lee, Richard Henry, and the Stamp Act, 6; mentioned, 4, 61, 67, 103

L'Enfant, Pierre Charles, 365

Leslie, General, invades Virginia, 58-59

Lewis, Frederick, commands forces at Williamsburg, 15

Lewis, Miss, 62

Lewis, Torbet, 62

Lewis, William B., promotes Jackson's candidacy, 455; and his canard on Clay, 462; mentioned, 489

Lincoln, Benjamin, advocated "black scheme," 50; mentioned, 51

Livingston, G., 158

Livingston, Mrs. Edward, describes Mrs. Monroe, 370

Livingston, Robert R., and the Louisiana Purchase, 187 ff. *passim;* attitude of toward Monroe in negotiation of Louisiana Purchase Treaty, 192 ff. *passim,* 206; visits London, 206-7; and Monroe's Spanish mission, 208 ff. *passim;* mentioned, 127

Livingston, Governor William, brother-in-law of Lord Stirling, 32, 41, 47

Logan, George, 142, 152

London Times, on Monroe's last message to Congress, 467

Lord Howick's Orders, 228-29

Louisiana Purchase, 183 ff.; western boundary of, 320

Love, Richard, 270

Lowell, Francis Cabot, 277

Lowndes, William, on internal improvements, 389; mentioned, 242

MACAULAY, Alexander, quoted on Monroe as councillor, 65

McCulloch v. Maryland, and power of states to tax federal banks, 334

MacGregor, Gregor, headed pirates on Amelia Island, 297 ff. *passim*

McHenry, James, dismissed from Cabinet, 176

McIlhany, James, 477

McKean, Judge, 156

McKeever, Isaac, 306, 307

McLane, Allen, 40

McLean, John, Monroe writes to on financial difficulties, 475, 476; relation of to Monroe, 480-82

Macon, Nathaniel, 224, 255

McQueen, Francis and Peter, 306

McWilliams, Major, 36

Madison, James, beginning of friendship of with Monroe, 81; aided Monroe's career, 97; at Virginia Ratifying Convention, 98 ff. *passim;* on Patrick Henry, 102; and the public debt, 108; intimacy of with Jefferson, 113; correspondence of with Monroe and Jefferson on party strategy, 117; on Monroe's first mission to France, 128; secretary of state, 180; on Louisiana matter, 185 ff. *passim;* on British alliance, 215 ff. *passim;* Randolph attacks, 220 ff. *passim;* and Monroe's English mission, 224 ff. *passim;* and the *Chesapeake* incident, 232 f.; on Jefferson and the Rose negotiations, 238; orders occupation of West Florida, 242;' announces revoking of Milan and Berlin decrees, 242; troubles of between France and England, 244; invites Monroe to become secretary of state, 245; dismisses Robert Smith as secretary of state, 247; differs from Monroe on France and England, 248; "secret"

[569]

Index

message of to Congress, 256; and the British invasion of Washington, 261 ff. *passim;* appoints Monroe acting secretary of war, 271; voluminous correspondence of with Monroe and Jefferson, 292; and Second U. S. Bank, 332; on Cumberland Road, 390-91; on Cuban question, 408; advises Monroe on message containing Monroe Doctrine, 437; and Adams' presidential campaign, 483; in Virginia's Constitutional Convention of 1829, 478; mentioned, 7, 9, 67, 107, 118, 204, 330, 437, and *passim*

Madison, Mrs. James (Dolly), on the British invasion, 263; forced to flee from Washington, 270, 357; popularity of, 359 ff. *passim;* mentioned, 204, 264

Madison, James, cousin of President James Madison, 6; as president of William and Mary, 9

Manufactures, new era in, 330. *See also* Commerce

Marbois. *See* Barbé-Marbois

Marion, Francis, 52

Marshall, John, schoolmate of James Monroe, 7-8; leads Culpeper Minute Men, 13; at Great Bridge, 14; in Monroe's company, 20; at Valley Forge, 38; with Monroe on Executive Council, 65; friendship of with Monroe, 65, 66, 78-79; financial difficulties of, 77-78; at Virginia Ratifying Convention, 100 ff. *passim;* opposed Monroe for senator, 109; secretary of state, 176; opposed Embargo, 237; administered oath of office to Monroe, 284, 355; and *McCulloch v. Maryland* case, 334; on Monroe's presidency, 468; administers oath of office to Adams, 470; mentioned, 179, 354, 478

Mason, Anne, 61

Mason, George, and session of western lands, 73; mentioned, 61

Mason, John, 409

Mason, Stevens Thomson, 179

Massachusetts Peace Society, congratulates Alexander on Holy Alliance, 424

Mathews, George, 258

Meade, Richard Kidder, 14

Mercer, George, 25

Mercer, Hugh, 62, 483
Mercer, Mrs. Isabella Gordon, 62
Mercer, John Francis, 24, 44
Merry, Anthony, on Washington, D. C., 201-2; offended by Jefferson's lack of ceremony, 203-4; mentioned, 276
Merry, Mrs. Anthony, 204
Metternich, 419
Middleton, Arthur C., 372
Miranda, Francisco de, career of, 293-94
Mississippi, free navigation of, Monroe champion of, 80 ff.; and Monroe's first mission to France, 129, 136, 143
Missouri, debates on admission of, 342 ff., 344
Missouri Compromise, 324, 339 ff.
Monmouth, battle of, 40 ff.
Monroe, Andrew, brother of James Monroe, 150, 505
Monroe, Eliza, daughter of James Monroe, 148, 154, 191. *See also* Hay, Eliza Monroe
Monroe, Elizabeth, sister of James Monroe, 505
Monroe, Elizabeth Jones, mother of James Monroe, 6-7

MONROE, JAMES
Boyhood and youth
At William and Mary College, 6, 9, 15; parents of, 6-7, 503-5; boyhood home and early schooling of, 7-8
Military career
Member of military company in Williamsburg, 12; helps remove arms from Palace, 13-14; made 2nd lieutenant in Third Virginia Regiment, 14; and Charles Lee, 16, 44; goes with regiment to New York, 19 ff.; in battle of White Plains, 21; in retreat across New Jersey, 22 ff.; crosses the Delaware, 25 ff.; on guard duty night before Trenton, 27-28; wounded at Trenton, 29 f.; promoted to captain, 31; at home of Judge Wyncoop, 31; additional aide to Lord Stirling, 32; in battle of Germantown, 33 ff. *passim;* at Brandywine, 33; promoted major, 35, 36; takes oath of allegiance at Valley Forge, 36; in battle of Monmouth, 40 ff. *passim;* early love af-

[570]

Index

fair of, 47 ff.; appointed lieutenant colonel of Virginia militia, 52; unable to raise regiment, studies law with Jefferson, 53, 54-55; appointed military commissioner by Jefferson, 56-57; colonel of "emergency regiment," 58; staff officer of Muhlenberg during Arnold's invasion, 59; unable to secure further military employment, 60-61; attends Peace Ball in Fredericksburg, 61, 62

Member of Virginia Assembly
Member of General Assembly and member of Executive Council, 64-65; friendship of with John Marshall, 65, 66, 78-79

Member of Congress of the Confederation
Member of Fourth Congress of the Confederation, 66 ff. *passim;* on proposed federal buildings, 68-69; as champion of the West, 70 ff.; attends Congress in Trenton, 76 ff.; tours western country, 75-77; financial difficulties of, 77-78; for free navigation of the Mississippi, 80 ff., *passim;* friendship of with Madison, 81; distrusts Jay, 80-81, 83; on problems of frontier, 81-82; fears secession of "East," 83-85; interest of in Indians, 87-88, 464 ff.; chairman of commerce committees and others, 86-87, 88, 89, 90; interested in getting western lands for Revolutionary veterans, 88; marriage of, 92 ff.; attends Congress in New York, 92

Lawyer
Practices law in Fredericksburg, Virginia, 93-94; elected to town council, 94-95; compared with Madison and Jefferson, 95; corresponds with Madison and Jefferson on changes in national government, 95; member of Virginia ratifying convention, 97 ff. *passim;* defeated by Madison for U. S. Senate, 103; buys property in Charlottesville, 104-5; close association of with Jefferson, 105-6; disagrees with Jefferson on public debt, 107

United States Senator
In U. S. Senate, 108 ff.; attempts to abolish secret sessions of Congress, 111-12, 124; member of committee to amend Virginia constitution, 112; in Federalist-Republican controversy, 116-17; drawn into unpleasant Hamilton episode, 118; and Genêt, 120 ff. *passim;* on Washington's neutrality stand, 121-22; opposed to sending Federalist envoy to British court, 125

First Mission to France
Goes to France, 127 ff.; attitude of toward Jay Treaty, 142-43; and the Algerian pirates, 144-45; gets Tom Paine out of prison, 148-49; recalled from France, 151 ff., 155; victim of party politics, 155 ff. *passim;* and Reynolds affair, 156 ff.; prospective duel of with Hamilton, 165 ff.; publishes *A View . . .,* 172

Governor of Virginia
Elected governor, 173 ff.; and Negro insurrection, 174-75; and colonization plan for Negroes, 175; death of only son of, 175-76; in 1779 party's chief tactician, 177; suspected Federalist plot to choose president, 178 ff.; and the Louisiana Purchase, 183 ff.

Diplomatic missions
Special envoy to France, 185 ff.; presented to Napoleon, 195-96; London mission of in 1803-4, 198 ff.; writes Livingston on Louisiana Purchase, 206; Spanish mission of, 208 ff.; in London, 215 ff., 220 ff.; rejects Randolph's plan to make him president, 220 ff., 237; and the *Chesapeake* incident, 231; returns to U. S., 236 ff.

Governor of Virginia
Becomes reconciled with Jefferson, 239; and the New Republicans, 240 ff.; again governor of Virginia, 244; holds Republican party together, 243, 245

Secretary of State
Appointed by Madison, 245 ff.; differs from Madison on France and England, 248; quoted on South American affairs, 249-50; relations of with South America, 295-96; on approaching war with Great Britain, 252-53; in war of 1812, 254 ff.; in agreement with Clay on war, 258

Acting Secretary of War
Appointed by Madison, 259-60;

Index

characterized by Sérurier, 262; and defense of Washington, 266 ff. *passim;* wins public favor, 273-74

Secretary of War
Meets financial and military problems of preparing national defense, 275 ff.

President of U. S.
First administration of, 281 ff.; first inaugural address of, 282-83; makes northern tour, 285 ff.; receives LL.D. from Harvard, 288; evaluates northern tour, 289; foreign problems of, 292 ff.; corresponds with Madison and Jefferson, 292; deals with South American affairs, 297 ff.; and Seminole War, 303 ff. *passim;* and Jackson's capture of Spanish towns in Florida, 311 ff.; and handling of Spanish affairs, 318; delays occupation of Florida, 323; on early danger of disunity, 324-25; makes tour of southern states, 334 ff.; favors deportation of free Negroes, 340; and the Missouri question, 343 ff. *passim;* social problems of in Washington, 358 ff.; elected to second term as president, 352; second inaugural of, 354 ff.; appearance and dress of, 354, 359, 375; as White House host, 370; and Jackson as governor of Florida, 377-78, 383; organizes government of Florida, 379; and internal improvements, 386 ff. *passim,* 392 ff., 396, 397, 398; and the Rhea letter, 394 ff., 495 ff.; and recognition of South American republics, 399 ff., 403-4, 406; on Cuba, 411; and Russian claims, 414 ff. *passim;* and formulation of Monroe Doctrine, 436; amends Adams' reply to Canning, 441; last of the Virginia dynasty, 452 ff., 463 ff.; urges strong navy and improved harbor defenses, 464; abstains from participating in presidential campaign, 455-56, 477, 482; and Lafayette, 459; unable to get money owed him by Congress, 460, 472 ff.; attends Adams' inauguration, 470-71

Retirement
Declines Lafayette's aid, 476; appointed regent of University of Virginia, 477; declined to serve as Governor of Virginia, 477-78; presides at Virginia constitutional convention, 478-79; besought to take sides in presidential race, 482, 483; urges Calhoun away from nullification, 488; involved again in Calhoun-Jackson feud, 489; reviews again matter of Jackson's letter, 491; life of at Oak Hill, 492; death of wife of, 493; sells Oak Hill and goes to New York to live with Gouverneurs, 493-94; life of in New York, 494; in last illness forced again to deny having seen Rhea letter, 495 ff.; death of, 498-99

Monroe, Mrs. James (Elizabeth Kortright), Marriage of, 92 ff.; in Paris, 148, 154; travels with sick son, 175; *la belle Américaine,* 205; in London, 205; at estate in Loudoun County, 285; at second inaugural, 356; as First Lady, 359 ff.; compared with Mrs. Madison, 360 ff.; suffers from Washington epidemics, 365-66; outlives her first unpopularity, 368; as White House hostess, 368-69; grieved by Eliza's feud with S. L. Gouverneur, 374; description of in 1825, 376; illness of, 471; death of, 493

Monroe, lieutenant James, Monroe's nephew, accompanies Monroe on southern tour, 335

Monroe, Joseph Jones, brother of James Monroe, 150, 505

Monroe, Maria Hester, daughter of James Monroe, 360; marries S. L. Gouverneur, 370 ff.

Monroe, Spence, father of James Monroe, 6, 7

Monroe, Spence, brother of James Monroe, 505

Monroe Doctrine, European background of, 417 ff.; formulation of in Cabinet sessions, 433 ff.; idea of incorporating statement in Message to Congress Monroe's alone, 444-46; presented to Congress as part of Annual Message, 447; quoted in part, 447-48; Monroe's part in evaluated, 448 ff.

Monrovia, named for Monroe, 340
Montpellier, Madison's home, 284
Morgan, Daniel, 56
Morris, Gouverneur, on the character

[572]

Index

of Congress, 80-81; and Monroe's first mission to France, 127 ff. *passim;* on Washington, D. C., 201

Muhlenberg, Frederick, and the Reynolds affair, 156 ff. *passim;* and Monroe-Hamilton interview, 163 ff. *passim;* mentioned, 123, 149

Muhlenberg, John Peter Gabriel, ordered to Virginia to organize defense, 55; organizes defense against Leslie, 58; mentioned, 44, 56

Mulgrave, Lord, 216

NAPOLEON, and Monroe's Spanish mission, 212; attitude of toward U. S. in 1811, 251; and the Louisiana Purchase, 187 ff. *passim;* gives Armstrong note concerning revoking of Berlin and Milan decrees, 241-42; mentioned, 209

Nash, Abner, 56

National capital, location of, 68

National Intelligencer, on Monroe's New Year's Day reception, 358-59; mentioned, 313

Neely, William, 25

Negro, free, problem of, 339 ff.; and the Missouri Compromise, 349

Negroes, uprising of in Virginia, 174-75; in Seminole War, 302 ff.

Nelson, Hugh, 406

Nelson, Thomas, commands Virginia militia, 58, 61

Neutrality, problems of during Napoleonic wars, 119 ff.; Washington's proclamation of, 120, 121; Jefferson and, 200-1

Neuville, Hyde de, French minister, and Florida negotiations, 309, 310; and Mrs. Hay, 361

New Haven *Herald,* on Monroe's northern tour, 286-87

New Republicans, and Monroe, 242 ff. *passim*

New States movement, 71

Nicholas, Henry, 11

Nicholas, Robert Carter, 11

Nicholas, Wilson Cary, 237, 179

Nicholls, Edward, 302, 307, 313

Nicholson, Joseph, 222, 224, 255

Niles, Hezekiah, interest of in South American affairs, 400

Niles' Register, quoted on Monroe's first inauguration, 281; on Monroe's first message to Congress, 328; on Russian claims, 414; approves spirit of Holy Alliance, 424; on Lafayette's visit, 460-61; on J. Q. Adams' tribute to Monroe, 471

Non-colonization, doctrine of due to Adams, 442; taken over by Monroe in Monroe Doctrine, 442; Calhoun on formulation of, 443

Non-importation Act, British resentment at, 222; goes into effect, 236

Norris, Captain, 263

Nullification, Calhoun's espousal of doctrine of, 487-88

OAK HILL, description of, 471-72; mentioned, 105, 376

Octagon House, (Tayloe house), temporary capital, 274

Ogg, F. A., cited on Monroe's official instructions as Jefferson's envoy to France, 186-87

Ohio Associates, 74-75

Old Republicans, and Monroe, 225

Onis, Don Luis de, Spanish envoy to U. S., 295 ff. *passim;* and Florida negotiations, 308 ff. *passim,* 320 ff. *passim;* mentioned, 408

Oregon territory, 412

PAGE, Mann, 12, 109

Paine, Thomas, and *Common Sense,* effect of in Virginia, 15; quoted on retreat across New Jersey, 23-24; quoted on banks of Delaware, 26; on battle of Germantown, 34; at Valley Forge, 38; *The Rights of Man* by, 116; makes trouble for Monroe, 148-49, 155

Pakenham, Sir Edward, attacks New Orleans, 278-79

Panic of 1819, 330-31

Parker, Josiah, 61, 63

Patriot, the, praises Monroe, 287

Paulding, Hiram, 285

Peace Ball, Monroe attends, 61-62

Peale, Rembrandt, 67

Pendleton, Edmund, 4, 12, 14, 107

Perceval, Spencer, on American trade, 233; mentioned, 230, 257

Pickens, Andrew, 52

Pickering, Timothy, and Monroe's handling of the Jay Treaty in France, 143 ff. *passim;* reprimands Monroe for handling of Jay Treaty in France, 151; criticizes Monroe,

[573]

Index

152-53; Monroe's epistolary battle with, 170 ff.; dismissed from Cabinet, 176; opposed to administration on accepting British peace terms, 277; mentioned, 146, 155, 165

Pinckney, Charles Cotesworth, succeeded Monroe in Paris, 153; as minister to Spain, 210-11

Pinckney, Thomas, as envoy to Spain, 144; Hamilton's plan to elect, 177; and Treaty of San Lorenzo el Real, 184; accompanies Monroe on southern tour, 355; mentioned, 149

Pinkney, William, colleague of Monroe in England, 221 ff. *passim;* abandons post in London, 248; and the Missouri debates, 344; mentioned, 292, 408

Pitt, William, on the Louisiana Purchase, 199

Pizarro, José, and Florida negotiations, 308, 310

Plessis, Chevalier du, 34

Plumer, William, Jr., on Monroe's difficult position as to the Missouri bill, 347-48; votes against Monroe for president, 352

Poindexter, George, supports Jackson, 319

Poinsett, Joel R., 249

Polignac, Prince, and Canning, 436

Polly, case of, 216

Porter, Peter B., entertains Monroe on northern tour, 289

Porterfield, Colonel, of Virginia, 57

Potts, Isaac, house of, Washington's headquarters, 38

Prevost, Augustine, 52

Prevost, Mrs., later wife of Aaron Burr, 47, 514

Public debt, funding of, 106 ff.

Pueyrredón, Juan Martín de, 400

Putnam, Israel, in command at Philadelphia, 24; plans of for Revolutionary veterans, 74-75, 88

RALEIGH TAVERN, Williamsburg, center of social life, 4-5; mentioned, 15, 17

Rall, Colonel Johann Gottlieb, at Trenton, 24 ff. *passim;* surprise of, 28 ff.

Randolph, Edmund, Governor of Virginia, attended Constitutional Convention, 96; at Virginia Ratifying Convention, 98 ff. *passim*

Randolph, John, Secretary of State, and Monroe's first mission to France, 127 ff. *passim;* casts Monroe in role of successor to Jefferson, 220 ff.; opposed to Embargo, 237; opposes draft in War of 1812, 275; opposes Clay on internal improvements, 398; mentioned, 236, 478

Randolph, Peyton, 4, 11, 12

Ravenel, Mrs., on Monroe's visit to South Carolina, 335

Reed, Joseph, quoted, 24-25

Republican (Democratic-Republican) party, attitude of toward West, contrasted with that of Federalist party, 79 ff.; in Congress attacks centralization of power in Federal government, 112; Jefferson, takes over leadership of, 123; during Monroe's administration, 452; versus Federalists, 115, 177 ff.; on "right of deposit" at New Orleans, 185 ff.

Reynolds, James, and Hamilton, 156 ff.

Reynolds, Mrs. James, and Hamilton, 157 ff. *passim*

Rhea, John, and the Rhea letter, 304 ff. *passim;* no reference to in long Jackson-Monroe correspondence after Florida affair, 316; resurrected in Jackson's feud with Crawford and Calhoun, 317; injected into presidential campaign after Monroe's retirement, 486

Richlieu, plan of for South America, 416

Richmond, burned by Benedict Arnold, 59

Richmond Examiner, 179

Ringgold, Tench, visits Monroe at Oak Hill, 472; Monroe visits in Washington, 480; mentioned, 489

"Right of deposit," at New Orleans, a party issue, 185-86

Roane, Spencer, 393

Robespierre, Maximilien, Monroe on fall of, 129

Rochambeau, Count de, 190

Rodgers, John, and *Little Belt,* 249; mentioned, 285

Rodney, Caesar A., 297

Rogers, Mr., of Baltimore, married Hortensia Hay, 492

Rose, George, British envoy to Washington, concerning *Chesapeake* in-

Index

cident, 233; negotiations of embarrassing to Jefferson, 238
Ross, James, resolution of, 186
Rush, Richard, Monroe appoints to Court of St. James's, 292; in Cabinet meetings, 297 ff. *passim;* and Canning, on possible rapprochment of England and U. S., 431; and Canning discuss joint action on question of Spanish-American colonies, 433 ff. *passim;* insists on British recognition of South American republics before entering upon any joint action, 434
Russell, Jonathan, on Napoleon, 251; and beginning of War of 1812, 258; member of commission to negotiate peace, 276 ff. *passim;* mentioned, 406
Russia, and Napoleon's Continental System, 252; claims of to western coast of North America, 413; U. S. relations with during Monroe's administration, 412 ff.; owned vast areas on North American continent, 425; strong declaration urged in Cabinet against intervention by in South America, 440
Rutherford, Griffith, 57
Rutledge, John, 52

SAINT-JUST, Louis de, 129
Salem *Register,* on Monroe's northern tour, 289
Sanchez, Mr., agent from Cuba, 409
Scarborough, Mr., Monroe's host in Savannah, 336
Schoepf, Johann David, describes Virginia legislature in *Travels in the Confederation in 1783 and 1784,* 66
Schouler, James, on William B. Giles, 111
Schuyler, Philip, 159
Scott, Alexander, 295, 379
Scott, Charles, commands Virginia line in South Carolina, 54
Scott, Sir William, rude to Monroe, 204; decision of in *Essex* case, 216
Seaton, Mrs. William, on British invasion, 263; on Washington society, 367-68; on Maria Hester Monroe's wedding, 373
Seccession, Monroe's fears of as result of conflicting sectional interests, 83-85
Sectional conflict, on western lands, 79 ff.

Sectional rivalry, development of between North and South, 340 ff.
Sedgwick, Theodore, 123, 124, 162, 177
Seminole controversy, ending of, 319
Seminole War, 302 ff.
Sérurier, Count de, French minister to U. S., and Monroe, in 1811, 250-51, 259; characterizes Monroe, 262; at diplomatic dinner, 364; mentioned, 255, 256
Session of western lands, 73 ff.
Shirt Men, enter Williamsburg, 13
Skipwith, Mr., Monroe's assistant in France, 191
Slavery, William Byrd on, 71; a cause of sectional differences, 339 ff.
Slave trade, early attempts to end, 339
Smith, Adam, Monroe quotes, 89
Smith, Matthew, 34
Smith, Mrs. Samuel Harrison, on fear of British invasion, 263; on the fall of the Capital, 269, 270
Smith, Robert, secretary of state, 245; dismissed by Madison, 247; and East Florida, 258
Smith, Samuel, and presidential election, 352
Smith, Steuben, 379
South America, when Monroe became secretary of state, 249; résumé of relations with Spain and U. S., 293 ff.
South American affairs, used by Clay to embarrass Monroe, 317; as affected by U. S. ownership of Florida, 323; prospect of European intervention in, 425
South American republics, recognition of, 399 ff.
Southard, S. L., in Cabinet during Monroe Doctrine discussions, 439; on Jackson and Monroe, 482
South, the, in the Revolution, 16 ff., 51-52; interests of early opposed to the "Eastern" states, 80 ff.
Spain, and the navigation of lower Mississippi, 80-81
Spoils System, beginning of, 350
Stansbury, General, at battle of Bladensburg, 268 ff. *passim*
States' rights, Monroe, with Jefferson, strongly on side of, 112; and the Virginia dynasty, 201
St. Cecilia Ball, Monroe attends, 335
St. Clair, Arthur, 24

Index

Sterett, Lieutenant Colonel, at battle of Bladensburg, 268
Steuben, Frederick William, Baron von, trains American army at Valley Forge, 38; at battle of Monmouth, 43; during Arnold's invasion, 59; mentioned, 62
Stevens, Edward, 58
Stewart, Charles, 263
Stirling, Lady, 47
Stirling, Lord (William Alexander), in retreat across New Jersey, 22 f.; guards Delaware fords, 25; sketch of, 32-33; at battle of Germantown, 34; headquarters of at Reading, Pa., 35; takes oath of allegiance at Valley Forge, 36; social life of, 36; brilliant artillerist, 37; at battle of Monmouth, 40 ff. *passim*; in camp at White Plains, 46-47; mentioned, 24, 55, 64
Story, Joseph, on Monroe's opposition to federally supported internal improvements, 395
Sullivan, John, led column at Trenton, 29; mentioned, 24
Sullivan, William, on end of War of 1812, 280
Sumter, Thomas, 52

TALIAFERRO, John, 92
Talleyrand, and the Louisiana Purchase, 187 ff. *passim*, 209 f.; and Monroe's Spanish mission, 212, 213, 217
Tallmadge, Benjamin, supports Jackson, 319
Tallmadge, James, 342
Tarleton, Sir Banastre, 56; reaches Charlottesville, 60
Taylor, John, of Caroline, persuades Monroe to accept position of secretary of state, 245; mentioned, 224, 243
Taylor, John W., in Missouri debates, 342, 344
Tazewell, Little Waller, 224, 237, 243, 478
Tertium Quids, 224
Thompson, Robert, 25
Thornton, Captain, 266
Ticknor, George, on Washington, D. C., 366-67
Tilsit Alliance, 252
Tomkins, D. D., vice-president, 281, 282, 286, 330, 363

Torres, Manuel, Colombian agent, 400; and the recognition of his country, 404, 405, 408
Toussaint L'Ouverture, 174
Transportation, importance and problems of, 387 ff.
Travel, in Monroe's day, 75-77
Treaty of Peace (1783), 68
Trenton, battle of, 23 ff., 28 ff.
Trevelyan, Sir George Otto, quoted on Colonel Rall, 24
Troup, Robert, 177
Trumbull, John, emissary of John Jay to Monroe, 140 ff. *passim*
Tucker, Judge, describes Maria Hester Monroe, 371
Tupper, Benjamin, plans of for revolutionary veterans, 88
Turreau de Linièrs, Baron, 218
Tuyll, Baron de, announces Russian Tsar's refusal to recognize South American republics, 438; reply to framed in Cabinet, 442; mentioned, 414, 415
Tyler, John, 477

UNITED States Bank, Republican nationalist faction opposed to rechartering of, 243; second, 332 ff.
U. S. Navy, started, 124
Upshur, Abel Parker, 478

VALLEY Forge, American army at, 37 ff.
Van Buren, Jackson's secretary of state, 489; mentioned, 484, 495
Van Ness, Albertina, 372
Van Ness, General, 264, 265
Vaughn, Sir Charles, 364
Venable, Mr., and the Reynolds affair, 157 ff. *passim*, 163 ff. *passim*
Vidal, Nicholas, 382
Virginia Dynasty, 282
Virginia Gazette, quoted, 11, 17
Virginia legislature in 1782, described by Schoepf, 66
Vives, Francisco Dionisio, Spanish envoy to deal with Florida treaty, 325-26

WALKER, Robert, 6
Wallace, Gustavus Browne, 61
Wallace, William Browne, 62
"War Hawks," urge war with Great Britain, 250, 256
War of 1812, 254 ff.; begun because of

Index

slow communications, 257; events leading up to, 248 ff.; outbreak of hostilities, responsibility for, 259

Washington, George, took command of Continental Army, 15-16; in New York in 1776, 19 ff.; retreats to Manhattan Island, 20; at battle of Harlem Heights, 21 ff. *passim;* retreat of across New Jersey, 22 ff.; quoted, 25, 26; crosses Delaware, 26 ff.; at Valley Forge, 37 ff. *passim;* decided to attack Clinton's column on its way northward from Philadelphia, 40; at battle of Monmouth, 41 ff. *passim;* writes letter recommending Monroe, 45, 51; joins Gates's army at White Plains, 46; resigns commission before Congress meeting in Annapolis, 67; and his Potomac-Ohio development, 71, 81, 86; and session of western lands, 73; opposed to free navigation of Mississippi, 85-86; proclaims stand on neutrality, 120, 121; and Monroe's first mission to France, 128 ff., 137 ff.; and the Jay Treaty, 142-43; and Monroe's recall, 151 ff.; toast to in Paris, 155; death of, 174; mentioned, 4, 7, 9, 15, 17, 55, 64, 155, 335

Washington, Mrs. Mary Ball, 61

Washington, William, commanded Monroe's company, 20; on guard duty with Monroe on night before Trenton, 27; wounded at Trenton, 29 f.; mentioned, 25, 56

Washington, D. C., in early 1800's, 201 ff.; in War of 1812, 261 ff.; during Monroe's two administrations, 354 ff., 365 ff.

Watson, Judge E. R., on Monroe, 493

Wayne, Anthony, at Valley Forge, 38; at battle of Monmouth, 41 ff. *passim;* captures Stony Point, 53; mentioned, 62

Wealth of Nations, Monroe quotes on "balance of trade," 89

Weedon, Colonel George, commanded Third Virginia Regiment, 20; quoted, 23; commands troops in defense of Virginia, 58; mentioned, 61

Weedon's Tavern, Fredericksburg, 61

Wellesley, Sir Henry, and Florida negotiations, 310

Wellesley, Richard, 248

Wellington, Duke of, 280

West, the (transmontane eighteenth-century frontiers), relations of to the Confederation, views on, 71; Monroe's services for, 79 ff.; rising political importance of, 386-87; criticizes Monroe for his stand on internal improvements, 396

Westward, 386

White, Hugh Lawson, 379, 482

White House, rebuilt after fire, 290; described by Axel Klinkowström, 357; Lafayette guest at, 459

White Plains, battle of, 21

Wilkinson, James, quoted on Monroe and William Washington, 29; and the Conway Cabal, 35-36; mentioned, 27, 265

Williamsburg, Va., in 1774, 3 ff.; and the outbreak of the Revolution, 10 ff.; host to Virginia Convention of May 15, 17; capital moved from, 54

Willis, Mrs., of Willis Hill, 62

Winder, William Henry, in command of defenses of Capital, 265 ff. *passim;* refuses to act as agent for Buenos Aires, 400

Wirt, William, Monroe's attorney-general, 291; and Jackson's course in Florida, 313; on constitutionality of Missouri bill, 349; approved Monroe's stand on internal improvements, 395; in Cabinet during Monroe Doctrine discussions, 439; consulted on the Rhea letter in Monroe's last illness, 496

Wolcott, Oliver, advises Monroe's recall, 151; and the Reynolds affair, 157 ff. *passim;* resigns from Cabinet, 176; on Washington, D. C., 202

Woodbine, George, 302, 307, 313

Woodford, William, commands Virginia line in South Carolina, 54; mentioned, 14, 15, 56, 61

Wyncoop, Judge, host to wounded Monroe, 30

Wythe, George, as teacher of law, 53; mentioned, 6

YORK, Penna., Congress in session at, 39

Yrujo, Marquis de Casa, 211